THE
MACROECONOMY
TODAY

SIXTEENTH EDITION

Mc
Graw
Hill

The McGraw-Hill Series Economics

THE
MACROECONOMY
TODAY

SIXTEENTH EDITION

Bradley R. Schiller

Karen Gebhardt

McGraw
Hill

THE MACROECONOMY TODAY, SIXTEENTH EDITION

Published by McGraw Hill LLC, 1325 Avenue of the Americas, New York, NY 10121. Copyright ©2022 by McGraw Hill LLC. All rights reserved. Printed in the United States of America. Previous editions ©2019, 2016, and 2013. No part of this publication may be reproduced or distributed in any form or by any means, or stored in a database or retrieval system, without the prior written consent of McGraw Hill LLC, including, but not limited to, in any network or other electronic storage or transmission, or broadcast for distance learning.

Some ancillaries, including electronic and print components, may not be available to customers outside the United States.

This book is printed on acid-free paper.

2 3 4 5 6 7 8 9 LWI 26 25 24 23 22

ISBN 978-1-264-27358-4 (bound edition)
MHID 1-264-27358-4 (bound edition)
ISBN 978-1-264-27361-4 (loose-leaf)
MHID 1-264-27361-4 (loose-leaf)

Portfolio Manager: *Anke Weekes*
Lead Product Developer: *Kelly Delso*
Content Project Managers: *Kathryn D. Wright, Ann Courtney, and Emily Windelborn*
Senior Buyer: *Laura Fuller*
Senior Designer: *Matt Diamond*
Content Licensing Specialist: *Traci Vaske*
Cover Image: *city vector/Shutterstock*
Compositor: *Aptara®, Inc.*

All credits appearing on page are considered to be an extension of the copyright page.

Library of Congress Cataloging-in-Publication Data

Names: Schiller, Bradley R., 1943- author. | Gebhardt, Karen, author.
Title: The macroeconomy today / Bradley R. Schiller, with Karen Gebhardt.
Description: Sixteenth edition. | New York, NY : McGraw Hill Education,
    [2022] | Includes index.
Identifiers: LCCN 2020047133 | ISBN 9781264273584 (hardcover) | ISBN
    9781264273614 (spiral bound)
Subjects: LCSH: Macroeconomics.
Classification: LCC HB172.5 .S3425 2022 | DDC 339—dc23
LC record available at https://lccn.loc.gov/2020047133

Bradley R. Schiller has more than four decades of experience teaching introductory economics at American University, the University of Nevada, the University of California (Berkeley and Santa Cruz), and the University of Maryland. He has given guest lectures at more than 300 colleges ranging from Fresno, California, to Istanbul, Turkey. Dr. Schiller's unique contribution to teaching is his ability to relate basic principles to current socioeconomic problems, institutions, and public policy decisions. This perspective is evident throughout *The Macroeconomy Today.*

Dr. Schiller derives this policy focus from his extensive experience as a Washington consultant. He has been a consultant to most major federal agencies, many congressional committees, political candidates, and presidents. In addition, he has evaluated scores of government programs and helped design others. His studies of poverty, discrimination, training programs, tax reform, pensions, welfare, Social Security, and lifetime wage patterns have appeared in both professional journals and popular media. Dr. Schiller is also a frequent commentator on economic policy for television and radio, and his commentary has appeared in *The Wall Street Journal, The Washington Post, The New York Times,* and *Los Angeles Times,* among other major newspapers.

Courtesy of Bradley R. Schiller

Dr. Schiller received his Ph.D. from Harvard and his B.A. degree, with great distinction, from the University of California (Berkeley). On his days off, Dr. Schiller is on the tennis courts, the ski slopes, or the crystal-blue waters of Lake Tahoe.

Dr. Karen Gebhardt is a faculty member in the Department of Economics and is the Director of the Online Economics Program at the University of Colorado Boulder. Dr. Gebhardt has a passion for teaching economics. She regularly instructs courses in all modalities (online, on campus, hybrid, remote) from introductory courses in macro- and microeconomics, to upper-division courses in microeconomics, international trade, and managerial economics and graduate courses in environmental economics and public finance.

She is an early adopter of teaching with technology and advocates strongly for it because she sees the difference it makes in student engagement and learning. Dr. Gebhardt was the recipient of the Water Pik Excellence in Education Award in 2006 and was awarded the Best Teacher Award in 2015 while she was at Colorado State University.

Courtesy of Karen Gebhardt

Dr. Gebhardt's research interests, publications, and presentations involve the economics and online education and the economics of human–wildlife interaction. Before returning to academia, she worked as an economist at the U.S. Department of Agriculture/Animal and Plant Health Inspection Service/Wildlife Services/National Wildlife Research Center, conducting research related to the interactions of humans and wildlife. Her current research focuses on using data to improve student learning outcomes in economics education with an emphasis on improving grades and completion rates in online courses.

In her free time, Dr. Gebhardt enjoys learning about new teaching methods that integrate technology and going rock climbing and camping in the Colorado Rockies and beyond.

CURRENT, POLICY FOCUSED, READABLE

Every edition of *The Macroeconomy Today* has offered a level of currency that no other text has matched. Maintaining that front-page advantage has been particularly important to this edition. First and foremost is the integration of the coronavirus pandemic into the narrative. The pandemic – and the responses to it – changed the behavior and performance of economies around the world. Among other things, the pandemic prompted breathtaking expansions in the scope and magnitude of fiscal and monetary policy options. It also focused more attention on the supply side of the economy, especially the potential for external shocks to shut down production. We have seen how the pandemic changed both consumer and producer behavior – and wreaked havoc on domestic and international financial markets. The pandemic also changed political priorities, contributing to President Biden's 2020 Election. This edition examines those developments and their implications for ongoing policy and personal decision-making. This 16th edition offers the latest data on U.S. economic performance, global comparisons, policy initiatives, court cases, and political controversies over economic policy and priorities. Among the more visible updates are the following:

Current

The Macroeconomy Today was one of the first economics textbooks to supplement the narrative with boxed illustrations of institutional and policy applications of core concepts. The goal has always been to help students see the relevance of studying economics to themselves and the world around them. Schiller and Gebhardt make sure students understand the challenges of economic policy and the consequences of specific actions like tariffs, tax changes, emergency lockdowns, and supply subsidies (like vaccines). They provide a balanced discussion of these issues, allowing students to recognize and assess different perspectives on critical issues. This Policy focus is reinforced by (a) attaching explanatory captions to every boxed insert, (b) referencing all of the boxed material in the body of the text, and (c) referencing the boxed material in end-of-chapter discussions questions and problems. Even the photos are captioned, to assure that students see their relevance.

Policy Focused

Front Page Economics. The *Front Page Economics* boxes are used to illustrate domestic applications of core concepts that make economics ever more relevant today. Student-focused examples cover everything from government stimulus checks and unemployment bonuses to the impact of low interest rates and higher stock markets on output and jobs. Some of the 20 new *Front Page Economics* stories are:

- "Trump Blasts GM Plant Closing" spotlights challenges of achieving full employment in Chapter 6.
- "Economy Craters, Unemployment Surges" with COVID lockdowns in Chapter 8
- "U.S. Leading Indicators Plummet" showcases forecasting potential in Chapter 9.
- "Congress OKs $2 Trillion Aid Package" describes CARES fiscal tools in Chapter 11.
- "Fed Slashes Rates to Zero" highlights monetary stimulus in Chapter 14.

World View. The *World View* boxes focus on global illustrations of core concepts that allow students to see economics in action beyond U.S. borders to help them become an educated global citizen. Among the 16 new *World View* boxes in this edition are:

- "GDP and Happiness" contrasts per capita income and well-being in Chapter 5.
- "Budget Imbalances Common" shows deficits in other nations in Chapter 12.
- "Zimbabwe Raises Key Interest Rate to 70%" illustrates real vs. nominal interest rates Chapter 15.

- "Cyclone IDAI Destroys Mozambique Port City" highlights the potential of supply-side shocks in Chapter 16.
- "Who Wins, Who Loses from Strong Dollar?" illustrates impacts of currency changes in Chapter 20.

Decisions for Tomorrow. At the end of every chapter, students are challenged to use critical thinking skills to apply core concepts to a real-world phenomenon. The challenges may relate to public policy issues or life situations. All of these provocative questions not only challenge students to apply critical thinking but also to recognize the relevancy of core principles to the real world. Notice that all of the *Decisions* are posed as questions. The intent here is to encourage classroom discussion and debate. Among the *Decisions* challenges in this edition are:

- "What Is the Cost of Going Green?" explores opportunity costs in Chapter 1.
- "Bring Jobs Back!" looks at the threats and benefits of outsourcing in Chapter 6.
- "Is the World Ready for Libra?" examines the nature of money in Chapter 13.
- "Hands On or Hands Off?" lays out basic macro policy options in Chapter 18.
- "Who Wins Trade Wars?" looks at the impacts of trade wars in Chapter 19.

All of the *Decisions* are posed as questions to encourage classroom discussion.

Questions for Discussion. End-of-chapter questions are common in textbooks. What distinguishes the *questions* in *The Macroeconomy Today* is their explicit integration with the core narrative and the boxed features in each chapter. There are 80 new questions in this 16th edition.

Problems. *Problems* are also provided at the end of each chapter. Like the *Questions for Discussion*, the *Problems* are closely integrated with chapter material and often require the student to review a boxed feature and apply data contained therein. There are 227 new problems (!) in this 16th edition.

Readable

The one adjective invariably used to describe *The Macroeconomy Today* is "readable." Professors often express a bit of shock when they realize that students actually enjoy reading the text. The writing style is lively and issue-focused. Unlike any other text on the market, every boxed feature, every graph, and every table is explained and analyzed. Every feature is also referenced in the text, so students actually learn the material rather than skipping over it. Because readability is ultimately in the eye of the beholder, you might ask a couple of students to read and compare a parallel chapter in *The Macroeconomy Today* and in another text. This is a test *The Macroeconomy Today* usually wins.

Robust Integration with Connect

Connect is designed to support teaching and learning goals through providing graded and ungraded activities that can be integrated into a lecture, or assigned as part of a discussion board or problem set. Activities such as assignable discussion, graphing, and algorithmic problems; interactive graphs; and videos make it easy to enhance learning with just a few clicks. One unique feature of this text is that Schiller and Gebhardt personally have created the text-specific Connect content, leveraging their combined 60 years of teaching undergraduate face-to-face, online, hybrid, and remote courses to help you improve *your* students' learning. The author team assures that the text and all supplemental materials are harmonized and robustly integrated with Connect, providing peace of mind for both the professor and students.

Remote Proctoring & Browser-Locking Capabilities

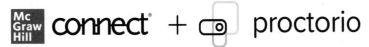

New remote proctoring and browser-locking capabilities, hosted by Proctorio within Connect, provide control of the assessment environment by enabling security options and verifying the identity of the student.

Seamlessly integrated within Connect, these services allow instructors to control students' assessment experience by restricting browser activity, recording students' activity, and verifying students are doing their own work.

Instant and detailed reporting gives instructors an at-a-glance view of potential academic integrity concerns, thereby avoiding personal bias and supporting evidence-based claims.

CHAPTER-BY-CHAPTER CHANGES: PURPOSE, APPROACH, AND UPDATES

Every chapter of this edition has been thoroughly reviewed and subjected to careful revision, editing, and updating. The following paragraphs provide a quick overview of each chapter and a list of the most notable updates.

Chapter 1: Economics: The Core Issues introduces the core issues of What, How, and For Whom goods and services are produced. It also highlights debates of how those decisions are made—by free markets, by governments, or by some mix of both. The intent is to give students a sense that "the economy" is not an abstract phenomenon but instead a vital determinant of our collective well-being. Heritage Organization "free market" 2020 rankings illustrate how different economies are structured and global military spending levels illustrate some of the "guns vs. butter" outcomes that result. A new "Decisions for Tomorrow" feature highlights the goals and trade-offs of the "Green revolution."

Chapter 2: The U.S. Economy: A Global View is uniquely designed to give students an empirical perspective on the dimensions of the U.S. economy—specifically, what we produce, how we produce, and for whom we produce. Within each of these dimensions, comparisons are provided to the rest of the world, giving students a truly global view of how the U.S. economy stacks up. This is a critical foundation for informing students about the economic world we want them to understand.

Chapter 3: Supply and Demand introduces the core elements of the market mechanism. It does this in a much more empirical context, however, than most texts. Illustrations include a Front Page Economics story on the pricing of Disney+ subscriptions, a World View on the supply shifts due to the 2019 missile attacks on Saudi oil fields, a World View on Venezuelan price controls, and a discussion of how the coronavirus pandemic prompted alleged price gouging. The end-of-chapter Decisions for Tomorrow feature confronts students with the deadly consequences of prohibiting the purchase and sale of human organs.

Chapter 4: The Role of Government focuses on the justifications for government intervention and the institutions—federal, state, and local—that have been developed to perform those functions. The chapter not only details the scope of government(s) but also looks at public perceptions about how well the public sector performs. A World View on Israel's "Iron Dome" missile defense (a public good), a Front Page Economics on vaping bans (externalities), and a Front Page Economics on public confidence in government enliven the discussion. The end-of-chapter Decisions for Tomorrow feature highlights the short-comings of collective decision making, including public choice theory.

Chapter 5: National Income Accounting emphasizes the circularity of output and income flows while highlighting their relevance to policy decisions. The contrast between economic and social indices of well-being are discussed and illustrated with a new World View on global happiness rankings. Another World View contrasts specific dimensions of our living standards with those of poorer nations—a comparison that adds real substance to cross-country statistical GDP comparisons.

Chapter 6: Unemployment not only introduces the standard measures of unemployment but also illustrates the socioeconomic costs of that macro failure. The spike in joblessness caused by the coronavirus helps illustrate the differences between jobless and unemployment measures. The Decisions for Tomorrow feature on "Is Outsourcing Really Bad?" discusses the motivations and consequences of President Trump's campaign against outsourcing.

Chapter 7: Inflation not only describes how inflation is measured but, importantly, discusses the socioeconomic costs of rising price levels. A World View on the Venezuelan bolivar underscores the destructive force of runaway inflation.

Chapter 8: The Business Cycle is the starting point for macro theory. The intent of this chapter is to describe the nature of business cycles, review their history, and preview some of the salient theories about their origins. The aggregate demand/aggregate supply model is also introduced in this chapter as a common framework for illustrating and contrasting different perspectives on macro (in)stability. The coronavirus pandemic serves as a timely illustration of how external shocks can derail an economy.

Chapter 9: Aggregate Demand focuses on the nature and building blocks of the aggregate demand curve. The novelty of this presentation is the construction of the AD curve with horizontal rather than vertical increments $[C + I + G + (X - M)]$, a nuance that greatly facilitates later illustrations of the income multiplier. Front Page Economics stories about the 2019/2020 wealth effects of a (then-)rising stock market and another about the March 2020 reversal of the leading economic indicators add real-world flavor.

Chapter 10: Self-Adjustment or Instability? confronts the central question of whether laissez-faire economies self-adjust or not. The multiplier is introduced—and illustrated in the context of the AD/AS model with sequential, horizontal shifts of the AD curve. This novel approach is much more intuitive than the traditional Keynesian-cross approach and lends itself to simple mathematical and graphical exercises. Data on the variability of consumer and investor spending help illustrate the potential for macro instability.

Chapter 11: Fiscal Policy examines the potential of tax, spending, and transfer policies to shift the AD curve in desired directions. The unique interpretation of Keynesian theory in the context of the AD/AS model permits the illustration of both output and price-level effects of fiscal interventions. Explicit, mathematical guidelines for designing fiscal interventions are derived. And, of course, the chapter examines the impact of the 2017 tax cuts and the 2020 coronavirus recovery rebates, and the massive increase in unemployment-benefit transfers.

Chapter 12: Deficits and Debt describes the nature, origins, history, and consequences of federal budget deficits and the resulting national debt. The distinction between cyclical and structural deficits is emphasized. Global comparisons of debt/GDP ratios are provided along with information about the ownership of the debt. The 2019–2021 suspension of the debt ceiling and the impact of the coronavirus stimulus package are discussed.

Chapter 13: Money and Banks focuses on the nature and origins of what we call "money," then explains why money is so critical to the functioning of any economy. The content and purpose of T-accounts are carefully explained, as is the process of money creation. Data on the structure of interest rates help illustrate the price of holding money. The Decisions for Tomorrow feature examines the potential of Facebook's Libra or other cryptocurrencies to displace traditional money.

Chapter 14: The Federal Reserve System starts by introducing Jerome Powell and the structure of the Fed. It then describes each of the Fed's major policy tools and illustrates how each can be used. A World View on China's reserve-requirement cuts helps illustrate the use of monetary tools and creates a nice mathematical exercise. The critical role of bond markets in open-market operations is carefully described—and illustrated with a new Front Page Economics on bond-market gyrations. The Decisions for Tomorrow feature examines the potential of crowdfunding to bypass traditional banks.

Chapter 15: Monetary Policy reviews the tools of monetary policy and illustrates their potential for altering macro outcomes, contrasting Keynesian and Monetarist views in the process. The chapter also discusses the constraints on policy impact and highlights the velocity of money as a critical arbiter of effectiveness. Last, but far from least, the chapter reviews and assesses recent Fed policy, including its "whatever it takes" response to the coronavirus pandemic.

Chapter 16: Supply-Side Policy: Short-Run Options emphasizes that demand-focused policies are not the only game in town—that the AS curve is also a critical determinant of macro outcomes. The chapter starts by looking at different opinions about the shape of the AS curve, and then delves into factors and policy tools that can shift the AS curve. The elasticity of supply and its determinants are highlighted. The impact of the coronavirus, tariffs, and tax cuts on the AS curve are all discussed.

Chapter 17: Growth and Productivity: Long-Run Possibilities takes a longer view of economic growth. It looks at global growth experiences, and then examines how savings, productivity advance, population dynamics, and public policy choices affect growth trajectories. The Decisions for Tomorrow feature asks whether limitless growth is possible—or even desirable.

Chapter 18: Theory versus Reality is a unique capstone chapter that offers students a review and synthesis of central macro concepts. It summarizes the basic tools of fiscal, monetary, and supply-side policy; reviews their usage in recent years; and examines the macro performance that resulted. An extended discussion of the obstacles that constrain policy effectiveness helps explain the gap between theoretical potential and economic reality. Students love this chapter.

Chapter 19: International Trade not only explains the theory of comparative advantage but also examines the opposition to free trade and the trade barriers that result. President Trump's trade wars with China and his national security argument about TikTok are discussed, followed by a Decisions feature on "Who Wins Trade Wars?" The USMCA is reviewed, as are the latest data on trade flows. World Views on the dumping of Korean cigarettes and competition from wine imports and a Front Page Economics on the cost of sugar quotas keep the discussion lively.

Chapter 20: International Finance goes beyond the mechanics of exchange-rate determination to identify the gainers and losers from exchange-rate fluctuations. A World View on the effects of the 2014–2020 appreciation of the U.S. dollar helps illustrate those redistributive effects (and the opposition thereto). The collapse of the Venezuelan bolivar adds further insight. A World View on the weakest global currencies is insightful as well.

Chapter 21: Global Poverty draws attention to the persistent depravation that still afflicts nearly 40 percent of the world's population. The discussion begins with a comparison of U.S. poverty thresholds with official global poverty measures. A survey of global poverty incidence is followed by an analysis of causation and potential remedies.

Student Problem Set

We firmly believe that students must *work* with key concepts in order to really learn them. Weekly homework assignments are *de rigueur* in our own classes. To facilitate homework assignments, we have prepared the student problem set at the end of each chapter. These sets include built-in numerical and graphing problems that build on the tables, graphs, and boxed material that align with each chapter's learning objectives. Students cannot complete all the problems without referring to material in the chapter. This increases the odds of students actually *reading* the chapter, the tables, and the boxed applications.

The student problem set at the end of each chapter is reproduced in Connect. This really helps students transition between the written material and online supplements. It also means that the online assignments are totally book-specific.

NEW AND IMPROVED SUPPLEMENTS

The following ancillaries are available for quick download and convenient access via the Instructor Resource material available through McGraw-Hill Connect: PowerPoint Presentations, Accessible PowerPoint Presentations, Instructor's Manual, Solution's Manual, and Test Builder Access.

ACKNOWLEDGMENTS

This 16th edition of *The Macroeconomy Today* represents a continuing commitment to disseminate the core principles of economics to a broad swath of college students.

Like earlier editions, it has benefited greatly from the continuing stream of ideas and suggestions from both instructors and students. For all that feedback we are most grateful. Among those who have contributed to this and prior editions are the following instructors:

Reviewers

Cynthia E. Abadie
Southwest Tennessee Community College

Mark Abajian
San Diego Mesa College

Steve Abid
Grand Rapids Community College

Ercument G. Aksoy
Los Angeles Valley College

Mauro Cristian Amor
Northwood University

Catalina Amuedo-Dorantes
San Diego State University

Dr. Michael Aubry
Cuyamaca College

Gerald Baumgardner
Penn College

Mack A. Bean
Franklin Pierce University

Adolfo Benavides
Texas A&M University-Corpus Christi

Anoop Bhargava
Finger Lakes Community College

Joerg Bibow
Skidmore College

Eugenie Bietry
Pace University

John Bockino
Suffolk County Community College

Peter Boelman
Norco College

Walter Francis Boyle
Fayetteville Technical Community College

Amber Brown
Grand Valley State University

Don Bumpass
Sam Houston State University

Suparna Chakraborty
Baruch College, CUNY

Stephen J. Conroy
University of San Diego

Sherry L. Creswell
Kent State University

Manabendra Dasgupta
University of Alabama-Birmingham

Antony Davies
Duquesne University

Diane de Freitas
Fresno City College

Diana Denison
Red Rocks Community College

Alexander Deshkovski
North Carolina Central University

John A. Doces
Bucknell University

Ishita Edwards
Oxnard College

Eric R. Eide
Brigham Young University

Yalcin Ertekin
Trine University

Ali Faegh
Houston Community College-Northwest

Kelley L. Fallon
Owensboro Community & Technical College

Frank Garland
Tri-County Technical College

Leroy Gill
The Ohio State University

Michael G. Goode
Central Piedmont Community College

Paul Graf
Indiana University

Barnali Gupta
Miami University

Sheila Amin Gutierrez de Pineres
University of Texas–Dallas

Jonatan Jelen
City College of New York

Hyojin Jeong
Lakeland Community College

Barbara Heroy John
University of Dayton

Ken Knox, Ph.D.
Eastern Gateway Community College

Tim Kochanski
Portland State University

David E. Laurel
South Texas College

Raymond Lawless
Quinsigamond Community College

Richard B. Le
Cosumnes River College

Jim Lee
Texas A&M University–Corpus Christi

Sang H. Lee
Southeastern Louisiana University

Minghua Li
Franklin Pierce University

Yan Li
University of Wisconsin–Eau Claire

Paul Lockard
Black Hawk College

Rotua Lumbantobing
North Carolina State University

Paula Manns
Atlantic Cape Community College

Shah Mehrabi
Montgomery College

Jeanette Milius
Iowa Western Community College

Norman C. Miller
Miami University

Stanley Robert Mitchell
McLennan Community College

Dr. Victor Moussoki
Lone Star College

Stephen K. Nodine
Tri-County Technical College

Phacharaphot Nuntramas
San Diego State University

Seth Ari Roberts
Frederick Community College

Michael J. Ryan
Western Michigan University

Craig F. Santicola
Westmoreland County Community College

Rolando A. Santos
Lakeland Community College

Theodore P. Scheinman
Mt. Hood Community College

James K. Self
Indiana University–Bloomington

Warren Smith
Palm Beach State College–Lake Worth

Marilyn K. Spencer
Texas A&M University–Corpus Christi

Irina Nikolayevna Strelnikova
Red Rocks Community College

Michael Swope
Wayne County Community College

Gary Lee Taylor
South Dakota State University

Deborah L. Thorsen
Palm Beach State College

Ngoc-Bich Tran
San Jacinto College

Markland Tuttle
Sam Houston State University

Roger E. Wehr
University of Texas–Arlington

Kenneth Lewis Weimer
Kellogg Community College

Selin Yalcindag
Mercyhurst College

Erik Zemljic
Kent State University

We would like to express our sincere appreciation to Gregory Gilpin of Montana State University and Christina Esparza-Luna at Hartnell College for preparing the PowerPoint Presentations, Christopher Blake of Emory University, Deborah Thorsen of Palm Beach State College, Emily Bello, and Stephen Slice of University of South Carolina for their contributions in revising the Testbank, Dan Mizak of Frostburg University for authoring the Instructor's Manual, and Jody Lotz for her detailed edit of the Connect content, as well as Mark Wilson of West Virginia State University, Joseph Euculano of Wilmington University, and Susan Bell of Seminole State College for their careful accuracy review. The text itself and all the accompanying supplements could not make it to the marketplace without the prodigious efforts of the production team at McGraw-Hill. In this regard, we want to extend special thanks to Kelly Delso, who managed the product development process required to produce a text today. Anke Weekes served once again as a valued portfolio director of the entire project. Let us conclude by thanking all the instructors and students who are going to use *The Macroeconomy Today* as an introduction to economic principles. We will welcome any reactions and suggestions you'd like to pass on for future editions.

—**Bradley R. Schiller**

—**Karen Gebhardt**

Instructors: Student Success Starts with You

Tools to enhance your unique voice

Want to build your own course? No problem. Prefer to use our turnkey, prebuilt course? Easy. Want to make changes throughout the semester? Sure. And you'll save time with Connect's auto-grading too.

65%
Less Time Grading

Laptop: McGraw Hill; Woman/dog: George Doyle/Getty Images

Study made personal

Incorporate adaptive study resources like SmartBook® 2.0 into your course and help your students be better prepared in less time. Learn more about the powerful personalized learning experience available in SmartBook 2.0 at **www.mheducation.com/highered/connect/smartbook**

Affordable solutions, added value

Make technology work for you with LMS integration for single sign-on access, mobile access to the digital textbook, and reports to quickly show you how each of your students is doing. And with our Inclusive Access program you can provide all these tools at a discount to your students. Ask your McGraw Hill representative for more information.

Padlock: Jobalou/Getty Images

Solutions for your challenges

A product isn't a solution. Real solutions are affordable, reliable, and come with training and ongoing support when you need it and how you want it. Visit **www. supportateverystep.com** for videos and resources both you and your students can use throughout the semester.

Checkmark: Jobalou/Getty Images

SUPPORT AT every step

Students: Get Learning that Fits You

Effective tools for efficient studying

Connect is designed to make you more productive with simple, flexible, intuitive tools that maximize your study time and meet your individual learning needs. Get learning that works for you with Connect.

Study anytime, anywhere

Download the free ReadAnywhere app and access your online eBook or SmartBook 2.0 assignments when it's convenient, even if you're offline. And since the app automatically syncs with your eBook and SmartBook 2.0 assignments in Connect, all of your work is available every time you open it. Find out more at **www.mheducation.com/readanywhere**

> *"I really liked this app—it made it easy to study when you don't have your textbook in front of you."*
>
> - Jordan Cunningham,
>   Eastern Washington University

Calendar: owattaphotos/Getty Images

Everything you need in one place

Your Connect course has everything you need—whether reading on your digital eBook or completing assignments for class, Connect makes it easy to get your work done.

Learning for everyone

McGraw Hill works directly with Accessibility Services Departments and faculty to meet the learning needs of all students. Please contact your Accessibility Services Office and ask them to email accessibility@mheducation.com, or visit **www.mheducation.com/about/accessibility** for more information.

Because learning changes everything.®

Connect Economics Asset Alignment with Bloom's Taxonomy

Schiller/Gebhardt The Macroeconomy Today 16e

We Take Students Higher

As a learning science company, we create content that supports higher order thinking skills. Within Connect®, we tag assessments accordingly so you can filter your search, assign it, and receive reporting on it. These content asset types can be associated with one or more levels of Bloom's Taxonomy.

The chart below shows a few of the key assignable economics assets with *McGraw Hill Connect* aligned with Bloom's Taxonomy. Take your students higher by assigning a variety of applications, moving them from simple memorization to concept application.

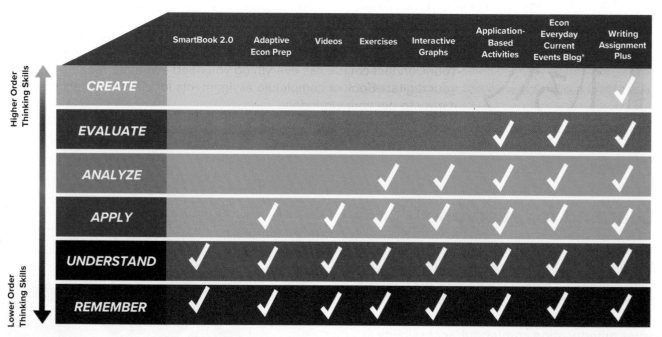

Higher Order / Lower Order Thinking Skills	SmartBook 2.0	Adaptive Econ Prep	Videos	Exercises	Interactive Graphs	Application-Based Activities	Econ Everyday Current Events Blog*	Writing Assignment Plus
CREATE								✓
EVALUATE						✓	✓	✓
ANALYZE				✓	✓	✓	✓	✓
APPLY		✓	✓	✓	✓	✓	✓	✓
UNDERSTAND	✓	✓	✓	✓	✓	✓	✓	✓
REMEMBER	✓	✓	✓	✓	✓	✓	✓	✓

* Outside of Connect.

SmartBook 2.0

Adaptively aids students to study more efficiently by highlighting where in the chapter to focus, asking review questions and pointing them to passages in the text until they understand. Assignable and assessable

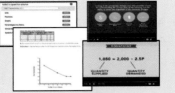

Adaptive Econ Prep

Math and graphing preparedness assignments help students refresh important prerequisite topics necessary to be successful in economics. New Adaptive Econ Prep Tool provides students just-in-time math and graphing remediation that are prerequisite to success in Economics courses and adapt to each student.

Videos

Tutorial videos provide engaging explanations to help students grasp challenging concepts. Application videos bring economics to life with relevant, real world examples. All videos include closed captioning for accessibility and are assignable with assessment questions for improved retention.

Exercises

Exercises with algorithmic variations provide ample opportunities for students to practice and hone quantitative skills. Graphing Exercises provide opportunities for students to draw, interact with, manipulate, and analyze graphs.

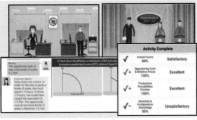

Interactive Graphs

Interactive Graphs provide visual displays of real data and economic concepts for students to manipulate. All graphs are accompanied by assignable Assessment questions and feedback to guide students through the experience of learning to read and interpret graphs and data.

Application-Based Activities

Immersive real-life scenarios engage students and put them in the role of everyday economists. Students practice their economic thinking and problem-solving skills as they apply course concepts and see the implications of their decisions as they go. Each activity is designed as a 15-minute experience, unless students eagerly replay for a better outcome.

ECON Everyday Current Events Blog

Our Econ Everyday blog saves instructors time bringing current, student-centered content into their course all semester long. Short articles, written for principles-level students, is tagged by topic to bring currency into your course. We also provide discussion questions to help you drive the conversation forward. Visit www.econeveryday.com and subscribe for updates.

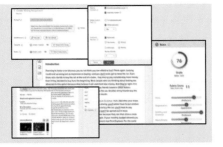

Writing Assignment Plus

Writing Assignment Plus delivers a learning experience that helps students improve their written communication skills and conceptual understanding. Faculty can assign, monitor, grade, and provide feedback on writing projects efficiently. Built-in grammar and writing review helps students improve writing quality while an originality check helps students correct central plagiarism before submission. End result? Improved workplace skills of writing in critical thinking.

CONTENTS IN BRIEF

CONTENTS

THE
MACROECONOMY TODAY

SIXTEENTH EDITION

Mc
Graw
Hill

ZUMA Press, Inc./Alamy Stock Photo

Jeff Chiu/AP Images

Glow Images

Pe3k/Shutterstock

LADO/Shutterstock

Hisham F. Ibrahim/Getty Images

PART

1

THE ECONOMIC CHALLENGE

People in Equatorial Guinea want more food, better shelter, and access to safe drinking water. Will they get it? That depends on how well their economy grows and how the fruits of economic growth are distributed. The same is true for middle-class Americans. We want better homes, newer cars, stylish clothes, the latest tech toys, more exotic vacations, and effective vaccines. Will we get these things? Again, that depends on how well the economy grows and how the fruits of economic growth are distributed.

These first few chapters look at what "the economy" is and how it grows. What are the *limits* to the production of goods and services? How does the interplay of market forces and government policy determine how much output will actually be produced and who will get it? How does a nation's capacity to produce goods and services *increase*—so that we can have *more* of the things we want? How will those goods be distributed?

1

"The Economist in Chief"

ZUMA Press, Inc./Alamy Stock Photo

CHAPTER 1

Economics: The Core Issues

LEARNING OBJECTIVES

After reading this chapter, you should know

LO1-1 What scarcity is.

LO1-2 How scarcity creates opportunity costs.

LO1-3 What the production possibilities curve represents.

LO1-4 The three core economic questions that every society must answer.

LO1-5 How market and government approaches to economic problems differ.

People understand that the president of the United States is the Commander in Chief of the armed forces. The president has the ultimate responsibility to decide when and how America's military forces will be deployed. He issues the orders that military officers must carry out. He is given credit for military successes and blame for military failures. He can't "pass the buck" down the line of command.

Less recognized is the president's role as "Economist in Chief." The president is held responsible not just for the *military* security of the United States, but for its *economic* security as well. Although he doesn't have the command powers in the economic arena that he has in the military arena, people expect him to take charge of the economy. They expect the Economist in Chief to keep the economy growing, to create jobs for everyone who wants one, and to prevent prices from rising too fast. Along the way, they expect the Economist in Chief to protect the environment, assure economic justice for all, and protect America's position in the global economy.

That is a tall order, especially in view of the president's limited constitutional powers to make economic policy decisions. The president can propose tax changes, spending priorities, and international trade deals, but the U.S. Congress must approve those policies. The economy is also buffeted by international and natural forces that no president can control. This was abundantly clear in 2020 when the "invisible enemy" of COVID-19 attacked the U.S. and derailed an otherwise prosperous economy. But no matter. Voters hold the Economist in Chief responsible for economic misfortunes, whether or not he is able to single-handedly prevent them, and give him credit for economic success.

What everyone ultimately wants is a prosperous and growing economy: an economy in which people can find good jobs, enjoy rising living standards and wealth, get the education they desire, and enjoy an array of creature comforts. And we want to enjoy this good life while protecting the environment, caring for the poor, and pursuing world peace.

How are we going to get all this? Is "the economy" some sort of perpetual motion machine that will keep churning out more goods and services every year? Clearly not. During the Great Recession of 2008–2009, the economy churned out less output, eliminated jobs, and reduced living standards and wealth. A lot of college graduates had to move back home when they couldn't find jobs. What went wrong?

Even after the Great Recession ended in June 2009, economic pain persisted. The growth of the economy was agonizingly slow, and unemployment remained high for another six years. Was that much distress really necessary? Couldn't the Economist in Chief have fixed these problems? These questions were debated intensely in the 2016 presidential election. Donald Trump promised "to make America great again" by creating more jobs, building more bridges and roads, strengthening the armed forces, and limiting both illegal immigration and unfair foreign competition. Voters decided to give him the opportunity to serve as an Economist in Chief.

The 2020 elections were largely a referendum on President Trump's performance as Economist in Chief. Voters gave Trump high marks for the growth of the economy during his first three years in office. Millions of new jobs had been created, incomes were up, wages were higher, and unemployment had fallen to record lows. Unfortunately, the coronavirus pandemic that swept across the world in early 2020 wiped out nearly all of those prior gains. In November 2020 the U.S. economy was still struggling to regain its footing: millions of Americans were still out of work, incomes were depressed, and people were fearful of a COVID-19 resurgence. They decided to vote for a new Economist in Chief.

The challenge for President Biden is to accelerate the economic recovery, while assuring people that the U.S. is well prepared to deal with any future viral attacks.

To succeed requires a knowledge of what makes an economy tick. How are prices, wages, employment, and other economic outcomes actually determined? Does Wall Street run the system? How about selfish, greedy capitalists? The banks? Or maybe foreign nations? Are incompetent bureaucrats and self-serving politicians the root of our occasional woes? Who, in fact, calls the shots?

The goal of this course is to understand how the economy works. To that end, we want to determine how *markets*—the free-wheeling exchange of goods and services—shape economic outcomes—everything from the price of this text to the national unemployment rate. Then we want to examine the role that government can and does play in (re)shaping economic performance. Do we need the government to assure adequate wages, fair prices, access to health care, or equal educational opportunities? Or can market forces alone give us these desirable outcomes? Once we've explored these issues, we'll be in a better position to evaluate what the Economist in Chief *can* do—and what he *should* do. We'll also better understand how we can make better economic decisions for ourselves.

Limited Resources

We'll start our inquiry with some harsh realities. In a world of unlimited resources, we could have all the goods we desired. We'd have time to do everything we wanted and enough money to buy everything we desired. We could produce enough to make everyone rich while protecting the environment and exploring the universe. The Economist in Chief could deliver everything voters asked for. Unfortunately, we don't live in that utopia: **We live in a world of limited resources.** Those limits are the root of our economic problems. They force us to make difficult decisions about how *best* to use our time, our money, and our resources. These are *economic* decisions.

In this first chapter, we'll examine how the problem of limited resources arises and the kinds of choices it forces us to make. As we'll see, **three core choices confront every nation:**

- **WHAT to produce with our limited resources.**
- **HOW to produce the goods and services we select.**
- **FOR WHOM goods and services are produced—that is, who should get them.**

We also have to decide who should answer these questions. Should people take care of their own health and retirement, or should the government provide a safety net of health care and pensions? Should the government regulate airfares or let the airlines set prices? Should Microsoft decide what features get included in a computer's operating system, or should the government make that decision? Should Facebook decide what personal information is protected, what posts should be permitted, or which ads can be targeted, or should the government make those decisions? Should interest rates be set by private banks alone, or should the government try to control interest rates? The battle over *who* should answer the core questions is often as contentious as the questions themselves.

THE ECONOMY IS US

To learn how the economy works, let's start with a simple truth: *The economy is us.* "The economy" is simply an abstraction referring to the grand sum of all our production and consumption activities. What we collectively produce is what the economy produces; what we collectively consume is what the economy consumes. In this sense, the concept of "the economy" is no more difficult than the concept of "the family." If someone tells you that the Jones family has an annual income of $42,000, you know that the reference is to the collective earnings of all the Joneses. Likewise, when someone reports that the nation's income is $22 trillion per year—as it now is—we should recognize that the reference is to the grand total of everyone's income. If we work fewer hours or get paid less, both family income *and* national income decline.

The same relationship between individual behavior and aggregate behavior applies to specific outputs. If we as individuals insist on driving cars rather than taking public transportation, the economy will produce millions of cars each year and consume vast quantities of oil. If we prefer to stream movies rather than watch them in theaters, then the economy will build fewer theaters and expand streaming services. If more consumers choose plant-based burgers rather than beef burgers, then cattle farms will shrink and plant processing expands. We also make choices on a collective level. We "produce" over $700 billion of national defense (e.g., military personnel, ships, planes, etc.) every year. This is a *choice* we make. If we want a different outcome, then we have to make a different choice. In each case, the output of the economy reflects the collective behavior of the 340 million individuals who participate in the U.S. economy.

We may not always be happy with the output of the economy, but we can't ignore the link between individual action and collective outcomes. If the highways are clogged and the air is polluted, we can't blame someone else for the transportation choices we made.

SCARCITY: THE CORE PROBLEM

Although we can change economic outcomes, we can't have everything we want. If you go to the mall with $20 in your pocket, you can buy only so much. The money in your pocket sets a *limit* to your spending.

The output of the entire economy is also limited. The limits in this case are set not by the amount of money in people's pockets, but by the resources available for producing goods and services. Everyone wants more housing, new schools, better transit systems, and a new car. We also want to explore space and bring safe water to the world's poor. But even a country as rich as the United States can't produce everything people want. So, like every other nation, we have to grapple with the core problem of **scarcity**—the fact that **there aren't enough resources available to satisfy all our desires.**

scarcity: Lack of enough resources to satisfy all desired uses of those resources.

Factors of Production

The resources used to produce goods and services are called **factors of production.** *The four basic factors of production are*

- *Land.*
- *Labor.*
- *Capital.*
- *Entrepreneurship.*

factors of production: Resource inputs used to produce goods and services, e.g., land, labor, capital, entrepreneurship.

These are the *inputs* needed to produce desired *outputs.* To produce this text, for example, we needed paper, printing presses, a building, and lots of labor. We also needed people with good ideas who could put it together. To produce the education you're getting in this class, we need not only a text but a classroom, a teacher, a blackboard, and maybe a computer as well. **Without factors of production, we simply can't produce anything.**

Land. The first factor of production, land, refers not just to the ground but to all natural resources. Crude oil, water, air, and minerals are all included in our concept of "land."

Labor. Labor too has several dimensions. It's not simply a question of how many bodies there are. When we speak of labor as a factor of production, we refer to the skills and abilities to produce goods and services. Hence, both the quantity and the quality of human resources are included in the "labor" factor.

Capital. The third factor of production is capital. In economics the term **capital** refers to final goods produced for use in further production. The residents of fishing villages in southern Thailand, for example, braid huge fishing nets. The sole purpose of these nets is to catch more fish. The nets themselves become a factor of production in obtaining the final goods (fish) that people desire. Thus, they're regarded as *capital.* Blast furnaces used to make steel and desks used to equip offices are also capital inputs.

capital: Final goods produced for use in the production of other goods, such as equipment and structures.

Entrepreneurship. The more land, labor, and capital we have, the more we can produce potential output. A farmer with 10,000 acres, 12 employees, and six tractors can grow more crops than a farmer with half those resources. But there's no guarantee that he will. The farmer with fewer resources may have better ideas about what to plant, when to irrigate, or how to harvest the crops. *It's not just a matter of what resources you have but also of how well you use them.* This is where the fourth factor of production—**entrepreneurship**—comes in. The entrepreneur is the person who sees the opportunity for new or better products and brings together the resources needed for producing them. If it weren't for entrepreneurs, Thai fishers would still be using sticks to catch fish. Without entrepreneurship, farmers would still be milking their cows by hand. If someone hadn't thought of a way to miniaturize electronic circuits, you wouldn't be able to text your friends.

entrepreneurship: The assembling of resources to produce new or improved products and technologies.

The role of entrepreneurs in economic progress is a key issue in the market versus government debate. The British economist John Maynard Keynes argued that free markets unleash the "animal spirits" of entrepreneurs, propelling innovation, technology, and growth. Critics of government regulation argue that government interference in the marketplace, however well intentioned, tends to stifle those very same animal spirits.

Limits to Output

No matter how an economy is organized, there's a limit to how much it can produce. The most evident limit is the amount of resources available for producing goods and services. One reason the United States can produce so much is that it has nearly 4 million square miles of land. Tonga, with less than 300 square miles of land, will never produce as much. The United States also has a population of more than 340 million people. That's a lot less than China (1.4 billion) but far larger than 200 other nations (Tonga has a population of less than 110,000). So an abundance of raw resources gives us the potential to produce a lot of output. But that greater production capacity isn't enough to satisfy all our desires. We're constantly scrambling for additional resources to build more houses, make better movies, and provide more health care. That imbalance between available resources and our wish list is one of the things that make the job of Economist in Chief so difficult: He can't deliver everything people want.

The science of **economics** helps us frame these choices. In a nutshell, economics is the study of how people use scarce resources. How do you decide how much time to spend studying? How does Google decide how many workers to hire? How does Tesla decide whether to use its factories to produce sport utility vehicles or sedans? What share of a nation's resources should be devoted to space exploration, the delivery of health care services, or pollution control? In every instance, **alternative ways of using scarce labor, land, and capital resources are always available, and we have to choose one use over another.**

economics: The study of how best to allocate scarce resources among competing uses.

OPPORTUNITY COSTS

Scientists have long sought to explore every dimension of space. President Kennedy initiated a lunar exploration program that successfully landed men on the moon on July 20, 1969. That only whetted the appetite for further space exploration. President George W. Bush initiated a program to land people on Mars, using the moon as a way station. Scientists believe that the biological, geophysical, and technical knowledge gained from the exploration of Mars will improve life here on Earth. But should we do it? In a world of unlimited resources, the answer would be an easy "yes." But we don't live in that world.

Every time we use scarce resources in one way, we give up the opportunity to use them in other ways. If we use more resources to explore space, we have fewer resources available for producing earthly goods. The forgone earthly goods represent the **opportunity costs** of a Mars expedition. *Opportunity cost is what is given up to get something else.* Even a so-called free lunch has an opportunity cost. The resources used to produce the lunch could have been used to produce something else. A trip to Mars has a much higher opportunity cost. President Obama decided those opportunity costs were too high: He scaled back the Mars programs to make more resources available for Earthly uses (like education, highway construction, and energy development). President Trump agreed. While calling space exploration "wonderful," he observed, "Right now, we have bigger problems—we've got to fix our potholes." He reallocated scarce resources from space exploration to domestic infrastructure (roads, bridges, airports).

Your economics class also has an opportunity cost. The building space used for your economics class can't be used to show movies at the same time. Your professor can't lecture (produce education) and repair motorcycles simultaneously. The decision to use these scarce resources (capital, labor) for an economics class implies producing less of other goods.

Even reading this text is costly. That cost is not measured in dollars and cents. The true (economic) cost is, instead, measured in terms of some alternative activity. What would you like to be doing right now? The more time you spend reading this text, the less time you have available for other uses of your time. The opportunity cost of reading this text is the best alternative use of your scarce time. If you are missing your favorite TV show, we'd say that show is the opportunity cost of reading this text. It is what you gave up to do this assignment. Hopefully, the benefits you get from studying will outweigh that cost. Otherwise, this wouldn't be the best way to use your scarce time.

opportunity cost: The most desired goods or services that are forgone in order to obtain something else.

Guns vs. Butter

One of the most difficult choices nations must make about resource use entails defense spending. After the September 11, 2001, terrorist attacks on the World Trade Center and Pentagon, American citizens overwhelmingly favored an increase in military spending. Even the unpopularity of the wars in Iraq and Afghanistan didn't quell the desire for more national defense. But national defense, like Mars exploration, requires the use of scarce resources; Americans wanted to feel *safe*. But there is a *cost* to assuring safety: The 1.4 million men and women who serve in the armed forces aren't available to build schools, program computers, or teach economics. Similarly, the land, labor, capital, and entrepreneurship devoted to producing military hardware aren't available for producing civilian goods. An *increase* in national defense implies more sacrifices of civilian goods and services. How many schools, hospitals, or cars are we willing to sacrifice in order to "produce" more national security? This is the "guns versus butter" dilemma that all nations confront.

PRODUCTION POSSIBILITIES

The opportunity costs implied by our every choice are easy to visualize. Suppose a nation can produce only two goods, trucks and tanks. To keep things simple, assume that labor (workers) is the only factor of production needed to produce either good. Although other

Production Options		
	Output of Trucks per Day	Output of Tanks per Day
Option A	5	0
Option B	4	2.0
Option C	3	3.0
Option D	2	3.8
Option E	1	4.5
Option F	0	5.0

TABLE 1.1

A Production Possibilities Schedule

As long as resources are limited, their use entails an opportunity cost. In this case, resources (labor) used to produce trucks can't be used for tank assembly at the same time. Hence, the forgone tanks are the opportunity cost of additional trucks. If all our resources were used to produce trucks (*Option A*), no tanks could be assembled. To produce tanks, we have to reduce truck production.

factors of production (land, machinery) are also needed in actual production, ignoring them for the moment does no harm. Assume further that we have a total of only 10 workers available per day to produce either trucks or tanks. That's a tiny workforce, but it makes the math a lot easier.

Our initial problem is to determine the *limits* of output. How many trucks or tanks *can* be produced in a day with available resources (our 10 workers)?

Before going any further, notice how opportunity costs emerge. If we use all 10 workers to manufacture trucks, how can we produce any tanks? All our workers will be busy building trucks; no one will be available to assemble tanks. In this case, forgone tanks would be the *opportunity cost* of a decision to employ all our resources in truck production.

We still don't know how many trucks could be produced with 10 workers or exactly how many tanks would be forgone by such a decision. To get these answers, we need more details about the production processes involved—specifically, how many workers are required to manufacture either good.

The Production Possibilities Curve

Table 1.1 summarizes the hypothetical choices, or **production possibilities,** that we confront in this case. Suppose we wanted to produce only trucks (i.e., no tanks). Row *A* of the table shows the *maximum* number of trucks we could produce. We have 10 workers available. Suppose it takes 2 workers to manufacture a truck in a day. Then, the *maximum* number of trucks we can produce is 5 per day.

Producing five trucks per day leaves no workers available to produce tanks. Our 10 available workers are all being used to produce trucks. Look at option *A* of Table 1.1; we've got "butter" (trucks) but no "guns" (tanks). If we want tanks, we roll back truck production. The remainder of Table 1.1 illustrates the trade-offs we confront in this simple case. By cutting truck production from five to four trucks per day (Option *B*), we reduce labor use in truck production from 10 workers to 8. That leaves 2 workers available for other uses, including the production of tanks.

If we employ these 2 workers to assemble tanks, we can build two tanks a day. We would then end up on row *B* of the table with four trucks and two tanks per day. What's the opportunity cost of these two tanks? It's the one additional truck (the fifth truck) that we could have produced but didn't.

As we proceed down the rows of Table 1.1, the nature of opportunity costs becomes apparent. Each additional tank built implies the loss (opportunity cost) of truck output. Likewise, every truck produced implies the loss of some tank output.

Choices, Choices These trade-offs between truck and tank production are illustrated in the production possibilities curve of Figure 1.1. *Each point on the production possibilities curve depicts an alternative mix of output* that could be produced. In this case, each point represents

production possibilities: The alternative combinations of final goods and services that could be produced in a given period with all available resources and technology.

FIGURE 1.1

A Production Possibilities Curve

A production possibilities curve (PPC) describes the various output combinations that could be produced in a given time period with available resources and technology. It represents a menu of output choices an economy confronts.

Point *B* indicates that we could produce a *combination* of four trucks and two tanks per day. Alternatively, we could produce one less truck and a third tank by moving to point *C*.

Points *A, D, E,* and *F* illustrate still other output combinations that *could* be produced. This curve is a graphic illustration of the production possibilities schedule in Table 1.1.

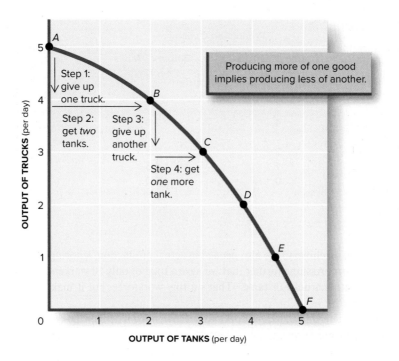

a different combination of trucks and tanks that we could produce in a single day using all available resources (10 workers in this case).

Notice in particular how points *A* through *F* in Figure 1.1 represent the choices described in each row of Table 1.1. At point *A*, we're producing five trucks per day and no tanks. As we move down the curve from point *A*, we're producing fewer trucks and more tanks. At point *B*, truck production has dropped from five to four vehicles per day while tank assembly has increased from zero to two. In other words, we've given up one truck to get two tanks assembled. The opportunity cost of those tanks is the one truck that is given up. A production possibilities curve, then, is simply a graphic summary of production possibilities, as described in Table 1.1. As such, *the production possibilities curve illustrates two essential principles*:

- *Scarce resources.* There's a limit to the amount of output we can produce in a given time period with available resources and technology. In this case, we can't produce more than 5 tanks or 5 trucks.
- *Opportunity costs.* We can obtain additional quantities of any particular good only by reducing the potential production of another good. To get more trucks, we have to produce fewer tanks, and vice versa.

In an economy as vast as the United States, we can, of course, produce millions of trucks and millions of tanks. But that doesn't change the basic principles. Every tank produced uses resources that could have been used to produce something else. This principle helps explain why both presidents Obama and Trump chose to devote fewer resources to space exploration. They felt the opportunity costs (such as reduced education or less infrastructure) were simply too high.

Opportunity costs made headlines again in 2020. When the potential severity of the COVID-19 pandemic became evident, there was a sense of desperation about the availability of ventilators, the breathing machines that severely ill patients needed. The availability of hand sanitizers was also an urgent concern. How could we get *more* of these essential medical supplies? The answer in part was to change the *mix* of output. Auto companies altered their production lines to produce ventilators. Distilleries altered their whiskey-making process in order to produce more high-proof ethanol, the key ingredient in hand sanitizers. By changing production in these ways, the nation moved to a more desirable mix of output (the WHAT outcome).

Increasing Opportunity Costs

The shape of the production possibilities curve reflects another limitation on our choices. Notice how opportunity costs increase as we move along the production possibilities curve. When we cut truck output from five to four (step 1, Figure 1.1), we get two tanks (step 2). When we cut truck production further, however (step 3), we get only one tank per truck given up (step 4). The opportunity cost of tank production is increasing. This process of increasing opportunity cost continues. By the time we give up the last truck (row *F*), tank output increases by only 0.5: We get only half a tank for the last truck given up. These increases in opportunity cost are reflected in the outward bend of the production possibilities curve.

Why do opportunity costs increase? Mostly because it's difficult to move resources from one industry to another. It's easy to transform trucks to tanks on a blackboard. In the real world, however, resources don't adapt so easily. Workers who assemble trucks may not have the right skills for tank assembly. As we continue to transfer labor from one industry to the other, we start getting fewer tanks for every truck we give up.

The difficulties entailed in transferring labor skills, capital, and entrepreneurship from one industry to another are so universal that we often speak of the *law* of *increasing opportunity cost.* This law says that we must give up ever-increasing quantities of other goods and services in order to get more of a particular good. The law isn't based solely on the limited versatility of individual workers. The *mix* of factor inputs makes a difference as well. Truck assembly requires less capital than tank assembly. In a pinch, wheels can be mounted on a truck almost completely by hand, whereas tank treads require more sophisticated machinery. As we move labor from truck assembly to tank assembly, available capital may restrict our output capabilities.

The Cost of North Korea's Military

The production possibilities curve illustrates why the core economic decision about WHAT to produce is so difficult: We can't have everything we want and, worse yet, getting more of one thing implies getting less of something else. We are forced to make difficult choices.

Consider, for example, North Korea's decision to maintain a large military. North Korea is a relatively small country: Its population of 26 million ranks 50th in the world. Yet North Korea maintains the fourth-largest army in the world and continues to develop a nuclear weapons capability. To do so, it allocates as much as 20 percent of all its resources to feeding, clothing, and equipping its military forces. As a consequence, there aren't enough resources available to produce food. Without adequate machinery, seeds, fertilizer, or irrigation, North Korea's farmers can't produce enough food to feed the population (see World View "North Korean Food Rations Cut"). As Figure 1.2 illustrates, the opportunity cost of "guns" in Korea is a lot of needed "butter."

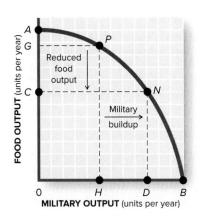

FIGURE 1.2

The Cost of War

North Korea devotes as much as 20 percent of its output to the military. The opportunity cost of this decision is reduced output of food. As the military expands from 0*H* to 0*D,* food output drops from 0*G* to 0*C.*

WORLD VIEW

WORLD'S LARGEST ARMIES

Rank	Country	Active Military
1	China	2,183,000
2	India	1,362,000
3	United States	1,282,000
4	North Korea	1,280,000
5	Russia	1,014,000
6	Pakistan	654,000
7	South Korea	525,000
8	Iran	523,000
9	Turkey	510,600
10	Vietnam	482,000

Source: U.S. Central Intelligence Agency 2019.

CRITICAL ANALYSIS: Nations "produce" national defense by employing land, labor, and capital in their armed forces. The **opportunity cost** of those "guns" is less "butter."

What is the opportunity cost of North Korea's army?

Ed Jones/AFP/Getty Images

During World War II, the United States confronted a similar trade-off. In 1944 nearly 40 percent of all U.S. output was devoted to the military. Civilian goods were so scarce that they had to be rationed. Staples like butter, sugar, and gasoline were doled out in small quantities. Even golf balls were rationed. In North Korea, golf balls would be a luxury even without a military buildup. As the share of North Korea's output devoted to the military increased, even basic food production became more difficult. (See World View "North Korean Food Rations Cut.")

WORLD VIEW

NORTH KOREAN FOOD RATIONS CUT

The United Nations estimates that 40 percent of North Korea's population—10.4 million people—experienced "food insecurity" in 2019. Most North Koreans depend on government-supplied food rations of rice, potatoes, and kimchi (fermented cabbage). Due to the worst harvests in a decade, however, the government slashed daily food rations from 380 grams (13.4 ounces) of food to only 300 grams (10.6 ounces). That is only half of the U.N. recommendation of at least 600 grams per day.

Source: United Nations Food and Agriculture Organization and news reports of May–November 2019.

NORTH KOREA RESUMES MISSILE LAUNCHES

After an 18-month hiatus, North Korea resumed ballistic missile launches in May. Since then, they have fired off seven more missiles, including one from a reputed submarine. Although keeping his promise not to test long-range missiles while continuing nuclear negotiations with President Trump, Kim Jong-un has vowed to strengthen North Korea's military capabilities. Analysts estimate that North Korea is now spending close to $2 billion a year on its nuclear and missile programs.

Source: Media reports, May–December 2019.

CRITICAL ANALYSIS: North Korea's inability to feed itself is partly due to maintaining its large army: Resources used for the military aren't available for producing food (**opportunity costs**).

Percentage of Output Allocated to Military

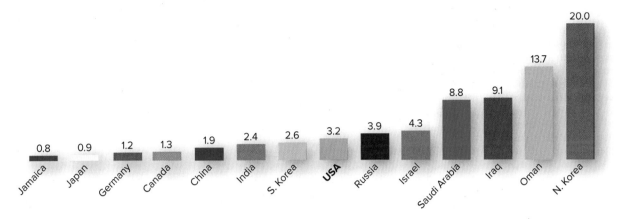

FIGURE 1.3
The Military Share of Output

The share of total output allocated to the military indicates the opportunity cost of maintaining an army. North Korea has the highest cost, using one-fifth of its resources for military purposes. Although China and the United States have much larger armies, their military share of output is much smaller.

Source: Stockholm International Peace Research Institute and U.S. Central Intelligence Agency (2018 data).

Figure 1.3 illustrates how other nations divide available resources between military and civilian production. The $650 billion the United States now spends on national defense absorbs only 3.2 percent of total output. This made the opportunity costs of the post-9/11 military buildup and the wars in Iraq and Afghanistan less painful. By contrast, North Korea's commitment to military spending (20 percent) implies a very high opportunity cost.

Efficiency

Not all of the choices on the production possibilities curve are equally desirable. They are, however, all *efficient*. **Efficiency** means squeezing *maximum* output out of available resources. Every point of the PPC satisfies this condition. Although the *mix* of output changes as we move around the production possibilities curve (Figures 1.1 and 1.2), at every point we are getting as much *total* output as physically possible. Because efficiency in production means simply getting the most from what you've got, **every point on the production possibilities curve is efficient.** At every point on the curve, we are using all available resources in the best way we know how.

efficiency: Maximum output of a good from the resources used in production.

Inefficiency

There's no guarantee, of course, that we'll always use resources so efficiently. *A production possibilities curve shows* **potential** *output, not* **actual** *output.* If we're inefficient, actual output will be less than that potential. This happens. In the real world, workers sometimes loaf on the job. Or they call in sick and go to a baseball game instead of working. Managers don't always give the clearest directions or stay in touch with advancing technology. Even students sometimes fail to put forth their best effort on homework assignments. This kind of slippage can prevent us from achieving maximum production. When that happens, we end up *inside* the PPC rather than *on* it.

Point *Y* in Figure 1.4 illustrates the consequences of inefficient production. At point *Y*, we're producing only three trucks and two tanks. This is less than our potential. We could assemble a third tank without cutting back truck production (point *C*). Or we could get an extra truck without sacrificing any tank output (point *B*). Instead we're producing *inside* the production possibilities curve at point *Y*. **Whenever we're producing inside the production possibilities curve, we are forgoing the opportunity of producing (and consuming) additional output.**

FIGURE 1.4

**Points Inside and Outside
the PPC Curve**

Points outside the production possibilities curve (point *X*) are unattainable with available resources and technology. Points inside the PPC (point *Y*) represent the incomplete use of available resources. Only points on the PPC (*A, B, C*) represent maximum use of our production capabilities.

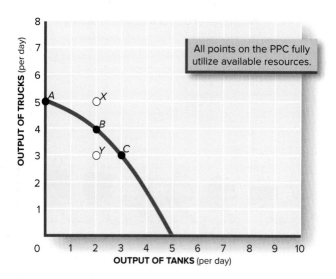

Unemployment

We can end up inside the production possibilities curve by utilizing resources inefficiently or simply by not using all available resources. This happened repeatedly in the Great Recession of 2008–2009. In October 2009, more than 15 million Americans were unemployed (see Front Page Economics "Jobless Workers Outnumber Manufacturing Workers"). These men and women were ready, willing, and available to work, but no one hired them. As a result, we were stuck *inside* the PPC, producing less output than we could have (like point *Y* in Figure 1.4). The same problem surfaced in 2020 when the COVID-19 pandemic threw millions of Americans out of work and pushed the economy well below its production possibilities. The goal of U.S. economic policy is to create more jobs and keep the United States on its production possibilities curve.

Economic Growth

The challenge of getting to the production possibilities curve increases with each passing day. People are born every day. As they age, they enter the labor force as new workers. In the United States, over 1 million new workers enter the marketplace every year. They want jobs,

---

FRONT PAGE ECONOMICS

JOBLESS WORKERS OUTNUMBER MANUFACTURING WORKERS

The number of jobless workers last month surpassed 15 million, according to the U.S. Bureau of Labor Statistics. The number of unemployed persons has risen every month since mid-2007 and is now double the level of unemployment that existed when the Great Recession started. Those 15 million *unemployed* workers now exceed the number of workers actually holding jobs in U.S. manufacturing.

Source: U.S. Bureau of Labor Statistics, October 2009.

CRITICAL ANALYSIS: In 2009 the U.S. economy was producing inside its production possibilities curve (like point *Y* in Figure 1.4), leaving millions of workers jobless and total output well below its potential. Our goal is to produce at a point on the PPC (**efficiency**).

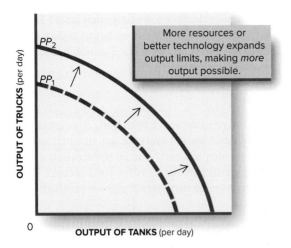

FIGURE 1.5

Growth: Increasing Production Possibilities

A production possibilities curve is based on *available* resources and technology. If more resources or better technology becomes available, production possibilities will increase. This economic growth is illustrated by the *shift* from PP_1 to PP_2.

and we want the output they can produce. Technology keeps advancing every year, too. That means every worker can produce *more* output. These increases in available labor and technology keep pushing the production possibilities curve outward. This **economic growth** is a good thing in the sense that it allows us to produce more goods and raise living standards. With economic growth, countries can have more guns *and* more butter (see Figure 1.5). But to get the benefits of that growth, we have to keep creating more and more jobs: We are always chasing a moving target. Nations that fail to achieve that growth risk declining living standards, as population growth exceeds output growth. That is a common problem in many of the world's poorest nations.

economic growth: An increase in output (real GDP); an expansion of production possibilities.

THREE BASIC DECISIONS

Production possibilities define the output choices that a nation confronts. From these choices, every nation must make some basic decisions. As we noted at the beginning of this chapter, the three core economic questions are

* *WHAT to produce.*
* *HOW to produce.*
* *FOR WHOM to produce.*

What

There are millions of points along a production possibilities curve, and each one represents a different mix of output. Unfortunately, we can choose only *one* of these points at any time. The point we choose determines what mix of output actually gets produced. That choice determines how many guns are produced, and how much butter—or how many space expeditions are taken and how many sewage treatment facilities get built.

The production possibilities curve itself doesn't tell us which mix of output is best; it just lays out a menu of available choices. It's up to us to pick out the one and only mix of output that will be produced at a given time. This WHAT decision is a fundamental decision every nation must make.

How

Decisions must also be made about HOW to produce. Should we generate electricity by burning coal, smashing atoms, or harnessing solar power? Should we harvest ancient forests even if that destroys endangered owls or other animal species? Should we dump municipal and industrial waste into nearby rivers, or should we dispose of it in some other way? Should we use children to harvest crops and stitch clothes, or should we use only adult labor? There are lots of different ways of producing goods and services, and someone has to make a decision about which production methods to use. The HOW decision is a question not just of efficiency but of social values as well.

For Whom

After we've decided what to produce and how, we must address a third basic question: FOR WHOM? Who is going to get the output produced? Should everyone get an equal share? Should everyone wear the same clothes and drive identical cars? Should some people get to enjoy seven-course banquets while others forage in garbage cans for food scraps? How should the goods and services an economy produces be distributed? Are we satisfied with the way output is now distributed?

THE MECHANISMS OF CHOICE

Answers to the questions of WHAT, HOW, and FOR WHOM largely define an economy. But who formulates the answers? Who actually decides which goods are produced, what technologies are used, or how incomes are distributed?

The Invisible Hand of a Market Economy

Adam Smith had an answer back in 1776. In his classic work *The Wealth of Nations*, the Scottish economist Smith said the "invisible hand" determines what gets produced, how, and for whom. The invisible hand he referred to wasn't a creature from a science fiction movie but, instead, a characterization of the way markets work.

Consider the decision about how many cars to produce in the United States. Who makes that decision? There's no "auto czar" who dictates how many vehicles will be produced this year. Not even General Motors can make such a decision. Instead, the *market* decides how many cars to produce. Millions of consumers signal their desire to have a car by browsing the Internet, visiting showrooms, and buying cars. Their purchases flash a green light to producers, who see the potential to earn more profits. To do so, they'll increase auto output. If consumers stop buying cars, profits will disappear. Producers will respond by reducing output, laying off workers, and even closing factories, as they did during the recession of 2008–2009 and again in 2020.

Notice how the invisible hand moves us along the production possibilities curve. If consumers demand more cars, the mix of output will include more cars and fewer of other goods. If auto production is scaled back, the displaced autoworkers will end up producing other goods and services, changing the mix of output in the opposite direction. In this scenario, consumers and producers are collectively deciding WHAT the economy will produce.

Adam Smith's invisible hand is now called the **market mechanism.** Notice that it doesn't require any direct contact between consumers and producers. Communication is indirect, transmitted by market prices and sales. Indeed, *the essential feature of the market mechanism is the price signal*. If you want something and have sufficient income, you can buy it. If enough people do the same thing, the total sales of that product will rise, and perhaps its price will as well. Producers, seeing sales and prices rise, will want to exploit this profit potential. To do so, they'll attempt to acquire a larger share of available resources and use it to produce the goods we desire. That's how the "invisible hand" works.

The market mechanism can also answer the HOW question. To maximize their profits, producers seek the lowest-cost method of producing a good. By observing prices in the marketplace, they can identify the cheapest method and adopt it.

The market mechanism can also resolve the FOR WHOM question. A market distributes goods to the highest bidder. Individuals who are willing and able to pay the most for a product tend to get it in a pure market economy. That's why someone else—not you—is driving the newest McLaren 720S.

market mechanism: The use of market prices and sales to signal desired outputs (or resource allocations).

How does the market decide who gets this car?

somchai choochat/Shutterstock

Adam Smith was so impressed with the ability of the market mechanism to answer the basic WHAT, HOW, and FOR WHOM questions that he urged government to "leave it alone" **(laissez faire). Adam Smith believed the price signals and responses of the marketplace were likely to do a better job of allocating resources than any government could.**

laissez faire: The doctrine of "leave it alone," of nonintervention by government in the market mechanism.

Government Intervention

The laissez-faire policy Adam Smith favored has always had its share of critics. The German economist Karl Marx emphasized how free markets tend to concentrate wealth and power in the hands of the few at the expense of the many. As he saw it, unfettered markets permit the capitalists (those who own the machinery and factories) to enrich themselves while the proletariat (the workers) toil long hours for subsistence wages. **Marx argued that the government not only had to intervene but had to *own* all the means of production**—the factories, the machinery, the land—in order to avoid savage inequalities. In *Das Kapital* (1867) and the revolutionary *Communist Manifesto* (1848), he laid the foundation for a communist state in which the government would be the master of economic outcomes.

The British economist John Maynard Keynes offered a less drastic solution. The market, he conceded, was pretty efficient in organizing production and building better mousetraps. However, individual producers and workers had no control over the broader economy. The cumulative actions of so many economic agents could easily tip the economy in the wrong direction. A completely unregulated market might veer off in one direction and then another as producers all rushed to increase output at the same time or throttled back production in a herdlike manner. The government, Keynes reasoned, could act like a pressure gauge, letting off excess steam or building it up as the economy needed. With the government maintaining overall balance in the economy, the market could live up to its performance expectations. While assuring a stable, full-employment environment, the government might also be able to redress excessive inequalities. **In Keynes's view, government should play an active but not all-inclusive role in managing the economy.**

Conservatives vs. Liberals

These historical views shed perspective on today's political debates. The core of most debates is some variation of the WHAT, HOW, or FOR WHOM questions. Much of the debate is how these questions should be answered. Conservatives favor Adam Smith's laissez-faire approach, with minimal government interference in the markets. Liberals, by contrast, think government intervention is needed to improve market outcomes. Conservatives resist workplace regulation, price controls, and minimum wages because such interventions might impair market efficiency. Liberals argue that such interventions temper the excesses of the market and promote both equity and efficiency.

World Opinion. The debate over how best to manage the economy is not unique to the United States. **Countries around the world confront the same choice between reliance on the market and reliance on the government.** Public opinion clearly favors the market system, as World View "Market Reliance vs. Government Reliance?" documents. Yet few countries have ever relied exclusively on either the markets or the government to manage their economy.

Degrees of Market Reliance. The World View "Index of Economic Freedom" categorizes nations by the extent of their actual market reliance. Hong Kong scores high on this index because its tax rates are relatively low, the public sector is comparatively small, and there are few restrictions on private investment or trade. By contrast, North Korea scores extremely low because the government owns all property, directly allocates resources, sets wages, rations food, and limits trade. In other words, Hong Kong is the most market-reliant; North Korea is the most government-reliant.

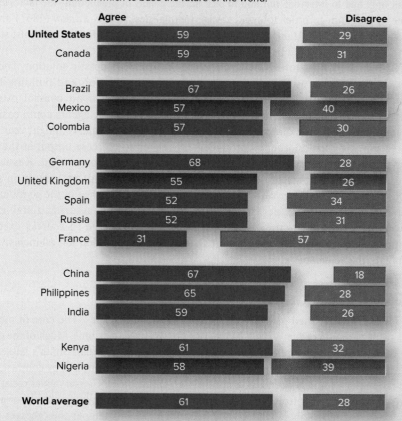

WORLD VIEW

MARKET RELIANCE VS. GOVERNMENT RELIANCE?

A public opinion poll conducted in countries from around the world found a striking global consensus that the free market economic system is best. In all but one country polled, a majority or plurality agreed with the statement that "the free enterprise system and free market economy is the best system on which to base the future of the world."

Source: GlobeScan Toronto–London–San Francisco 2010.

The free enterprise system and free market economy is the best system on which to base the future of the world.

	Agree	Disagree
United States	59	29
Canada	59	31
Brazil	67	26
Mexico	57	40
Colombia	57	30
Germany	68	28
United Kingdom	55	26
Spain	52	34
Russia	52	31
France	31	57
China	67	18
Philippines	65	28
India	59	26
Kenya	61	32
Nigeria	58	39
World average	61	28

CRITICAL ANALYSIS: Most people around the world believe that markets do a good job of answering the core questions of WHAT, HOW, and FOR WHOM. They favor a **laissez-faire** approach, albeit with government safeguards.

The Heritage rankings simply *describe* differences in the extent of market/government reliance across different nations. By themselves, they don't tell us which mix of market and government reliance is best. Moreover, the individual rankings change over time. In 1989 Russia began a massive transformation from a state-controlled economy to a more market-oriented economy. Some of the former Soviet republics (e.g., Estonia) became relatively free, while others (e.g., Turkmenistan) still rely on extensive government control of the economy. China has greatly expanded the role of private markets in the last 20 years, and Cuba is grudgingly moving in the same direction in fits and starts. Venezuela has moved in the opposite direction, with sharply increased government control of production and prices.

WORLD VIEW

INDEX OF ECONOMIC FREEDOM

Singapore ranks number one among the world's nations in economic freedom. It achieves that status with low tax rates, free-trade policies, minimal government regulation, and secure property rights. These and other economic indicators place Singapore at the top of the Heritage Foundation's 2020 country rankings by the degree of "economic freedom." The "most free" and the "least free" (repressed) economies on the list of 186 countries are listed here:

Greatest Economic Freedom	Least Economic Freedom
Singapore	North Korea
Hong Kong	Venezuela
New Zealand	Cuba
Australia	Eritrea
Switzerland	Republic of Congo
Ireland	Bolivia
United Kingdom	Zimbabwe
Denmark	Sudan

Source: *2020 Index of Economic Freedom*, Washington, DC: Heritage Foundation, 2020.

CRITICAL ANALYSIS: Nations differ in how much they rely on the **market mechanism** or government intervention to shape economic outcomes. Nations that rely the least on government intervention score highest ("most free") on this Index of Economic Freedom.

Notice that the United States is not on the World View list. Although the United States relies heavily on private markets to make WHAT, HOW, and FOR WHOM decisions, it lags behind Hong Kong, Canada, and other nations on the Heritage Index. In 2020 the United States came in 17th, down a notch from earlier years. That modest decline was largely due to the increased international trade barriers erected by President Trump. This tug-of-war between more government regulation and more market reliance continues—in both public opinion and the U.S. Congress.

A Mixed Economy

No one advocates *complete* dependence on markets, nor *total* government control of economic resources. Neither Adam Smith's invisible hand nor the governments' very visible hand always works perfectly. As a result, *the United States, like most nations, uses a combination of market signals and government directives to direct economic outcomes.* The resulting compromises are called **mixed economies.**

The reluctance of countries around the world to rely exclusively on either market signals or government directives is due to the recognition that both mechanisms can and do fail on occasion. As we've seen, market signals are capable of answering the three core questions of WHAT, HOW, and FOR WHOM. But the answers may not be the best possible ones.

mixed economy: An economy that uses both market signals and government directives to allocate goods and resources.

Market Failure

When market signals don't give the best possible answers to the WHAT, HOW, and FOR WHOM questions, we say that the market mechanism has *failed.* Specifically, **market failure** means that the invisible hand has failed to achieve the best possible outcomes. If the market fails, we end up with the wrong (*sub*optimal) mix of output, too much unemployment, polluted air, or an inequitable distribution of income.

market failure: An imperfection in the market mechanism that prevents optimal outcomes.

In a market-driven economy, for example, producers will select production methods based on cost. Cost-driven production decisions, however, may encourage a factory to spew pollution into the environment rather than to use cleaner but more expensive methods of production. The resulting pollution may be so bad that society ends up worse off as a result of the extra production. In such a case we may need government intervention to force better answers to the WHAT and HOW questions.

We could also let the market decide who gets to consume cigarettes. In that laissez-faire situation, anyone with enough money to buy a pack of cigarettes would then be entitled to smoke. What if, however, children aren't experienced enough to balance the risks of smoking against the pleasures? What if nonsmokers are harmed by secondhand smoke? In this case as well, the market's answer to the FOR WHOM question might not be optimal.

After the experience with the coronavirus in 2020, nearly everyone recognized that markets alone cannot assure optimal outcomes. While secondhand smoke is a significant problem for unregulated markets, COVID-19 contagion is far more deadly. If we had relied on free choice to determine how much social distancing or treatment was undertaken, many more people would have died from COVID-19. There was near universal consensus that government intervention (regulation, subsidized care, etc.) was needed to get better results.

Then there is the question of fairness. What if the market mechanism distributed incomes so unequally that some people couldn't afford basic necessities while others engaged in conspicuous consumption? Would that be *fair?* The market itself doesn't worry about fairness, but society might. In that event, we might want the government to intervene to change the answer to the FOR WHOM question.

Government Failure

Clearly, government intervention might be needed to correct market failures. If successful, the resulting mix of market signals and government directives would be an improvement over a purely market-driven economy. But government intervention may fail as well. **Government failure** occurs when government intervention fails to improve market outcomes or actually makes them worse.

Government failure often occurs in unintended ways. For example, the government may intervene to force an industry to clean up its pollution. The government's directives may impose such high costs that the industry closes factories and lays off workers. Some cutbacks in output might be appropriate, but they could also prove excessive. The government might also mandate pollution control technologies that are too expensive or even obsolete. None of this has to happen, but it might. If it does, government failure will have worsened economic outcomes.

The government might also fail if it interferes with the market's answer to the FOR WHOM question. For 50 years, communist China distributed goods by government directive, not market performance. Incomes were more equal, but uniformly low. To increase output and living standards, China turned to market incentives. As entrepreneurs responded to these incentives, living standards rose dramatically—even while inequality increased. That surge in living standards made the vast majority of Chinese believers in the power of free markets (see the World View appearing earlier in this chapter).

Excessive taxes and transfer payments can also worsen economic outcomes. If the government raises taxes on the rich to pay welfare benefits for the poor, neither the rich nor the poor may see much purpose in working. In that case, the attempt to give everybody a "fair" share of the pie might end up shrinking the size of the pie. If that happened, society could end up worse off.

Seeking Balance

None of these failures has to occur. But they might. *The challenge for any society is to minimize economic failures by selecting the appropriate balance of market signals and government directives.* This isn't an easy task. To begin with, it requires that we share some common perspectives about what mix of output is best, what the balance between production and environmental

government failure:
Government intervention that fails to improve economic outcomes.

protection should be, and how much inequality is fair. On a more mundane level, it also requires that we know how markets work and why they sometimes fail. We also need to know what policy options the government has and how and when they might work. That's a lot to ask for.

WHAT ECONOMICS IS ALL ABOUT

Understanding how economies function is the basic purpose of studying economics. We seek to know how an economy is organized, how it behaves, and how successfully it achieves its basic objectives. Then, if we're lucky, we can discover better ways of attaining those same objectives.

Ends vs. Means

Economists don't formulate an economy's objectives. Instead they focus on the *means* available for achieving given *goals.* In 1978, for example, the U.S. Congress identified "full employment" as a major economic goal. Congress then directed future presidents (and their economic advisers) to formulate policies that would enable us to achieve full employment. The economist's job is to help design policies that will best achieve this and other economic goals.

The same distinction between ends and means is integral to your own life. Your *goal* (the ends) may be to achieve a specific career. The immediate question is how best to achieve that goal (the means). Should you major in economics? Take computer science? Study art history? Surely, you hope that the course choices you make will best help you attain your career goals. Economists can help select those courses based on studies of other students, their majors, and their career outcomes.

Normative vs. Positive Analysis

The distinction between ends and means is mirrored in the difference between *normative* analysis and *positive* analysis. Normative analysis incorporates subjective judgments about what *ought* to be done. Positive analysis focuses on how things might be done without subjective judgments of what is "best." The Heritage Index of Economic Freedom (World View), for example, constitutes a *positive* analysis to the extent that it objectively describes global differences in the extent of market reliance. That effort entails collecting, sorting, and ranking mountains of data. Heritage slides into *normative* analysis when it suggests that market reliance is tantamount to "economic freedom" and inherently superior to more government intervention—that markets are good and governments are bad.

Debates over the core FOR WHOM question likewise reflect both positive and normative analysis. A positive analysis would observe that the U.S. incomes are very "unequal," with the richest 20 percent of the population getting half of all income (see table in Figure 2.3). That's an observable fact—that is, positive analysis. To characterize that same distribution as "inequitable" or "unfair" is to transform (positive) fact into (normative) judgment. Economists are free, of course, to offer their judgments but must be careful to distinguish positive and normative perspectives.

Macro vs. Micro

The study of economics is typically divided into two parts: macroeconomics and microeconomics. **Macroeconomics** focuses on the behavior of an entire economy—the "big picture." In macroeconomics we worry about such national goals as full employment, control of inflation, and economic growth, without worrying about the well-being or behavior of specific individuals or firms. The essential concern of macroeconomics is to understand and improve the performance of the economy as a whole.

Microeconomics is concerned with the details of this big picture. In microeconomics we focus on the individuals, firms, and government agencies that actually compose the larger economy. Our interest here is in the behavior of individual economic actors. What are their goals? How can they best achieve these goals with their limited resources? How will they respond to various incentives and opportunities?

macroeconomics: The study of aggregate economic behavior, of the economy as a whole.

microeconomics: The study of individual behavior in the economy, of the components of the larger economy.

A primary concern of *macro*economics, for example, is to determine how much money, *in total,* consumers will spend on goods and services. In *micro*economics, the focus is much narrower. In micro, attention is paid to purchases of *specific* goods and services rather than just aggregated totals. Macro likewise concerns itself with the level of *total* business investment, while micro examines how *individual* businesses make their investment decisions.

Although they operate at different levels of abstraction, macro and micro are intrinsically related. Macro (aggregate) outcomes depend on micro behavior, and micro (individual) behavior is affected by macro outcomes. One can't fully understand how an economy works until one understands how all the individual participants behave. But just as you can drive a car without knowing how its engine is constructed, you can observe how an economy runs without completely disassembling it. In macroeconomics we observe that the car goes faster when the accelerator is depressed and that it slows when the brake is applied. That's all we need to know in most situations. At times, however, the car breaks down. When it does, we have to know something more about how the pedals work. This leads us into micro studies. How does each part work? Which ones can or should be fixed?

Our interest in microeconomics is motivated by more than our need to understand how the larger economy works. The "parts" of the economic engine are people. To the extent that we care about the well-being of individuals, we have a fundamental interest in microeconomic behavior and outcomes. In this regard, we examine how individual consumers and business firms seek to achieve specific goals in the marketplace. The goals aren't always related to output. Gary Becker won the 1992 Nobel Prize in Economics for demonstrating how economic principles also affect decisions to marry, to have children, to engage in criminal activities—or even to complete homework assignments in an economics class.

Theory vs. Reality

The economy is much too vast and complex to describe and explain in one course (or one lifetime). We need to simplify it. To do so, we focus on basic relationships, ignoring annoying details. We develop basic principles of economic behavior and then use those principles to predict and explain economic events. This means that we formulate theories, or *models,* of economic behavior and then use those theories to evaluate and design economic policy.

Our model of consumer behavior assumes, for example, that people buy less of a good when its price rises. In reality, however, people *may* buy *more* of a good at increased prices, especially if those high prices create a certain snob appeal or if prices are expected to increase still further. In predicting consumer responses to price increases, we typically ignore such possibilities by *assuming* that the price of the good in question is the *only* thing that changes. This assumption of "other things remaining equal" (unchanged) (in Latin, *ceteris paribus*) allows us to make straightforward predictions. If instead we described consumer responses to increased prices in any and all circumstances (allowing everything to change at once), every prediction would be accompanied by a book full of exceptions and qualifications. We'd look more like lawyers than economists.

ceteris paribus: The assumption of nothing else changing.

Although the assumption of *ceteris paribus* makes it easier to formulate economic theory and policy, it also increases the risk of error. If other things do change in significant ways, our predictions (and policies) may fail. But like weather forecasters, we continue to make predictions, knowing that occasional failure is inevitable. In so doing, we're motivated by the conviction that it's better to be approximately right than to be dead wrong.

Imperfect Knowledge. One last word of warning before you read further. Economics claims to be a science in pursuit of basic truths. We want to understand and explain how the economy works without getting tangled up in subjective value judgments. This may be an impossible task. First, it's not clear where the truth lies. For more than 200 years economists have been arguing about what makes the economy tick. None of the competing theories has performed spectacularly well. Indeed, few economists have successfully predicted major economic events with any consistency. Even annual forecasts of inflation, unemployment, and output are regularly in error. Worse still, never-ending arguments about what caused a major economic event continue long after it occurs. In fact, economists are still arguing over the primary causes of the Great Depression of the 1930s!

In view of all these debates and uncertainties, don't expect to learn everything there is to know about the economy today in this text or course. Our goals are more modest. We want to develop a reasonable perspective on economic behavior, an understanding of basic principles. With this foundation, you should acquire a better view of how the economy works. Daily news reports on economic events should make more sense. Congressional debates on tax and budget policies should take on more meaning. You may even develop some insights that you can apply toward running a business, planning a career, or simply managing your scarce time and money more efficiently.

DECISIONS FOR **TOMORROW**

What Is the Cost of Going Green?

People are worried about the future of the planet. Continued population and production growth have raised concerns about global warming. The earth's temperature has risen over time, and scientists are worried that the warming trend is accelerating. In 2018, the United Nations warned that weather patterns will become more extreme, droughts will spread, and the solar ice field will melt if we don't curb the greenhouse gas emissions that are a root cause of global warming. Those warnings have spawned calls for "going green," that is, replacing carbon-based energy sources with clean, renewable, and zero-emissions energy sources like wind and solar. A proposed Green New Deal calls for the complete elimination of carbon-based energy by 2030.

Are wind farms a free good?
xxlphoto/123RF

That is a tall order. The United States now gets 80 percent of its energy from coal, petroleum, and natural gas—all carbon-based fuels. We get another 10 percent from nuclear power. Only 10 percent or so comes from renewable sources like wind and solar. So, while everyone might share the goal of an emissions-free future, we have to ask how we get from here to there.

Opportunity Costs. It's easy to get excited about a solar-powered future. But before we jump on the solar bandwagon, we have to at least consider the costs involved. Sure, the sun's rays are free. But you need a lot of capital investment to harness that solar power. Solar panels on the roof don't come free. Nor do solar-powered electrical charging stations, solar power plants, or the electrical grids that distribute electricity to users. To develop a nationwide, complete solar power infrastructure would cost *trillions* of dollars. That's only the beginning. We'd also have to change the technology embedded in our transportation systems, office buildings, homes, and even farms. Retrofitting existing infrastructure would cost billions of dollars. Building new transportation systems would cost even more. The dollar cost of "going green" would be tens of trillions.

In economics we don't think in terms of papers dollars, but instead in terms of opportunity costs. Paper money doesn't build solar panels; it takes real factors of production—land, labor, capital, and entrepreneurship. Those resources—worth trillions of dollars—could be used to produce something else. If we invested that many resources in medical technology, we might cure cancer, find an antidote for the COVID-19 virus, and maybe even eradicate the flu. Investing that many resources in education might make college not only more enjoyable but a lot more productive as well. To invest all those resources in renewable energy implies that "going green" trumps all other social goals. That's a *normative* judgment that not everyone embraces. Many people worry more about their education, their homes, national defense, and the nation's infrastructure than the harm that conventional energy sources inflict on the environment. In deciding whether and how intensively to develop clean energy, we have to assess opportunity costs—what goods and services we implicitly forsake in order to "go green."

SUMMARY

- Scarcity is a basic fact of economic life. Factors of production (land, labor, capital, entrepreneurship) are scarce in relation to our desires for goods and services.   **LO1-1**
- All economic activity entails opportunity costs. Factors of production (resources) used to produce one output cannot simultaneously be used to produce something else. When we choose to produce one thing, we forsake the opportunity to produce some other good or service.   **LO1-2**
- A production possibilities curve (PPC) illustrates the limits to production—the various combinations of goods and services that could be produced in a given period if all available resources and technology are used efficiently. The PPC also illustrates opportunity costs—what is given up to get more of something else.   **LO1-3**
- The bent shape of the PPC reflects the law of increasing opportunity costs: Increasing quantities of any good can be obtained only by sacrificing ever-increasing quantities of other goods.   **LO1-3**
- Inefficient or incomplete use of resources will fail to attain production possibilities. Additional resources or better technologies will expand them. This is the essence of economic growth.   **LO1-3**
- Every country must decide WHAT to produce, HOW to produce, and FOR WHOM to produce with its limited resources.   **LO1-4**
- The study of economics focuses on the broad question of resource allocation. Macroeconomics is concerned with allocating the resources of an entire economy to achieve aggregate economic goals (e.g., full employment). Microeconomics focuses on the behavior and goals of individual market participants.   **LO1-4**
- The WHAT, HOW, and FOR WHOM choices can be made by the market mechanism or by government directives. Most nations are mixed economies, using a combination of these two choice mechanisms.   **LO1-5**
- Market failure exists when market signals generate suboptimal outcomes. Government failure occurs when government intervention worsens economic outcomes. The challenge for economic theory and policy is to find the mix of market signals and government directives that best fulfills our social and economic goals.   **LO1-5**

Key Terms

scarcity	production possibilities	market failure
factors of production	efficiency	government failure
capital	economic growth	macroeconomics
entrepreneurship	market mechanism	microeconomics
economics	laissez faire	*ceteris paribus*
opportunity cost	mixed economy	

Questions for Discussion

1. What opportunity costs did you incur in reading this chapter? If you read another chapter today, would your opportunity cost (per chapter) increase? Explain.   **LO1-2**
2. How much time *could* you spend on homework in a day? How much do you spend? How do you decide?   **LO1-2**
3. What's the real cost of a "free lunch," as mentioned in the discussion of "Opportunity Costs?"   **LO1-2**
4. How might a nation's production possibilities be affected by the following?   **LO1-3**
   (*a*) Discovery of a new oil field.
   (*b*) A decrease in immigration.
   (*c*) An increase in military spending.
   (*d*) More job training.
5. What was the opportunity cost of more hand sanitizers during the COVID-19 crisis?   **LO1-2**
6. Who would go to college in a completely private (market) college system? How does government intervention change this FOR WHOM outcome?   **LO1-4**
7. Why do people around the world have so much faith in free markets (World View "Market Reliance vs. Government Reliance?")?   **LO1-5**
8. What is the connection between North Korea's missile program and its hunger problem? (World View "North Korean Food Rations Cut")   **LO1-2**
9. Explain why there are limits to output and how these limits force economies to make trade-offs.   **LO1-1**
10. If climate change was in fact the greatest threat to society, should all our resources be used to combat it? What percentage of our output should be devoted to the pursuit of a carbon-neutral economy?   **LO1-2**

PROBLEMS FOR CHAPTER 1

LO1-2 1. According to Table 1.1 (or Figure 1.1), what is the opportunity cost of the second truck produced?

LO1-3 2. (*a*) Compute the opportunity cost in forgone consumer goods (millions of pounds of butter) for each additional unit of military output produced (number of planes):

Military output	0	1	2	3	4	5
Consumer goods output	100	95	80	60	35	0
Opportunity cost		—	—	—	—	—

(*b*) As military output increases, are opportunity costs increasing, decreasing, or remaining constant?

LO1-3 3. According to Figure 1.2, how much food production is sacrificed when North Korea moves from point *P* to point *N*?

LO1-2 4. (*a*) If the average North Korean farmer produces 1,500 pounds of food per year, what is the opportunity cost, in pounds of food, of North Korea's army (World View "World's Largest Armies")?

(*b*) If a person needs at least 500 pounds of food per year to survive, how many people could have been fed with the forgone food output?

LO1-2 5. What is the opportunity cost (in civilian output) of a defense buildup that raises military spending from 3.2 to 3.4 percent of a $22 trillion economy?

LO1-5 6. According to Figure 1.3, what percent of output consists of nonmilitary goods in
(*a*) Jamaica?
(*b*) Russia?

LO1-3 7. According to the figure below (similar to Figure 1.4),
(*a*) At which point(s) is this society producing some of each type of output but producing inefficiently?
(*b*) At which point(s) is this society producing the most output possible with the available resources and technology?
(*c*) At which point(s) is the output combination unattainable with available resources and technology?
(*d*) Show the change that would occur if the resources of this society increased. Label this curve PPC₂.
(*e*) Show the change that would occur with a huge natural disaster that destroyed one-third of production capacity. Label this curve PPC₃.

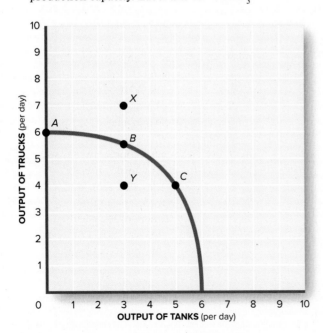

LO1-3   8. You have only 20 hours per week to use for either study time or fun time. Suppose the relationship between study time, fun time, and grades is shown in this table:

Fun time (hours per week)	16	12	8	4	0
Study time (hours per week)	0	4	8	12	16
Grade point average	*0*	*1.0*	*2.0*	*3.0*	*4.0*

(*a*) Draw the (linear) production possibilities curve on a graph that represents the alternative uses of your time.

(*b*) On the same graph, show the combination of study time and fun time that would get you a 2.0 grade average.

(*c*) What is the cost, in lost fun time, of raising your grade point average from 2.0 to 3.0?

LO1-5   9. According to the World View "Market Reliance vs. Government Reliance?," which nation has
(*a*) The highest level of faith in the market system?
(*b*) The lowest level of faith in the market system?

LO1-2   10. If a student literally had "nothing else to do,"
(*a*) What would be the opportunity cost of doing this homework?
(*b*) What is the likelihood of that?

LO1-1   11. According to the World View "World's Largest Armies," what percent of the total population is serving in the military in
(*a*) The United States (population = 340 million)?
(*b*) North Korea (population = 25 million)?
(*c*) China (population = 1.4 billion)?

LO1-2   12. *Decisions for Tomorrow:* What is the opportunity cost of investing $1 trillion in clean energy technology?

USING GRAPHS

Economists like to draw graphs. In fact, we didn't even make it through the first chapter without a few graphs. This appendix looks more closely at the way graphs are drawn and used. The basic purpose of a graph is to illustrate a relationship between two *variables.* Consider, for example, the relationship between grades and studying. In general, we expect that additional hours of study time will lead to higher grades. Hence, we should be able to see a distinct relationship between hours of study time and grade point average.

Suppose that we actually surveyed all the students taking this course with regard to their study time and grade point averages. The resulting information can be compiled in a table such as Table A.1.

According to the table, students who don't study at all can expect an F in this course. To get a C, the average student apparently spends 8 hours a week studying. All those who study 16 hours a week end up with an A in the course.

These relationships between grades and studying can also be illustrated on a graph. Indeed, the whole purpose of a graph is to summarize numerical relationships.

We begin to construct a graph by drawing horizontal and vertical boundaries, as in Figure A.1. These boundaries are called the *axes* of the graph. On the vertical axis (often called the *y*-axis), we measure one of the variables; the other variable is measured on the horizontal axis (the *x*-axis).

In this case, we shall measure the grade point average on the vertical axis. We start at the *origin* (the intersection of the two axes) and count upward, letting the distance between horizontal lines represent half (0.5) a grade point. Each horizontal line is numbered, up to the maximum grade point average of 4.0.

TABLE A.1

Hypothetical Relationship of Grades to Study Time

Study Time (Hours per Week)	Grade Point Average
16	4.0 (A)
14	3.5 (B+)
12	3.0 (B)
10	2.5 (C+)
8	2.0 (C)
6	1.5 (D+)
4	1.0 (D)
2	0.5 (F+)
0	0.0 (F)

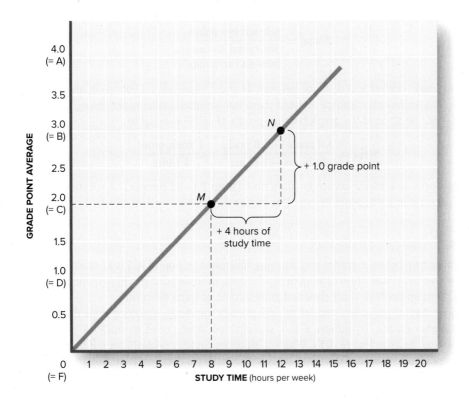

FIGURE A.1

The Relationship of Grades to Study Time

The upward (positive) slope of the curve indicates that additional studying is associated with higher grades. The average student (2.0, or C grade) studies 8 hours per week. This is indicated by point *M* on the graph.

The number of hours each week spent doing homework is measured on the horizontal axis. We begin at the origin again and count to the right. The *scale* (numbering) proceeds in increments of 1 hour, up to 20 hours per week.

When both axes have been labeled and measured, we can begin illustrating the relationship between study time and grades. Consider the typical student who does 8 hours of homework per week and has a 2.0 (C) grade point average. We illustrate this relationship by first locating 8 hours on the horizontal axis. We then move up from that point a distance of 2.0 grade points, to point *M*. Point *M* tells us that 8 hours of study time per week are typically associated with a 2.0 grade point average.

The rest of the information in Table A.1 is drawn (or *plotted*) on the graph the same way. To illustrate the average grade for people who study 12 hours per week, we move upward from the number 12 on the horizontal axis until we reach the height of 3.0 on the vertical axis. At that intersection, we draw another point (point *N*).

Once we've plotted the various points describing the relationship of study time to grades, we may connect them with a line or curve. This line (curve) is our summary. In this case, the line slopes upward to the right—that is, it has a *positive* slope. This slope indicates that more hours of study time are associated with *higher* grades. Were higher grades associated with *less* study time, the curve in Figure A.1 would have a *negative* slope (downward from left to right).

Slopes

The upward slope of Figure A.1 tells us that higher grades are associated with increased amounts of study time. That same curve also tells us *by how much* grades tend to rise with study time. According to point *M* in Figure A.1, the average student studies 8 hours per week and earns a C (2.0 grade point average). To earn a B (3.0 average), students apparently need to study an average of 12 hours per week (point *N*). Hence, an increase of 4 hours of study time per week is associated with a 1-point increase in grade point average. This relationship between *changes* in study time and *changes* in grade point average is expressed by the steepness, or *slope*, of the graph.

The slope of any graph is calculated as

$$\text{Slope} = \frac{\text{Vertical distance between two points}}{\text{Horizontal distance between two points}}$$

In our example, the vertical distance between *M* and *N* represents a change in grade point average. The horizontal distance between these two points represents the change in study time. Hence, the slope of the graph between points *M* and *N* is equal to

$$\text{Slope} = \frac{3.0 \text{ grade} - 2.0 \text{ grade}}{12 \text{ hours} - 8 \text{ hours}} = \frac{1 \text{ grade point}}{4 \text{ hours}}$$

In other words, a 4-hour increase in study time (from 8 to 12 hours) is associated with a 1-point increase in grade point average (see Figure A.1).

Shifts

The relationship between grades and studying illustrated in Figure A.1 isn't inevitable. It's simply a graphical illustration of student experiences, as revealed in our hypothetical survey. The relationship between study time and grades could be quite different.

Suppose that the university decided to raise grading standards, making it more difficult to achieve higher grades. To achieve a C, a student now would need to study 12 hours per week, not just 8 (as in Figure A.1). Whereas students could previously get a B by studying 12 hours per week, now they'd have to study 16 hours to get that grade.

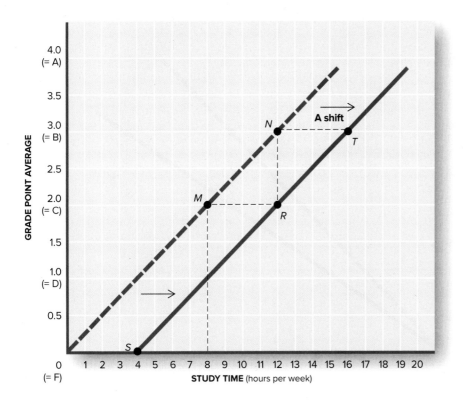

FIGURE A.2
A Shift

When a relationship between two variables changes, the entire curve *shifts*. In this case, a tougher grading policy alters the relationship between study time and grades. To get a C, one must now study 12 hours per week (point *R*), not just 8 hours (point *M*).

Figure A.2 illustrates the new grading standards. Notice that the new curve lies to the right of the earlier curve. We say that the curve has *shifted* to reflect a change in the relationship between study time and grades. Point *R* indicates that 12 hours of study time now "produce" a C, not a B (point *N* on the old curve). Students who now study only 4 hours per week (point *S*) will fail. Under the old grading policy, they could have at least gotten a D. *When a curve shifts, the underlying relationship between the two variables has changed.*

A shift may also change the slope of the curve. In Figure A.2, the new grading curve is parallel to the old one; it therefore has the same slope. Under either the new grading policy or the old one, a 4-hour increase in study time leads to a 1-point increase in grades. Therefore, the slope of both curves in Figure A.2 is

$$\text{Slope} = \frac{\text{Vertical change}}{\text{Horizontal change}} = \frac{1}{4}$$

This too may change, however. Figure A.3 illustrates such a possibility. In this case, zero study time still results in an F. But now the payoff for additional studying is reduced. Now it takes 6 hours of study time to get a D (1.0 grade point), not 4 hours as before. Likewise, another 4 hours of study time (to a total of 10) raise the grade by only two-thirds of a point. It takes 6 hours to raise the grade a full point. The slope of the new line is therefore

$$\text{Slope} = \frac{\text{Vertical change}}{\text{Horizontal change}} = \frac{1}{6}$$

The new curve in Figure A.3 has a smaller slope than the original curve and so lies below it. What all this means is that it now takes a greater effort to improve your grade.

FIGURE A.3

A Change in Slope

When a curve shifts, it may change its slope as well. In this case, a new grading policy makes each higher grade more difficult to reach. To raise a C to a B, for example, one must study 6 additional hours (compare points *J* and *K*). Earlier it took only 4 hours to move the grade scale up a full point. The slope of the line has declined from 0.25 (= 1 ÷ 4) to 0.17 (= 1 ÷ 6).

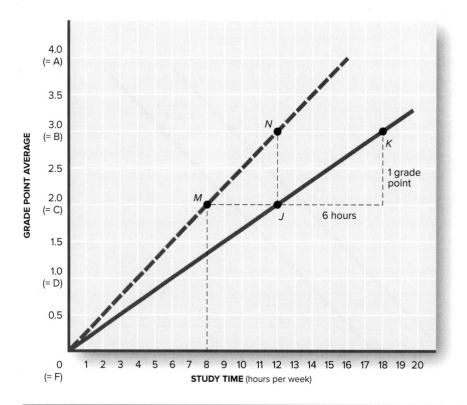

Linear vs. Nonlinear Curves

In Figures A.1–A.3 the relationship between grades and studying is represented by a straight line—that is, a *linear curve*. A distinguishing feature of linear curves is that they have the same (constant) slope throughout. In Figure A.1 it appears that *every* 4-hour increase in study time is associated with a 1-point increase in average grades. In Figure A.3 it appears that every 6-hour increase in study time leads to a 1-point increase in grades. But the relationship between studying and grades may not be linear. Higher grades may be more difficult to attain. You may be able to raise a C to a B by studying 4 hours more per week. But it may be harder to raise a B to an A. According to Figure A.4, it takes an additional 8 hours of studying to raise a B to an A. Thus, the relationship between study time and grades is *nonlinear* in Figure A.4; the slope of the curve changes as study time increases. In this case, the slope decreases as study time increases. Grades continue to improve, but not so fast, as more and more time is devoted to homework. You may know the feeling.

Causation

Figure A.4 doesn't by itself guarantee that your grade point average will rise if you study 4 more hours per week. In fact, the graph drawn in Figure A.4 doesn't prove that additional study ever results in higher grades. The graph is only a summary of empirical observations. It says nothing about cause and effect. It could be that students who study a lot are smarter to begin with. If so, then less able students might not get higher grades if they studied harder. In other words, the *cause* of higher grades is debatable. At best, the empirical relationship summarized in the graph may be used to support a particular theory (e.g., that it pays to study more). Graphs, like tables, charts, and other statistical media, rarely tell their own story; rather, they must be *interpreted* in terms of some underlying theory or expectation.Appendix

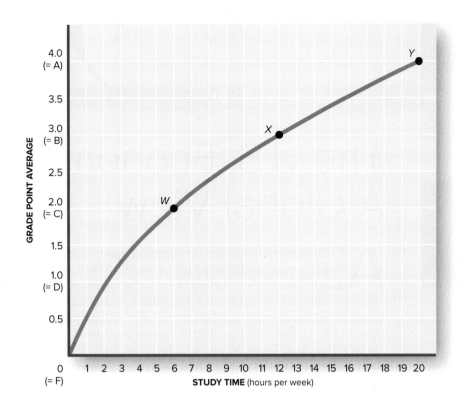

FIGURE A.4

A Nonlinear Relationship

Straight lines have a constant slope, implying a constant relationship between the two variables. But the relationship (and slope) may vary. In this case, it takes 6 extra hours of study to raise a C (point *W*) to a B (point *X*) but 8 extra hours to raise a B to an A (point *Y*). The slope decreases as we move up the curve.

Design Credit: Shutterstock

Jeff Chiu/AP Images

Glow Images   Pe3k/Shutterstock

The economy produces diverse goods and services.

LEARNING
OBJECTIVES

After reading this chapter, you should know

LO2-1 The relative size of the U.S. economy.

LO2-2 How the U.S. output mix has changed over time.

LO2-3 How the United States is able to produce so much output.

LO2-4 How incomes are distributed in the United States and elsewhere.

The U.S. Economy: A Global View

All nations must confront the central economic questions of WHAT to produce, HOW to produce, and FOR WHOM to produce it. However, the nations of the world approach these issues with vastly different production possibilities. China, Canada, the United States, Russia, and Brazil have more than *3 million* square miles of land each. All that land gives them far greater production possibilities than Dominica, Tonga, Malta, or Lichtenstein, each of which has less than 300 square miles of land. The population of China totals more than 1.4 billion people, nearly five times that of the United States, and 25,000 times the population of Greenland. Obviously, these nations confront very different output choices.

In addition to vastly uneven production possibilities, the nations of the world use different mechanisms for deciding WHAT, HOW, and FOR WHOM to produce. Belarus, Romania, North Korea, and Cuba still rely heavily on central planning. By contrast, Singapore, New Zealand, Ireland, and the United States permit the market mechanism to play a dominant role in shaping economic outcomes.

With different production possibilities and mechanisms of choice, you'd expect economic outcomes to vary greatly across nations. And they do. This chapter assesses how the U.S. economy stacks up. Specifically,

- **WHAT goods and services does the United States produce?**
- **HOW is that output produced?**
- **FOR WHOM is the output produced?**

In each case, we want to see not only how the United States has answered these questions but also how America's answers compare with those of other nations.

WHAT AMERICA PRODUCES

The United States has less than 5 percent of the world's population and only 12 percent of the world's arable land, yet it produces 20 percent of the world's output.

GDP Comparisons

World View "Comparative Output (GDP)" shows how total U.S. production compares with that of other nations. Every country produces a different mix of output. So, it's impossible to compare output in purely *physical* terms (e.g., so many cars, so many fish, etc.). But we can make comparisons based on the *value* of output. We do this by computing the

WORLD VIEW

COMPARATIVE OUTPUT (GDP)

The United States is by far the world's largest economy. Its annual output of goods and services is one and a half times larger than China's, three times Japan's, and more than all of the European Union's. The output of Third World countries is only a tiny fraction of U.S. output.

Source: The World Bank (Atlas method).

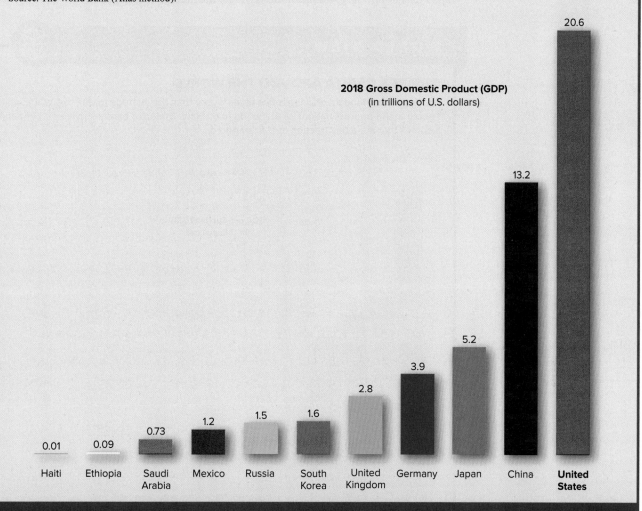

2018 Gross Domestic Product (GDP)
(in trillions of U.S. dollars)

Haiti	Ethiopia	Saudi Arabia	Mexico	Russia	South Korea	United Kingdom	Germany	Japan	China	United States
0.01	0.09	0.73	1.2	1.5	1.6	2.8	3.9	5.2	13.2	20.6

CRITICAL ANALYSIS: The market value of output (GDP) is a basic measure of an economy's size. The U.S. economy is far larger than any other and accounts for more than one-fifth of the entire world's output of goods and services.

total market value of all the goods and services a nation produces in a year—what we call **gross domestic product (GDP).** In effect, GDP is the "pie" of output we bake each year.

In 2019 the U.S. economy baked a huge pie—one containing more than $21 trillion worth of goods and services. That was far more output than any other nation produced. The second-largest economy, China, produced only two-thirds that much. Japan came in third, with about a third of U.S. output. Cuba, by contrast, produced less than $100 *billion* of output, less than the state of Mississippi. Russia, which is regarded as a superpower, produced only $1.5 trillion. The entire 27-member European Union produces less output than the United States.

Per Capita GDP. What makes the U.S. share of world output so remarkable is that we do it with so few people. The U.S. population of 340 million amounts to less than 5 percent of

gross domestic product (GDP): The total market value of all final goods and services produced within a nation's borders in a given time period.

the world's total (7.8 billion). Yet we produce more than 20 percent of the world's output. That means we're producing a lot of output *per person*. China, by contrast, has the opposite ratios: 18 percent of the world's population producing 17 percent of the world's output. So China is producing a lot of output but relatively less *per person*.

This people-based measure of economic performance is called **per capita GDP**. Per capita GDP is simply a nation's total output divided by its total population. It doesn't tell us how much any specific person gets. *Per capita GDP is an indicator of how much output the average person would get if all output were divided evenly among the population.* In effect, GDP per capita tells us how large a slice of the GDP pie the average citizen gets.

per capita GDP: The dollar value of GDP divided by total population; average GDP.

WORLD VIEW

GDP PER CAPITA AROUND THE WORLD

The American standard of living is five times higher than the average for the rest of the world. People in the poorest nations of the world (e.g., Haiti, Ethiopia) barely survive on per capita incomes that are a tiny fraction of U.S. standards.

Source: The World Bank.

GDP per Capita (2018) (in U.S. dollars)

Country	GDP per Capita
United States	63,080
Germany	47,090
Canada	44,940
Japan	41,310
South Korea	30,600
Saudi Arabia	21,600
World average	11,124
Russia	10,230
China	9,460
Mexico	9,180
Cuba	7,480
India	2,020
Nigeria	1,960
Haiti	800
Ethiopia	790

CRITICAL ANALYSIS: Per capita GDP is a measure of output that reflects average living standards. America's exceptionally high **per capita GDP** implies access to far more goods and services than people in other nations have.

In 2019 per capita GDP in the United States was roughly $64,000. That means the average U.S. citizen could have consumed $64,000 worth of goods and services. That's a staggering amount by global standards—five times the average for the rest of the world. World View "GDP per Capita around the World" provides a global perspective on just how "rich" America is. Notice how much more output the average American has than a person in India or, worse yet, Haiti. The gap between U.S. living standards and those in other nations is startling. According to the World Bank, 40 percent of the people on Earth subsist on incomes of less than $3 a day—a level completely unimaginable to the average American. *Homeless* people in the United States enjoy a higher living standard than billions of poor people in other nations (see chapter titled "Global Poverty"). In this context, it's easy to understand why the rest of the world envies (and sometimes resents) America's prosperity.

GDP Growth. What's even more startling about global comparisons is that the GDP gap between the United States and the world's poor nations keeps growing. The reason for that is **economic growth.** With few exceptions, U.S. output increases nearly every year: The pie keeps getting larger. *On average, U.S. output has grown by roughly 3 percent a year, nearly three times faster than population growth (1 percent).* So the U.S. pie is growing faster than the number of people coming to the table. Hence, not only does *total* output keep rising, but *per capita* output keeps rising as well (see Figure 2.1). Even the Great Recession of 2008–2009 and the 2020 coronavirus pandemic hardly made a dent in this pattern of ever-rising incomes.

economic growth: An increase in output (real GDP); an expansion of production possibilities.

Poor Nations. People in the world's poorest countries aren't so fortunate. China's economy has grown exceptionally fast in the last 20 years, propelling it to second place in the global GDP rankings. But in many other nations, total output has actually *declined* year after year, further depressing living standards. Notice in Table 2.1, for example, what's been happening in Libya. From 2000 to 2018, Libya's output of goods and services (GDP) *declined* by an average of 1.2 percent a year. As a result, total Libyan output in 2018 was 25 percent *smaller* than in 2000. During those same years, the Libyan population kept growing—by 1.2 percent a year. So the Libyan pie was shrinking every year even as the number of people coming to the table was increasing. As a result, Libya's per capita GDP fell below $7,000 a year.

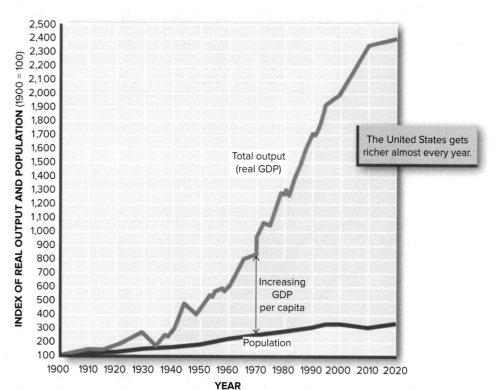

FIGURE 2.1

U.S. Output and Population Growth Since 1900

Over time, the growth of output in the United States has greatly exceeded population growth. As a consequence, GDP per capita has grown tremendously. GDP per capita was five times higher in 2000 than in 1900.

Source: U.S. Department of Labor.

TABLE 2.1

GDP Growth vs. Population Growth

The relationship between GDP growth and population growth is very different in rich and poor countries. The populations of rich countries are growing very slowly, and gains in per capita GDP are easily achieved. In the poorest countries, the population is still increasing rapidly, making it difficult to raise living standards. Notice how per capita incomes are *declining* in some lower-income countries (such as Libya and Haiti).

	Average Growth Rate (2000–2018) of		
	GDP	**Population**	**Per Capita GDP**
High-income countries			
United States	1.7	0.8	0.9
Canada	1.9	1.0	0.9
Japan	0.7	0.0	0.7
France	1.1	0.6	0.5
Middle-income countries			
China	9.5	0.5	9.0
India	6.8	1.4	5.4
Libya	−1.2	1.2	−2.4
Low-income countries			
Burundi	3.1	3.1	0.0
Haiti	1.4	1.5	−0.1
Ethiopia	9.8	2.8	7.0

Source: The World Bank, data.worldbank.org.

Burundi is another interesting case study of the relationship between output growth and population growth. Notice in Table 2.1 that Burundi's economy grew nearly twice as fast as the U.S. economy for 20 years. But Burundi's population increased just as fast as GDP. As a result, Burundians experienced *zero* improvement in living standards, while American per capita GDP was increasing at a 0.9 percent annual clip.

The Mix of Output

Regardless of how much output a nation produces, the *mix* of output always includes both *goods* (such as cars, big-screen TVs, and potatoes) and *services* (like this economics course, visits to a doctor, video streaming, or a professional baseball game). A century ago, about two-thirds of U.S. output consisted of farm goods (37 percent), manufactured goods (22 percent), and mining (9 percent). Since then, more than 25 *million* people have left the farms and taken jobs in other sectors. As a result, today's mix of output is completely reversed: ***Eighty percent of U.S. output now consists of services, not goods*** (see Figure 2.2).

The *relative* decline in goods production (manufacturing, farming) doesn't mean that we're producing *fewer* goods today than in earlier decades. Quite the contrary. While some industries such as iron and steel have shrunk, others, such as chemicals, publishing, and

FIGURE 2.2

The Changing Mix of Output

Two hundred years ago, almost all U.S. output came from farms. Today 80 percent of output consists of services, not farm or manufactured goods.

Source: U.S. Department of Commerce.

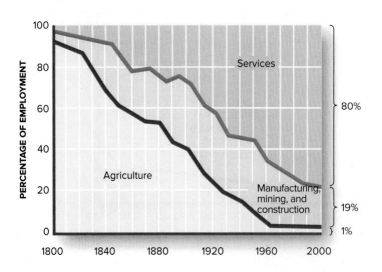

telecommunications equipment, have grown tremendously. The result is that manufacturing output has increased fourfold since 1950. The same kind of thing has happened in the farm sector, where output keeps rising even though agriculture's *share* of total output has declined. It's just that our output of *services* has increased so much faster.

Development Patterns. The transformation of the United States into a service economy is a reflection of our high incomes. In Ethiopia, where the most urgent concern is to keep people from starving, more than 50 percent of output still comes from the farm sector. Poor people don't have enough income to buy dental services, vacations, or even an education, so the mix of output in poor countries is weighted toward goods, not services.

HOW AMERICA PRODUCES

Regardless of how much output a nation produces, every nation ultimately depends on its resources—its **factors of production**—to produce goods and services. So *differences* in GDP must be explained in part by HOW those resources are used.

Human Capital

We've already observed that America's premier position in global GDP rankings isn't due to the number of humans within our borders. We have far fewer bodies than China or India, yet we produce far more output than either of those nations. What counts for production purposes is not just the *number* of workers a nation has, but the *skills* of those workers—what we call **human capital.**

Over time, the United States has invested heavily in human capital. In 1940 only 1 out of 20 young Americans graduated from college; today more than 40 percent of young people are college graduates. High school graduation rates have jumped from 38 percent to more than 85 percent in the same period. In the poorest countries, fewer than half of youth ever *attend* high school, much less graduate (see World View "The Education Gap between Rich and Poor Nations"). As a consequence, the United Nations estimates that 1.2 billion people—a sixth of

factors of production: Resource inputs used to produce goods and services, e.g., land, labor, capital, entrepreneurship.

human capital: The knowledge and skills possessed by the workforce.

WORLD VIEW

THE EDUCATION GAP BETWEEN RICH AND POOR NATIONS

Virtually all Americans attend high school and roughly 85 percent graduate. In poor countries, relatively few workers attend high school and even fewer graduate. Half the workers in the world's poorest nations are illiterate.

Source: The World Bank, WDI2017 Data Set, data.worldbank.org.

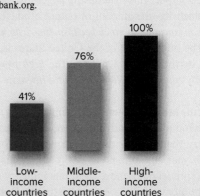

Enrollment in Secondary Schools (percentage of school-age youth attending secondary schools)

	Low-income countries	Middle-income countries	High-income countries
	41%	76%	100%

CRITICAL ANALYSIS: The high productivity of the American economy is explained in part by the quality of its labor resources, its **human capital.** Workers in poorer, less-developed countries get much less education and training.

Critical analysis: An abundance of capital equipment and advanced technology make American farmers and workers far more **productive** than workers in poor nations.
(*left*): Barry Barker/McGraw Hill; (*right*): Photo by Jeff Vanuga, USDA Natural Resources Conservation Service

humanity—are unable to read a book or even write their own names. Without even functional literacy, such workers are doomed to low-productivity jobs. Despite low wages, they are not likely to "steal" many jobs from America's highly educated and trained workforce.

Capital Stock

America has also accumulated a massive stock of capital—more than $80 *trillion* worth of machinery, factories, and buildings. As a result of all this prior investment, U.S. production tends to be very **capital-intensive.** The contrast with *labor-intensive* production in poorer countries is striking. A farmer in India still works mostly with his hands and crude implements, whereas a U.S. farmer works with computers, automated irrigation systems, and mechanized equipment (see the photos above). Russian business managers don't have the computer networks or telecommunications systems that make U.S. business so efficient. In Haiti and Ethiopia, even telephones, indoor plumbing, and dependable sources of power are scarce.

capital-intensive: Production processes that use a high ratio of capital to labor inputs.

High Productivity

When you put educated workers together with sophisticated capital equipment, you tend to get more output. This relationship largely explains why the United States has such a lead in worker **productivity**—the amount of output produced by the average worker. *American households are able to consume so much because American workers produce so much.* It's really that simple.

The huge output of the United States is thus explained not only by a wealth of resources but by their quality as well. *The high productivity of the U.S. economy results from using highly educated workers in capital-intensive production processes.*

productivity: Output per unit of input—for example, output per labor-hour.

Factor Mobility. Our continuing ability to produce the goods and services that consumers demand also depends on our agility in *reallocating* resources from one industry to another. Every year, some industries expand and others contract. Thousands of new firms start up each year, and almost as many others disappear. In the process, land, labor, capital, and entrepreneurship move from one industry to another in response to changing demands and technology. In 1975 Federal Express, Dell Computer, Staples, Oracle, and Amgen didn't exist. Walmart was still a small retailer. Starbucks was selling coffee on Seattle street corners, and the founders of Google, Facebook, and Snapchat weren't even born. Today these companies employ millions of people. These workers came from other firms and industries that weren't growing as fast.

Technological Advance. One of the forces that keep shifting resources from one industry to another is continuing advances in technology. Advances in technology can be as sophisticated as microscopic miniaturization of electronic circuits or as simple as the reorganization of production processes. Either phenomenon increases the productivity of the workforce and potential output. *Whenever technology advances, an economy can produce more output with existing resources;* its **production possibilities** curve shifts outward (see Figure 1.5).

Outsourcing and Trade. The same technological advances that fuel economic growth also facilitate *global* resource use. Telecommunications have become so sophisticated and inexpensive that phone workers in India or Grenada can answer calls directed to U.S. companies. Likewise, programmers in India can work online to write computer code, develop software, or perform accounting chores for U.S. corporations. Although such "outsourcing" is often viewed as a threat to U.S. jobs, it is really another source of increased U.S. output. By outsourcing routine tasks to foreign workers, U.S. workers are able to focus on higher-value jobs. U.S. computer engineers do less routine programming and more systems design. U.S. accountants do less cost tabulation and more cost analysis. By utilizing foreign resources in the production process, U.S. workers are able to pursue their *comparative advantage* in high-skill, capital-intensive jobs. In this way, both productivity and total output increase. Although some U.S. workers suffer temporary job losses in this process, the overall economy gains.

Role of Government

In assessing HOW goods are produced and economies grow, we must also take heed of the role the government plays. As we noted in Chapter 1, the amount of economic freedom varies greatly among the 200-plus nations of the world. Moreover, the Heritage Foundation has documented a positive relationship between the degree of economic freedom and economic growth. Quite simply, when entrepreneurs are unfettered by regulation or high taxes, they are more likely to design and produce better mousetraps. When the government owns the factors of production, imposes high taxes, or tightly regulates output, there is little opportunity or incentive to design better products or pursue new technology. This is one reason why more market-reliant economies grow faster than others.

Recognizing the importance of market incentives doesn't force us to reject all government intervention. No one really advocates the complete abolition of government. On the contrary, the government plays a critical role in establishing a framework in which private businesses can operate. Among its many roles are these:

- *Providing a legal framework.* One of the most basic functions of government is to establish and enforce the rules of the game. In some bygone era, maybe a person's word was sufficient to guarantee delivery or payment. Businesses today, however, rely more on written contracts. The government gives legitimacy to contracts by establishing the rules for such pacts and by enforcing their provisions. In the absence of contractual rights, few companies would be willing to ship goods without prepayment (in cash). Even the incentive to write texts would disappear if government copyright laws didn't forbid unauthorized photocopying. By establishing ownership rights, contract rights, and other rules of the game, the government lays the foundation for market transactions.
- *Protecting the environment.* The government also intervenes in the market to protect the environment. The legal contract system is designed to protect the interests of a buyer and a seller who wish to do business. What if, however, the business they contract for harms third parties? How are the interests of persons who *aren't* party to the contract to be protected?

  Numerous examples abound of how unregulated production may harm third parties. Earlier in the century, the steel mills around Pittsburgh blocked out the sun with clouds of sulfurous gases that spewed out of their furnaces. Local residents were harmed every time they inhaled. In the absence of government intervention, such side effects would be common. Decisions on how to produce would be based on costs alone, not on how the environment is affected. However, such negative **externalities**—spillover costs imposed on the broader community—affect our collective well-being.

production possibilities: The alternative combinations of final goods and services that could be produced in a given period with all available resources and technology.

externalities: Costs (or benefits) of a market activity borne by a third party; the difference between the social and private costs (benefits) of a market activity.

monopoly: A firm that produces the entire market supply of a particular good or service.

To reduce the external costs of production, the government limits air, water, and noise pollution and regulates environmental use.

- *Protecting consumers.* The government also uses its power to protect the interests of consumers. One way to do this is to prevent individual business firms from becoming too powerful. In the extreme case, a single firm might have a **monopoly** on the production of a specific good. As the sole producer of that good, a monopolist could dictate the price, the quality, and the quantity of the product. In such a situation, consumers would likely end up paying too much for too little.

  To protect consumers from monopoly exploitation, the government tries to prevent individual firms from dominating specific markets. Antitrust laws prohibit mergers or acquisitions that would threaten competition. The U.S. Department of Justice and the Federal Trade Commission also regulate pricing practices, advertising claims, and other behavior that might put consumers at an unfair disadvantage in product markets.

  Government also regulates the safety of many products. Consumers don't have enough expertise to assess the safety of various medicines, for example. If they rely on trial and error to determine drug safety, they might not get a second chance. To avoid this calamity, the government requires rigorous testing of new drugs, food additives, and other products.

- *Protecting labor.* The government also regulates how labor resources are used in the production process. In most poor nations, children are forced to start working at very early ages, often for minuscule wages. They often don't get the chance to go to school or to stay healthy. In Africa, 40 percent of children under age 14 work to survive or to help support their families. In the United States, child labor laws and compulsory schooling prevent minor children from being exploited. Government regulations also set standards for workplace safety, minimum wages, fringe benefits, and overtime provisions.

Striking a Balance

All these and other government interventions are designed to change the way resources are used. Such interventions reflect the conviction that the market alone might not always select the best possible way of producing goods and services. There's no guarantee, however, that government regulation of HOW goods are produced always makes us better off. Excessive regulation may inhibit production, raise product prices, and limit consumer choices. As noted in Chapter 1, *government* failure might replace *market* failure, leaving us no better off—possibly even worse off. This possibility underscores the importance of striking the right balance between market reliance and government regulation.

FOR WHOM AMERICA PRODUCES

As we've seen, America produces a huge quantity of output, using high-quality labor and capital resources. That leaves one basic question unanswered: FOR WHOM is all this output produced?

How many goods and services one gets largely depends on how much income one has to spend. The U.S. economy uses the market mechanism to distribute most goods and services. Those who receive the most income get the most goods. This goes a long way toward explaining why millionaires live in mansions and homeless people seek shelter in abandoned cars. This is the kind of stark inequality that fueled Karl Marx's denunciation of capitalism. Even today, people wonder how some Americans can be so rich while others are so poor.

U.S. Income Distribution

income quintile: One-fifth of the population, rank-ordered by income (e.g., top fifth).

Figure 2.3 illustrates the actual distribution of income in the United States. For this illustration the entire population is sorted into five groups of equal size, ranked by income. In this depiction, all the rich people are in the top **income quintile;** the poor are in the lowest quintile. To be in the top quintile in 2019, a household needed at least $143,000 of income. All the households in the lowest quintile had incomes under $28,000.

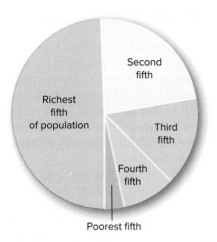

FIGURE 2.3

The U.S. Distribution of Income

The richest fifth of U.S. households gets half of all the income—a huge slice of the income pie. By contrast, the poorest fifth gets only a sliver.

Income Quintile	2019 Income	Average Income	Share of Total Income (%)
Highest fifth	Above $143,000	$254,400	51.9
Second fifth	$86,000–143,000	$111,100	22.7
Third fifth	$54,000–86,000	$ 68,900	14.1
Fourth fifth	$28,000–54,000	$ 40,700	8.3
Lowest fifth	$0–28,000	$ 15,300	3.1

Source: U.S. Department of Commerce, Bureau of the Census (averages rounded to thousands of dollars; 2019 data).

The most striking feature of Figure 2.3 is how large a slice of the income pie rich people get: ***The top 20 percent (quintile) of U.S. households get half of all U.S. income.*** By contrast, the poorest 20 percent (quintile) of U.S. households get only a sliver of the income pie— about 3 percent. Those grossly unequal slices explain why nearly half of all Americans believe the nation is divided into "haves" and "have nots." In the 2020 presidential campaigns, there was a lot of talk about changing the answer to the FOR WHOM question with new taxes on the rich and more subsidies and wage floors for the poor.

Critical analysis: The market distributes income (and, in turn, goods and services) according to the resources an individual owns and how well they are used. If the resulting inequalities are too great, government intervention may be desired to change the **FOR WHOM** outcome.

TerryJ/Getty Images; Philip Pilosian/Shutterstock

Global Inequality

As unequal as U.S. incomes are, income disparities are actually greater in many other countries. Ironically, income inequalities are often greatest in the poorest countries. The richest *tenth* of U.S. families gets 30 percent of America's income pie. The richest tenth of South Africa's families gets a far greater share (51 percent) of that nation's income (see World View "Global Inequalities"). Given the small size of South Africa's pie, the *bottom* tenth of South African families is left with mere crumbs. As we'll see in the chapter titled "Global Poverty," 40 percent of South Africa's population lives in "severe poverty," defined by the World Bank as an income of less than $3 a day.

Comparisons across countries would manifest even greater inequality. As we saw earlier, Third World GDP per capita is far below U.S. levels. As a consequence, even *poor people in the United States receive far more goods and services than the* average *household in most low-income countries.*

WORLD VIEW

GLOBAL INEQUALITIES

Inequality tends to diminish as a country develops. In poor, developing nations, the richest tenth of the population typically gets 40 to 50 percent of all income. In developed countries, the richest tenth gets 20 to 30 percent of total income.

Source: The World Bank, 2020.

Share of Total Income Received by Top Tenth

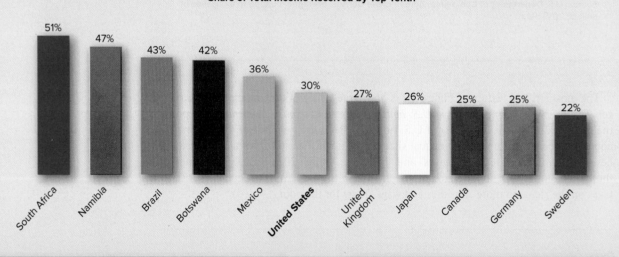

South Africa	51%
Namibia	47%
Brazil	43%
Botswana	42%
Mexico	36%
United States	30%
United Kingdom	27%
Japan	26%
Canada	25%
Germany	25%
Sweden	22%

CRITICAL ANALYSIS: The **FOR WHOM** question is reflected in the distribution of income. Although the U.S. distribution of income is unequal, inequalities are much more severe in most poor nations.

DECISIONS FOR TOMORROW

Can We Eliminate Global Poverty?

Global answers to the basic questions of WHAT, HOW, and FOR WHOM have been shaped by market forces and government intervention. Obviously, the answers aren't fully satisfactory.

Millions of Americans still struggle to make ends meet. Worse yet, nearly 3 *billion* people around the world live in abject poverty—with incomes of less than $3 a day. More

Continued

CHAPTER 2: THE U.S. ECONOMY: A GLOBAL VIEW 41

than a sixth of the world's population are illiterate, nearly half have no access to sanitation facilities, and a fifth are chronically malnourished.

Then there is a staggering amount of pollution, rampant inequalities, inadequate education, and insufficient health care for billions of people.

The United Nations wants us to fashion better answers for the WHAT, HOW, and FOR WHOM questions. In September 2015 the U.N. adopted a set of 17 specific goals for sustainable development and a 15-year timeline for achieving them. Ending world poverty and eliminating world hunger are the first two on the list. High on the list is also the goal of reducing inequalities across income groups, gender, and race. Protecting the environment and slowing climate change are additional goals.

Can the world meet all these goals? Perhaps. But it will take a lot of resources and even more political will. Consider just the first goal of ending global poverty.

The rich nations of the world have enough resources to wipe out global poverty. But they're not willing to give them up. People in rich nations also have aspirations: They want higher living standards in the economy tomorrow. They already enjoy more comforts than people in poor nations even dream of. But that doesn't stop them from wanting more consumer goods, better schools, improved health care, a cleaner environment, and greater economic security. So the needs of the world's poor typically get lower priority.

How about the poor nations themselves? Couldn't they do a better job of mobilizing and employing their own resources to accelerate economic growth? Governments in many poor nations are notoriously self-serving and corrupt. Private property is often at risk of confiscation and contracts hard to enforce. This discourages the kind of investment poor nations desperately need. The unwillingness of rich nations to open their markets to the exports of poor nations also puts a lid on income growth.

In reality, an array of domestic and international policies has perpetuated global poverty. Developing a better mix of market-based and government-directed policies is the prerequisite for ending global poverty. Although some progress has been made in reducing poverty in the last few years, few believe that we will achieve the goal of eradicating extreme poverty in the next 10 years. In 2019, the U.N. itself projected that 6 percent of the world's population will still be in extreme poverty in the year 2030. Can we do better than that? How?

SUMMARY

- Answers to the core WHAT, HOW, and FOR WHOM questions vary greatly across nations. These differences reflect varying production possibilities, productivity, and values. **LO2-1, LO2-3, LO2-4**
- Gross domestic product (GDP) is the basic measure of how much an economy produces. The United States produces roughly $20 trillion of output per year, more than one-fifth of the world's total. **LO2-1**
- Per capita GDP is a nation's total output divided by its population. It indicates the average standard of living. The U.S. GDP per capita is five times the world average. **LO2-1**
- The high level of U.S. per capita GDP reflects the high productivity of U.S. workers. Abundant capital, education, technology, training, and management all contribute to high productivity. The relatively high degree of U.S. economic freedom (market reliance) is

- also an important cause of superior economic growth. **LO2-3**
- More than 80 percent of U.S. output consists of services, including government services. This is a reversal of historical ratios and reflects the relatively high incomes in the United States. Poor nations produce much higher proportions of food and manufactured goods. **LO2-2**
- U.S. incomes are distributed very unequally, with households in the highest income class (quintile) receiving more than 10 times more income than low-income households. Incomes are even less equally distributed in most poor nations. **LO2-4**
- The mix of output, production methods, and the income distribution continues to change. The WHAT, HOW, and FOR WHOM answers in tomorrow's economy will depend on the continuing interplay of (changing) market signals and (changing) government policy. **LO2-2, LO2-3, LO2-4**

Key Terms

gross domestic product (GDP)	human capital	externalities
per capita GDP	capital-intensive	monopoly
economic growth	productivity	income quintile
factors of production	production possibilities	

Questions for Discussion

1. Americans already enjoy living standards that far exceed world averages. Do we have enough? Should we even try to produce more? **LO2-1**

2. Why is per capita GDP so much higher in the United States than in Haiti? **LO2-3**

3. Can we continue to produce more output every year? Is there a limit? **LO2-3**

4. The U.S. farm population has shrunk by more than 25 million people since 1900. Where did all the people go? Why did they move? **LO2-2**

5. Is the relative decline in U.S. farming and manufacturing (Figure 2-2) a good thing or a bad thing? **LO2-2**

6. How many people are employed by your local or state government? Are they producing goods or services? Can you name some? What is the opportunity cost of that output? **LO2-1**

7. Where do growing companies like Netflix and Peloton get their employees? What were those workers doing before? **LO2-2**

8. Should the government try to equalize incomes more by raising taxes on the rich and giving more money to the poor? How might such redistribution affect total output and growth? **LO2-4**

9. Why are incomes so much more unequal in poor nations than in rich ones? **LO2-4**

10. What more can be done to reduce global poverty? **LO2-3**

LO2-1 1. In 2018 the world's total output (real GDP) was roughly $84 trillion. What percent of this total was produced
    (*a*) By the three largest economies (World View "Comparative Output (GDP)")?
    (*b*) By the three smallest economies in that World View?

LO2-1 2. According to the World View "GDP per Capita around the World," how does per capita GDP in the following countries "stack up" against America's (in percentage terms)
    (*a*) Canada
    (*b*) Mexico
    (*c*) India

LO2-4 3. In 1980, America's GDP per capita was approximately $30,000 (measured in today's dollars). How much higher in percentage terms was America's GDP per capita in 2018 (see World View "GDP per Capita around the World")?

LO2-3 4. (*a*) How much more output does the $22 trillion U.S. economy produce when GDP increases by 1.0 percent?
    (*b*) By how much does this increase per capita income if the population is 340 million?

LO2-1 5. According to Table 2.1, how fast does total output (GDP) have to grow each year in order to increase per capita GDP in
    (*a*) the United States?
    (*b*) Japan?
    (*c*) Burundi?

LO2-3 6. (*a*) If Haiti's per capita GDP of $800 were to DOUBLE every decade (an annual growth rate of 7.2 percent), what would Haiti's per capita GDP be in 30 years?
    (*b*) Compare (a) to the U.S. per capita GDP in 2018 (World View "GDP per Capita around the World)?

LO2-2 7. U.S. real gross domestic product increased from $13 trillion in 2000 to $19 trillion in 2019. During that same time period, the share of manufactured goods (e.g., cars, appliances) fell from 16 percent to 11 percent. What was the dollar value of manufactured output
    (*a*) In 2000?
    (*b*) In 2019?
    (*c*) In percentage terms, by how much did the dollar value of manufacturing output change?

LO2-4 8. Using the data in Figure 2.3,
    (*a*) Compute the average income of U.S. households.
    If all incomes were equalized by government taxes and transfer payments,
    (*b*) How much would the average household in the highest income quintile pay in taxes?
    (*c*) What *percent* of income would the average household in the highest income quintile pay in tax?
    (*d*) How much would the average household in the lowest quintile receive in transfer payments?

LO2-3 9. If 160 million workers produced America's GDP in 2018 (World View "Comparative Output (GDP)"), how much output did the average worker produce?

LO2-1 10. Assuming the 2019 per capita GDP growth rate is equal to the average growth rate (2000–2018) provided in Table 2.1, estimate 2019 per capita GDP for each of the following countries using data from World View "GDP per Capita around the World."
    (*a*) China
    (*b*) Canada
    (*c*) Haiti

PROBLEMS FOR CHAPTER 2 (cont'd)

LO2-2   11. Using the data from the Data Tables, calculate
            (*a*) the federal government's share of total output in 1998, 2008, and 2018.
            (*b*) the state and local government's share of total output in 1998, 2008, and 2018.

LO2-2   12. ***Decisions for Tomorrow:*** How much more output per year will have to be produced in the world
            just to provide the 3 billion "severely" poor population with $1 more income per day?

LADO/Shutterstock

CHAPTER 3

Supply and Demand

LEARNING OBJECTIVES

After reading this chapter, you should know

LO3-1 The nature and determinants of market demand.

LO3-2 The nature and determinants of market supply.

LO3-3 How market prices and quantities are established.

LO3-4 What causes market prices to change.

LO3-5 How government price controls affect market outcomes.

On Saturday, September 14, 2019, ten unmanned drones attacked the Saudi Arabian oil facilities in Abqaiq. The resulting damage temporarily crippled Saudi Arabia's production capabilities—taking out 5.7 million barrels of oil per day. That damage represented about 50 percent of Saudi Arabia's daily production and about 5 percent of the entire world's capacity. Overnight, the U.S. price of unleaded, regular gasoline jumped by 3 cents, to $2.59 a gallon. A week later, the price was higher still, at $2.65 a gallon. The outcry from American motorists over "price gouging" was immediate: They thought it unfair for oil companies to charge higher prices. Those outcries prompted President Trump to announce that he was authorizing the sale of oil from America's Strategic Petroleum Reserve, an underground store of 645 million barrels of oil.

A similar price spike occurred when the World Health Organization declared a worldwide coronavirus pandemic on January 30, 2020. That declaration prompted people to stock up on surgical masks and hand sanitizers that might reduce the chances of COVID-19 infections. Within days, the price of an 8-ounce bottle of Purell hand sanitizer shot up from $3 to $16. The price of surgical masks increased as much as 166 percent on Amazon. Here again, a market shock had thrown demand and supply temporarily out of kilter. To restrain the resulting price hikes, the Surgeon General of the United States said that most people didn't need surgical masks (demand) and the federal government started selling surgical masks from its emergency medical stockpiles (supply). Mask manufacturers also increased production. As the market adjusted to the coronavirus threat, mask and sanitizer prices receded.

Economists took the spike in gasoline prices in stride. They pointed out that the price increase was the natural result of "supply and demand." The world was *demanding* just as much oil on Sunday, September 15 (about 100 million barrels per day) as it had on September 14. But the drone attacks had reduced the *supply* of oil by 5.7 million barrels. A price increase was inevitable. But economists also pointed out that the price jump was likely to be temporary. The Saudis would soon repair their production facilities and other nations (including the United States) would increase production to cover the Saudi shortfall. And that's exactly what happened. By the end of 2019, gasoline prices had fallen back to $2.49 a gallon. No oil had been taken out of the Strategic Petroleum Reserve. No congressional hearings had been conducted. And no oil companies had been charged with price gouging. The market forces of supply and demand had simply adjusted to changing circumstances.

45

The goal of this chapter is to explain how supply and demand really work. How do *markets* establish the prices of gasoline, surgical masks, and other products? Why do prices change so often? More broadly, how does the market mechanism decide WHAT to produce, HOW to produce, and FOR WHOM to produce? Specifically,

* **What determines the price of a good or service?**
* **How does the price of a product affect its production and consumption?**
* **Why do prices and production levels often change?**

Once we've seen how unregulated markets work, we'll observe how government intervention may alter market outcomes—for better or worse.

MARKET PARTICIPANTS

A good way to start figuring out how markets work is to see who participates in them. The answer is simple: just about every person and institution on the planet. Domestically, nearly 340 million consumers, about 25 million business firms, and tens of thousands of government agencies participate directly in the U.S. economy. Millions of international buyers and sellers also participate in U.S. markets.

Maximizing Behavior

All these market participants enter the marketplace to pursue specific goals. Consumers, for example, come with a limited amount of income to spend. Their objective is to buy the most desirable goods and services that their limited budgets will permit. We can't afford *everything* we want, so we must make *choices* about how to spend our scarce dollars. Our goal is to *maximize* the utility (satisfaction) we get from our available incomes.

Businesses also try to maximize in the marketplace. In their case, the quest is for maximum *profits*. Business profits are the difference between sales receipts and total costs. To maximize profits, business firms try to use resources efficiently in producing products that consumers desire.

The public sector also has maximizing goals. The economic purpose of government is to use available resources to serve public needs. The resources available for this purpose are limited too. Hence, local, state, and federal governments must use scarce resources carefully, striving to maximize the general welfare of society. International consumers and producers pursue these same goals when participating in our markets.

Market participants sometimes lose sight of their respective goals. Consumers sometimes buy impulsively and later wish they'd used their income more wisely. Likewise, a producer may take a two-hour lunch, even at the sacrifice of maximum profits. And elected officials sometimes put their personal interests ahead of the public's interest. In all sectors of the economy, however, ***the basic goals of utility maximization, profit maximization, and welfare maximization explain most market activity.***

Specialization and Exchange

We are driven to buy and sell goods and services in the market by two simple facts. First, most of us are incapable of producing everything we want to consume. Second, even if we *could* produce all our own goods and services, it would still make sense to *specialize,* producing only one product and *trading* it for other desired goods and services.

Suppose you were capable of growing your own food, stitching your own clothes, building your own shelter, and even writing your own economics text. Even in this little utopia, it would still make sense to decide how *best* to expend your limited time and energy, relying on others to fill in the gaps. If you were *most* proficient at growing food, you would be best off spending your time farming. You could then *exchange* some of your food output for the clothes, shelter, and books you wanted. In the end, you'd be able to consume *more* goods than if you'd tried to make everything yourself.

Our economic interactions with others are thus necessitated by two constraints:

1. Our absolute inability as individuals to produce all the things we need or desire.
2. The limited amount of time, energy, and resources we have for producing those things we could make for ourselves.

Together these constraints lead us to *specialize* and interact. Most of the interactions that result take place in the market.

International Trade. The same motivations foster international trade. The United States is *capable* of producing just about everything. But we've learned that it's cheaper to import bananas from Ecuador than to grow them in hothouses in Idaho. So we *specialize* in production, exporting tractors to Ecuador in exchange for imported bananas. Both nations end up consuming more products than they could if they had to produce everything themselves. That's why *global* markets are so vital to economic prosperity.

THE CIRCULAR FLOW

Figure 3.1 summarizes the kinds of interactions that occur among market participants. Note first that the figure identifies four separate groups of participants. Domestically, the rectangle labeled "Consumers" includes all 340 million consumers in the United States. In the "Business firms" box are grouped all the domestic business enterprises that buy and sell goods and services. The third participant, "Governments," includes the many separate agencies of the federal government, as well as state and local governments. Figure 3.1 also illustrates the role of global actors.

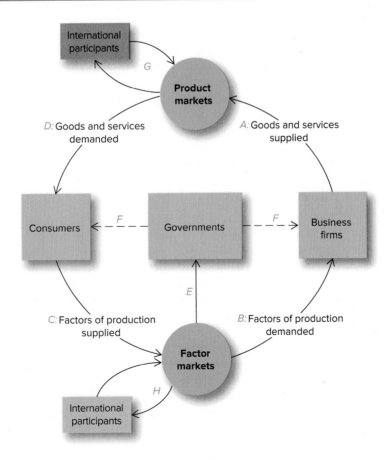

FIGURE 3.1

The Circular Flow

- *Business firms* supply goods and services to product markets (point *A*) and purchase factors of production in factor markets (*B*).

- *Individual consumers* supply factors of production such as their own labor (*C*) and purchase final goods and services (*D*).

- Federal, state, and local *governments* acquire resources in factor markets (*E*) and provide services to both consumers and business (*F*).

- *International participants* also take part by supplying imports, purchasing exports (*G*), and buying and selling factors of production (*H*).

The Two Markets

The easiest way to keep track of all this activity is to distinguish two basic markets. Figure 3.1 makes this distinction by portraying separate circles for product markets and factor markets. In **factor markets,** factors of production are exchanged. Market participants buy or sell land, labor, or capital that can be used in the production process. When you go looking for work, for example, you're making a factor of production—your labor—available to producers. The producers will hire you—purchase your services in the factor market—if you're offering the skills they need at a price they're willing to pay.

Interactions within factor markets are only half the story. At the end of a hard day's work, consumers go to the grocery store (or to a virtual store online) to buy desired goods and services—that is, to buy *products.* In this context, consumers again interact with business firms, this time purchasing goods and services those firms have produced. These interactions occur in **product markets.** Foreigners also participate in the product market by supplying goods and services (imports) to the United States and buying some of our output (exports).

The government sector also supplies services (e.g., education, national defense, highways). Most government services aren't explicitly sold in product markets, however. Typically, they're delivered "free," without an explicit price (e.g., public elementary schools, highways). This doesn't mean government services are truly free, though. There's still an **opportunity cost** associated with every service the government provides. Consumers and businesses pay that cost indirectly through taxes rather than directly through market prices.

In Figure 3.1, the arrow connecting product markets to consumers (D) emphasizes the fact that consumers, by definition, don't supply products. When individuals produce goods and services, they do so within the government or business sector. For instance, a doctor, a dentist, or an economic consultant functions in two sectors. When selling services in the market, this person is regarded as a "business"; when away from the office, he or she is regarded as a "consumer." This distinction is helpful in emphasizing that *the consumer is the final recipient of all goods and services produced.*

Locating Markets. Although we refer repeatedly to two kinds of markets in this text, it would be a little foolish to go off in search of the product and factor markets. Neither market is a single, identifiable structure. The term *market* simply refers to a place or situation where an economic exchange occurs—where a buyer and seller interact. The exchange may take place on the street, in a taxicab, over the phone, by mail, or in cyberspace. In some cases, the market used may in fact be quite distinguishable, as in the case of a Walmart store, the Chicago Commodity Exchange, or a state employment office. But whatever it looks like, *a market exists wherever and whenever an exchange takes place.*

Dollars and Exchange

Figure 3.1 neglects one critical element of market interactions: dollars. Each arrow in the figure actually has two dimensions. Consider again the arrow (D) linking consumers to product markets: It's drawn in only one direction because consumers, by definition, don't provide goods and services directly to product markets. But they do provide something: dollars. If you want to obtain something from a product market, you must offer to pay for it (typically with cash, check, or debit or credit card). Consumers exchange dollars for goods and services in product markets.

The same kinds of exchange occur in factor markets. When you go to work, you exchange a factor of production (your labor) for income, typically a paycheck. Here again, the path connecting consumers to factor markets (C) really goes in two directions: one of real resources, the other of dollars. Consumers receive wages, rent, and interest for the labor, land, and capital they bring to the factor markets. Indeed, nearly *every market transaction involves an exchange of dollars for goods (in product markets) or resources (in factor markets).* Money is thus critical in facilitating market exchanges and the specialization the exchanges permit.

---

factor market: Any place where factors of production (e.g., land, labor, capital) are bought and sold.

---

product market: Any place where finished goods and services (products) are bought and sold.

---

opportunity cost: The most desired goods or services that are forgone in order to obtain something else.

In markets people exchange money for products.

Ariel Skelley/Blend Images/Getty Images

Supply and Demand

In every market transaction, there must be a buyer and a seller. The seller is on the **supply** side of the market; the buyer is on the **demand** side. As noted earlier, we *supply* resources to the market when we look for a job–that is, when we offer our labor in exchange for income. We *demand* goods when we shop in a supermarket–that is, when we're prepared to offer dollars in exchange for something to eat. Business firms may *supply* goods and services in product markets at the same time they're *demanding* factors of production in factor markets. Whether one is on the supply side or the demand side of any particular market transaction depends on the nature of the exchange, not on the people or institutions involved.

supply: The ability and willingness to sell (produce) specific quantities of a good at alternative prices in a given time period, *ceteris paribus.*

demand: The willingness and ability to buy specific quantities of a good at alternative prices in a given time period, *ceteris paribus.*

DEMAND

To get a sense of how the demand side of market transactions works, we'll focus first on a single consumer. Then we'll aggregate to illustrate *market* demand.

Individual Demand

We can begin to understand how market forces work by looking more closely at the behavior of a single market participant. Let us start with Tom, a senior at Clearview College. Tom has majored in everything from art history to government in his five years at Clearview. He didn't connect to any of those fields and is on the brink of academic dismissal. To make matters worse, his parents have threatened to cut him off financially unless he gets serious about his course work. By that, they mean he should enroll in courses that will lead to a job after graduation. Tom thinks he has found the perfect solution: web design. Everything associated with the Internet pays big bucks. Or at least so Tom thinks. And his parents would definitely approve. So Tom has enrolled in web design courses.

Unfortunately for Tom, he never developed computer skills. Until he got to Clearview College, he thought mastering Sony's latest alien-attack video game was the pinnacle of electronic wizardry. Tom didn't have a clue about "cookies," "wireframe," "responsive design," or the other concepts the web design instructor outlined in the first lecture.

Given his circumstances, Tom was desperate to find someone who could tutor him in web design. But desperation is not enough to secure the services of a web architect. In a market-based economy, you must also be willing to *pay* for the things you want. Specifically, ***a demand exists only if someone is willing and able to pay for the good***–that is, exchange dollars for a good or service in the marketplace. Is Tom willing and able to *pay* for the tutoring he so obviously needs?

Desiring a Gucci bag is not the same as demanding one.

gilaxia/Getty Images

Let us assume that Tom has some income and is willing to spend some of it to get a tutor. With these assumptions, we can claim that Tom is a participant in the *market* for web design services; he is a potential consumer.

But how much is Tom willing to pay? Surely Tom is not prepared to exchange *all* his income for help in mastering web design. After all, Tom could use his income to buy more desirable goods and services. If he spent all his income on a web tutor, that help would have an extremely high *opportunity cost.* He would be giving up the opportunity to spend that income on things he really likes. He'd pass his web design class but have little else. It doesn't sound like a good idea.

It seems more likely that there are *limits* to the amount Tom is willing to pay for web design tutoring. These limits will be determined by how much income Tom has to spend and how many other goods and services he must forsake to pay for a tutor.

Tom also knows that his grade in web design will depend in part on how much tutoring service he buys. He can pass the course with only a few hours of design help. If he wants a better grade, however, the cost is going to escalate quickly.

Naturally, Tom wants it all: an A in web design and a ticket to higher-paying jobs. But here again, the distinction between *desire* and *demand* is relevant. He may *desire* to master web design, but his actual proficiency will depend on how many hours of tutoring he is willing to *pay* for.

The Demand Schedule

demand schedule: A table showing the quantities of a good a consumer is willing and able to buy at alternative prices in a given time period, *ceteris paribus.*

We assume, then, that when Tom starts looking for a tutor, he has some sense of how much money he is willing to spend. He might have in mind some sort of **demand schedule,** like that described in Figure 3.2. According to row *A* of this schedule, Tom is willing and able to buy only 1 hour of tutoring service per semester if he must pay $50 an hour. At such a high price, he will learn just enough web design to pass the course.

At lower prices, Tom would behave differently. According to Figure 3.2, Tom would purchase *more* tutoring services if the price per hour were *less.* Indeed, we see from row *I* of the demand schedule that Tom is willing to purchase 20 hours per semester—the whole bag of design tricks—if the price of tutoring gets as low as $10 per hour.

Notice that the demand schedule doesn't tell us anything about *why* this consumer is willing to pay specific prices for various amounts of tutoring. Tom's expressed willingness to pay for web design tutoring may reflect a desperate need to finish a web design course, a lot of income to spend, or a relatively small desire for other goods and services. All the demand schedule tells us is what the consumer is *willing and able* to buy, for whatever reasons.

Also, observe that the demand schedule doesn't tell us how many hours of design help the consumer will *actually* buy. Figure 3.2 simply states that Tom is *willing and able* to pay for 1 hour of tutoring per semester at $50 per hour, for 2 hours at $45 each, and so on. How much tutoring he purchases will depend on the actual price of such services in the market. Until we know that price, we cannot tell how much service will be purchased. Hence, *"demand" is an expression of consumer buying intentions, of a willingness to buy, not a statement of actual purchases.*

The Demand Curve

demand curve: A curve describing the quantities of a good a consumer is willing and able to buy at alternative prices in a given time period, *ceteris paribus.*

A convenient summary of buying intentions is the **demand curve,** a graphical illustration of the demand schedule. The demand curve in Figure 3.2 tells us again that this consumer is willing to pay for only 1 hour of tutoring per semester if the price is $50 per hour (point *A*), for 2 if the price is $45 (point *B*), for 3 at $40 an hour (point *C*), and so on. Once we know what the market price of tutoring actually is, a glance at the demand curve tells what quantity a consumer will buy at any given price.

A common feature of demand curves is their downward slope. *As the price of a good falls, people purchase more of it.* In Figure 3.2, the quantity of tutoring demanded increases (moves rightward along the horizontal axis) as the price per hour decreases (moves down the vertical axis). This inverse relationship between price and quantity is so common that

Tom's Demand Schedule		
	Price of Tutoring (per Hour)	Quantity of Tutoring Demanded (Hours per Semester)
A	$50	1
B	45	2
C	40	3
D	35	5
E	30	7
F	25	9
G	20	12
H	15	15
I	10	20

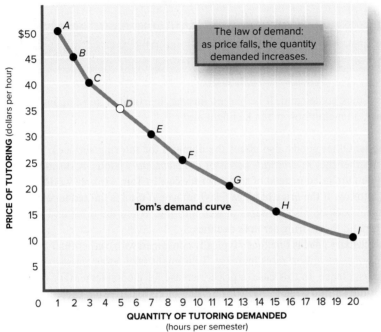

The law of demand: as price falls, the quantity demanded increases.

Tom's demand curve

PRICE OF TUTORING (dollars per hour)

QUANTITY OF TUTORING DEMANDED (hours per semester)

FIGURE 3.2
A Demand Schedule and Curve

A demand schedule indicates the quantities of a good a consumer is able and willing to buy at alternative prices (*ceteris paribus*). The **demand schedule** here indicates that Tom would buy 5 hours of web tutoring per semester if the price were $35 per hour (row *D*). If web tutoring were less expensive (rows *E–I*), Tom would purchase a larger quantity.

A **demand curve** is a graphical illustration of a demand schedule. Each point on the curve refers to a specific quantity that will be demanded at a given price. If, for example, the price of web tutoring were $35 per hour, this curve tells us the consumer would purchase 5 hours per semester (point *D*). If web tutoring cost $30 per hour, 7 hours per semester would be demanded (point *E*). Each point on the curve corresponds to a row in the schedule.

we refer to it as the **law of demand.** Disney used this law to assure that its launch of the Disney+ streaming service would be a success (see Front Page Economics "Pricing Disney+").

law of demand: The quantity of a good demanded in a given time period increases as its price falls, *ceteris paribus*.

Determinants of Demand

The demand curve in Figure 3.2 has only two dimensions—quantity demanded (on the horizontal axis) and price (on the vertical axis). This seems to imply that the amount of tutoring demanded depends only on the price of that service. This is surely not the case. A consumer's willingness and ability to buy a product at various prices depend on a variety of forces. *The determinants of market demand include*

- *Tastes* (desire for this and other goods).
- *Income* (of the consumer).
- *Other goods* (their availability and price).
- *Expectations* (for income, prices, tastes).
- *Number of buyers.*

Tastes and Incomes. Tom's "taste" for tutoring has nothing to do with taste buds. *Taste* is just another word for desire. In this case, Tom's taste for web design services is clearly acquired. If he didn't have to pass a web design course, he would have no desire for related

FRONT PAGE ECONOMICS

PRICING DISNEY+

Disney decided it wanted to provide streaming services directly to customers, rather than renting its library of films and television shows to other streaming services like Netflix. But how successful would a streaming service be? In other words, what did the demand for a "Disney+" streaming service look like? Disney knew that the number of subscribers would depend not just on the attractiveness of the Disney archives, but also on the subscription price. After doing some market research, Disney decided to launch Disney+ at a price of $6.99 a month (or $69.99 per year). When Disney+ was launched on November 12, 2019, 10 million people signed up on the first day—a resounding success!

Source: News reports October–December 2019.

CRITICAL ANALYSIS: The **law of demand** dictates that a larger quantity will be demanded at lower prices. To secure millions of initial subscribers, Disney priced its streaming service low.

---

services and thus no demand. If he had no **income,** he couldn't *demand* any web design tutoring either, no matter how much he might *desire* it.

Other Goods. Other goods also affect the demand for tutoring services. Their effect depends on whether they're *substitute* goods or *complementary* goods. A **substitute good** is one that might be purchased instead of tutoring services. In Tom's simple world, pizza is a substitute for tutoring. If the price of pizza fell, Tom would use his limited income to buy more pizzas and cut back on his purchases of web tutoring. When the price of a substitute good falls, the demand for tutoring services declines.

A **complementary good** is one that's typically consumed with, rather than instead of, tutoring. If text prices or tuition rates increase, Tom might take fewer classes and demand *less* web design assistance. In this case, a price increase for a complementary good causes the demand for tutoring to decline. When the price of coffee goes up, the demand for cream goes down. When theater ticket prices go down, the demand for popcorn goes up.

Expectations. Expectations also play a role in consumer decisions. If Tom expected to flunk his web design course anyway, he probably wouldn't waste any money getting tutorial help; his demand for such services would disappear. On the other hand, if he expects a web tutor to determine his college fate, he might be more willing to buy such services.

Number of Buyers. Tom may not be the only one in need of tutoring. The demand for tutoring depends on the number of students who are in a similar situation.

Ceteris Paribus

If demand is in fact such a multidimensional decision, how can we reduce it to only the two dimensions of price and quantity? In Chapter 1 we first encountered this *ceteris paribus* trick. To simplify their models of the world, economists focus on only one or two forces at a time and *assume* nothing else changes. We know a consumer's tastes, income, other goods, and expectations all affect the decision to hire a tutor. But we want to focus on the relationship between quantity demanded and price. That is, we want to know what *independent* influence price has on consumption decisions. To find out, we must isolate that one influence, price, and assume that the determinants of demand remain unchanged.

The *ceteris paribus* assumption is not as farfetched as it may seem. People's tastes, income, and expectations do not change quickly. Also, the prices and availability of other goods don't change all that fast. Hence, a change in the *price* of a product may be the only factor that prompts an immediate change in quantity demanded.

---

substitute goods: Goods that substitute for each other; when the price of good *x* rises, the demand for good *y* increases, *ceteris paribus.*

complementary goods: Goods frequently consumed in combination; when the price of good *x* rises, the demand for good *y* falls, ceteris paribus.

ceteris paribus: The assumption of nothing else changing.

The ability to predict consumer responses to a price change is important. What would happen, for example, to enrollment at your school if tuition doubled? Must we guess? Or can we use demand curves to predict how the quantity of applications will change as the price of college goes up? *Demand curves show us how changes in market prices alter consumer behavior.* We used the demand curve in Figure 3.2 to predict how Tom's web design ability would change at different tutorial prices. Disney used its knowledge of consumer demand to set the subscription price for Disney+ (see Front Page Economics "Pricing Disney+").

Shifts in Demand

Although demand curves are useful in predicting consumer responses to market signals, they aren't infallible. The problem is that *the determinants of demand can and do change.* When they do, a specific demand curve may become obsolete. A *demand curve (schedule) is valid only so long as the underlying determinants of demand remain constant.* If the *ceteris paribus* assumption is violated—if tastes, income, other goods, or expectations change—the ability or willingness to buy will change. When this happens, the demand curve will **shift** to a new position.

Suppose, for example, that Tom won $1,000 in the state lottery. This windfall would increase his ability to pay for tutoring services. Figure 3.3 shows the effect on Tom's demand. The old demand curve, D_1, is no longer relevant. Tom's lottery winnings enable him to buy *more* tutoring at any price, as illustrated by the new demand curve, D_2. According to this

shift in demand: A change in the quantity demanded at any (every) price.

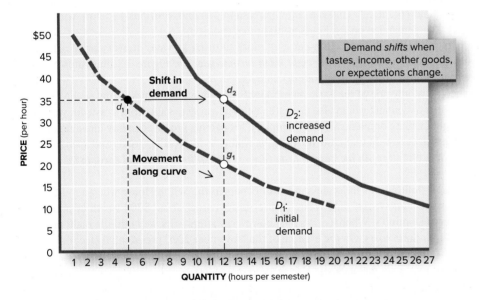

	Quantity Demanded (Hours per Semester)		
	Price (per Hour)	Initial Demand	After Increase in Income
A	$50	1	8
B	45	2	9
C	40	3	10
D	35	5	12
E	30	7	14
F	25	9	16
G	20	12	19
H	15	15	22
I	10	20	27

FIGURE 3.3
Shifts vs. Movements

A demand curve shows how a consumer responds to price changes. If the determinants of demand stay constant, the response is a *movement* along the curve to a new quantity demanded. In this case, when price falls from $35 to $20 per hour, the quantity demanded increases from 5 (point d_1), to 12 (point g_1).

If the determinants of demand *change,* the entire demand curve *shifts.* In this case, a rise in income increases demand. With more income, Tom is willing to buy 12 hours at the initial price of $35 (point d_2), not just the 5 hours he demanded before the lottery win (point d_1).

What would you buy if you won?
McGraw Hill

new curve, lucky Tom is now willing and able to buy 12 hours per semester at the price of $35 per hour (point d_2). This is a large increase in demand; previously (before winning the lottery), he demanded only 5 hours at that price (point d_1).

With his higher income, Tom can buy more tutoring services at every price. Thus, *the entire demand curve shifts to the right when income goes up.* Figure 3.3 illustrates both the old (pre-lottery) and new (post-lottery) demand curves.

Income is only one of the basic determinants of demand. Changes in any of the other determinants of demand would also cause the demand curve to shift. Tom's taste for web tutoring might increase dramatically, for example, if his parents promised to buy him a new car for passing web design. In that case, he might be willing to forgo other goods and spend more of his income on tutors. *An increase in taste (desire) also shifts the demand curve to the right.*

Pizza and Politics. A similar demand shift occurs at the White House when a political crisis erupts. On an average day, White House staffers order about $300 worth of pizza from the nearby Domino's. When a crisis hits, however, staffers work well into the night and their demand for pizza soars. On the evening of the November 2020 presidential elections, White House staffers ordered more than $1,000 worth of pizza! Political analysts now use pizza deliveries to predict major White House announcements.

Movements vs. Shifts

It's important to distinguish shifts of the demand curve from movements along the demand curve. *Movements along a demand curve are a response to price changes for that good.* Such movements assume that determinants of demand are unchanged. By contrast, *shifts of the demand curve occur when the determinants of demand change.* When tastes, income, other goods, or expectations are altered, the basic relationship between price and quantity demanded is changed (shifts).

For convenience, movements along a demand curve and shifts of the demand curve have their own labels. Specifically, take care to distinguish

- *Changes in quantity demanded:* movements along a given demand curve in response to price changes of that good.
- *Changes in demand:* shifts of the demand curve due to changes in tastes, income, other goods, or expectations.

Tom's behavior in the web tutoring market will change if either the price of tutoring changes (a movement) or the underlying determinants of his demand are altered (a shift).

Notice in Figure 3.3 that he ends up buying 12 hours of web tutoring if either the price of tutoring falls (to $20 per hour, leading him to point d_1) or his income increases (leading him to point d_2). Demand curves help us predict those market responses.

Market Demand

Whatever we say about demand for web design tutoring on the part of one wannabe web master, we can also say about every student at Clearview College (or, for that matter, about all consumers). Some students have no interest in web design and aren't willing to pay for related services: They don't participate in the web tutoring market. Other students want such services but don't have enough income to pay for them: They too are excluded from the web tutoring market. A large number of students, however, not only have a need (or desire) for web tutoring but also are willing and able to purchase such services.

What we start with in product markets, then, is many individual demand curves. Fortunately, it's possible to combine all the individual demand curves into a single **market demand.** The aggregation process is no more difficult than simple arithmetic. Suppose that you would be willing to buy 1 hour of tutoring per semester at a price of $80 per hour. George, who is also desperate to learn web design, would buy 2 at that price; and I would buy none because my publisher (McGraw-Hill) creates a web page for my book. What would our combined (market) demand for hours of tutoring be at that price? Collectively, we would be willing to buy a total of 3 hours of tutoring per semester if the price were $80 per hour. Our combined willingness to buy—our collective market demand—is nothing more than the sum of our individual demands. The same kind of aggregation can be performed for all consumers, leading to a summary of the total *market* demand for a specific good or service. Thus, *market demand is determined by the number of potential buyers and their respective tastes, incomes, other goods, and expectations.*

market demand: The total quantities of a good or service people are willing and able to buy at alternative prices in a given time period; the sum of individual demands.

The Market Demand Curve

Figure 3.4 provides the basic market demand schedule for a situation in which only three consumers participate in the market. It illustrates the same market situation with demand curves. The three individuals who participate in the market demand for web tutoring at Clearview College obviously differ greatly, as suggested by their respective demand schedules. Tom's demand schedule is portrayed in the first column of the table (and is identical to the one we examined in Figure 3.2). George is also desperate to acquire some job skills and is willing to pay relatively high prices for web design tutoring. His demand is summarized in the second column under Quantity Demanded in the table.

The third consumer in this market is Lisa. Lisa already knows the nuts and bolts of web design, so she isn't so desperate for tutorial services. She would like to upgrade her skills, however, especially in animation and e-commerce applications. But her limited budget precludes paying a lot for help. She will hire a tutor only if the price falls to $30 per hour. Should tutors cost less, she'd even buy quite a few hours of web design tutoring.

The differing circumstances of Tom, George, and Lisa are expressed in their individual demand schedules (Figure 3.4). To determine the *market* demand for tutoring from this information, we simply add these three separate demands. The end result of this aggregation is, first, a *market* demand schedule (last column in the table) and, second, the resultant *market* demand curve (Figure 3.4d). These market summaries describe the various quantities of tutoring that Clearview College students are *willing and able* to purchase each semester at various prices.

What price? How much web tutoring will be purchased each semester? Knowing how much help Tom, George, and Lisa are willing to buy at various prices doesn't tell you how much they're *actually* going to purchase. To determine the actual consumption of web tutoring, we have to know something about prices and supplies. Which of the many different prices illustrated in Figures 3.3 and 3.4 will actually prevail? How will that price be determined?

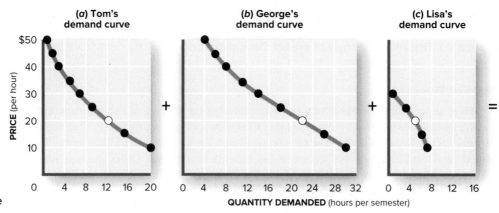

FIGURE 3.4

Construction of the Market Demand Curve

Market demand represents the combined demands of all market participants.

To determine the total quantity of web tutoring demanded at any given price, we add the separate demands of the individual consumers. Row *G* of this schedule indicates that a *total* quantity of 39 hours per semester will be demanded at a price of $20 per hour.

This same conclusion is reached by adding the individual demand curves, leading to point *G* on the market demand curve (see graph *d*).

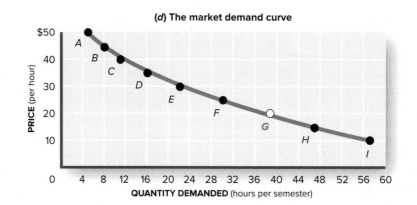

	Price (per Hour)	Quantity of Tutoring Demanded (Hours per Semester)					
		Tom	+	George	+	Lisa	=	Market Demand
A	$50	1		4		0		5
B	45	2		6		0		8
C	40	3		8		0		11
D	35	5		11		0		16
E	30	7		14		1		22
F	25	9		18		3		30
G	20	12		22		5		39
H	15	15		26		6		47
I	10	20		30		7		57

SUPPLY

market supply: The total quantities of a good that sellers are willing and able to sell at alternative prices in a given time period, *ceteris paribus*.

To understand how the price of web tutoring is established, we must also look at the other side of the market: the *supply* side. We need to know how many hours of tutoring services people are willing and able to *sell* at various prices—that is, the **market supply.** As on the demand side, the *market supply* depends on the behavior of all the individuals willing and able to supply web tutoring at some price.

Determinants of Supply

Let's return to the Clearview campus for a moment. What we need to know now is how much tutorial help people are willing and able to provide. Generally speaking, web design can be fun, but it can also be drudge work, especially when you're doing it for someone else. Hosting services like Weebly, Squarespace, and GoDaddy have made setting up a website easier and more creative. And the cloud and Wi-Fi access have made the job more convenient. But teaching someone else to design web pages is still work. So why does anyone do it? Easy answer: for the money. People offer (supply) tutoring services to earn income that they, in turn, can spend on the goods and services *they* desire.

How much money must be offered to induce web designers to do a little tutoring depends on a variety of things. The ***determinants of market supply include***

- *Technology.*
- *Factor costs.*
- *Other goods.*
- *Taxes and subsidies.*
- *Expectations.*
- *Number of sellers.*

Technology. The technology of web design, for example, is always getting easier and more creative. With a program like Weebly, for example, it's very easy to create a bread-and-butter web page. A continuous stream of new software programs (e.g., Wordpress, DreamWeaver) keeps stretching the possibilities for graphics, animation, interactivity, and content. These technological advances mean that web design services can be supplied more quickly and cheaply. They also make *teaching* web design easier. As a result, they induce people to supply *more* tutoring services at every price.

Factor Costs. How much web design service is offered at any given price also depends on the cost of factors of production. If the software programs needed to create web pages are cheap (or, better yet, free), web designers can afford to charge lower prices. If the required software inputs are expensive, however, they will have to charge more for their services.

Other Goods. Other goods can also affect the willingness to supply web design services. If you can make more income waiting tables than you can tutoring lazy students, why would you even boot up the computer? As the prices paid for other goods and services change, they will influence people's decision about whether to offer web services.

Taxes. In the real world, the decision to supply goods and services is also influenced by the long arm of Uncle Sam. Federal, state, and local governments impose **taxes** on income earned in the marketplace. When tax rates are high, people get to keep less of the income they earn. Once taxes start biting into paychecks, some people may conclude that tutoring is no longer worth the hassle and withdraw from the market.

Expectations. Expectations are also important on the supply side of the market. If web designers expect higher prices, lower costs, or reduced taxes, they may be more willing to learn new software programs. On the other hand, if they have poor expectations about the future, they may just find something else to do.

Number of Sellers. Finally, we note that the number of potential sellers will affect the quantity of service offered for sale at various prices. If there are lots of willing tutors on campus, a lot of tutorial service will be available at reasonable prices.

All these considerations—factor costs, technology, taxes, expectations—affect the decision to offer web services at various prices. In general, we assume that web architects will be willing to provide more tutoring if the per-hour price is high and less if the price is low. In other words, there is a **law of supply** that parallels the law of demand. *The law of supply says that larger quantities will be offered for sale at higher prices.* Here again, the laws rest on the *ceteris paribus* assumption: The quantity supplied increases at higher prices *if* the determinants of supply are constant. *Supply curves are upward-sloping to the right,* as shown in Figure 3.5. Note how the *quantity supplied* jumps from 39 hours (point *d*) to 130 hours (point *h*) when the price of web service doubles (from $20 to $40 per hour).

law of supply: The quantity of a good supplied in a given time period increases as its price increases, *ceteris paribus*.

FIGURE 3.5

Market Supply

The market supply curve indicates the *combined* sales intentions of all market participants—that is, the total quantities they are willing and able to sell at various prices.

If the price of tutoring were $45 per hour (point *i*), the *total* quantity of services supplied would be 140 hours per semester. This quantity is determined by adding the supply decisions of all individual producers. In this case, Ann supplies 93 hours, Bob supplies 33, and Carlos supplies the rest.

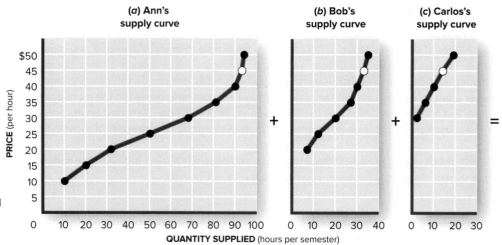

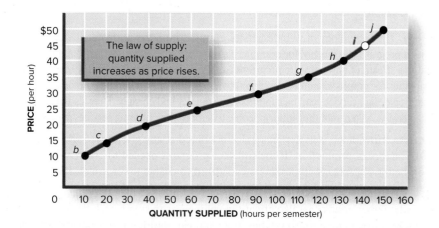

	Price per Hour	Quantity of Tutoring Supplied by				
		Ann	+	Bob	+	Carlos	=	Market
j	$50	94		35		19		148
i	45	93		33		14		140
h	40	90		30		10		130
g	35	81		27		6		114
f	30	68		20		2		90
e	25	50		12		0		62
d	20	32		7		0		39
c	15	20		0		0		20
b	10	10		0		0		10

Market Supply

Figure 3.5 also illustrates how *market* supply is constructed from the supply decisions of individual sellers. In this case, only three web masters are available. Ann is willing to provide a lot of tutoring at low prices, whereas Bob requires at least $20 an hour. Carlos won't talk to students for less than $30 an hour.

By adding the quantity each tutor is willing to offer at every price, we can construct the market supply curve. Notice in Figure 3.5 how the quantity supplied to the market at $45 (point *i*) comes from the individual efforts of Ann (93 hours), Bob (33 hours), and Carlos (14 hours). *The market supply curve is just a summary of the supply intentions of all producers.*

None of the points on the market supply curve (Figure 3.5) tells us how much web tutoring is *actually* being sold on the Clearview campus. ***Market supply is an expression of sellers' intentions—an offer to sell—not a statement of actual sales.*** My next-door neighbor may be willing to sell his 2014 Honda Civic for $18,000, but most likely he'll never find a buyer at that price. Nevertheless, his *willingness* to sell his car at that price is part of the *market supply* of used cars.

Shifts of Supply

As with demand, there's nothing sacred about any given set of supply intentions. Supply curves *shift* when the underlying determinants of supply change. Thus, ***it is important to distinguish***

- *Changes in quantity supplied:* movements along a given supply curve in response to price changes of that good.
- *Changes in supply:* shifts of the supply curve due to changes in technology, factor costs, other goods, taxes and subsidies, or expectations.

Our Latin friend *ceteris paribus* is once again the decisive factor. If the price of a product is the only variable changing, then we can ***track changes in quantity supplied along the supply curve.*** But if *ceteris paribus* is violated—if technology, factor costs, the profitability of producing other goods, tax rates, expectations, or the number of sellers changes—then ***changes in supply are illustrated by shifts of the supply curve.***

The World View "Gas Prices Jump in Wake of Saudi Attack" illustrates how a supply shift pushed up gasoline prices in September 2019. As noted at the beginning of this chapter, drone strikes on Saudi oil facilities reduced Saudi Arabia's ability to produce (supply) oil. As the market supply curve shifted to the left, the price of gasoline rose.

WORLD VIEW

GAS PRICES JUMP IN WAKE OF SAUDI ATTACK

The Saudi Arabian oil processing plants in Abqaiq were hit by drone strikes, shutting down about half of the Kingdom's production capacity. Early estimates put the damage at about 5.7 million barrels of oil per day, roughly half of Saudi output. Crude oil prices jumped as much as $8 per barrel and U.S. gasoline prices jumped by 9 cents a gallon, according to the U.S. Energy Information Agency.

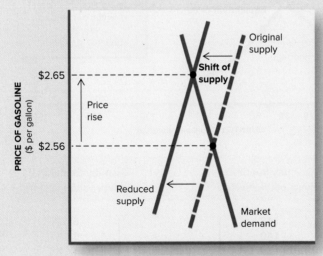

Source: News reports, September–December 2019.

CRITICAL ANALYSIS: When factor costs or availability worsens, the supply curve **shifts** to the left. Such leftward supply-curve shifts push prices up the market demand curve.

The coronavirus outbreak in 2020 had similar effects across a broad spectrum of industries. Thousands of American companies import needed components and materials from China. General Electric, for example, imports critical parts for its production of aircraft engines, CT scanners, X-ray machines, and other products. Pharmaceutical companies get critical ingredients from China to produce blood pressure, depression, and Alzheimer's disease medicines. Phantom Fireworks, a small company in Youngstown, Ohio, needs Chinese rockets and firecrackers for its July 4 celebrations. When the coronavirus shut down production facilities in China, the *market supply* of these products was reduced. The resulting leftward supply shift raised input prices and reduced production in U.S. factories.

EQUILIBRIUM

That spike in gasoline prices after the Saudi attacks offers some clues to how the forces of supply and demand set—and change—market prices. For a closer look at how those forces work, we'll return to Clearview College for a moment. How did supply and demand resolve the WHAT, HOW, and FOR WHOM questions in that web tutoring market?

Figure 3.6 helps answer that question by bringing together the market supply and demand curves we've already examined (Figures 3.4 and 3.5). When we put the two curves together, we see that *only one price and quantity combination is compatible with the intentions of both buyers and sellers. This equilibrium occurs at the intersection of the supply and demand curves.*

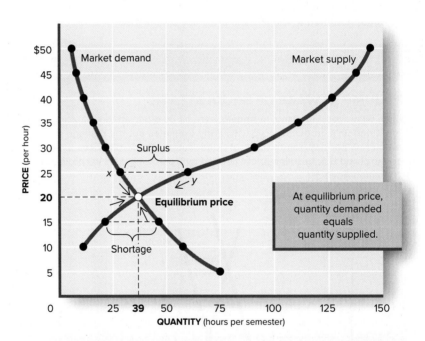

FIGURE 3.6

Equilibrium Price

The intersection of the demand and supply curves establishes the *equilibrium* price and quantity. Only at equilibrium is the quantity demanded equal to the quantity supplied. In this case, the equilibrium price is $20 per hour, and 39 hours is the equilibrium quantity.

At above-equilibrium prices, a market *surplus* exists—the quantity supplied exceeds the quantity demanded. At prices below equilibrium, a market *shortage* exists.

Price (per Hour)	Quantity Supplied (Hours per Semester)		Quantity Demanded (Hours per Semester)	
$50	148		5	
45	140		8	
40	130	Market surplus	11	Nonequilibrium prices create surpluses or shortages.
35	114		16	
30	90		22	
25	62		30	
20	39	Equilibrium	39	
15	20	Market shortage	47	
10	10		57	

Notice in Figure 3.6 where that intersection occurs—at the price of $20 and the quantity of 39 hours. So $20 is the **equilibrium price:** Campus tutors will sell a total of 39 hours of tutoring per semester—the same amount that students wish to buy at that price. Those 39 hours of tutoring service will be part of WHAT is produced in the economy.

equilibrium price: The price at which the quantity of a good demanded in a given time period equals the quantity supplied.

Market Clearing

An equilibrium doesn't imply that everyone is happy with the prevailing price or quantity. Notice in Figure 3.6, for example, that some students who want to buy tutoring services don't get any. These would-be buyers are arrayed along the demand curve *below* the equilibrium. Because the price they're *willing* to pay is less than the equilibrium price of $20, they don't get any web design help. The market's FOR WHOM answer includes only those students willing and able to pay the equilibrium price.

Likewise, some would-be sellers are frustrated by this market outcome. These wannabe tutors are arrayed along the supply curve *above* the equilibrium. Because they insist on being paid *more* than the equilibrium price of $20 per hour, they don't actually sell anything.

Although not everyone finds satisfaction in the market equilibrium, that unique outcome is efficient. *The equilibrium price and quantity reflect a compromise between buyers and sellers. No other compromise yields a quantity demanded that's exactly equal to the quantity supplied.*

The Invisible Hand. The equilibrium price isn't determined by any single individual. Rather, it's determined by the collective behavior of many buyers and sellers, each acting out his or her own demand or supply schedule. It's this kind of impersonal price determination that gave rise to Adam Smith's characterization of the market mechanism as "the invisible hand." In attempting to explain how the **market mechanism** works, the famed 18th-century economist noted a remarkable feature of market prices. The market behaves as if some unseen force (the invisible hand) were examining each individual's supply or demand schedule and then selecting a price that assured an equilibrium. In practice, the process of price determination isn't so mysterious: It's a simple process of trial and error.

market mechanism: The use of market prices and sales to signal desired outputs (or resource allocations).

Disequilibrium: Surplus and Shortage

Market Surplus. To appreciate the power of the market mechanism, consider interference in its operation. Suppose, for example, that campus tutors banded together and agreed to charge a minimum price of $25 per hour, five dollars more than the equilibrium price. By establishing a **price floor,** a minimum price for their services, the tutors hope to increase their incomes. Their goal won't be achieved. Figure 3.6 illustrates the consequences of this *dis*equilibrium pricing. At $25 per hour, campus tutors would be offering more than 39 hours of tutoring. How much more? Move up the market supply curve from the equilibrium price until you hit the price of $25. At that price, tutors are prepared to offer the quantity indicated by point *y*. What's wrong with that point? Students in need of tutoring aren't willing to buy that much tutoring at that price. The market demand curve tells us Tom, George, and Lisa are willing to buy only the smaller quantity indicated by point *x* at the price of $25 per hour. We have a discrepancy between the quantity suppliers want to sell and the quantity consumers want to buy. This is a *dis*equilibrium.

price floor: Lower limit set for the price of a good.

In this case, the disequilibrium creates a **market surplus:** More tutoring is being offered for sale than consumers are willing to purchase at the available price. As Figure 3.6 indicates, at a price of $25 per hour, a market surplus of 32 hours per semester exists. Under these circumstances, campus tutors would be spending many idle hours at their keyboards waiting for customers to appear. Their waiting will be in vain because the quantity of web tutoring demanded will not increase until the price of tutoring falls. That is the clear message of the demand curve. As would-be tutors get this message, they'll reduce their prices. They really have no other choice.

market surplus: The amount by which the quantity supplied exceeds the quantity demanded at a given price; excess supply.

As sellers' asking prices decline, the quantity demanded will increase. This concept is illustrated in Figure 3.6 by the movement along the demand curve from point *x* to lower prices and greater quantity demanded. As we move down the market demand curve, the *desire* for web design help doesn't change, but the quantity people are *able and willing to buy* increases. When the price falls to $20 per hour, the quantity demanded will finally equal the quantity supplied. This is the *equilibrium* illustrated in Figure 3.6.

Market Shortage. A very different sequence of events would occur if a market shortage existed. Suppose someone were to spread the word that web tutoring services were available at only $15 per hour. Tom, George, and Lisa would be standing in line to get tutorial help, but campus web designers wouldn't be willing to supply the quantity demanded at that price. As Figure 3.6 confirms, at $15 per hour, the quantity demanded (47 hours per semester) greatly exceeds the quantity supplied (20 hours per semester). In this situation, we speak of a **market shortage**—that is, an excess of quantity demanded over quantity supplied. At a price of $15 an hour, the shortage amounts to 27 hours of tutoring services.

When a market shortage exists, not all consumer demands can be satisfied. Some people who are *willing* to buy web help at the going price ($15) won't be able to do so. To get the help they want, Tom, George, Lisa, or some other consumer will offer to pay a *higher* price, thus initiating a move up the demand curve in Figure 3.6. The higher prices offered will in turn induce enterprising tutors to work more hours, thus ensuring an upward movement along the market supply curve. Notice, again, that the *desire* to tutor web design hasn't changed; only the quantity supplied has responded to a change in price. As this process continues, the quantity supplied will eventually equal the quantity demanded (39 hours in Figure 3.6).

Price Gouging? In the midst of a crisis, it is often difficult to wait for the market to adjust to an abrupt disequilibrium. Consider what happened to the price of hand sanitizers when the coronavirus swept across the country. Suddenly, everyone wanted hand sanitizers to ward off the COVID-19 virus. The explosion of demand sent the price of hand sanitizers soaring. Consumers cried foul and asked the government to step in and prevent price gouging.

Economists would argue that the price hikes were an important step in satisfying consumer demands. On the demand side, the higher price discouraged people from buying more sanitizer than they needed (hoarding). More importantly, the high prices were an incentive for producers to increase the quantity supplied. Soap companies increased production, while companies that had never produced sanitizers before (like Jim Beam, the whiskey distiller) jumped into the market. If the government prohibited price gouging,

> **market shortage:** The amount by which the quantity demanded exceeds the quantity supplied at a given price; excess demand.

WORLD VIEW

VENEZUELA'S FOOD CRISIS

Venezuelans are starving. According to the Food and Agriculture Organization (FAO), 21.2 percent of Venezuelans are suffering from hunger. Thirty percent of children are malnourished. There simply isn't enough food to go around.

Price controls are a major culprit. In 2003, then-president Hugo Chavez declared war on "speculators" who were increasing food prices. He imposed price controls on basic foods and medicines. Price controls were tightened by his successor, Nicolas Maduro, in the Fair Prices Act of 2014 and again in the Constitutional Law of Agreed Prices passed in November 2017.

The price ceilings make food seem affordable. But food is hard to find. The price ceilings make production and importation of food unprofitable. The government distributes some basic food rations every month. But people have to wait hours in line to get access to more food, often in vain. Rice, flour, coffee, toilet paper, diapers, sugar, and medicine are in short supply. Black markets, occasional food riots, and cross-border smuggling bring some relief but not enough. Over four million Venezuelans have fled the country since 2014. Those left behind are hungry all the time.

Source: News reports of 2017–2019.

CRITICAL ANALYSIS: Price controls increase the quantity demanded but reduce the quantity supplied. The end result is a **market shortage** that leaves consumers frustrated (and hungry).

those market adjustments wouldn't have occurred and the sanitizer shortage would have persisted longer.

In Venezuela, the government's determination to prevent any sort of price gouging has had debilitating effects. The socialist government has tried to keep food prices low by imposing **price ceilings** on everything from rice to sanitary napkins. As the accompanying World View "Venezuela's Food Crisis" notes, those price controls have led to widespread hunger.

price ceiling: An upper limit imposed on the price of a good.

Self-Adjusting Prices. What we observe, then, is that *whenever the market price is set above or below the equilibrium price, either a market surplus or a market shortage will emerge.* To overcome a surplus or shortage, buyers and sellers will change their behavior. Sellers will have to compete for customers by reducing prices when a market surplus exists. If a shortage exists, buyers will compete for service by offering to pay higher prices. Only at the *equilibrium* price will no further adjustments be required.

Sometimes the market price is slow to adjust, and a disequilibrium persists. This is often the case with tickets to rock concerts, football games, and other one-time events. People initially adjust their behavior by standing in ticket lines for hours, or hopping on the Internet, hoping to buy a ticket at the below-equilibrium price. The tickets are typically resold ("scalped"), however, at prices closer to equilibrium. This is a common occurrence at major college sporting events such as the Final Four basketball championships (see Front Page Economics "March Madness Becomes Sadness").

FRONT PAGE ECONOMICS

MARCH MADNESS BECOMES SADNESS

Ticket prices for the college basketball championships always skyrocket when the 68-team draw is announced. And they jump even further as the Final Four teams emerge. The year 2020 was no different. The 700 floor seats that are sold to students for $40 apiece were already reselling for as much as $4,670 in early January. If the history of March Madness is a guide, those tickets could have sold for more than $10,000 each once the Final Four teams were known. In 2020, however, there wasn't a Final Four: Fear of the coronavirus convinced the NCAA to cancel that year's tournament. The only madness was among those fans that paid scalpers' prices for tickets that got only $40 refunds.

Source: Media reports, March 10–14, 2020.

CRITICAL ANALYSIS: When tickets are sold initially at below-equilibrium prices, a market **shortage** is created. Scalpers resell tickets at prices closer to equilibrium, reaping a profit in the process.

Business firms can discover equilibrium prices by trial and error. If consumer purchases aren't keeping up with production, a firm may conclude that its price is above the equilibrium price. To get rid of accumulated inventory, the firm will have to lower its price. In the happier situation where consumer purchases are outpacing production, a firm might conclude that its price was a trifle too low and give it a nudge upward. In either case, the equilibrium price can be established after a few trials in the marketplace.

Changes in Equilibrium

No equilibrium price is permanent. The equilibrium price established in the Clearview College tutoring market, for example, was the unique outcome of specific demand and supply schedules. Those schedules themselves were based on our assumption of *ceteris paribus.* We assumed that the "taste" (desire) for web design assistance was given, as were consumers'

Why do stores ever have sales?
Ron Zmiri/123RF

incomes, the price and availability of other goods, and expectations. Any of these determinants of demand could change. When one does, the demand curve has to be redrawn. Such a shift of the demand curve will lead to a new equilibrium price and quantity. Indeed, *the equilibrium price will change whenever the supply or demand curve shifts.*

A Demand Shift We can illustrate how equilibrium prices change by taking one last look at the Clearview College tutoring market. Our original supply and demand curves, together with the resulting equilibrium (point E_1), are depicted in Figure 3.7. Now suppose that all the professors at Clearview begin requiring class-specific web pages from each student. The

FIGURE 3.7

Changes in Equilibrium

If demand or supply changes (shifts), market equilibrium will change as well.

　Demand shift: In (*a*), the rightward shift of the demand curve illustrates an increase in demand. When demand increases, the equilibrium price rises (from E_1 to E_2).

　Supply shift: In (*b*), the leftward shift of the supply curve illustrates a decrease in supply. This raises the equilibrium price to E_3.

　Demand and supply curves shift only when their underlying determinants change—that is, when *ceteris paribus* is violated.

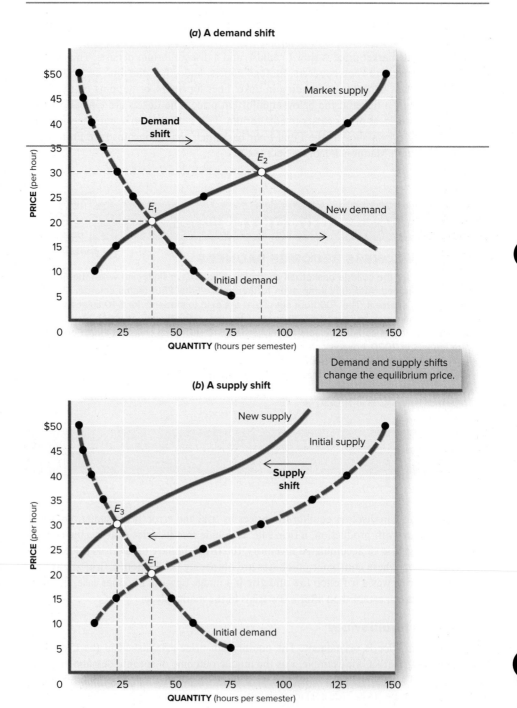

(a) A demand shift

(b) A supply shift

Demand and supply shifts change the equilibrium price.

increased need (desire) for web design ability will affect market demand. Tom, George, and Lisa will be willing to buy more web tutoring at every price than they were before. That is, the *demand* for web services has increased. We can represent this increased demand by a rightward *shift* of the market demand curve, as illustrated in Figure 3.7a.

Note that the new demand curve intersects the (unchanged) market supply curve at a new price (point E_2); the equilibrium price is now $30 per hour and 90 hours of tutoring are bought. This new equilibrium price will persist until either the demand curve or the supply curve shifts again.

A Supply Shift. Figure 3.7b illustrates a *supply* shift. The decrease (leftward shift) in supply might occur if some on-campus tutors got sick. Or approaching exams might convince would-be tutors that they have no time to spare. *Whenever supply decreases (shifts left), price tends to rise,* as in Figure 3.7b.

Lots of Shifts. In the real world, demand and supply curves are constantly shifting. A change in the weather can alter the supply and demand for food, vacations, and baseball games. A new product can change the demand for old products. A foreign crisis can alter the supply, demand, and price of oil (see World View "Gas Prices Jump in Wake of Saudi Attack"). And a virus can lead to extreme changes in ticket prices to sporting events (see Front Page Economics "March Madness Becomes Sadness"). Look for and remember these shifts:

Type of Shift	Name	Effect on Price	Effect on Quantity
Rightward shift of demand	"Increase in demand"	Price increase	Quantity increase
Leftward shift of demand	"Decrease in demand"	Price decrease	Quantity decrease
Rightward shift of supply	"Increase in supply"	Price decrease	Quantity increase
Leftward shift of supply	"Decrease in supply"	Price increase	Quantity decrease

When you see a price change, one or more of these shifts must have occurred.

MARKET OUTCOMES

Notice how the market mechanism resolves the basic economic questions of WHAT, HOW, and FOR WHOM.

WHAT

The WHAT question refers to the mix of output society produces. How much web tutorial service will be included in that mix? The answer at Clearview College was 39 hours of tutoring per semester. This decision wasn't reached in a referendum, but instead in the market equilibrium (Figure 3.6). In the same way but on a larger scale, millions of consumers and a handful of auto producers decide to include 17 million or so cars and trucks in each year's mix of output. Auto manufacturers use rebates, discounts, and variable interest rates to induce consumers to buy the same quantity that auto manufacturers are producing.

HOW

The market mechanism also determines HOW goods are produced. Profit-seeking producers will strive to produce web designs and automobiles in the most efficient way. They'll use market prices to decide not only WHAT to produce but also what resources to use in the production process. If new software simplifies web design—and is priced low enough—tutors will use it. Likewise, auto manufacturers will use robots rather than humans on the assembly line if robots reduce costs and increase profits.

FOR WHOM

Finally, the invisible hand of the market will determine who gets the goods produced. At Clearview College, who got web tutoring? Only those students who were willing and able to pay $20 per hour for that service. FOR WHOM are all those automobiles produced each year? The answer is the same: those consumers who are willing and able to pay the market price for a new car.

Optimal, Not Perfect

Not everyone is happy with these answers, of course. Tom would like to pay only $10 an hour for a tutor. And some of the Clearview students don't have enough income to buy any tutoring. They think it's unfair that they have to design their own web pages while rich students can have someone else do their design work for them. Students who can't afford cars are even less happy with the market's answer to the FOR WHOM question.

Although the outcomes of the marketplace aren't perfect, they're often optimal. Optimal outcomes are the best possible given our incomes and scarce resources. Sure, we'd like everyone to have access to tutoring and to drive a new car. But there aren't enough resources available to create such a utopia. So we have to ration available tutors and cars. The market mechanism performs this rationing function. People who want to supply tutoring or build cars are free to make that choice. And consumers are free to decide how they want to spend their income. In the process, we expect market participants to make decisions that maximize their own well-being. If they do, then we conclude that everyone is doing as well as possible, given their available resources.

DECISIONS FOR TOMORROW

Should We Allow the Sale of Human Organs?

As you were reading this chapter, dozens of Americans were dying from failed organs. More than 100,000 Americans are waiting for life-saving kidneys, livers, lungs, and other vital organs. They can't wait long, however. Every day at least 20 of these organ-diseased patients die. The clock is always ticking.

Modern technology can save most of these patients. Vital organs can be transplanted, extending the life of diseased patients. How many people are saved, however, depends on how well the organ "market" works.

The Supply of Organs. The only cure for liver disease and some other organ failures is a replacement organ. More than 50 years ago, doctors discovered that they could transplant an organ from one individual to another. Since then, medical technology has advanced to the point where organ transplants are exceptionally safe and successful. The constraint on this life-saving technique is the *supply* of transplantable organs.

Although more than 2 million Americans die each year, most deaths do not create transplantable organs. Only 20,000 or so people die in circumstances—such as brain death after a car crash—that make them suitable donors for life-saving transplants. Additional kidneys can be "harvested" from live donors (we have two kidneys but can function with only one; this is not true for liver, heart, or pancreas).

You don't have to die to supply an organ. Instead, you become a donor by agreeing to release your organs after death. The agreement is typically certified on a driver's license and sometimes on a bracelet or "dog tag." This allows emergency doctors to identify potential organ supplies.

People become donors for many reasons. Moral principles, religious convictions, and humanitarianism all play a role in the donation decision. It's the same with blood donations: People give blood (while alive!) because they want to help save other individuals.

Continued

Market Incentives. Monetary incentives could also play a role. When blood donations are inadequate, hospitals and medical schools *buy* blood in the marketplace. People who might not donate blood come forth to *sell* blood when a price is offered. In principle, the same incentive might increase the number of *organ* donors. If offered cash now for a postmortem organ, would the willingness to donate increase? The law of supply suggests it would. Offer $1,000 in cash for signing up, and potential donors will start lining up. Offer more, and the quantity supplied will increase further.

Zero Price Ceiling. The government doesn't permit this to happen. In 1984 Congress forbade the purchase or sale of human organs in the United States (the National Organ Transplantation Act). In part, the prohibition was rooted in moral and religious convictions. It was also motivated by equity concerns—the FOR WHOM question. If organs could be bought and sold, then the rich would have a distinct advantage in living.

The prohibition on market sales is effectively a **price ceiling** set at zero. As a consequence, the only available organs are those supplied by altruistic donors—people who are willing to supply organs at a zero price. The quantity supplied can't be increased with (illegal) price incentives. In general, *price ceilings have three predictable effects: they*

> **price ceiling:** An upper limit imposed on the price of a good.

- *Increase the quantity demanded.*
- *Decrease the quantity supplied.*
- *Create a market shortage.*

The Deadly Shortage Figure 3.8 illustrates the consequences of this price ceiling. At a price of zero, only the quantity q_a of "altruistic" organs is available (roughly one-third of the potential supply). But the quantity q_d is demanded by all the organ-diseased individuals. The market shortage $q_d - q_a$ tells us how many patients will die.

Economists contend that many of these deaths are unnecessary. A University of Pennsylvania study showed that the quantity of organs supplied *doubled* when payment was offered. Without the government-set price ceiling, more organ-diseased patients would live. Figure 3.8 shows that q_E people would get transplants in a market-driven system. In the government-regulated system, only the quantity of q_a of transplants can occur.

Why does the government impose price controls that condemn more people to die? Because it feels the market unfairly distributes available organs. Only people who can afford the price p_E end up living in the market-based system—a feature regulators say is unfair. In the absence of the market mechanism, however, the government must set other rules for who gets the even smaller quantity of organs supplied. That rationing system may be unfair as well.

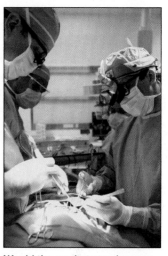

Would the market supply more organs?

ERproductions Ltd/Blend Images LLC

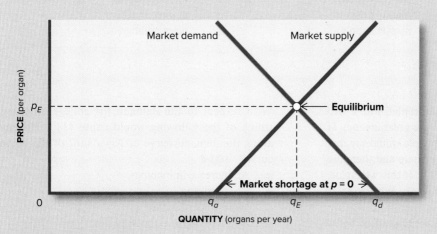

FIGURE 3.8

Organ Transplant Market

A market in human organs would deliver the quantity q_E at a price of p_E. The government-set price ceiling ($p = 0$) reduces the quantity supplied to q_a.

SUMMARY

- People participate in the marketplace by offering to buy or sell goods and services, or factors of production. Participation is motivated by the desire to maximize utility (consumers), profits (business firms), or the general welfare (government) from the limited resources each participant has. **LO3-1, LO3-2**
- All market transactions involve the exchange of either factors of production or goods and services. Although the actual exchanges can occur anywhere, they take place in product markets or factor markets, depending on what is being exchanged. **LO3-1, LO3-2**
- People willing and able to buy a particular good at some price are part of the market demand for that product. All those willing and able to sell that good at some price are part of the market supply. Total market demand or supply is the sum of individual demands or supplies. **LO3-1, LO3-2**
- Supply and demand curves illustrate how the quantity demanded or supplied changes in response to a change in the price of that good, if nothing else changes *(ceteris paribus)*. Demand curves slope downward; supply curves slope upward. **LO3-1, LO3-2**
- Determinants of market demand include the number of potential buyers and their respective tastes (desires), incomes, other goods, and expectations. If any of these determinants changes, the demand curve shifts. Movements along a demand curve are induced only by a change in the price of that good. **LO3-4**
- Determinants of market supply include factor costs, technology, profitability of other goods, expectations, tax rates, and number of sellers. Supply shifts when these underlying determinants change. **LO3-4**
- The quantity of goods or resources actually exchanged in each market depends on the behavior of all buyers and sellers, as summarized in market supply and demand curves. At the point where the two curves intersect, an equilibrium price—the price at which the quantity demanded equals the quantity supplied—is established. **LO3-3**
- A distinctive feature of the market equilibrium is that it's the only price-quantity combination acceptable to buyers and sellers alike. At higher prices, the quantity supplied is more than buyers are willing to purchase (a market surplus); at lower prices, the amount demanded exceeds the quantity supplied (a market shortage). Only the equilibrium price clears the market. **LO3-3**
- Price ceilings are disequilibrium prices imposed on the marketplace. Such price controls create an imbalance between quantities demanded and supplied, resulting in market shortages. **LO3-5**

Key Terms

factor market	law of demand	law of supply
product market	substitute goods	equilibrium price
opportunity cost	complementary goods	market mechanism
supply	*ceteris paribus*	price floor
demand	shift in demand	market surplus
demand schedule	market demand	market shortage
demand curve	market supply	price ceiling

Questions for Discussion

1. In our story of Tom, the student confronted with a web design assignment, we emphasized the great urgency of his desire for web tutoring. Many people would say that Tom had an "absolute need" for web help and therefore was ready to "pay anything" to get it. If this were true, what shape would his demand curve have? Why isn't this realistic? **LO3-1**
2. If Disney+ had been priced at $9.99 instead of $6.99 what would have happened to (a) market demand, (b) the quantity demanded? Why was the initial price so important? (see Front Page Economics "Pricing Disney+")? **LO3-1**
3. With respect to the demand for college enrollment, which of the following would cause (1) a movement along the demand curve or (2) a shift of the demand curve? **LO3-4**
   a. An increase in incomes.
   b. Lower tuition.
   c. More student loans.
   d. An increase in textbook prices.
4. What happens to Netflix subscriptions when the price of Amazon Prime changes? **LO3-5**
5. Why are scalpers typically able to resell tickets to the Final Four basketball games at such high prices (Front

Page Economics "March Madness Becomes Sadness")? **LO3-2**

6. In Figure 3.8, why is the organ demand curve downward-sloping rather than vertical? **LO3-1**

7. The shortage in the organ market (Figure 3.8) requires a nonmarket rationing scheme. Who should get the available (q_a) organs? Is this fairer than the market-driven distribution? **LO3-5**

8. What would happen in the apple market if the government set a *minimum* price of $10.00 per apple? What might motivate such a policy? **LO3-5**

9. When the price of hand sanitizers shot up in March 2020, the attorneys general of 33 states demanded that sellers stop price gouging. How would a price ceiling have affected the availability and distribution of hand sanitizers, compared to an uncontrolled market? **LO3-5**

10. Is there a shortage of on-campus parking at your school? How might the shortage be resolved? **LO3-3**

PROBLEMS FOR CHAPTER 3

LO3-1 1. According to Figure 3.3, at what price would Tom buy 12 hours of web tutoring?
(*a*) Without a lottery win.
(*b*) With a lottery win.

LO3-3 2. According to Figures 3.5 and 3.6, what would the new equilibrium price of tutoring services be if Ann decided to stop tutoring?

LO3-1 3. Suppose Disney+ changes its monthly subscription price from $7 to $9 per month. Graphically show the impact of this price change in the following markets:
(*a*) Popcorn, pizza, and other movie snacks.
(*b*) Netflix.

LO3-3 4. If the quantity demanded increases by 2 million for every $1 reduction in the subscription price,
(*a*) How many initial subscribers would Disney+ have gotten at a price of $8.99 (see Front Page Economics "Pricing Disney+")?
(*b*) Is this a movement along the demand curve or a shift in demand?

5. If Netflix loses 4 million subscribers for every $1 reduction in the Disney+ subscription price,
(*a*) How many more subscribers would Netflix have lost if Disney+ were initially priced at $4.99 a month (see Front Page Economics "Pricing Disney+")?
(*b*) Is this a movement along the demand curve or a shift in demand?

LO3-3 6. According to Front Page Economics "March Madness Becomes Sadness"
(*a*) What was the initial student price of a ticket to the NCAA finals?
(*b*) In January 2020, was there an equilibrium, a shortage, or a surplus of tickets?
(*c*) In March 2020, was there an equilibrium, a shortage, or a surplus of tickets?

LO3-3 7. Given the following data on gasoline supply and demand,
(*a*) What is the equilibrium price?
(*b*) Suppose the current price is $4. At this price, how much of a shortage or surplus exists?

Price per gallon	$5.00	$4.00	$3.00	$2.00	$1.00		$5.00	$4.00	$3.00	$2.00	$1.00
Quantity demanded (gallons per day)						Quantity supplied (gallons per day)					
Al	1	2	3	4	5	Firm A	3	3	2	2	1
Betsy	0	1	1	1	2	Firm B	7	5	3	3	2
Casey	2	2	3	3	4	Firm C	6	4	3	3	1
Daisy	1	3	4	4	6	Firm D	6	5	3	2	0
Eddie	1	2	2	3	5	Firm E	4	2	2	2	1
Market total	—	—	—	—	—	Market total	—	—	—	—	—

LO3-2 8. Illustrate using a supply and demand graph what happened to gasoline prices in World View "Gas Prices Jump in Wake of Saudi Attack."
(*a*) Which curve shifted?
(*b*) Which direction did that curve shift (left or right)?
(*c*) Did price increase or decrease?
(*d*) Did quantity increase or decrease?

LO3-4 9. Illustrate using a supply and demand graph what happened to Netflix resulting from new competition (see Front Page Economics "Pricing Disney+").
(*a*) Which curve shifted?
(*b*) Which direction did that curve shift (left or right)?
(*c*) Did price increase or decrease?
(*d*) Did quantity increase or decrease?

PROBLEMS FOR CHAPTER 3 (cont'd)

LO3-5 10. Which curve shifts and in which direction when the following events occur in the domestic car market?
   (*a*) The U.S. economy falls into a recession.
   (*b*) U.S. autoworkers go on strike.
   (*c*) Imported cars become more expensive.
   (*d*) The price of gasoline increases.

LO3-5 11. Use the following data to draw supply and demand curves and illustrate the answers for (*a*)–(*c*) on your graph.

Price	$ 8	7	6	5	4	3	2	1
Quantity demanded	2	3	4	5	6	7	8	9
Quantity supplied	10	9	8	7	6	5	4	3

   (*a*) What is the equilibrium price?
   (*b*) Suppose the current price is $7,
       (*i*) What kind of disequilibrium situation results?
       (*ii*) How large is this surplus or shortage?
   (*c*) Suppose the current price is $3,
       (*i*) What disequilibrium situation results?
       (*ii*) How large is this surplus or shortage?

LO3-5 12. *Decisions for Tomorrow:* In Figure 3.8, when a price ceiling of zero is imposed, does
   (*a*) The quantity of organs demanded increase?
   (*b*) The market demand increase?
   (*c*) The quantity of organs supplied decrease?
   (*d*) The market supply increase?
   (*e*) The equilibrium price change?

LO3-5 13. *Decisions for Tomorrow:* According to Figure 3.8,
   (*a*) How many organs are supplied at a zero price?
   (*b*) How many people die in the government-regulated economy where there is a price ceiling = $0?
   (*c*) How many people die in the market-driven economy?

Design Credit: Shutterstock

71

4

The Role of Government

The market has a keen ear for private wants, but a deaf ear for public needs.

—Robert Heilbroner

Hisham F. Ibrahim/Getty Images

LEARNING OBJECTIVES

After reading this chapter, you should know

LO4-1 The nature and causes of market failure.

LO4-2 How the public sector has grown.

LO4-3 Which taxes finance state, local, and federal governments.

LO4-4 The meaning of government failure.

Governments play a huge role in the economy today—not just the massive federal government, but also the 50 state governments, the 3,142 county governments, the 35,000 city governments, and thousands of school, sanitation, transportation, utility, and other special districts. Together, these various governments directly account for more than a fifth of our economic output and exercise significant influence on all WHAT, HOW, and FOR WHOM answers.

Public opinion polls consistently reveal that Americans feel that the government sector has grown too large. Yet, the same polls show that people want the government to do more things, fix more problems, and regulate more activities. To decide whether the government sector should be larger or smaller, we've got to understand its economic functions better. That is the goal of this chapter.

Laissez faire? We know by now that markets do work: The interaction of supply and demand in product markets *does* generate goods and services. Likewise, the interaction of supply and demand in labor markets *does* yield jobs, wages, and a distribution of income. As we've observed, the market is capable of determining WHAT goods to produce, HOW, and FOR WHOM.

But are the market's answers good enough? Is the mix of output produced by unregulated markets the best possible mix? Will producers choose the production process that protects the environment? Will the market-generated distribution of income be fair enough? Will there be enough jobs for everyone who wants one?

In reality, markets don't always give us the best possible outcomes. Markets dominated by a few powerful corporations may charge excessive prices, limit output, provide poor service, or even retard technological advance. In the quest for profits, producers may sacrifice the environment for cost savings. In unfettered markets, some people may not get life-saving health care, basic education, or even adequate nutrition. When markets generate such undesirable outcomes, government intervention may be needed to ensure better answers to the WHAT, HOW, and FOR WHOM questions.

This chapter identifies the circumstances under which such government intervention is desirable. To this end, we answer the following questions:

- **Under what circumstances do markets fail?**
- **How can government intervention help?**
- **How much government intervention is desirable?**

As we'll see, there's substantial agreement about how and when markets fail to give us the best WHAT, HOW, and FOR WHOM answers. But there's much less agreement about whether government intervention improves the situation. Indeed, an overwhelming majority of Americans are ambivalent about government intervention. They want the government to "fix" the mix of output, protect the environment, and ensure an adequate level of income for everyone. But voters are equally quick to blame government meddling for many of our economic woes.

laissez faire: The doctrine of "leave it alone," of non-intervention by government in the market mechanism.

MARKET FAILURE

We can visualize the potential for government intervention by focusing on the WHAT question. Our goal is clear: produce the best possible mix of output with existing resources. We illustrated this goal earlier with production possibilities curves. Figure 4.1 assumes that of all the possible combinations of output we could produce, the unique combination at point *X* represents the most desirable one. In other words, it's the **optimal mix of output,** the one that maximizes our collective social utility. We haven't yet figured out how to pinpoint that optimal mix; we're simply using the arbitrary point *X* in Figure 4.1 to represent that best possible outcome.

Ideally, the **market mechanism** would lead us to point *X*. Price signals in the marketplace are supposed to move factors of production from one industry to another in response to consumer demands. If we demand more health care—offer to buy more at a given price—more resources (labor) will be allocated to health care services. Similarly, a fall in demand will encourage health care practitioners (doctors, nurses, and the like) to find jobs in another industry. *Changes in market prices direct resources from one industry to another, moving us along the perimeter of the production possibilities curve.*

Where will the market mechanism take us? Will it move resources around until we end up at the optimal point *X?* Or will it leave us at another point on the production possibilities curve with a *sub*optimal mix of output? (If point *X* is the *optimal,* or best possible, mix, all other output mixes must be *sub*optimal.)

We use the term **market failure** to refer to situations in which the market generates imperfect (suboptimal) outcomes. If the invisible hand of the marketplace produces a mix of output that's different from the one society most desires, then it has failed. *Market failure implies that the forces of supply and demand haven't led us to the best point on the*

optimal mix of output: The most desirable combination of output attainable with existing resources, technology, and social values.

market mechanism: The use of market prices and sales to signal desired outputs (or resource allocations).

market failure: An imperfection in the market mechanism that prevents optimal outcomes.

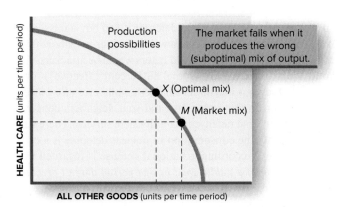

FIGURE 4.1

Market Failure

We can produce any mix of output on the production possibilities curve. Our goal is to produce the optimal (best possible) mix of output, as represented by point *X*. Market forces, however, might produce another combination, like point *M*. In that case, the market fails—it produces a *sub*optimal mix of output.

production possibilities curve. Such a failure is illustrated by point *M* in Figure 4.1. Point *M* is assumed to be the mix of output generated by market forces. Notice that the market mix (*M*) doesn't represent the optimal mix, which is assumed to be at point *X*. We get less health care and more of other goods than are optimal. The market in this case *fails;* we get the wrong answer to the WHAT question.

Market failure opens the door for government intervention. If the market can't do the job, we need some form of *nonmarket* force to get the right answers. In terms of Figure 4.1, we need something to change the mix of output—to move us from point *M* (the market mix of output) to point *X* (the optimal mix of output). Accordingly, *market failure establishes a basis for government intervention.* We look to the government to push market outcomes closer to the ideal.

Causes of Market Failure. Because market failure is the justification for government intervention, we need to know how and when market failure occurs. *The four specific sources of market failure are*

- *Public goods.*
- *Externalities.*
- *Market power.*
- *Inequity.*

We will first examine the nature of these problems, then see why government intervention is called for in each case.

Public Goods

The market mechanism does a good job of signaling consumer demands for various goods and services. By offering to pay for goods, we express our preferences about WHAT to produce. However, this mode of communication is socially efficient only if the benefits of consuming a particular good are available only to the individuals who purchase that product.

Consider doughnuts, for example. When you eat a doughnut, you alone get the satisfaction from its sweet, greasy taste—that is, you derive a private benefit. No one else benefits from your consumption of a doughnut: The doughnut you purchase in the market is yours alone to consume; it's a **private good.** Accordingly, your decision to purchase the doughnut will be determined only by your anticipated satisfaction, your income, and your opportunity costs.

No Exclusion. Most of the goods and services produced in the public sector are different from doughnuts—and not just because doughnuts look, taste, and smell different from "star wars" missile shields. When you buy a doughnut, you exclude others from consumption of that product. If Dunkin' Donuts sells you a particular pastry, it can't supply the same pastry to someone else. If you devour it, no one else can. In this sense, the transaction and product are completely private.

The same exclusiveness is not characteristic of national defense. If you buy a missile defense system to thwart enemy attacks, there's no way you can exclude your neighbors from the protection your system provides. Either the missile shield deters would-be attackers—like Israel's "Iron Dome" (see World View "Israel's 'Iron Dome' 86 Percent Effective")—or it doesn't. In the former case, both you and your neighbors survive happily ever after; in the latter case, we're all blown away together. In that sense, you and your neighbors consume the benefits of a missile shield *jointly.* National defense isn't a divisible service. There's no such thing as exclusive consumption here. The consumption of nuclear defenses is a communal feat, no matter who pays for them. Accordingly, national defense is regarded as a **public good** in the sense that *consumption of a public good by one person doesn't preclude consumption of the same good by another person.* By contrast, a doughnut is a private good because if I eat it, no one else can consume it.

private good: A good or service whose consumption by one person excludes consumption by others.

public good: A good or service whose consumption by one person does not exclude consumption by others.

WORLD VIEW

ISRAEL'S "IRON DOME" 86 PERCENT EFFECTIVE

The fragile peace between Israel and its Arab neighbors never lasts very long. The surest sign of a peace breakdown is a barrage of rockets fired by Hamas into Israel. Since 2011, however, Israel has had the advantage in these skirmishes. Its "Iron Dome" defense system is designed to intercept and destroy incoming missiles and mortars. Between 2011 and 2019, Israel claims to have intercepted and destroyed 1,500 incoming projectiles. In May 2019 Israel successfully intercepted 86 percent of a one-day, 600-rocket barrage fired off by Hamas. This defense doesn't come cheap, however: Each interceptor costs about $100,000.

Source: News reports, May 2019.

CRITICAL ANALYSIS: An air-defense system is a **public good,** as consumption of its services by one individual does not preclude consumption by others. Nonpayers cannot be excluded from its protection.

The Free-Rider Dilemma. The communal nature of public goods creates a dilemma. If you and I will *both* benefit from nuclear defenses, which one of us should buy the missile shield? I'd prefer that *you* buy it, thereby giving me protection at no direct cost. Hence, I may profess no desire for a missile shield, secretly hoping to take a **free ride** on your market purchase. Unfortunately, you too have an incentive to conceal your desire for national defenses. As a consequence, neither one of us may step forward to *demand* a missile shield in the marketplace. We'll both end up defenseless.

Flood control is also a public good. No one in the valley wants to be flooded out. But each landowner knows that a flood control dam will protect *all* the landowners, regardless of who pays. Either the entire valley is protected or no one is. Accordingly, individual farmers and landowners may say they don't want a dam and aren't willing to pay for it. Everyone is waiting and hoping that someone else will pay for flood control. In other words, everyone wants a *free ride.* Thus, if we leave it to market forces, no one will *demand* flood control, and all the property in the valley will be washed away.

The difference between public goods and private goods rests on *technical considerations,* not political philosophy. ***The central question is whether we have the technical capability to exclude nonpayers.*** In the case of national defense or flood control, we simply don't have that capability. Even city streets have the characteristics of public goods. Although theoretically we could restrict the use of streets to those who paid to use them, a tollgate on every corner would be exceedingly expensive and impractical. Here again, joint or public consumption appears to be the only feasible alternative. As Front Page Economics "Firefighters Watch as Home Burns to the Ground" on local firefighting emphasizes, the technical capability to exclude nonpayers is the key factor in identifying "public goods."

To the list of public goods we could add snow removal, the administration of justice (including prisons), the regulation of commerce, the conduct of foreign relations, airport security, and even Fourth of July fireworks. These services—which cost tens of *billions* of dollars and employ thousands of workers—provide benefits to everyone, no matter who pays for them. In each instance it's technically impossible or prohibitively expensive to exclude nonpayers from the services provided.

Underproduction of Public Goods. The free riders associated with public goods upset the customary practice of paying for what you get. If I can get all the national defense, flood control, and laws I want without paying for them, I'm not about to complain. I'm perfectly happy to let you pay for the services while we all consume them.

You may feel the same way. Why should you pay for these services if you can consume just as much of them when your neighbors foot the whole bill? It might seem selfish not to pay

free rider: An individual who reaps direct benefits from someone else's purchase (consumption) of a public good.

Flood control is a public good.
Department of Commerce/NOAA

FRONT PAGE ECONOMICS

FIREFIGHTERS WATCH AS HOME BURNS TO THE GROUND

OBION COUNTY, Tenn.—Imagine your home catches fire, but the local fire department won't respond, then watches it burn. That's exactly what happened to a local family tonight.

A local neighborhood is furious after firefighters watched as an Obion County, Tennessee, home burned to the ground.

The homeowner, Gene Cranick, said he offered to pay whatever it would take for firefighters to put out the flames but was told it was too late. They wouldn't do anything to stop his house from burning.

WPSD Local 6/AP Images

Each year, Obion County residents must pay $75 if they want fire protection from the city of South Fulton. But the Cranicks did not pay.

The mayor said if homeowners don't pay, they're out of luck.

—Jason Hibbs

©WPSD Local 6, Paducah, KY, September 30, 2010. Used with permission.

CRITICAL ANALYSIS: A product is a **public good** only if nonpayers *cannot* be excluded from its consumption. Firefighters in Tennessee proved that fire protection is not inherently a public good: They let the nonpaying homeowner's house burn down!

your share of the cost of providing public goods. But you'd be better off in a material sense if you spent your income on doughnuts, letting others pick up the tab for public services.

Because the link between paying and consuming is broken, public goods can't be peddled in the supermarket. People are reluctant to buy what they can get free. Hence, *if public goods were marketed like private goods, everyone would wait for someone else to pay.* The end result might be a total lack of public services. This is the kind of dilemma Robert Heilbroner had in mind when he spoke of the market's "deaf ear" (see the quote at the beginning of this chapter).

The production possibilities curve in Figure 4.2 illustrates the dilemma created by public goods. Suppose that point *A* represents the optimal mix of private and public goods. It's the mix of goods and services we'd select if everyone's preferences were known and reflected in production decisions. The market mechanism won't lead us to point *A*, however, because the *demand* for public goods will be hidden. If we rely on the market, nearly everyone will withhold demand for public goods, waiting for a free ride to point *A*. As a result, we'll get a smaller quantity of public goods than we really want. The market mechanism will leave us at point *B*, with few, if any, public goods. Because point *A* is assumed to be optimal, point *B* must be *suboptimal* (inferior to point *A*). The market fails: We can't rely on the market mechanism to allocate enough resources to the production of public goods, no matter how much they might be desired.

Note that we're using the term "public good" in a peculiar way. To most people, "public good" refers to any good or service the government produces. In economics, however, the meaning is much more restrictive. The term "public good" refers only to those nonexcludable goods and services that must be consumed jointly, both by those who pay for them and by those who don't. Public goods can be produced by either the government or the private sector. Private goods can be produced in either sector as well. The problem is that *the market tends to underproduce public goods and overproduce private goods.* If we want more public goods, we need a *nonmarket* force—government intervention—to get them. The government will have to force people to pay taxes, then use the tax revenues to pay for the production of national defense, flood control, snow removal, and other public goods.

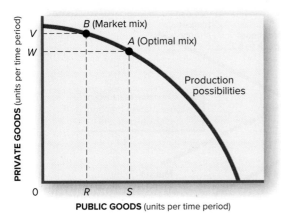

FIGURE 4.2

**Underproduction
of Public Goods**

Suppose point *A* represents the optimal mix of output—that is, the mix of private and public goods that maximizes society's welfare. Because consumers won't demand purely public goods in the marketplace, the price mechanism won't allocate so many resources to their production. Instead the market will tend to produce a mix of output like point *B*, which includes fewer public goods (*OR*) than are optimal (*OS*).

Externalities

The free-rider problem associated with public goods is an important justification for government intervention. It's not the only justification, however. A second justification for intervention arises from the tendency of costs or benefits of some market activities to "spill over" onto third parties.

Consider the case of cigarettes. The price someone is willing to pay for a pack of cigarettes reflects the amount of satisfaction a smoker anticipates from its consumption. If that price is high enough, tobacco companies will produce the cigarettes demanded. That is how market-based price signals are supposed to work. In this case, however, the price paid isn't a satisfactory signal of the product's desirability. The smoker's pleasure is offset in part by nonsmokers' *dis*pleasure. In this case, smoke literally spills over onto other consumers, causing them discomfort, ill health, and even death (see World View "Secondhand Smoke Kills 600,000 People a Year"). Yet their loss isn't reflected in the market price: The harm caused to nonsmokers is *external* to the market price of cigarettes.

The term **externalities** refers to all costs or benefits of a market activity borne by a third party—that is, by someone other than the immediate producer or consumer. *Whenever externalities are present, market prices aren't a valid measure of a good's value to society.* As a

externalities: Costs (or benefits) of a market activity borne by a third party; the difference between the social and private costs (benefits) of a market activity.

WORLD VIEW

SECONDHAND SMOKE KILLS MORE THAN 600,000 PEOPLE A YEAR

Secondhand smoke globally kills more than 600,000 people each year, accounting for 1 percent of all deaths worldwide.

Researchers estimate that annually secondhand smoke causes about 379,000 deaths from heart disease, 165,000 deaths from lower respiratory disease, 36,900 deaths from asthma, and 21,400 deaths from lung cancer.

Hannah Maule-Finch/Image Source/Corbis

Children account for about 165,000 of the deaths. Forty percent of children and 30 percent of adults regularly breathe in secondhand smoke.

Source: World Health Organization

CRITICAL ANALYSIS: The health risks imposed on nonsmokers via passive smoke represent an **external cost.** The market price of cigarettes doesn't reflect costs borne by third parties.

FIGURE 4.3
Externalities

The market responds to consumer demands, not externalities. Smokers demand q_M cigarettes at the equilibrium price of $7. But external costs on nonsmokers ($2 per pack) imply that the *social* demand for cigarettes is less than (below) *market* demand. The socially optimal level of output is q_O, less than the market output q_M.

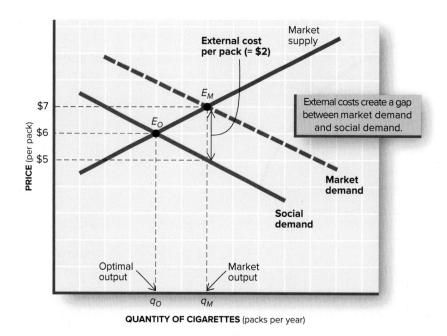

consequence, the market will fail to produce the right mix of output. Specifically, *the market will underproduce goods that yield external benefits and overproduce those that generate external costs.*

External Costs. Figure 4.3 shows how external costs—*negative* externalitites—cause the market to overproduce cigarettes. The market demand curve includes only the wishes of smokers—that is, people who are willing and able to purchase cigarettes. The forces of market demand and supply result in an equilibrium at E_M in which Q_M cigarettes are produced and consumed. The market price of $7 reflects the value of those cigarettes to smokers.

The well-being of *non*smokers isn't reflected in the market equilibrium. To take the *non*smokers' interests into account, we must subtract the external costs imposed on *them* from the value that *smokers* put on cigarettes. In general,

$$\text{Social demand} = \text{Market demand} \pm \text{Externalities}$$

In this case, the externality is a *cost,* so we must *subtract* the external cost from market demand to get a full accounting of social demand. Suppose that the external costs associated with secondhand smoke work out to $2 a pack. That implies that the social value of a pack of cigarettes is $5.

$$\begin{array}{ccccc} \text{Social value} & = & \text{Market value} & - & \text{External Costs} \\ \$5 & = & \$7 & - & \$2 \end{array}$$

Yet, the market equilibrium depicted in Figure 4.3 doesn't reflect this social calculation.

What we need is a *second* demand curve, one that takes into account the well-being of both the smokers and the nonsmokers. We call this second curve the "social demand" curve. To locate this curve in Figure 4.3, we subtract the amount of external cost ($2) from every price on the market demand curve. Hence, the social demand curve lies below the market demand curve in this case. What the social demand curve tells us is how much society would be willing and able to pay for cigarettes if the preferences of *both* smokers and nonsmokers were taken into account.

The social demand curve in Figure 4.3 creates a social equilibrium at E_O. At this juncture, we see that the socially *optimal* quantity of cigarettes is q_O, not the larger market-generated level at q_M. In this sense, the market produces too many cigarettes.

Many people have tried to extend the restrictions on cigarettes to vaping. At first blush, the argument seems plausible, as vape (aerosol) clouds look like exhaled smoke. But studies have concluded that vape clouds might be a nuisance, but they don't pose secondhand health risks (see Front Page Economics "The Health Risks of Vaping"). So vaping restrictions have to be based on other market-failure arguments.

FRONT PAGE ECONOMICS

THE HEALTH RISKS OF VAPING

Vaping has become a popular alternative to smoking, especially among teenagers. In 2019, roughly one out of three teenagers reported vaping. Most teens used flavored pods or cartridges, especially mint-flavored ones produced by JUUL, the industry leader. Concerned with the health risks of vaping, several cities and states sought bans on vaping. Even President Trump suggested that flavored pods should be prohibited.

These government interventions aren't based on the externalities argument, however. Vape clouds do contain some nicotine, fine particles, and trace amounts of toxins associated with cancer. But the levels of these contaminants are so low that they pose no risk to third parties. The bans on vaping are motivated by the health risks to vapers themselves, not to nonvapers.

Source: News reports of September–November 2019.

CRITICAL ANALYSIS: The **externality** explanation for market failure focuses on third-party effects of market transactions. Vaping doesn't pose significant secondhand risks.

Negative externalities also exist in production. A power plant that burns high-sulfur coal damages the surrounding environment. Yet the damage inflicted on neighboring people, vegetation, and buildings is external to the cost calculations of the firm. Because the cost of such pollution is not reflected in the price of electricity, the firm will tend to produce more electricity (and pollution) than is socially desirable. To reduce this imbalance, the government has to step in and change market outcomes.

External Benefits. Externalities can also be beneficial. A product may generate external *benefits* rather than external *costs*. Your college is an example. The students who attend your school benefit directly from the education they receive. That's why they (and you) are willing to pay for tuition, books, and other services. The students in attendance aren't the only beneficiaries of this educational service, however. The research that a university conducts may yield benefits for a much broader community. The values and knowledge students acquire may also be shared with family, friends, and coworkers. These benefits would all be *external* to the market transaction between a paying student and the school. Positive externalities also arise from immunizations against infectious diseases: The person getting immunized obviously benefits, but so do all the people with whom that person comes into contact. Other people (third parties) benefit when you get vaccinated.

If a product yields external benefits, the social demand is greater than the market demand. In this case, the social value of the good *exceeds* the market price (by the amount of external benefit). Accordingly, society wants *more* of the product than the market mechanism alone will produce at any given price. To get that additional output, the government may have to intervene with subsidies or other policies. We conclude then that *the market fails by*

- *Overproducing goods that have external costs.*
- *Underproducing goods that have external benefits.*

If externalities are present, the market won't produce the optimal mix of output. To get that optimal mix, we need government intervention.

The need for government intervention was dramatically apparent during the coronavirus pandemic. The coronavirus pandemic that started in Wuhan, China, in December 2019 swept across the globe like wildfire. Within three months' time, over 1 million cases were reported in 151 nations (see Front Page Economics "COVID-19 Cases Surpass 1 Million"). One of the most critical factors in the spread of the COVID-19 virus was its contagiousness: People with the virus were infecting others with whom they came into contact. More often than not, the people harboring the virus didn't even know they were affected, much less contagious. So, they weren't likely to pay for tests or treatments or voluntarily take precautions that would reduce the spread of the virus. Yet, tests, self-isolation, and treatment would generate a positive—life-saving—externality. But too few people were willing to do it on their own. This was a deadly situation. In response, governments everywhere mandated "social distancing" to reduce infectious contact and offered free tests and treatments. Many governments also ordered people to shelter in place. The motivation there was not only to protect affected individuals, but also to prevent individuals from spreading the virus to others—that is, create positive externalities.

FRONT PAGE ECONOMICS

COVID-19 CASES SURPASS 1 MILLION

Confirmed cases of the coronavirus worldwide surpassed one million this week. Data collected by researchers at the Johns Hopkins University reveal that the number of confirmed cases has risen to 1,011,490 worldwide, with 52,863 confirmed deaths. In the United States, the case count stands at 242,182, with 5,850 deaths. Experts say the number of confirmed cases likely understates the actual incidence of COVID-19 infections due to incomplete reporting. They also expect the case and death tolls to rise in the coming weeks despite increasingly stringent mitigation efforts.

Source: Media reports of April 2–5, 2020.

CRITICAL ANALYSIS: An infectious disease is a classic case of an **externality**. If people isolate themselves or take other preventive measures, they are benefiting third parties. When market participants won't exercise enough caution, the government can force behavior changes that create positive externalities.

Market Power

In the case of both public goods and externalities, the market fails to achieve the optimal mix of output because the price signal is flawed. The price consumers are willing and able to pay for a specific good doesn't reflect all the benefits or cost of producing that good.

The market may fail, however, even when the price signals are accurate. The *response* to price signals, rather than the signals themselves, may be flawed.

Restricted Supply. Market power is often the cause of a flawed response. Suppose that there were only one airline company in the world. This single seller of airline travel would be a **monopoly**—that is, the only producer in that industry. As a monopolist, the airline could charge extremely high prices without worrying that travelers would flock to a competing airline. At the same time, the high prices paid by consumers would express the importance of that service to society. Ideally, those high prices would act as a signal to producers to build and fly more planes—to change the mix of output. But a monopolist doesn't have to cater to every consumer's whim. It can rake in those high prices without increasing service, thereby obstructing our efforts to achieve an optimal mix of output.

Monopoly is the most severe form of **market power.** More generally, market power refers to any situation in which a single producer or consumer has the ability to alter the market

monopoly: A firm that produces the entire market supply of a particular good or service.

market power: The ability to alter the market price of a good or service.

price of a specific product. If the publisher (McGraw-Hill) charges a high price for this book, you'll have to pay the tab. McGraw-Hill has market power because there are relatively few economics texts and your professor has required you to use this one. You don't have power in the textbook market because your decision to buy or not won't alter the market price of this text. You're only one of the million students who are taking an introductory economics course this year.

The market power McGraw-Hill possesses is derived from the copyright on this text. No matter how profitable textbook sales might be, no one else is permitted to produce or sell this particular book. Patents are another common source of market power because they also preclude others from making or selling a specific product. Market power may also result from control of resources, restrictive production agreements, or efficiencies of large-scale production.

Whatever the source of market power, the direct consequence is that one or more producers attain discretionary power over the market's response to price signals. They may use that discretion to enrich themselves rather than to move the economy toward the optimal mix of output. In this case, the market will again fail to deliver the most desired goods and services.

The mandate for government intervention in this case is to prevent or dismantle concentrations of market power. That's the basic purpose of **antitrust** policy. Another option is to *regulate* market behavior. This was one of the goals of the antitrust case against Microsoft. The government was less interested in breaking Microsoft's near monopoly on operating systems than in changing the way Microsoft behaved. Google is now under the same kind of pressure to change its search protocols in order to permit greater competition.

In some cases, it may be economically efficient to have one large firm supply an entire market. Such a situation arises in **natural monopoly,** where a single firm can achieve economies of scale over the entire range of market output. Utility companies, local telephone service, subway systems, and cable all exhibit such scale (size) efficiencies. In these cases, a monopoly *structure* may be economically desirable. The government may have to regulate the *behavior* of a natural monopoly, however, to ensure that consumers get the benefits of that greater efficiency.

With nearly 90 percent of the online search market, Google has great market power.

Annette Shaff/Shutterstock

antitrust: Government intervention to alter market structure or prevent abuse of market power.

natural monopoly: An industry in which one firm can achieve economies of scale over the entire range of market supply.

Inequity

Public goods, externalities, and market power all cause resource misallocations. Where these phenomena exist, the market mechanism will fail to produce the optimal mix of output in the best possible way.

Beyond the questions of WHAT and HOW to produce, we're also concerned about FOR WHOM output is produced. The market answers this question by distributing a larger share of total output to those with the most income. Although this result may be efficient, it's not necessarily equitable. As we saw in Chapter 2, the market mechanism may enrich some people while leaving others to seek shelter in abandoned cars. If such outcomes violate our vision of equity, we may want the government to change the market-generated distribution of income.

Taxes and Transfers. The tax-and-transfer system is the principal mechanism for redistributing incomes. The idea here is to take some of the income away from those who have "too much" and give it to those whom the market has left with "too little." Taxes are levied to take back some of the income received from the market. Those tax revenues are then redistributed via transfer payments to those deemed needy, such as the poor, the aged, and the unemployed. **Transfer payments** are income payments for which no goods or services are exchanged. They're used to bolster the incomes of those for whom the market itself provides too little. In the 2020 presidential campaigns, Democrats championed the notion of changing the market's answer to the FOR WHOM question with higher taxes on the rich and more transfers to the poor.

transfer payments: Payments to individuals for which no current goods or services are exchanged, like Social Security, welfare, and unemployment benefits.

merit good: A good or service society deems everyone is entitled to some minimal quantity of.

Merit Goods. Often our vision of what is "too little" is defined in terms of specific goods and services. There is a widespread consensus in the United States that everyone is entitled to some minimum levels of shelter, food, and health care. These are regarded as **merit goods,** in the sense that everyone merits at least some minimum provision of such goods. When the market does not distribute that minimum provision, the government is called on to fill the gaps. In this case, the income transfers take the form of *in-kind* transfers (e.g., food stamps, housing vouchers, Medicaid) rather than *cash* transfers (e.g., welfare checks, Social Security benefits).

Some people argue that we don't need the government to help the poor—that private charity alone will suffice. Unfortunately, private charity alone has never been adequate. One reason private charity doesn't suffice is the "free-rider" problem. If I contribute heavily to the poor, you benefit from safer streets (fewer muggers), a better environment (fewer slums and homeless people), and a clearer conscience (knowing that fewer people are starving). In this sense, the relief of misery is a *public* good. Were I the only taxpayer to benefit substantially from the reduction of poverty, then charity would be a private affair. As long as income support substantially benefits the public at large, then income redistribution is a *public* good, for which public funding is appropriate. This is the *economic* rationale for public income redistribution activities. To this rationale one can add such moral arguments as seem appropriate.

Macro Instability

The micro failures of the marketplace imply that we may end up at the wrong point on the production possibilities curve or inequitably distributing the output produced. There's another basic question we've swept under the rug, however. How do we get to the production possibilities curve in the first place? To reach the curve, we must utilize all available resources and technology. Can we be confident that the invisible hand of the marketplace will use all available resources? That confidence was shattered in 2008–2009 when total output contracted and **unemployment** soared. Millions of people who were willing and able to work but unable to find jobs demanded that the government intervene to increase output and create more jobs. The market had failed.

And what about prices? Price signals are a critical feature of the market mechanism. But the validity of those signals depends on some stable measure of value. What good is a doubling of salary when the price of everything you buy doubles as well? Generally, rising prices will enrich people who own property and impoverish people who rent. That's why we strive to avoid **inflation**—a situation in which the *average* price level is increasing.

Historically, the marketplace has been wracked with bouts of both unemployment and inflation. These experiences have prompted calls for government intervention at the macro level. *The goal of macro intervention is to foster economic growth—to get us on the production possibilities curve (full employment), maintain a stable price level (price stability), and increase our capacity to produce (growth).*

unemployment: The inability of labor force participants to find jobs.

inflation: An increase in the average level of prices of goods and services.

....

GROWTH OF GOVERNMENT

The potential micro and macro failures of the marketplace provide specific justifications for government intervention. We do need government to provide public goods, compensate for externalities, limit the excesses of market power, and redistribute incomes more fairly. We can't rely completely on a private, market-based economy to generate optimal answers to the WHAT, HOW, and FOR WHOM questions.

The question then becomes, "How well does the government respond to these needs?" We'll start answering this question by looking at what the government now does and how it has grown.

Federal Growth

Until the 1930s the federal government's role was largely limited to national defense (a public good), enforcement of a common legal system (also a public good), and provision of postal service (equity). The Great Depression of the 1930s spawned a new range of government activities, including welfare and Social Security programs (equity), minimum wage laws and workplace standards (regulation), and massive public works (public goods and externalities). In the 1950s the federal government also assumed a greater role in maintaining macroeconomic stability (macro failure), protecting the environment (externalities), and safeguarding the public's health (externalities and equity).

These increasing responsibilities have greatly increased the size of the public sector. In 1902 the federal government employed fewer than 350,000 people and spent a mere $650 *million*. Today, the federal government employs nearly 4 million people and spends nearly $5 *trillion* a year.

Direct Expenditure. Figure 4.4 summarizes the growth of the public sector since 1930. Let's focus on the federal government, depicted with the orange line. Back in 1930 the federal share of total spending was close to zero. That share grew in the 1930s and skyrocketed during World War II. Federal purchases of goods and services for the war accounted for more than 40 percent of total output during the 1943–1944 period. The federal share of total U.S. output fell abruptly after World War II, rose again during the Korean War (1950–1953), and has declined slightly since then.

The decline in the federal share of total output is somewhat at odds with most people's perception of government growth. This discrepancy is explained by two phenomena. First, people see the *absolute* size of the government growing every year. But we're focusing here on the *relative* size of the public sector. From 1950 until 2008, the public sector grew a bit more slowly than the private sector, slightly reducing its relative size. The trend was interrupted in 2008–2011, when the private sector shrank and the federal government undertook massive stimulus spending. Since then, the federal government's share of total output has hovered around 6.5 percent. President Trump's stepped-up spending on national defense has increased that share by only one decimal point.

Income Transfers. The federal share of output depicted in Figure 4.4 looks small (6.6 percent) because it doesn't include *all* federal spending. As noted above, Uncle Sam *spends* nearly $5 trillion a year. But the majority of that spending is for income transfers, not direct

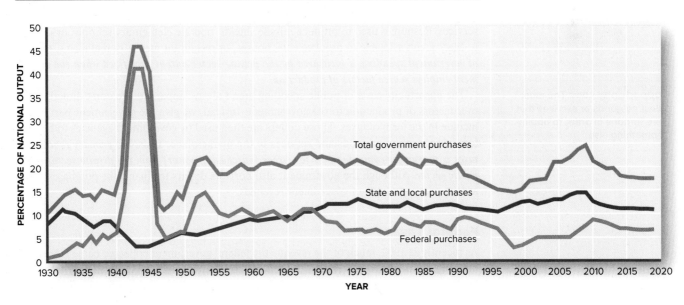

FIGURE 4.4

Government Growth

During World War II the public sector purchased nearly half of the total U.S. output. Since the early 1950s the public sector share of total output has been closer to 20 percent. Within the public sector, however, there's been a major shift: Since 1970,

state and local claims on resources (now 11 percent) have exceeded the federal share (now 6.5 percent).

Source: U.S. Bureau of Economic Analysis.

expenditure on goods and services. Figure 4.4 only counts direct expenditure on things like national defense, transportation systems, education, and other real goods—the things that are included in the WHAT outcome of the economy. By contrast, income transfers go to people who themselves decide how to spend that money—and thus what gets produced. Hence, income transfers don't directly alter the mix of output. Their effect is primarily *distributional* (the FOR WHOM question), not *allocative* (the WHAT question). Were income transfers included, the relative size and growth of the federal government would be larger than Figure 4.4 depicts. This is because ***most of the growth in federal spending has come from increased income transfers, not purchases of goods and services.***

State and Local Growth

State and local spending on goods and services has followed a very different path. Prior to World War II, state and local governments dominated public sector spending. During the war, however, the share of total output going to state and local governments fell, hitting a low of 3 percent in that period (Figure 4.4).

State and local spending caught up with federal spending in the mid-1960s and has exceeded it ever since. Today ***more than 80,000 state and local government entities buy much more output than Uncle Sam and employ five times as many people.*** Education is a huge expenditure at lower levels of government. Most direct state spending is on colleges; most local spending is for elementary and secondary education. The fastest-growing areas for state expenditure are prisons (public safety) and welfare. At the local level, sewage and trash services are claiming an increasing share of budgets.

TAXATION

Whatever we may think of any specific government expenditure, we must recognize one basic fact of life: We pay for government spending. We pay not just in terms of tax *dollars* but in the more fundamental form of a changed mix of output. Government expenditures on goods and services absorb factors of production that could be used to produce consumer goods. The mix of output changes toward *more* public services and *fewer* private goods and services. Resources used to produce missile shields, operate elementary schools, or journey to Mars aren't available to produce cars, houses, or restaurant meals. In real terms, ***the cost of government spending is measured by the private sector output sacrificed when the government employs scarce factors of production.***

The **opportunity costs** of public spending aren't always apparent. We don't directly hand over factors of production to the government. Instead, we give the government part of our income in the form of taxes. Those dollars are then used by government agencies to buy factors of production or goods and services in the marketplace. Thus, ***the primary function of taxes is to transfer command over resources (purchasing power) from the private sector to the public sector.*** Although the government also borrows dollars to finance its purchases, taxes are the primary source of government revenues.

opportunity cost: The most desired goods or services that are forgone in order to obtain something else.

Federal Taxes

As recently as 1902, much of the revenue the federal government collected came from taxes imposed on alcoholic beverages. The federal government didn't have authority to collect income taxes. As a consequence, *total* federal revenue in 1902 was only $653 million.

Income Taxes. All that changed, beginning in 1915. The Sixteenth Amendment to the U.S. Constitution granted the federal government authority to collect *income* taxes. The government now collects more than $1.8 *trillion* in that form alone each year. Although the federal government still collects taxes on alcoholic beverages, the individual income tax has become the largest single source of government revenue (see Figure 4.5).

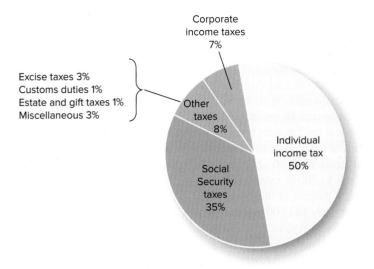

Corporate
income taxes
7%

Excise taxes 3%
Customs duties 1%
Estate and gift taxes 1%
Miscellaneous 3%

Other
taxes
8%

Social
Security
taxes
35%

Individual
income tax
50%

FIGURE 4.5

Federal Taxes

Taxes transfer purchasing power from the private sector to the public sector. The largest federal tax is the individual income tax. The second-largest source of federal revenue is the Social Security payroll tax.

Source: Office of Management and Budget, FY2020 data.

In theory, the federal income tax is designed to be **progressive**—that is, to take a larger *fraction* of high incomes than of low incomes. In 2020, for example, a single person with less than $9,875 of taxable income was taxed at 10 percent. People with incomes of $40,126–$85,525 confronted a 24 percent tax rate on their additional income. The marginal tax rate got as high as 37 percent for people earning more than $518,400 in income. Thus, *people with high incomes not only pay more taxes but also pay a larger* **fraction** *of their income in taxes.*

> **progressive tax:** A tax system in which tax rates rise as incomes rise.

Social Security Taxes. The second major source of federal revenue is the Social Security payroll tax. People working now transfer part of their earnings to retired workers by making "contributions" to Social Security. There's nothing voluntary about these "contributions"; they take the form of mandatory payroll deductions. In 2020, each worker paid 7.65 percent of his or her wages to Social Security, and employers contributed an equal amount. As a consequence, the government collected more than $1.3 trillion from this tax.

At first glance, the Social Security payroll tax looks like a **proportional tax**—that is, a tax that takes the *same* fraction of every taxpayer's income. But this isn't the case. The Social Security (FICA) tax isn't levied on every payroll dollar. Incomes above a certain ceiling ($132,900 in 2020) aren't taxed. As a result, workers with *really* high salaries turn over a smaller fraction of their incomes to Social Security than do low-wage workers. This makes the Social Security payroll tax a **regressive tax.**

> **proportional tax:** A tax that levies the same rate on every dollar of income.

> **regressive tax:** A tax system in which tax rates fall as incomes rise.

Corporate Taxes. The federal government taxes the profits of corporations as well as the incomes of consumers. But there are far fewer corporations (less than 2 million) than consumers (340 million), and their profits are small in comparison to total consumer income. In 2020, the federal government collected less than $300 billion in corporate income taxes, despite the fact that it imposed a top tax rate of 21 percent on corporate profits.

Excise Taxes. The last major source of federal revenue is excise taxes. Like the early taxes on whiskey, excise taxes are sales taxes imposed on specific goods and services. The federal government taxes not only liquor ($13.50 per gallon) but also gasoline (18.4 cents per gallon), cigarettes ($1.01 per pack), air fares (7.5 percent), firearms (10–11 percent), gambling (0.25 percent), and a variety of other goods and services. Such taxes not only discourage production and consumption of these goods by raising their price and thereby reducing the quantity demanded; they also raise a substantial amount of revenue.

State and Local Revenues

Taxes. State and local governments also levy taxes on consumers and businesses. In general, cities depend heavily on property taxes, and state governments rely heavily on sales taxes. Although nearly all states and many cities also impose income taxes, effective tax rates are so low (averaging less than 2 percent of personal income) that income tax revenues are much less than sales and property tax revenues.

Like the Social Security payroll tax, state and local taxes tend to be *regressive*—that is, they take a larger share of income from the poor than from the rich. Consider a 4 percent sales tax, for example. It might appear that a uniform tax rate like this would affect all consumers equally. But people with lower incomes tend to spend most of their income on goods and services. Thus, most of their income is subject to sales taxes. By contrast, a person with a high income can afford to save part of his or her income and thereby shelter it from sales taxes.

Consider a family that earns $40,000 and spends $30,000 of it on taxable goods and services. This family will pay $1,200 in sales taxes when the tax rate is 4 percent. In effect, then, they are handing over 3 percent of their *income* ($1,200 ÷ $40,000) to the state. Now consider a family that makes only $12,000 and spends $11,500 of it for food, clothing, and shelter. That family will pay $460 in sales taxes in the same state. Their total tax is smaller, but it represents a much larger *share* (3.8 versus 3.0 percent) of their income.

Local property taxes are also regressive because poor people devote a larger portion of their incomes to housing costs. Hence, a larger share of a poor family's *income* is subject to property taxes. State lotteries are also regressive for the same reason (see Front Page Economics "State Lotteries: A Tax on the Uneducated and the Poor"). Low-income players spend 1.4 percent of their incomes on lottery tickets while upper-income players devote only 0.1 percent of their income to lottery purchases.

FRONT PAGE ECONOMICS   NEWS

STATE LOTTERIES: A TAX ON THE UNEDUCATED AND THE POOR

Americans now spend over $85 billion a year on lottery tickets. That's more than we spend on sporting events, books, video games, movies, and music *combined*. That spending works out to about $650 a household.

Poor people are proportionally the biggest buyers of lottery tickets. Households with less than $25,000 of income spend $1,100 a year on lottery tickets. By contrast, households with more than $50,000 of income buy only $300 of lottery tickets each year.

Education also affects lottery spending: 2.7 percent of high school dropouts are compulsive lottery players, while only 1.1 percent of college grads play compulsively. Because lottery games are a sucker's game to start with—payouts average less than 60 percent of sales—lotteries are effectively a regressive tax on the uneducated and the poor.

Source: Research on lottery sales.

CRITICAL ANALYSIS: Poor people spend a larger percentage of their income on lottery tickets than do rich people. This makes lotteries a **regressive** source of government revenue.

GOVERNMENT FAILURE

government failure:
Government intervention that fails to improve economic outcomes.

Some government intervention in the marketplace is clearly desirable. The market mechanism can fail for a variety of reasons, leaving a laissez-faire economy short of its economic goals. But how much government intervention is desirable? Communist nations once thought that complete government control of production, consumption, and distribution decisions was the surest path to utopia. They learned the hard way that *not only markets but governments as well can fail.* In this context, **government failure** means that government intervention fails to move us closer to our economic goals.

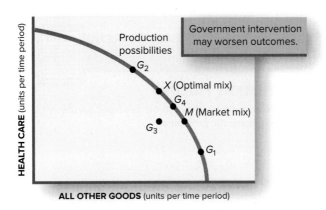

FIGURE 4.6
Government Failure

When the market produces a suboptimal mix of output like point *M*, the goal of government is to move output to the social optimum (point *X*). A move to G_4 would be an improvement in the mix of output. But government intervention *may* move the economy to points G_1, G_2, or G_3—all reflecting government failure.

Consider again our collective goal of producing the optimal mix of output. In Figure 4.6, this goal is again illustrated by point *X* on the production possibilities curve. Point *M* on the curve reminds us that the market may fail to generate that optimal answer to the WHAT question. This is why we want the government to intervene. We want the government to move the mix of output from point *M* to point *X*.

We have no guarantee that government intervention will yield the desired move. Government intervention might unwittingly move us to point G_1, making matters worse. Or the government might overreact, sending us to point G_2. Red tape and onerous regulation might even force us to point G_3, *inside* the production possibilities curve (with less total output than at point *M*). All those possibilities (G_1, G_2, G_3) represent government failure. **Government intervention is desirable only to the extent that it** *improves* **market outcomes** (e.g., G_4).

We face a similar risk when the government intervenes in the HOW and FOR WHOM questions. Regulations imposed on an industry may reduce output with little or no environmental improvements. Taxes and transfers intended to make the distribution of income fairer may actually have the opposite effect. These things won't necessarily happen, but they *could*. Even when outcomes improve, government failure may occur if the costs of government intervention exceed the benefits of an improved output mix, cleaner production methods, or a fairer distribution of income.

DECISIONS FOR TOMORROW

Can We Trust Government to Fix Things?

Two things are obvious from our discussion of the government sector. First, market failures provide an economic justification for government intervention. When the market alone gives us the wrong answers to the WHAT, HOW, and FOR WHOM questions, we need someone to adjust those answers. That "someone" is the government.

Second, we recognize that government intervention doesn't always succeed. The government may change market outcomes in the wrong direction, making things worse. Or it may generate a miniscule improvement in market outcomes, but at too high a price. In these cases, we end up with government failure—outcomes no better, and possibly worse, than the market alone would generate.

Public Opinion. Taxpayers seem to have strong opinions about government failure. A 2019 poll asked people how confident they were that the federal government could

Continued

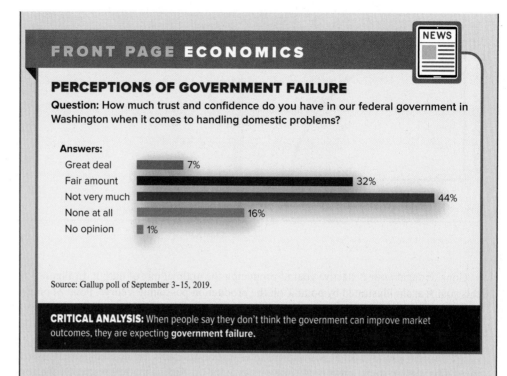

PERCEPTIONS OF GOVERNMENT FAILURE

Question: How much trust and confidence do you have in our federal government in Washington when it comes to handling domestic problems?

Answers:
- Great deal — 7%
- Fair amount — 32%
- Not very much — 44%
- None at all — 16%
- No opinion — 1%

Source: Gallup poll of September 3–15, 2019.

CRITICAL ANALYSIS: When people say they don't think the government can improve market outcomes, they are expecting **government failure.**

successfully tackle important problems. As Front Page Economics "Perceptions of Government Failure" reveals, 60 percent of Americans don't have such confidence. In other words, they *expect* government failure.

People also feel that the federal government *wastes* their tax dollars. The average taxpayer now believes that state governments waste 42 cents out of each dollar, while the federal government wastes 51 cents out of each tax dollar!

Government "waste" implies that the public sector isn't producing as many services as it could with the resources at its disposal. Such inefficiency implies that we're producing somewhere *inside* our production possibilities curve rather than on it (e.g., point G_3 in Figure 4.6). If the government is wasting resources this way, we can't possibly be producing the optimal mix of output.

Opportunity Cost

Even if the government wasn't wasting resources, it might still be guilty of government failure. Notice in Figure 4.6 that points G_1 and G_2 are on the production possibilities curve. So resources aren't being "wasted." But those points still represent suboptimal outcomes. In reality, *the issue of government failure encompasses two distinct questions:*

- *Efficiency:* Are we getting as much service as we could from the resources we allocate to government?
- *Opportunity cost:* Are we giving up too many private sector goods in order to get those services?

When assessing government's role in the economy, *we must consider not only what governments do but also what we give up to allow them to do it.* Everyone wants better schools, more access to health care, improved roads and transit systems, and secure national defenses. But each of those things comes with a price tag. When the government employs resources to produce goods that society wants, it takes resources from the production of other goods. Again, we are looking for the optimal *mix* of output, not just better schools, roads, and other public services.

Who Should Decide? You don't have to be a genius to find the optimal mix of output in Figure 4.6—it's clearly marked. In practice, establishing the optimal size of the public sector isn't so easy. We rarely have complete information about people's preferences, the social value of specific goods, or the precise opportunity costs incurred. So, while economists can talk in theoretical terms about the optimal mix of output, they aren't really equipped to locate it with any precision. Nor are they any better positioned to tell us which distribution of income is the most fair.

Ballot Box Economics. In practice, we rely on political mechanisms to decide what to produce in the public sector and how to redistribute incomes. *Voting mechanisms substitute for the market mechanism in allocating resources to the public sector and deciding how to use them.* Some people have even suggested that the variety and volume of public goods are determined by the most votes, just as the variety and volume of private goods are determined by the most dollars. Thus, governments choose the level and mix of output (and related taxation) that seem to command the most votes.

Sometimes the link between the ballot box and output decisions is very clear and direct. State and local governments, for example, are often compelled to get voter approval before building another highway, school, housing project, or sewage plant. *Bond referenda* are direct requests by a government unit for voter approval of specific public spending projects (e.g., roads, schools). In 2018, for example, nine state governments sought voter approval for $12 billion of new borrowing to finance specific public projects (schools, hospitals, etc.).

Bond referenda are more the exception than the rule. Bond referenda account for less than 1 percent of state and local expenditures (and no federal expenditures). As a consequence, voter control of public spending is typically much less direct. At best, voters get the opportunity every two years to elect congressional representatives and every four years a president. Promises about future spending and taxes typically play a major role in those elections. But election campaigns rarely get into the details of government spending and often fail to deliver on campaign promises.

Public Choice Theory. The tenuous link between the ballot box and economic policy creates another mechanism for decision making—namely, self-interest. In principle, government officials are supposed to serve the people. It doesn't take long, however, before officials realize that the public is indecisive about what it wants and takes little interest in government's day-to-day activities. With such latitude, government officials can set their own agendas. Those agendas may give higher priority to personal advancement than to the needs of the public. Agency directors may foster new programs that enlarge their mandate, enhance their visibility, and increase their prestige or income. Members of Congress may likewise pursue legislative favors like tax breaks for supporters more diligently than they pursue the general public interest. In such cases, the probability of attaining the socially optimal mix of output declines.

The theory of **public choice** emphasizes the role of self-interest in public decision making. Public choice theory essentially extends the analysis of market behavior to political behavior. Public officials are assumed to have specific personal goals (for example, power, recognition, wealth) that they'll pursue in office. *A central tenet of public choice theory is that bureaucrats are just as selfish (utility maximizing) as everyone else.*

Public choice theory provides a neat and simple explanation for public sector decision making. But critics argue that the theory provides a woefully narrow view of public servants. Some people do selflessly pursue larger, public goals, such critics argue, and ideas can overwhelm self-interest. Steven Kelman of Harvard, for example, argues that narrow self-interest can't explain the War on Poverty of the 1960s, the tax revolt of the 1970s, or the deregulation movement of the 1980s. These tidal changes in public policy reflect the power of ideas, not simple self-interest. Public choice theory tells us how many decisions about government are made; it doesn't tell us how they should be made. The role of government in the economy tomorrow will depend less on self-interest and more on how much we trust *markets* to generate optimal outcomes or trust government intervention to *improve* on market failures.

public choice: Theory of public sector behavior emphasizing rational self-interest of decision makers and voters.

SUMMARY

- Government intervention in the marketplace is justified by market failure—that is, suboptimal market outcomes. **LO4-1**
- The micro failures of the market originate in public goods, externalities, market power, and an inequitable distribution of income. These flaws deter the market from achieving the optimal mix of output or distribution of income. **LO4-1**
- Public goods are those that can't be consumed exclusively; they're jointly consumed regardless of who pays. Because everyone seeks a free ride, no one demands public goods in the marketplace. Hence, the market underproduces public goods. **LO4-1**
- Externalities are costs (or benefits) of a market transaction borne by a third party. Externalities create a divergence between social and private costs or benefits, causing suboptimal market outcomes. The market overproduces goods with external costs and underproduces goods with external benefits. **LO4-1**
- Market power enables a producer to thwart market signals and maintain a suboptimal mix of output. Antitrust policy seeks to prevent or restrict market power. The government may also regulate the behavior of powerful firms. **LO4-1**

- The market-generated distribution of income may be unfair. This inequity may prompt the government to intervene with taxes and transfer payments that redistribute incomes. **LO4-1**
- The macro failures of the marketplace are reflected in unemployment and inflation. Government intervention is intended to achieve full employment and price stability. **LO4-1**
- The federal government expanded greatly in the 1930s and during World War II, but its share of output has shrunk in recent decades. Recent growth in federal spending has been on income transfers, not output. **LO4-2**
- State and local governments purchase more output (11 percent of GDP) than the federal government (6.5 percent) and employ five times as many workers. **LO4-2**
- Income and payroll taxes provide most federal revenues. States get most revenue from sales taxes; local governments rely on property taxes. **LO4-3**
- Government failure occurs when intervention doesn't move toward the optimal mix of output (or income). Failure may result from outright waste (operational inefficiency) or from a misallocation of resources. **LO4-4**
- All government activity must be evaluated in terms of its opportunity cost—that is, the *private* goods and services forgone to make resources available to the public sector. **LO4-4**

Key Terms

laissez faire	monopoly	opportunity cost
optimal mix of output	market power	progressive tax
market mechanism	antitrust	proportional tax
market failure	natural monopoly	regressive tax
private good	transfer payments	government failure
public good	merit good	public choice
free rider	unemployment	
externalities	inflation	

Questions for Discussion

1. If vaping doesn't entail external costs, what is the theoretical basis for restricting vape consumption (see Front Page Economics "The Health Risks of Vaping")? **LO4-1**
2. If the United States wanted to build an "Iron Dome" missile system, how much would you willingly contribute to its cost? Could it be financed with crowd funding? (World View "Israel's 'Iron Dome' 86 Percent Effective") **LO4-1**
3. If everyone seeks a free ride, what mix of output will be produced in Figure 4.2? Why would anyone voluntarily contribute to the purchase of public goods like flood control or snow removal? **LO4-1**

4. Should the firefighters have saved the house in Front Page Economics "Firefighters Watch as Home Burns to the Ground"? What was the justification for their belated intervention? **LO4-1**
5. Why might Fourth of July fireworks be considered a public good? Who should pay for them? What about airport security? **LO4-1**
6. What is the specific market failure justification for government spending on (*a*) public universities, (*b*) health care, (*c*) trash pickup, (*d*) highways, (*e*) police, and (*f*) solar energy? Would a purely private economy produce any of these services? **LO4-1**

7. If smoking generates external costs, should smoking simply be outlawed? How about cars that pollute?   **LO4-1**

8. The government now spends more than $1 trillion a year on Social Security benefits. Why don't we leave it to individuals to save for their own retirement?   **LO4-1**

9. What government actions might cause failures like points G_1, G_2, and G_3 in Figure 4.6? Can you give examples?   **LO4-4**

10. How does Sirius Satellite deter nonsubscribers from listening to its transmissions? Does this make radio programming a private good or a public good?   **LO4-1**

11. Which taxes hit the poor hardest—those of local, state, or federal governments?   **LO4-3**

12. Why wouldn't market participants take the optimal amount of precautionary actions in a virus pandemic?   **LO4-1**

PROBLEMS FOR CHAPTER 4

LO4-1   1. In Figure 4.2, by how much is the market
- (a) Overproducing private goods?
- (b) Underproducing public goods?

LO4-1   2. (a) Use Figure 4.3 to illustrate on the accompanying production possibilities curve the optimal mix of output (X)

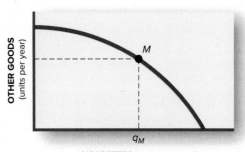

CIGARETTES (packs per year)

    (b) Does the optimal mix include more or fewer "other goods"?

LO4-1   3. Assume that the product depicted below generates external costs in consumption of $3 per unit.
- (a) What is the market price (market value) of the product?
- (b) Draw the social demand curve.
- (c) What is the socially optimal output?
- (d) By how much does the market overproduce this good?

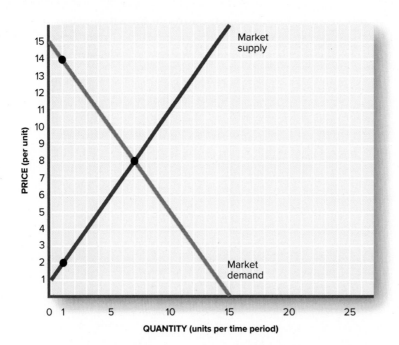

LO4-1   4. (a) Draw the market demand curve, social demand curve, and the supply curve for flu shots.
- (b) Based on your graph, does society want more or less people to get a flu shot?

LO4-1   5. If the average adult produces $30,000 of output per year, how much global output is lost annually as a result of adult deaths from secondhand smoke, according to World View "Secondhand Smoke Kills More Than 600,000 People a Year?"

PROBLEMS FOR CHAPTER 4 (cont'd)

LO4-3 6. (*a*) Assuming an 8 percent sales tax is levied on all consumption, complete the following table:

Income	Consumption	Sales Tax	Percentage of Income Paid in Taxes
$10,000	$11,000	_____	_____
20,000	20,000	_____	_____
40,000	36,000	_____	_____
80,000	60,000	_____	_____

   (*b*) Is the sales tax progressive or regressive?

LO4-4 7. If a new home can be constructed for $150,000, what is the opportunity cost of federal defense spending, measured in terms of private housing? (Assume a defense budget of $750 billion.)

LO4-1 8. Suppose the following data represent the market demand for college education:

Tuition (per year)	$40,000	$35,000	$30,000	$25,000	$20,000	$15,000	$10,000	$5,000
Enrollment demanded (in millions per year)	1	2	3	4	5	6	7	8

   (*a*) If tuition is set at $15,000, how many students will enroll?

   Now suppose that society gets an external benefit of $5,000 for every enrolled student.

   (*b*) Draw the social and market demand curves for this situation on the graph below.
   (*c*) What is the socially optimal level of enrollment at the same tuition price of $15,000?
   (*d*) If the government were to intervene and subsidize college education, how large of a subsidy is needed per student each year to achieve this optimal outcome?

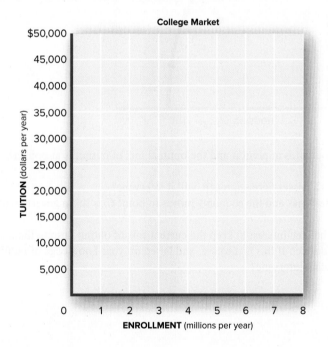

College Market

LO4-1 9. Suppose the market demand for cigarettes is given in the following table.

Price per pack	$10	$9	$8	$7	$6	$5	$4	$3
Quantity demanded (million packs per year)	2	4	6	8	10	12	14	16

PROBLEMS FOR CHAPTER 4 (cont'd)

Suppose further that smoking creates external costs valued at $2 per pack.

(a) Graph the social and market demand curves.

If cigarettes are priced at $7 a pack,
(b) What is the quantity demanded in the market?
(c) What is the socially optimal quantity?
(d) If the government were to intervene and tax cigarettes, how large of a tax is needed per pack to achieve this optimal outcome?

LO4-3 10. According to Front Page Economics "State Lotteries: A Tax on the Uneducated and the Poor," what percentage of income is spent on lottery tickets by
(a) A low-income family with income of $20,000 per year?
(b) An middle-income family with income of $60,000 per year?

LO4-3 11. *Decisions for Tomorrow:* The following production possibilities curve shows the trade-off between housing and all other goods.

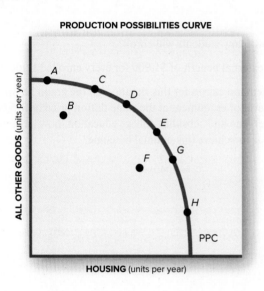

PRODUCTION POSSIBILITIES CURVE

(a) If the market mix of output is at point *A* and the optimal mix of output is at point *D*, does a market failure exist?
(b) If the government has a laissez-faire approach, will it intervene?
(c) If the government intervenes and the economy moves to point *C*, is this a government failure?
(d) Suppose a politician has self-interest to keep the current mix of output despite the need for more housing in her district. If this is the case, and based on your knowledge of public choice theory, will the politician intervene?

Design Credit: Shutterstock

PART

2

MEASURING MACRO OUTCOMES

Monty Rakusen/Digital Vision/Punchstock

Michael S. Williamson/Getty Images

John Alphonse/Brand X Pictures/Getty Images

Macroeconomics focuses on the performance of the entire economy rather than on the behavior of individual participants (a micro concern). The central concerns of macroeconomics are (1) the short-term business cycle and (2) long-term economic growth. In the long run, the goal is to expand the economy's capacity to produce goods and services, thereby raising future living standards. In the short run, the emphasis is on fully using available capacity, thereby maximizing output and minimizing unemployment. Chapters 5 through 7 focus on the measurement tools used to gauge the nation's macroeconomic performance (both short run and long run). Also examined are the social and economic damage caused by the problems of unemployment and inflation.

Monty Rakusen/Digital Vision/Punchstock

5

National Income Accounting

After reading this chapter, you should know

LO5-1 What GDP measures—and what it doesn't.

LO5-2 The difference between real and nominal GDP.

LO5-3 Why aggregate income equals aggregate output.

LO5-4 The major submeasures of output and income.

A favorite cliché of policymakers in Washington is that government likes to tackle only those problems it can measure. Politicians need visible results. They want to be able to brag to their constituents about the miles of new highways built, the number of students who graduated, the number of families that left welfare, and the number of unemployed workers who found jobs. To do this, they must be able to measure economic outcomes.

The Great Depression of the 1930s was a lesson in the need for better measures of economic performance. There were plenty of anecdotes about factories closing, farms failing, and people selling apples on the streets. But nobody knew the dimensions of the nation's economic meltdown until millions of workers had lost their jobs. The need for more timely information about the health of the national economy was evident. From that experience, a commitment to **national income accounting**—the measurement of aggregate economic activity—emerged. During the 1930s the economist Simon Kuznets (who later received a Nobel Prize for his work) and the U.S. Department of Commerce developed an accounting system to gauge the economy's health. That national accounting system now churns out reams of data that track the economy's performance. They answer such questions as

- **How much output is being produced? What is it being used for?**
- **How much income is being generated in the marketplace?**
- **What's happening to prices and wages?**

It's tempting, of course, to ignore all these measurement questions, especially because they tend to be rather dull. But if we avoid measurement problems, we severely limit our ability to understand how well (or poorly) the economy is performing. We also limit our ability to design policies for improving economic performance.

National income accounting also provides a useful perspective on the way the economy works. It shows how factor markets relate to product markets, how output relates to income, and how consumer spending and business investment relate to production. It also shows how the flow of taxes and government spending affect economic outcomes.

MEASURES OF OUTPUT

The array of goods and services we produce is truly massive, including everything from professional baseball (a service) to guided-missile systems (a good). All these products are part of our total output; the first data challenge is to find a summary measure of all these diverse products.

Itemizing the amount of each good or service produced each year won't solve our measurement problem. The resulting list would be so long that it would be both unwieldy and meaningless. We couldn't even add it up because it would contain diverse goods measured in a variety of different units (e.g., miles, packages, pounds, quarts). Nor could we compare one year's output to another's. Suppose that last year we produced 3 billion oranges, 2 million bicycles, and 700 rock concerts, whereas this year we produced 4 billion oranges, 4 million bicycles, and 600 rock concerts. Which year's output was larger? With more of some goods, but less of others, the answer isn't obvious.

national income accounting: The measurement of aggregate economic activity, particularly national income and its components.

Gross Domestic Product

To facilitate our accounting tasks, we need some mechanism for organizing annual output data into a more manageable summary. The mechanism we use is price. *Each good and service produced and brought to market has a price. That price serves as a measure of value for calculating total output.*

Consider again the problem of determining how much output was produced this year and last. There's no obvious way to answer this question in physical terms alone. But once we know the price of each good, we can calculate the *value* of output produced. The total dollar value of final output produced each year is called the **gross domestic product (GDP).** GDP is simply the sum of all final goods and services produced for the market in a given time period, with each good or service valued at its market price.

gross domestic product (GDP): The total market value of all final goods and services produced within a nation's borders in a given time period.

Table 5.1 illustrates the use of prices to value total output in two hypothetical years. If oranges were 40 cents each last year and 3 billion oranges were produced, then the *value* of orange production last year was $1,200 million ($0.40 × 3 billion). In the same manner, we can determine that the value of bicycle production was $200 million and the value of rock concerts was $700 million. By adding these figures, we can say that the value of last year's production—last year's GDP—was $2,100 million (Table 5.1*a*).

Now we're in a position to compare one year's output to another's. Table 5.1*b* shows that the use of prices enables us to say that the *value* of this year's output is $2,600 million. Hence,

Retailers count sales in dollars, not physical products.

Erik Isakson/Blend Images LLC

TABLE 5.1

The Measurement of Output

It's impossible to add up all output in *physical* terms. Accordingly, total output is measured in *monetary* terms, with each good or service valued at its market price. GDP refers to the total *market value* of all goods and services *produced* in a given time period.

According to the numbers in this table, the total *value* of the oranges, bicycles, and rock concerts produced "last" year was $2.1 billion and $2.6 billion "this" year. So, we can say that *total output* increased.

Output	Amount
a. Last Year's Output	
In physical terms:	
Oranges	3 billion
Bicycles	3 million
Rock concerts	700
Total	?
In monetary terms:	
3 billion oranges @ $0.40 each	$1,200 million
2 million bicycles @ $100 each	200 million
700 rock concerts @ $1 million each	700 million
Total	$2,100 million
b. This Year's Output	
In physical terms:	
Oranges	4 billion
Bicycles	4 million
Rock concerts	600
Total	?
In monetary terms:	
4 billion oranges @ $0.40 each	$1,600 million
4 million bicycles @ $100 each	400 million
600 rock concerts @ $1 million each	600 million
Total	$2,600 million

total output has increased from one year to the next. ***The use of prices to value market output allows us to summarize output activity and to compare the output of one period with that of another.***

GDP vs. GNP. The concept of GDP is of relatively recent use in U.S. national income accounts. Prior to 1992, most U.S. statistics focused on gross *national* product, or GNP. Gross *national* product refers to the output produced by American-owned factors of production, regardless of where they're located. Gross *domestic* product refers to output produced within America's borders. Thus, GNP would include some output from an Apple computer factory in Singapore but exclude some of the output produced by a Honda factory in Ohio. In an increasingly global economy, where factors of production and ownership move easily across international borders, the calculations of GNP became ever more complex. It also became a less dependable measure of the nation's economic health. ***GDP is geographically focused, including all output produced within a nation's borders regardless of whose factors of production are used to produce it.*** Apple's output in Singapore ends up in Singapore's GDP; the cars produced at Honda's Ohio plant are counted in America's GDP.

International Comparisons. The geographic focus of GDP facilitates international comparisons of economic activity. Is China's output as large as that of the United States? How could you tell? China produces a mix of output different from ours, making *quantity*-based comparisons difficult. We can compare the *value* of output produced in each country, however. The World View "Comparative Output (GDP)" in Chapter 2 shows that the value of America's GDP is much larger than China's.

GDP per Capita. International comparisons of total output are even more vivid in *per capita terms.* GDP per capita relates the total value of annual output to the number of people who share that output; it refers to the average GDP per person. In 2020, America's total GDP of $21 trillion was shared by 340 million citizens. Hence, our average, or *per capita,* GDP was nearly $62,000. By contrast, the average GDP for the rest of the world's inhabitants was only $12,000. In these terms, America's position as among the richest countries in the world clearly stands out.

Statistical comparisons of GDP across nations are abstract and lifeless. They do, however, convey very real differences in the way people live. World View "Global Inequalities"

GDP per capita: Total GDP divided by total population; average GDP.

WORLD VIEW

GLOBAL INEQUALITIES

The 705 million residents of the world's low-income nations such as Afghanistan and Malawi have comparatively few goods and services. Their average income (per capita GDP) is only $841 a year, a mere 1.9 percent of the average income of the 1.2 billion residents in high-income nations such as the United States, Japan, and Germany. It's not just a colossal *income* disparity; it's also a disparity in the quality and even the duration of life.

Some examples:

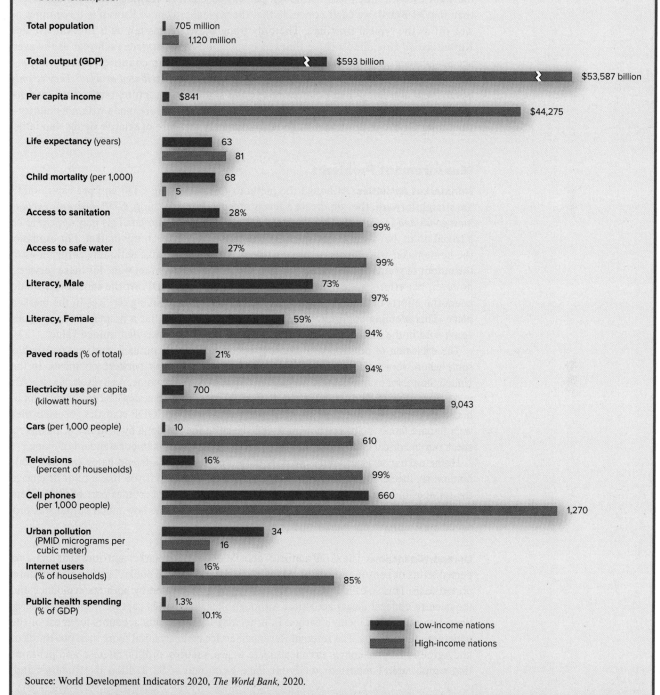

	Low-income nations	High-income nations
Total population	705 million	1,120 million
Total output (GDP)	$593 billion	$53,587 billion
Per capita income	$841	$44,275
Life expectancy (years)	63	81
Child mortality (per 1,000)	68	5
Access to sanitation	28%	99%
Access to safe water	27%	99%
Literacy, Male	73%	97%
Literacy, Female	59%	94%
Paved roads (% of total)	21%	94%
Electricity use per capita (kilowatt hours)	700	9,043
Cars (per 1,000 people)	10	610
Televisions (percent of households)	16%	99%
Cell phones (per 1,000 people)	660	1,270
Urban pollution (PMID micrograms per cubic meter)	34	16
Internet users (% of households)	16%	85%
Public health spending (% of GDP)	1.3%	10.1%

Source: World Development Indicators 2020, *The World Bank,* 2020.

CRITICAL ANALYSIS: Hidden behind dry statistical comparisons of **per capita GDP** lie very tangible and dramatic differences in the way people live. Low GDP per capita reflects a lot of deprivation.

examines some everyday realities of living in a poor nation, compared with a rich nation. Disparities in per capita GDP mean that people in low-income countries have little access to telephones, televisions, paved roads, schools, or even safe water. They also die a lot younger than do people in rich countries.

But even the World View fails to fully convey how tough life is for people at the *bottom* of the income distribution in both poor and rich nations. Per capita GDP isn't a measure of what every citizen is getting. In the United States, millions of individuals have access to far more goods and services than our *average* per capita GDP, while millions of others must get by with much less. Although per capita GDP in Kuwait is three times larger than that of Brazil, we can't conclude that the typical citizen of Kuwait is three times as well off as the typical Brazilian. The only thing these figures tell us is that the average Kuwaiti *could have* almost three times as many goods and services each year as the average Brazilian *if* GDP were distributed in the same way in both countries. ***Measures of per capita GDP tell us nothing about the way GDP is actually distributed or used: They're only a statistical average.*** When countries are quite similar in structure, institutions, and income distribution, however—or when historical comparisons are made within a country—per capita GDP can be viewed as a rough-and-ready measure of relative living standards.

Measurement Problems

Nonmarket Activities. Although the methods for calculating GDP and per capita GDP are straightforward, they do create a few problems. For one thing, ***GDP measures exclude most goods and services that are* produced *but not* sold *in the market.*** This may appear to be a trivial point, but it isn't. Vast quantities of output never reach the market. For example, the homemaker who cleans, washes, gardens, shops, and cooks definitely contributes to the output of goods and services. Because she's not paid a market wage for these services, however, her efforts are excluded from the calculation of GDP. At the same time, we do count the efforts of those workers who sell identical homemaking services in the marketplace. This seeming contradiction is explained by the fact that a homemaker's services aren't sold in the market and therefore carry no explicit, market-determined value.

The exclusion of homemakers' services from the GDP accounts is particularly troublesome when we want to compare living standards over time or between countries. In the United States, for example, most women now work outside the home. As a result, households make greater use of *paid* domestic help (e.g., child care, housecleaning). Accordingly, a lot of housework and child care that were previously excluded from GDP statistics (because they were unpaid family help) are now included (because they're done by paid help). In this respect, our historical GDP figures may exaggerate improvements in our standard of living.

Homemaking services aren't the only output excluded. If a friend helps you with your homework, the services never get into the GDP accounts. But if you hire a tutor or engage the services of a term paper–writing agency, the transaction becomes part of GDP. Here again, the problem is simply that we have no way to determine how much output was produced until it enters the market and is purchased.[1]

Unreported Income. The GDP statistics also fail to capture market activities that aren't reported to tax or census authorities. Many people work "off the books," getting paid in unreported cash. This so-called underground economy is motivated by both tax avoidance and the need to conceal illegal activities. Although illegal activities capture most of the headlines, tax evasion on income earned in otherwise legal pursuits accounts for most of the underground economy. The Internal Revenue Service estimates that more than two-thirds of underground income comes from legitimate wages, salaries, profits, interest, and pensions that simply aren't reported. As Front Page Economics "$2 Trillion in 'Underground'

---

[1]The U.S. Commerce Department does, however, *estimate* the value of some nonmarket activities (e.g., food grown by farmers for their own consumption, the rental value of home ownership) and includes such estimates in GDP calculations.

FRONT PAGE ECONOMICS

$2 TRILLION IN "UNDERGROUND" ECONOMY

Day laborers expect to be paid in cash at the end of the day. Babysitters, lawn mowers, and painters also prefer cash payments, as do nearly all illegal (undocumented) migrants. Lots of renters also pay their rent in cash. None of these "underground" transactions get reported to the IRS. As a result, there is no information to feed into the national income accounts. The IRS estimates the size of this underground economy at $2 trillion—or about 11 percent of total output (GDP).

Although most people think the underground economy consists primarily of criminal activity—drugs, prostitution, gambling, loan sharking—the lion's share of the shadow economy is comprised of legal (noncriminal) activity that is transacted in cash and not reported. A University of Michigan study identified some of the most prominent participants in the underground economy:

	Estimated Percentage of Services Supplied by the Underground Economy
Lawn maintenance	90
Domestic help	83
Child care	49
Home repair/improvements	34
Laundry/sewing services	25
Appliance repair	17
Car repairs	13
Haircuts/beauty service	8
Catering	8

Data from University of Michigan Institute for Social Research, U.S. Department of Labor.

Source: U.S. Internal Revenue Service.

CRITICAL ANALYSIS: GDP statistics include only the value of reported market transactions. Unreported transactions in the underground economy can't be counted and may therefore distort perceptions of economic activity.

Economy" indicates, unreported income is particularly common in the service sector. People who mow lawns, clean houses, paint walls, pick apples, or provide child care services are apt to get paid in cash that isn't reported. The volume of such mundane transactions greatly exceeds the underground income generated by drug dealers, prostitutes, or illegal gambling.

Value Added

Not every reported market transaction gets included at full value in GDP statistics. If it did, the same output would get counted over and over. The problem here is that **the production of goods and services typically involves a series of distinct stages**. Consider the production of a bagel, for example. For a bagel to reach Einstein's or some other bagel store, the farmer must grow some wheat, the miller must convert it to flour, and the baker must make bagels with it. Table 5.2 illustrates this chain of production.

Notice that each of the four stages of production depicted in Table 5.2 involves a separate market transaction. The farmer sells to the miller (stage 1), the miller to the baker (stage 2), the baker to the bagel store (stage 3), and, finally, the store to the consumer (stage 4). If we added up the separate value of each market transaction, we'd come to the conclusion that $1.75 of output had been produced. In fact, though, only one bagel has been produced, and it's worth only 75 cents. Hence, we should increase GDP—the value of output—only by 75 cents.

How many producers does it take to supply a bagel?

Foodcollection

Stages of Production	Value of Transaction	Value Added
1. Farmer grows wheat, sells it to miller.	$0.12	$0.12
2. Miller converts wheat to flour, sells it to baker.	0.28	0.16
3. Baker bakes bagel, sells it to bagel store.	0.60	0.32
4. Bagel store sells bagel to consumer.	0.75	0.15
Total	$1.75	$0.75

intermediate goods: Goods or services purchased for use as input in the production of final goods or in services.

value added: The increase in the market value of a product that takes place at each stage of the production process.

To get an accurate measure of GDP, we must distinguish between *intermediate* goods and *final* goods. **Intermediate goods** are goods purchased for use as input in further stages of production. Final goods are the goods produced at the end of the production sequence, for use by consumers (or other market participants). In this case, the wheat, the flour, and the bagel from the baker are intermediate goods. Only when the bagel is sold to the customer is it a final good.

We can compute the value of *final* output in one of two ways. The easiest way would be to count only market transactions entailing final sales (stage 4 in Table 5.2). To do this, however, we'd have to know who purchased each good or service in order to know when we had reached the end of the process. Such a calculation would also exclude any output produced in stages 1, 2, and 3 in Table 5.2 but not yet reflected in stage 4.

Another way to calculate GDP is to count only the **value added** at each stage of production. Consider the miller, for example. He sells 28 cents of flour to the baker, but he doesn't really contribute $0.28 worth of production to total output. His contribution to output is only $0.16. The other $0.12 reflected in the price of his flour represents the contribution of the farmer who grew the wheat.

It's the same story with the baker. He sells a bagel for $0.60. But the baker *adds* only $0.32 to the value of output, as part of his output ($0.28) was purchased from the miller. By considering only the value *added* at each stage of production, we eliminate double counting and potential overstatements of GDP. As Table 5.2 confirms, we can determine that value of final output by summing up the value added at each stage of production. (Note that $0.75 is also the price of a bagel sold to the final consumer.)

Real vs. Nominal GDP

Our perceptions of total output can also be distorted by prices. Imagine what would happen to our calculations of GDP if all prices were to double from one year to the next. Suppose that the price of oranges, as shown in Table 5.1 for this year, rose from $0.40 to $0.80, the price of bicycles to $200, and the price of rock concerts to $2 million each. How would such price changes alter measured GDP? Obviously, the price increases would double the dollar *value* of final output. Measured GDP would rise from $2,600 million to $5,200 million.

Unfortunately, the measured increase in GDP is a mirage. There has been no increase in the *quantity* of goods and services available to us. We're still producing the same quantities shown in Table 5.1; only the prices of those goods have changed. Hence, *changes in GDP brought about by changes in the price level give us a distorted view of real economic activity.* We wouldn't think that our standard of living had improved just because price increases had raised *measured* GDP from $2,600 million to $5,200 million.

To distinguish increases in the *quantity* of goods and services from increases in their *prices,* we must construct a measure of GDP that takes into account price level changes. We do so by distinguishing between *real* GDP and *nominal* GDP. **Nominal GDP** is the value of final output measured in *current* prices, whereas **real GDP** is the value of output measured in *constant* prices. *To calculate real GDP, we adjust the market value of goods and services for changing prices.*

nominal GDP: The value of final output produced in a given period, measured in the prices of that period (current prices).

real GDP: The value of final output produced in a given period, adjusted for changing prices.

Note, for example, that in Table 5.1 prices were unchanged from one year to the next: Oranges cost $0.40 both last year and this year. When prices in the marketplace are constant, interyear comparisons of output are simple. It's only when prices change that comparisons become more complicated. As we just saw, if all prices doubled from last year to this year, this year's *nominal* GDP would rise to $5,200 million. But these price increases wouldn't alter the quantity of goods produced. In other words, *real* GDP, valued at constant prices, would remain at $2,600 million. Thus, ***the distinction between nominal and real GDP is important whenever the price level changes.***

Because the price level does change every year, both real and nominal GDP are regularly reported. Nominal GDP is computed simply by adding the *current* dollar value of production. Real GDP is computed by making an adjustment for changes in prices from year to year.

Zero Growth. Consider the GDP statistics for 2007 and 2008, as displayed in Table 5.3. The first row shows *nominal* GDP in each year: Nominal GDP increased by $307 billion between 2007 and 2008 (row 2). At first blush, this 2.2 percent increase in GDP looks impressive; that works out to roughly $1,000 more output for every U.S. citizen.

But output didn't really grow that much. Row 3 indicates that *prices* increased by 2.2 percent from year to year. This wiped out the entire increase in the value of output. *Real* GDP actually decreased from 2007 to 2008!

Row 4 in Table 5.3 adjusts the GDP comparison for the change in prices. We represent the price increase as an index, with a base of 100. Thus, a price increase of 2.2 percent raises the base of 100 to 102.2. So the price level change can be expressed as 102.2/100.0, or 1.022.

To convert the *nominal* value of GDP in 2008 to its *real* value, we need only a little division. As row 4 of Table 5.3 shows, we divide the nominal GDP of $14,369 by the indexed price change (1.022) and discover that *real* GDP in 2008 was only $14,060 billion. Hence, *real* GDP actually decreased by $2 billion in 2008 (row 5).

Notice in Table 5.3 that in 2007 real and nominal GDP are identical because we're using that year as the basis of comparison. We're comparing performance in 2008 to that of the 2007 **base year.** Real GDP can be expressed in the prices of any particular year; whatever year is selected serves as the base for computing price level and output changes. In Table 5.3 we used 2007 as the base year for computing real GDP in subsequent years. The general formula for computing real GDP is

$$\text{Real GDP in year } t = \frac{\text{Nominal GDP in year } t}{\text{Price index}}$$

This is the formula we used in row 4 of Table 5.3 to compute real GDP in 2008, valued at 2007 base year prices.

The distinction between nominal and real GDP becomes critical when more distant years are compared. In the 80 years between 1933 and 2013, for example, prices rose by an incredible 1,300 percent. But what about real output? Did real output increase that much? Unfortunately not. When we value 2013 output at base year 1933 prices, *real* GDP turns out to be only $1,200 billion, not the *nominal* $16,800 billion seen in Table 5.4.

base year: The year used for comparative analysis; the basis for indexing price changes.

	2007	2008
1. Nominal GDP (in billions)	$14,062	$14,369
2. Change in nominal GDP		+$307
Inflation adjustment:		
3. Change in price level, 2007 to 2008		2.2%
4. Real GDP in 2007 dollars	$14,062	$14,060
$\left(= \dfrac{\text{Nominal GDP}}{\text{Price index}} \right)$		$\left(= \dfrac{\$14,369}{1.022} \right)$
5. Change in real GDP		−$2

TABLE 5.3

Computing Real GDP

Real GDP is the inflation-adjusted value of nominal GDP. Between 2007 and 2008, *nominal* GDP increased by $307 billion (row 2). All of this gain was due to rising prices (row 3). After adjusting for inflation, *real* GDP actually decreased by $2 billion (row 5).

TABLE 5.4

Real vs. Nominal GDP:
A Historical View

Suppose we want to determine how much better off the average American was in 2013, as measured in terms of new goods and services, than people were during the Great Depression. To do this, we'd compare GDP per capita in 2013 with GDP per capita in 1933. The following data make that comparison.

	Nominal GDP	Population	Nominal per Capita GDP
1933	$ 57 billion	126 million	$ 452
2013	16,800 billion	310 million	54,194

In 1933 the nation's nominal GDP of $57 billion was shared by 126 million Americans, yielding a *per capita* GDP of $452. By contrast, nominal GDP in 2013 was more than 300 times larger, at $16,800 billion. This vastly larger GDP was shared by 310 million people, giving us a per capita GDP of $54,194. Hence, it would appear that our standard of living in 2013 was 120 times higher than the standard of 1933.

But this increase in *nominal* GDP vastly exaggerates the gains in our material well-being. The average price of goods and services—the *price level*—increased by 1,300 percent between 1933 and 2013. The goods and services you might have bought for $1 in 1933 cost $14 in 2013. In other words, we needed a lot more dollars in 2013 to buy any given combination of real goods and services.

To compare our *real* GDP in 2013 with the real GDP of 1933, we have to adjust for this tremendous jump in prices (inflation). We do so by measuring both years' output in terms of *constant* prices. Because prices went up, on average, fourteenfold between 1933 and 2013, we simply divide the 2013 *nominal* output by 14. The calculation is

$$\text{Real GDP in 2013 (in 1933 prices)} = \frac{\text{Nominal 2013 GDP}}{\text{Price index}}$$

By arbitrarily setting the level of prices in the base year 1933 at 100 and noting that prices have increased fourteenfold since then, we can calculate

$$\text{Price Index} = \frac{\text{2013 price level}}{\text{1933 price level}} = \frac{1400}{100} = 14.0$$

and, therefore,

$$\text{Real GDP in 2013 (1933 prices)} = \frac{\$16,800}{14.0}$$
$$= \$1,200 \text{ billion}$$

With a population of 310 million, this left us with real GDP per capita of $3,870 in 2013—as measured in base year 1933 dollars. This was nearly nine times the *real* per capita GDP of the depression ($452), but not nearly so great an increase as comparisons of *nominal* GDP suggest.

Table 5.4 also depicts the divergence between the *nominal* growth of per capita GDP and the real growth. In *nominal* terms, our growth looks spectacular, with per capita income in 2013 a whopping 120 times larger than 1933 levels. In *real* terms, however, the income gain is a much less spectacular 9 times larger.

Figure 5.1 shows how nominal and real GDP have changed just since 2000. Real GDP is calculated here on the basis of the level of prices prevailing in 2012. So 2012 is the *base year* in this case. (Note that real and nominal GDP are identical in that base year.) The dollar value of output produced each year has risen considerably faster than the quantity of output, reflecting persistent increases in the price level—that is, **inflation.**

Notice also how inflation can obscure actual *declines* in real output. Real GDP actually declined in 2008 even though *nominal* GDP rose.

Chain-Weighted Price Adjustments. Although the distinction between real and nominal GDP is critical in measuring the nation's economic health, the procedure for making inflation adjustments isn't perfect. When we use the prices of a specific year as the base for computing real GDP, we're implicitly freezing *relative* prices as well as *average* prices. Over

---

inflation: An increase in the average level of prices of goods and services.

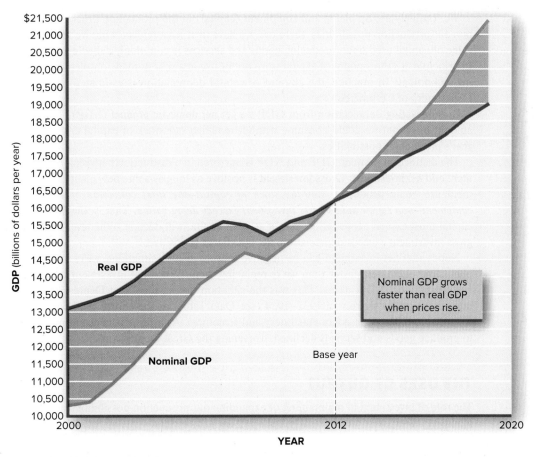

FIGURE 5.1

Changes in GDP: Nominal vs. Real

Increases in *nominal* GDP reflect higher prices as well as more output. Increases in *real* GDP reflect more output only. To measure these real changes, we must value each year's output in terms of common base prices. In this figure the base year is 2012. Nominal GDP rises faster than real GDP as a result of inflation.

Source: U.S. Bureau of Economic Analysis.

time, however, relative prices change markedly. Computer prices, for example, have fallen sharply in recent years in both absolute and relative terms. During the same period, unit sales of computers have increased by 20 to 25 percent a year. If we used the higher computer prices of five years ago to compute that sales growth, we'd greatly exaggerate the *value* of today's computer output. If we use today's prices, however, we'll underestimate the value of output produced in the past. To resolve this problem, the U.S. Department of Commerce uses a *chain-weighted* price index to compute real GDP. Instead of using the prices of a *single* base year to compute real GDP, *chain-weighted indexes use a moving average of price levels in consecutive years as an inflation adjustment.* When chain-weighted price adjustments are made, real GDP still refers to the inflation-adjusted value of GDP but isn't expressed in terms of the prices prevailing in any specific base year.

Net Domestic Product

Changes in real GDP from one year to the next tell us how much the economy's output is growing. Some of that growth, however, may come at the expense of future output. Recall that our **production possibilities** determine how much output we can produce with available factors of production and technology. If we use up some of these resources to produce this year's output, future production possibilities may shrink. *Next year we won't be able to produce as much output unless we replace factors of production we use this year.*

production possibilities: The alternative combinations of final goods and services that could be produced in a given period with all available resources and technology.

depreciation: The consumption of capital in the production process; the wearing out of plant and equipment.

net domestic product (NDP): GDP less depreciation.

investment: Expenditures on (production of) new plants, equipment, and structures (capital) in a given time period, plus changes in business inventories.

gross investment: Total investment expenditure in a given time period.

net investment: Gross investment less depreciation.

We routinely use up plants and equipment (capital) in the production process. To maintain our production possibilities, therefore, we have to at least replace what we've used. The value of capital used up in producing goods and services is commonly called **depreciation**.[2] In principle, it's the amount of capital worn out by use in a year or made obsolete by advancing technology. In practice, the amount of capital depreciation is estimated by the U.S. Department of Commerce.

By subtracting depreciation from GDP we get **net domestic product (NDP)**. This is the amount of output we could consume without reducing our stock of capital and thus next year's production possibilities.

The distinction between GDP and NDP is mirrored in a distinction between *gross* investment and *net* **investment. Gross investment** is positive as long as some new plants and equipment are being produced. But *the stock of capital—the total collection of plants and equipment—won't grow unless gross investment exceeds depreciation.* That is, the *flow* of new capital must exceed depreciation, or our *stock* of capital will decline. Whenever the rate of gross investment exceeds depreciation, **net investment** is positive.

Notice that net investment can be negative as well; in such situations, we're wearing out plants and equipment faster than we're replacing them. When net investment is negative, our capital stock is shrinking. This was the situation during the Great Depression. Gross investment fell so sharply in 1932–1934 (see Data Tables at the end of the book) that it wasn't even replacing used-up machinery and structures. As a result, the economy's ability to produce goods and services declined, worsening the Great Depression.

THE USES OF OUTPUT

The role of investment in maintaining or expanding our production possibilities helps focus attention on the uses to which GDP is put. It's not just the total value of annual output that matters; it's also the use that we make of that output. *The GDP accounts also tell us what mix of output we've selected—that is, society's answer to the core issue of WHAT to produce.*

Consumption

The major uses of total output conform to the four sets of market participants we encountered in Chapter 2—namely, consumers, business firms, government, and foreigners. Those goods and services used by households are called *consumption goods* and range all the way from doughnuts to phone services. Included in this category are all goods and services households purchase in product markets. Presently, *consumer spending claims more than two-thirds of our annual output.*

Investment

Investment goods represent another use of GDP. Investment goods are the plants, machinery, and equipment we produce. Net changes in business inventories and expenditures for residential construction are also counted as investment. To produce any of these investment goods, we must use scarce resources that could be used to produce something else. Investment spending claims about one-sixth of our total output.

Government Spending

The third major use of GDP is the *public sector*. Federal, state, and local governments purchase resources to police the streets, teach classes, write laws, and build highways. The resources purchased by the government sector are unavailable for either consumption or investment purposes. At present, government spending on goods and services (*not* income transfers) claims roughly one-fifth of total output.

[2]The terms *depreciation, capital consumption allowance,* and *consumption of fixed capital* are used interchangeably. The depreciation charges firms commonly make, however, are determined in part by income tax regulations and thus may not accurately reflect the amount of capital consumed.

Net Exports

Finally, remember that some of the goods and services we produce each year are used abroad rather than at home. That is, we **export** some of our output to other countries, for whatever use they care to make of it. Thus, GDP—the value of output produced—will be larger than the sum of our own consumption, investment, and government purchases to the extent that we succeed in exporting goods and services.

We **import** goods and services as well. A flight to London on British Air is an imported service; a Jaguar is an imported good. These goods and services aren't part of America's GDP because they weren't produced within our borders. In principle, these imports never enter the GDP accounts. In practice, however, it's difficult to distinguish imports from domestic-made products, especially when goods include value added from both foreign and domestic producers. Even "American-made" cars typically incorporate parts manufactured in Japan, Mexico, Thailand, Britain, Spain, or Germany, with final assembly here in the United States. Should that car be counted as an "American" product or as an import? Rather than try to sort out all these products and parts, the U.S. Commerce Department simply subtracts the value of all imports from the value of total spending. **Thus, exports are *added* to GDP and imports are *subtracted*.** The difference between the two expenditure flows is called **net exports**.

GDP Components

Once we recognize the components of output, we discover a simple method for computing GDP. *The value of GDP can be computed by adding up the expenditures of market participants.* Specifically, we note that

$$GDP = C + I + G + (X - M)$$

where C = consumption expenditure
I = investment expenditure
G = government expenditure
X = exports
M = imports

This approach to GDP accounting emphasizes the fact that **all the output produced in the economy must be claimed by someone.** If we know who's buying our output, we know how much was produced and what uses were made of it. This is the answer to the WHAT question.

MEASURES OF INCOME

There's another way of looking at GDP. Instead of looking at who's *buying* our output, we can look at who's *being paid* to produce it. Like markets themselves. *GDP accounts have two sides: One side focuses on expenditure (the demand side) and the other side focuses on income (the supply side).*

We've already observed (see Figure 3.1) that every market transaction involves an *exchange* of dollars for a good or resource. Moreover, the *value* of each good or resource is measured by the amount of money exchanged for it (its market price). Hence, *the total value of market incomes must equal the total value of final output, or GDP.* In other words, one person's expenditure always represents another person's income.

Figure 5.2 illustrates the link between spending on output and incomes. This is a modified version of the circular flow we saw in Chapter 3. The spending that flows into the product market gets funneled into the factor market, where resources are employed to produce the goods people want. The expenditure then flows into the hands of business owners, workers, landlords, and other resource owners. With the exception of sales taxes and depreciation, all spending on output becomes income to factors of production.

The equivalence of output and income isn't dependent on any magical qualities possessed by money. Were we to produce only one product—say, wheat—and pay everyone in bushels

FIGURE 5.2

Output = Income

The spending that establishes the value of output also determines the value of income. With minor exceptions, the market value of income must equal the market value of output.

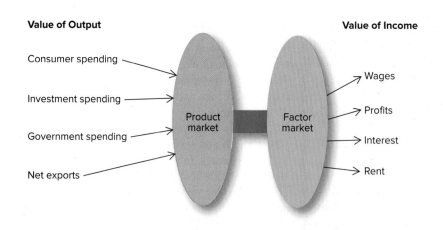

and pecks, total income would still equal total output. People couldn't receive in income more wheat than we produced. On the other hand, all the wheat produced would go to *someone.* Hence, one could say that the production possibilities of the economy define not only the limits to *output,* but also the limits to real *income.* The amount of income actually generated in any year depends on the production and expenditure decisions of consumers, firms, and government agencies.

Table 5.5 shows the actual flow of output and income in the U.S. economy during 2019. Total output is made up of the four components of GDP: consumption, investment, government goods and services, and net exports. The figures on the left side of Table 5.5 indicate that consumers spent nearly $15 trillion, businesses spent almost $4 trillion on plant and equipment, governments also spent nearly $4 trillion, and net exports were a *negative* $600 billion (imports exceeded exports). Our total output value (GDP) was thus $21.4 trillion in 2019. That was one-fifth of the *world's* output.

The right side of Table 5.5 indicates who received the income generated from these market transactions. ***Every dollar spent on goods and services provides income to someone.*** It may go to a worker (as wage or salary) or to a business firm (as profit and depreciation allowance). It may go to a landlord (as rent), to a lender (as interest), or to government (as taxes on production and imports). None of the dollars spent on goods and services disappears into thin air.

National Income

Although it may be exciting to know that we collectively received more than $21 trillion of income in 2019, it might be of more interest to know who actually got all that income. After

TABLE 5.5

The Equivalence of Expenditure and Income (in Billions of Dollars)

The value of total expenditure must equal the value of total income. Why? Because every dollar spent on output becomes a dollar of income for someone.

Expenditure		Income	
C: Consumer goods and services	$14,561	Wages and salaries	$11,434
		Corporate profits	2,075
I: Investment in plants, equipment, and		Proprietors' income	1,658
		Rents	778
inventory	3,744	Interest	645
G: Government goods		Taxes on output and	
and services	3,754	imports	1,494
X: Exports	2,504	Depreciation	3,463
M: Imports	(3,136)	Statistical discrepancy	(120)
GDP: Total value of output	$21,427 =	Total value of income	$21,427

Source: U.S. Department of Commerce (2019 data).

all, in addition to the 340 million pairs of outstretched palms among us, millions of businesses and government agencies were also competing for those dollars and the goods and services they represent. By charting the flow of income through the economy, we can see FOR WHOM our output was produced.

Depreciation. The annual income flow originates in product market sales. Purchases of final goods and services create a flow of income to producers and, through them, to factors of production. But a major diversion of sales revenues occurs immediately as a result of depreciation charges made by businesses. As we noted earlier, some of our capital resources are used up in the process of production. For the most part, these resources are owned by business firms that expect to be compensated for such investments. Accordingly, they regard some of the sales revenue generated in product markets as reimbursement for wear and tear on capital plants and equipment. They therefore subtract *depreciation charges* from gross revenues in calculating their incomes. Depreciation charges reduce GDP to the level of *net domestic product (NDP)* before any income is available to current factors of production. As we saw earlier,

$$NDP = GDP - Depreciation$$

Net Foreign Factor Income. Remember that some of the income generated in U.S. product markets belongs to foreigners. Wages, interest, and profits paid to foreigners are not part of U.S. income. So we need to subtract that outflow.

Recall also that U.S. citizens own factors of production employed in other nations (e.g., a Ford plant in Mexico; a McDonald's outlet in Singapore). This creates an *in*flow of income to U.S. households. To connect the value of U.S. output to U.S. incomes, we must add back in the net inflow of foreign factor income.

Once depreciation charges are subtracted from GDP and net foreign factor income added, we're left with **national income (NI),** which is the total income earned by U.S. factors of production. Thus,

$$NI = NDP + Net\ foreign\ factor\ income$$

As Table 5.6 illustrates, our national income in 2019 was $18.1 trillion, nearly 85 percent of GDP.

national income (NI): Total income earned by current factors of production: GDP less depreciation and indirect business taxes, plus net foreign factor income.

TABLE 5.6

The Flow of Income, 2019

Income Flow	Amount (in Billions)
Gross domestic product (GDP)	$21,427
Less depreciation	(3,463)
Net domestic product (NDP)	17,964
Plus net foreign factor income	296
Less statistical discrepancy	(105)
National income (NI)	18,155
Less indirect business taxes*	(1,420)
Less corporate profits	(2,075)
Less interest and miscellaneous payments	(645)
Less Social Security taxes	(1,420)
Plus transfer payments	3,172
Plus capital income	2,835
Personal income (PI)	18,602
Less personal taxes	(2,182)
Disposable income (DI)	16,420

*Taxes on production and imports.
Source: U.S. Department of Commerce.

The revenue generated from market transactions passes through many hands. Households end up with disposable income equal to about 75 percent of GDP, after depreciation and taxes are taken out and net interest and transfer payments are added back in. Disposable income is either spent (consumption) or saved by households.

Personal Income

There are still more revenue diversions as the GDP flow makes its way to consumer households.

Indirect Business Taxes. Another major diversion of the income flow occurs at its point of origin. When goods are sold in the marketplace, their purchase price is typically encumbered with some sort of sales tax. Thus, some of the revenue generated in product markets disappears before any factor of production gets a chance to claim it. These taxes on production and imports—often referred to as *indirect business taxes*—must be deducted from national income because they don't represent payment to factors of production. That revenue goes to the government.

Corporate Profits. Theoretically, all the income corporations receive represents income for their owners—the households who hold stock in the corporations. But the flow of income through corporations to stockholders is far from complete. First, corporations have to pay taxes on their profits. Accordingly, a chunk of corporate revenue goes into the public treasury rather than into private bank accounts. Second, corporate managers typically find some urgent need for cash. As a result, another chunk of (after-tax) profits is retained by the corporation rather than passed on to the stockholders in the form of dividends. In Table 5.6 the net result is attained by subtracting all corporate profits from national income, then adding back dividends paid to households in the category "capital income."

Payroll Taxes and Transfers. Still another deduction must be made for *Social Security taxes*. Nearly all people who earn a wage or salary are required by law to pay Social Security contributions. In 2020, the Social Security tax rate for workers was 7.65 percent of the first $132,900 of earnings received in the year. Workers never see this income because it is withheld by employers and sent directly to the U.S. Treasury. Thus, the flow of national income is reduced considerably before it becomes **personal income (PI),** the amount of income received by households before payment of personal taxes.

> **personal income (PI):** Income received by households before payment of personal taxes.

Not all of our adjustments to national income are negative. Households receive income in the form of transfer payments from the public treasury. More than 60 million people receive monthly Social Security checks, for example, and another 14 million receive some form of public welfare. These income transfers represent income for the people who receive them.

Capital Income. People also receive interest payments and dividend checks. These forms of capital income provide another source of personal income. Accordingly, our calculation of personal income is as follows:

> *National income* (= income earned by factors of production)
> *less*   indirect business taxes
>   corporate profits
>   interest and miscellaneous payments
>   Social Security taxes
> *plus*   transfer payments
>   capital income
> *equals* **personal income** (= income received by households)

As you can see, **the flow of income generated in production is significantly reduced before it gets into the hands of individual households.** Even then, households don't get to keep all of their income. Uncle Sam and his state and local cousins want a piece of those paychecks, dividends, rents, and other incomes. They get their piece through the mechanism of personal income taxes. Typically, those taxes are withheld by employers so that workers never

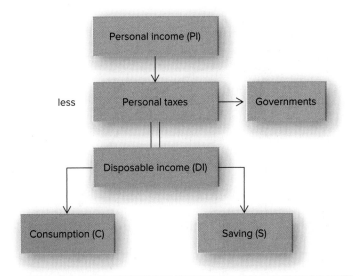

FIGURE 5.3
Where Does the Money Go?

Personal income (PI) refers to that portion of the income generated in production that ends up in the hands of private households (after businesses and governments take their shares). But we don't get to keep all that money: Households must pay personal taxes on that income. After paying income taxes, households are left with their after-tax **disposable income (DI).** We can then spend our DI on consumer goods and services—or save (not spend) it.

even see their entire income. What's left from paychecks after personal income taxes are withheld is called **disposable income (DI),** which is the amount of income consumers may themselves spend (dispose of). Thus,

disposable income (DI): After-tax income of households; personal income less personal taxes.

$$\text{Disposable income} = \text{Personal income} - \text{Personal taxes}$$

Disposable income is the end of the accounting line. As Table 5.6 shows, households end up with roughly 75 percent of the revenues generated from final market sales (GDP).

Once consumers get this disposable income in their hands, they face two choices. They may choose to *spend* their disposable income on consumer goods and services. Or they may choose to *save* it. These are the only two choices in GDP accounting. **Saving,** in this context, simply refers to disposable income that isn't spent on consumption. We don't care whether savings are hidden under a mattress, deposited in the bank, or otherwise secured. All we want to know is what portion of disposable income is spent. Thus, *all disposable income is, by definition, either consumed or saved; that is,*

saving: That part of disposable income not spent on current consumption; disposable income less consumption.

$$\text{Disposable income} = \text{Consumption} + \text{Saving}$$

Figure 5.3 summarizes these last steps.

THE FLOW OF INCOME

Figure 5.4 summarizes the broader relationship between expenditure and income. The essential point again is that every dollar spent on goods and services flows into somebody's hands. Thus, *the dollar value of output will always equal the dollar value of income.* Specifically, total income (GDP) ends up distributed in the following way:

- To *households* in the form of disposable income.
- To *business* in the form of retained earnings and depreciation allowances.
- To *government* in the form of taxes.

Income and Expenditure

The annual flow of income to households, businesses, and government is part of a continuing process. Households rarely stash their disposable income under the mattress; they spend

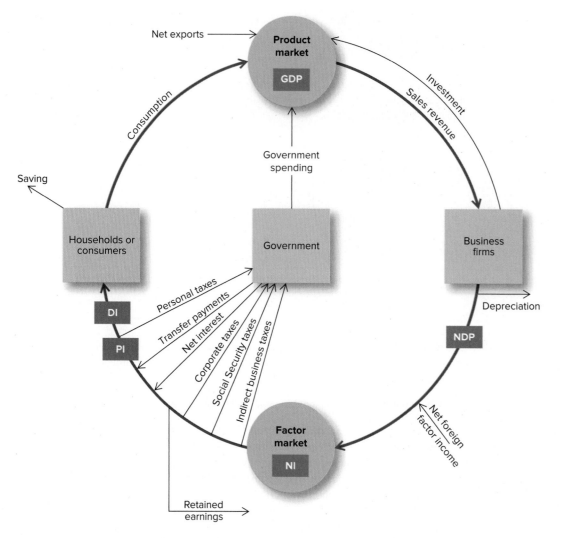

FIGURE 5.4

The Circular Flow of Spending and Income

GDP represents the dollar value of final output sold in the product market. The revenue stream flowing from GDP works its way through NDP, NI, and PI before reaching households in the form of smaller DI. DI is in turn either spent or saved by consumers. This consumption, plus investment, government spending, and net exports, continues the circular flow.

most of it on consumption. This spending adds to GDP in the next round of activity, thereby helping to keep the flow of income moving.

Business firms also have a lot of purchasing power tied up in retained earnings and depreciation charges. This income, too, may be recycled—returned to the circular flow—in the form of business investment.

Even the income that flows into public treasuries finds its way back into the marketplace as government agencies hire police officers, soldiers, and clerks, or they buy goods and services. Thus, *the flow of income that starts with GDP ultimately returns to the market in the form of new consumption (C), investment (I), and government purchases (G).* A new GDP arises, and the flow starts all over. In later chapters, we examine in detail these *expenditure* flows, with particular emphasis on their ability to keep the economy producing at its full potential.

DECISIONS FOR TOMORROW

Will More GDP Make Us Happier?

Money, money, money—it seems that's all we talk about. Why don't we talk about important things like beauty, virtue, or the quality of life? Will the economy of tomorrow be filled with a glut of products but devoid of real meaning? Do the GDP accounts tell us anything we really want to know about the quality of life? If not, why should we bother to examine them?

Intangibles. All the economic measures discussed in this chapter are important indexes of individual and collective welfare; they tell us something about how well people are living. They don't, however, capture the completeness of the way in which we view the world or the totality of what makes our lives satisfying. A clear day, a sense of accomplishment, even a smile can do more for a person's sense of well-being than can favorable movements in the GDP accounts. Or as the economist John Kenneth Galbraith put it, "In a rational lifestyle, some people could find contentment working moderately and then sitting by the street—and talking, thinking, drawing, painting, scribbling, or making love in a suitably discreet way. None of these requires an expanding economy."[3]

The emphasis on economic outcomes arises not from ignorance of life's other meanings but from the visibility of the economic outcomes. We all realize that well-being arises from both material and intangible pleasures. But the intangibles tend to be elusive. It's not easy to gauge individual happiness, much less to ascertain the status of our collective satisfaction. We have to rely on measures we can see, touch, and count. As long as material goods have a positive impact to our well-being, they at least serve a useful purpose.

In some situations, however, more physical output may actually worsen our collective welfare. If increased automobile production raises congestion and pollution levels, the rise in GDP occasioned by those additional cars is a misleading index of society's welfare. In such a case, the rise in GDP might actually mask a *decrease* in the well-being of the population. We might also wonder whether more casinos, more prisons, more telemarketing, more divorce litigation, and more Prozac—all of which contribute to GDP growth—are really valid measures of our well-being. Exclusive emphasis on measurable output would clearly be a mistake in many cases.

Index of Well-Being. Researchers at the Institute for Innovation in Social Policy at Vassar College have devised an alternative index of well-being. Their Index of Social Health includes a few economic parameters (such as unemployment and weekly earnings) but puts more emphasis on sociological behavior (such as child abuse, teen suicides, crime, poverty, and inequality). They claim that this broader view offers a more meaningful guidepost to everyday life than GDP measures of material wealth. According to their calculations, life has gotten worse, not better, as GDP has increased (see Front Page Economics "Material Wealth vs. Social Health").

World Happiness Index. The United Nations also tries to gauge the correlation between GDP and happiness. Rather than collecting statistics on social problems, the UN simply asks people to rate their own happiness. Based on those self-assessments, the UN ranks nations on the basis of their "happiness." The accompanying World View "GDP and Happiness" shows that Finland is the world's happiest country. The United States comes in at 19th place, and South Sudan emerges as the world's most unhappy place.

[3]Cited in Leonard Silk, *Nixonomics,* 2nd ed. (New York: Praeger, 1973), p. 163.

Continued

MATERIAL WEALTH VS. SOCIAL HEALTH

National income accounts are regularly reported and widely quoted. They do not, however, adequately reflect the nation's *social* performance. To measure more accurately the country's social health, a Vassar College team of social scientists devised an Index of Social Health with 16 indicators, including infant mortality, drug abuse, health insurance coverage, and poverty among the aged. According to this index, America's social health increased only 6 percent from 1990 to 2011, despite a 34 percent increase in real GDP per capita.

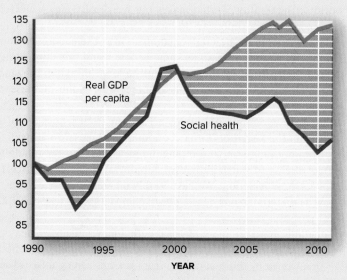

Source: Data from Institute for Innovation in Social Policy (Vassar College).

CRITICAL ANALYSIS: The **national income accounts** emphasize material well-being. They are an important, but not a complete, gauge of our societal welfare.

Although the happiest nations all enjoy high living standards, GDP per capita is not the decisive factor in perceived happiness. Social support networks, healthy life expectancies, personal freedom, and perceptions of corruption all affect reported happiness. That helps explain why the United States and Hong Kong aren't closer to the top of the happiness rankings, despite having such high incomes.

Both the Index of Social Health and the World Happiness Index underscore the fact that *social welfare* and *economic welfare* aren't always synonymous. The GDP accounts tell us whether our economic welfare has increased, as measured by the value of goods and services produced. They don't tell us how highly we value additional goods and services relative to nonmarket phenomena. Nor do they even tell us whether important social costs were incurred in the process of production. These judgments must be made outside the market; they're social decisions.

Finally, note that any given level of GDP can encompass many combinations of output. Choosing WHAT to produce is still a critical question, even after the goal of *maximum* production has been established. The quality of life in the economy tomorrow will depend on what specific mix of goods and services we include in GDP.

WORLD VIEW

GDP AND HAPPINESS

The United Nations again ranked the world's nations on the basis of self-perceived happiness. Finland emerged as the happiest place on Earth and South Sudan as the most unhappy.

Rank	Nation	GDP per Capita
1	Finland	$47,970
2	Denmark	56,410
3	Norway	68,310
4	Iceland	55,190
5	Netherlands	56,890
9	Canada	47,490
19	United States	63,390
23	Mexico	19,360
76	Hong Kong	67,700
156	South Sudan	1,550

Source: United Nations World Happiness Report 2019 and World Bank Development Indicators, 2019.

CRITICAL ANALYSIS: Per capita GDP is a measure of material living standards. While income is an important influence on happiness, it is not the only factor that counts.

SUMMARY

- National income accounting measures annual output and income flows. The national income accounts provide a basis for assessing our economic performance, designing public policy, and understanding how all the parts of the economy interact. **LO5-1**
- The most comprehensive measure of output is gross domestic product (GDP), the total market value of all final goods and services produced within a nation's borders during a given period. **LO5-1**
- In calculating GDP, we include only the value added at each stage of production. This value-added procedure eliminates the double counting that results when business firms buy intermediate goods from other firms and include those costs in their selling price. **LO5-1**
- To distinguish physical changes in output from monetary changes in its value, we compute both nominal and real GDP. Nominal GDP is the value of output expressed in *current* prices. Real GDP is the value of output expressed in *constant* prices (the prices of some *base year*). **LO5-2**
- Each year some of our capital equipment is worn out in the process of production. Hence, GDP is larger than the amount of goods and services we could consume without reducing our production possibilities. The amount of capital used up each year is referred to as *depreciation*. **LO5-4**

- By subtracting depreciation from GDP, we derive net domestic product (NDP). The difference between NDP and GDP is also equal to the difference between *gross* investment—the sum of all our current plant and equipment expenditures—and *net* investment—the amount of investment over and above that required to replace worn-out capital. **LO5-4**
- All the income generated in market sales (GDP) is received by someone. Therefore, the value of aggregate output must equal the value of aggregate income. **LO5-3**
- The sequence of flows involved in this process is
  GDP
  less depreciation
  equals **NDP**
  plus net foreign factor income
  equals national income (**NI**)
  less indirect business taxes,
      corporate profits,
      interest payments, and
      Social Security taxes
  plus transfer payments and
      capital income
  equals personal income (**PI**)
  less personal income taxes
  equals disposable income (**DI**) **LO5-3**

- The incomes received by households, business firms, and governments provide the purchasing power required to buy the nation's output. As that purchasing power is spent, further GDP is created and the circular flow continues. **LO5-3**

Key Terms

national income accounting	inflation	imports
gross domestic product (GDP)	production possibilities	net exports
GDP per capita	depreciation	national income (NI)
intermediate goods	net domestic product (NDP)	personal income (PI)
value added	investment	disposable income (DI)
nominal GDP	gross investment	saving
real GDP	net investment	
base year	exports	

Questions for Discussion

1. The manuscript for this text was typed for free by a friend. Had I hired an administrative assistant to do the same job, GDP would have been higher, even though the amount of output would have been identical. Why is this? Does this make sense? **LO5-1**

2. According to Table 5.3, GDP grew from $14.062 trillion in 2007 to $14.369 trillion in 2008, yet the quantity of output actually decreased. How is this possible? **LO5-2**

3. Does Walmart compute its sales in physical terms? Why or why not? **LO5-1**

4. Can we increase consumption in a given year without cutting back on either investment or government services? Under what conditions? **LO5-4**

5. Why is it important to know how much output is being produced? Who uses such information? **LO5-1**

6. What jobs are likely part of the underground economy? **LO5-1**

7. Clear-cutting a forest adds to GDP the value of the timber, but it also destroys the forest. How should we value that loss? **LO5-1**

8. Is the Index of Social Health, discussed in Front Page Economics "Material Wealth vs. Social Health," a better barometer of well-being than GDP? What are its relative advantages or disadvantages? **LO5-1**

9. More than 4 million websites sell a combined $100 billion of pornography a year. Should these sales be included in (*a*) GDP and (*b*) an index of social welfare? **LO5-1**

10. Are you better off today than a year ago? How do you gauge your well-being? **LO5-1**

11. Why must the value of total expenditure equal the value of total income? **LO5-3**

PROBLEMS FOR CHAPTER 5

LO5-1 1. Suppose that furniture production encompasses the following stages:

Stage 1: Trees are sold to lumber company.	$ 800
Stage 2: Lumber is sold to furniture company.	$2,000
Stage 3: Furniture company sells furniture to retail store.	$5,000
Stage 4: Furniture store sells furniture to consumer.	$9,000

    (*a*) What is the value added at each stage?
    (*b*) How much does this output contribute to GDP?
    (*c*) How would answer (*b*) change if the lumber were imported from Canada?

LO5-2 2. Suppose this year's nominal GDP is $1,000 billion and price level is 100. If nominal GDP increases by 2 percent and the price level goes up by 3 percent next year, calculate next year's:
    (*a*) Nominal GDP
    (*b*) Price level
    (*c*) Real GDP

LO5-2 3. What was real per capita GDP in 1933 measured in 2013 prices? (Use the data in Table 5.4 to compute your answer.)

LO5-3 4. If all prices were to double overnight, what would be the
    (*a*) Change in real GDP?
    (*b*) Change in nominal GDP?

LO5-3 5. Based on the following data,

Consumption	$200 billion
Depreciation	20
Retained earnings	12
Gross investment	30
Imports	60
Exports	50
Net foreign factor income	10
Government purchases	80

    (*a*) How much is GDP?
    (*b*) How much is net investment?
    (*c*) How much is national income?

LO5-4 6. Using the data in Table 5.5, what share of U.S. total income in 2019 consisted of
    (*a*) Wages and salaries?
    (*b*) Corporate profits?

LO5-2 7. Nominal GDP was $9,817 billion in 2000 and $21,433 billion in 2019. The chain-weighted price deflator (price index) for GDP was 78.1 in 2000 and 112.3 in 2019.
    (*a*) Calculate real GDP for 2019 using 2000 prices.
    (*b*) By how much did real GDP increase between 2000 and 2019?
    (*c*) By how much did nominal GDP increase between 2000 and 2019?

LO5-4 8. According to Table 5.5, calculate the following as a percentage of GDP for 2019:
    (*a*) Personal consumption expenditures.
    (*b*) Gross private investment.
    (*c*) Total government purchases.
    (*d*) Exports.
    (*e*) Imports.

PROBLEMS FOR CHAPTER 5 (cont'd)

LO5-2   9. Using the data in the endpapers related to nominal GDP and the chain-weighted price deflators for gross domestic product,
     (*a*) Calculate the percentage change in *nominal* GDP between 2010 and 2019.
     (*b*) Calculate Real GDP in 2019 at prices of 2010.
     (*c*) Calculate the percentage change in *real* GDP between 2010 and 2019.
     (*d*) What is the percentage change in *nominal* GDP between 2010 and 2019 attributed to changing prices?
     (*e*) What is the percentage change in nominal GDP between 2010 and 2019 attributed to a growing economy?

LO5-2   10. Using the data in the endpapers related to nominal GDP, real GDP, and total population, answer the questions for the time period 2010–2019:
     (*a*) Calculate nominal and real GDP per capita for 2010 and 2019.
     (*b*) By what percentage did *nominal* per capita GDP increase?
     (*c*) By what percentage did *real* GDP per capita increase?

LO5-1   11. *Decisions for Tomorrow*: According to Front Page Economics "Material Wealth vs. Social Health,"
     (*a*) Do per capita GDP data overstate or understate the rise in U.S. well-being since 1990?
     (*b*) How do you know?

Michael S. Williamson/Getty Images

Unemployment

LEARNING OBJECTIVES

After reading this chapter, you should know

LO6-1 How unemployment is measured.

LO6-2 The socioeconomic costs of unemployment.

LO6-3 The major types of unemployment.

LO6-4 The meaning of "full employment."

George H. had worked at the General Motors factory in Lordstown, Ohio, for 18 years. Now he was 46 years old with a wife and three children. With his base salary of $48,200 and the performance bonus he received nearly every year, he was doing pretty well. He had his own home, two cars, company-paid health insurance for the family, and a growing nest egg in the company's pension plan. The H. family wasn't rich, but they were comfortable and secure.

Or so they thought. Overnight the H. family's comfort was shattered. On March 6, 2019, GM announced it was closing the plant permanently. George H., along with 1,500 fellow workers, was permanently laid off. The weekly paychecks stopped immediately; the pension nest egg was in doubt. Although GM offered job transfers to plants in other states, George H. couldn't just pack up and go. He had kids in school, parents nearby, and a house that would be hard to sell in a depressed community. He was stuck. Within a few weeks, George H. was on the street looking for a new job—an experience he hadn't had since high school. The unemployment benefits the state and union provided didn't come close to covering the mortgage payment, groceries, insurance, and other necessities. The H. family quickly used up its savings, including the $5,000 set aside for the children's college education.

George H. stayed unemployed for months. His wife found a part-time waitressing job, and his oldest son went to work rather than college. George himself ultimately found a warehousing job that paid only half as much as his previous job.

In the recession of 2008–2009 and its aftermath, more than *8 million* workers lost their jobs as companies "downsized," "restructured," or simply closed. The abrupt lockdown of the American economy in response to the coronavirus pandemic in early 2020 threw even more people out of work. Not all these displaced workers fared as badly as George H. and his family. But the job loss was a painful experience for every one of those displaced workers. That's the human side of an economic downturn.

The pain of joblessness is not confined to those who lose their jobs. In recessions, students discover that jobs are hard to find in the summer. No matter how good their grades are or how nice their résumés look, some graduates just don't get any job offers in a recession. Even people with jobs feel some economic pain: Their paychecks shrink when hours or wages are scaled back.

In this chapter, we take a closer look at the problem of unemployment, focusing on the following questions:

- **When is a person "unemployed"?**
- **What are the costs of unemployment?**
- **What's an appropriate policy goal for "full employment"?**

As we answer these questions, we'll develop a sense of why full employment is a major goal of macro policy and begin to see some of the obstacles we face in achieving it.

THE LABOR FORCE

To assess the dimensions of our unemployment problems, we first need to decide who wants a job. Millions of people are jobless, yet they're not part of our unemployment problem. Full-time students, young children playing with their toys, and older people living in retirement are all jobless. We don't expect them to be working, so we don't regard them as part of the unemployment problem. We're not trying to get *everybody* a job, just those people who are ready and willing to work.

To distinguish those people who want a job from those who don't, we separate the entire population into two distinct groups. One group consists of *labor force participants;* the other group encompasses all *nonparticipants.*

labor force: All persons over age 16 who are either working for pay or actively seeking paid employment.

Labor Force. The **labor force** includes everyone age 16 and older who is actually working plus all those who aren't working but are actively seeking employment. Individuals are also counted as employed in a particular week if their failure to work is due to vacation, illness, labor dispute (strike), or bad weather. All such persons are regarded as "with a job but not at work." Also, unpaid family members working in a family enterprise (farming, for example) are counted as employed. *Only those people who are either employed or actively seeking work are counted as part of the labor force.* People who are neither employed *nor* actively looking for a job are referred to as *nonparticipants.* As Figure 6.1 shows, only half the U.S. population participates in the labor force.

Nonparticipants. Note that our definition of labor force participation excludes most household and volunteer activities. People who choose to devote their energies to household responsibilities or to unpaid charity work aren't counted as part of the labor force, no matter how hard they work. Because they are neither in paid employment nor seeking such employment in the marketplace, they are regarded as outside the labor market (nonparticipants or out of the labor force). But if they decide to seek a paid job outside the home, we say that they are "entering the labor force." Students too are typically out of the labor force until they leave school. They *"enter"* the labor force when they go looking for a job, either during the summer or after graduation. People *"exit"* the labor force when they go back to school, return to household activities, go to prison, or retire. These entries and exits keep changing the size and composition of the labor force.

labor force participation rate: The percentage of the working-age population working or seeking employment.

Participation rates. Over time, the labor force grows pretty much in step with population growth, as Figure 6.2 illustrates. Within that pattern, however, there has been a dramatic change in **labor force participation rates**. Back in the 1950s, only one out of three women

FIGURE 6.1

The Labor Force, 2019

Only half the total U.S. population participates in the civilian labor force. The rest of the population is too young, in school, at home, retired, or otherwise unavailable.

Unemployment statistics count only those participants who aren't currently working but are actively seeking paid employment. Nonparticipants are neither employed nor actively seeking employment.

Source: U.S. Bureau of Labor Statistics.

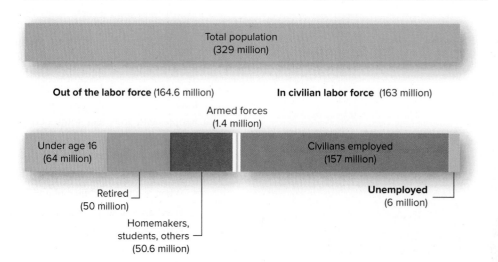

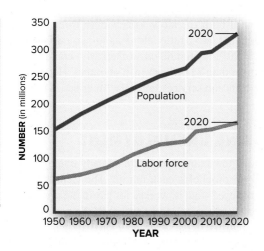

Participation Rates (Age 16 and Older)		
Year	Men	Women
1950	86.4	33.9
1960	83.3	37.7
1970	79.7	43.3
1980	77.4	51.5
1990	76.4	57.5
2000	74.7	60.0
2010	71.2	58.6
2020	69.2	57.4

FIGURE 6.2

A Growing Labor Force

The labor force expands as births and immigration increase. A big increase in the participation rate of women after 1950 also added to labor force growth.

Source: U.S. Bureau of Labor Statistics.

held a job outside the home; their participation rate was way below that of men. Since then, however, women have entered the labor market in droves, while the participation rate of men has actually declined.

Labor Force Growth

The labor force continues to grow each year along with population increases and continuing immigration. These sources add more than 2 million persons to the labor force every year. This is both good news and bad news. The good news is that labor force growth expands our **production possibilities,** enabling us to produce more output with each passing year. The bad news is that we've got to create at least 2 million *more* jobs every year to ensure that labor force participants can find a job. If we don't, we'll end up *inside* the production possibilities curve, as at point *F* in Figure 6.3.

Unemployment

If we end up inside the production possibilities curve, we are not producing at capacity. We're also not using all available resources, including labor force participants. This gives rise to the problem of **unemployment:** People who are willing and able to work aren't being hired. At point *F* in Figure 6.3 would-be workers are left unemployed; potential output isn't produced. Everybody suffers.

Okun's Law; Lost Output. Arthur Okun quantified the relationship between unemployment and the production possibilities curve. According to the original formulation of **Okun's law,** each additional 1 percent of unemployment translated into a loss of 3 percent in real output. More recent estimates of Okun's law put the ratio at about 1 to 2, largely due to the changing

production possibilities: The alternative combinations of final goods and services that could be produced in a given period with all available resources and technology.

unemployment: The inability of labor force participants to find jobs.

Okun's law: One percent more unemployment is estimated to equal 2 percent less output.

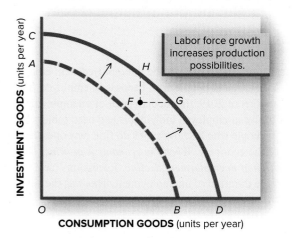

FIGURE 6.3

Labor Force Growth

The amount of labor available for work—the *labor force*—is a prime determinant of a nation's production possibilities. As the labor force grows, so does the capacity to produce. To produce at capacity, however, the labor force must be fully employed. At point *F*, resources are unemployed.

composition of both the labor force (more women and teenagers) and output (more services). Using that 1-to-2 ratio allows us to put a dollar value on the aggregate cost of unemployment. In 2019 the 6 milllion workers who couldn't find jobs (see Figure 6.1) could have produced more than $1 *trillion* worth of output. Hence, their unemployment implied a loss of $3,000 of goods and services for every American. That's a high cost for macro failure.

MEASURING UNEMPLOYMENT

To determine how many people are actually unemployed, the U.S. Census Bureau surveys about 60,000 households each month. The Census interviewers first determine whether a person is employed—that is, worked for pay in the previous week (or didn't work due to illness, vacation, bad weather, or a labor strike). If the person is not employed, he or she is classified as either *unemployed* or *out of the labor force.* To make that distinction, the Census interviewers ask whether the person actively looked for work in the preceding four weeks. *If a person is not employed but is actively seeking a job, he or she is counted as unemployed.* Individuals neither employed nor actively seeking a job are counted as outside the labor force (nonparticipants).

The Unemployment Rate

unemployment rate: The proportion of the labor force that is unemployed.

In 2019, an average of 6 million persons were counted as unemployed in any month. These unemployed individuals accounted for 3.7 percent of our total labor force in that year. Accordingly, the average **unemployment rate** in 2019 was 3.7 percent.

$$\text{Unemployment rate} = \frac{\text{Number of unemployed people}}{\text{Labor force}}$$
$$\text{in 2019} = \frac{6,000,000}{163,000,000} = 3.7\%$$

The Census surveys reveal not only the total amount of unemployment in the economy but also which groups are suffering the greatest unemployment. Typically, teenagers just entering the labor market have the greatest difficulty finding (or keeping) jobs. They have no job experience and relatively few marketable skills. Employers are reluctant to hire them, especially if they must pay a government-set minimum wage. As a consequence, teenage unemployment rates are typically three times higher than adult unemployment rates (see Figure 6.4).

Minority workers also experience above-average unemployment. Notice in Figure 6.4 that Black and Hispanic unemployment rates are much higher than white workers' unemployment rates. In 2019 Black teenagers had an extraordinary unemployment rate of 21 percent—five times the national average.

Education. Education also affects the chances of being unemployed. If you graduate from college, your chances of being unemployed drop sharply, regardless of gender or race. Advancing technology and a shift to services from manufacturing have put a premium on better-educated workers. Very few people with master's or doctoral degrees stand in unemployment lines.

The Duration of Unemployment

Although high school dropouts are three times more likely to be unemployed than college graduates, they don't *stay* unemployed. In fact, most people who become unemployed find jobs in 2–3 months. In the robust labor market of 2019, the median spell of unemployment was 9.1 weeks (Table 6.1). Only one out of five unemployed individuals had been jobless for as long as 6 months (27 weeks or longer). People who lose their jobs do find new ones; how fast that happens depends on the state of the economy. *When the economy is growing, both unemployment rates and the average duration of unemployment decline.* Recessions have the opposite effect—raising both the rate and the duration of unemployment. This was the situation in 2020 when the COVID-19 lockdowns kept people unemployed longer.

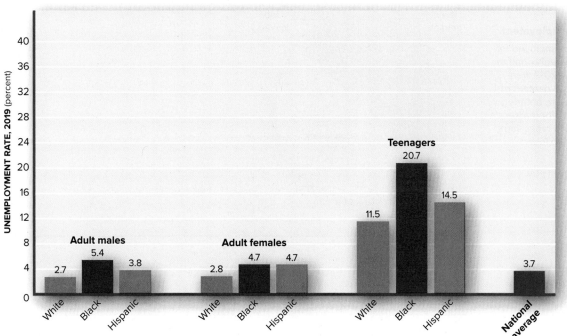

FIGURE 6.4

Unemployment Varies by Race and Sex

Minority groups, teenagers, and less-educated individuals experience higher rates of unemployment. Teenage unemployment rates are particularly high, especially for Black and Hispanic youth.

Source: U.S. Department of Labor (2019 data).

Reasons for Unemployment

The reason a person becomes unemployed also affects the length of time the person stays jobless. A person just entering the labor market might need more time to identify job openings and develop job contacts. By contrast, an autoworker laid off for a temporary plant closing can expect to return to work quickly. Figure 6.5 depicts these and other reasons for unemployment. In 2019, roughly one of every two unemployed persons was a job loser (laid off or fired), and only one in seven was a job leaver (quit). The rest were new entrants (primarily teenagers) or reentrants (primarily mothers returning to the workforce). Like the duration of unemployment, the reasons for joblessness are very sensitive to economic conditions. In really bad years like 2008–2010 and 2020, most of the unemployed are job losers, and they remain out of work a long time.

Discouraged Workers

Unemployment statistics don't tell the complete story about the human costs of a sluggish economy. When unemployment persists, job seekers become increasingly frustrated. After

Duration	Percentage of Unemployed
Less than 5 weeks	34.8%
5 to 14 weeks	29.8
15 to 26 weeks	14.3
27 weeks or more	21.1
Median duration	9.1 weeks

Source: U.S. Bureau of Labor Statistics (2019 data).

TABLE 6.1

Duration of Unemployment

The severity of unemployment depends on how long the spell of joblessness lasts. About half of unemployed workers return to work quickly, but many others remain unemployed for 6 months or longer.

FIGURE 6.5

Reasons for Unemployment

People become unemployed for various reasons. Roughly half of the unemployed in 2019 were job losers. About 40 percent of the unemployed were entering or reentering the labor market in search of a job. In recessions, the proportion of job losers shoots up.

Source: U.S. Labor Department.

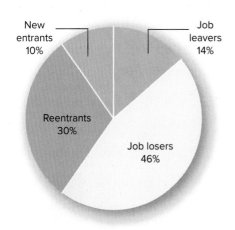

discouraged worker: An individual who isn't actively seeking employment but would look for or accept a job if one were available.

underemployment: People seeking full-time paid employment who work only part time or are employed at jobs below their capability.

repeated rejections, job seekers often get so discouraged that they give up the search and turn to their families, friends, or public welfare for income support. When the Census Bureau interviewer asks whether they're actively seeking employment, such **discouraged workers** are apt to reply no. Yet they'd like to be working, and they'd probably be out looking for work if job prospects were better.

Discouraged workers aren't counted as part of our unemployment problem because they're technically out of the labor force. The Labor Department estimates that nearly 400,000 individuals fell into this uncounted class of discouraged workers in 2019. That's on top of the 6 million officially counted as unemployed because they were still actively seeking jobs. In years of higher unemployment, this number increases sharply.

Underemployment

Some people can't afford to be discouraged. Many people who become jobless have family responsibilities and bills to pay. Like George H. and the other workers who lost jobs at GM's Lordstown plant, they simply can't afford to drop out of the labor force. Instead they're compelled to take some job—any job—just to keep body and soul together. The resultant job may be part-time or full-time and may pay very little. Nevertheless, any paid employment is sufficient to exclude the person from the count of the unemployed, though not from a condition of **underemployment.**

Underemployed workers represent labor resources that aren't being fully utilized. They're part of our unemployment problem, even if they're not officially counted as *unemployed.* In 2019, nearly 5 million workers were underemployed in the U.S. economy.

The Phantom Unemployed

Although discouraged and underemployed workers aren't counted in official unemployment statistics, some of the people who *are* counted probably shouldn't be. Many people report that they're actively seeking a job even when they have little interest in finding employment. To some extent, public policy actually encourages such behavior. For example, welfare recipients are often required to look for a job, even though some welfare mothers would prefer to spend all their time raising their children. Their resultant job search is likely to be perfunctory at best. Similarly, most states require people receiving unemployment benefits (see Front Page Economics "Unemployment Benefits Not for Everyone") to provide evidence that they're looking for a job, even though some recipients may prefer a brief period of joblessness. Here again, reported unemployment may conceal labor force nonparticipation.

FRONT PAGE ECONOMICS

UNEMPLOYMENT BENEFITS NOT FOR EVERYONE

In 2019, more than 5 million people collected unemployment benefits averaging $370 per week. But don't rush to the state unemployment office yet—not all unemployed people are eligible.

To qualify for weekly unemployment benefits, you must have worked a substantial length of time and earned some minimum amount of wages, both determined by your state. Furthermore, you must have a "good" reason for having lost your last job. Most states will not provide benefits to students (or their professors!) during summer vacations, to professional athletes in the off-season, or to individuals who quit their last jobs.

If you qualify for benefits, the amount of benefits you receive each week will depend on your previous wages. In most states, the benefits are equal to about one-half of the previous weekly wage, up to a state-determined maximum. The maximum benefit in 2019 ranged from $235 in Mississippi to a high of $795 in Massachusetts.

Unemployment benefits are financed by a tax on employers and can continue for as long as 26 weeks. During periods of high unemployment, eligibility may be extended another 13 weeks or more by the U.S. Congress. In 2010–2011, benefits were available for up to 99 weeks.

In the recession of 2020 the *federal* government added $600 per week to the benefits authorized by individual *states*, substantially increasing unemployment benefits temporarily.

Source: U.S. Employment and Training Administration.

CRITICAL CONCEPTS: Some of the income lost due to unemployment is replaced by unemployment insurance benefits. Not all **unemployed** persons are eligible, however, and the duration of benefits is limited.

THE HUMAN COSTS

Our measures of unemployment are a valuable index to a serious macro problem. However, they don't adequately convey how devastating unemployment can be for individual workers and their families.

Lost Income. The most visible impact of unemployment on individuals is the loss of income. Even short spells of joblessness can force families to tighten their belts and fall behind on bills (see Front Page Economics "The Real Costs of Joblessness"). For workers who've been unemployed for long periods, such losses can spell financial disaster. Typically, an unemployed person must rely on a combination of savings, income from other family members, and government unemployment benefits for financial support. After these sources of support are exhausted, public welfare is often the only legal support left.

Lost Confidence. Not all unemployed people experience such a financial disaster, of course. College students who fail to find summer employment are unlikely to end up on welfare the following semester. Similarly, teenagers and others looking for part-time employment won't suffer great economic losses from unemployment. Nevertheless, the experience of unemployment—of not being able to find a job when you want one—can be painful. This sensation isn't easily forgotten, even after one has finally found employment.

Social Stress. It is difficult to measure all the intangible effects of unemployment on individual workers. Studies have shown, however, that joblessness causes more crime, more health problems, more divorces, and other problems (see Front Page Economics "The Real Costs of Joblessness"). Such findings underscore the notion that prolonged unemployment poses a real danger. Like George H., the worker discussed at the beginning of this chapter, many unemployed workers simply can't cope with the resulting stress. Thomas Cottle, a lecturer at Harvard Medical School, stated the case more bluntly: "I'm now convinced that unemployment is *the* killer disease in this country—responsible for wife beating, infertility, and even tooth decay."

NEWS

FRONT PAGE ECONOMICS

THE REAL COSTS OF JOBLESSNESS

Workers who lose their jobs not only lose paychecks but also experience a variety of personal and social setbacks, including

Increased family stress
77%

Postponed medical care for financial reasons
57%

Cut back spending on food
56%

Reduced spending on children
46%

Fell behind on rent
46%

Sold personal possessions
36%

Other family member started job or increased hours
26%

Interrupted education
23%

Lost telephone service
22%

Had to stop paying for child care or elder care
12%

Source: National Employment Law Project.

CRITICAL ANALYSIS: The **cost of unemployment** is not measured in lost wages alone. Prolonged unemployment also impairs health, social relationships, and productivity.

Lost Lives. German psychiatrists have also observed that unemployment can be hazardous to your health. They estimate that the anxieties and other nervous disorders that accompany one year of unemployment can reduce life expectancy by as much as five years. In Japan, the suicide rate jumped by more than 50 percent when the economy plunged into recession. In New Zealand, suicide rates are twice as high for unemployed workers as they are for employed ones. A University of Oxford study estimated that the economic downturn of 2008–2010 triggered more than 10,000 suicides in the United States and Europe.

DEFINING FULL EMPLOYMENT

In view of the economic and social losses associated with unemployment, it's not surprising that *full employment* is one of our basic macroeconomic goals. You may be surprised to learn, however, that *"full"* **employment isn't the same thing as** *"zero"* **unemployment.** There are in fact several reasons for regarding some degree of unemployment as inevitable and even desirable.

Seasonal Unemployment

seasonal unemployment: Unemployment due to seasonal changes in employment or labor supply.

Some joblessness is virtually inevitable as long as we continue to grow crops, build houses, or go skiing at certain seasons of the year. At the end of each such season, thousands of workers must go searching for new jobs, experiencing some **seasonal unemployment** in the process.

Seasonal fluctuations also arise on the supply side of the labor market. Teenage unemployment rates, for example, rise sharply in the summer as students look for temporary jobs. To avoid such unemployment completely, we'd either have to keep everyone in school or ensure that all students went immediately from the classroom to the workroom. Neither alternative is likely, much less desirable.[1]

Frictional Unemployment

There are other reasons for expecting a certain amount of inevitable unemployment. Many workers have sound financial or personal reasons for leaving one job to look for another. In the process of moving from one job to another, a person may well miss a few days or even weeks of work without any serious personal or social consequences. On the contrary, people who spend more time looking for work may find *better* jobs.

The same is true of students first entering the labor market. It's not likely that you'll find a job the moment you leave school. Nor should you necessarily take the first job offered. If you spend some time looking for work, you're more likely to find a job you like. The job search period gives you an opportunity to find out what kinds of jobs are available, what skills they require, and what they pay. Accordingly, a brief period of job search may benefit labor market entrants and the larger economy. The unemployment associated with these kinds of job searches is referred to as **frictional unemployment.**

frictional unemployment: Brief periods of unemployment experienced by people moving between jobs or into the labor market.

Three factors distinguish frictional unemployment from other kinds of unemployment. First, enough jobs exist for those who are frictionally unemployed—that is, there's adequate *demand* for labor. Second, individuals who are frictionally unemployed have the skills required for available jobs. Third, the period of job search will be relatively short. Under these conditions, frictional unemployment resembles an unconventional game of musical chairs. There are enough chairs of the right size for everyone, and people dance around them for only a brief period.

No one knows for sure just how much of our unemployment problem is frictional. Most economists agree, however, that friction alone is responsible for an unemployment rate of 2 to 3 percent. Accordingly, our definition of *"full employment"* should allow for at least this much unemployment.

Structural Unemployment

For many job seekers, the period between jobs may drag on for months or even years because they don't have the skills that employers require. Imagine, for example, the predicament of steelworkers. During the 1980s, the steel industry contracted as consumers demanded fewer and lighter-weight cars and as construction of highways, bridges, and buildings slowed. In the process, more than 300,000 steelworkers lost their jobs. Most of these workers had a decade or more of experience and substantial skill. But the skills they'd perfected were no longer in demand. They couldn't perform the jobs available in computer software, biotechnology, or other expanding industries. Although there were enough job vacancies in the labor market, the steelworkers couldn't fill them. These workers were victims of **structural unemployment.**

structural unemployment: Unemployment caused by a mismatch between the skills (or location) of job seekers and the requirements (or location) of available jobs.

The same kind of structural displacement hit the construction industry from 2007 to 2010. The housing market collapsed, leaving millions of homes unsold and even unfinished. Tens of thousands of carpenters, electricians, and plumbers lost their jobs. These displaced workers soon discovered that their highly developed skills were no longer in demand. They couldn't fill job openings in the growing health care, financial, or Internet industries.

Teenagers from urban slums also suffer from structural unemployment. Most poor teenagers have an inadequate education, few job-related skills, and little work experience. For

[1]Seasonal variations in employment and labor supply not only create some unemployment in the annual averages but also distort monthly comparisons. Unemployment rates are always higher in February (when farming and housing construction come to a virtual standstill) and June (when a mass of students go looking for summer jobs). The Labor Department adjusts monthly unemployment rates according to this seasonal pattern and reports "seasonally adjusted" unemployment rates for each month. Seasonal adjustments don't alter *annual* averages, however.

them, almost all decent jobs are "out of reach." As a consequence, they remain unemployed far longer than can be explained by frictional forces.

Structural unemployment violates the second condition for frictional unemployment: that the job seekers can perform the available jobs. Structural unemployment is analogous to a musical chairs game in which there are enough chairs for everyone, but some of them are too small to sit on. It's a more serious concern than frictional unemployment and incompatible with any notion of full employment.

Cyclical Unemployment

cyclical unemployment: Unemployment attributable to a lack of job vacancies—that is, to an inadequate level of aggregate demand.

The fourth type of unemployment is **cyclical unemployment**—joblessness that occurs when there simply aren't enough jobs to go around. Cyclical unemployment exists when the number of workers demanded falls short of the number of persons supplied (in the labor force). This isn't a case of mobility between jobs (frictional unemployment) or even of job seekers' skills (structural unemployment). Rather, it's simply an inadequate level of demand for goods and services and thus for labor. Cyclical unemployment resembles the most familiar form of musical chairs, in which the number of chairs is always less than the number of players.

The Great Depression is the most striking example of cyclical unemployment. The dramatic increase in unemployment rates that began in 1930 (see Figure 6.6) wasn't due to any increase in friction or sudden decline in workers' skills. Instead the high rates of unemployment that persisted for a *decade* were caused by a sudden decline in the market demand for goods and services. How do we know? Just notice what happened to our unemployment rate when the demand for military goods and services increased in 1941!

Slow Growth. Cyclical unemployment can emerge even when the economy is expanding. Keep in mind that the labor force is always growing due to population growth and continuing immigration. If these additional labor force participants are to find jobs, the economy must grow. Specifically, *the economy must grow at least as fast as the labor force to avoid cyclical unemployment.* When economic growth slows below this threshold, unemployment rates start to rise.

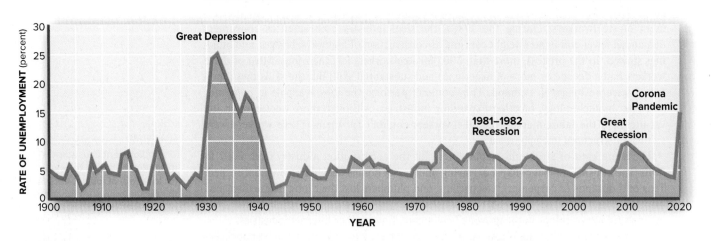

FIGURE 6.6
The Unemployment Record

Unemployment rates reached record heights (25 percent) during the Great Depression. In more recent decades, the unemployment rate has varied from under 4 percent in full-employment years to 10 percent in the recession years of 1982, 2009, and 2020. Keeping the labor force fully employed is a primary macro policy goal. This proved to be impossible in early 2020, when the coronavirus pandemic virtually shut down the economy and threw millions of workers off their jobs.

Source: U.S. Labor Department.

The Full-Employment Goal

In later chapters we examine the causes of cyclical unemployment and explore some potential policy responses. At this point, however, we just want to establish a macro policy goal. In the Employment Act of 1946, Congress committed the federal government to pursue a goal of "maximum" employment but didn't specify exactly what that rate was. Presumably, this meant avoiding as much cyclical and structural unemployment as possible while keeping frictional unemployment within reasonable bounds. As guidelines for public policy, these perspectives are a bit vague.

Inflationary Pressures. The first attempt to define *full employment* more precisely was undertaken in the early 1960s. At that time the Council of Economic Advisers (itself created by the Employment Act of 1946) decided that our proximity to full employment could be gauged by watching *prices.* As the economy approached its production possibilities, labor and other resources would become increasingly scarce. As market participants bid for these remaining resources, wages and prices would start to rise. Hence, ***rising prices are a signal that employment is nearing capacity.***

After examining the relationship between unemployment and inflation, the Council of Economic Advisers decided to peg full employment at 4 percent unemployment. The unemployment rate could fall below 4 percent. If it did, however, price levels would begin to rise at an accelerating rate. Hence, this threshold came to be regarded as an **inflationary flashpoint:** a level of output that would trigger too much inflation. Thus, 4 percent unemployment was seen as an acceptable compromise of our employment and price goals.

During the 1970s and early 1980s, this view of our full-employment potential was considered overly optimistic. Unemployment rates stayed far above 4 percent, even when the economy expanded. Moreover, inflation began to accelerate at higher levels of unemployment.

In view of these factors, the Council of Economic Advisers later raised the level of unemployment thought to be compatible with price stability. In 1983 the Reagan administration concluded that the "inflation-threshold" unemployment rate was between 6 and 7 percent.

Changed Labor Force. The quest for low unemployment got easier in the 1990s, largely due to changes in the labor force. The number of teenagers declined by 3 million between 1981 and 1993. The upsurge in women's participation in the labor force also leveled off. High school and college attendance and graduation rates increased. And welfare programs were reformed in ways that encouraged more work. All these structural changes made it easier to reduce unemployment rates without increasing inflation. As a result, the unemployment-rate threshold for **full employment** was set at 4–6 percent. Hence, we recognize that *full employment entails 4–6 percent unemployment, not zero percent unemployment.*

The "Natural" Rate of Unemployment

The ambiguity about which rate of unemployment might trigger an upsurge in inflation has convinced some analysts to abandon the inflation-based concept of full employment. They prefer to specify a "natural" rate of unemployment that doesn't depend on inflation trends. In this view, the natural rate of unemployment consists of frictional and structural components only. It's the rate of unemployment that will prevail in the long run. In the short run, both the unemployment rate and the inflation rate may go up and down. However, the economy will tend to gravitate toward the long-run **natural rate of unemployment.**

Although the natural rate concept avoids specifying a short-term inflation trigger, it too is subject to debate. As we've seen, the *structural* determinants of unemployment (e.g., age and composition of the labor force) change over time. When structural forces change, the level of natural unemployment presumably changes as well.

Congressional Targets

Although most economists agree that an unemployment rate of 4–6 percent is consistent with either natural or full employment, Congress has set tougher goals for macro policy.

inflationary flashpoint: The rate of output at which inflationary pressures intensify; the point on the AS curve where slope increases sharply.

full employment: The lowest rate of unemployment compatible with price stability, variously estimated at between 4 percent and 6 percent unemployment.

natural rate of unemployment: The long-term rate of unemployment determined by structural forces in labor and product markets.

According to the Full Employment and Balanced Growth Act of 1978 (commonly called the Humphrey-Hawkins Act), our national goal is to attain a 4 percent rate of unemployment. The act also requires a goal of 3 percent inflation. There was an escape clause, however. In the event that both goals couldn't be met, the president could set higher, provisional definitions of full employment.

THE HISTORICAL RECORD

Our greatest failure to achieve full employment occurred during the Great Depression. As Figure 6.6 shows, as much as one-fourth of the labor force was unemployed in the 1930s.

Unemployment rates fell dramatically during World War II. In 1944, virtually anyone who was ready and willing to work quickly found a job; the civilian unemployment rate hit a rock-bottom 1.2 percent.

Since 1950 the unemployment rate has fluctuated from a low of 2.8 percent during the Korean War (1953) to a high of 10.8 percent during the 1981–1982 recession. From 1982 to 1989 the unemployment rate receded, but it shot up again in the 1990–1991 recession.

From 1995 to 2007 the unemployment rate stayed in a fairly narrow range and actually dipped below 5 percent in 2007. But the Great Recession of 2008–2009 wiped out that gain, sending the unemployment rate to near-record heights once again (see Front Page Economics "Unemployment Rate Hits a 26-Year High"). The unemployment rate started declining as the economy recovered, but the return to full employment was agonizingly slow.

FRONT PAGE ECONOMICS

UNEMPLOYMENT RATE HITS A 26-YEAR HIGH

The nation's unemployment rate climbed to 10.2 percent in October, the highest rate since 1983. Nonfarm payrolls dropped another 190,000 last month, adding to 22 consecutive months of job losses. The biggest job losses were in manufacturing, construction, and retail employment.

Since the recession began over 7.3 million jobs have been lost. The unemployment rate has more than doubled from 4.9 percent in December 2007 to its current level of 10.2 percent.

In October, 35.6 percent of unemployed persons were jobless for 27 weeks or more, while 20 percent of the unemployed were jobless for 5 weeks or less.

Source: U.S. Bureau of Labor Statistics, November 10, 2009.

CRITICAL ANALYSIS: When the economy contracts, millions of workers lose jobs, and the unemployment rate rises—sometimes sharply. This is largely due to **cyclical unemployment.**

Coronavirus Lockdown. By the beginning of 2020, the national unemployment rate had fallen all the way to 3.7 percent, one of the lowest in history. But the coronavirus that struck the United States in early 2020 changed the employment situation overnight. Workers were told to stay home and businesses were ordered to shut down. Within days, millions of workers were displaced. In just 5 weeks, more than 20 million workers filed for unemployment benefits (see Front Page Economics "Unemployment Spikes to 14.7 Percent as Lockdown Persists"). The unemployment rate jumped from 3.5 percent in February to 4.4 percent in March, then to 14.7 in April, the highest level since the Great Depression (see Figure 6.6). Even those numbers understated the extent of the employment losses. Workers who stayed employed but had their hours drastically reduced were not counted as unemployed. Neither were those workers who didn't start actively seeking another job. But they all experienced the pain of the economic disruption.

FRONT PAGE ECONOMICS

UNEMPLOYMENT SPIKES TO 14.7 PERCENT AS LOCKDOWN PERSISTS

The unemployment rate for the nation spiked upwards in April, to a decades-long high of 14.7 percent. With the national social distancing timeframe extended to April 30, millions of restaurants, theaters, malls, and other businesses remained closed last month, suspending jobs for millions of American workers. The U.S. Labor Department reported this morning that 23 million Americans were officially unemployed in April, an increase of nearly 16 million from the prior month. Unemployment rates at these levels haven't been seen since the Great Depression of the 1930s. With some states starting to reopen, officials expect the worst of the unemployment crisis may be over.

Source: U.S. Bureau of Labor Statistics, May 8, 2020.

CRITICAL ANALYSIS: When an economy shuts down, millions of workers lose their jobs and the **unemployment** rate increases—sometimes sharply.

DECISIONS FOR TOMORROW

Is Outsourcing Really Bad?

GM's decision to close the Lordstown, Ohio, auto plant angered President Trump. Shortly after GM's announcement, Trump took to Twitter to lambaste both GM and its UAW union. In a March 17, 2019, tweet, President Trump said, "GM let our country down" and went on to insist that "GM must get their Lordstown Ohio plant open . . . FAST." As he saw it, GM and other U.S. corporations were exporting jobs by closing factories in the United States and building plants in Mexico, China, and elsewhere. He demanded that U.S. companies "bring back jobs" by building new plants and retrofitting old ones on American soil (see Front Page Economics "Trump Blasts GM Plant Closing").

Outsourcing. GM and other U.S. companies respond that their decisions on **outsourcing** are based on simple economics. If cars can be produced in Mexico at lower cost than in Ohio, GM needs to move production to Mexico. GM and other companies point out that this kind of outsourcing not only reduces production costs, but also lowers consumer prices—a benefit for everyone.

> **outsourcing:** The relocation of production to foreign countries.

U.S. companies are also quick to point out that outsourcing frees up American labor that can be used in other jobs—especially higher-paying jobs. Apple, for example, outsources virtually all of its cell phone production to China. But it still employs 90,000 workers in its American offices and 271 retail stores. It also retains 9,000 U.S.-based suppliers, who collectively employ nearly 2 million American workers. For the most part, these are well-paid jobs in design, engineering, marketing work, and retail. Apple emphasizes that all these jobs are made possible by the ability of the company to outsource lower-wage manufacturing jobs that create highly popular cell phones, ear buds, and other products.

Companies also emphasize that the number of outsourced jobs is quite small. The total number of outsourced jobs averages less than 300,000 per year. That amounts to only 0.002 percent of all U.S. jobs and only 3 percent of total U.S. *un*employment. So even in the worst case, outsourcing can't be a major explanation for U.S. unemployment.

Insourcing. We also have to recognize that outsourcing of U.S. jobs has a counterpart in the "insourcing" of foreign production. The German Mercedes Benz company builds cars in Alabama to reduce production and distribution costs. In the process, German

Continued

FRONT PAGE ECONOMICS

TRUMP BLASTS GM PLANT CLOSING

President Trump reacted angrily to GM's decision to close its Lordstown, Ohio, assembly plant. Accusing GM of "letting our country down," he demanded that GM "must get their Lordstown Ohio plant open FAST." Trump even called Mary Barra, GM's CEO, on Sunday, expressing his disappointment over the closure decision and asking her to move quickly to sell or revamp the auto plant. He insisted that GM "bring back jobs" that it had outsourced to its factories in Mexico.

President Trump pushed companies to keep factories open.

MARK LYONS/EPA-EFE/Shutterstock

Source: News accounts of March 16–17, 2019.

CRITICAL ANALYSIS: Outsourcing often causes visible job losses at specific factories and stores. But **outsourcing** may also create jobs through cost savings, higher productivity, and changing consumption patterns.

autoworkers lose some jobs to U.S. autoworkers. In addition to this direct investment, foreign nations and firms hire U.S. workers to design, build, and deliver a wide variety of products. According to the U.S. Bureau of Economic Analysis, foreign companies employ more than 8 million Americans in U.S.-based factories and offices. In other words, *trade in both products and labor resources is a two-way street*. Looking at the flow of jobs in only one direction distorts the jobs picture.

Productivity and Growth. Even the gross flow of outsourced jobs is not all bad. The cost savings realized by U.S. firms due to outsourcing increase U.S. profits. Those profits may finance new investment in U.S. product markets, thereby creating new jobs. More jobs may be gained than lost as a result. Outsourcing routine tasks to foreign workers also raises the productivity of U.S. workers by allowing U.S. workers to focus on more complex and high-value tasks. In other words, outsourcing promotes specialization and higher productivity both here and abroad. *Production possibilities expand, not contract, with outsourcing.*

Consumer Spending. Outsourcing also has an impact on the *demand* side of the market. When outsourcing leads to lower prices for flat-screen TVs, consumers end up spending less on televisions. What do they do with their savings? Typically, they spend the money they saved on their TV purchase by buying something else. So, demand for *other* goods and services increases, leading to more jobs in other industries. That is the nature of a dynamic economy.

The Displaced Workers. All these economic arguments are of no consolation to George H. and the other workers who lost their jobs when GM closed the Lordstown factory. They are out of work in Ohio, in part because GM can produce cars more cheaply in Mexico. While GM and U.S. consumers may be better off with outsourced cars, George H. and his fellow workers are clearly worse off. The fact that they live in an important electoral district was not lost on President Trump.

The challenge for economic policy is not to put a halt to outsourcing and insourcing, but to find new jobs for workers displaced by changing patterns of production and consumption. Stopping the outsourcing of jobs won't achieve our full-employment goal and may even worsen income and job prospects in the economy tomorrow.

SUMMARY

- To understand unemployment, we must distinguish the labor force from the larger population. Only people who are working (employed) or spend some time looking for a job (unemployed) are participants in the labor force. People neither working nor looking for work are outside the labor force.   **LO6-1**
- The labor force grows every year due to population growth and immigration. This growth increases production possibilities but also necessitates continued job creation.   **LO6-1**
- The economy (output) must grow at least as fast as the labor force to keep the unemployment rate from rising. Unemployment implies that we're producing inside the production possibilities curve rather than on it.   **LO6-1**
- The macroeconomic loss imposed by unemployment is reduced output of goods and services. Okun's law suggests that 1 percentage point in unemployment is equivalent to a 2 percentage point decline in output.   **LO6-2**
- The human cost of unemployment includes not only financial losses but social, physical, and psychological costs as well.   **LO6-2**
- Unemployment is distributed unevenly: Minorities, teenagers, and the less educated have much higher rates of

unemployment. Also hurt are discouraged workers–those who've stopped looking for work–and those working at part-time or menial jobs because they can't find full-time jobs equal to their training or potential.   **LO6-1**
- There are four types of unemployment: seasonal, frictional, structural, and cyclical.   **LO6-3**
- Because some seasonal and frictional unemployment is inevitable and even desirable, full employment is not defined as zero unemployment. These considerations, plus fear of inflationary consequences, result in full employment being defined as an unemployment rate of 4–6 percent.   **LO6-4**
- The natural rate of unemployment is based on frictional and structural forces, without reference to short-term price (inflation) pressures.   **LO6-4**
- Unemployment rates got as high as 25 percent in the 1930s. Since 1960 the unemployment rate has ranged from 3.4 to 10.8 percent.   **LO6-1**
- Outsourcing of U.S. production directly reduces domestic employment. But the indirect effects of higher U.S. productivity, profits, and global competitiveness may create even more jobs.   **LO6-3**

Key Terms

labor force	discouraged worker	inflationary flashpoint
labor force participation rate	underemployment	full employment
production possibilities	seasonal unemployment	natural rate of unemployment
unemployment	frictional unemployment	outsourcing
Okun's law	structural unemployment	
unemployment rate	cyclical unemployment	

Questions for Discussion

1. In April 2020, the coronavirus lockdown reduced the number of *employed* people by 22,369,000 but increased the number of *unemployed* persons by only 15,938,000. How is this possible?   **LO6-1**
2. If more teenagers stay in school longer, what happens to (*a*) production possibilities? (*b*) unemployment rates?   **LO6-1**
3. When the housing industry implodes, what do construction workers do?   **LO6-3**
4. What type of unemployment did the GM workers experience when their Lordstown plant closed? (See Chapter introduction.)   **LO6-3**
5. When the GM plant in Ohio closed (see Chapter introduction), how was the local economy affected?   **LO6-3**
6. Why is frictional unemployment deemed desirable?   **LO6-3**
7. Why do people expect inflation to heat up when the unemployment rate approaches 4 percent?   **LO6-4**
8. How might prolonged unemployment cause (*a*) spousal abuse? (*b*) tooth decay?   **LO6-2**
9. President Trump suggested that Apple Corporation should move its iPhone manufacturing back from China into the United States. Is this a good idea? What impact would it have on employment, wages, and prices?   **LO6-4**
10. How can the outsourcing of U.S. computer jobs generate new U.S. jobs in construction or retail trade? (See Front Page Economics "Trump Blasts GM Plant Closing.")   **LO6-4**

LO6-1 1. According to Figure 6.1,
  (a) What percentage of the civilian labor force was employed?
  (b) What percentage of the civilian labor force was unemployed?
  (c) What percentage of the *population* was employed in civilian jobs?

LO6-1 2. If the unemployment rate in 2019 had been 4.7 percent instead of 3.7 percent (Figure 6.1),
  (a) How many more workers would have been unemployed?
  (b) How many fewer would have been employed?

LO6-1 3. Between 2000 and 2019 (see Data Tables), by how much did
  (a) The labor force change?
  (b) Unemployment change?
  (c) Employment change?

LO6-1 4. If the labor force of 165 million people is growing by 1.2 percent this year, how many new jobs have to be created each month to keep unemployment from increasing?

LO6-1 5. Between 1980 and 2020, by how many percentage points did the labor force participation rate (Figure 6.2) of
  (a) Men change?
  (b) Women change?

LO6-2 6. According to Okun's law, how much output (real GDP) was lost in 2009 when the nation's unemployment rate increased from 5.8 percent to 9.8 percent?

LO6-1 7. Suppose the following data describe a nation's population:

	Year 1	Year 2
Population	320 million	330 million
Labor force	150 million	160 million
Unemployment rate	6 percent	6 percent

  (a) How many people are unemployed in each year?
  (b) How many people are employed in each year?

LO6-1 8. Based on the data in the previous problem, in Year 2, what happens to each of the following when 1 million job seekers become "discouraged workers"?
  (a) Number of unemployed persons.
  (b) Unemployment rate.
  (c) Number of employed persons.

LO6-1 9. According to Front Page Economics "Unemployment Rate Hits a 26-Year High," in October 2009
  (a) How many people were in the labor force?
  (b) How many people were employed?

LO6-1 10. In 2019, how many of the 700,000 Black teenagers who participated in the labor market
  (a) Were unemployed?
  (b) Were employed?
  (c) Would have been employed if they had the same unemployment rate as white teenagers? (See Figure 6.4 for needed info.)

LO6-4 11. On a graph, illustrate both the unemployment rate and the real GDP growth rate for 2009–2019. (The data required for this exercise can be found in the Data Tables at the end of the book.)
  (a) In how many years was "full employment" achieved? (Use the current benchmark.)
  (b) Unemployment and growth rates tend to move in opposite directions. Which appears to change direction first?
  (c) In how many years does the unemployment rate increase even when output is increasing?

LO6-4 12. (*a*) What was the unemployment rate in 2019?
(*b*) How many more jobs were needed to bring the unemployment rate down to 3 percent?

LO6-3 13. *Decisions for Tomorrow:* For each situation described here, determine the type of unemployment:
(*a*) Steelworkers losing their jobs due to outsourcing.
(*b*) A college graduate waiting to accept a job that allows her to utilize her level of education.
(*c*) The Great Recession of 2008–2009.
(*d*) A homemaker entering the labor force.

Design Credit: Shutterstock

John Alphonse/Brand X Pictures/Getty Images

Inflation

LEARNING OBJECTIVES

After reading this chapter, you should know

LO7-1 How inflation is measured.

LO7-2 Why inflation is a socioeconomic problem.

LO7-3 The meaning of "price stability."

LO7-4 The broad causes of inflation.

Germany set a record in 1923 that no other nation wants to beat. In that year, prices in Germany rose a *trillion* times over. Prices rose so fast that workers took "shopping breaks" to spend their twice-a-day paychecks before they became worthless. Menu prices in restaurants rose while people were still eating! Accumulated savings became worthless, as did outstanding loans. People needed sacks of currency to buy bread, butter, and other staples. With prices more than doubling every *day,* no one could afford to save, invest, lend money, or make long-term plans. In the frenzy of escalating prices, production of goods and services came to a halt, unemployment rose tenfold, and the German economy all but collapsed.

Hungary had a similar episode of runaway inflation in 1946, as did Japan. More recently, Venezuela, Russia, Bulgaria, Brazil, Zaire, Yugoslavia, Argentina, and Uruguay have all witnessed at least a tenfold jump in prices in a single year. Zimbabwe came close to breaking Germany's record in 2008, with an inflation rate of *231 million* percent (see World View "Zimbabwe's Trillion-Dollar Currency.")

The United States has never experienced such a price frenzy. During the Revolutionary War, prices did double in one year, but that was a singular event. In the last decade, U.S. prices have risen only 0 to 4 percent a year. Despite this enviable record, Americans still worry a lot about inflation. In response to this anxiety, every president since Franklin Roosevelt has expressed a determination to keep prices from rising. In 1971 the Nixon administration took drastic action to stop inflation. With prices rising an average of only 3 percent, President Nixon imposed price controls on U.S. producers to keep prices from rising any faster. For 90 days all wages and prices were frozen by law—price increases were prohibited. For three more years, wage and price increases were limited by legal rules.

In 1990 U.S. prices were rising at a 6 percent clip—twice the pace that triggered the 1971–1974 wage and price controls. Calling such price increases "unacceptable," Federal Reserve Chairman Alan Greenspan set a goal of *zero* percent inflation. In pursuit of that goal, the Fed slowed economic growth so much that the economy fell into a recession. The Fed did the same thing again in early 2000.

In later chapters we'll examine how the Fed and other policymakers slow the economy down or speed it up. Before looking at the levers of macro policy, however, we need to examine our policy goals. Why is inflation so feared? How much inflation is unacceptable? To get a handle on this basic issue, we'll ask and answer the following questions:

- **What kind of price increases are referred to as *inflation?***
- **Who is hurt (or helped) by inflation?**
- **What is an appropriate goal for *price stability?***

As we'll discover, inflation is a serious problem, but not for the reasons most people cite. We'll also see why deflation—falling prices—isn't so welcome either.

WHAT IS INFLATION?

Most people associate **inflation** with price increases for specific goods and services. The economy isn't necessarily experiencing inflation, however, every time the price of a cup of coffee goes up. We must distinguish the phenomenon of inflation from price increases for specific goods. *Inflation is an increase in the average level of prices, not a change in any specific price.*

inflation: An increase in the average level of prices of goods and services.

The Average Price

Suppose you wanted to know the average price of fruit in the supermarket. Surely you wouldn't have much success in seeking out an average fruit—nobody would be quite sure what you had in mind. You might have some success, however, if you sought out the prices of apples, oranges, cherries, and peaches. Knowing the price of each kind of fruit, you could then compute the average price of fruit. The resultant figure wouldn't refer to any particular product but would convey a sense of how much a typical basket of fruit might cost. By repeating these calculations every day, you could then determine whether fruit prices, *on average,* were changing. On occasion, you might even notice that apple prices rose while orange prices fell, leaving the *average* price of fruit unchanged.

The same kinds of calculations are made to measure inflation in the entire economy. We first determine the average price of all output—the average price level—and then look for changes in that average. A rise in the average price level is referred to as inflation.

The average price level may fall as well as rise. A decline in average prices—**deflation**—occurs when price decreases on some goods and services outweigh price increases on all others. This happened in Japan in 1995 and again in 2003. Such deflations are rare, however: The United States has not experienced any general deflation since 1940.

deflation: A decrease in the average level of prices of goods and services.

Relative Prices vs. the Price Level

Because inflation and deflation are measured in terms of average price levels, it's possible for individual prices to rise or fall continuously without changing the average price level. We already noted, for example, that the price of apples can rise without increasing the average price of fruit, so long as the price of some other fruit, such as oranges, falls. In such circumstances, **relative prices** are changing, but not *average* prices. An increase in the *relative* price of apples simply means that apples have become more expensive in comparison with other fruits (or any other goods or services).

relative price: The price of one good in comparison with the price of other goods.

How would you compute the average price of fruit?
gioiak2/123RF

TABLE 7.1

Prices That Have Fallen

Inflation refers to an increase in the *average* price level. It doesn't mean that *all* prices are rising. In fact, many prices fall, even during periods of general inflation.

Item	Early Price	2020 Price
Long-distance telephone call (per minute)	$ 6.90 (1915)	$ 0.02
Pocket electronic calculator	200.00 (1972)	1.99
Digital watch	2,000.00 (1972)	1.99
Pantyhose	2.16 (1967)	1.29
Ballpoint pen	0.89 (1965)	0.29
DVD player	800.00 (1997)	19.99
Laptop computer	3,500.00 (1986)	149.99
Airfare (New York–Paris)	490.00 (1958)	277.00
Microwave oven	400.00 (1972)	35.00
Contact lenses	275.00 (1972)	15.79
Television (19-inch, color)	469.00 (1980)	59.99
Compact disk player	1,000.00 (1985)	14.99
Digital camera	748.00 (1994)	15.95
Digital music player (MP3)	399.00 (2001)	22.99
Cell phone	3,595.00 (1983)	9.99
Smartphone	400.00 (1999)	39.99
E-reader	398.00 (2007)	19.99

Changes in relative prices may occur in a period of stable average prices, or in periods of inflation or deflation. In fact, in an economy as vast as ours—in which literally millions of goods and services are exchanged in the factor and product markets—*relative prices are always changing.* Indeed, relative price changes are an essential ingredient of the market mechanism. Recall from Chapter 3 what happens when the market price of web design services rises relative to other goods and services. This (relative) price rise alerts web architects (producers) to increase their output, cutting back on other production or leisure activities.

A general inflation—an increase in the *average* price level—doesn't perform this same market function. If all prices rise at the same rate, price increases for specific goods are of little value as market signals. In less extreme cases, when most but not all prices are rising, changes in relative prices do occur but aren't so immediately apparent. Table 7.1 reminds us that some prices fall even during periods of general inflation.

....

REDISTRIBUTIVE EFFECTS OF INFLATION

The distinction between relative and average prices helps us determine who's hurt by inflation—and who's helped. Popular opinion notwithstanding, it's simply not true that everyone is worse off when prices rise. *Although inflation makes some people worse off, it makes other people better off.* Some people even get rich when prices rise!

The micro consequences of inflation are reflected in redistributions of income and wealth, not general declines in either measure of our economic welfare. These redistributions occur because people buy different combinations of goods and services, own different assets, and sell distinct goods or services (including labor). The impact of inflation on individuals therefore depends on how prices change for the goods and services each person actually buys or sells.

Price Effects

Price changes are the most visible consequence of inflation. If you've been paying tuition, you know how painful a price hike can be. Fifteen years ago the average tuition at public colleges and universities was $1,000 per year. Today the average tuition exceeds $9,600 for in-state residents. At private universities, tuition has increased eightfold in the past 10 years to more than $33,000 (see Front Page Economics "College Tuition Up Again"). You don't need a whole course in economics to figure out the implications of these tuition hikes. To stay in college, you (or your parents) must forgo increasing amounts of other goods and services. You end up being worse off because you can't buy as many goods and services as you could before tuition went up.

COLLEGE TUITION UP AGAIN

College gets more expensive—again. In-state tuition at public four-year colleges rose 2.3 percent in 2019–2020, to an average of $10,440 per year. Out-of-state students paid an average of $26,820 to attend.

Private four-year colleges also saw even bigger price hikes: 3.4 percent—to an average of $36,880. Tuition prices have been outpacing general inflation rates for many years.

Source: The College Board.

CRITICAL ANALYSIS: Tuition increases reduce the **real income** of students. How much you suffer from inflation depends on what happens to the prices of the products you purchase.

The effect of tuition increases on your economic welfare is reflected in the distinction between nominal income and real income. **Nominal income** is the amount of money you receive in a particular time period; it's measured in current dollars. **Real income,** by contrast, is the purchasing power of that money, as measured by the quantity of goods and services your dollars will buy. If the number of dollars you receive every year is always the same, your *nominal income* doesn't change—but your *real income* will rise or fall with price changes.

Suppose your parents agree to give you $8,000 a year while you're in school. Out of that $8,000 you must pay for your tuition, room and board, books, and everything else. The budget for your first year at school might look like this:

nominal income: The amount of money income received in a given time period, measured in current dollars.

real income: Income in constant dollars; nominal income adjusted for inflation.

FIRST YEAR'S BUDGET

Nominal income	$8,000
Consumption	
Tuition	$4,000
Room and board	2,600
Books	600
Everything else	800
Total	$8,000

After paying for all your essential expenses, you have $800 to spend on clothes, entertainment, or anything else you want. That's not exactly living high, but it's not poverty.

Now suppose tuition increases to $4,500 in your second year, while all other prices remain the same. What will happen to your nominal income? Nothing. Unless your parents take pity on you, you'll still be getting $8,000 a year. Your nominal income is unchanged. Your *real* income, however, will suffer. This is evident in the second year's budget:

SECOND YEAR'S BUDGET

Nominal income	$8,000
Consumption	
Tuition	$4,500
Room and board	2,600
Books	600
Everything else	300
Total	$8,000

You now have to use more of your income to pay tuition. This means you have less income to spend on other things. Because room and board and books still cost $3,200 per year, there's only one place to cut: the category of "everything else." After tuition increases, you can spend only $300 per year on movies, clothes, pizzas, and dates—not $800 as in the "good old days." This $500 reduction in purchasing power represents a *real* income loss.

Even though your *nominal* income is still $8,000, you have $500 less of "everything else" in your second year than you had in the first.

Although tuition hikes reduce the real income of students, nonstudents aren't hurt by such price increases. In fact, if tuition *doubled,* nonstudents really wouldn't care. They could continue to buy the same bundle of goods and services they'd been buying all along. Tuition increases reduce the real incomes only of people who go to college.

Two basic lessons about inflation are to be learned from this sad story:

- *Not all prices rise at the same rate during an inflation.* In our example, tuition increased substantially while other prices remained steady. Hence, the "average" price increase wasn't representative of any particular good or service. Typically some prices rise rapidly, others rise only modestly, and some actually fall.
- *Not everyone suffers equally from inflation.* This follows from our first observation. Those people who consume the goods and services that are rising faster in price bear a greater burden of inflation; their real incomes fall further. Other consumers bear a lesser burden, or even none at all, depending on how fast the prices rise for the goods they enjoy.

Table 7.2 illustrates some of the price changes that occurred in 2019. The average rate of inflation was only 2.3 percent. This was little solace to motorists, however, who confronted gasoline price increases of 12.8 percent. On the other hand, price reductions on eggs, televisions, and coffee spared consumers of these products from the pain of the *average* inflation rate. Even college students got a little relief on textbook prices.

Income Effects

Even if all prices rose at the *same* rate, inflation would still redistribute income. The redistributive effects of inflation originate in not only *expenditure* patterns but also *income* patterns. Some people have fixed incomes that *don't* go up with inflation. Fixed-income groups include retired people who depend primarily on private pensions and workers with multiyear contracts that fix wage rates at preinflation levels. Lenders (like banks) that have lent funds at fixed interest rates also suffer real income losses when price levels rise. They continue to receive interest payments fixed in *nominal* dollars that have increasingly less *real* value. All these market participants experience a declining share of real income (and output) in inflationary periods.

Not all market participants suffer a real income decline when prices rise. Some people's nominal income rises *faster* than average prices, thereby boosting their *real* incomes. Keep in mind that there are two sides to every market transaction. **What looks like a price to a buyer looks like an income to a seller.** Lettuce growers profited from the 7.6 percent rise in lettuce prices in 2019. When students pay 1.9 percent higher tuition, the university takes in more income. It is able to buy *more* goods and services (including faculty, buildings, and library books) after a period of inflation than it could before. When the price of this text

TABLE 7.2

Price Changes in 2019

The average rate of inflation conceals substantial differences in the price changes of specific products. The impact of inflation on individuals depends in part on which goods and services are consumed. People who buy goods whose prices are rising fastest lose more real income. In 2019 people who needed health insurance or drove a lot were particularly hard-hit by inflation.

Prices That Rose (%)		Prices That Fell (%)	
Heath insurance	+20.5%	Televisions	−20.8%
Gasoline	+12.8	Peanut butter	−6.0
Lettuce	+7.6	Oranges	−5.5
Cigarettes	+5.9	Apples	−4.8
Hot dogs	+4.2	Eggs	−4.6
College tuition	+1.9	College textbooks	−3.1
Bananas	+0.6	Coffee	−1.4

Average inflation rate: +2.3%

Source: U.S. Bureau of Labor Statistics.

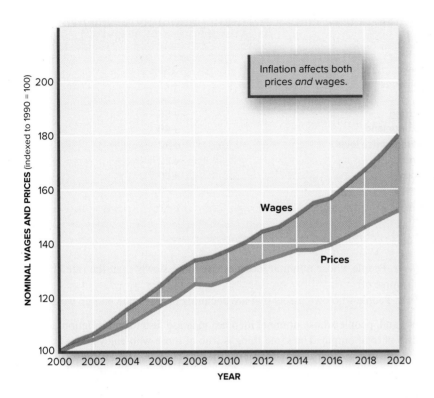

FIGURE 7.1

Nominal Wages and Prices

Inflation implies not only higher prices but higher incomes as well. In fact, average wages increase along with average prices. They rise even faster than prices when productivity increases.

Source: U.S. Bureau of Labor Statistics.

goes up, my *nominal* income goes up. If the text price rises faster than other prices, my *real* income increases as well. In either case, you lose (sorry!).

Once we recognize that nominal incomes and prices don't all increase at the same rate, it makes no sense to say that "inflation hurts everybody." ***If prices are rising, incomes must be rising too.*** In fact, on *average,* incomes rise just as fast as prices. Notice in Figure 7.1 that inflation increased *prices* by 52 percent from 2000 to 2020. However, *wages* more than kept pace—at least on average. That fact is of little comfort, however, to those whose wages didn't keep pace; they end up losing real income in the inflation game.

Wealth Effects

Still more winners and losers of the inflation game are selected on the basis of the assets they hold. Suppose you deposit $100 in a savings account on January 1, where it earns 5 percent interest. At the end of the year you'll have more nominal wealth ($105) than you started with ($100). But what if all prices have doubled in the meantime? In that case, your $105 will buy you no more at the end of the year than $52.50 would have bought you at the beginning. Inflation in this case reduces the *real* value of your savings, and you end up worse off than those individuals who spent all their income earlier in the year!

Table 7.3 shows how the value of various assets has changed. Between 1991 and 2001, the average price level increased 32 percent. The average value of stocks, diamonds, and homes rose much faster than the price level, increasing the *real* value of those assets. Farmland prices rose too, but just a bit more than average prices. People who owned bonds, silver, and gold weren't so lucky; their *real* wealth declined.

Redistributions

By altering relative prices, incomes, and the real value of wealth, inflation turns out to be a mechanism for redistributing incomes and wealth. ***The redistributive mechanics of inflation include***

- *Price effects.* People who buy products that are increasing in price the fastest end up worse off.

TABLE 7.3

The Real Story of Wealth

Households hold their wealth in many different forms. As the value of various assets changes, so does a person's wealth. Between 1991 and 2001, inflation was very good to people who held stocks. By contrast, the real value of bonds, gold, and silver fell.

Asset	Change in Value (%), 1991–2001
Stocks	+250%
Diamonds	+71
Oil	+66
Housing	+56
U.S. farmland	+49
Average price level	+32
Silver	+22
Bonds	+20
Stamps	−9
Gold	−29

- *Income effects*. People whose nominal incomes rise more slowly than the rate of inflation end up worse off.
- *Wealth effects*. People who own assets that are declining in real value end up worse off.

On the other hand, people whose nominal incomes increase faster than inflation end up with larger shares of total output. The same thing is true of those who enjoy goods that are rising slowest in price or who hold assets whose real value is increasing. In this sense, ***inflation acts just like a tax, taking income or wealth from one group and giving it to another***. But we have no assurance that this particular tax will behave like Robin Hood, taking from the rich and giving to the poor. In reality, inflation often redistributes income in the opposite direction.

Social Tensions

Because of its redistributive effects, inflation also increases social and economic tensions. Tensions—between labor and management, between government and the people, and among consumers—may overwhelm a society and its institutions. As Gardner Ackley of the University of Michigan observed, "A significant real cost of inflation is what it does to morale, to social coherence, and to people's attitudes toward each other." "This society," added Arthur Okun, "is built on implicit and explicit contracts. . . . They are linked to the idea that the dollar means something. If you cannot depend on the value of the dollar, this system is undermined. People will constantly feel they've been fooled and cheated."[1] This is how the middle class felt in Germany in 1923 and in China in 1948, when the value of their savings was wiped out by sudden and unanticipated inflation. A surge in prices also stirred social and political tensions in Russia as it moved from a price-controlled economy to a market-driven economy in the 1990s. The same kind of sociopolitical tension arose in Zimbabwe in 2008–2009 (see World View "Zimbabwe's Trillion-Dollar Currency") and in Venezuela in 2015–2019. On a more personal level, psychotherapists report that "inflation stress" leads to more frequent marital spats, pessimism, diminished self-confidence, and even sexual insecurity. Some people turn to crime as a way of solving the problem.

Money Illusion

Even people whose nominal incomes keep up with inflation often feel oppressed by rising prices. People feel that they *deserve* any increases in wages they receive. When they later discover that their higher (nominal) wages don't buy any additional goods, they feel cheated. They feel worse off, even though they haven't suffered any actual loss of real income. This phenomenon is called **money illusion.** People suffering from money illusion are forever reminding us that they used to pay only $5 to see a movie or $20 for a textbook. What they forget is that nominal *incomes* were also a lot lower in the "good old days" than they are today.

money illusion: The use of nominal dollars rather than real dollars to gauge changes in one's income or wealth.

[1]Quoted in *Business Week*, May 22, 1978, p. 118.

WORLD VIEW

ZIMBABWE'S TRILLION-DOLLAR CURRENCY

Imagine the price of coffee *doubling* every day. Or the price of a textbook soaring from $100 to $12,800 in a single week! Sounds unbelievable. But that was the day-to-day reality in Zimbabwe in 2008–2009, when the inflation rate reached an astronomical 231 *million* percent.

The Zimbabwean currency lost so much value that people needed a sackful to buy a loaf of bread. To facilitate commerce, the Zimbabwe central bank printed the world's first $100 *trillion* banknote. Within a week, that $100 trillion note was worth about 33 U.S. dollars—enough to buy six loaves of bread.

Tsvangirayi Mukwazhi/AP Images

Source: News reports, January 2009.

CRITICAL ANALYSIS: Hyperinflation renders a currency useless for market transactions. The economy contracts, and social tensions rise.

MACRO CONSEQUENCES

Although microeconomic redistributions of income and wealth are the primary consequences of inflation, inflation has *macroeconomic* effects as well.

Uncertainty

One of the most immediate consequences of inflation is uncertainty. When the average price level is changing significantly in either direction, economic decisions become more difficult. Even something as simple as ordering a restaurant meal is more difficult if menu prices are changing (as they did during Germany's 1923 runaway inflation). In Zimbabwe, postponing bread purchases cost a *billion* Zimbabwean dollars a day (see World View "Zimbabwe's Trillion-Dollar Currency"). The $100 trillion banknote issued in January 2009 was worthless two months later.

Inflation makes longer-term decisions even more difficult. Should you commit yourself to four years of college, for example, if you aren't certain that you or your parents will be able to afford the full costs? In a period of stable prices, you can be fairly certain of what a college education will cost. But if prices are rising, you can't be sure how large the bill will be. Under such circumstances, some individuals may decide not to enter college rather than risk the possibility of being driven out later by rising costs.

Price uncertainties affect production decisions as well. Imagine a firm that wants to build a new factory. Typically the construction of a factory takes two years or more, including planning, site selection, and actual construction. If construction costs change rapidly, the firm may find that it's unable to complete the factory or to operate it profitably. Confronted with this added uncertainty, the firm may decide not to build a new plant. This deprives the economy of new investment and expanded production possibilities.

Speculation

Inflation threatens not only to reduce the level of economic activity but to change its very nature. If you really expect prices to rise, it makes sense to buy goods and resources now for resale later. If prices rise fast enough, you can make a handsome profit. These are the kinds of thoughts that motivate people to buy houses, precious metals, commodities, and other assets. But such speculation, if carried too far, can detract from the production process. If speculative profits become too easy, few people will engage in production; instead everyone will be buying and selling existing goods. People may even be encouraged to withhold resources from the production process, hoping to sell them later at higher prices. Such speculation may fuel **hyperinflation** as spending accelerates and production declines. This happened in Germany in the 1920s, in China in 1948–1949, in Russia in the early 1990s, and in Zimbabwe in 2007–2009. No one wanted to hold Zimbabwean dollars or trade for them. Farmers preferred to hold their crops rather than sell them. With the price of a loaf of bread increasing by a billion Zimbabwean dollars a day, why would a baker want to *sell* his bread? Producers chose to hold rather than sell their products. The resulting contraction in supply caused a severe decline in output.

hyperinflation: Inflation rate in excess of 200 percent, lasting at least one year.

Bracket Creep

Another reason that savings, investment, and work effort decline when prices rise is that taxes go up, too. Federal income tax rates are *progressive;* that is, tax rates are higher for larger incomes. The intent of these progressive rates is to redistribute income from rich to poor. However, inflation tends to increase *everyone's* income. In the process, people are pushed into higher tax brackets and confront higher tax rates. The process is referred to as **bracket creep.** In recent years, bracket creep has been limited by the inflation indexing of personal income tax rates and a reduction in the number of tax brackets. However, Social Security payroll taxes and most state and local taxes aren't indexed.

bracket creep: The movement of taxpayers into higher tax brackets (rates) as nominal incomes grow.

Deflation Dangers

Ironically, a *falling* price level—a deflation—might not make people happy either. In fact, a falling price level can do the same kind of harm as a rising price level. When prices are falling, people on fixed incomes and long-term contracts gain more *real* income. Lenders win and borrowers lose. People who hold cash or bonds win; home owners and stamp collectors lose. Deflation simply reverses the kinds of redistributions caused by inflation.

A falling price level also has similar macro consequences. Time horizons get shorter. Businesses are more reluctant to borrow money or to invest. People lose confidence in themselves and public institutions when declining price levels deflate their incomes and assets.

MEASURING INFLATION

In view of the macro and micro consequences of price level changes, the measurement of inflation serves two purposes: to gauge the average rate of inflation and to identify its principal victims.

Consumer Price Index

Consumer Price Index (CPI): A measure (index) of changes in the average price of consumer goods and services.

The most common measure of inflation is the **Consumer Price Index (CPI).** As its name suggests, the CPI is a mechanism for measuring changes in the average price of consumer goods and services. It's analogous to the fruit price index we discussed earlier. The CPI refers not to the price of any particular good but to the average price of all consumer goods.

By itself, the "average price" of consumer goods isn't a useful number. But once we know the average price of consumer goods, we can observe whether that average rises—that is, whether inflation is occurring. By observing the extent to which prices increase, we can calculate the **inflation rate.**

inflation rate: The annual percentage rate of increase in the average price level; (Price Level$_{\text{Year 2}}$ − Price Level$_{\text{Year 1}}$)/ Price Level$_{\text{Year 1}}$.

The Market Basket. We can get a better sense of how inflation is measured by observing how the CPI is constructed. The process begins by identifying a market basket of goods and services the typical consumer buys. For this purpose, the Bureau of Labor Statistics surveys a large sample of families every year to determine what goods and services consumers actually buy. Figure 7.2 summarizes the results of the 2018 survey, which reveal that 32.8 cents out of every consumer dollar is spent on housing (shelter, furnishings, and utilities), 12.9 cents on food, and another 15.9 cents on transportation. Only 5.3 cents of every consumer dollar is spent on entertainment.

Within these broad categories of expenditure, the Bureau of Labor Statistics itemizes specific goods and services. The details of the expenditure survey show, for example, that private expenditures for reading and education account for only 2.5 percent of the typical consumer's budget, less than is spent on alcoholic beverages, tobacco, and gambling. It also shows that we spend 7 cents out of every dollar on fuel, to drive our cars (3.7 cents) and to heat and cool our houses (3.6 cents).

Price of the Basket. Once we know what the typical consumer buys, it's relatively easy to calculate the average price of a market basket. The Bureau of Labor Statistics actually goes shopping in 85 cities across the country, recording the prices of the 184 items that make up the typical market basket. Approximately 19,000 stores are visited, and 60,000 landlords, renters, and home owners are surveyed—every month!

As a result of these massive, ongoing surveys, the Bureau of Labor Statistics can tell us what's happening to consumer prices. Suppose, for example, that the market basket cost $100 last year and that the same basket of goods and services cost $110 this year. On the basis of those two shopping trips, we could conclude that consumer prices had risen by 10 percent in one year.

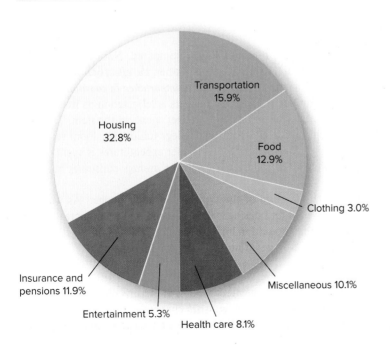

FIGURE 7.2
The Market Basket

To measure changes in average prices, we must first know what goods and services consumers buy. This diagram, based on consumer surveys, shows how the typical urban consumer spends each dollar. Housing, transportation, and food account for more than two-thirds of consumer spending.

Source: U.S. Bureau of Labor Statistics, Consumer Expenditure Survey (2018 data).

TABLE 7.4

Computing Changes in the CPI

The impact of any price change on the average price level depends on the importance of an item in the typical consumer budget—its **item weight**.

The Consumer Expenditure Survey of 2018 revealed that the average household spends 1.52 cents of every consumer dollar on college tuition. Households without college students don't pay any tuition, of course. And your family probably devotes *more* than 1.52 cents of each consumer dollar to tuition. On *average,* however, 1.52 cents is the proportion of each dollar spent on tuition. This figure is the *item weight* of tuition in computing the CPI.

The impact on the CPI of a price change for a specific good is calculated as follows:

Item weight × Percentage change in price of item = Percentage change in CPI

Suppose that tuition prices suddenly go up 20 percent. What impact will this single price increase have on the CPI? In this case, where tuition is the only price that increases, the impact on the CPI will be only 0.30 percent (0.0152 × 20), as illustrated below. Thus, a very large increase in the price of tuition (20 percent) has a tiny impact (0.30 percent) on the *average* price level.

Housing, on the other hand, accounts for 32.8 percent of consumer expenditures. Thus, if housing prices increase 20 percent, and housing is the only price that increases, the impact on the CPI will be 6.56 percent, as shown below.

The relative importance of an item in consumer budgets—its item weight—is a key determinant of its inflationary impact.

Item	Item Weight	×	Price Increase for the Item	=	Impact on the CPI
College tuition	0.0152		20%		0.30%
Housing	0.328		20		6.56

base year: The year used for comparative analysis; the basis for indexing price changes.

Price Changes. In practice, the CPI is usually expressed in terms of what the market basket cost in a specific **base year.** The price level in the base year is arbitrarily designated as 100. In the case of the CPI, the average price level for the period 1982–1984 is usually used as the base for computing price changes. Hence, the price index for that base year is set at 100. In January 2020, the CPI registered 258. In other words, it cost $258 in 2020 to buy the same market baskets that cost only $100 in the base year. Prices had increased by an average of 158 percent over that period. Each month the Bureau of Labor Statistics updates the CPI, telling us how the current cost of that same basket compares to its cost between 1982 and 1984.

Item Weights

item weight: The percentage of total expenditure spent on a specific product; used to compute inflation indexes.

Table 7.4 illustrates how changes in the official CPI are computed. Notice that all price changes don't have the same impact on the inflation rate. Rather, *the effect of a specific price change on the inflation rate depends on the product's relative importance in consumer budgets*.

The relative importance of a product in consumer budgets is reflected in its **item weight,** which refers to the percentage of a typical consumer budget spent on the item. Table 7.4 shows the item weights for college tuition and housing. College tuition may loom very large in your personal budget, but only 1.5 percent of *all* consumer expenditures is spent on college tuition. Hence, the item weight for college tuition in the *average* consumer budget is only 0.0152.

Housing costs absorb a far larger share of the typical consumer budget. As was first observed in Figure 7.2, the item weight for housing is 0.328. Accordingly, rent increases have a much larger impact on the CPI than do tuition hikes. Notice in Table 7.4 how a 20 percent hike in tuition has a tiny impact on average inflation, whereas a 20 percent hike in housing prices adds a lot to the CPI.

core inflation rate: Changes in the CPI, excluding food and energy prices.

The Core Rate. Every month the Labor Department reports the results of its monthly price surveys. In its news releases, the department distinguishes changes in the "core" price level from the broader, all-inclusive CPI. The **core inflation rate** excludes changes in food and energy prices, which have a lot of month-to-month variation. A freeze in California or Florida can cause a temporary spike in produce prices; a hurricane in the Gulf can do the same thing to oil prices. These temporary price shocks, however, may not reflect price trends. By excluding volatile food and energy prices from the core rate, we hope to get a more accurate monthly reading of consumer price trends.

Producer Price Indexes

In addition to the Consumer Price Index, there are three Producer Price Indexes (PPIs). The PPIs keep track of average prices received by *producers*. One index includes crude materials, another covers intermediate goods, and the last covers finished goods. The three PPIs don't include all producer prices but primarily those in mining, manufacturing, and agriculture. Like the CPI, changes in the PPIs are identified in monthly surveys.

Over long periods of time, the PPIs and the CPI generally reflect the same rate of inflation. In the short run, however, the PPIs usually increase before the CPI because it takes time for producers' price increases to be reflected in the prices that consumers pay. For this reason, the PPIs are watched closely as a clue to potential changes in consumer prices.

The GDP Deflator

The broadest price index is the GDP deflator. The GDP deflator covers all output, including consumer goods, investment goods, and government services. Unlike the CPI and PPIs, the **GDP deflator** isn't based on a fixed "basket" of goods or services. Rather, it allows the contents of the basket to change with people's consumption and investment patterns. The GDP deflator therefore isn't a pure measure of price change. Its value reflects both price changes and market responses to those price changes, as reflected in new expenditure patterns. Hence, the GDP deflator typically registers a lower inflation rate than the CPI.

GDP deflator: A price index that refers to all goods and services included in GDP.

Real vs. Nominal GDP. The GDP deflator is the price index used to adjust nominal GDP statistics for changing price levels. Recall that **nominal GDP** refers to the *current* dollar value of output, whereas **real GDP** denotes the *inflation-adjusted* value of output. These two measures of output are connected by the GDP deflator:

nominal GDP: The value of final output produced in a given period, measured in the prices of that period (current prices).

$$\text{Real GDP in year } t = \frac{\text{Nominal GDP in year } t}{\text{Price index}} = \frac{\text{Nominal GDP in year } t}{\text{GDP deflator}}$$

real GDP: The value of final output produced in a given period, adjusted for changing prices.

The nominal values of GDP were approximately $10 trillion in 2000 and $21 trillion in 2020. At first blush, this would suggest that output more than doubled over those 20 years. However, the price level rose by about 50 percent between those years. Hence, *real* GDP in 2020 in the base-year prices of 2000 was

$$\frac{\text{2020 real GDP}}{\text{(in 2000 prices)}} = \frac{\text{Nominal GDP}}{\text{Price index}} = \frac{\$21 \text{ trillion}}{\frac{150}{100}} = \frac{\$21 \text{ trillion}}{1.5} = \$14 \text{ trillion}$$

In reality, then, output increased by only 40 percent (from $10 trillion to $14 trillion) from 2000 to 2020. **Changes in real GDP are a good measure of how output and living standards are changing. Nominal GDP statistics, by contrast, mix up output and price changes.**

THE GOAL: PRICE STABILITY

In view of the inequities, anxieties, and real losses caused by inflation, it's not surprising that price stability is a major goal of economic policy. As we observed at the beginning of this chapter, every U.S. president since Franklin Roosevelt has decreed price stability to be a foremost policy goal. Unfortunately, few presidents (or their advisers) have stated exactly what they mean by "price stability." Do they mean *no* change in the average price level? Or is some upward creep in the price index acceptable?

price stability: The absence of significant changes in the average price level; officially defined as a rate of inflation of less than 3 percent.

A Numerical Goal

An explicit numerical goal for **price stability** was established for the first time in the Full Employment and Balanced Growth Act of 1978. According to that act, the goal of economic policy is to hold the rate of inflation under 3 percent.

Unemployment Concerns

Why did Congress choose 3 percent inflation rather than zero inflation as the benchmark for price stability? One reason was concern about unemployment. To keep prices from rising, the government might have to restrain spending in the economy. Such restraint could lead to cutbacks in production and an increase in joblessness. In other words, **there might be a trade-off between inflation and unemployment.** From this perspective, a little bit of inflation might be the "price" the economy has to pay to keep unemployment rates from rising.

Recall how the same kind of logic was used to define the goal of full employment. The fear there was that price pressures would increase as the economy approached its production possibilities. This suggested that some unemployment might be the "price" the economy has to pay for price stability. Accordingly, the goal of "full employment" was defined as the lowest rate of unemployment *consistent with stable prices.* The same kind of thinking is apparent here. The amount of inflation regarded as tolerable depends in part on the effect of anti-inflation strategies on unemployment rates. After reviewing our experiences with both unemployment and inflation, Congress concluded that 3 percent inflation was a safe target.

Quality Changes

The second argument for setting our price stability goal above zero inflation relates to our measurement capabilities. The Consumer Price Index isn't a perfect measure of inflation. In essence, the CPI simply monitors the price of specific goods over time. Over time, however, the goods themselves change, too. Old products become better as a result of *quality improvements.* A flat-screen TV set costs more today than a TV did in 1955, but today's television also delivers a bigger, clearer picture, in digital sound and color, and with a host of on-screen programming options. Hence, increases in the price of TV sets tend to exaggerate the true rate of inflation: Most of the higher price represents more product.

The same is true of automobiles. The best-selling car in 1958 (a Chevrolet Bel Air) had a list price of only $2,618. That makes a 2020 Chevy Camaro look awfully expensive at $27,800. The quality of today's cars is much better, however. Improvements since 1958 include seat belts, air bags, variable-speed windshield wipers, electronic ignitions, rear-window defrosters, radial tires, antilock brakes, emergency flashers, remote-control mirrors, crash-resistant bodies, a doubling of fuel mileage, a 100-fold decrease in exhaust pollutants, and global positioning systems. As a result, today's higher car prices also buy cars that are safer, cleaner, and more comfortable.

The U.S. Bureau of Labor Statistics does adjust the CPI for quality changes. Such adjustments inevitably entail subjective judgments, however. Critics are quick to complain that the CPI overstates inflation because quality improvements are undervalued.

New Products

The problem of measuring quality improvements is even more difficult in the case of new products. The computers and word processors used today didn't exist when the Census Bureau conducted its 1972–1973 survey of consumer expenditure. The 1982–1984 expenditure survey included those products but not still newer ones such as the cell phone. The omission of cell phones caused the CPI to overstate the rate of inflation. The consumer expenditure survey of 1993–1995 included cell phones but not digital cameras, DVD players, flat-screen TVs, or MP3 players—all of which have had declining prices (Table 7.1). As a result, there's a significant (though unmeasured) element of error in the CPI insofar as it's intended to gauge changes in the average prices paid by consumers. The goal of 3 percent inflation allows for such errors. The 2010 survey didn't include Alexa or other cloud-based virtual assistants.

New products like Alexa complicate inflation measures.

rclassenlayouts/Getty images

Year	CPI	Year	CPI	Year	CPI	Year	CPI
1800	17.0	1900	8.3	1950	24.1	1982–1984	100.0
1825	11.3	1920	20.0	1960	29.6	1990	130.5
1850	8.3	1930	16.7	1970	38.8	2000	172.8
1875	11.0	1940	14.0	1980	82.4	2020	258.0

Note: Data from 1915 forward reflect the official all-items Consumer Price Index, which used the pre-1983 measure of shelter costs. Estimated indexes for 1800 through 1900 are drawn from several sources.
Source: U.S. Bureau of Labor Statistics.

TABLE 7.5

Two Centuries of Price Changes

Before World War II, the average level of prices rose in some years and fell in others. Since 1945, prices have risen continuously. The Consumer Price Index has more than doubled since 1982–1984. It stood at 258 in January 2020.

THE HISTORICAL RECORD

In the long view of history, the United States has done a good job of maintaining price stability. On closer inspection, however, our inflation performance is very uneven. Table 7.5 summarizes the long view, with data going back to 1800. The base period for pricing the market basket of goods is again 1982–1984. Notice that the same market basket cost only $17 in 1800. Consumer prices increased 500 percent in 183 years. But also observe how frequently the price level *fell* in the 1800s and again in the 1930s. These recurrent deflations held down the long-run inflation rate. Because of these periodic deflations, average prices in 1945 were at the same level as in 1800! Since then, however, prices have risen almost every year.

Figure 7.3 provides a closer view of our more recent experience with inflation. In this figure we transform annual changes in the CPI into percentage rates of inflation. The CPI increased from 72.6 to 82.4 during 1980. This 9.8-point jump in the CPI translates into a

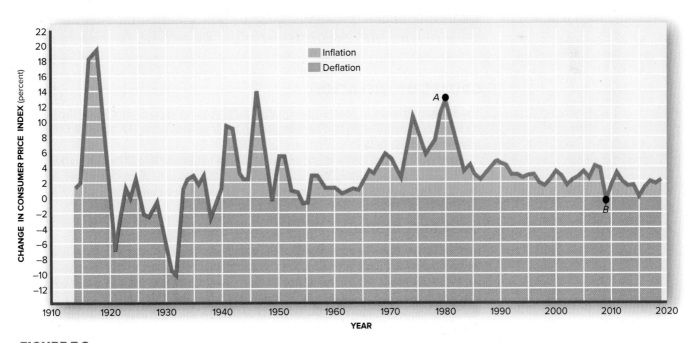

FIGURE 7.3

Annual Inflation Rates

During the 1920s and 1930s, consumer prices fell significantly, causing a general deflation. Since the Great Depression, however, average prices have risen almost every year. But the annual rate of price increases has varied widely: The highest rate of inflation was 13.5 percent in 1980 (point *A*); the lowest rate (−0.4 percent) occurred in 2009 (point *B*).

Source: U.S. Bureau of Labor Statistics.

13.5 percent rate of inflation (9.8 ÷ 72.6 = 0.135). This inflation rate, represented by point *A* in Figure 7.3, was the highest in a generation. Since then, prices have continued to increase, but at much slower rates. These low rates of inflation in the United States are far below the pace in most nations. Venezuela provides a stark contrast in recent inflation rates (see World View "Venezuela's New Bolivar").

CAUSES OF INFLATION

The evident variation in year-to-year inflation rates requires explanation. So do the horrify-ing bouts of hyperinflation that have erupted in other nations at various times. What causes price levels to rise or fall?

In the most general terms, this is an easy question to answer. Recall that all market trans-actions entail two converging forces, namely *demand* and *supply*. Accordingly, any explana-tion of changing price levels must be rooted in one of these two market forces.

Demand-Pull Inflation

Excessive pressure on the demand side of the economy is often the cause of inflation. Suppose the economy was already producing at capacity but that consumers were willing and able to buy even more goods. With accumulated savings or easy access to credit, consumers could end up trying to buy more output than the economy was producing. This would be a classic case of "too much money chasing too few goods." As consumers sought to acquire more goods, store shelves (inventory) would begin to empty. Seeing this, producers would begin raising prices. The end result would be a demand-driven rise in average prices, or demand-pull inflation.

Cost-Push Inflation

The pressure on prices could also originate on the supply side. When Hurricane Harvey destroyed oil-producing facilities in the Gulf (August 2017), oil prices increased abruptly, raising transportation and production costs in a broad array of industries. To cover these higher costs, producers raised output prices. When tropical cyclone Idai hit Zimbabwe in March 2019, it destroyed thousands of homes, roads, bridges, farms, and other productive facilities in that already-poor nation. As market participants scurried for the remaining output, prices rose across the board. The same thing happened in Haiti in January 2010, when an earthquake destroyed production facilities and transportation routes, making goods scarce and increasingly more expensive.

PROTECTIVE MECHANISMS

Whatever the *causes* of inflation, market participants don't want to suffer the consequences. Even at a relatively low rate of inflation, the real value of money declines over time. If prices rise by an average of just 4 percent a year, the real value of $1,000 drops to $822 in 5 years and to only $676 in 10 years (see Table 7.6). *Low rates of inflation don't have the drama of hyperinflation, but they still redistribute real wealth and income.*

COLAs

Market participants can protect themselves from inflation by *indexing* their nominal incomes, as is done with Social Security benefits, for example. In any year that the rate of inflation exceeds 3 percent, Social Security benefits go up *automatically* by the same percentage as the inflation rate. This **cost-of-living adjustment (COLA)** ensures that nominal benefits keep pace with the rising prices.

cost-of-living adjustment (COLA): Automatic adjustments of nominal income to the rate of inflation.

Landlords often protect their real incomes with COLAs as well, by including in their leases provisions that automatically increase rents by the rate of inflation. COLAs are also common in labor union agreements, government transfer programs (like food stamps), and many other contracts. In every such case, *a COLA protects real income from inflation.*

| | Annual Inflation Rate | | | | |
Year	2%	4%	6%	8%	10%
2021	$1,000	$1,000	$1,000	$1,000	$1,000
2022	980	962	943	926	909
2023	961	925	890	857	826
2024	942	889	840	794	751
2025	924	855	792	735	683
2026	906	822	747	681	621
2027	888	790	705	630	564
2028	871	760	665	584	513
2029	853	731	627	540	467
2030	837	703	592	500	424
2031	820	676	558	463	386

TABLE 7.6

Inflation's Impact, 2021–2031

In the past 40 years, the U.S. rate of inflation ranged from a low of −0.4 percent to a high of 13.5 percent. Does a range of 14 percentage points really make much difference? One way to find out is to see how a specific sum of money will shrink in real value in a decade.

Here's what would happen to the real value of $1,000 from January 1, 2021, to January 1, 2031, at different inflation rates. At 2 percent inflation, $1,000 held for 10 years would be worth $820. At 10 percent inflation, that same $1,000 would buy only $386 worth of goods in the year 2031.

ARMs

Cost-of-living adjustments have also become more common in loan agreements. As we observed earlier, debtors win and creditors lose when the price level rises. Suppose a loan requires interest payments equal to 5 percent of the amount (principal) borrowed. If the rate of inflation jumps to 7 percent, prices will be rising faster than interest is accumulating. Hence, the **real interest rate**—the inflation-adjusted rate of interest—will actually be negative. The interest payments made in future years will buy fewer goods than can be bought today.

real interest rate: The nominal interest rate minus the anticipated inflation rate.

The real rate of interest is calculated as

$$\textbf{Real interest rate} = \textbf{Nominal interest rate} - \textbf{Anticipated rate of inflation}$$

In this case, the nominal interest rate is 5 percent and inflation is 7 percent. Hence, the *real* rate of interest is *minus* 2 percent.

The distinction between real and nominal interest rates isn't too important if you're lending or borrowing money for just a couple of days. But the distinction is critical for long-term loans like home mortgages. Mortgage loans typically span a period of 25 to 30 years. If the inflation rate stays higher than the nominal interest rate during this period, the lender will end up with less *real* wealth than was initially lent.

To protect against such losses, the banking industry offers home loans with adjustable interest rates. An **adjustable-rate mortgage (ARM)** stipulates an interest rate that changes during the term of the loan. A mortgage paying 5 percent interest in a stable (3 percent inflation) price environment may later require 9 percent interest if the inflation rate jumps to 7 percent. Such an adjustment would keep the real rate of interest at 2 percent. These and other inflation-indexing mechanisms underscore the importance of measuring price changes accurately.

adjustable-rate mortgage (ARM): A mortgage (home loan) that adjusts the nominal interest rate to changing rates of inflation.

DECISIONS FOR TOMORROW

Is a Little Inflation a Good Thing?

Despite evidence to the contrary, most people still believe that "inflation hurts everybody." In fact, the distaste for inflation is so strong that sizable majorities say they prefer low inflation and high unemployment to the combination of high inflation and low unemployment. A study by Yale economist Robert Shiller confirmed that *money illusion* contributes to this sentiment: People *feel* worse off when they have to pay higher prices, even if their nominal incomes are keeping pace with (or exceeding) the rate of inflation. Politically, this implies a policy bias toward keeping inflation under control, even at the sacrifice of high unemployment and slower economic growth.

There are times, however, when a little inflation might be a good thing. In the wake of the Great Recession of 2008–2009, the rate of inflation fell to zero. Investors and home purchasers could borrow money at unprecedented low rates. Yet market participants were still reluctant to borrow and spend. So the economy was frustratingly slow to recover.

What if, however, people thought prices were going to rise? If prospective home buyers expected housing prices to go up, they'd be more willing to purchase a new home. If investors thought prices were going up, they'd want to get in the game while prices were still low. In other words, *expectations of rising prices can encourage more spending.* A little inflation might actually be a virtue in such circumstances.

Governments around the world are aware that a little inflation might actually be more desirable than zero inflation. Indeed, central bankers in the United States and Europe lamented the fact that inflation rates were below their "target' rates in 2016–2019. In response, they initiated policies to push inflation rates higher, thereby hoping to stimulate more spending.

The challenge for the economy tomorrow is to find the optimal rate of inflation—the one that's just high enough to encourage more spending, but not so high as to raise the specter of an **inflationary flashpoint.** No one wants to experience a Zimbabwean-type hyperinflation or even a less drastic bout of accelerating inflation. So, we have to embrace a little inflation with extreme caution—motivating market participants but keeping inflationary expectations under control. That's not always easy.

inflationary flashpoint: The rate of output at which inflationary pressures intensify; the point on the AS curve where slope increases sharply.

SUMMARY

- Inflation is an increase in the average price level. Typically it's measured by changes in a price index such as the Consumer Price Index (CPI). **LO7-1**
- At the micro level, inflation redistributes income by altering relative prices, income, and wealth. Because not all prices rise at the same rate and because not all people buy (and sell) the same goods or hold the same assets, inflation doesn't affect everyone equally. Some individuals actually gain from inflation, whereas others suffer a loss of real income or wealth. **LO7-2**
- At the macro level, inflation threatens to reduce total output because it increases uncertainties about the future and thereby inhibits consumption and production decisions. Fear of rising prices can also stimulate spending, forcing the government to take restraining action that threatens full employment. Rising prices also encourage speculation and hoarding, which detract from productive activity. **LO7-2**
- Fully anticipated inflation reduces the anxieties and real losses associated with rising prices. However, few people can foresee actual price patterns or make all the necessary adjustments in their market activity. **LO7-2**
- The U.S. goal of price stability is defined as an inflation rate of less than 3 percent per year. This goal recognizes potential conflicts between zero inflation and full employment as well as the difficulties of measuring quality improvements and new products. **LO7-3**
- From 1800 to 1945, prices both rose and fell, leaving the average price level unchanged. Since then, prices have risen nearly every year but at widely different rates. **LO7-3**
- Inflation is caused by either excessive demand (demand-pull inflation) or structural changes in supply (cost-push inflation). **LO7-4**
- Cost-of-living adjustments (COLAs) and adjustable-rate mortgages (ARMs) help protect real incomes from inflation. Universal indexing, however, wouldn't eliminate inflationary redistributions of income and wealth. **LO7-2**

Key Terms

inflation	bracket creep	nominal GDP
deflation	Consumer Price Index (CPI)	real GDP
relative price	inflation rate	price stability
nominal income	base year	cost-of-living adjustment (COLA)
real income	item weight	real interest rate
money illusion	core inflation rate	adjustable-rate mortgage (ARM)
hyperinflation	GDP deflator	inflationary flashpoint

Questions for Discussion

1. Why would farmers rather store their output than sell it during periods of hyperinflation? How does this behavior affect prices? **LO7-2**
2. How might rapid inflation affect college enrollments? **LO7-2**
3. Who gains and who loses from rising house prices? **LO7-2**
4. Who gained and who lost from the price changes in Table 7.2? What happened to the price of driving? **LO7-2**
5. Whose real wealth (see Table 7.3) declined in the 1990s? Who else might have lost real income or wealth? Who gained as a result of inflation? **LO7-2**
6. If *all* prices increased at the same rate (i.e., no *relative* price changes), would inflation have any redistributive effects? **LO7-2**
7. Would it be advantageous to borrow money if you expected prices to rise? Would you want a fixed-rate loan or one with an adjustable interest rate? **LO7-2**
8. Are people worse off when the price level rises as fast as their income? Why do people often feel worse off in such circumstances? **LO7-2**
9. What benefit came from changing Venezuela's currency in August 2018 (World View "Venezuela's New Bolivar")? Why didn't that change stop inflation? **LO7-4**
10. Could demand-pull inflation occur before an economy was producing at capacity? How? **LO7-4**
11. How much do higher gasoline prices contribute to inflation? **LO7-1**

LO7-1   1. According to World View "Zimbabwe's Trillion-Dollar Currency," what was the price of a loaf of bread in Zimbabwe, measured in
     (*a*) U.S. dollars?
     (*b*) Zimbabwean dollars?

LO7-1   2. How did the pace of college tuition hikes compare to the 2019 rate of inflation (Table 7.2)?

LO7-1   3. Using the Consumer Price Index (CPI) shown below:

Year	Index
2007	207.3
2008	215.3
2009	214.5
2010	218.1
2011	224.9
2012	229.6
2013	233.0
2014	236.7
2015	237.0
2016	240.0
2017	245.1
2018	251.1
2019	255.7

     (*a*) Calculate the inflation rate for 2007–2008, 2008–2009, 2014–2015, and 2015–2016.
     (*b*) Which years had inflation?
     (*c*) Which years had deflation?

LO7-2   4. If tuition keeps increasing at the same rate as in 2019–2020 (see Front Page Economics "College Tuition Up Again"), how much will it cost to complete a degree at a private college in four years (2019–2023)?

LO7-1   5. Suppose you'll have an annual nominal income of $40,000 for each of the next three years, and the inflation rate is 5 percent per year.
     (*a*) Find the real value of your $40,000 salary for each of the next three years.
     (*b*) If you have a COLA in your contract, and the inflation rate is 5 percent, what is the real value of your salary for each year?

LO7-2   6. Suppose you borrow $1,000 of principal that must be repaid at the end of two years, along with interest of 5 percent a year. If the annual inflation rate turns out to be 10 percent,
     (*a*) What is the real rate of interest on the loan?
     (*b*) What is the real value of the principal repayment?
     (*c*) Who loses, the debtor or the creditor?

LO7-1   7. If apples, oranges, and bananas are weighted equally in a "fruit price index" and no other fruit changed prices (see Table 7.2),
     (*a*) By how much did fruit prices rise or fall in 2019?
     (*b*) Is a consumer better or worse off if he loves eating these fruit?

LO7-1 8. To better understand how inflation is measured, pretend that the following table describes the typical consumer's complete market basket for the year. Compute the item weights for each product.

Item	Quantity	Unit Price	Item Weight
Coffee	20 pounds	$ 7	_____
Tuition	1 year	4,000	_____
Pizza	150 pizzas	10	_____
Streaming TV	12 months	30	_____
Vacation	1 week	350	_____
		Total:	_____

LO7-1 9. To better understand how inflation is measured, suppose the prices listed in the table for Problem 8 changed from one year to the next, as shown here. Use the rest of the table to compute the average inflation rate for this hypothetical complete market basket.

Item	Unit Price		Percentage Change in Price	×	Item Weight (calculated in Problem 8)	=	Inflation Impact
	Last Year	This Year					
Coffee	$ 7	$ 14	_____		_____		_____
Tuition	4,000	4,500	_____		_____		_____
Pizza	10	12	_____		_____		_____
Streaming TV	30	36	_____		_____		_____
Vacation	350	300	_____		_____		_____
					Average inflation:		_____

LO7-1 10. Use the item weights in Figure 7.2 to determine the percentage change in the CPI that would result from a(n)
(*a*) 20 percent increase in entertainment prices.
(*b*) 8 percent decrease in transportation costs.
(*c*) Doubling of clothing prices.
(*Note:* Review Table 7.4 for assistance.)

LO7-1 11. When Disney's Magic Kingdom in Orlando, Florida, opened in 1971, the price of admission was $3.50. In 2020 the ticket price was $109. The CPI index was at 40.5 in 1971 and 261 in 2020.
(*a*) By how much did the nominal price of a Disney ticket increase from 1971 to 2020?
(*b*) What was the 1971 price in the dollars of 2020?
(*c*) By how much did the real price of a ticket increase between 1971 and 2020?

LO7-1 12. According to Table 7.3, what happened during the period shown to the
(*a*) Nominal price of gold?
(*b*) Real price of gold?

LO7-3 13. On a graph, illustrate both the inflation rate and the real GDP growth rate for 2009–2019. (The data required for this exercise can be found in the Data Tables at the end of the book.)
(*a*) In how many years was the official goal of price stability met?
(*b*) In what years was inflation the lowest? The highest?

LO7-4 14. *Decisions for Tomorrow:* If home prices are expected to rise in the future, will you be more or less likely to buy a house now?

Design Credit: Shutterstock

PART 3

CYCLICAL INSTABILITY

AP Images

Ariel Skelley/Blend Images/Getty Images

Ingram Publishing

One of the central concerns of macroeconomics is the short-run business cycle—recurrent episodes of expansion and contraction of the nation's output. These cycles affect jobs, prices, economic growth, and international trade and financial balances. Chapters 8 through 10 focus on the nature of the business cycle and the underlying market forces that can cause both macroeconomic gain and macroeconomic pain.

AP Images

The Business Cycle

In 1929 it looked as though the sun would never set on the U.S. economy. For eight years in a row, the U.S. economy had been expanding rapidly. During the Roaring Twenties, the typical American family drove its first car, bought its first radio, and went to the movies for the first time. With factories running at capacity, virtually anyone who wanted to work found a job readily.

Everyone was optimistic. In his Acceptance Address in November 1928, President-elect Herbert Hoover echoed this optimism by declaring, "We in America today are nearer to the final triumph over poverty than ever before in the history of any land. . . . We shall soon with the help of God be in sight of the day when poverty will be banished from this nation."

The booming stock market seemed to confirm this optimistic outlook. Between 1921 and 1927 the stock market's value more than doubled, adding billions of dollars to the wealth of U.S. households and businesses. The stock market boom accelerated in 1927, causing stock prices to double again in less than two years. The roaring stock market made it look easy to get rich in America.

The party ended abruptly on October 24, 1929. On what came to be known as Black Thursday, the stock market crashed. In a few short hours, the market value of U.S. corporations tumbled in the most frenzied selloff ever seen (see Front Page Economics "Market in Panic as Stocks Are Dumped in 12,894,600-Share Day"). The next day President Hoover tried to assure America's stockholders that the economy was "on a sound and prosperous basis." But despite his assurances, the stock market continued to plummet. The following Tuesday (October 29) the pace of selling quickened. By the end of the year, more than $40 billion of wealth had vanished in the Great Crash. Rich men became paupers overnight; ordinary families lost their savings, their homes, and even their lives.

The devastation was not confined to Wall Street. The financial flames engulfed farms, banks, and industry. Between 1930 and 1935, millions of rural families lost their farms. Automobile production fell from 4.5 million cars in 1929 to only 1.1 million in 1932. So many banks were forced to close that newly elected President Roosevelt had to declare a "bank holiday" in March 1933: He closed all of the nation's banks for five days to curtail the outflow of cash to anxious depositors.

Throughout these years, the ranks of the unemployed continued to swell. In October 1929, only 3 percent of the workforce was unemployed. A year later the total was more than 9 percent. Still things got worse. By 1933, more than one-fourth of the labor force was unable to find work. People slept in the streets, scavenged for food, and sold apples on Wall Street.

FRONT PAGE ECONOMICS

MARKET IN PANIC AS STOCKS ARE DUMPED IN 12,894,600-SHARE DAY; BANKERS HALT IT

Effect Is Felt on the Curb and throughout Nation—Financial District Goes Wild

The stock markets of the country tottered on the brink of panic yesterday as a prosperous people, gone suddenly hysterical with fear, attempted simultaneously to sell a record-breaking volume of securities for whatever they would bring.

The result was a financial nightmare, comparable to nothing ever before experienced in Wall Street. It rocked the financial district to its foundations, hopelessly overwhelmed its mechanical facilities, chilled its blood with terror.

In a society built largely on confidence, with real wealth expressed more or less inaccurately by pieces of paper, the entire fabric of economic stability threatened to come toppling down.

Into the frantic hands of a thousand brokers on the floor of the New York Stock Exchange poured the selling orders of the world. It was sell, sell, sell—hour after desperate hour until 1:30 p.m.

—Laurence Stern

Source: Laurence Stern, *The World,* October 25, 1929.

CRITICAL ANALYSIS: Stock markets are a barometer of confidence in the economy. If people have doubts about the economy, they're less willing to hold stocks. The crash of 1929 mirrored and worsened consumer confidence. The subsequent Great Depression was the deepest **recession** the country has ever seen.

The Great Depression seemed to last forever. In 1933 President Roosevelt lamented that one-third of the nation was ill-clothed, ill-housed, and ill-fed. Thousands of unemployed workers marched to the Capitol to demand jobs and aid. In 1938, nine years after Black Thursday, nearly 20 percent of the workforce was still idle.

The Great Depression shook not only the foundations of the world economy but also the self-confidence of the economics profession. No one had predicted the Depression, and few could explain it. The ensuing search for explanations focused on three central questions:

- **How stable is a market-driven economy?**
- **What forces cause instability?**
- **What, if anything, can the government do to promote steady economic growth?**

The basic purpose of **macroeconomics** is to answer these questions—to *explain* how and why economies grow and what causes the recurrent ups and downs of the economy that characterize the **business cycle.** In this chapter we introduce the theoretical model economists use to describe and explain the short-run business cycle. We'll also preview some of the policy options the government might use to dampen those cycles, including the slew of actions taken in 2008–2009 to reverse another macro downturn: the Great Recession of 2008–2009. And we'll examine how the coronavirus pandemic upended economies around the world in 2020, the economic devastation it caused, and the policy responses that tried to contain it.

macroeconomics: The study of aggregate economic behavior, of the economy as a whole.

business cycle: Alternating periods of economic growth and contraction.

STABLE OR UNSTABLE?

Prior to the 1930s, macro economists thought there could never be a Great Depression. The economic thinkers of the time asserted that a market-driven economy was inherently stable. There was no need for government intervention.

laissez faire: The doctrine of "leave it alone," of nonintervention by government in the market mechanism.

law of demand: The quantity of a good demanded in a given time period increases as its price falls, *ceteris paribus.*

Say's law: Supply creates its own demand.

Classical Theory

This **laissez-faire** view of macroeconomics seemed reasonable at the time. During the 19th century and the first 30 years of the 20th, the U.S. economy experienced some bad years in which the nation's output declined and unemployment increased. But most of these episodes were relatively short-lived. The dominant feature of the Industrial Era was *growth:* an expanding economy with more output, more jobs, and higher incomes nearly every year.

A Self-Regulating Economy. In this environment, classical economists, as they later became known, propounded an optimistic view of the macro economy. *According to the classical view, the economy "self-adjusts" to deviations from its long-term growth trend.* Producers might occasionally reduce their output and throw people out of work, but these dislocations would cause little damage. If output declined and people lost their jobs, the internal forces of the marketplace would quickly restore prosperity. *Economic downturns were viewed as temporary setbacks, not permanent problems.*

The cornerstones of classical optimism were flexible prices and flexible wages. If producers couldn't sell all their output at current prices, they had two choices. Either (1) they could reduce the rate of output and throw some people out of work or (2) they could reduce the price of their output, thereby stimulating an increase in the quantity demanded. Classical economists liked the second option. According to the **law of demand,** price reductions cause an increase in unit sales. If prices fall far enough, everything can be sold. Thus, flexible prices—prices that would drop when consumer demand slowed—virtually guaranteed that all output could be sold. No one would have to lose a job because of weak consumer demand.

Flexible prices had their counterpart in factor markets. If some workers were temporarily out of work, they'd compete for jobs by offering their services at lower wages. As wage rates declined, producers would find it profitable to hire more workers. Ultimately, flexible wages would ensure that everyone who wanted a job would have a job.

These optimistic views of the macro economy were summarized in Say's law. **Say's law**—named after the 19th-century economist Jean-Baptiste Say—decreed that "supply creates its own demand." Whatever was produced would be sold. All workers who sought employment would be hired. *Unsold goods and unemployed labor could emerge in this classical system, but both would disappear as soon as people had time to adjust prices and wages.* There could be no Great Depression—no protracted macro failure—in this classical view of the world.

Macro Failure. The Great Depression was a stunning blow to classical economists. At the onset of the Depression, classical economists assured everyone that the setbacks in production and employment were temporary and would soon vanish. Andrew Mellon, Secretary of the U.S. Treasury, expressed this optimistic view in January 1930, just a few months after the stock market crash. Assessing the prospects for the year ahead, he said, "I see nothing . . . in the present situation that is either menacing or warrants pessimism. . . . I have every confidence that there will be a revival of activity in the spring and that during the coming year the country will make steady progress."[1] Merrill Lynch, one of the nation's largest brokerage houses, was urging that people should buy stocks. But the Depression deepened. Indeed, unemployment grew and persisted *despite* falling prices and wages (see Figure 8.1). The classical self-adjustment mechanism simply didn't work.

The Keynesian Revolution

The Great Depression effectively destroyed the credibility of classical economic theory. As the British economist John Maynard Keynes pointed out in 1935, classical economists

> were apparently unmoved by the lack of correspondence between the results of their theory and the facts of observation:—a discrepancy which the ordinary man has not failed to observe. . . .
> The celebrated optimism of [classical] economic theory . . . is . . . to be traced, I think, to their having neglected to take account of the drag on prosperity which can be exercised by an insufficiency of effective demand. For there would obviously be a natural tendency towards the optimum

---

[1]David A. Shannon, *The Great Depression* (Englewood Cliffs, NJ: Prentice Hall, 1960), p. 4.

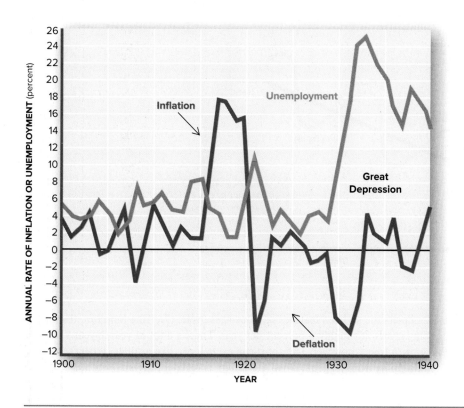

FIGURE 8.1

Inflation and Unemployment, 1900–1940

In the early 1900s, falling price levels (deflation) appeared to limit increases in unemployment. Periods of high unemployment also tended to be brief. These experiences bolstered the confidence of classical economists in the stability of the macro economy. Say's law seemed to work.

In the 1930s, unemployment rates rose to unprecedented heights and stayed high for a decade. Falling wages and prices (deflation) did not restore full employment. This macro failure prompted calls for new theories and policies to control the business cycle.

Source: U.S. Bureau of the Census, *The Statistics of the United States, 1957.*

employment of resources in a Society which was functioning after the manner of the classical postulates. It may well be that the classical theory represents the way in which we should like our Economy to behave. But to assume that it actually does so is to assume our difficulties away.[2]

Inherent Instability. Keynes went on to develop an alternative view of how the macro economy works. Whereas the classical economists viewed the economy as inherently stable, *Keynes asserted that a market-driven economy is inherently unstable.* Small disturbances in output, prices, or unemployment were likely to be magnified, not muted, by the invisible hand of the marketplace. The Great Depression was not a unique event, Keynes argued, but a calamity that would recur if we relied on the market mechanism to self-adjust.

Government Intervention. In Keynes's view, the inherent instability of the marketplace required government intervention. When the economy falters, we can't afford to wait for some assumed self-adjustment mechanism but must instead intervene to protect jobs and income. The government can do this by "priming the pump": buying more output, employing more people, providing more income transfers, and making more money available. When the economy overheats, the government must cool it down with higher taxes, spending reductions, and less money.

Keynes's denunciation of classical theory didn't end the macroeconomic debate. On the contrary, economists continue to wage fierce debates about the inherent stability of the economy. Those debates—which became intense again in 2008–2009 and 2020–2021—fill the pages of the next few chapters. But before examining them, let's first take a quick look at the economy's actual performance since the Great Depression.

HISTORICAL CYCLES

The upswings and downturns of the business cycle are gauged in terms of changes in total output. An economic upswing, or expansion, refers to an increase in the volume of goods and services produced. An economic downturn, or contraction, occurs when the total volume of production declines.

[2]John Maynard Keynes, *The General Theory of Employment: Interest and Money* (London, UK: Macmillan, 1936), pp. 33–34.

FIGURE 8.2

The Business Cycle

The model business cycle resembles a roller coaster. Output first climbs to a peak, then decreases. After hitting a trough, the economy recovers, with real GDP again increasing.

A central concern of macroeconomic theory is to determine whether a recurring business cycle exists and, if so, what forces cause it.

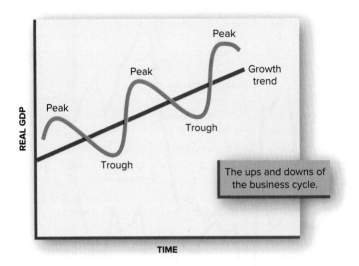

The ups and downs of the business cycle.

Figure 8.2 depicts the stylized features of a business cycle. Over the long run, the output of the economy grows at roughly 3 percent per year. There's a lot of year-to-year variation around this growth trend, however. The short-run cycle looks like a roller coaster, climbing steeply, then dropping from its peak. Once the trough is reached, the upswing starts again.

In reality, business cycles aren't as regular or as predictable as Figure 8.2 suggests. The U.S. economy has experienced recurrent upswings and downswings, but of widely varying length, intensity, and frequency.

Figure 8.3 illustrates the actual performance of the U.S. economy since 1929. Changes in total output are measured by changes in **real GDP,** the inflation-adjusted value of all goods

real GDP: The value of final output produced in a given period, adjusted for changing prices.

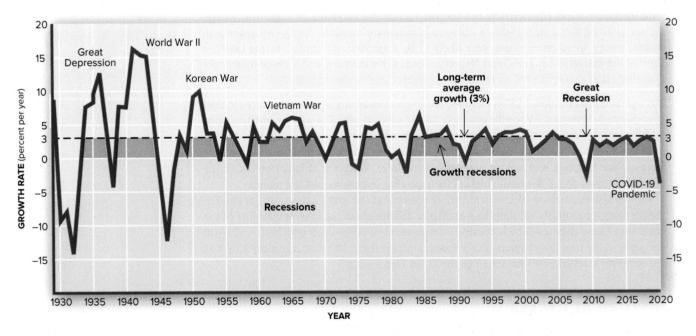

FIGURE 8.3

The Business Cycle in U.S. History

From 1929 to 2020, real GDP increased at an average rate of 3 percent a year. But annual growth rates have departed widely from that average. Years of above-average growth seem to alternate with years of sluggish growth (*growth recessions*) and actual decreases in total output (*recessions*).

Source: U.S. Department of Commerce.

and services produced. From a long-run view, the growth of real GDP has been impressive: Real GDP today is 20 times larger than it was in 1929. Americans now consume a vastly greater variety of goods and services, and in greater quantities, than earlier generations ever dreamed possible.

Our long-term success in raising living standards is clouded, however, by a spate of short-term macro setbacks. On closer inspection, *the growth path of the U.S. economy isn't a smooth, rising trend but a series of steps, stumbles, and setbacks*. This short-run instability is evident in Figure 8.3. The dashed horizontal line across the middle of the chart represents the long-term *average* growth rate of the U.S. economy. From 1929 through 2020, the U.S. economy expanded at an average rate of 3 percent per year. But Figure 8.3 clearly shows that we didn't grow so nicely every year. There were lots of years when real GDP grew by less than 3 percent. Worse still, there were many years of *negative* growth, with real GDP *declining* from one year to the next. These successive short-run contractions and expansions are the essence of the business cycle.

The Great Depression

The most prolonged departure from our long-term growth path occurred during the Great Depression. Between 1929 and 1933, total U.S. output steadily declined. Notice in Figure 8.3 how the growth rate is negative in each of these years. During these four years of negative growth, real GDP contracted a total of nearly 30 percent. Investments in new plant and equipment virtually ceased. Economies around the world came to a grinding halt (see World View "Global Depression").

The U.S. economy rebounded in April 1933 and continued to expand for three years (see the positive growth rates in Figure 8.3). By 1937, however, the rate of output was still below

WORLD VIEW

GLOBAL DEPRESSION

The Great Depression wasn't confined to the U.S. economy. Most other countries suffered substantial losses of output and employment over a period of many years. Between 1929 and 1932, industrial production around the world fell 37 percent. The United States and Germany suffered the largest losses, while Spain and the Scandinavian countries lost only modest amounts of output.

Some countries escaped the ravages of the Great Depression altogether. The Soviet Union, largely insulated from Western economic structures, was in the midst of Stalin's forced industrialization drive during the 1930s. China and Japan were also relatively isolated from world trade and finance and so suffered less damage from the Depression.

Country	Decline in Industrial Output
Germany	−47%
United States	−46
France	−31
Chile	−22
Great Britain	−17
Spain	−12
Norway	−7
Japan	−2

CRITICAL ANALYSIS: International trade and financial flows tie nations together. When the U.S. economy tumbled into a **recession** in the 1930s, other nations lost export sales. Such interactions made the Great Depression a worldwide calamity.

that of 1929. Then things got worse again. During 1938 and 1939 output again contracted and more people lost their jobs. **At the end of the 1930s, GDP per capita was lower than it had been in 1929.**

World War II

World War II greatly increased the demand for goods and services and ended the Great Depression. During the war years, real GDP grew at unprecedented rates–almost 19 percent in a single year (1942). Virtually everyone was employed, either in the armed forces or in the factories. Throughout the war, America's productive capacity was strained to the limit.

The Postwar Years

After World War II, the U.S. economy resumed a pattern of alternating growth and contraction. The contracting periods are called *recessions.* Specifically, we use the term **recession** to mean a decline in real GDP that continues for at least two successive quarters. As Table 8.1 indicates, there have been 12 recessions since 1944. The most severe postwar recession occurred immediately after World War II ended. Sudden cutbacks in defense production caused GDP to decline sharply in 1945. That postwar recession was relatively brief, however. Pent-up demand for consumer goods and a surge in investment spending helped restore full employment.

The 1980s and 1990s

The 1980s started with two recessions, the second lasting 16 months (July 1981–November 1982). Despite the onset of a second recession at midyear, real GDP actually increased in 1981. But the growth rate was so slow (1.9 percent) that the number of unemployed workers actually rose that year. This kind of experience is called a **growth recession**–the economy grows, but at a slower rate than the long-run (3 percent) average. Thus,

- *A growth recession occurs when the economy expands too slowly* (0–2 percent).
- *A recession occurs when real GDP actually contracts.*
- *A depression is an extremely deep and long recession.*

In November 1982 the U.S. economy began an economic expansion that lasted more than seven years. During that period, real GDP increased by more than $1 trillion, and nearly 20 million new jobs were created.

recession: A decline in total output (real GDP) for two or more consecutive quarters.

growth recession: A period during which real GDP grows but at a rate below the long-term trend of 3 percent.

TABLE 8.1

Business Slumps

The U.S. economy has experienced 15 business slumps since 1929. In the post–World War II period, these downturns have been much less severe than the Great Depression. The typical recession lasts around 10 months.

Dates	Duration (Months)	Percentage Decline in Real GDP	Peak Unemployment Rate
Aug. 1929–Mar. 1933	43	35.4%	24.9%
May 1937–June 1938	13	9.4	20.0
Feb. 1945–Oct. 1945	8	23.8	4.3
Nov. 1948–Oct. 1949	11	9.9	7.9
July 1953–May 1954	10	10.0	6.1
Aug. 1957–Apr. 1958	8	14.3	7.5
Apr. 1960–Feb. 1961	10	7.2	7.1
Dec. 1969–Nov. 1970	11	8.1	6.1
Nov. 1973–Mar. 1975	16	14.7	9.0
Jan. 1980–July 1980	6	8.7	7.6
July 1981–Nov. 1982	16	12.3	10.8
July 1990–Feb. 1991	8	2.2	6.5
Mar. 2001–Nov. 2001	8	0.6	5.6
Dec. 2007–June 2009	18	4.1	10.0
Mar. 2020-May 2020	3	32.0	14.7

In the 20 years from 1986 to 2006 the U.S. economy grew quite well. There was only one year (1991) in which total output contracted (a recession) and only seven years of below 3 percent growth (growth recessions).

Great Recession of 2008–2009

That 20-year string of economic growth was broken in 2008. In mid-2007 home prices and stock market prices started falling, sapping consumer wealth and confidence. A credit crisis made loans hard to obtain. Sales of homes, autos, and other big-ticket items plummeted, causing GDP to again contract (see Front Page Economics "Sharpest Economic Decline in 26 Years"). The Great Recession of 2008–2009 was the worst since 1981–1982. The unemployment rate peaked at 10 percent when 15 million workers were unable to find jobs.

FRONT PAGE ECONOMICS

SHARPEST ECONOMIC DECLINE IN 26 YEARS

It's all bad news on the economic front. The government reported yesterday that the U.S. economy suffered its biggest decline in 26 years in the last quarter of 2008. According to the Department of Commerce, gross domestic product (GDP) fell at an annual rate of 3.8 percent—the largest drop since the first quarter of 1982. Spending was down across the board, especially in the critical area of big-ticket durable goods (down 22 percent). Economists are worried that the plunge in spending will continue, pushing the U.S. economy into another recession.

Source: News reports of January 30, 2009.

CRITICAL ANALYSIS: Everyone agrees that **business cycles** happen and the macro economy can contract on occasion. The debate is whether such contractions self-correct or require government intervention.

Sluggish Recovery. Even after the Great Recession officially ended in June 2009, economic growth was excruciatingly slow. Notice in Figure 8.3 how the economy stayed in the "growth recession" range from 2010 to 2016. The best year of that recovery (2015) exhibited only 2.9 percent growth; the worst year (2011) had a snail's pace of 1.6 percent GDP growth. As a result, unemployment stayed high for five years and receded only when millions of would-be workers stopped looking for work and left the labor force. The appeal of Donald Trump's 2016 campaign promise to "make America great again" was partly the hope that different economic policies would accelerate economic growth. Tax cuts enacted in 2017 did in fact accelerate growth, although GDP growth stayed a bit below the long-run average of 3 percent.

Coronavirus Shutdowns. The coronavirus pandemic that swept across the globe threw the U.S. economy completely off its growth track in 2020. In response to the pandemic, governments at all levels issued orders for consumers to shelter in place and for all nonessential businesses to close their doors. The decline in output was immediate and severe, pushing the economy into recession. More than 20 million Americans became unemployed in the span of only two months, while total output plunged by more than 30 percent in the same time. It was a quick but deep recession. A massive policy response kept the economy from plunging further and about half of the lost jobs returned within a couple of months. Extraordinary biotech advances fueled optimism that the economy would rebound strongly in 2021–2022 once the pandemic was eradicated.

A MODEL OF THE MACRO ECONOMY

The bumpy growth record of the U.S. economy lends some validity to the notion of a recurring business cycle. Every decade seems to contain at least one boom or bust cycle. But the historical record doesn't really answer our key questions. Are business cycles *inevitable?* Can we do anything to control them? *Keynes and the classical economists weren't debating whether business cycles occur but whether they are an appropriate target for government intervention.* That debate continues.

To determine whether and how the government should try to control the business cycle, we first need to understand its origins. What causes the economy to expand or contract? What market forces dampen (self-adjust) or magnify economic swings?

Figure 8.4 sets the stage for answering these questions. This diagram provides a bird's-eye view of how the macro economy works. This basic macro model emphasizes that the performance of the economy depends on a surprisingly small set of determinants.

Macro Outcomes. On the right side of Figure 8.4 the primary measures of macroeconomic performance are arrayed. These basic *macro outcomes include*

- *Output:* total value of goods and services produced (real GDP).
- *Jobs:* levels of employment and unemployment.
- *Prices:* average price of goods and services (inflation).
- *Growth:* year-to-year expansion in production capacity.
- *International balances:* international value of the dollar; trade and payment balances with other countries.

These macro outcomes define our economic welfare; we measure our economic well-being in terms of the value of output produced, the number of jobs created, price stability, and rate of economic expansion. We also seek to maintain a certain balance in our international trade and financial relations. The economy's performance is rated by the "scores" on these five macro outcomes.

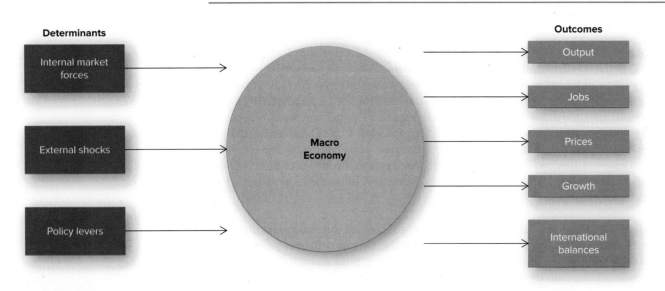

FIGURE 8.4
The Macro Economy

The primary outcomes of the macro economy are output of goods and services (GDP), jobs, prices, economic growth, and international balances (trade, currency). These outcomes result from the interplay of internal market forces such as population growth, innovation, and spending patterns; external shocks such as wars, weather, pandemics, and trade disruptions; and policy levers such as tax, budget, and regulatory decisions.

Macro Determinants. On the left side of Figure 8.4 three very broad forces that shape macro outcomes are depicted. These *determinants of macro performance are*

- *Internal market forces:* population growth, spending behavior, invention and innovation, and the like.
- *External shocks:* wars, natural disasters, pandemics, terrorist attacks, trade disruptions, and so on.
- *Policy levers:* tax policy, government spending, changes in the availability of money, and regulation, for example.

In the absence of external shocks or government policy, an economy would still function: It would still produce output, create jobs, develop prices, and maybe even grow. The U.S. economy operated with minimal government intervention for much of its history. Even today, many less developed countries operate in relative isolation from government or international events. In these situations, macro outcomes depend exclusively on internal market forces.

The crucial macro controversy is whether pure, market-driven economies are inherently stable or unstable. The GDP contraction described in the preceding Front Page Economics wouldn't have surprised classical economists. They knew the economy could sometimes stumble, but they believed the economy would quickly recover from any such setbacks. They saw no need for the box in Figure 8.4 labeled "policy levers." Keynes, by contrast, argued that policy levers were both effective and necessary. Without such intervention, Keynes believed, the economy was doomed to bouts of repeated macro failure.

Modern economists hesitate to give policy intervention that great a role. Nearly all economists recognize that policy intervention affects macro outcomes. But there are great arguments about just how effective any policy lever is. Some economists even echo the classical notion that policy intervention may be either ineffective or, worse still, inherently *de*stabilizing.

AGGREGATE DEMAND AND SUPPLY

To determine which views of economic performance are valid, we need to examine the inner workings of the macro economy. All Figure 8.4 tells us is that macro outcomes depend on certain identifiable forces. But the figure doesn't reveal *how* the determinants and outcomes are connected. What's in the mysterious circle labeled "Macro Economy" at the center of Figure 8.4?

When economists peer into the mechanics of the macro economy, they see the forces of supply and demand at work. All the macro outcomes depicted in Figure 8.4 are the result of market transactions—an interaction between supply and demand. Hence, *any influence on macro outcomes must be transmitted through supply or demand.*

By conceptualizing the inner workings of the macro economy in supply and demand terms, economists have developed a remarkably simple model of how the economy works.

Aggregate Demand

Economists use the term *aggregate demand* to refer to the collective behavior of all buyers in the marketplace. Specifically, **aggregate demand (AD)** refers to the various quantities of output (real GDP) that all people, taken together, are willing and able to buy at alternative price levels in a given period. Our view here encompasses the collective demand for *all* goods and services rather than the demand for any single good.

To understand the concept of aggregate demand better, imagine that everyone is paid on the same day. With their incomes in hand, people then enter the product market. The question becomes, how much output will people buy?

To answer this question, we have to know something about prices. If goods and services are cheap, people will be able to buy more with their available income. On the other hand, high prices will limit both the ability and willingness to purchase goods and services. Note that we're talking here about the *average* price level, not the price of any single good.

Figure 8.5 illustrates this simple relationship between average prices and real spending. The horizontal axis depicts the various quantities of (real) output that might be purchased. The vertical axis shows various price levels that might exist.

aggregate demand (AD): The total quantity of output (real GDP) demanded at alternative price levels in a given time period, *ceteris paribus.*

FIGURE 8.5

Aggregate Demand

Aggregate demand refers to the total output (real GDP) demanded at alternative price levels, *ceteris paribus.* The vertical axis measures the average level of all prices rather than the price of a single good. Likewise, the horizontal axis refers to the real quantity of all goods and services, not the quantity of only one product.

The downward slope of the aggregate demand curve is due to the real balances, foreign trade, and interest rate effects.

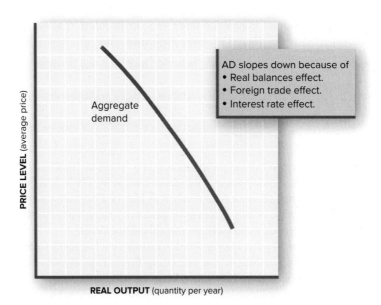

The aggregate demand curve illustrates how the real value of purchases varies with the average level of prices. The downward slope of the aggregate demand curve suggests that with a given (constant) level of income, people will buy more goods and services at lower price levels. Why would this be the case? *Three separate reasons explain the downward slope of the aggregate demand curve:*

- *The real balances effect.*
- *The foreign trade effect.*
- *The interest rate effect.*

Real Balances Effect. The most obvious explanation for the downward slope of the aggregate demand curve is that cheaper prices make dollars more valuable. Suppose you had $1,000 in your savings account. How much output could you buy with that savings balance? That depends on the price level. At current prices, you could buy $1,000 worth of output. But what if the price level rose? Then your $1,000 wouldn't stretch as far. *The real value of money is measured by how many goods and services each dollar will buy.* When the *real* value of your savings declines, your ability to purchase goods and services declines as well.

Suppose inflation pushes the price level up by 25 percent in a year. What will happen to the real value of your savings balance? At the end of the year, you'll have

$$\begin{aligned} \text{Real value of savings} \atop \text{at year-end} &= \frac{\text{Savings balance}}{\dfrac{\text{Price level at year-end}}{\text{Price level at year-start}}} \\ &= \frac{\$1,000}{\dfrac{125}{100}} = \frac{\$1,000}{1.25} \\ &= \$800 \end{aligned}$$

In effect, inflation has wiped out a chunk of your purchasing power. At year's end, you can't buy as many goods and services as you could have at the beginning of the year. The *quantity* of output you demand will decrease. In Figure 8.5 this would be illustrated by a movement up the aggregate demand curve to higher prices and reduced purchases.

A declining price level (deflation) has the opposite effect. Specifically, lower price levels make you "richer": **the cash balances you hold in your pocket, in your bank account, or under your pillow are worth more when the price level falls**. As a result, you can buy *more* goods, even though your *nominal income* hasn't changed.

Lower price levels increase the purchasing power of other dollar-denominated assets as well. Bonds, for example, rise in value when the price level falls. This may tempt consumers to sell some bonds and buy more goods and services. With greater real wealth, consumers might also decide to save less and spend more of their current income. In either case, the quantity of goods and services demanded at any given income level will increase. These real balances effects create an inverse relationship between the price level and the real value of output demanded—that is, *a downward-sloping aggregate demand curve.*

Foreign Trade Effect. The downward slope of the aggregate demand curve is reinforced by changes in imports and exports. Consumers have the option of buying either domestic or foreign goods. A decisive factor in choosing between them is their relative price. If the average price of U.S.-produced goods is rising, Americans may buy more imported goods and fewer domestically produced products. Conversely, falling price levels in the United States may convince consumers to buy more "made in the USA" output and fewer imports.

International consumers are also swayed by relative price levels. When U.S. price levels decline, overseas tourists flock to Disney World. Global consumers also buy more U.S. wheat, airplanes, and computers when our price levels decline. Conversely, a rise in the relative price of U.S. products deters foreign buyers. These changes in import and export flows contribute to the downward slope of the aggregate demand curve.

Interest Rate Effect. Changes in the price level also affect the amount of money people need to borrow. At lower price levels, consumer borrowing needs are smaller. As the demand for loans diminishes, interest rates tend to decline as well. This "cheaper" money stimulates more borrowing and loan-financed purchases. These interest rate effects reinforce the downward slope of the aggregate demand curve, as illustrated in Figure 8.5.

Aggregate Supply

Although lower price levels tend to increase the volume of output *demanded,* they have the opposite effect on the aggregate quantity *supplied.* As we observed, our production possibilities are defined by available resources and technology. Within those limits, however, producers must decide how much output they're *willing* to supply. Their **supply decisions are influenced by changes in the price level.**

Profit Effect. The primary motivation for supplying goods and services is the chance to earn a profit. Producers can earn a profit so long as the prices they receive for their output exceed the costs they pay in production. Hence, *changing price levels will affect the profitability of supplying goods.*

If the price level declines, profits tend to drop. In the short run, producers are saddled with some relatively constant costs like rent, interest payments, negotiated wages, and inputs

Lower park prices attract throngs of foreign visitors.
Joshua Rainey/123RF

already contracted for. If output prices fall, producers will be hard-pressed to pay these fixed costs, much less earn a profit. Their response will be to reduce the rate of output.

Higher output prices have the opposite effect. Because many costs are relatively constant in the short run, higher prices for goods and services tend to widen profit margins. As profit margins widen, producers will want to produce and sell more goods. Thus, *we expect the rate of output to increase when the price level rises.* This expectation is reflected in the upward slope of the aggregate supply curve in Figure 8.6. **Aggregate supply (AS)** reflects the various quantities of real output that firms are willing and able to produce at alternative price levels in a given time period.

aggregate supply (AS): The total quantity of output (real GDP) producers are willing and able to supply at alternative price levels in a given time period, *ceteris paribus.*

Cost Effect. The upward slope of the aggregate supply curve is also explained by rising costs. The profit effect depends on some costs remaining constant when the average price level rises. Not all costs will remain constant, however. Producers may have to pay overtime wages, for example, to increase output, even if *base* wages are constant. Tight supplies of other inputs may also unleash cost increases. Such cost pressures tend to multiply as the rate of output increases. As time passes, even costs that initially stayed constant may start creeping upward.

All these cost pressures will make producing output more expensive. Producers will be willing to supply additional output only if prices rise at least as fast as costs.

The upward slope of the aggregate supply curve in Figure 8.6 illustrates this cost effect. Notice how the aggregate supply curve is practically horizontal at low rates of aggregate output and then gets increasingly steeper. At high output levels the aggregate supply curve almost turns straight up. This changing slope reflects the fact that *cost pressures are minimal at low rates of output but intense as the economy approaches capacity.*

Macro Equilibrium

When all is said and done, what we end up with here is two rather conventional-looking supply and demand curves. But these particular curves have special significance. Instead of describing the behavior of buyers and sellers in a single product market, *aggregate supply and demand curves summarize the market activity of the whole (macro) economy.* These curves tell us what *total* amount of goods and services will be supplied or demanded at various price levels.

These graphic summaries of buyer and seller behavior provide some important clues about the economy's performance. The most important clue is point *E* in Figure 8.7, where

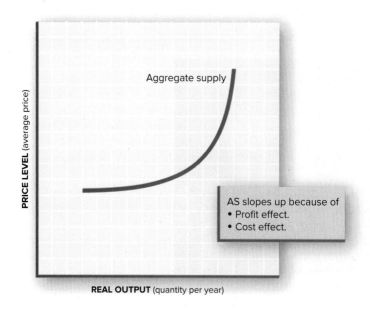

FIGURE 8.6

Aggregate Supply

Aggregate supply is the real value of output (real GDP) producers are willing and able to bring to the market at alternative price levels, *ceteris paribus.* The upward slope of the aggregate supply curve reflects both profit effects (the lure of widening profit margins) and cost effects (increasing cost pressures).

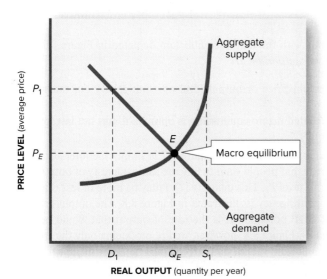

FIGURE 8.7
Macro Equilibrium

The aggregate demand and supply curves intersect at only one point (*E*). At that point, the price level (*P$_E$*) and output (*Q$_E$*) combination is compatible with both buyers' and sellers' intentions. The economy will gravitate to those equilibrium price (*P$_E$*) and output (*Q$_E$*) levels. At any other price level (e.g., *P$_1$*), the behavior of buyers and sellers is incompatible.

the aggregate demand and supply curves intersect. This is the only point at which the behavior of buyers and sellers is compatible. We know from the aggregate demand curve that people are willing and able to buy the quantity Q_E when the price level is at P_E. From the aggregate supply curve we know that businesses are prepared to sell quantity Q_E at the price level P_E. Hence, buyers and sellers are willing to trade exactly the same quantity (Q_E) at that price level. We call this situation **macro equilibrium**—the unique combination of prices and output compatible with *both* buyers' and sellers' intentions.

Disequilibrium. To appreciate the significance of macro equilibrium, suppose that another price or output level existed. Imagine, for example, that prices were higher, at the level P_1 in Figure 8.7. How much output would people want to buy at that price level? How much would business want to produce and sell?

The aggregate demand curve tells us that people would want to buy only the quantity D_1 at the higher price level P_1. In contrast, business firms would want to sell a larger quantity, S_1. This is a *dis*equilibrium situation in which the intentions of buyers and sellers are incompatible. The aggregate *quantity supplied* (S_1) exceeds the aggregate *quantity demanded* (D_1). Accordingly, a lot of goods will remain unsold at price level P_1.

Market Responses. To sell these goods, producers will have to reduce their prices. As prices drop, producers will decrease the volume of goods sent to market. At the same time, the quantities that consumers seek to purchase will increase. This adjustment process will continue until point *E* is reached and the quantities demanded and supplied are equal. At that point, the lower price level P_E will prevail.

The same kind of adjustment process would occur if a lower price level first existed. At lower prices, the aggregate quantity demanded would exceed the aggregate quantity supplied. The resulting shortages would permit sellers to raise their prices. As they did so, the aggregate quantity demanded would decrease, and the aggregate quantity supplied would increase. Eventually we would return to point *E,* where the aggregate quantities demanded and supplied are equal.

Equilibrium is unique; it's the only price level-output combination that is mutually compatible with aggregate supply and demand. In terms of graphs, it's the only place where the aggregate supply and demand curves intersect. At point *E* there's no reason for the level of output or prices to change. The behavior of buyers and sellers is compatible. By contrast, any other level of output or prices creates a *dis*equilibrium that requires market adjustments. All other price and output combinations, therefore, are unstable. They won't last. Eventually the economy will return to point *E*.

equilibrium (macro): The combination of price level and real output that is compatible with both aggregate demand and aggregate supply.

Macro Failures

There are two potential problems with the macro equilibrium depicted in Figure 8.7. The *two potential problems with macro equilibrium are*

- *Undesirability:* The equilibrium price or output level may not satisfy our macroeconomic goals.
- *Instability:* Even if the designated macro equilibrium is optimal, it may not last long.

Undesirability. The macro equilibrium depicted in Figure 8.7 is simply the intersection of two curves. All we know for sure is that people want to buy the same quantity of output that businesses want to sell at the price level P_E. This quantity (Q_E) may be more or less than our full-employment capacity. This contingency is illustrated in Figure 8.8. The output level Q_F represents our **full-employment GDP** potential. It is the rate of output that would be produced if we were fully employed. In Figure 8.8, however, we are producing only the smaller quantity Q_E. In this case, the equilibrium rate of output (Q_E) falls far short of capacity production Q_F. We've failed to achieve our goal of full employment.

Similar problems may arise from the equilibrium price level. Suppose that P^* represents the most desired price level. In Figure 8.8, we see that the equilibrium price level P_E exceeds P^*. If market behavior determines prices, the price level will rise above the desired level. The resulting increase in the average level of prices is what we call **inflation.**

It could be argued, of course, that our apparent macro failures are simply an artifact. We could have drawn the aggregate supply and demand curves to intersect at point F in Figure 8.8. At that intersection we'd have both price stability and full employment. Why didn't we draw them there, instead of intersecting at point E?

On the graph we can draw curves anywhere we want. In the real world, however, *only one set of aggregate supply and demand curves will correctly express buyers' and sellers' behavior.* We must emphasize here that these real-world curves may *not* intersect at point F, thus denying us price stability or full employment, or both. That is the kind of **market failure** illustrated in Figure 8.8.

Instability. Figure 8.8 is only the beginning of our macro worries. Suppose that the real-world AS and AD curves actually intersected in the perfect spot (point F). That is, imagine that macro equilibrium yielded the optimal levels of both employment and prices. If this happened, could we stop fretting about the state of the economy?

Unhappily, even a "perfect" macro equilibrium doesn't ensure a happy ending. Real-world AS and AD curves aren't permanently locked into their respective positions. They can *shift*— and they will whenever the behavior of buyers and sellers changes.

---

full-employment GDP: The value of total market output (real GDP) produced at full employment.

inflation: An increase in the average level of prices of goods and services.

market failure: An imperfection in the market mechanism that prevents optimal outcomes.

FIGURE 8.8

An Undesired Equilibrium

Equilibrium establishes only the level of prices and output compatible with both buyers' and sellers' intentions. These outcomes may not satisfy our policy goals. In this case, the equilibrium price level (P_E) is too high (above P^*), and the equilibrium output rate (Q_E) falls short of full employment (Q_F).

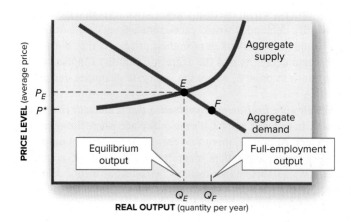

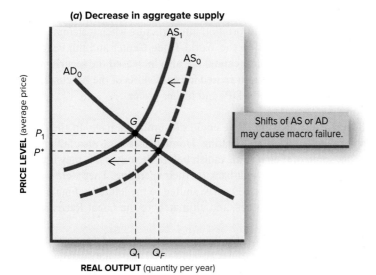

(a) Decrease in aggregate supply

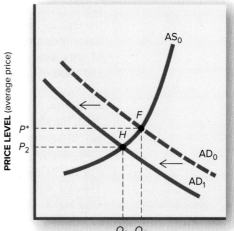

(b) Decrease in aggregate demand

Shifts of AS or AD may cause macro failure.

FIGURE 8.9
Macro Disturbances

(a) **Aggregate supply shifts** A decrease (leftward shift) of the aggregate supply curve reduces real GDP and raises average prices. When supply shifts from AS_0 to AS_1, the equilibrium moves from F to G. At G, output is lower and prices are higher than at F. Such a supply shift may result from higher import prices, natural disasters, changes in tax policy, or other events.

(b) **Aggregate demand shifts** A decrease (leftward shift) in aggregate demand reduces output and price levels. When demand shifts from AD_0 to AD_1, both real output and the price level decline. A fall in demand may be caused by decreased export demand, changes in expectations, higher taxes, or other events.

AS Shifts. The coronavirus pandemic of 2020 was a dramatic example of how an AS shift can destabilize an economy. Before the pandemic hit, the U.S. economy was at a full-employment equilibrium, as illustrated by point F in Figure 8.9a. Then the virus struck. The immediate effect of the pandemic was seen in increased illness and death, which took a toll on the labor force. Then governments around the world shut down production facilities as part of the COVID-19 containment strategy (see Front Page Economics "Trump Extends Stay-at-Home Guidelines"). Suddenly, a lot less output was available at any given price level. In other words, the AS curve shifted abruptly to the left, as shown in Figure 8.9a. The end result was a shift of macro equilibrium from its full-employment level to a much lower level.

FRONT PAGE ECONOMICS

TRUMP EXTENDS STAY-AT-HOME GUIDELINES

President Trump extended his stay-at-home guidelines until April 30. In a Rose Garden press conference yesterday, President Trump said the containment measures first announced on March 15 would be extended for another 30 days. The guidelines advise people to avoid social gatherings of more than 10 people, to work from home if possible, to cease discretionary travel, to steer clear of bars and restaurants, and to practice social distancing. While recognizing the toll this was taking on the economy, the president said he was persuaded by health experts who warn of mounting death rates if containment efforts are relaxed.

Source: Media reports of March 30, 2020.

CRITICAL ANALYSIS: An **external shock** can shift the AS curve to the left, causing reduced output. In this case, both the virus and the response to it reduced aggregate supply.

Other natural disasters have similar but much smaller impacts. Hurricane Harvey, for example, destroyed a lot of production and transportation infrastructure when it slammed into the Gulf in 2017. The 2001 terrorist attacks on the World Trade Center and the Pentagon not only destroyed a lot of human and physical capital but also increased the security costs of subsequent transportation. These actions also caused leftward shifts of the AS curve. The end result of such shifts is less output (lower GDP) and higher prices.

AD Shifts. A shift of the aggregate demand curve could do similar damage. In the fall of 2008, the stock and credit markets took a real beating. Home prices were also falling rapidly. Consumers were seeing some of their wealth vanish before their eyes. As they became increasingly anxious about their future, they cut back on their spending. They were willing to buy *less* output at any given price level; the AD curve shifted to the left, as in Figure 8.9*b*. This AD shift led to lower output, falling prices, and ultimately to the Great Recession of 2008–2009.

The coronavirus pandemic had similar effects. On the one hand, it reduced aggregate supply via mandatory lockdowns and health concerns. But it also impacted aggregate demand. Workers who couldn't get to their jobs lost paychecks. Businesses that had to close lost revenue and profits. With incomes falling, market participants had less to spend. And worries about future income made them even less likely to go shopping. The consequence was a leftward shift of AD that caused another recession and sent unemployment to its highest levels since the Great Depression of the 1930s (see Front Page "Economy Craters; Unemployment Surges").

FRONT PAGE

ECONOMY CRATERS; UNEMPLOYMENT SURGES

The government confirmed today what everyone already knows: COVID-19 devastated the economy in the second quarter of this year. According to the U.S. Bureau of Economic Analysis, GDP plunged by a record-breaking 34.8 percent in the April-June quarter. Since the pandemic first hit the economy, over 40 million Americans have lost their jobs and filed for unemployment benefits. The nation's unemployment rate rose to 14.7 percent, the highest since the 1930s. Economists are hoping that that the federal government's massive infusion of money will turn things around in the coming months. But that may depend on progress in the battle against COVID-19.

Source: U.S. Bureau of Economic Analysis July 31, 2020

CRITICAL CONCEPTS: Leftward shifts of the AS or AD curves cause the economy to contract and unemployment to increase. The coronavirus pandemic caused both curves to shift leftward.

Multiple Shifts. The situation gets even crazier when the aggregate supply and demand curves shift repeatedly in different directions. A leftward shift of the AD curve can cause a recession, as the rate of output falls. A later rightward shift of the AD curve can cause a recovery, with real GDP (and employment) again increasing. Shifts of the aggregate supply curve can cause similar upswings and downswings. Thus, *business cycles are likely to result from recurrent shifts of the aggregate supply and demand curves.*

COMPETING THEORIES OF SHORT-RUN INSTABILITY

Figures 8.8 and 8.9 hardly inspire optimism about the macro economy. Figure 8.8 suggests that the odds of the market generating an equilibrium at full employment and price stability are about the same as finding a needle in a haystack. Figure 8.9 suggests that if we're lucky enough to find the needle, we'll probably drop it again.

The classical economists had no such worries. As we saw earlier, they believed that the economy would gravitate toward full employment. Keynes, on the other hand, worried that the macro equilibrium might start out badly and get worse in the absence of government intervention.

The AS/AD model doesn't really settle this controversy. It does, however, provide a convenient framework for comparing these and other theories about how the economy works. Essentially, *macro controversies focus on the shape of aggregate supply and demand curves and the potential to shift them.* With the right shape—or the correct shift—any desired equilibrium could be attained. As we'll see, there are differing views as to whether and how this happy outcome might come about. These differing views can be classified as demand-side explanations, supply-side explanations, or some combination of the two.

Demand-Side Theories

Keynesian Theory. Keynesian theory is the most prominent of the demand-side theories. Keynes argued that a deficiency of spending would tend to depress an economy. This deficiency might originate in consumer saving, inadequate business investment, or insufficient government spending. Whatever its origins, the lack of spending would leave goods unsold and production capacity unused. This contingency is illustrated in Front Page Economics "Sharpest Economic Decline in 26 Years" and here by point E_1 in Figure 8.10a. Notice that the equilibrium at E_1 leaves the economy at Q_1, below its full-employment potential (Q_F). Thus, *Keynes concluded that inadequate aggregate demand would cause persistently high unemployment.*

Keynes developed his theory during the Great Depression, when the economy seemed to be stuck at a very low level of equilibrium output, far below full-employment GDP. The only way to end the Depression, he argued, was for someone to start demanding more goods. He advocated a big hike in government spending—a rightward AD shift—to start the economy moving toward full employment. At the time his advice was largely ignored. When the United States mobilized for World War II, however, the sudden surge in government spending shifted the aggregate demand curve sharply to the right, restoring full employment (e.g., a reverse shift from AD_1 to AD_0 in Figure 8.10a). In times of peace, Keynes also advocated changing government taxes and spending to shift the aggregate demand curve in whatever direction is desired.

Monetary Theories. Another demand-side theory emphasizes the role of money in financing aggregate demand. Money and credit affect the ability and willingness of people to buy goods and services. If credit isn't available or is too expensive, consumers won't be able to buy as many cars, homes, or other expensive products. "Tight" money might also curtail business investment. In these circumstances, aggregate demand might prove to be inadequate, as illustrated in Figure 8.10a. In this case, an increase in the money supply and/or lower interest rates might help shift the AD curve into the desired position.

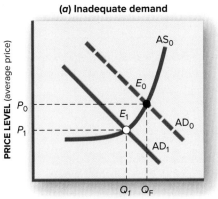

(a) Inadequate demand

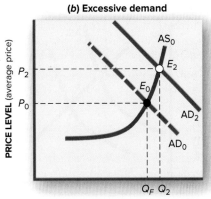

(b) Excessive demand

FIGURE 8.10

Demand-Side Theories

Inadequate demand may cause unemployment. In part (a), the demand AD_1 creates an equilibrium at E_1. The resulting output Q_1 falls short of full employment Q_F.

In part (b), excessive aggregate demand causes inflation. The price level rises from P_0 to P_2 when aggregate demand expands to AD_2. Demand-side theories emphasize how inadequate or excessive AD can cause macro failures.

Both the Keynesian and monetarist theories also regard aggregate demand as a prime suspect for inflationary problems. In Figure 8.10b, the curve AD_2 leads to an equilibrium at E_2. At first blush, that equilibrium looks desirable, as it offers more output (Q_2) than the full-employment threshold (Q_F). Notice, however, what's happening to prices: The price level rises from P_0 to P_2. Hence, *excessive aggregate demand may cause inflation.*

The more extreme monetary theories attribute all our macro successes and failures to management of the money supply. According to these *monetarist* theories, the economy will tend to stabilize at something like full-employment GDP. Thus, only the price level will be affected by changes in the money supply and resulting shifts of aggregate demand. We'll examine the basis for this view in a moment. At this juncture we simply note that *both Keynesian and monetarist theories emphasize the potential of aggregate-demand shifts to alter macro outcomes.*

Supply-Side Theories

Figure 8.11 illustrates an entirely different explanation of the business cycle. Notice that the aggregate *supply* curve is on the move in Figure 8.11. The initial equilibrium is again at point E_0. This time, however, aggregate demand remains stationary, while aggregate supply shifts. The resulting decline of aggregate supply causes output and employment to decline (to Q_3 from Q_F).

Figure 8.11 tells us that aggregate supply may be responsible for downturns as well. Our failure to achieve full employment may result from the unwillingness of producers to provide more goods at existing prices. That unwillingness may originate in simple greed, in rising costs, in resource shortages, or in government taxes and regulation. Inadequate investment in infrastructure (e.g., roads, sewer systems) or skill training may also limit supply potential. Whatever the cause, if the aggregate supply curve is AS_1 rather than AS_0, full employment will not be achieved with the demand AD_0.

The inadequate supply illustrated in Figure 8.11 causes not only unemployment but inflation as well. At the equilibrium E_3, the price level has risen from P_0 to P_3. Hence, a decrease in aggregate supply can cause multiple macro problems. On the other hand, an increase—a rightward shift—in aggregate supply can move us closer to both our price-stability and full-employment goals. Chapter 16 examines the many ways of inducing such a shift.

Eclectic Explanations

Not everyone blames either the demand side or the supply side exclusively. *The various macro theories tell us that either AS or AD can cause us to achieve or miss our policy goals.* These theories also demonstrate how various shifts of the aggregate supply and demand curves can achieve any specific output or price level. One could also shift *both* the AS and AD curves to explain unemployment, inflation, or recurring business cycles. Such eclectic explanations of macro failure draw from both sides of the market.

FIGURE 8.11

Supply-Side Theories

Inadequate supply can keep the economy below its full-employment potential and cause prices to rise as well. AS_1 leads to equilibrium output Q_3 and increases the price level from P_0 to P_3. Supply-side theories emphasize how AS shifts can worsen or improve macro outcomes.

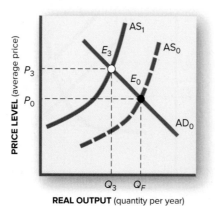

LONG-RUN SELF-ADJUSTMENT

Some economists argue that these various theories of short-run instability aren't only confusing but also pointless. As they see it, what really matters is the *long*-run trend of the economy, not *short*-run fluctuations around those trends. In their view, month-to-month or quarter-to-quarter fluctuations in real output or prices are just statistical noise. The *long*-term path of output and prices is determined by more fundamental factors.

This emphasis on long-term outcomes is reminiscent of the classical theory: the view that the economy will self-adjust. A decrease in aggregate demand is only a *temporary* problem. Once producers and workers make the required price and wage adjustments, the economy will return to its long-run equilibrium growth path.

The monetarist theory we encountered a moment ago has a similar view of long-run stability. According to the monetarist theory, the supply of goods and services is determined by institutional factors such as the size of the labor force and technology. These factors determine a "natural" rate of output that's relatively immune to short-run fluctuations in aggregate demand. If this argument is valid, the long-run aggregate supply curve is vertical, not sloped.

Figure 8.12 illustrates the classical/monetarist view of long-run stability. The vertical long-run AS curve is anchored at the natural rate of output Q_N. The natural rate Q_N is itself determined by demographics, technology, market structure, and the institutional infrastructure of the economy.

If the long-run AS curve is really vertical, as the classical and monetarist theories assert, some startling conclusions follow. The most startling implication is that ***shifts of the aggregate demand curve affect prices but not output in the long run.*** Notice in Figure 8.12 how the shift from AD$_1$ to AD$_2$ raises the price level (from P_1 to P_2) but leaves output anchored at Q_N.

What has happened here? Didn't we suggest earlier that an increase in aggregate demand would spur producers to increase output? And aren't rising prices an extra incentive for doing so?

Monetarists concede that *short-run* price increases tend to widen profit margins. This profit effect is an incentive to increase the rate of output. In the *long run,* however, costs are likely to catch up with rising prices. Workers will demand higher wages, landlords will increase rents, and banks will charge higher interest rates as the price level rises. Hence, a rising price level has only a *temporary* profit effect on supply behavior. In the *long run,* cost effects will dominate. In the *long run,* a rising price level will be accompanied by rising costs, giving producers no special incentive to supply more output. Accordingly, output will revert to its natural rate Q_N.

Classical economists use the vertical AS curve to explain also how the economy self-adjusts to temporary setbacks. If AD declines from AD$_2$ to AD$_1$ in Figure 8.12, the economy

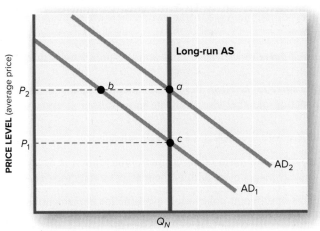

REAL OUTPUT (quantity per year)

FIGURE 8.12

The "Natural" Rate of Output

Monetarists and neoclassical theorists assert that the level of output is fixed at the natural rate Q_N by the size of the labor force, technology, and other institutional factors. As a result, fluctuations in aggregate demand affect the price level but not real output.

may move from point *a* to point *b,* leaving a lot of unsold output. As producers respond with price cuts, however, the volume of output demanded increases as the economy moves from point *b* to point *c.* At point *c,* full employment is restored. Thus, flexible prices (and wages) enable the economy to maintain the natural rate of output Q_N.

Short- vs. Long-Run Perspectives

All this may well be true. But as Keynes pointed out, it's also true that "in the long run we are all dead." How long are we willing to wait for the promised "self-adjustment"? In the Great Depression, people waited for 10 years—and still saw no self-adjustment. In 2020 people were scared that they might not live into the long run; they wanted the government to act quickly.

Whatever the long run may hold, it's in the short run that we must consume, invest, and find a job. However stable and predictable the long run might be, short-run variations in macro outcomes will determine how well we fare in any year. Moreover, *the short-run aggregate supply curve is likely to be upward-sloping,* as shown in our earlier graphs. This implies that both aggregate supply and aggregate demand influence short-run macro outcomes.

By distinguishing between short-run and long-run aggregate supply curves, competing economic theories achieve a standoff. Theories that highlight the necessity of policy intervention emphasize the importance of short-run macro outcomes. People *care* about short-run changes in job prospects and prices. If inflation or unemployment is too high, voters insist that "Washington" fix the problem—now.

Theories that emphasize the "natural" stability of the market point to the predictability of long-run outcomes. They prefer to let the economy self-adjust rather than risk government intervention that might worsen macro outcomes. Even if these theories are true, however, the duration of acceptable "short-" and "long-" run periods remains controversial.

DECISIONS FOR TOMORROW

What Ends a Recession?

The AS/AD model is a convenient summary of how the macro economy works. A market-driven economy will gravitate to an equilibrium that is compatible with the behavior of both buyers (AD) and sellers (AS). As we've observed, however, that short-run macro equilibrium may not be consistent with our economic goals. That was certainly the case in the Great Recession of 2008–2009, when the equilibrium rate of output was less than full-employment output. People expected newly elected President Obama—the new Economist in Chief—to do something about it. What *could* he do?

Policy Strategies. The beauty of the AS/AD model is that it highlights the strategic options for coping with a recession. In the AS/AD framework, there are really only *three strategy options for macro policy:*

- *Shift the aggregate demand curve to the right.* Find and use policy tools that will stimulate total spending.
- *Shift the aggregate supply curve to the right.* Find and implement policy levers that reduce the cost of production or otherwise stimulate more output at every price level.
- *Laissez faire.* Don't interfere with the market; let markets self-adjust.

The first two strategies assume some form of government intervention is needed to end a recession. The third strategy places more faith in the market's ability to self-adjust.

Policy Tools. There are a host of different policy tools available for implementing any given AS/AD strategy, as President Obama discovered.

- *Classical Laissez Faire*. The laissez-faire strategy advocated by classical economists requires no tools, of course. Classical economists count on the self-adjustment mechanisms of the market—flexible prices and wages—to bring a quick end to recessions. Falling home prices would ultimately spur more sales; declining wages would encourage more hiring. In this view, AS and AD curves "naturally" shift back into an optimal position, where full employment (Q_F) prevails.
- *Fiscal Policy*. Keynes rejected this hands-off approach. He advocated using the federal budget as a policy tool. The government can shift the AD curve to the right by spending more money. Or it can cut taxes, leaving consumers with more income to spend. These budgetary tools are the hallmark of fiscal policy. Specifically, **fiscal policy** is the use of government tax and spending powers to alter economic outcomes.
- *Monetary Policy*. The budget isn't the only tool in the interventionist toolbox. Interest rates and the money supply can also shift the AD curve. Lower interest rates encourage consumers to buy more big-ticket items like cars, homes, and appliances—purchases typically financed with loans. Businesses also take advantage of lower interest rates to buy more loan-financed plant and equipment. **Monetary policy** refers to the use of money and credit controls to alter economic outcomes.
- *Supply-Side Policy*. Fiscal and monetary tools are used to fix the AD side of the macro economy. **Supply-side policy** pursues a different strategy: It uses tools that shift the aggregate supply curve. Tax incentives that encourage more work, saving, or investment are in the supply-side toolbox. So are deregulation actions that make it easier or cheaper to supply products.
- *Trade Policy*. International trade and money flows offer yet another option for shifting aggregate supply and demand. A reduction in trade barriers makes imports cheaper and more available. This shifts the aggregate supply to the right, reducing price pressures at every output level. Reducing the international value (exchange rate) of the dollar lowers the relative price of U.S.-made goods, thereby encouraging foreigners to buy more U.S. exports. Hence, trade policy is another tool in the macroeconomic toolbox.

Taking Action. President Obama never really considered following the do-nothing-and-wait classical approach. He had been elected in November 2008 on the promise of change for the better. In his view, that meant using the available array of activist policy tools to get the economy moving again. His first major intervention was a massive fiscal policy package of increased government spending and tax cuts—the kind of policy Keynes advocated. Over the next five years, President Obama, Congress, and the Federal Reserve used additional policy tools to push the economy out of the Great Recession. Some worked; some didn't. In subsequent chapters we'll examine which tools worked, which didn't, and why.

fiscal policy: The use of government taxes and spending to alter macroeconomic outcomes.

monetary policy: The use of money and credit controls to influence macroeconomic outcomes.

supply-side policy: The use of tax incentives, (de)regulation, and other mechanisms to increase the ability and willingness to produce goods and services.

SUMMARY

- The long-term growth rate of the U.S. economy is approximately 3 percent a year. But output doesn't increase 3 percent every year. In some years real GDP grows much faster; in other years growth is slower. Sometimes GDP actually declines (recession).   **LO8-1**
- Short-run variations in GDP growth are a central focus of macroeconomics. Macro theory tries to explain the alternating periods of growth and contraction that characterize the business cycle; macro policy attempts to control the cycle.   **LO8-1**

- Classical economists thought the economy would self-adjust, eliminating the need for government intervention. Keynes said the market economy was inherently unstable, necessitating government intervention to attain full employment.   **LO8-2**
- The primary outcomes of the macro economy are output, prices, jobs, and international balances. The outcomes result from the interplay of internal market forces, external shocks, and policy levers.   **LO8-3**

- All the influences on macro outcomes are transmitted through aggregate supply or aggregate demand. Aggregate demand refers to the rates of output people are willing to purchase at various price levels. Aggregate supply is the rate of output producers are willing to supply at various price levels. **LO8-4**
- Aggregate supply and demand determine the equilibrium rate of output and prices. The economy will gravitate to that unique combination of output and price levels. **LO8-4**
- The market-driven macro equilibrium may not satisfy our employment or price goals. Macro failure occurs when the economy's equilibrium isn't optimal. **LO8-4**
- Macro equilibrium may be disturbed by changes in aggregate supply (AS) or aggregate demand (AD). Such changes are illustrated by shifts of the AS and AD curves, and they lead to a new equilibrium. **LO8-5**

- Competing economic theories try to explain the shape and shifts of the aggregate supply and demand curves, thereby explaining the business cycle. Specific theories tend to emphasize demand or supply influences. **LO8-2**
- In the long run the AS curve tends to be vertical, implying that changes in aggregate demand affect prices but not output. In the short run, however, the AS curve is sloped, making macro outcomes sensitive to both supply and demand. **LO8-4**
- Macro policy options range from laissez faire (the classical approach) to various strategies for shifting either the aggregate demand curve or the aggregate supply curve. **LO8-5**

Key Terms

macroeconomics	recession	inflation
business cycle	growth recession	market failure
laissez faire	aggregate demand (AD)	fiscal policy
law of demand	aggregate supply (AS)	monetary policy
Say's law	equilibrium (macro)	supply-side policy
real GDP	full-employment GDP	

Questions for Discussion

1. If business cycles were really inevitable, what purpose would macro policy serve? **LO8-2**
2. What events might prompt consumers to demand fewer goods at current prices? **LO8-4**
3. If equilibrium is compatible with both buyers' and sellers' intentions, how can it be undesirable? **LO8-4**
4. How did the sharp rise in the 2017–2019 stock market affect aggregate demand? **LO8-4**
5. What exactly did Say mean when he said that "supply creates its own demand"? **LO8-2**
6. What's wrong with the classical theory of self-adjustment? Why didn't sales and employment increase in 1929–1933 in response to declining prices and wages (see Figure 8.1)? **LO8-2**
7. What might have caused real GDP to decline so dramatically in (a) 1929 and (b) 1946 (see Figure 8.3)? What caused output to increase again in each case? **LO8-5**
8. How would a sudden jump in U.S. prices affect (a) imports from Mexico, (b) exports to Mexico, and (c) U.S. aggregate demand? **LO8-5**
9. Why might rising prices stimulate short-run production but have no effect on long-run production? **LO8-4**
10. President Trump sought to increase economic growth by cutting taxes and reducing regulation of production. How did these two initiatives affect the AS and AD curves? **LO8-4**

LO8-4 1. In Figure 8.7,
    (*a*) How much output is unsold at the price level P_1?
    (*b*) At what price level is all output produced sold?

LO8-3
LO8-4 2. In Figure 8.8, what price level will induce people to buy all the output produced at full employment?

LO8-4 3. Suppose you have $5,000 in savings when the price level index is 100.
    (*a*) If inflation pushes the price level up by 10 percent, what will be the real value of your savings?
    (*b*) What is the real value of your savings if the price level *declines* by 5 percent?

LO8-4 4. Use the following information to draw aggregate demand (AD) and aggregate supply (AS) curves on the following graph. Both curves are assumed to be straight lines.

Price Level	Output Demanded	Output Supplied
800	0	$800
100	$700	100

    (*a*) At what rate of real output does equilibrium occur?
    (*b*) What curve (AD or AS) would have shifted if a new equilibrium were to occur at an output level of 600 and a price level of $600?
    (*c*) What curve would have shifted if a new equilibrium were to occur at an output level of 600 and a price level of $200?

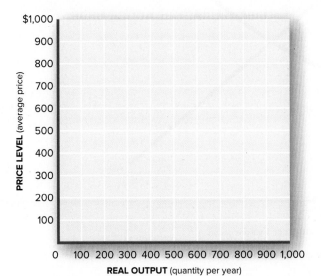

LO8-1 5. According to Front Page Economics "Sharpest Economic Decline in 26 Years,"
    (*a*) By what percentage did GDP decline in 2008?
    (*b*) At that rate, how much output would have been lost in the $14 trillion economy of 2008?
    (*c*) How much income did this represent for each of the 300 million U.S. citizens?

LO8-1 6. According to Table 8.1,
    (*a*) What was the largest percentage GDP decline in a post–Great Depression U.S. recession?
    (*b*) What was
        (*i*) The longest post–Great Depression recession?
        (*ii*) The recession that had the smallest percentage decline in real GDP post–Great Depression?

LO8-5 7. If the AS curve shifts to the left, what happens to
    (*a*) The equilibrium rate of output?
    (*b*) The equilibrium price level?

LO8-5 8. If the AD curve shifts to the left, what happens to
    (*a*) The equilibrium rate of output?
    (*b*) The equilibrium price level?

LO8-5 9. Assume that the accompanying graph depicts aggregate supply and demand conditions in an economy. Full employment occurs when $5 trillion of real output is produced.
    (*a*) What is the equilibrium rate of output?
    (*b*) How far short of full employment is the equilibrium rate of output?
    (*c*) Illustrate a shift of aggregate demand that would change the equilibrium rate of output to $5 trillion. Label the new curve AD_2.
    (*d*) What is the price level at this full-employment equilibrium?

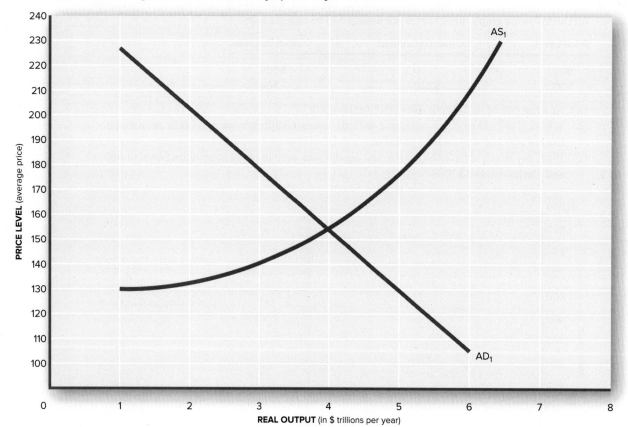

LO8-2 10. *Decisions for Tomorrow:* Graphically show an economy in a recession. What are the
    (*a*) Classical strategy options for macro policy?
    (*b*) Keynesian strategy options for macro policy?
    (*c*) Supply-side strategy options for macro policy?

LO8-5 11. *Decisions for Tomorrow:* Identify the following policies as either fiscal, monetary, supply-side or trade policy and determine whether the aggregate demand or aggregate supply curve would shift to the left or right if the policy was enacted.
    (*a*) Increasing trade barriers.
    (*b*) Tax cut for businesses that invest in new technologies.
    (*c*) Tax cuts for households.
    (*d*) Higher interest rates.
    (*e*) Increased infrastructure spending.
    (*f*) Reducing tariffs (taxes on imports) and easing import regulations.

Design Credit: Shutterstock

LEARNING OBJECTIVES

After reading this chapter, you should know

LO9-1 What the major components of aggregate demand are.

LO9-2 What the consumption function tells us.

LO9-3 The determinants of investment spending.

LO9-4 How and why AD shifts occur.

LO9-5 How and when macro failure occurs.

CHAPTER 9

Aggregate Demand

The spring of 2020 was a scary time for the U.S. economy. The coronavirus pandemic that swept across the world was forcing businesses to close. In the month of March over 10 *million* American workers lost their jobs. The automobile factories shut down, malls closed, sporting events were canceled, airplane schedules were slashed, and movie theaters and concerts were shut down. Even the beaches were closed. All but "essential" workers were ordered to stay home.

The abrupt lockdown of the economy was necessitated by a global health emergency. But it had devastating effects on the economy. With the loss of jobs came sudden and sharp declines in household incomes. People couldn't afford to continue spending as much as they had before. Millions of Americans worried that they couldn't pay monthly mortgage payments on their homes or the minimum payments on their credit cards.

The recession of 2020 was a stark reminder about economic cycles. After all, 2019 had been a very good year for the U.S. economy. At the end of 2019 the national unemployment rate was near a historic low, incomes were at an all-time high, the stock market was breaking records on the upside, and expectations for the future of the economy were overwhelmingly optimistic. No one was anticipating a recession—much less a pandemic.

Although the 2020 downturn was unique in its origins, it followed the pattern of earlier recessions. In the previous chapter we saw how an economy slips into a recession and also how it recovers. The key to both events is often the aggregate demand (AD) curve. When AD declines (shifts left), the equilibrium level of real GDP falls below the full-employment level—a recession. To escape from recession, AD must increase (shift right). To continue growing, we need still more rightward shifts of aggregate demand. Simple enough in theory. But how can we make this happen in the real world?

To answer that question, we've got to know more about the details of aggregate demand. In this and the next two chapters we delve into those details. We confront the same questions the Economist in Chief and his economic advisers have to consider:

· **What are the components of aggregate demand?**
· **What determines the level of spending for each component?**
· **Will there be enough demand to maintain full employment?**

By working through the demand side of the macro economy, we'll get a better view of what might cause business cycles and what might cure them. Later on we'll examine the aggregate supply side more closely as well.

MACRO EQUILIBRIUM

In Chapter 8 we got a bird's-eye view of how macro equilibrium is established. Producers have some notion of how much output they're willing and able to produce at various price levels. Likewise, consumers, businesses, governments, and foreign buyers have some notion of how much output they're willing and able to buy at different price levels. These forces of **aggregate demand** and **aggregate supply** confront each other in the marketplace. Eventually, sellers and buyers discover that only one price level and output combination is acceptable to *both* sides. This is the price–output combination we designate as **(macro) equilibrium.** At equilibrium, the rate of output equals the rate of spending. Producers have no reason to change production levels. In the absence of macro disturbances, the economy will gravitate toward that equilibrium.

The Desired Adjustment

Figure 9.1 illustrates again this general view of macro equilibrium. In the figure, aggregate supply (AS) and demand (AD_1) establish an equilibrium at E_1. At this particular equilibrium, the value of real output is Q_E. Notice Q_E is significantly short of the economy's full-employment potential at Q_F. Accordingly, the economy depicted in Figure 9.1 is producing below capacity and thus is saddled with excessive unemployment. This is the kind of situation the U.S. economy confronted in 2008–2009 and again in 2020.

All economists recognize that such a *short-run* macro failure is possible. We also realize that the unemployment problem depicted in Figure 9.1 would disappear if either the AD or AS curve shifted rightward. A central macro debate is over whether the curves *will* shift on their own (self-adjust). If not, the government might have to step in and do some heavy shifting.

Components of Aggregate Demand

To assess the possibilities for self-adjustment, we need to examine the nature of aggregate demand more closely. Who's buying the output of the economy? What factors influence their purchase decisions? Why aren't people buying more output?

We can best understand the nature of aggregate demand by breaking it down into its various components. *The four components of aggregate demand are*

- *Consumption (C).*
- *Investment (I).*

aggregate demand (AD): The total quantity of output (real GDP) demanded at alternative price levels in a given time period, *ceteris paribus*.

aggregate supply (AS): The total quantity of output (real GDP) producers are willing and able to supply at alternative price levels in a given time period, *ceteris paribus*.

equilibrium (macro): The combination of price level and real output that is compatible with both aggregate demand and aggregate supply.

FIGURE 9.1

Escaping a Recession

Aggregate demand (AD) might be insufficient to ensure full employment (Q_F), as illustrated by the intersection of AD_1 and the aggregate supply curve. The question is whether and how AD will increase—that is, *shift* rightward—say, to AD_2. To answer these questions, we must examine the components of aggregate demand.

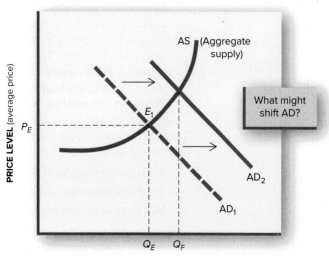

- *Government spending (G).*
- *Net exports (X − M).*

Each of these components represents a stream of spending that contributes to aggregate demand. What we want to determine is how these various spending decisions are made. We also want to know what factors might *change* the level of spending, thereby *shifting* aggregate demand.

CONSUMPTION

Consider first the largest component of aggregate demand, namely, **consumption.** Consumption refers to expenditures by households (consumers) on final goods and services. As we observed in Chapter 5, *consumer expenditures account for more than two-thirds of total spending.* Hence, whatever factors alter consumer behavior are sure to have an impact on aggregate demand.

consumption: Expenditure by consumers on final goods and services.

Income and Consumption

The aggregate demand curve tells us that consumers will buy more output at lower price levels with a *given* amount of income. But what if *incomes* themselves were to change? If incomes were to increase, consumers would have more money to spend at any given price level. This could cause a rightward *shift* of the AD curve, exactly the kind of move a recessionary economy (e.g., Figure 9.1) needs.

As far as the British economist John Maynard Keynes was concerned, this was a no-brainer. Experience shows that *consumers tend to spend most of whatever income they have.* This is apparent in Figure 9.2: Year after year, consumer spending has risen in tandem with income.

Disposable income is the key concept here. As noted in Chapter 5, **disposable income** is the amount of income consumers actually take home after all taxes have been paid, transfers

disposable income (DI): After-tax income of households; personal income less personal taxes.

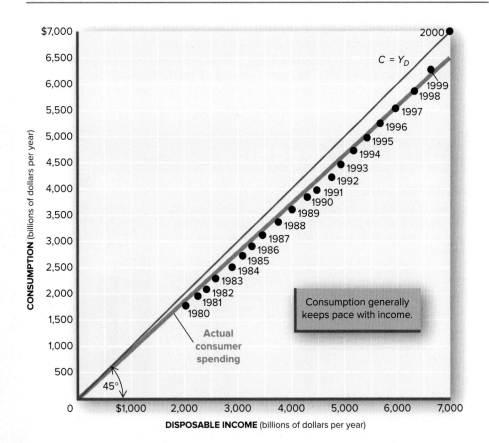

FIGURE 9.2

U.S. Consumption and Income

The points on the graph indicate the actual rates of U.S. disposable income and consumption for the years 1980–2000. By connecting these dots, we can approximate the long-term consumption function. Clearly, consumption rises with income. Indeed, consumers spend almost every extra dollar they receive.

(e.g., Social Security benefits) have been received, and depreciation charges and retained earnings have been subtracted (see Table 5.6).

What will consumers do with their disposable income? There are only two choices: They can either spend their disposable income on consumption or save (not spend) it. At this point we don't care what form household **saving** might take (e.g., cash under the mattress, bank deposits, stock purchases); all we want to do is distinguish that share of disposable income spent on consumer goods and services from the remainder that is *not* spent. By definition, then, *all disposable income is either consumed (spent) or saved (not spent);* that is,

$$\text{Disposable income} = \text{Consumption} + \text{Saving}$$
$$(Y_D) \qquad\qquad (C) \qquad\qquad (S)$$

saving: That part of disposable income not spent on current consumption; disposable income less consumption.

Consumption vs. Saving

To figure out how much consumer spending will actually occur, we need to know what fraction of disposable income will be consumed and how much will be saved. There are two ways of looking at this decision: first in terms of *averages,* and then in terms of *marginal* decisions.

APC. The proportion of *total* disposable income spent on consumer goods and services is referred to as the **average propensity to consume (APC).** To determine the APC, we simply observe how much consumers spend in a given time period out of that period's disposable income. In 2019, for example, the disposable income of U.S. households amounted to more than $16 trillion. Out of this amount, consumers spent nearly every available dollar, saving a measly $1.3 trillion. Accordingly, we may calculate the average propensity to consume as

average propensity to consume (APC): Total consumption in a given period divided by total disposable income.

$$\text{APC} = \frac{\text{Total consumption}}{\text{Total disposable income}} = \frac{C}{Y_D}$$

For 2019 this works out to

$$\text{APC} = \frac{\$15,122 \text{ billion}}{\$16,420 \text{ billion}} = 0.92$$

In other words, U.S. consumers spent just about every nickel they received in 2019. Specifically, consumers spent, on average, 92 cents out of every dollar of income. Only 8 cents out of every disposable dollar was saved. (How much do *you* save?)

The relatively high APC in the United States distinguishes our consumer-oriented economy. In some years, the U.S. APC has even *exceeded* 1.0 on occasion, forcing U.S. households to finance some of their consumption with credit or past savings (see Front Page Economics "Overspending").

FRONT PAGE ECONOMICS

OVERSPENDING

Four out of ten Americans admit to overspending—spending more money than they earn. Young adults are particularly prone to overspending. Seniors are a bit more cautious with their wallets.

Source: Lutheran Brotherhood/Yankelovich Partners Survey of 1,010 Adults in January 2001.

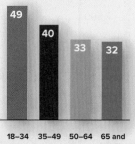

PERCENTAGE OF ADULTS WHO SAY THEY SPEND MORE THAN THEY EARN

CRITICAL ANALYSIS: When consumer spending exceeds disposable income, consumer **saving** is negative; households are *dissaving.* Dissaving is financed with credit or prior savings.

The Marginal Propensity to Consume

If consumers *always* spent 92 cents out of every income dollar, predicting consumer spending would be an easy task. But life is never that simple; consumer behavior changes from time to time. This led Keynes to develop a second measure of consumption behavior called the *marginal* propensity to consume. The **marginal propensity to consume (MPC)** tells us how much consumer expenditure will *change* in response to *changes* in disposable income. With the delta symbol, Δ, representing "change in," MPC can be written as

$$\text{MPC} = \frac{\textbf{Change in consumption}}{\textbf{Change in disposable income}} = \frac{\Delta C}{\Delta Y_D}$$

To calculate the marginal propensity to consume, we could ask how consumer spending in 2019 was affected by the *last* dollar of disposable income. That is, how did consumer spending change when disposable income increased from \$16,419,999,999,999 to \$16,420,000,000,000?

Suppose consumer spending increased by only 80 cents when this last \$1.00 was received. In that case, we'd calculate the *marginal* propensity to consume as

$$\text{MPC} = \frac{\Delta C}{\Delta Y_D} = \frac{\$0.80}{\$1.00} = 0.8$$

Notice that the MPC in this particular case (0.8) is lower than the APC (0.92). This is important. Suppose we had incorrectly assumed that consumers would always spend \$0.92 of every dollar's income. Then we'd have expected the rate of consumer spending to rise by 92 cents as the last dollar was received. In fact, however, the rate of spending increased by only 80 cents. In other words, consumers responded to an *increase* in their income differently than past averages implied.

No one would be upset if our failure to distinguish the APC from the MPC led to an error of only 12 cents in forecasts of consumer spending. After all, the rate of consumer spending in the U.S. economy now exceeds \$15 *trillion* per year! But those same trillion-dollar dimensions make the accuracy of the MPC that much more important. Annual *changes* in disposable income entail hundreds of billions of dollars. When we start playing with those sums—the actual focus of economic policymakers—the distinction between APC and MPC is significant.

The Marginal Propensity to Save

Once we know how much of their income consumers will spend, we also know how much they'll save. Remember that all *disposable income is, by definition, either consumed (spent on consumption) or saved.* Saving is just whatever income is left over after consumption expenditures. Accordingly, if the MPC is 0.80, then 20 cents of each additional dollar are being saved and 80 cents are being spent (see Figure 9.3). The **marginal propensity to save (MPS)**—the fraction of each additional dollar saved (that is, *not* spent)—is simply

$$\text{MPS} = 1 - \text{MPC}$$

marginal propensity to consume (MPC): The fraction of each additional (marginal) dollar of disposable income spent on consumption; the change in consumption divided by the change in disposable income.

marginal propensity to save (MPS): The fraction of each additional (marginal) dollar of disposable income not spent on consumption; 1 − MPC.

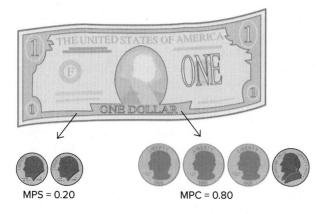

MPS = 0.20   MPC = 0.80

FIGURE 9.3
MPC and MPS

The marginal propensity to consume (MPC) tells us what portion of an extra dollar of income will be spent. The remaining portion is, by definition, "saved." The MPC and MPS help us predict consumer behavior.

TABLE 9.1
Average and Marginal Propensities to Consume

MPC. The marginal propensity to consume (MPC) is the *change* in consumption that accompanies a *change* in disposable income; that is,

$$MPC = \frac{\Delta C}{\Delta Y_D}$$

MPS. The marginal propensity to save (MPS) is the fraction of each additional (marginal) dollar of disposable income *not* spent—that is, saved. This is summarized as

$$MPS = \frac{\Delta S}{\Delta Y_D}$$

MPS equals 1 − MPC because every additional dollar is either spent (consumed) or not spent (saved).

APC. The average propensity to consume is the proportion of *total* disposable income that's spent on consumption. It is computed as

$$APC = \frac{C}{Y_D}$$

APS. The average propensity to save is $\frac{S}{Y_D}$ and must equal 1 − APC.

As Table 9.1 illustrates, if we know how much of their income consumers spend, we also know how much of it they save.

THE CONSUMPTION FUNCTION

The MPC, MPS, APC, and APS are simply statistical measures of observed consumer behavior. They tell us what consumers are doing in product markets. That is useful, but what we really want to know is what drives these measures. If we know, then we'll be in a position to *predict* rather than just *observe* consumer behavior. This ability would be of immense value in anticipating and controlling short-run business cycles.

Autonomous Consumption

Keynes had several ideas about the determinants of consumption. Although he observed that consumer spending and income were highly correlated (Figure 9.2), he knew consumption wasn't *completely* determined by current income. In extreme cases, this is evident. People who have no income in a given period continue to consume goods and services. They finance their purchases by dipping into their savings accounts (past income) or using credit (future income) instead of spending current income. We also observe that people's spending sometimes changes even when income doesn't, suggesting that income isn't the only determinant of consumption. Other, *non*income determinants of consumption include

What percent of their incomes will these shoppers spend?

Ariel Skelley/Getty Images

- *Expectations:* People who anticipate a pay raise, a tax refund, or a birthday check often start spending that money even before they get it. Conversely, workers who anticipate being laid off tend to save more and spend less than usual. Hence, expectations may alter consumer spending before income itself changes. This was painfully evident in early 2020 when workers feared not only for their health but also for their jobs. They were in no mood to buy new cars, exotic vacations, or anything else.
- *Wealth effects:* The amount of wealth an individual owns also affects a person's ability and willingness to consume. A homeowner may take out a home equity loan to buy a flat-screen TV, a vacation, or a new car. In this case, consumer spending is being financed by wealth, not current income. *Changes* in wealth will also change consumer behavior. When the stock market rises, stockholders respond by saving less and spending more of their current income. This **wealth effect** was particularly evident in the late 1990s, when a persistent rise in the stock market helped fuel a consumption spree (and a negative savings rate). When the stock market plunged by 50 percent in 2008–2009, consumers cut back their spending sharply. The same thing happened in early 2020.

wealth effect: A change in consumer spending caused by a change in the value of owned assets.

Changes in housing prices have a similar effect. A five-year surge in housing prices made consumers feel rich in 2002–2006. Many homeowners tapped into those higher prices by borrowing money with home-equity loans. They used those loans to increase their consumption. When housing prices started declining in 2007, this source of consumer finance dried up. As we've already noted, this negative wealth effect contributed to the 2008–2009 recession.

- *Credit:* The availability of credit allows people to spend more than their current income. Here again, changes in credit availability or cost (interest rates) may alter consumer behavior. When banks curtailed credit in 2008, consumers had to stop buying cars and homes. When interest rates later fell, auto sales rose again.
- *Taxes:* Taxes are the wedge between total income and disposable income. The tax cuts enacted in 2017 put more income into consumer hands. Tax rebates in early 2008 had the same effect: These tax reductions stimulated more aggregate demand at existing price levels. Were income taxes to go up, disposable incomes and consumer spending would decline.

Income-Dependent Consumption

In recognition of these many determinants of consumption, Keynes distinguished between two kinds of consumer spending: (1) spending *not* influenced by current income and (2) spending that *is* determined by current income. This simple categorization is summarized as

$$\text{Total consumption} = \frac{\text{Autonomous}}{\text{consumption}} + \text{Income-dependent consumption}$$

where **autonomous consumption** refers to that portion of consumption spending that is independent of current income. The level of autonomous spending depends instead on expectations, wealth, credit, taxes, and other nonincome influences.

These various determinants of consumption are summarized in an equation called the **consumption function,** which is written as

$$C = a + bY_D$$

where C = current consumption

    a = autonomous consumption

    b = marginal propensity to consume

    Y_D = disposable income

At first blush, the consumption function is just a mathematical summary of consumer behavior. It has important *predictive* power, however. *The consumption function tells us*

- *How much consumption will be included in aggregate demand at the prevailing price level.*
- *How the consumption component of AD will change (shift) when incomes change.*

One Consumer's Behavior

To see how the consumption function works, consider the plight of Justin, a college freshman who has no income. How much will Justin spend? Obviously he must spend *something;* otherwise, he'll starve. At a very low rate of income—in this case, zero—consumer spending depends less on current income than on basic survival needs, past savings, and credit. The *a* in the consumption function expresses this autonomous consumption; let's assume it's $50 per week. Thus, the weekly rate of consumption expenditure in this case is

$$C = \$50 + bY_D$$

Notice again that Justin has no income. So how is he able to spend $50 a week? Taking money out of his bank account (past savings), perhaps. Or using his credit card—hoping to be able to pay it off later.

Now suppose that Justin finds a job and begins earning $100 per week. Will his spending be affected? For sure. The $50 per week he'd been spending didn't buy much. Now that he's earning

autonomous consumption: Consumer spending not dependent on current income.

consumption function: A mathematical relationship indicating the rate of desired consumer spending at various income levels.

a little income, Justin will want to improve his lifestyle. That is, *we expect consumption to rise with income.* The marginal propensity to consume tells us how fast spending will rise.

Suppose Justin responds to the newfound income by increasing his consumption from $50 per week to $125. The *change* in his consumption is therefore $75. Dividing this *change* in his consumption ($75) by the *change* in income ($100) reveals that his marginal propensity to consume is 0.75.

Predictive Power. Once we know the level of autonomous consumption ($50 per week) and the marginal propensity to consume (0.75), we can predict consumer behavior with uncanny accuracy. In this case, Justin's consumption function is

$$C = \$50 + 0.75Y_D$$

With these numerical values we can advance from simple observation (what he's spending now) to prediction (what he'll spend at different income levels). Figure 9.4 summarizes this predictive power.

We've already noted that Justin will spend $125 per week when his income is only $100. This observation is summarized in row *B* of the table in Figure 9.4 and by point *B* on the graph.

FIGURE 9.4

A Consumption Function

The rate of consumer spending (*C*) depends on autonomous consumption and disposable income (Y_D). The marginal propensity to consume indicates how much consumption will *increase* with each *added* dollar of income. In this case, when disposable income rises from $100 to $200, consumption increases by $75 (from point *B* to point *C*). The MPC = 0.75.

The consumption function can be expressed in an equation, a table, or a graph. Point *B* on the graph, for example, corresponds to row *B* in the table. Both indicate that this consumer desires to spend $125 per week when his income is $100 per week. The difference between income and consumption equals (dis)saving.

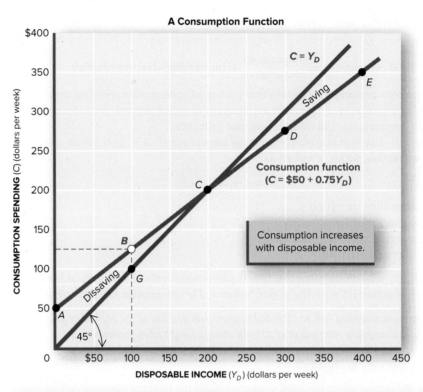

A Consumption Function

		Consumption ($C = \$50 + 0.75Y_D$)		
	Disposable Income (Y_D)	Autonomous Consumption +	Income-Dependent Consumption =	Total Consumption
A	$ 0	$50	$ 0	$ 50
B	100	50	75	125
C	200	50	150	200
D	300	50	225	275
E	400	50	300	350
F	500	50	375	425

Notice that his spending exceeds his income by $25 at this point. The other $25 is still being begged, borrowed, or withdrawn from savings. Without peering further into Justin's personal finances, we simply say that he's **dissaving** $25 per week. *Dissaving occurs whenever current consumption exceeds current income.* As Front Page Economics "Overspending" revealed, dissaving is common in the United States, especially among younger people who are "livin' large."

If Justin's income continues to rise, he'll stop dissaving at some point. Perhaps he'll even start saving enough to pay back all the people who have sustained him through these difficult months. Figure 9.4 shows just how and when this will occur.

The 45-Degree Line. The green line in Figure 9.4, with a 45-degree angle, represents all points where consumption and income are exactly equal ($C = Y_D$). Recall that Justin currently has an income of $100 per week. By moving up from the horizontal axis at $Y_D = \$100$, we see all his consumption choices. Were he to spend exactly $100 on consumption, he'd end up on the 45-degree line at point G. But we already know he doesn't stop there. Instead he proceeds further to point B. At point B the consumption function lies *above* the 45-degree line, so Justin's spending exceeds his income; dissaving is occurring.

Observe, however, what happens when his disposable income rises to $200 per week (row C in the table in Figure 9.4). The upward slope of the consumption function (see graph) tells us that consumption spending will rise with income. In fact, *the slope of the consumption function equals the marginal propensity to consume.* In this case, we see that when income increases from $100 to $200, consumption rises from $125 (point B) to $200 (point C). Thus, the *change* in consumption ($75) equals three-fourths of the *change* in income. The MPC is still 0.75.

Point C has further significance. At an income of $200 per week Justin is no longer dissaving. At point C his spending exactly equals his income. As a result, he is neither saving nor dissaving; he is breaking even. That is, disposable income equals consumption, so saving equals zero. Notice that point C lies *on* the 45-degree line, where current consumption equals current income.

What would happen to spending if income increased still further? According to Figure 9.4, Justin will start *saving* once income exceeds $200 per week. To the right of point C, the consumption function always lies below the 45-degree line. If spending is less than income, saving must be positive.

The Aggregate Consumption Function

Repeated studies of consumers suggest that there's nothing remarkable about Justin. The consumption function we've constructed for him can be used to depict all consumers simply by changing the numbers involved. Instead of dealing in hundreds of dollars per week, we now play with trillions of dollars per year. But the basic relationship is the same. As we observed earlier in Figure 9.2, we can predict consumer spending if we know how much

FRONT PAGE ECONOMICS

DISPOSABLE INCOME AND OUTLAYS: FEBRUARY 2020

Disposable income increased $89 billion, or 0.5 percent, in February, according to the Bureau of Economic Analysis. Personal spending increased $28 billion.

(in $ billions)	January 2020	February 2020
Disposable income..................	16,765	16,854
Personal outlays.....................	15,441	15,469
Personal savings....................	1,324	1,385

Source: U.S. Bureau of Economic Analysis.

CRITICAL ANALYSIS: When household incomes increase, consumer spending increases as well. The **marginal propensity to consume** summarizes this relationship.

dissaving: Consumption expenditure in excess of disposable income; a negative saving flow.

income consumers have. That's why there are no surprises in Front Page Economics "Disposable Income and Outlays: February 2020," which confirms that when disposable income increased in February 2020, people increased both their consumption spending and their saving. (What was the MPC? The MPS?)

Shifts of the Consumption Function

Although the consumption function is a handy device for predicting consumer behavior, it's not infallible. People change their behavior. Neither autonomous consumption (the a in the consumption function) nor the marginal propensity to consume (the b in $C = a + bY_D$) is set in stone. Whenever one of these parameters changes, the entire consumption function moves. *A change in "a"* shifts *the consumption function up or down; a change in "b"* alters the slope *of the function.*

Consider first the value for a. We know that autonomous consumption depends on wealth, credit, expectations, taxes, and price levels. If any of these nonincome determinants changes, the value of the a in the consumption function will change as well.

The plunge in consumer confidence that occurred in March 2020 illustrates how consumer behavior can change abruptly. As Front Page Economics "Consumer Confidence Falls Abruptly" relates, consumer confidence declined sharply in March 2020 after months of steady increases. In March, fewer than one out of five consumers felt the economy would improve over the following six months. With such dismal expectations, they became more cautious about spending their income. That caution caused autonomous consumption to decline from a_1 to a_2 in Figure 9.5, *shifting* the consumer function downward.

FRONT PAGE ECONOMICS

NEWS

CONSUMER CONFIDENCE FALLS ABRUPTLY

The Conference Board reported yesterday that consumer confidence has taken a sharp turn for the worse. The Board's closely watched Consumer Confidence Index fell from 132.6 (1985 = 100) in February to 120.0 in March. The confidence decline was attributed to the rapid spread of COVID-19 cases, the surge in unemployment, and the extreme volatility of financial markets. Expectations for the future also declined, with only 18.2 percent of consumers expecting the economy to improve over the next six months. The extent of the drop in confidence portends a severe contraction in the economy in the coming months.

Source: Media reports, March 31, 2020.

CRITICAL ANALYSIS: When consumer confidence declines, **autonomous spending** drops and the consumption function shifts downward (as in Figure 9.5). This causes a leftward shift of the AD curve (as in Figure 9.6).

FIGURE 9.5

A Shift in the Consumption Function

Consumers' willingness to spend current income is affected by their confidence in the future. If consumers become more worried or pessimistic, autonomous consumption may decrease from a_1 to a_2. This change will shift the entire consumption function downward.

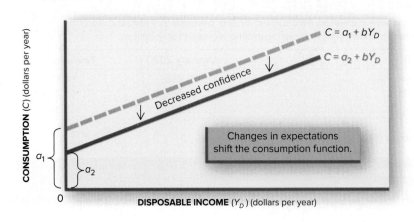

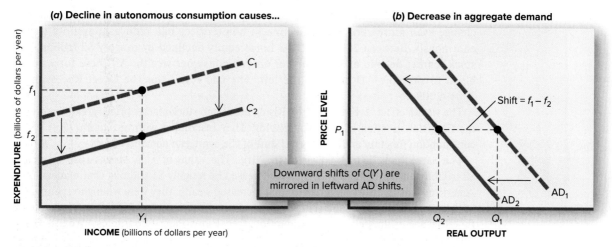

FIGURE 9.6

AD Effects of Consumption Shifts

A downward shift of the consumption function implies that households want to spend less of their income. Here, consumption at the income level Y_1 decreases from f_1 to f_2. This decreased expenditure is reflected in a leftward shift of the aggregate demand curve. At the initial price level P_1, consumers demanded Q_1 output. At that same price level, consumers now demand less output, $Q_2 = [Q_1 - (f_1 - f_2)]$.

Shifts of Aggregate Demand. Shifts of the consumption function are reflected in shifts of the aggregate demand curve. Consider again the March 2020 downward shift of the consumption function. A decrease in consumer spending at any given income level implies a decrease in aggregate demand as well. Recall that the aggregate demand curve depicts how much real output will be demanded at various price levels, *with income held constant.* When the consumption function shifts downward, households spend less of their income. Hence, less real output is demanded at any given price level. To summarize,

- *A downward shift of the consumption function implies a leftward shift of the aggregate demand curve.*
- *An upward shift of the consumption function implies an increase (a rightward shift) in aggregate demand.*

These relationships are illustrated in Figure 9.6.

Notice in the graph on the left how the downward shift of the consumption function reduces consumer spending from f_1 to f_2 at the unchanged income Y_1. That decrease in consumption $(f_1 - f_2)$ is reflected in an equivalent decline in aggregate demand, as illustrated by the leftward shift of the AD curve in the graph on the right.

AD Shift Factors

Keep in mind what we're doing here. Our goal is to predict consumer spending. We want to know how much consumer spending will contribute to AD at any given price level. We get that information from the consumption function. That information helps us position the AD curve correctly. Then we want to know what might cause the AD curve to *shift*. We now know that *the AD curve will shift if consumer incomes change, if autonomous consumption changes,* or if the MPC changes. Hence, *the AD curve will shift in response to*

- *Changes in income.*
- *Changes in expectations* (consumer confidence).
- *Changes in wealth.*
- *Changes in credit conditions.*
- *Changes in tax policy.*

As we've seen, a recession can change incomes quickly. Consumer confidence can change even more abruptly. A decline in home prices can reduce household wealth enormously. Between 2006 and 2008 home equity declined by roughly $2 trillion. The stock market decline of 2008 further eroded consumer wealth. All these forces combined to shift the AD curve to the left. The end result was the Great Recession of 2008–2009.

The wealth effect reversed in 2014. Rising home and stock-market prices greatly improved the financial situation of U.S. households. They responded with an *upward* shift of the consumption function and a *rightward* shift of the aggregate demand curve.

The same thing happened again in 2019. The value of U.S. stocks rose by nearly $8 trillion and the value of U.S. homes increased by roughly $1 trillion. That made a lot of American consumers wealthier. With that increased wealth, they were willing to spend more of their income on goods and services. That resulted in an *upward* shift of the consumption function and ultimately more production (see Front Page Economics "Wealth Effect Boosts Spending").

FRONT PAGE ECONOMICS

WEALTH EFFECT BOOSTS SPENDING

The stock market surge of 2019 was a boon to consumption. According to estimates by Moody's Analytics, every dollar of increased consumer wealth increases consumer spending by 4.5 cents. The stock market surge of $8 trillion in 2019 sent consumers on a spending spree. The greatest beneficiaries were travel spending and furniture and appliance purchases. As Mark Zandi, Moody's chief economist, observed, "the U.S. stock market has been the jet fuel for the economy."

Source: News reports of January 2020.

CRITICAL ANALYSIS: Consumer spending depends not only on current income but also on household wealth. Rising stock-market and housing values generate a wealth effect that shifts AD to the right.

Unfortunately, the consumption spree fueled by rising wealth in 2019 ended abruptly in early 2020. The coronavirus pandemic that swept the globe led to drastic changes in market behavior that depressed consumer sentiment, incomes, and wealth. In March 2020 the U.S. stock market lost all of its 2019 gains, reversing the wealth effect and curtailing consumer spending.

Shifts and Cycles

Shifts of the AD curve can be a good thing (as in 2019) or a bad thing (as in 2020), depending on the state of the economy. They can also cause macro instability, especially if they alternately expand and contract, giving rise to short-run business cycles.

What we've observed here is that those aggregate demand shifts may originate in consumer behavior. Changes in consumer confidence, in wealth, or in credit conditions alter the rate of consumer spending. If consumer spending increases abruptly, demand-pull inflation may follow. If consumer spending slows abruptly, a recession may occur.

Knowing that consumer behavior *might* cause macro problems is a bit worrisome. But it's also a source of policy power. What if we *want* AD to increase in order to achieve full employment? Our knowledge of consumer-based AD shift factors gives us huge clues about which macro policy tools to look for.

INVESTMENT

Consumption is only one of four AD components. To determine where AD is and whether it might shift, we need to examine the other components of spending as well.

Determinants of Investment

As we observed in Chapter 5, investment spending accounts for roughly 15 percent of total output. That spending includes not only expenditures on new plant, equipment, and business software (all referred to as *fixed investment*) but also spending on inventories (called *inventory investment*). Residential construction is also counted in investment statistics because houses and apartment buildings continue to produce housing services for decades. All these forms of **investment** represent a demand for output; they are part of aggregate demand.

Expectations. Expectations play a critical role in investment decisions. No firm wants to purchase a new plant or equipment unless it is convinced people will later buy the output produced by that plant and that equipment. Nor do producers want to accumulate inventories of goods unless they expect consumers to eventually buy them. Thus, *favorable expectations of future sales are a necessary condition for investment spending.*

Interest Rates. A second determinant of investment spending is the rate of interest. Business firms typically borrow money to purchase plants and equipment. The higher the rate of interest, the costlier it is to invest. Accordingly, *we anticipate a lower rate of investment spending when interest rates are high, and more investment at lower rates,* ceteris paribus.

Technology and Innovation. A third determinant of investment is changes in technology and innovation. When scientists learned how to miniaturize electronic circuitry, an entire new industry of electronic calculators, watches, and other goods sprang to life. In this case, the demand for investment goods shifted to the right as a result of improved miniaturized circuits and imaginative innovation (the use of the new technology in pocket calculators). More recently, technological advances and cost reductions in cloud infrastructure have stimulated an investment spree in data storage centers, mobile devices, and fiber optic networks.

The Investment Function. The curve I_1 in Figure 9.7 depicts the general shape of the investment function. To find the rate of investment spending in this figure, we first have to know the rate of interest. At an interest rate of 8 percent, for example, we expect to see $150 billion of investment (point A in Figure 9.7). At 6 percent interest, we'd expect $300 billion of investment (point B).

investment: Expenditures on (production of) new plants, equipment, and structures (capital) in a given time period, plus changes in business inventories.

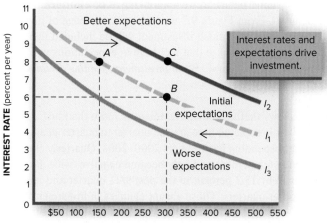

PLANNED INVESTMENT SPENDING (billions of dollars per year)

FIGURE 9.7

Investment Demand

The rate of desired investment depends on expectations, the rate of interest, and innovation. A *change* in expectations will *shift* the investment demand curve. A change in the rate of interest will lead to *movements* along the existing investment demand curve.

In this case, an increase in investment beyond the initial $150 billion per year (point *A*) may be triggered by lower interest rates (point *B*) or improved expectations (point *C*).

Shifts of Investment

As was the case with consumer spending, predicting investment spending isn't quite as easy as it first appears. Any specific investment function (like I_2 in Figure 9.7) is based on a specific set of investor expectations about future sales and profits. Those expectations can change, however.

Altered Expectations. Business expectations are essentially a question of confidence in future sales. An upsurge in current consumer spending could raise investor expectations for future sales, shifting the investment function rightward (to I_2). New business software might induce a similar response. New business tax breaks might have the same effect. If any of these things happened, businesses would be more eager to invest. They'd borrow more money at any given interest rate (e.g., point C in Figure 9.7) and use it to buy more plants, equipment, and inventory.

Business expectations could worsen as well. Imagine you were the CEO of a company contemplating a major expansion. Then you read a story about plunging consumer confidence, as in Front Page Economics "Consumer Confidence Falls Abruptly." Would you rethink your plans? Probably. That's what U.S. businesses did in early 2020 (see Front Page Economics "Factory Orders Hit 11-Year Low"). When *business* expectations worsen, investments get postponed or canceled. Suddenly there's less investment spending at any given interest rate. This investment shift is illustrated by the curve I_3 in Figure 9.7.

FRONT PAGE ECONOMICS

FACTORY ORDERS HIT 11-YEAR LOW

The Institute of Supply Management reported that manufacturing activity declined in March. Even more alarming is the drop in new orders for manufacturing equipment. The ISM's subindex for new orders fell from 49.8 in February to 42.2 in March, the lowest level since March of 2009. The drop in new orders was attributed to the COVID-19 pandemic that has shut down consumer demand, brought the transportation industry screeching to a near halt, and shuttered businesses across the country.

Source: Media reports of April 1–2, 2020.

CRITICAL ANALYSIS: Business investment is based more on expected future sales than on current sales and income. When **expectations** for future sales growth diminish, investment spending on plants, equipment, and inventory drops.

AD Shifts. As was the case with consumer behavior, we are looking at investor behavior to help us understand aggregate demand. From Figure 9.7 we see that knowledge of investor expectations and interest rates will tell us how much investment will be included in aggregate demand at the current price level. We also see that a change in expectations will alter investment behavior and thereby *shift* the AD curve. ***When investment spending declines, the aggregate demand curve shifts to the left.***

Empirical Instability. Figure 9.8 shows that unstable investment is more than just a theoretical threat to macro stability. What is depicted here are the quarter-to-quarter changes in both consumer spending and investor spending for the years 2000–2008. Quarterly changes in *consumer* spending never exceeded 6.5 percent and only became negative twice. By contrast, *investment* spending plummeted by 13.3 percent in the post-9/11 quarter and jumped by more than 14 percent in three other quarters. Those abrupt changes in investment (and related AD shifts) were a major cause of the 2001 recession as well as the Great Recession of 2008–2009.

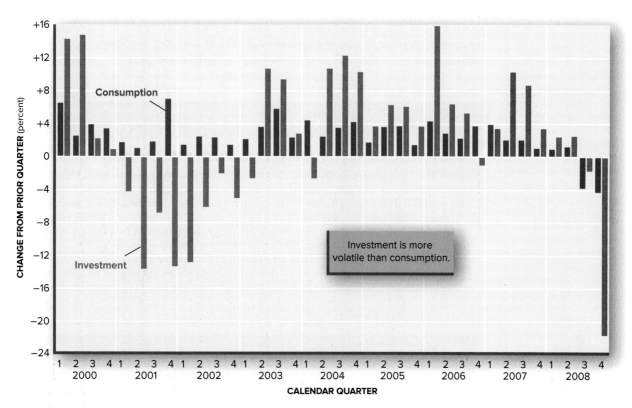

FIGURE 9.8

Volatile Investment Spending

Investment spending fluctuates more than consumption. Shown here are the quarter-to-quarter changes in the real rate of spending for fixed investment (excluding residential construction and inventory changes) and total consumption. Notice the sharp drops in investment spending just prior to the March 2001 recession and the plunge in investment that occurred in 2008. Consumption spending is far less volatile.

Source: *U.S. Bureau of Economic Analysis* (quarterly data seasonally adjusted).

GOVERNMENT AND NET EXPORT SPENDING

The apparent volatility of investment spending heightens rather than soothes anxiety about short-run macro instability. Together, consumption and investment account for more than 80 percent of total output. As we have seen, the investment component of aggregate demand can be both uncertain and unstable. The consumption component of aggregate demand may shift abruptly as well. Such shifts can sow the seeds of macro failure. Will the other components of aggregate demand improve the odds of macro success? What determines the level of government and net export spending? How stable are they?

Government Spending

At present, the government sector (federal, state, and local) spends more than $4 trillion on goods and services, all of which is part of aggregate demand (unlike income transfers, which are not).

Pro-cyclical State/Local Spending. As we observed in Chapter 5, about two-thirds of all government spending occurs at the state and local levels. That nonfederal spending is limited by tax receipts because state and local governments can't deficit-spend (borrow). As a consequence, state and local spending is slightly pro-cyclical, with expenditure rising as the economy (and tax receipts) expands and declining when the economy (and tax receipts) slumps. (See Front Page Economics "State/Local Belt Tightening Hurts Economy.") This doesn't augur well for macro stability, much less "self-adjustment." *If consumption and investment spending decline, the subsequent decline in state and local government spending will aggravate rather than offset the leftward shift of the AD curve.*

FRONT PAGE ECONOMICS

STATE/LOCAL BELT TIGHTENING HURTS ECONOMY

State and local governments have cut spending at the worst possible time. They had no choice: State and local governments can't finance their expenditures with debt; their spending is limited by tax receipts. And those receipts nosedived when the economy plunged into recession. State sales tax revenues fell by 17 percent in 2009 and income tax receipts fell by 27 percent. Falling home prices cut deeply into the property tax base that cities and counties depend on. So, they had no choice but to cut spending and lay off workers.

State and local governments laid off nearly 600,000 workers from 2008 through 2011. Thirty-four states cut spending on K–12 education, 43 states cut college budgets, and 31 reduced spending on health programs. All these cutbacks deepened the economy's downturn.

Source: Brookings Institution.

CRITICAL ANALYSIS: A recession reduces tax revenues, forcing state and local governments to cut spending. This **pro-cyclical** effect deepens a recession.

Countercyclical Federal Spending. Federal spending on goods and services isn't so constrained by tax receipts. Uncle Sam can *borrow* money, thereby allowing federal spending to exceed tax receipts. In fact, the federal government typically operates "in the red," with large annual budget deficits. This gives the federal government a unique *counter*cyclical power. If private sector spending and incomes decline, federal tax revenues will fall in response. Unlike state and local governments, however, the federal government can *increase* its spending despite declining tax revenues. In other words, Uncle Sam can help reverse AD shifts by changing its own spending. This is exactly the kind of government action that Keynes advocated and President Obama pursued in 2009–2011. We will examine its potential to stabilize the economy more closely in Chapter 11.

Net Exports

The fourth and final source of aggregate demand is net exports. Our gross exports depend on the spending behavior of foreign consumers and businesses. If foreign consumers and investors behave like Americans, their demand for U.S. products will be subject to changes in *their* income, expectations, wealth, and other factors. In the Asian currency crisis of 1997–1999, this was alarmingly evident: Once incomes in Asia began falling, U.S. exports to Asia of rice, corn, lumber, computers, and other goods and services fell sharply. So did the number of Asian students applying to U.S. colleges (a demand for U.S.-produced educational services). This decline in export spending represented a leftward shift of U.S. aggregate demand. Strong GDP growth in India and China has had the opposite effect in recent years.

Imports, too, can be unstable, and for the same reasons. Most U.S. imports are consumer goods and services. Imports, therefore, get caught up in the ebb and flow of consumer spending. When consumer confidence slips or the stock market dips, import spending declines along with the rest of consumption (and investment). As a consequence, *net* exports can be both uncertain and unstable, creating further shifts of aggregate demand.

The AD Curve Revisited

Figure 9.9 illustrates how the four components of spending come together to determine aggregate demand. From the consumption function, we determine how much output

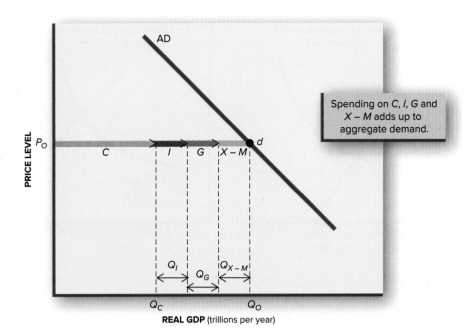

FIGURE 9.9

Building an AD Curve

The quantity of output demanded at the prevailing price level originates in the spending decisions of consumers (*C*), investors (*I*), government (*G*), and net exports (*X − M*). By adding up the intended spending of these market participants, we can see how much output (Q_O) will be demanded at the current price level (P_O). Thus, point *d* is the first building block in the construction of the AD curve.

The slope of the AD curve above and below point *d* is based on the responses of real balances, interest rates, and foreign trade to changing price levels (see Chapter 8).

consumers will demand at the prevailing price level P_O. In this case, they demand Q_C of output, as illustrated on the horizontal axis of the graph.

Once we know how much output consumers want to purchase (*QG*), we add investment demand Q_I, as revealed in Figure 9.7 and investor surveys. Local, state, and federal budgets will tell us how much output (*QG*) the government intends to buy. Net exports complete the computation. When we add them all up, we see that output Q_O will be demanded at the prevailing price level P_O. The result of this calculation is illustrated by point *d* on the aggregate demand curve: Market participants will demand the quantity Q_O at the price level of P_O.

We now know that the AD curve must go through point *d*. But how much output will be demanded at other price levels? The rest of the AD curve reflects how the quantity of output demanded will change if the price level rises or falls (i.e., the real balances, interest rate, and foreign trade effects discussed in Chapter 8).

MACRO FAILURE

In principle, the construction of the AD curve is simple. In practice, it requires an enormous amount of information about the intentions and behavior of market participants. Let's assume for the moment, however, that we have all that information and can therefore accurately depict the AD curve. What then?

Once we know the shape and position of the AD curve, we can put it together with the AS curve and locate macro equilibrium. Here's where our macro problems may emerge. As we noted earlier, *there are two chief concerns about macro equilibrium:*

1. *Undesirability: The market's macro equilibrium might not give us full employment or price stability.*
2. *Instability: Even if the market's macro equilibrium were perfectly positioned (i.e., with full employment and price stability), it might not last.*

Undesired Equilibrium

Figure 9.10*a* depicts the perfect macro equilibrium that everyone hopes for. Aggregate demand and aggregate supply intersect at E_1. At that macro equilibrium, we get both full employment (Q_F) and price stability (P^*)—an ideal situation.

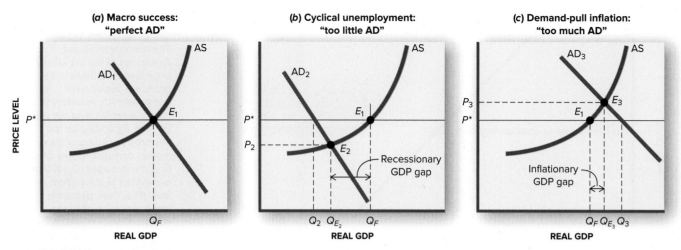

FIGURE 9.10

Macro Failures

Keynesian theory emphasizes that the combined spending decisions of consumers, investors, governments, and net exporters may not be compatible with the desired full employment (Q_F)–price stability (P^*) equilibrium (as they are in panel *a*). Aggregate demand may be too small (panel *b*) or too great (panel *c*), causing cyclical unemployment (*b*) or demand-pull inflation (*c*). Worse yet, even a desirable macro equilibrium (*a*) may be upset by abrupt shifts of aggregate demand.

Keynes didn't think such a perfect outcome was likely. Why should aggregate demand intersect with aggregate supply exactly at point E_1? As we've observed, consumers, investors, government, and foreigners make independent spending decisions, based on many influences. Why should all these decisions add up to just the right amount of aggregate demand? Keynes didn't think they would. ***Because market participants make independent spending decisions, there's no reason to expect that the sum of their expenditures will generate exactly the right amount of aggregate demand.*** Instead, there's a high likelihood that we'll confront an imbalance between desired spending and full-employment output levels—that is, too much or too little aggregate demand.

full-employment GDP: The value of total market output (real GDP) produced at full employment.

equilibrium GDP: The value of total output (real GDP) produced at macro equilibrium (AS = AD).

recessionary GDP gap: The amount by which equilibrium GDP falls short of full-employment GDP.

cyclical unemployment: Unemployment attributable to a lack of job vacancies—that is, to an inadequate level of aggregate demand.

Recessionary GDP Gap. Figure 9.10*b* illustrates one of the undesired equilibriums that Keynes worried about. **Full-employment GDP** is still at Q_F and stable prices are at the level P^*. In this case, however, the rate of output demanded at price level P^* is only Q_2, far short of full-employment GDP (Q_F). How could this happen? Quite simple: The spending plans of consumers, investors, government, and export buyers don't generate enough aggregate demand at current (P^*) prices.

The economy depicted in Figure 9.10*b* is in trouble. At full employment, a lot more output would be produced than market participants would be willing to buy. As unsold inventories rose, production would get cut back, workers would get laid off, and prices would decline. Eventually, the economy would settle at E_2, where AD$_2$ and AS intersect. **Equilibrium GDP** would be equal to QE_2 and the equilibrium price level would be at P_2.

E_2 is clearly not a happy equilibrium. What particularly concerned Keynes was the **recessionary GDP gap,** the amount by which equilibrium GDP falls short of full-employment GDP. In Figure 9.10*b*, the recessionary GDP gap equals Q_F minus QE_2. This gap represents unused productive capacity: lost GDP and unemployed workers. It is the breeding ground of **cyclical unemployment,** the kind of situation President Obama confronted in 2009, President Trump in 2020, and President Biden in 2021.

Figure 9.11 illustrates this dilemma with more numerical details on aggregate demand. The table depicts the demand for GDP at different price levels by consumers, investors, government, and net export buyers. Full-employment GDP is set at $10 trillion and the

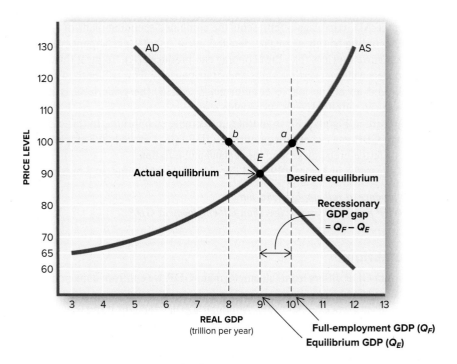

FIGURE 9.11
A Recessionary GDP Gap

The level of aggregate demand depends on the spending behavior of market participants. In this case, the level of GDP demanded at current ($P = 100$) prices ($8 trillion) is less than full-employment GDP ($10 trillion). More output is being produced (point *a*) than purchased (point *b*) at prevailing prices. This results in a lower *equilibrium* GDP ($9 trillion).

The resulting recessionary GDP gap of $1 trillion ($= Q_F - Q_E$) causes unemployment. The price level also declines from 100 to 90.

	Real GDP Demanded (in $ trillions) by:					
Price Level	Consumers +	Investors +	Government +	Net Exports =	Aggregate Demand	Aggregate Supply
130	3.0	0.25	1.5	0.25	5.0	12.0
120	3.5	0.50	1.5	0.50	6.0	11.5
110	4.0	0.75	1.5	0.75	7.0	11.0
100	4.5	1.0	1.5	1.0	8.0	10.0
90	5.0	1.25	1.5	1.25	9.0	9.0
80	5.5	1.50	1.5	1.50	10.0	7.0
70	6.0	1.75	1.5	1.75	11.0	5.0
60	6.5	2.0	1.5	2.0	12.0	3.0

price level at 100. Producers are hoping to sell all the output produced, as indicated by point *a* on the graph. As is evident, however, the quantity of output demanded at that price level is only $8 trillion (point *b* in Figure 9.11). This shortfall of aggregate demand will lead to output and price reductions, pushing the economy downward to the equilibrium GDP at point *E*. At that AS = AD intersection, the *equilibrium* GDP is at $9 trillion, with a price level of 90. The recessionary GDP gap is therefore $1 trillion ($Q_F - Q_E$). The economy's output is $1 trillion less than its full-employment potential. This recessionary gap spells job losses and economic misery.

Inflationary GDP Gap. Aggregate demand won't always fall short of potential output. But Keynes saw it as a distinct possibility. He also realized that aggregate demand might even *exceed* the economy's full-employment/price stability capacity. This contingency is illustrated in Figure 9.10*c*.

In Figure 9.10c, the AD_3 curve again represents the combined spending plans of all market participants. According to this aggregate demand curve, market participants demand more output (Q_3) at current prices than the economy can produce (Q_F). To meet this excessive demand, producers will use overtime shifts and strain capacity. This will push prices up. The economy will end up at the macro equilibrium E_3. At E_3 the price level is higher (inflation) and short-run output exceeds sustainable levels.

What we end up with in Figure 9.10c is another undesirable equilibrium. In this case, we have an **inflationary GDP gap,** wherein equilibrium GDP (QE_3) exceeds full-employment GDP (Q_F). This is a fertile breeding ground for **demand-pull inflation.**

The GDP gaps illustrated in Figure 9.10b and c are clearly troublesome. In a nutshell,

- *The goal is to produce at full employment, but*
- *Equilibrium GDP may be greater or less than full-employment GDP.*

inflationary GDP gap: The amount by which equilibrium GDP exceeds full-employment GDP.

demand-pull inflation: An increase in the price level initiated by excessive aggregate demand.

Unstable Equilibrium

Whenever equilibrium GDP differs from full-employment GDP, we confront a macro failure (unemployment or inflation).

Things need not always work out so badly. Although Keynes thought it improbable, the spending plans of market participants *might* generate the perfect amount of aggregate demand, leaving the economy at the desired macro equilibrium depicted in Figure 9.10a. In Figure 9.10a, *equilibrium* GDP equals *full-employment* GDP. Unfortunately, that happy outcome might not last.

As we've observed, market participants may change their spending behavior abruptly. The stock market may boom or bust, shifting the consumption component of aggregate demand. Changed sales forecasts (expectations) may alter investment plans. Crises in foreign economies may disrupt export sales. A terrorist attack or outbreak of war may rock everybody's boat. Any of these events will cause the aggregate demand curve to shift. When this happens, the AD curve will get knocked out of its "perfect" position in Figure 9.10a, sending us to undesirable outcomes like 9.10b and 9.10c. Recurrent shifts of aggregate demand could even cause a **business cycle.**

business cycle: Alternating periods of economic growth and contraction.

Macro Failures

Economies can get into macro trouble from the supply side of the market place as well, as we'll see later (Chapter 16). Keynes's emphasis on demand-side inadequacies serves as an early warning of potential macro failure, however. *If aggregate demand is too little, too great, or too unstable, the economy will not reach and maintain the goals of full employment and price stability.*

Self-Adjustment?

As we noted earlier, not everyone is as pessimistic as Keynes was about the prospects for macro bliss. The critical question is not whether undesirable outcomes might *occur* but whether they'll *persist.* In other words, the seriousness of any short-run macro failure depends on how markets *respond* to GDP gaps. If markets self-adjust, as classical economists asserted, then macro failures would be temporary.

How might markets self-adjust? If investors stepped up *their* spending whenever consumer spending faltered, the right amount of aggregate demand could be maintained. Such self-adjustment requires that some components of aggregate demand shift in the right direction at just the right time. In other words, *macro self-adjustment requires that any shortfalls in one component of aggregate demand be offset by spending in another component.* If such offsetting shifts occurred, then the desired macro equilibrium in Figure 9.10a could be maintained. Keynes didn't think that likely, however, for reasons we'll explore in the next chapter.

DECISIONS FOR TOMORROW

Can Macro Failures Be Predicted?

The Index of Leading Economic Indicators. Keynes's theory of macro failure gave economic policymakers a lot to worry about. If Keynes was right, abrupt changes in aggregate demand could ruin even the best of economic times. Even if he was wrong about the ability of the economy to self-adjust, sudden shifts of aggregate demand could cause a lot of temporary pain. To minimize such pain, **policymakers need some way of peering into the future—to foresee shifts of aggregate demand.** With such a crystal ball, they might be able to take defensive actions and keep the economy on track.

Market participants have developed all kinds of crystal balls for anticipating AD shifts. The Foundation for the Study of Cycles has identified 4,000 different crystal balls people use to foretell changes in spending. They include the ratio of used car to new car sales (it rises in economic downturns); the number of divorce petitions (it rises in bad times); animal population cycles (they peak just before economic downturns); and even the optimism/pessimism content of popular music (a reflection of consumer confidence).

One of the more conventional crystal balls is the Leading Economic Index (LEI). The index includes 10 gauges that are supposed to indicate in what direction the economy is moving. What's appealing about the LEI is the plausible connection between its components and future spending. Equipment orders, for example, are one of the leading indicators (number 5 in Table 9.2). This seems reasonable because businesses don't order equipment unless they later plan to buy it. The same is true of building permits (indicator 6); people obtain permits only if they plan to build something. Hence, both indicators appear to be dependable signs of future investment. That's why an uptick in the LEI is viewed as good news for the economy and a downtick can be a harbinger of economic woes (see Front Page Economics "U.S. Leading Indicators Plummet").

Unfortunately, the leading indicators aren't a perfect crystal ball. Equipment orders are often canceled. Building plans get delayed or abandoned. Hence, shifts of aggregate demand still occur without warning. No crystal ball could predict a terrorist strike or the timing and magnitude of a natural disaster. Compared to other crystal balls, however, the LEI has a pretty good track record—and a very big audience. It helps investors and policymakers foresee what aggregate demand in the economy tomorrow might look like.

Indicator	Expected Impact
1. Average workweek	Hours worked per week typically increase when greater output and sales are expected.
2. Unemployment claims	Initial claims for unemployment benefits reflect changes in industry layoffs.
3. New orders	New orders for consumer goods trigger increases in production and employment.
4. Delivery times	The longer it takes to deliver ordered goods, the greater the ratio of demand to supply.
5. Equipment orders	Orders for new equipment imply increased production capacity and higher anticipated sales.
6. Building permits	A permit represents the first step in housing construction.
7. Stock prices	Higher stock prices reflect expectations of greater sales and profits.
8. Money supply	Faster growth of the money supply implies a pickup in aggregate demand.
9. Interest rates	Larger differences between long- and short-term rates indicate faster growth.
10. Consumer confidence	Optimism spurs more consumer spending.

TABLE 9.2

The Leading Economic Indicators

Everyone wants a crystal ball to foresee economic events. In reality, forecasters must reckon with very crude predictors of the future. One of the most widely used predictors is the Leading Economic Index, which includes 10 factors believed to predict economic activity 3 to 6 months in advance. Changes in the leading indicators are used to forecast changes in GDP.

The leading indicators rarely move in the same direction at the same time. They're weighted together to create the index. Up-and-down movements of the index are reported each month by the nonprofit Conference Board.

Continued

FRONT PAGE ECONOMICS

U.S. LEADING INDICATORS PLUMMET

The Conference Board's Leading Economic Index (LEI) for the United States dropped precipitously in March, signaling trouble for the economy in the months ahead. The LEI had been rising steadily for months, fueling optimism for the economy in 2020. But the coronavirus shattered all forecasts. After hitting a high of 111.7 (2016 = 100) in February, the Index dropped to 104.2 in March, a decline of 6.7 percent. That was the largest decline in the 60-year history of the LEI. Widespread reductions across a number of leading indicators point to a deteriorating economic outlook for the remainder of 2020.

Source: Conference Board, April 2020.

CRITICAL ANALYSIS: Market participants try to predict the economic outlook with measurable indicators like new orders and building permits.

SUMMARY

- Macro failure occurs when the economy fails to achieve full employment and price stability. **LO9-5**
- Too much or too little aggregate demand can cause macro failure. Too little aggregate demand causes cyclical unemployment; too much aggregate demand causes demand-pull inflation. **LO9-5**
- Aggregate demand reflects the spending plans of consumers (C), investors (I), government (G), and foreign buyers (net exports $= X - M$). **LO9-1**
- Consumer spending is affected by nonincome (autonomous) factors and current income, as summarized in the consumption function: $C = a + bY_D$. **LO9-2**
- Autonomous consumption (a) depends on wealth, expectations, taxes, credit, and price levels. Income-dependent consumption depends on the marginal propensity to consume (MPC), the b in the consumption function. **LO9-2**

- Consumer saving is the difference between disposable income and consumption (that is, $S = Y_D - C$). All disposable income is either spent (C) or saved (S). **LO9-1**
- The consumption function shifts up or down when autonomous influences such as wealth and expectations change. **LO9-2**
- The AD curve shifts left or right whenever the consumption function shifts up or down. **LO9-4**
- Investment spending depends on interest rates, expectations for future sales, and innovation. *Changes* in investment spending will also shift the AD curve. **LO9-3**
- Government spending and net exports are influenced by a variety of cyclical and noncyclical factors and may also change abruptly. **LO9-1**
- Even a "perfect" macro equilibrium may be upset by abrupt shifts of spending behavior. Recurrent shifts of the AD curve may cause a business cycle. **LO9-5**

Key Terms

aggregate demand (AD)
aggregate supply (AS)
equilibrium (macro)
consumption
disposable income (DI)
saving
average propensity to consume (APC)
marginal propensity to consume (MPC)
marginal propensity to save (MPS)

wealth effect
autonomous consumption
consumption function
dissaving
investment
full-employment GDP
equilibrium GDP
recessionary GDP gap
cyclical unemployment

inflationary GDP gap
demand-pull inflation
business cycle
aggregate expenditure
recessionary gap
expenditure equilibrium
inflationary gap

Questions for Discussion

1. What percentage of last month's income did you spend? How much more would you spend if you won a $1,000 lottery prize? Why might your average and marginal propensities to consume differ?   **LO9-2**

2. Why do rich people have a higher marginal propensity to save than poor people?   **LO9-2**

3. How do households dissave? Where do they get the money to finance their extra consumption? Can everyone dissave at the same time?   **LO9-2**

4. Why would an *employed* consumer cut spending when other workers were being laid off (see Front Page Economics "Consumer Confidence Falls Abruptly")?   **LO9-2**

5. According to Front Page Economics "Factory Orders Hit 11-Year Low," why did U.S. businesses cut investment spending in early 2020? Was this a rational response?   **LO9-3**

6. Why is the APC in the United States so much higher than that in China or Japan?   **LO9-2**

7. Why are declining housing permits considered a negative leading indicator? (See Front Page Economics "U.S. Leading Indicators Plummet.")   **LO9-5**

8. Why wouldn't market participants always want to buy all the output produced?   **LO9-5**

9. If an inflationary GDP gap exists, what will happen to business inventories. How will producers respond?   **LO9-5**

10. How might a "perfect" macro equilibrium (Figure 9.10*a*) be affected by (*a*) a stock market crash, (*b*) rising home prices, (*c*) a recession in Canada, and (*d*) a spike in oil prices?   **LO9-1, LO9-5**

PROBLEMS FOR CHAPTER 9

LO9-2 1. If the proportion of the total disposable income spent on consumer goods and services is 93 percent and if consumers spend 85 percent of each additional dollar, what is
 (*a*) The APC?
 (*b*) The APS?
 (*c*) The MPC?
 (*d*) The MPS?

LO9-2 2. According to Front Page Economics "Disposable Income and Outlays: February 2020," between January and February by how much did
 (*a*) Disposable income increase?
 (*b*) Consumption increase?
 (*c*) Savings increase?
 (*d*) What was the MPC?
 (*e*) What was the MPS?
 (*f*) What was the APC for February?

LO9-2 3. On the accompanying graph, draw the consumption function $C = \$300 \text{ billion} + 0.50Y_D$.
LO9-4
 (*a*) At what level of income do households begin to save?
    Designate that point on the graph with the letter *A*.
 (*b*) By how much does consumption increase when income rises $100 billion beyond point *A?*
    Designate this new level of consumption with point *B*.

LO9-4 4. Illustrate on the following two graphs the impact of decreased consumer confidence.

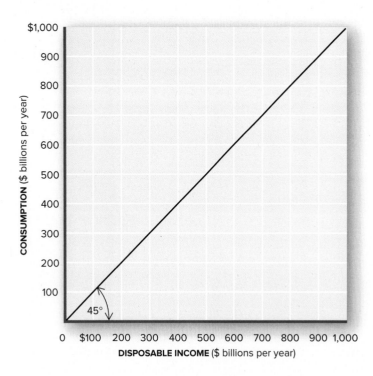

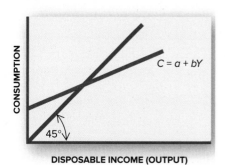

What direction did
(*a*) The consumption function shift?
(*b*) AD shift?

LO9-4 5. If every $1,000 increase in the real price of homes adds 6 cents to annual consumer spending (the "wealth effect"),
- (a) By how much did consumption *decline* when home prices fell by $2 trillion in 2006–2008?
- (b) In which direction did the consumption function shift?
- (c) In which direction did the AD curve shift?

LO9-4 6. Identify which direction the consumption function ($C(Y)$) and aggregate demand (AD) curves will shift when:
- (a) Consumer confidence increases.
- (b) Income taxes go up.
- (c) Interest rates decline.
- (d) The stock market rises.
- (e) Home prices decline.

LO9-2 7. According to the Moody's Analytics analysis (see Front Page Economics "Wealth Effect Boosts Spending"), by how much did consumer spending increase due to the stock market rise in 2019?

LO9-3 8. Illustrate on the following graphs the impact of COVID-19 on investment plans (Front Page Economics "Factory Orders Hit 11-Year Low").

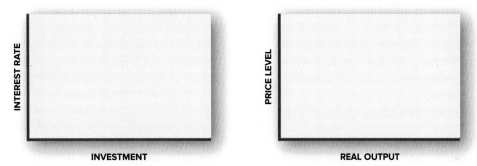

LO9-4 9. What was the range, in absolute percentage points, of the variation in quarterly growth rates between 2005 and 2008 of
- (a) Consumer spending?
- (b) Investment spending?
- (c) Which is more volatile?

(*Note:* See Figure 9.8 for data.)

LO9-5 10. Complete the following table:

Price Level	Consumers	+	Investors	+	Government	+	Net Exports	=	Aggregate Demand	Aggregate Supply
120	80		15		20		10		___	320
110	92		16		20		12		___	260
100	104		17		20		14		___	215
90	116		18		20		16		___	200
80	128		19		20		18		___	185
70	140		20		20		20		___	175
60	154		21		20		22		___	170

Real Output Demanded (in $ billions) by

- (a) What is the level of equilibrium GDP?
- (b) What is the equilibrium price level?
- (c) If full employment occurs at real GDP = $200 billion, what kind of GDP gap exists?
- (d) How large is that gap?
- (e) Which macro problem exists here (unemployment or inflation)?

PROBLEMS FOR CHAPTER 9 (cont'd)

LO9-1
LO9-5
11. On the following graph, draw the AD and AS curves with these data that lead to the desired full-employment equilibrium:

Price level	140	130	120	110	100	90	80	70	60	50
Real output										
Demanded	600	700	800	900	1,000	1,100	1,200	1,300	1,400	1,500
Supplied	1,200	1,150	1,100	1,050	1,000	950	900	800	600	400

(a) What is the full-employment equilibrium
    (i) Real output level?
    (ii) Price level?

Suppose aggregate demand decreases by $150 at all price levels.
(b) Draw the new AD curve.
(c) What is the new equilibrium
    (i) Output level?
    (ii) Price level?
(d) What macro problem has arisen in this economy: unemployment or inflation?

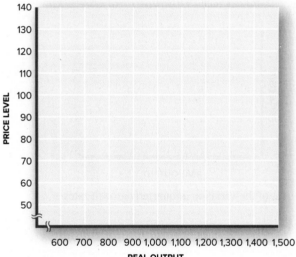

LO9-2 12. Given $C = \$2,000 + 0.84Y_D$.
    (a) How much is saved if Y_D is $40,000?
    (b) How much does consumption increase if Y_D increases by $1,000?

LO9-4 13. *Decisions for Tomorrow:* Predict the impact on aggregate demand if
    (a) The average workweek increased.
    (b) Consumer confidence lags.
    (c) Retailers are placing larger orders than in the past.

APPENDIX

THE KEYNESIAN CROSS

The Keynesian view of the macro economy emphasizes the potential instability of the private sector and the undependability of a market-driven self-adjustment. We have illustrated this theory with shifts of the AD curve and resulting real GDP gaps. The advantage of the AS/AD model is that it illustrates how both real output and the price level are simultaneously affected by AD shifts. At the time Keynes developed his theory of instability, however, inflation was not a threat. In the Great Depression, prices were *falling*. With unemployment rates reaching as high as 25 percent, no one worried that increased aggregate demand would push price levels up. The only concern was to get back to full employment.

Because inflation was not seen as an immediate threat, early depictions of Keynesian theory didn't use the AS/AD model. Instead, they used a different graph called the "Keynesian cross." *The Keynesian cross focuses on the relationship of total spending to the value of total output, without an explicit distinction between price levels and real output.* As we'll see, the Keynesian cross doesn't change any conclusions we've come to about macro instability. It simply offers an alternative, and historically important, framework for explaining macro outcomes.

Focus on Aggregate Expenditure

Keynes said that in a really depressed economy we could focus exclusively on the rate of *spending* in the economy without distinguishing between real output and price levels. All he worried about was whether **aggregate expenditure**—the sum of consumer, investor, government, and net export buyers' spending plans—would be compatible with the dollar value of full-employment output.

aggregate expenditure: The rate of total expenditure desired at alternative levels of income, *ceteris paribus*.

For Keynes, the critical question was how much each group of market participants would spend at different levels of nominal *income*. As we saw earlier, Keynes showed that consumer spending directly varies with the level of income. That's why the consumption function in Figure 9.4 had *spending* on the vertical axis and nominal *income* on the horizontal axis.

Figure 9A.1 puts the consumption function into the larger context of the macro economy. In this figure, the focus is exclusively on *nominal* incomes and spending. Y_F indicates the dollar

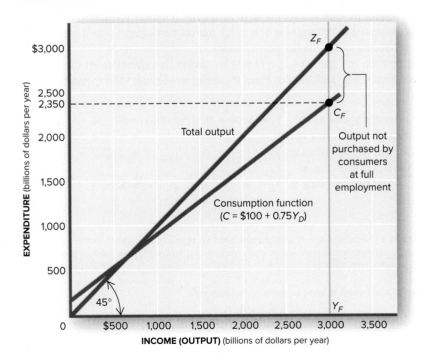

FIGURE 9A.1

The Consumption Shortfall

To determine how much output consumers will demand at full-employment output (Y_F), we refer to the consumption function. First, locate full-employment output on the horizontal axis (at Y_F). Then, move up until you reach the consumption function. In this case, the amount C_F (equal to $2,350 billion per year) will be demanded at full-employment output ($3,000 billion per year). This leaves $650 billion of output not purchased by consumers.

value of full-employment output at current prices. In this figure, $3,000 billion is assumed to be the value of Y_F. The 45-degree line shows all points where total spending equals total income.

The consumption function in Figure 9A.1 is the same one we used before, namely

$$C = \$100 + 0.75Y_D$$

Notice again that consumers *dissave* at lower income levels but *save* at higher income levels.

The Consumption Shortfall

What particularly worried Keynes was the level of intended consumption at full employment. At full employment, $3 trillion of income (output) is generated. But consumers plan to spend only

$$C = \$100 + 0.75(\$3,000 \text{ billion}) = \$2,350 \text{ billion}$$

and save the rest ($650 billion).[1] Were product market sales totally dependent on consumers, this economy would be in trouble: Consumer spending falls short of full-employment output. In Figure 9A.1, this consumption shortfall is the vertical difference between points Z_F and C_F.

Nonconsumer Spending

The evident shortfall in consumer spending need not doom the economy to macro failure. There are other market participants, and their spending will add to aggregate expenditure. Keynes, however, emphasized that the spending decisions of investors, governments, and net export buyers are made independently. They *might* add up to just the right amount—or they might not.

To determine how much other market participants might spend, we'd have to examine their behavior. Suppose we did so and ended up with the information in Figure 9A.2. The data in that figure reveal how many dollars will be spent at various income levels. By vertically stacking these expenditure components, we can draw an *aggregate* (total) expenditure curve as in Figure 9A.2. The aggregate expenditure curve shows how *total* spending varies with income.

A Recessionary Gap

Keynes used the aggregate expenditure curve to assess the potential for macro failure. He was particularly interested in determining how much market participants would spend if the economy were producing at full-employment capacity.

With the information in Figure 9A.2, it is easy to answer that question. At full employment (Y_F), total income is $3,000 billion. From the table, we see that total spending at that income level is

Consumer spending at	$Y_F = \$100 + 0.75(\$3,000)$	$= \$2,350$
Investment spending at	Y_F	$= \quad 150$
Government spending at	Y_F	$= \quad 200$
Net export spending at	Y_F	$= \quad\quad 50$
Aggregate spending at	Y_F	$= \$2,750$

---

[1]In principle, we first have to determine how much *disposable* income is generated by any given level of *total income*, then use the consumption function to determine how much consumption occurs. If Y_D is a constant percentage of Y, this two-step computation boils down to

$$Y_D = dY$$

where d = the share of total income received as disposable income, and

$$C = a + b(dY)$$
$$= a + (b \times d)Y$$

The term $(b \times d)$ is the marginal propensity to consume out of total income.

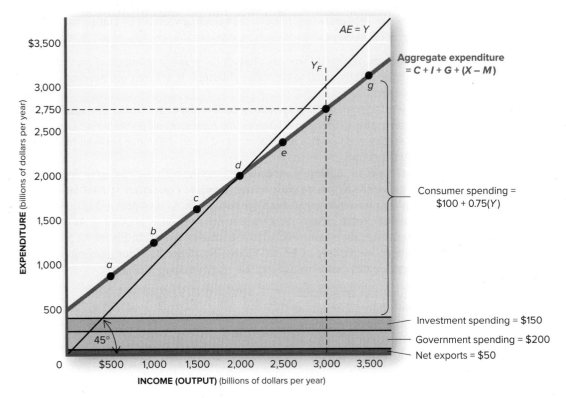

FIGURE 9A.2

Aggregate Expenditure

The aggregate expenditure curve depicts the desired spending of market participants at various income (output) levels. In this case, *I*, *G*, and (*X* − *M*) don't vary with income, but *C* does. Adding these four components gives us total desired spending.

If total income were $1,000 billion, desired spending would total $1,250 billion, as shown in row *b* in the table and by point *b* in the graph.

	At Income (Output) of	Consumers Desire to Spend	+	Investors Desire to Spend	+	Governments Desire to Spend	+	Net Export Spending	=	Aggregate Expenditure
a	$ 500	$ 475		$150		$200		$50		$ 875
b	1,000	850		150		200		50		1,250
c	1,500	1,225		150		200		50		1,625
d	2,000	1,600		150		200		50		2,000
e	2,500	1,975		150		200		50		2,375
f	3,000	2,350		150		200		50		2,750
g	3,500	2,725		150		200		50		3,125

In this case, we end up with less aggregate expenditure in product markets ($2,750 billion) than the value of full-employment output ($3,000 billion). This is illustrated in Figure 9A.2 by point *f* on the graph and row *f* in the table.

The economy illustrated in Figure 9A.2 is in trouble. If full employment were achieved, it wouldn't last. At full employment, $3,000 billion of output would be produced. But only $2,750 of output would be sold. There isn't enough aggregate expenditure at current price levels to sustain full employment. As a result, $250 billion of unsold output piles up in warehouses and on store shelves. That unwanted inventory is a harbinger of trouble.

The difference between full-employment output and desired spending at full employment is called a **recessionary gap.** Not enough output is willingly purchased at full employment to

recessionary gap: The amount by which aggregate spending at full employment falls short of full-employment output.

sustain the economy. Producers may react to the spending shortfall by cutting back on production and laying off workers.

A Single Equilibrium. You might wonder whether the planned spending of market participants would ever be exactly equal to the value of output. It will, but not necessarily at the rate of output we seek.

Figure 9A.3 illustrates where this **expenditure equilibrium** exists. Recall the significance of the 45-degree line in that figure. The 45-degree line represents all points where expenditure *equals* income. At any point on this line, there would be no difference between total spending and the value of output.

The juxtaposition of the aggregate expenditure function with the 45-degree line is called the Keynesian cross. *The Keynesian cross relates aggregate expenditure to total income (output) without explicit consideration of (changing) price levels.* As is evident in Figure 9A.3, the aggregate expenditure curve crosses the 45-degree line only once, at point *E*. At that point, therefore, desired spending is *exactly* equal to the value of output. In Figure 9A.3 this equilibrium occurs at an output rate of $2,000 billion. Notice in the accompanying table how much market participants desire to spend at that rate of output. We have

Consumer spending at $\quad Y_E = \$100 + 0.75(\$2,000) \quad = \$1,600$
Investment spending at $\quad Y_E \qquad\qquad\qquad\qquad\quad = \quad\;\, 150$
Government spending at $\ Y_E \qquad\qquad\qquad\qquad\quad = \quad\;\, 200$
Net export spending at $\quad Y_E \qquad\qquad\qquad\qquad\quad = \quad\quad\; 50$
Aggregate spending at $\quad Y_E \qquad\qquad\qquad\qquad\quad = \$2,000$

At Y_E we have spending behavior that's completely compatible with the rate of production. At this equilibrium rate of output, no goods remain unsold. At that one rate of output

---

expenditure equilibrium: The rate of output at which desired spending equals the value of output.

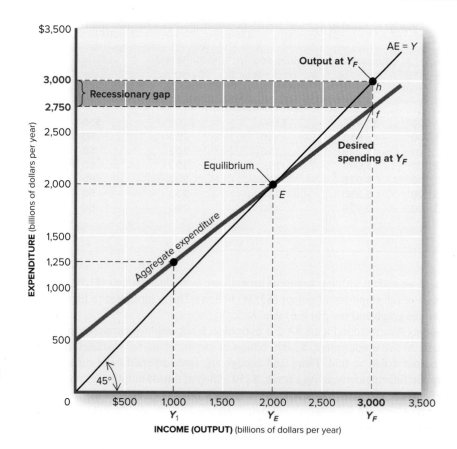

FIGURE 9A.3

Expenditure Equilibrium

There's only one rate of output at which desired expenditure equals the value of output. This expenditure equilibrium occurs at point *E*, where the aggregate expenditure and 45-degree lines intersect. At this equilibrium, $2,000 billion of output is produced and willingly purchased.

At full-employment output (Y_F = $3,000), aggregate expenditure is only $2,750 billion. This spending shortfall leaves $250 billion of output unsold. The difference between full-employment output (point *h*) and desired spending at full employment (point *f*) is called the recessionary gap.

where desired spending and the value of output are exactly equal, an expenditure equilibrium exists. *At macro equilibrium, producers have no incentive to change the rate of output because they're selling everything they produce.*

Macro Failure

Unfortunately, the equilibrium depicted in Figure 9A.3 isn't the one we hoped to achieve. At Y_E the economy is well short of its full-employment goal (Y_F).

The expenditure equilibrium won't always fall short of the economy's productive capacity. Indeed, market participants' spending desires could also *exceed* the economy's full-employment potential. This might happen if investors, the government, or foreigners wanted to buy more output or if the consumption function shifted upward. In such circumstances, an **inflationary gap** would exist. An inflationary gap arises when market participants want to buy more output than can be produced at full employment. The resulting scramble for goods may start a bidding war that pushes price levels even higher. This would be another symptom of macro failure.

inflationary gap: The amount by which aggregate spending at full employment exceeds full-employment output.

Two Paths to the Same Conclusion

The Keynesian analysis of aggregate *expenditure* looks remarkably similar to the Keynesian analysis of aggregate *demand*. In fact, it is: Both approaches lead to the same conclusions about macro instability. The key difference between the "old" (expenditure) analysis and the "new" (AD) analysis is the level of detail about macro outcomes. In the old aggregate expenditure analysis, the focus was simply on total spending, the product of output and prices. *In the newer AD analysis, the separate effects of macro instability on prices and real output are distinguished.*[2] In a world where changes in both real output and price levels are important, the AD/AS framework is more useful.

[2]This distinction is reflected in the differing definitions for the traditional *recessionary gap* (the *spending* shortfall at full-employment income) and the newer *recessionary real GDP gap* (the real output gap between full-employment GDP and equilibrium GDP).

Design Credit: Shutterstock

Ingram Publishing

CHAPTER 10

Self-Adjustment or Instability?

John Maynard Keynes took a dim view of a market-driven macro economy. He emphasized that (1) macro failure is likely to occur in such an economy and, worse yet, (2) macro failure isn't likely to go away. As noted earlier, the first prediction wasn't all that controversial. The classical economists had conceded the possibility of occasional recession or inflation. In their view, however, the economy would quickly self-adjust, restoring full employment and price stability. Keynes's second proposition challenged this view. The most distinctive, and frightening, proposition of Keynes's theory was that there would be no automatic self-adjustment; the economy could stagnate in *persistent* unemployment or be subjected to *continuing* inflation.

President Herbert Hoover was a believer in the market's ability to self-adjust. So was President George H.W. Bush. As Hoover and Bush Sr. waited for the economy to self-adjust, however, they both lost their reelection bids. President George W. Bush wasn't willing to take that chance. As soon as he was elected, he pushed tax cuts through Congress that boosted consumer disposable incomes and helped bolster a sagging economy. After the terrorist attacks of September 11, 2001, he called for even greater government intervention. Yet when the economy slowed down in his final year, he seemed willing to await the self-correcting forces of the marketplace.

President Obama embraced the Keynesian perspective from day 1. He explicitly rejected the "worn-out dogma" of classical theory and insisted that only dramatic government intervention could keep a bad economic situation from getting worse. He advocated massive spending programs to jump-start the recession-bound economy of 2008–2009.

President Trump also adopted the Keynesian approach. To accelerate economic growth and "make America great again," he pushed tax cuts for consumers and also tax cuts for businesses. Like Keynes, Trump believed tax cuts would lead to more spending, shifting the aggregate demand curve to the right. When the coronavirus pandemic later derailed the economy, president Trump at first thought the virus would quickly disappear and was willing to let market forces handle the problem. As the severity of the pandemic became clearer, however, he agreed with Congress to pull the Keynesian policy levers again, especially increased income transfers (tax rebates, unemployment benefits). President Biden initially pursued the same strategy.

These different presidential experiences don't resolve the self-adjustment debate; rather, they emphasize how important the debate is.

In this chapter, we'll focus on the *adjustment process*—that is, how markets *respond* to an undesirable equilibrium. We're especially concerned with the following questions:

- **Why does anyone think the market might self-adjust (returning to a desired equilibrium)?**
- **Why might markets *not* self-adjust?**
- **Could market responses actually *worsen* macro outcomes?**

LEAKAGES AND INJECTIONS

Chapter 9 demonstrated how the economy could end up at the wrong macro equilibrium—with too much or too little aggregate demand. Such an undesirable outcome might result from an initial imbalance between **aggregate demand** at the current price level and full-employment GDP. Or the economy could fall into trouble from a *shift* in aggregate demand that pushes the economy out of a desirable full-employment–price-stability equilibrium. Whatever the sequence of events might be, the bottom line is the same: Total spending doesn't match total output at the desired full-employment–price-stability level.

> **aggregate demand (AD):** The total quantity of output (real GDP) demanded at alternative price levels in a given time period, *ceteris paribus.*

The Circular Flow. The circular flow of income illustrates how such an undesirable outcome comes about. Recall that all income originates in product markets, where goods and services are sold. If the economy were producing at **full-employment GDP,** then enough income would be available to buy everything a fully employed economy produces. As we've seen, however, aggregate demand isn't so certain. It could happen that market participants choose *not* to spend all their income, leaving some goods unsold. Alternatively, they might try to buy *more* than full-employment output, pushing prices up.

> **full-employment GDP:** The value of total market output (real GDP) produced at full employment.

To see how such imbalances might arise, Keynes distinguished *leakages* from the circular flow and *injections* into that flow, as illustrated in Figure 10.1.

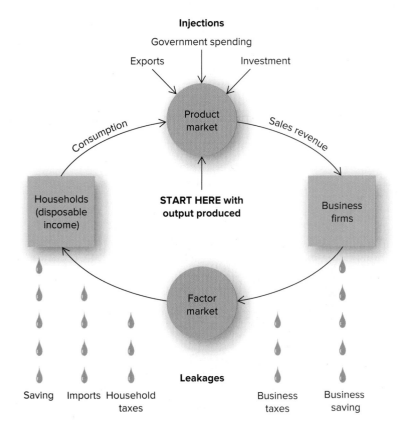

Injections

Government spending

Exports   Investment

Product market

Consumption

Sales revenue

Households (disposable income)

START HERE with output produced

Business firms

Factor market

Leakages

Saving   Imports Household taxes   Business taxes   Business saving

FIGURE 10.1

Leakages and Injections

The income generated in production doesn't return completely to product markets in the form of consumer spending. Consumer saving, imports, taxes, and business saving all leak from the circular flow, *reducing* potential aggregate demand. If this leakage isn't offset, some of the output produced will remain unsold.

Business investment, government purchases of goods and services, and exports inject spending into the circular flow, *adding* to aggregate demand. The focus of macro concern is whether injections will offset leakage at full employment.

---

leakage: Income not spent directly on domestic output but instead diverted from the circular flow—for example, saving, imports, taxes.

Consumer Saving

As we observed in Chapter 9, consumers typically don't spend *all* the income they earn in product markets; they *save* some fraction of it. This is the first leak in the circular flow. Some income earned in product markets isn't being instantly converted into spending. This circular flow **leakage** creates the potential for a spending shortfall.

Suppose the economy were producing at full employment, with $3,000 billion of output at the current price level, indexed at $P = 100$. This initial output rate is marked by point F in Figure 10.2. Suppose further that *all* of the income generated in product markets went directly to consumers (i.e., no taxes, no business retained earnings, etc.). This assumption puts consumers in an all-powerful position: Their spending decisions will determine whether the economy stays at full-employment (Q_F). The question then is whether consumers will *spend* enough to *maintain* full employment.

We already observed in Chapter 9 that such an outcome is unlikely. Typically, consumers *save* a small fraction of their incomes.

If the consumption function were $C_F = \$100$ billion $+ 0.75Y$, consumers will spend only

$$C_F = \$100 \text{ billion} + 0.75 \ (\$3,000 \text{ billion})$$
$$= \$2,350 \text{ billion}$$

at the current price level. This consumption behavior is illustrated in Figure 10.2 by the point C_F.

Consumers would demand *more* real output with their current income if prices were to fall (due to the real balances, foreign trade, and interest rate effects, discussed in Chapter 8). Hence, the consumption component of aggregate demand slopes downward from point C_F. Our immediate concern, however, focuses on how much (real) output consumers will purchase at the *current* price level. At the price level $P = 100$, consumers choose to save $650 billion, leaving consumption ($2,350 billion) far short of full-employment GDP ($3,000 billion).

The decision to save some fraction of household income isn't necessarily bad, but it does present a potential problem. Unless other market participants, such as business, government, and foreigners, buy this unsold output, goods will pile up on producers' shelves. As undesired inventory accumulates, producers will reduce the rate of output and unemployment will rise.

FIGURE 10.2

Leakage and AD

The disposable income consumers receive is only about 70 percent of total income (GDP) due to taxes and income held by businesses. Consumers also tend to save some of their disposable income and buy imported products. As a result of these leakages, consumers will demand less output at the current price level ($P = 100$) than the economy produces at full-employment GDP (Q_F). In this case, $3,000 billion of output (income) is produced (point F), but consumers demand only $2,350 billion of output at the price level $P = 100$ (point C_F).

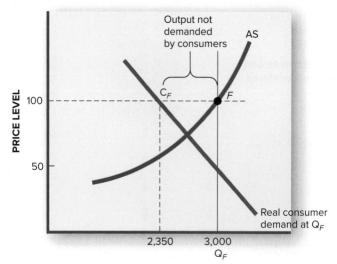

REAL GDP (in billions of dollars per year)

Imports and Taxes

Saving isn't the only source of leakage. *Imports also represent leakage from the circular flow.* When consumers buy imported goods, their spending leaves (that is, leaks out of) the domestic circular flow and goes to foreign producers. As a consequence, income spent on imported goods is not part of domestic aggregate demand.

In the real world, *taxes are a form of leakage as well.* A lot of revenue generated in market sales gets diverted into federal, state, and local government coffers. Sales taxes are taken out of the circular flow in product markets. Then payroll taxes and income taxes are taken out of paychecks. Households never get the chance to spend any of that income. They start with **disposable income,** which is much less than the total income generated in product markets. In 2019, disposable income was only $16.4 trillion while total income (GDP) was $21.4 trillion. Hence, consumers couldn't have bought everything produced that year with their current incomes even if they had saved nothing. Their disposable income was $5 trillion less than the value of output produced.

disposable income (DI): After-tax income of households; personal income less personal taxes.

Business Saving

The business sector also keeps some of the income generated in product markets. Businesses set aside some of their revenue to cover the costs of maintaining, repairing, and replacing plants and equipment. The revenue held aside for these purposes is called a *depreciation allowance.* In addition, corporations keep some part of total profit (retained earnings) for continuing business uses rather than paying all profits out to stockholders in the form of dividends. The total value of depreciation allowances and retained earnings is called **gross business saving.** The income businesses hold back in these forms represents further leakage from the circular flow—income that consumers never see and that doesn't automatically flow directly back into product markets.

gross business saving: Depreciation allowances and retained earnings.

Injections into the Circular Flow

Although leakage from the circular flow is a potential source of unemployment problems, we shouldn't conclude that the economy will sink as soon as consumers start saving some of their income, buy a few imports, or pay their taxes. Consumers aren't the only source of aggregate demand; business firms and government agencies also contribute to total spending. So do international consumers who buy our exports. So before we run out into the streets and scream, "The circular flow is leaking!" we need to look at what other market participants are doing.

The top half of Figure 10.1 completes the picture of the circular flow by depicting **injections** of new spending. When businesses buy plant and equipment, they add to the dollar value of product market sales. Government purchases and exports also inject spending into the product market. These *injections of investment, government, and export spending help offset leakage from saving, imports, and taxes.* As a result, there may be enough aggregate demand to maintain full employment at the current price level, even if consumers aren't spending every dollar of income.

injection: An addition of spending to the circular flow of income.

The critical issue for macro stability is whether spending injections will actually equal spending leakage at full employment. *Injections must equal leakages if all the output supplied is to equal the output demanded* (macro equilibrium). Ideally, the economy will satisfy this condition at full employment and we can stop worrying about short-run macro problems. If not, we've still got some work to do.

Self-Adjustment?

As we noted earlier, classical economists had no worries. They assumed that spending injections would always equal spending leakage. That was the foundation of their belief in the market's self-adjustment. The mechanism they counted on for equalizing leakages and injections was the interest rate.

FIGURE 10.3

Leakages and Injections

Macro equilibrium occurs only when leakages equal injections. Consumer saving and business investment are the primary flows in and out of the circular flow in a wholly private and closed economy. Hence, the relationship between saving and investment reveals whether a market-driven economy will self-adjust to a full-employment equilibrium.

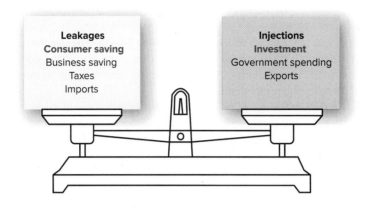

Flexible Interest Rates. Ignore all other injections and leakages for the moment and focus on just consumer saving and business investment (Figure 10.3). If consumer saving (a leakage) exceeds business investment (an injection), unspent income must be piling up somewhere (in bank accounts, for example). These unspent funds will be a tempting lure for business investors. Businesses are always looking for funds to finance expansion or modernization. So they aren't likely to leave a pile of consumer savings sitting idle. Moreover, the banks and other institutions that are holding consumer savings will be eager to lend more funds as consumer savings pile up. To make more loans, they can lower the interest rate. As we observed in Chapter 9 (Figure 9.7), lower interest rates prompt businesses to borrow and invest more. Hence, *classical economists concluded that if interest rates fell far enough, business investment (injections) would equal consumer saving (leakage).*

From this classical perspective, any spending shortfall in the macro economy would soon be closed by this self-adjustment of leakage and injection flows. If saving leakage increased, interest rates would drop, prompting an offsetting rise in investment injections. Aggregate demand would be maintained at full-employment GDP because investment spending would soak up all consumer saving. The *content* of AD would change (less *C*, more *I*), but the *level* would remain at full-employment GDP.

Changing Expectations. Keynes argued that classical economists ignored the role of expectations. As Figure 9.7 illustrated, the level of investment *is* sensitive to interest rates. But the whole investment function *shifts* when business expectations change. Keynes thought it preposterous that investment spending would *increase* in response to *declining* consumer sales. A *decline* in investment is more likely, Keynes argued.

Flexible Prices. The classical economists said self-adjustment was possible even without flexible interest rates. Flexible *prices* would do the trick. Look at Figure 10.2 again. It says consumers will demand only $2,350 billion of output *at the current price level.* But what if prices *fell?* Then consumers would buy more output. In fact, if prices fell far enough, consumers might buy *all* the output produced at full employment. In Figure 10.2, the price level $P = 50$ elicits such a response. (Notice how much output is demanded at the $P = 50$ price level.)

Expectations (Again). Keynes again chided the classical economists for their naïveté. Sure, a nationwide sale might prompt consumers to buy more goods and services. But how would businesses react? They had planned on selling Q_F amount of output at the price level $P = 100$. If prices must be cut in half to move their merchandise, businesses are likely to rethink their production and investment plans. Keynes argued that declining (retail) prices would prompt businesses to invest *less,* not more. This was a real fear in 2008–2009, as Front Page Economics "Everything Is on Sale and That's Not Good" suggests.

EVERYTHING IS ON SALE AND THAT'S NOT GOOD

The Bureau of Labor Statistics reported that consumer prices fell in October at their fastest pace in more than 60 years. Prices were down across the board—for cars, clothes, gasoline, and electronics. Housing prices also continued to drop.

Consumers might like the short-term rewards of a nationwide fire sale. But declining prices can eventually hurt. Declining prices squeeze the profit margins of producers, causing them to cut back production and lay off workers. Retailers become more hesitant to restock inventory. A kind of downward spiral may emerge that pushes both prices and production down. This is the kind of deflationary spiral that made the Great Depression of the 1930s so painful.

Source: U.S. Bureau of Labor Statistics and news accounts of December 2008.

CRITICAL ANALYSIS: Deflation does make products cheaper for consumers. But declining prices also reduce business revenues, profits, and sales **expectations**.

THE MULTIPLIER PROCESS

Keynes not only rejected the classical notion of self-adjustment; he also argued that things were likely to get *worse,* not better, once a spending shortfall emerged. This was the scariest part of Keynes's theory.

To understand Keynes's fears, imagine that the economy is initially at the desired full-employment GDP equilibrium, as represented again by point *F* in Figure 10.4. Included in that full-employment equilibrium GDP is

Consumption	=	$2,350 billion
Investment	=	400 billion
Government	=	150 billion
Net exports	=	100 billion
Aggregate demand at current price level	=	$3,000 billion

Everything looks good in this macro economy. This is pretty much how the U.S. economy looked in 2006–2007: We had full employment and price stability.

The 2007 Q4 Investment Decline

In the fourth quarter of 2007, the U.S. economy took a turn for the worse. The problem began in the housing industry. Housing prices had risen dramatically from 1998 to 2006. This surge in home prices had increased household wealth by trillions of dollars and prompted home builders to construct more new homes every year. These injections of investment spending helped keep GDP growing for a decade. But the party ended in July 2006 when home prices stopped rising. That made home builders rethink their construction plans. When home prices actually began falling in 2007, many home builders called it quits. In the fourth quarter of 2007, residential investment (home construction) declined by a staggering 29 percent (see Front Page Economics "Housing Starts Fall to 10-Year Low"), dragging total U.S. investment down by more than $50 billion. The die was cast: A recession was sure to follow.

FIGURE 10.4
AD Shift

When investment spending drops, aggregate demand shifts to the left. In the short run, this causes output and the price level to fall. The initial full-employment equilibrium at F is pushed to a new and lower equilibrium at point b.

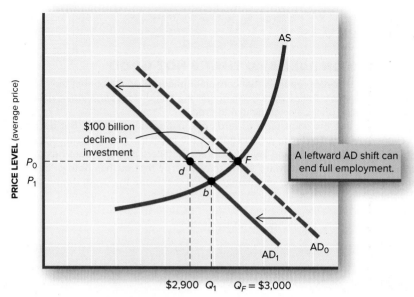

PRICE LEVEL (average price)

AS

$100 billion decline in investment

P_0
P_1

d
F

b

A leftward AD shift can end full employment.

AD_1 AD_0

$2,900 Q_1 $Q_F = $3,000

REAL OUTPUT (in billions of dollars per year)

FRONT PAGE ECONOMICS

NEWS

HOUSING STARTS FALL TO 10-YEAR LOW

Builders are scaling back. The Commerce Department reported yesterday that housing starts fell to a seasonally adjusted rate of 1.381 million homes, down from 1.471 million in June. This is the fewest number of new homes being built in more than 10 years. Housing permits were down as well, to a seasonally adjusted rate of only 1.373 million. All in all, the data point to a "pretty gloomy" outlook for the housing industry, according to a senior Wells Fargo economist.

Source: U.S. Department of Commerce and news reports of August 2007.

CRITICAL ANALYSIS: A drop in residential construction (investment) in 2007 shifted the AD curve to the left, as in Figure 10.4, throwing thousands of construction employees out of work. This started a series of consumption-based AD shifts in a sequence called the **multiplier process.**

Undesired Inventory. The plunge in residential construction was accompanied by a surge in the number of unsold new homes. Buyers were fleeing the housing market even faster than builders. So inventories of unsold new homes were rising despite the slowdown in construction.

Ironically, this additional inventory is counted as part of investment spending. (Recall that our definition of investment spending includes changes in business inventories.) This additional inventory was clearly undesired, however, as builders had planned on selling these homes.

To keep track of these unwanted changes in investment, we ***distinguish* desired *(or planned)* investment from actual *investment*.** *Desired* investment represents purchases of new plants and equipment plus any *desired* changes in business inventories. By contrast, *actual* investment represents purchases of new plants and equipment plus *actual* changes in business inventories, desired or otherwise. In other words,

$$\text{Actual investment} = \text{Desired investment} + \text{Undesired investment}$$

Falling Output and Prices. How are business firms likely to react when they see undesired inventory piling up in new housing developments, on car lots, or on store shelves? They could regard the inventory pileup as a brief aberration and continue producing at full-employment levels. But the inventory pileup might also set off sales alarms, causing businesses to alter their pricing, production, and investment plans. If that happens, they're likely to start cutting prices in an attempt to increase the rate of sales. Producers are also likely to reduce the rate of new output.

Figure 10.4 illustrates these two responses. Assume that investment spending declines by $100 billion at the existing price level P_0. This shifts the aggregate demand curve leftward from AD_0 to AD_1 and immediately moves the economy from point F to point d. At d, however, excess inventories prompt firms to reduce prices. As prices fall, the economy gravitates toward a new **equilibrium GDP** at point b. At point b, the rate of output (Q_1) is less than the full-employment level (Q_F), and the price level has fallen from P_0 to P_1. This economy is now in a recession, and the unemployment rate is rising.

equilibrium GDP: The value of total output (real GDP) produced at macro equilibrium (AS = AD).

Household Incomes

The decline in GDP depicted in Figure 10.4 isn't pretty. But Keynes warned that the picture would get uglier when *consumers* start feeling the impact of the production cutbacks. This is the scary part of the story.

So far we've treated the production cutbacks that accompany a GDP gap as a rather abstract problem. But the reality is that when production is cut back, people suffer. When producers decrease the rate of output, workers lose their jobs or face pay cuts, or both. Cutbacks in investment spending in 2007–2008 led to layoffs among home builders, mortgage companies, banks, equipment manufacturers, auto companies, and even hi-tech companies like Hewlett-Packard, IBM, Yahoo!, and Google. A decline in travel caused layoffs at airlines and aircraft manufacturers. As workers get laid off or have their wages cut, household incomes decline. Thus, *a reduction in investment spending implies a reduction in household incomes.*

Income-Dependent Consumption

We saw in Chapter 9 the kind of threat a reduction in household income poses. Those consumers who end up with less income won't be able to purchase as many goods and services as they did before. As a consequence, aggregate demand will fall further, leading to still larger stocks of unsold goods, more job layoffs, and further reductions in income. It's this sequence of events—called the *multiplier process*—that makes a sudden decline in aggregate demand so frightening. *What starts off as a relatively small spending shortfall quickly snowballs into a much larger problem.*

We can see the multiplier process at work by watching what happens to a $100 billion decline in investment spending as it makes its way around the circular flow. The process starts at step 1 in Figure 10.5, when investment is cut back by $100 billion. At first (step 2), the only thing that happens is that unsold goods appear (in the form of undesired inventories). Producers adjust to this problem by cutting back on production and laying off workers or reducing wages and prices (step 3). In either case, consumer income falls $100 billion per year shortly after the investment cutbacks occur (step 4).

How will consumers respond to this drop in disposable income? *If disposable income falls, we expect consumer spending to drop as well.* In fact, the consumption function tells us just how much spending will drop. The **marginal propensity to consume (MPC)** is the critical variable in this process. Because we've specified that $C = \$100$ billion $+ 0.75Y$, we expect consumers to reduce their spending by $0.75 for every $1.00 of lost income. In the present example, the loss of $100 billion of annual income will induce consumers to reduce their rate of spending by $75 billion per year ($0.75 \times \$100$ billion). This drop in spending is illustrated by step 5 in Figure 10.5.

The multiplier process doesn't stop here. A reduction in consumer spending quickly translates into more unsold output (step 6). As additional goods pile up on producers' shelves, we anticipate further cutbacks in production, employment, and disposable income (step 7).

marginal propensity to consume (MPC): The fraction of each additional (marginal) dollar of disposable income spent on consumption; the change in consumption divided by the change in disposable income.

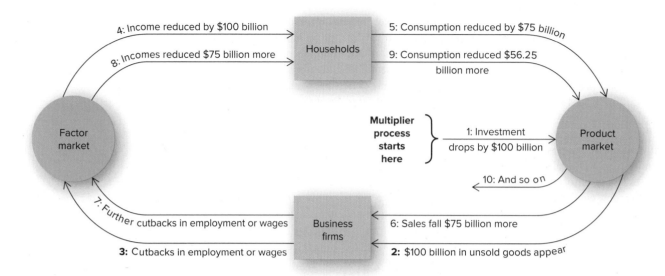

FIGURE 10.5

The Multiplier Process

A decline in investment (step 1) will leave output unsold (step 2) and may lead to a cutback in production and income (step 3). A reduction in total income (step 4) will in turn lead to a reduction in consumer spending (step 5). These additional cuts in spending cause a further decrease in income, leading to additional spending reductions, and so on. This sequence of adjustments is referred to as the *multiplier process.*

As disposable incomes are further reduced by job layoffs and wage cuts (step 8), more reductions in consumer spending are sure to follow (step 9). Again the marginal propensity to consume (MPC) tells us how large such reductions will be. With an MPC of 0.75, we may expect spending to fall by another $56.25 billion per year (0.75 × $75 billion) in step 9. This is exactly what was happening in 2008, as Front Page Economics "U.S. GDP Down 3.8% in Q4, Biggest Drop Since 1982" reports.

FRONT PAGE ECONOMICS

U.S. GDP DOWN 3.8% IN Q4, BIGGEST DROP SINCE 1982

WASHINGTON: The U.S. economy contracted at the fastest pace since 1982, a 3.8 percent rate of decline.

The decline in fourth-quarter gross domestic product (GDP) as estimated by the Commerce Department marked a sharp downward acceleration in economic activity after a 0.5 percent drop in the third quarter.

Christina Romer, chair of President Barack Obama's Council of Economic Advisors, warned the recession had spread to all sectors of the economy and highlights the need for a quick stimulus plan.

"This widespread decline emphasizes that the problems that began in our housing and financial sector have spread to nearly all areas of the economy," Romer said in a statement.

Source: AFP, January 30, 2009.

CRITICAL ANALYSIS: A decline in investment reduces consumer incomes and induces cutbacks in consumer spending. The resultant decline in consumption triggers further declines in income and spending (**multiplier process**).

Spending Cycles	Change in This Cycle's Spending and Income (Billions per Year)	Cumulative Decrease in Spending and Income (Billions per Year)	
First cycle: investment declines.	$100.00	$100.00	} ΔI
Second cycle: consumption drops by MPC × $100.	75.00	175.00	
Third cycle: consumption drops by MPC × $75.	56.25	231.25	
Fourth cycle: consumption drops by MPC × $56.25.	42.19	273.44	
Fifth cycle: consumption drops by MPC × $42.19.	31.64	305.08	} ΔC
Sixth cycle: consumption drops by MPC × $31.64.	23.73	328.81	
Seventh cycle: consumption drops by MPC × $23.73.	17.80	346.61	
Eighth cycle: consumption drops by MPC × $17.80.	13.35	359.95	
⋮	⋮	⋮	
nth cycle and beyond		400.00	

TABLE 10.1

The Multiplier Cycles

The circular flow of income implies that an initial drop in spending will lead to cumulative changes in consumer spending and income. Here, an initial decline in investment spending of $100 billion (first cycle) causes a cutback in consumer spending in the amount of $75 billion (second cycle). At each subsequent cycle, consumer spending drops by the amount MPC × prior change in income. Ultimately, total spending (and income) falls by $400 billion, or $[1/(1 - MPC)]$ × initial change in spending.

The Multiplier

The multiplier process continues to work until the reductions in income and sales become so small that no one's market behavior is significantly affected. We don't have to examine each step along the way. As you may have noticed, all the steps begin to look alike once we've gone around the circular flow a few times. Instead of examining each step, we can look ahead to see where they are taking us. Each time the multiplier process works its way around the circular flow, the reduction in spending equals the previous drop in income multiplied by the MPC. Accordingly, by pressing a few keys on a calculator, we can produce a sequence of events like that depicted in Table 10.1.

Ultimate Impact. The impact of the multiplier is devastating. The ultimate reduction in real spending resulting from the initial drop in investment isn't $100 billion per year but $400 billion! Even if one is accustomed to thinking in terms of billions and trillions, this is a huge drop in demand. What the multiplier process demonstrates is that the dimensions of an initial spending gap greatly understate the severity of the economic dislocations that will follow in its wake. *The eventual decline in spending will be much larger than the initial (autonomous) decrease in aggregate demand.* This was evident in the recession of 2008–2009, when layoffs snowballed from industry to industry (see Front Page Economics "Unemployment Spreading Fast across U.S. Industries"), ultimately leaving millions of people unemployed. In 2020, similar multiplier effects swept the economy into a downward spiral that threw millions of workers out of jobs.

Multiplier Formula. The ultimate impact of an AD shift on total spending can be determined by computing the change in income and consumption at each cycle of the circular flow. This is the approach summarized in Table 10.1, with each row representing a spending cycle. The entire computation can be simplified considerably by using a single figure, the multiplier. The **multiplier** tells us the extent to which the rate of total spending will change in response to an initial change in the flow of expenditure. The multiplier summarizes the

FRONT PAGE ECONOMICS

UNEMPLOYMENT SPREADING FAST ACROSS U.S. INDUSTRIES

The collapse of the housing industry has sent ripple effects across U.S. industries. The surge in construction unemployment is spilling over into other sectors of the economy at an alarming rate. In data released Friday, the Bureau of Labor Statistics reported that the unemployment rate has jumped by more than 2 percentage points over last year in 12 states. Job losses have spread beyond construction to a host of industries, including tourism and professional services. Economists now predict that the national unemployment rate, presently at 6.5 percent, will top 8 percent in the coming months.

Source: U.S. Bureau of Labor Statistics and news accounts, November 2008.

CRITICAL ANALYSIS: Cutbacks in production cause employee layoffs. The newly unemployed workers curtail *their* spending, causing sequential layoffs in other industries. These ripple effects give rise to the multiplier.

sequence of steps described in Table 10.1.[1] In its simplest form, the multiplier can be computed as

$$\text{Multiplier} = \frac{1}{1 - \text{MPC}}$$

In our example, the initial change in aggregate demand occurs when investment drops by $100 billion per year at full-employment output ($3,000 billion per year). Table 10.1 indicates that this investment drop-off will lead to a $400 billion reduction in the rate of total spending at the current price level. Using the multiplier, we arrive at the same conclusion by observing that

$$\begin{aligned}
\text{Total change in spending} &= \text{Multiplier} \times \text{Initial change in aggregate spending} \\
&= \frac{1}{1 - \text{MPC}} \times \$100 \text{ billion per year} \\
&= \frac{1}{1 - 0.75} \times \$100 \text{ billion per year} \\
&= 4 \times \$100 \text{ billion per year} \\
&= \$400 \text{ billion per year}
\end{aligned}$$

In other words, *the cumulative decrease in total spending ($400 billion per year) resulting from an abrupt decline in aggregate demand at full employment is equal to the initial decline ($100 billion per year) multiplied by the multiplier (4).*

Notice how the size of the multiplier depends on the value of the MPC: the larger the fraction (MPC) of income respent in each round of the circular flow, the greater the impact of any autonomous change in spending on cumulative aggregate demand. The cumulative process of spending adjustments can also have worldwide effects. As World View "Asian Economies Hurt by U.S. Recession" illustrates, Asia's economic growth slowed when the U.S. economy slumped in 2008–2009.

The same kind of global linkage occurred in 2020. Eighty percent of Mexico's exports go to the United States. When the COVID-19 lockdowns shut bars and restaurants across the U.S., Americans drank less tequila. They also reduced car purchases and drove less. The result was increased unemployment and lower incomes in Mexico's tequila, auto, and oil industries. The multiplier slid across national boundaries.

[1]The multiplier summarizes the geometric progression $1 + \text{MPC} + \text{MPC}^2 + \text{MPC}^3 + \cdots + \text{MPC}^n$, which equals $1/(1 - \text{MPC})$ when n becomes infinite.

MACRO EQUILIBRIUM REVISITED

The key features of the Keynesian adjustment process are

- *Producers cut output and employment when output exceeds aggregate demand at the current price level (leakage exceeds injections).*
- *The resulting loss of income causes a decline in consumer spending.*
- *Declines in consumer spending lead to further production cutbacks, more lost income, and still less consumption.*

Sequential AD Shifts

Figure 10.6 illustrates the ultimate impact of the multiplier process. Notice that the AD curve shifts *twice*. The first shift—from AD_0 to AD_1—represents the $100 billion drop in investment spending. As we saw earlier in Figure 10.4, this initial shift of aggregate demand will start the economy moving toward a new equilibrium at point *b*.

Along the way, however, the multiplier kicks in and things get worse. *The decline in household income caused by investment cutbacks sets off the multiplier process, causing sequential shifts of the AD curve.* We measure these multiplier effects at the initial price level of P_0. With a marginal propensity to consume of 0.75, we've seen that induced consumption ultimately declines by $300 billion when autonomous investment declines by $100 billion. In Figure 10.6 this is illustrated by the *second* shift of the aggregate demand curve, from AD_1 to AD_2. Notice that the horizontal distance between AD_1 and AD_2 is $300 billion. That represents the *cumulative* decline in consumer spending that results from repeated steps in the multiplier process. When added to the initial decline in investment spending ($100 billion), we get a $400 billion shift in AD.

Price and Output Effects

Although aggregate demand has fallen (shifted) by $400 billion, real output doesn't necessarily drop that much. *The impact of a shift in aggregate demand is reflected in both output and price changes.* This is evident in Figure 10.7, which is a close-up view of Figure 10.6. When AD shifts from AD_0 to AD_2, the macro equilibrium moves down the sloped AS curve to point *c*. At point *c* the new equilibrium output is Q_E and the new price level is P_E.

FIGURE 10.6

Multiplier Effects

A decline in investment spending reduces household income, setting off negative multiplier effects. Hence, the *initial* shift of AD₀ to AD₁ is followed by a series of aftershocks that ultimately ends up at AD₂. The shift from AD₁ to AD₂ represents reduced consumption.

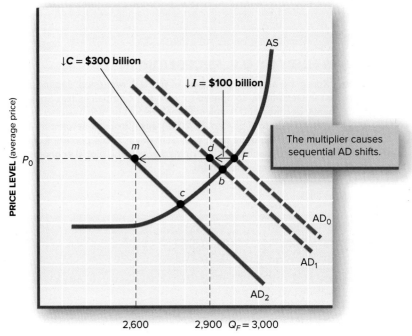

recessionary GDP gap: The amount by which equilibrium GDP falls short of full-employment GDP.

cyclical unemployment: Unemployment attributable to a lack of job vacancies—that is, to an inadequate level of aggregate demand.

Recessionary GDP Gap. As long as the aggregate supply curve is upward-sloping, the shock of any AD shift will be spread across output and prices. In Figure 10.7 the net effect on real output is shown as the real GDP gap. *The recessionary GDP gap equals the difference between equilibrium real GDP (Q_E) and full-employment real GDP (Q_F).* It represents the amount by which the economy is underproducing during a recession. As we noted in Chapter 9, this is a classic case of **cyclical unemployment.**

FIGURE 10.7

Recessionary GDP Gap

The real GDP gap is the difference between equilibrium GDP (Q_E) and full-employment GDP (Q_F). It represents the lost output due to a recession.

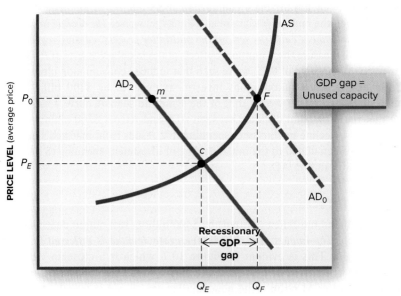

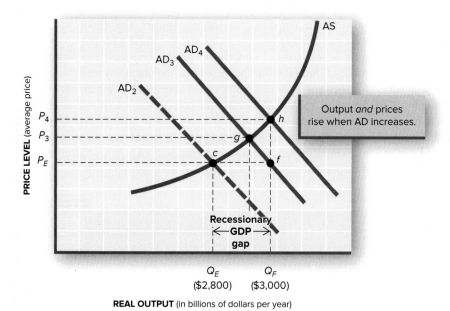

FIGURE 10.8

**The Unemployment–
Inflation Trade-Off**

If the short-run AS curve is
upward-sloping, an AD increase
will raise output *and* prices. If
AD increases by the amount of
the recessionary GDP gap only
(AD$_2$ to AD$_3$), full employment
(Q_F) won't be reached. Macro
equilibrium moves to point *g*,
not point *f.*

Short-Run Inflation–Unemployment Trade-Offs

Figure 10.7 not only illustrates how much output declines when AD falls but also provides an important clue about the difficulty of restoring full employment. Suppose the recessionary GDP gap were $200 billion, as illustrated in Figure 10.8. How much more AD would we need to get back to full employment?

Upward-Sloping AS. Suppose aggregate demand at the equilibrium price level (P_E) were to increase by exactly $200 billion (including multiplier effects), as illustrated by the shift to AD$_3$. Would that get us back to full-employment output? Not according to Figure 10.8. *When AD increases, both output and prices go up.* Because the AS curve is upward-sloping, the $200 billion shift from AD$_2$ to AD$_3$ moves the new macro equilibrium to point *g* rather than point *f.* We'd like to get to point *f* with full employment and price stability, but as demand picks up, producers are likely to raise prices. This leads us up the AS curve to point *g.* At point *g*, we're still short of full employment and have experienced a bit of inflation (an increased price level). *So long as the short-run AS is upward-sloping, there's a trade-off between unemployment and inflation.* We can get lower rates of unemployment (more real output) only if we accept some inflation.

"Full" vs. "Natural" Unemployment. The short-term trade-off between unemployment and inflation is the basis for the definition of "full" employment. We don't define full employment as *zero* unemployment; we define it as the rate of unemployment *consistent with price stability.* As noted in Chapter 6, **full employment** is typically defined as a 4 to 6 percent rate of unemployment. What the upward-sloping AS curve tells us is that *the closer the economy gets to capacity output, the greater the risk of inflation.* To get back to full employment in Figure 10.8, aggregate demand would have to increase to AD$_4$, with the price level rising to P_4.

Not everyone accepts this notion of full employment. As we saw in Chapter 8, neoclassical and monetarist economists prefer to focus on *long*-run outcomes. In their view, the long-run AS curve is vertical (see Figure 8.12). In that long-run context, there's no unemployment–inflation trade-off: An AD shift doesn't change the "natural" (institutional) rate of unemployment but does alter the price level. We'll examine this argument in Chapters 16 and 17.

The Coronavirus Shutdown. In early 2020 very few people were focused on long-run outcomes for the economy: The coronavirus had everyone riveted to short-term health dangers and the immediate risks to the economy. Although some people thought the economy could "ride

full employment: The lowest
rate of unemployment
compatible with price stability,
variously estimated at between
4 percent and 6 percent
unemployment.

out" the pandemic, the overwhelming consensus was that government intervention was a dire necessity. In response to the pandemic, governments around the world had shut down their economies, throwing millions of people out of work and devastating household incomes. In the United States, the Congressional Budget Office predicted that the unemployment rate would jump to 12 percent in April 2020 and that GDP would fall by as much as 10 percent (see Front Page Economics "CBO Foresees April Pain"). Unless the government intervened, multiplier effects could have pushed the economy into a long and deep recession. Although some of the leftward shift of the AD curve would have been absorbed by falling price levels, the residual loss in output and jobs was frightening. Congress responded to this outlook with a series of spending and tax initiatives that helped reverse the AD shifts (discussed in Chapter 11).

FRONT PAGE ECONOMICS

CBO FORESEES APRIL PAIN

The Congressional Budget Office has posted some numbers that may spark congressional action. The CBO sees the nation's unemployment rate jumping to 12 percent in April as the nation's factories, businesses, and entertainment venues shut down. Stay-at-home orders are keeping people not only from their jobs, but also from spending their incomes. CBO says the resulting GDP damage could be as much as 10 percent in April. These forecasts are a clarion call for Congress and the White House to pump up fiscal relief.

Source: Media reports March–April 2020.

CRITICAL ANALYSIS: When macro equilibrium is derailed, the choice is whether to let it adjust on its own or to ask the government to intervene. In early 2020 the decision was to intervene aggressively to reverse leftward shifts of the AD curve.

ADJUSTMENT TO AN INFLATIONARY GDP GAP

As we've observed, *a sudden shift in aggregate demand can have a cumulative effect on macro outcomes* that's larger than the initial imbalance. This multiplier process works both ways. Just as a *decrease* in investment (or any other AD component) can send the economy into a recessionary tailspin, an *increase* in investment might initiate an inflationary spiral.

Figure 10.9 illustrates the consequences of a sudden jump in investment spending. We start out again in the happy equilibrium (point F), where full employment (Q_F) and price stability (P_0) prevail. Initial spending consists of

$$C = \$2,350 \text{ billion} \qquad G = \$150 \text{ billion}$$
$$I = \$400 \text{ billion} \qquad X - M = \$100 \text{ billion}$$

Increased Investment

Then investors suddenly decide to step up the rate of investment. Perhaps their expectations for future sales have risen. Maybe new technology has become available that compels firms to modernize their facilities. Maybe they want to take advantage of President Trump's tax cuts and investment incentives. Whatever the reason, investors decide to raise the level of investment from \$400 billion to \$500 billion at the current price level (P_0). This change in investment spending shifts the aggregate demand curve from AD_0 to AD_5 (a horizontal shift of \$100 billion).

Inventory Depletion. One of the first things you'll notice when AD shifts like this is that available inventories shrink. Investors can step up their *spending* more quickly than firms can increase their *production*. A lot of the increased investment demand will have to be

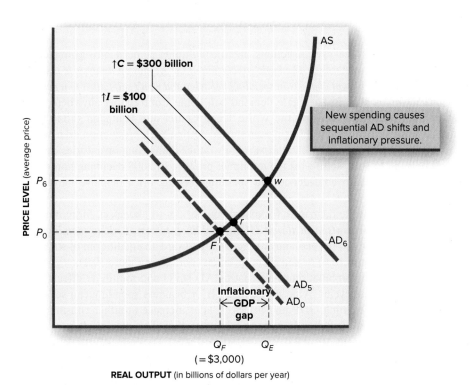

FIGURE 10.9
Demand-Pull Inflation
An increase in investment or other autonomous spending sets off multiplier effects shifting AD to the right. AD shifts to the right *twice*, first (AD$_0$ to AD$_5$) because of increased investment and then (AD$_5$ to AD$_6$) because of increased consumption. The increased AD moves the economy up the short-run AS curve, causing some inflation. How much inflation results depends on the slope of the AS curve.

satisfied from existing inventory. The decline in inventory is a signal to producers that it might be a good time to raise prices a bit. Thus, *inventory depletion is a warning sign of potential inflation.* As the economy moves up from point *F* to point *r* in Figure 10.9, that inflation starts to become visible.

Household Incomes

Whether or not prices start rising quickly, household incomes will get a boost from the increased investment. Producers will step up the rate of output to rebuild inventories and supply more investment goods (equipment and structures). To do so, they'll hire more workers or extend working hours. The end result for workers will be fatter paychecks.

Induced Consumption

What will households do with these heftier paychecks? By now, you know what the consumer response will be. The marginal propensity to consume prompts an increase in consumer spending. Eventually, consumer spending increases by a *multiple* of the initial income change. In this case, the consumption increase is $300 billion (see Table 10.1).

Figure 10.9 illustrates the results of the sequential AD shifts caused by multiplier-induced consumption. Notice how the AD curve ultimately shifts, from AD$_5$ to AD$_6$.

A New Equilibrium

The ultimate impact of the investment surge is reflected in the new equilibrium at point *w*. As before, the shift of AD has affected both real output and prices. Real output does increase beyond the full-employment level, but it does so only at the expense of accelerating inflation. This is a classic case of **demand-pull inflation.** The initial increase in investment was enough to kindle a little inflation. The multiplier effect worsened the problem by forcing the economy further along the ever-steeper AS curve. The **inflationary GDP gap** ends up as $Q_E - Q_F$.

demand-pull inflation: An increase in the price level initiated by excessive aggregate demand.

inflationary GDP gap: The amount by which equilibrium GDP exceeds full-employment GDP.

Booms and Busts

The Keynesian analysis of leakages, injections, and the multiplier paints a fairly grim picture of the prospects for macro stability. ***The basic conclusion of the Keynesian analysis is that the economy is vulnerable to abrupt changes in spending behavior and won't self-adjust to a desired macro equilibrium.*** A shift in aggregate demand can come from almost anywhere. The September 2001 terrorist attacks on the World Trade Center and Pentagon shook both consumer and investor confidence. Businesses started cutting back production even *before* inventories started piling up. Worsened *expectations* rather than rising inventories caused investment demand to shift, setting off the multiplier process. In 2008 declining home and stock prices curtailed both confidence and spending, setting off a negative multiplier process.

When the aggregate demand curve shifts, macro equilibrium will be upset. Moreover, ***the responses of market participants to an abrupt AD shift are likely to worsen rather than improve market outcomes.*** As a result, the economy may gravitate toward an equilibrium of stagnant recession (point *c* in Figure 10.6) or persistent inflation (point *w* in Figure 10.9).

As Keynes saw it, the combination of alternating AD shifts and multiplier effects also causes recurring business cycles. A drop in consumer or business spending can set off a recessionary spiral of declining GDP and prices. A later increase in either consumer or business spending can set the ball rolling in the other direction. This may result in a series of economic booms and busts.

DECISIONS FOR TOMORROW

How Important Is Consumer Confidence?

This chapter emphasized how a sudden change in investment might set off the multiplier process. Investors aren't the only potential culprits, however. A sudden change in government spending or exports could just as easily start the multiplier ball rolling. In fact, the whole process could originate with a change in *consumer* spending.

Consumer Confidence. Recall the two components of consumption: *autonomous* consumption and *induced* consumption. These two components may be expressed as

$$C = a + bY$$

We've seen that autonomous consumption (*a* in the equation) is influenced by *nonincome* factors, including consumer confidence. As we first observed in Chapter 8, *changes* in consumer confidence can therefore be an AD shift factor: a force that changes the value of autonomous consumption and thus shifts the AD curve to the right or left. A change in consumer confidence can change the marginal propensity to consume (*b* in the equation) as well, further shifting the AD curve.

These AD shifts can be substantial. According to the World Bank, every 1 percent change in consumer confidence alters autonomous consumption by $1.1 billion. That makes the 2007–2008 plunge in consumer confidence particularly scary. As Figure 10.10 illustrates, consumer confidence declined by more than 40 percent from the beginning of 2007 to the end of 2008. The drop in consumer confidence in early 2020 was also severe. That loss of confidence caused consumer spending to drop even further than the cutbacks induced by falling incomes.

Ironically, when consumers try to cope with recession by cutting their spending and saving more of their incomes, they actually make matters worse (see Front Page Economics "The Paradox of Thrift"). This "paradox of thrift" recognizes that what might make sense for an *individual* consumer doesn't necessarily make sense for *aggregate* demand.

The Official View: Always a Rosy Outlook. Because consumer spending vastly outweighs any other component of aggregate demand, the threat of abrupt changes in consumer

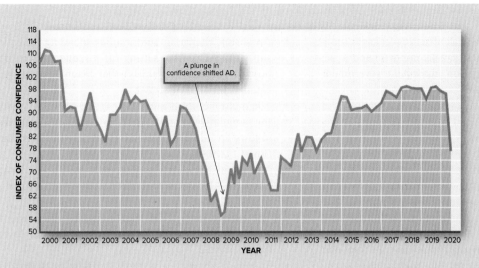

FIGURE 10.10

Consumer Confidence

Consumer confidence is affected by various financial, political, and international events. Changes in consumer confidence affect consumer behavior and thereby shift the AD curve right or left. The steep loss of confidence in 2007–2009 deepened and lengthened the Great Recession. In early 2020 confidence again declined sharply, falling from 100 in February to 72 in April.

Source: University of Michigan.

FRONT PAGE ECONOMICS

THE PARADOX OF THRIFT

With incomes falling and more job layoffs announced daily, American families are getting thrifty. They are cutting back on spending, reducing credit card debt, and even setting aside a little more money for the proverbial rainy day. This might be a sound financial strategy for individual households. But such thriftiness can drive the economy deeper into recession. It's what economists call the "paradox of thrift": Saving more money in a recession pulls the reins on spending just when the economy needs it the most.

Source: News accounts, January 2009.

CRITICAL ANALYSIS: When consumers become more pessimistic about their economy, they start saving more and spending less. This shifts AD leftward and deepens a **recession**.

behavior is serious. Recognizing this, public officials strive to maintain consumer confidence in the economy tomorrow, even when such confidence might not be warranted. That's why President Hoover, bank officials, and major brokerage houses tried to assure the public in 1929 that the outlook was still rosy. (Look back at the first few pages of Chapter 8.) The "rosy outlook" is still the official perspective on the economy tomorrow. The White House is always upbeat about prospects for the economy. If it weren't—if it were even to hint at the possibility of a recession—consumer and investor confidence might wilt. Then the economy might quickly turn ugly.

SUMMARY

- The circular flow of income has offsetting leakages (consumer saving, taxes, business saving, imports) and injections (autonomous consumption, investment, government spending, exports).   **LO10-1**
- When desired injections equal leakage, the economy is in equilibrium (output demanded = output supplied at prevailing price level).   **LO10-3**
- An imbalance of injections and leakages will cause the economy to expand or contract. An imbalance at full-employment GDP will cause cyclical unemployment or demand-pull inflation. How serious these problems become depends on how the market responds to the initial imbalance.   **LO10-3**
- Classical economists believed (flexible) interest rates and price levels would equalize injections and leakages (especially consumer saving and investment), restoring full-employment equilibrium.   **LO10-3**
- Keynes showed that spending imbalances might actually *worsen* if consumer and investor expectations changed.   **LO10-2**

- An abrupt change in autonomous spending (injections) shifts the AD curve, setting off a sequential multiplier process (further AD shifts) that magnifies changes in equilibrium GDP.   **LO10-2**
- The multiplier itself is equal to $1/(1 - MPC)$. It indicates the cumulative change (shift) in aggregate demand that follows an initial (autonomous) disruption of spending flows.   **LO10-2**
- As long as the short-run aggregate supply curve slopes upward, AD shifts will affect both real output and prices.   **LO10-2**
- The recessionary GDP gap measures the amount by which equilibrium GDP falls short of full-employment GDP.   **LO10-3**
- Sudden changes in consumer confidence shift the AD curve right or left and may destabilize the economy. To avoid this, policymakers always maintain a rosy outlook.   **LO10-3**

Key Terms

aggregate demand (AD)	injection	recessionary GDP gap
full-employment GDP	equilibrium GDP	cyclical unemployment
leakage	marginal propensity to consume	full employment
disposable income (DI)	(MPC)	demand-pull inflation
gross business saving	multiplier	inflationary GDP gap

Questions for Discussion

1. How might declining prices affect a firm's decision to borrow and invest? (See Front Page Economics "Housing Starts Fall to 10-Year Low".)   **LO10-3**
2. Why wouldn't investment and saving flows at full employment always be equal?   **LO10-1**
3. When unwanted inventories pile up in retail stores, how is production affected? What are the steps in this process?   **LO10-3**
4. How can equilibrium output exceed full-employment output (as in Figure 10.9)?   **LO10-3**
5. How might construction industry job losses affect incomes in the clothing and travel industries?   **LO10-2**
6. What forces might turn an economic bust into an economic boom? What forces might put an end to the boom?   **LO10-3**

7. Why might "belt-tightening" by consumers in a recession be unwelcome? (See Front Page Economics "The Paradox of Thrift.")   **LO10-3**
8. What is the "ripple effect" in Front Page Economics "Unemployment Spreading Fast across U.S. Industries?"   **LO10-2**
9. Will the price level always rise when AD increases? Why or why not?   **LO10-3**
10. What would have happened to the economy in 2020 if the government had not intervened in the coronavirus pandemic?   **LO10-3**

LO10-3 1. From 2007 to 2009, calculate the percentage change in
   (*a*) Real consumption.
   (*b*) Real investment.
   (*c*) Real government spending.
   (See Data Tables at the end of the book.)

2. Based on the following data (in billions of dollars),

	2016	2017	2018	2019
GDP	18,715	19,519	20,580	21,340
Disposable income	14,165	14,833	15,741	16,356
Consumption	12,749	13,312	13,999	14,511

LO10-1 Calculate
   (*a*) The MPC (2016–2017).
   (*b*) The APC in 2017.
   (*c*) The share of output devoted to consumer goods in 2017.

LO10-1 3. If the consumption function is $C = \$800$ billion $+ 0.8Y$,
   (*a*) What is the MPC?
   (*b*) How large is autonomous C?
   (*c*) How much do consumers spend with incomes of $4 trillion?
   (*d*) How much do they save?

LO10-2 4. If the marginal propensity to consume is 0.9,
   (*a*) What is the value of the multiplier?
   (*b*) What is the marginal propensity to save?

LO10-2 5. Suppose that investment demand increases by $400 billion and no leakages occur except household saving. Assume further that households have a marginal propensity to consume of 75 percent.
   (*a*) Compute four rounds of multiplier effects:

	Changes in This Cycle's Spending	Cumulative Change in Spending
First cycle	_____	_____
Second cycle	_____	_____
Third cycle	_____	_____
Fourth cycle	_____	_____

   (*b*) What will be the final cumulative impact on spending?

PROBLEMS FOR CHAPTER 10 (cont'd)

LO10-3   6. Illustrate in the following graph the impact of a sudden decline in consumer confidence that reduces autonomous consumption by $200 billion at the price level P_F. Assume MPC = 0.5.
   (a) What is the new equilibrium level of real output? (Don't forget the multiplier.)
   (b) How large is the real GDP gap?
   (c) Did average prices increase or decrease?

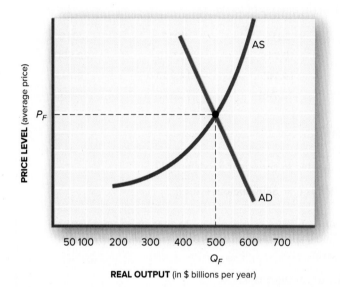

REAL OUTPUT (in $ billions per year)

LO10-1   7. By how much did annualized consumption decline in November 2008 when GDP was $14 trillion? (See Front Page Economics "U.S. GDP Down 3.8% in Q4, Biggest Drop Since 1982.")

LO10-2   8. If U.S. exports to Mexico decline by $20 billion, by how much will U.S. spending drop if our MPC is 0.75?

LO10-3   9. How large is the inflationary GDP gap in Figure 10.9?

LO10-2 10. The accompanying graph depicts a macro equilibrium. Answer the questions based on the
LO10-3   information in the graph.
   (a) What is the equilibrium rate of GDP?
   (b) If full-employment real GDP is $800, what problem does this economy have?
   (c) How large is the real GDP gap?

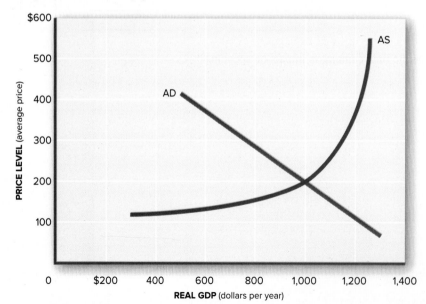

REAL GDP (dollars per year)

234

LO10-2 11. Calculate the total change in aggregate spending if investment increases by $200 billion and the marginal propensity to consume is 0.8.

LO10-2 12. The accompanying graph depicts a full-employment macro equilibrium. On the following graph,
   (*a*) Identify this full-employment equilibrium.
   (*b*) Show the initial change in aggregate demand when consumer spending falls by $50 billion.
   (*c*) Show the total impact on aggregate demand once multiplier effects are taken into account. Assume the marginal propensity to consume = 0.6.

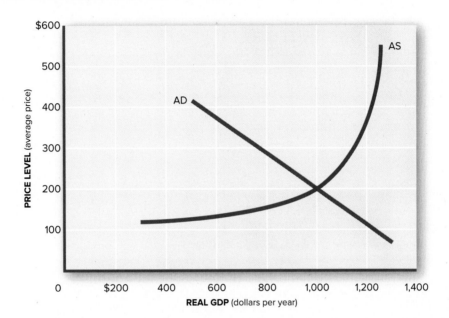

LO10-3 13. *Decisions for Tomorrow:* Refer to Figure 10.10 to describe the impact of changing consumer confidence on aggregate demand for the following years:
   (*a*) 2002
   (*b*) 2007–2008
   (*c*) 2020

Design Credit: Shutterstock

FISCAL POLICY TOOLS

Photodisc/Getty Images

NoDerog/iStock/360/Getty Images

The government's tax and spending activities influence economic outcomes. Keynesian theory emphasizes the market's lack of self-adjustment, particularly in recessions. If the market doesn't self-adjust, the government may have to intervene. Specifically, the government may have to use its tax and spending power (fiscal policy) to stabilize the macro economy at its full-employment equilibrium. Chapters 11 and 12 look closely at the policy goals, strategies, and tools of fiscal policy.

Photodisc/Getty Images

LEARNING OBJECTIVES

After reading this chapter, you should know

LO11-1 How and why the real GDP gap and the AD shortfall differ.

LO11-2 The tools of fiscal stimulus and their desired scope.

LO11-3 What AD excess measures.

LO11-4 The tools of fiscal restraint and their desired scope.

LO11-5 How the multiplier affects fiscal policy.

CHAPTER **11**

Fiscal Policy

The Keynesian theory of macro instability is practically a mandate for government intervention. From a Keynesian perspective, too little aggregate demand causes unemployment; too much aggregate demand causes inflation. If the market itself won't correct these imbalances, the federal government must. Keynes concluded that the government must intervene to manage the level of aggregate demand. This implies increasing aggregate demand when it's deficient and decreasing aggregate demand when it's excessive.

President Obama adopted the Keynesian prescription for ending a recession. Even before taking office, he developed a spending and tax cut package designed to stimulate aggregate demand and "get the country moving again." President Trump wasn't saddled with a recession when he took office but also adopted Keynesian policies to accelerate economic growth. President Biden also followed Keynes's advice. In this chapter we'll examine the fiscal policy tools an Economist in Chief has available, how they work, and what impact they are expected to have. The basic questions we address are

- **Can government spending and tax policies ensure full employment?**
- **What policy actions will help fight inflation?**
- **What are the risks of government intervention?**

As we'll see, the government's tax and spending activities affect not only the *level* of output and prices but the *mix* of output as well.

TAXES AND SPENDING

Article I of the U.S. Constitution empowers Congress "to lay and collect Taxes, Duties, Imposts and Excises, to pay the Debts and provide for the common Defence and general Welfare of the United States." Up until 1915, however, the federal government collected few taxes and spent little. In 1902 the federal government employed fewer than 350,000 people and spent a mere $650 million. Today the federal government employs more than 4 million people and spends nearly $5 trillion a year.

Government Revenue

The tremendous expansion of the federal government started with the Sixteenth Amendment to the U.S. Constitution (1913), which extended the government's taxing power to *incomes.* Prior to that, most government revenue came from taxes on imports, whiskey, and tobacco. Once the federal government got the power to tax incomes, it had the revenue base to finance increased expenditure.

Today the federal government collects nearly $5 trillion a year in tax revenues. About half of that revenue comes from individual income taxes (see Figure 4.5). Social Security payroll taxes are the second-largest revenue source, followed at a distance by corporate income taxes. The customs, whiskey, and tobacco taxes on which the federal government depended in 1902 now count for very little.

Government Expenditure

In 1902 federal government expenditures mirrored tax revenues: Both were small. Today things are different. The federal government now spends all of its much larger tax revenues—and more. Uncle Sam even borrows additional funds to pay for federal spending. In Chapter 12 we look at the implications of the budget deficits that help finance federal spending. In this chapter we focus on how government spending *directly* affects **aggregate demand**.

Purchases vs. Transfers. To understand how government spending affects aggregate demand, we must again distinguish between government *purchases* and *income transfers*. Government spending on defense, highways, and health care entails the purchase of real goods and services in product markets; they're part of aggregate demand. By contrast, the government doesn't buy anything when it mails out Social Security checks. Those checks simply transfer income from taxpayers to retired workers. **Income transfers** don't become part of aggregate demand until the transfer recipients decide to spend that income.

As we observed in Chapter 4, less than half of all federal government spending entails the purchase of goods and services. The rest of federal spending is either an income transfer or an interest payment on the national debt.

Fiscal Policy

The federal government's tax and spending powers give it a great deal of influence over aggregate demand. *The government can alter aggregate demand by*

- *Purchasing more or fewer goods and services.*
- *Raising or lowering taxes.*
- *Changing the level of income transfers.*

Fiscal policy entails the use of these three budget tools to influence macroeconomic outcomes. *From a macro perspective, the federal budget is a tool that can shift aggregate demand and thereby alter macroeconomic outcomes.* Figure 11.1 puts this tool into the framework of the basic AS/AD model.

aggregate demand (AD): The total quantity of output (real GDP) demanded at alternative price levels in a given time period, *ceteris paribus.*

income transfers: Payments to individuals for which no current goods or services are exchanged, such as Social Security, welfare, and unemployment benefits.

fiscal policy: The use of government taxes and spending to alter macroeconomic outcomes.

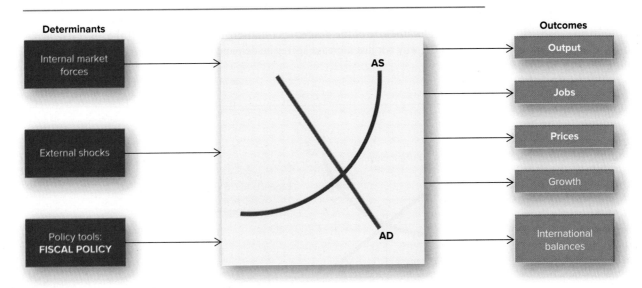

FIGURE 11.1

Fiscal Policy

Fiscal policy refers to the use of the government's tax and spending powers to alter macro outcomes. Fiscal policy works principally through shifts of the aggregate demand curve.

Although fiscal policy can be used to pursue any of our economic goals, we begin our study by exploring its potential to ensure full employment. We then look at its potential to maintain price stability. Along the way we also observe the potential of fiscal policy to alter the mix of output and the distribution of income.

FISCAL STIMULUS

equilibrium (macro): The combination of price level and real output that is compatible with both aggregate demand and aggregate supply.

The basic premise of fiscal policy is that the market's short-run macro equilibrium may not be a desirable one. This is clearly the case in Figure 11.2. **Macro equilibrium** occurs at Q_E, where $5.6 trillion of output is being produced. Full-employment GDP occurs at Q_F, where the real value of output is $6 trillion. Accordingly, the economy depicted in Figure 11.2 confronts a **recessionary GDP gap** of $400 billion. Unless something else happens, unemployment is sure to rise as the economy contracts from Q_F to Q_E.

recessionary GDP gap: The amount by which equilibrium GDP falls short of full-employment GDP.

Keynesian Strategy

The Keynesian model of the adjustment process helps us not only understand how an economy can get into such trouble but also see how it might get out. Keynes emphasized how the aggregate demand curve *shifts* with changes in spending behavior. He also emphasized how new injections of spending into the circular flow multiply into much larger changes in total spending via the multiplier process. *From a Keynesian perspective, the way out of recession is obvious: Get someone to spend more on goods and services.* Should desired spending increase, the aggregate demand curve would *shift* to the right, leading the economy out of recession. That additional spending could come from increased government purchases or from tax cuts that induce increased consumer or business spending. Any such **fiscal stimulus** could propel the economy out of recession.

fiscal stimulus: Tax cuts or spending hikes intended to increase (shift) aggregate demand.

Although the general strategy for Keynesian fiscal policy is clear, the scope of desired intervention isn't so evident. Two strategic policy questions must be addressed:

- By how much do we want to shift the AD curve to the right?
- How can we induce the desired shift?

The AD Shortfall

At first glance, the size of the desired AD shift might seem obvious. If the real GDP gap is $400 billion, why not just increase aggregate demand by that amount?

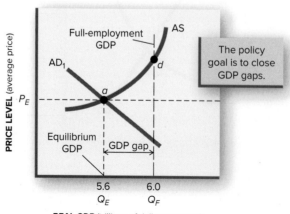

FIGURE 11.2

The Policy Goal

If the economy is in a recessionary equilibrium like point *a*, the policy goal is to increase output to full employment (Q_F). Keynes urged the government to use its tax and spending powers to shift the AD curve rightward.

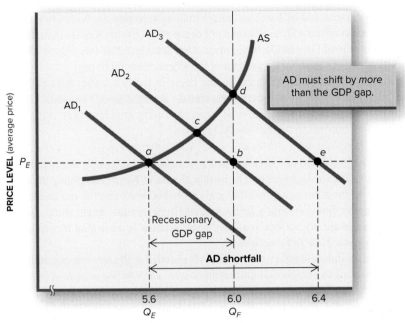

FIGURE 11.3
The AD Shortfall

If aggregate demand increased by the amount of the recessionary GDP gap, we would get a shift from AD$_1$ to AD$_2$. The resulting equilibrium would occur at point c, leaving the economy short of full employment (Q$_F$). (Some of the increased demand pushes up prices instead of output.)

To reach full-employment equilibrium (point d), the AD curve must shift to AD$_3$, thereby eliminating the entire AD shortfall. The AD shortfall—the horizontal distance between point a and point e—is the fiscal policy target for achieving full employment.

How Large a Shift?. Keynes thought that policy might just work. But it's not quite that simple, as Figure 11.3 illustrates. The intent of expansionary fiscal policy is to achieve full employment. In Figure 11.3, this goal would be attained at point b. So it looks like we could restore full employment simply by shifting AD to the right by $400 billion, as the curve AD$_2$ illustrates. The AD$_2$ curve does, in fact, pass through point b. That tells us that people would actually demand the full-employment output Q$_F$ at the price level P$_E$.

But where is the **aggregate supply (AS)** curve? We won't get an *equilibrium* at full employment unless the AD curve intersects with the AS curve at point b. What we see in Figure 11.3 is that the AD curve passes through point b, but the AS curve is nowhere close. So, the economy can't move to point b, as we would like.

So, where will this economy move to? The answer, as always, is to the intersection of the AD and AS curves. In this case, that *equilibrium* occurs at point c. At point c the new AD$_2$ curve intersects with the unchanged AS curve.

What's wrong with this new equilibrium? Simple: The *equilibrium* output associated with AD$_2$ is less than Q$_F$. Hence, *a rightward AD shift equal to the real GDP gap will leave the economy short of full employment* (at the equilibrium point c rather than the desired point b).

Price Level Changes. The failure of the AD$_2$ curve to restore full employment results from the upward slope of the AS curve. *When the AD curve shifts to the right, the economy moves up the aggregate supply (AS) curve, not horizontally to the right. As a result, both real output and the price level change.*

Figure 11.3 illustrates the consequences of the upward-sloping aggregate supply curve. When the aggregate demand curve shifts from AD$_1$ to AD$_2$, we expect cost pressures to increase, pushing the price level up the upward-sloping AS curve. At point c, the AS and AD$_2$ curves intersect, establishing a new equilibrium. At that equilibrium, the price level is higher than it was initially (P$_E$). Real output is higher as well. But at point c we are still short of the full-employment target (Q$_F$).

The Naïve Keynesian Model: Constant Prices. Under special circumstances, the job of restoring full employment wouldn't be that difficult. If there was no cost-push pressure as the economy expanded, the price level wouldn't rise when AD increased. In such an "inflation-free"

aggregate supply (AS): The total quantity of output (real GDP) producers are willing and able to supply at alternative price levels in a given time period, *ceteris paribus*.

environment, the AS curve would be *horizontal* rather than upward-sloping. With a horizontal AS curve, rightward shifts of the AD curve would not cause prices to rise. Keynes thought this was the case during the Great Depression, when prices were actually *falling* (see Figure 8.1). So he proposed shifting the AD curve by the amount of the recessionary GDP gap.

The assumption of a horizontal AS curve seems naïve in today's world. Although not every AD shift will raise prices, inflationary pressures do increase as AD expands. So, we should assume that the short-run AS curve is upward-sloping and take that slope into account when deciding how much to shift the AD curve.

The AD Shortfall. The likelihood of increasing price pressures doesn't imply that we should forsake fiscal stimulus. Figure 11.3 simply tells us that the naïve Keynesian policy prescription (increasing AD by the amount of the GDP gap) probably won't cure all our unemployment ills. It also suggests, however, that a *larger* dose of fiscal stimulus might work. *So long as the AS curve slopes upward, we must increase aggregate demand by more than the size of the recessionary GDP gap to achieve full employment.*

Figure 11.3 illustrates this new policy target. The **AD shortfall** is the amount of additional aggregate demand needed to achieve full employment *after allowing for price level changes.* Notice in Figure 11.3 that full employment (Q_F) is achieved only when the AD curve intersects the AS curve at point *d.* To get there, the aggregate demand curve must shift from AD$_1$ all the way to AD$_3$. So, the AD$_3$ curve, not the AD$_2$ curve, is our route to full employment.

Notice something else about the AD$_3$ curve. It not only passes through the equilibrium intersection at point *d* but continues on to point *e.* What's so special about point *e?* Point *e* is on a horizontal plane at the initial output price level of P_E. As such, it tells us something really important: It tells us how much additional output must be demanded at the *current* price level (P_E) to get us to the AD$_3$ curve. In other words, we need that much additional aggregate demand to achieve full employment. If we can't get to point *e* at current prices, we simply can't get to the desired point *d* at higher prices. We need to get to point *e* in order to reach full employment at point *d.*

The horizontal distance between point *a* and point *e* in Figure 11.3 is what we call "the AD shortfall." Aggregate demand must increase (shift) by the amount of the AD shortfall to achieve full employment. Thus, *the AD shortfall is the fiscal target.* In Figure 11.3 the AD shortfall amounts to $800 billion ($0.8 trillion). That's how much *additional* aggregate demand is required at current prices to reach full employment (Q_F).

Were we to increase AD by enough to attain full employment, it's apparent in Figure 11.3 that prices would increase as well. We'll examine this dilemma later; for the time being, we focus on the policy options for increasing aggregate demand by the desired amount.

More Government Spending

The simplest way to shift aggregate demand is to increase government spending. If the government were to step up its purchases of tanks, highways, schools, and other goods, the increased spending would add directly to aggregate demand. This would shift the AD curve rightward, moving us closer to full employment. Hence, *increased government spending is a form of fiscal stimulus.*

Multiplier Effects. It isn't necessary for the government to make up the entire shortfall in aggregate demand. Suppose that the fiscal target was to increase aggregate demand by $800 billion, the AD shortfall illustrated in Figure 11.3, by the distance between point *e* ($6.4 billion) and point *a* ($5.6 billion). At first blush, that much stimulus looks perfect for restoring full employment. But life is never that simple.

Were government spending to increase by $800 billion, the AD curve would actually shift *beyond* point *e* in Figure 11.3. In that case we'd quickly move from a situation of *inadequate* aggregate demand (point *a*) to a situation of *excessive* aggregate demand.

The origins of this apparent riddle lie in the circular flow of income. When the government buys more goods and services, it creates additional income for market participants.

AD shortfall: The amount of additional aggregate demand needed to achieve full employment after allowing for price-level changes.

The recipients of this income will, in turn, spend it. Hence, each dollar gets spent and respent many times. This is the multiplier adjustment process we encountered in Chapter 10. As a result of this process, *every dollar of new government spending has a multiplied impact on aggregate demand.*

How much "bang" the economy gets for each government "buck" depends on the value of the **multiplier**. Specifically,

$$\frac{\text{Total change}}{\text{in spending}} = \text{Mutiplier} \times \text{New spending injection}$$

The multiplier adds a lot of punch to fiscal policy. Suppose that households have a **marginal propensity to consume** equal to 0.75. In this case, the multiplier would have a value of 4, and each dollar of new government expenditure would increase aggregate demand by $4.

Sequential Shifts. Figure 11.4 illustrates that leveraged impact of government spending. Aggregate demand shifts from AD_1 to AD_2 when the government buys an additional $200 billion of output.

Multiplier effects then increase consumption spending by $600 billion more. This additional consumption shifts aggregate demand repeatedly, ultimately reaching AD_3. Thus, *the impact of fiscal stimulus on aggregate demand includes both the new government spending and all subsequent increases in consumer spending triggered by multiplier effects.* In Figure 11.4, the shift from AD_1 to AD_3 includes

AD_1 to AD_2: Shift due to $200 billion injection of new government spending.
AD_2 to AD_3: Shift due to multiplier-induced increases in consumption ($600 billion).

As a result of these initial and multiplier-induced shifts, aggregate demand at the current price level (P_E) increases by $800 billion. Thus,

$$\frac{\text{Cumulative increase}}{\text{(horizontal shift) in AD}} = \frac{\text{New spending}}{\text{injection}} + \frac{\text{Induced increase}}{\text{in consumption}}$$
$$\text{(fiscal stimulus)}$$
$$= \text{Multiplier} \times \text{Fiscal stimulus}$$
$$\text{(new spending injection)}$$

The second equation is identical to the first but is expressed in the terminology of fiscal policy. The "fiscal stimulus" is the "new spending injection" that sets the multiplier process in motion. The multiplier carries the ball from there.

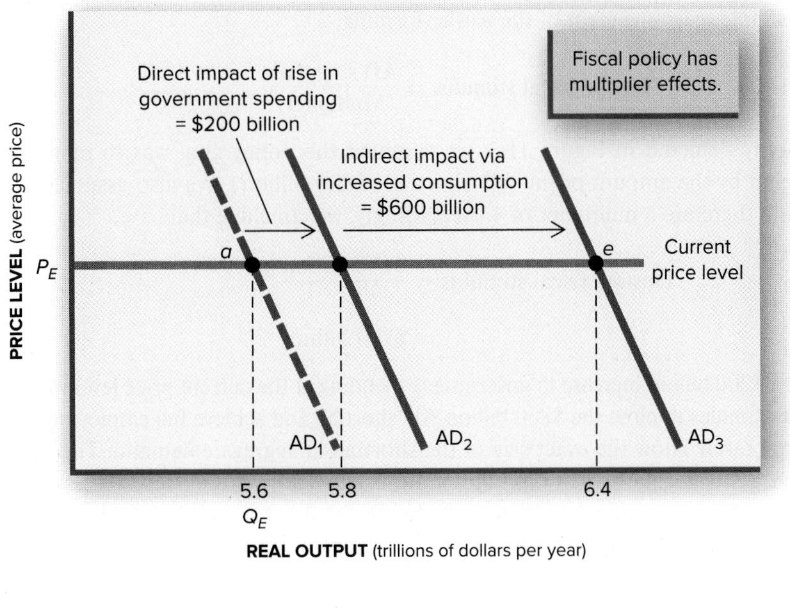

multiplier: The multiple by which an initial change in aggregate spending will alter total expenditure after an infinite number of spending cycles; 1/(1 − MPC).

marginal propensity to consume (MPC): The fraction of each additional (marginal) dollar of disposable income spent on consumption; the change in consumption divided by the change in disposable income.

FIGURE 11.4
Multiplier Effects

Fiscal stimulus will set off the multiplier process. As a result of this, aggregate demand will increase (shift) in two distinct steps: (1) the initial fiscal stimulus (AD_1 to AD_2) and (2) induced changes in consumption (AD_2 to AD_3). In this case, a $200 billion increase in government spending causes an $800 billion increase in aggregate demand at the *existing* price level.

The Desired Stimulus. Multiplier effects make changes in government spending a powerful policy lever. The multiplier also increases the risk of error, however. Just as too little fiscal stimulus may leave the economy in a recession, too much can rapidly lead to excessive spending and inflation. This was the dilemma President Trump confronted in his first year. He wanted a massive increase in infrastructure spending and a huge increase in military spending. With the economy virtually at full employment already, there was heightened concern that President Trump's spending plans would shift the AD curve so far to the right that it would accelerate price increases—i.e., move the economy up the ever-steeper AS curve (see Front Page Economics "Trump's Spending Proposals Stir Inflation Worries").

FRONT PAGE ECONOMICS

TRUMP'S SPENDING PROPOSALS STIR INFLATION WORRIES

Washington, DC. President Trump has said he wants a trillion-dollar program to repair America's roads, bridges, railroads, and airports. In addition to this step-up in infrastructure spending, he wants a multibillion-dollar increase in defense spending and expanded services for military veterans. Critics—even Republicans in Congress—are worried about how all this spending will affect the economy. With the economy already near full employment, such a massive increase in federal spending could put a lot of pressure on prices.

Source: Media reports, March 2017.

CRITICAL ANALYSIS: President Trump's initial budget proposals called for substantial increases in spending—spending that would **shift the AD curve** to the right. Critics worried that the intended AD shift was too great and might push price levels too high.

In 2020 Congress enacted even a larger stimulus program. But there was little concern about inflation then. At that time the economy was in a severe slump and unemployment was exceptionally high. In other words, the economy was operating on the lower, more horizontal section of the AS curve: a rightward shift of the AD curve was not likely to push price levels up.

Policy decisions would be a lot easier if we knew the exact dimensions of aggregate demand, as in Figure 11.3. With such perfect information about AD, AS, and the AD shortfall, we could easily calculate the required increase in the rate of government spending. The general formula for computing the *desired* stimulus (such as an increase in government spending) is a simple rearrangement of the earlier formula:

$$\text{Desired fiscal stimulus} = \frac{\text{AD shortfall}}{\text{Multiplier}}$$

In the economy depicted in Figure 11.3, we assumed the policy goal was to increase aggregate demand by the amount of the AD shortfall ($800 billion). We also assumed an MPC of 0.75 and therefore a multiplier of 4. Accordingly, we conclude that

$$\text{Desired fiscal stimulus} = \frac{\$800 \text{ billion}}{4}$$

$$= \$200 \text{ billion}$$

In other words, a $200 billion increase in government spending at the current price level would be enough fiscal stimulus to close the $800 billion AD shortfall and achieve full employment.

In practice, we rarely know the exact size of the shortfall in aggregate demand. The multiplier is also harder to calculate when taxes and imports enter the picture. Nevertheless, the foregoing formula does provide a useful rule of thumb for determining how much fiscal stimulus is needed to achieve any desired increase in aggregate demand.

Tax Cuts

There is no doubt that increased government spending can shift the AD curve to the right, helping to close a GDP gap. But increased government spending isn't the only way to get there. The increased demand required to raise output and employment levels from Q_E to Q_F could emerge from increases in autonomous consumption or investment as well as from increased government spending. An AD shift could also originate overseas, in the form of increased demand for our exports. In other words, any "big spender" would help, whether from the public sector or the private sector. Of course, the reason we're initially at Q_E instead of Q_F in Figure 11.3 is that consumers, investors, and export buyers have chosen *not* to spend as much as required for full employment.

Consumer and investor decisions are subject to change. Moreover, fiscal policy can encourage such changes. Congress not only buys goods and services but also levies taxes. By lowering taxes, the government increases the **disposable income** of the private sector. This was the objective of the 2008 Bush tax cuts, which gave all taxpayers a rebate of $300–600 in the summer of 2008. By putting $168 billion more after-tax income into the hands of consumers, Congress hoped to stimulate (shift) the consumption component of aggregate demand. President Obama used the tax cut tool as part of his 2009 stimulus package and again in 2011. President Trump pulled the same policy lever in 2017.

disposable income (DI): After-tax income of households; personal income less personal taxes.

Taxes and Consumption. An income tax cut directly increases the disposable income of consumers. The question here, however, is how a tax cut affects *spending*. By how much will consumption increase for every dollar of tax cuts?

The answer lies in the marginal propensity to consume. Consumers won't spend every dollar of tax cuts; they'll *save* some of the cut and spend the rest. The MPC tells us how the tax cut dollar will be split between saving and spending. If the MPC is 0.75, consumers will spend $0.75 out of every tax cut $1.00. In other words,

$$\text{Initial increase in consumption} = \text{MPC} \times \text{Tax cut}$$

If taxes were cut by $200 billion, the resulting shopping spree would amount to

$$\text{Initial increase in consumption} = 0.75 \times \$200 \text{ billion}$$
$$= \$150 \text{ billion}$$

Hence, *a tax cut that increases disposable incomes stimulates consumer spending.* A tax cut therefore shifts the aggregate demand curve to the right.

Multiplier Effects. The initial shopping spree induced by a tax cut is only the beginning of the story. Remember the multiplier! The new consumer spending creates additional income for producers and workers, who will then use *their* additional income to increase their own consumption. This will propel us along the multiplier path already depicted in Figure 11.4. The cumulative change in total spending will be

$$\frac{\text{Cumulative change}}{\text{in spending}} = \text{Multiplier} \times \frac{\text{Initial change}}{\text{in consumption}}$$

In this case, the cumulative change is

$$\frac{\text{Cumulative change}}{\text{in spending}} = \frac{1}{1 - \text{MPC}} \times \$150 \text{ billion}$$
$$= 4 \times \$150 \text{ billion}$$
$$= \$600 \text{ billion}$$

Here again we see that the multiplier increases the impact on aggregate demand of a fiscal policy stimulus. There's an important difference here, though. When we increased government spending by $200 billion, aggregate demand increased by $800 billion. When we cut

FIGURE 11.5

The Tax Cut Multiplier

Only part of a tax cut is used to increase consumption; the remainder is saved. Accordingly, the initial *spending* injection is less than the tax cut. This makes tax cuts less stimulative than government purchases of the same size. The multiplier still goes to work on that new consumer spending, however.

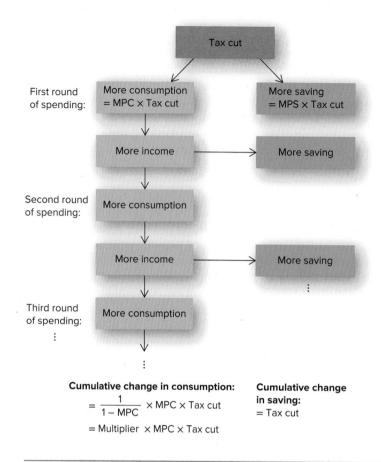

taxes by $200 billion, however, aggregate demand increases by only $600 billion. Hence, *a tax cut contains less fiscal stimulus than an increase in government spending of the same size.*

The lesser stimulative power of tax cuts is explained by consumer saving. Only part of a tax cut gets spent. Consumers save the rest. This is evident in Figure 11.5, which illustrates the successive rounds of the multiplier process. Notice that the tax cut is used to increase both consumption and saving, according to the MPC. Only that part of the tax cut that's used for consumption enters the circular flow as a spending injection. Hence, *the initial spending injection is less than the size of the tax cuts.* By contrast, every dollar of government purchases goes directly into the circular flow. Accordingly, tax cuts are less powerful than government purchases because the initial *spending* injection is smaller.

This doesn't mean we can't close the AD shortfall with a tax cut. It simply means that the desired tax cut must be larger than the required stimulus. It remains true that

$$\text{Desired fiscal stimulus} = \frac{\text{AD shortfall}}{\text{Multiplier}}$$

But now we're using a consumption shift as the fiscal stimulus rather than increased government spending. Hence, we have to allow for the fact that the initial surge in consumption (the fiscal stimulus) will be *less* than the tax cut. Specifically,

$$\text{Initial consumption injection} = \text{MPC} \times \text{Tax cut}$$

The fact that consumers will save some fraction of their tax cut forces us to perform one more calculation. We know how to compute the desired fiscal stimulus. Now we want to know how large of a tax cut will deliver that much stimulus. The answer lies in the following equation:

$$\text{Desired tax cut} = \frac{\text{Desired fiscal stimulus}}{\text{MPC}}$$

In the economy in Figure 11.3, we assumed that the desired stimulus is $200 billion and the MPC equals 0.75. Hence, the desired tax cut is

$$\text{Desired tax cut} = \frac{\$200 \text{ billion}}{0.75} = \$267 \text{ billion}$$

By cutting taxes $267 billion, we directly increase disposable income by the same amount. Consumers then increase their rate of spending by $200 billion (0.75 × $267 billion); they save the remaining $67 billion. As the added spending enters the circular flow, it starts the multiplier process, ultimately increasing aggregate demand by $800 billion per year.

This comparison of government purchases and tax cuts clearly reveals their respective power. What we've demonstrated is that *a dollar of tax cuts is less stimulative than a dollar of government purchases.* This doesn't mean that tax cuts are undesirable, just that they need to be larger than the desired injection of spending.

The different effects of tax cuts and increased government spending have an important implication for government budgets. Because some of the power of a tax cut "leaks" into saving, tax increases don't "offset" government spending of equal value. This unexpected result is described in Table 11.1.

TABLE 11.1

The Balanced Budget Multiplier

An increase in government spending paid for by an increase in taxes of equal size isn't really neutral. Such a "balanced budget" strategy actually shifts aggregate demand to the right. This box explains why.

Many taxpayers and politicians demand that any new government spending be balanced with new taxes. Such balancing at the margin, it's asserted, will keep the budget deficit from rising. It will also avoid undesired increases in aggregate demand. Unfortunately, that isn't true.

The reality is that changes in government spending (G) are more powerful than changes in taxes (T) or transfers. This implies that an increase in G seemingly "offset" with an equal rise in T will actually increase aggregate demand.

To see how this happens, suppose that the government decided to spend $50 billion on a fleet of space shuttles and to pay for them by raising income taxes by the same amount. Thus,

Change in G = + $50 billion per year
Change in T = + $50 billion per year
Change in budget balance = 0

How will this pay-as-you-go (balanced) budget initiative affect total spending?

The increased government spending represents an *injection* of $50 billion into the circular flow. But the higher taxes don't increase *leakage* by the same amount. Households will pay taxes by reducing *both* consumption and saving. The initial reduction in annual consumer spending equals only MPC × $50 billion.

The reduction in consumption is therefore less than the increase in government spending, implying a net increase in *aggregate* spending. The *initial* change in aggregate demand brought about by this balanced budget expenditure is

Initial increase in government spending = $50 billion
less Initial reduction in consumer spending = MPC × $50 billion
Net initial change in total spending = (1 − MPC) $50 billion

Like any other changes in the rate of spending, this initial increase in aggregate spending will start a multiplier process in motion. The *cumulative* change in expenditure will be much larger, as indicated by the multiplier. In this case, the cumulative (ultimate) change in total spending is

$$\text{Multiplier} \times \frac{\text{Initial change}}{\text{in spending per year}} = \frac{\text{Cumulative change}}{\text{in total spending}}$$

$$\frac{1}{1 - \text{MPC}} \times (1 - \text{MPC}) \, \$50 \text{ billion} = \$50 \text{ billion}$$

Thus, the balanced budget multiplier is equal to 1. In this case, a $50 billion increase in annual government expenditure combined with an equivalent increase in taxes actually increases aggregate demand by $50 billion per year.

Taxes and Investment. A tax cut may also be an effective mechanism for increasing *investment* spending. As we observed in Chapter 9, investment decisions are guided by expectations of future profit. If a cut in corporate taxes raises potential after-tax profits, it should encourage additional investment. Once additional investment spending enters the circular flow, it too has a multiplier effect.

In 1981 President Reagan convinced Congress not only to cut personal taxes $250 billion over a three-year period but also to cut business taxes another $70 billion. The resulting increase in both consumer spending and investment helped push the economy out of the 1981–1982 recession. President Clinton also embraced the notion of tax incentives for investment. He favored a tax credit for new investments in plants and equipment to increase the level of investment and set off multiplier effects for many years.

President George W. Bush pulled out all the tax cut stops. Immediately upon taking office in 2001, he convinced Congress to pass a $1.35 trillion tax cut for consumers, spread over several years. He followed that up with business tax cuts in 2002 and 2003. The cumulative impact of these tax cuts shifted AD significantly to the right and accelerated recovery from the 2001 recession. President Trump followed the same strategy, on an even grander scale. He convinced Congress to reduce the tax rate on corporations from 35 percent to 21 percent beginning in 2018. That sharp decline in corporate taxes left corporations with more profits to reinvest and a greater incentive for doing so.

Increased Transfers

A third fiscal policy option for stimulating the economy is to increase transfer payments. If Social Security recipients, welfare recipients, unemployment insurance beneficiaries, and veterans get larger benefit checks, they'll have more disposable income to spend. The resulting increase in consumption will boost aggregate demand. Thus, increases in unemployment benefits like those Congress approved in 2008–2010 and again in 2020 not only help jobless workers but also boost the macro economy.

Increased transfer payments don't, however, increase injections dollar-for-dollar. Here again, we have to recognize that consumers will save some of their additional transfer payments; only part (MPC) of the additional income will be injected into the spending stream. Hence, ***the initial fiscal stimulus (AD shift) of increased transfer payments is***

$$\text{Initial fiscal stimulus (injection)} = \text{MPC} \times \text{Increase in transfer payments}$$

This initial stimulus sets the multiplier in motion, shifting the aggregate demand curve repeatedly to the right.

Fiscal Stimulus Results

In the last decade or so, tax cuts have been used repeatedly to shift the AD curve to the right.

2009 Stimulus. When President Obama took office in January 2009, the U.S. economy was already deep into recession. There was a massive AD shortfall that someone had to fill. President Obama convinced Congress to authorize a $787 billion stimulus package that included increased government spending, tax cuts, and increased transfer payments. According to the Congressional Budget Office, that stimulus package had the desired effect: GDP growth accelerated by between 0.4 and 1.8 percentage points in 2009 and somewhere between 200,000 and 900,000 jobs were saved. Although both GDP and employment declined in 2009, the CBO said the declines would have been worse without the fiscal stimulus. In other words, the stimulus package did shift the AD curve to the right, but not far or fast enough to get back to full employment.

2017 Tax Cuts. When President Trump took office in January 2017, the U.S. economy was in far better shape. But Trump wanted even faster growth to "make America great again." He was convinced that tax cuts would be the key to faster GDP growth and job creation. He persuaded Congress to pass the Tax Cuts and Jobs Act in December 2017. Although

	2018	2019	2020	2021	2022
Real GDP acceleration (%)	0.3	0.6	0.8	0.9	1.0
Increase in employment (%)	0.2	0.5	0.6	0.7	0.7

Source: Congressional Budget Office (April 2018).

TABLE 11.2

Jobs Impact of the Stimulus

The success of a stimulus program can be measured by faster GDP growth and the number of jobs created in its wake. The Congressional Budget Office (CBO) estimated that the 2017 tax cuts had significant effects.

most of the tax cuts were directed at corporations and high-income households, the average middle-class household got a tax cut of $900 in 2018. This increase in disposable income spurred more consumer spending (via the MPC). Growth in consumer spending accelerated from 2.7 percent in 2017 to 3.0 percent in 2018, an AD shift of about $200 billion.

Table 11.2 shows how the initial shift of AD due to more consumer spending continued to impact the economy over subsequent years. According to the Congressional Budget Office, the GDP and jobs gains were actually larger in the second year (2019) than the first year (2018) following the tax cuts. That's because it took time for the new spending to get into the circular flow and set the multiplier process into motion.

2020 Coronavirus Relief. The projections of the Congressional Budget Office for multiplier effects stretching into 2020 and beyond (Table 11.2) were completely derailed by the coronavirus pandemic that shut down the U.S. economy in early 2020. A gigantic AD shortfall appeared almost overnight when the government shut down businesses across the country and advised consumers and workers to stay home. In March–April of 2020, GDP shrank and more than 22 million American workers lost their jobs. The fiscal response to the pandemic was quick and massive. Congress passed four stimulus bills to pump up aggregate demand, the largest of which was the Corona Aid, Relief, and Economic Security (CARES)

FRONT PAGE ECONOMICS

CONGRESS OKS $2 TRILLION AID PACKAGE

Washington, D.C. Congress approved a $2.2 trillion fiscal package to help cushion the blow of the COVID-19 shutdowns. With the unemployment rate expected to reach as high as 20 percent in the next couple of months, Congress acted swiftly to authorize massive relief. The Corona Aid, Relief, and Economic Security (CARES) Act includes:

Recovery Rebates: $293 billion in direct payments to individuals. The rebates are $1,200 per person, plus an additional $500 each for children under the age of 17. Payments will be directly deposited into taxpayer accounts in April.

Unemployment Benefit Supplements: $268 billion is authorized for federal supplements to state unemployment benefits. The supplement is equal to $600 a week, over and above each state's regular weekly benefit. The supplements are authorized for 16 weeks.

Payroll Protection Program: The PPP will provide loans to small businesses to keep employees on their payroll. If a business uses the PPP loan to retain employees for four months, the loan may be forgiven. Initial funding for the PPP is $377 billion.

Other provisions in the CARES Act provide money for hospitals, state and local governments, COVID-19 research, suspension of student loan payments, disaster relief, and emergency social and health services. CARES is expected to act as a lifeline to families and businesses whose incomes have vanished in the coronavirus shutdowns.

Source: Media reports of March 27–30, 2020.

CRITICAL ANALYSIS: When an AD shortfall appears, the government can use its tax and spending powers (fiscal stimulus) to shift AD to the right.

Act, authorized on March 27, 2020. As the Front Page Economics "Congress OKs $2 Trillion Aid Package" notes, the CARES act was focused primarily on direct aid to consumers in the form of tax rebates and vastly increased unemployment benefits.

What did Congress expect consumers to do with their recovery rebates and enhanced unemployment benefits? Spend them, of course. In the midst of a recession, it didn't seem likely that consumers would use their added disposable income to buy new cars or appliances. They were more likely to use the extra money to pay rent, mortgages, and credit card debt and buy groceries. So long as they spent the added income, however, they would set the multiplier process in motion and help blunt the downward spiral originating in the coronavirus pandemic.

FISCAL RESTRAINT

fiscal restraint: Tax hikes or spending cuts intended to reduce (shift) aggregate demand.

The objective of fiscal policy isn't always to increase aggregate demand. At times the economy may be expanding too fast, and **fiscal restraint** is more appropriate. In these overheated circumstances, policymakers will be more concerned about inflation than unemployment. Their objective will be to *reduce* aggregate demand, not to stimulate it.

The means available to the federal government for restraining aggregate demand emerge again from both sides of the budget. The difference here is that we use the budget tools in reverse. We now want to *reduce* government spending, *increase* taxes, or *decrease* transfer payments.

The AD Excess

As before, our first task is to determine how much we want aggregate demand to fall. To determine this, we must consult Figure 11.6. The initial equilibrium in this case occurs at point E_1, where the AS and AD_1 curves intersect. At that equilibrium, the unemployment rate falls below the rate consistent with full employment (Q_F) and we produce the output Q_1. The resulting strains on production push the price level to P_E, higher than we're willing to accept. Our goal is to maintain the price level at P_F, which is consistent with our notion of full employment *and* price stability.

inflationary GDP gap: The amount by which equilibrium GDP exceeds full-employment GDP.

In this case, we have an **inflationary GDP gap**—that is an equilibrium GDP that exceeds full-employment GDP. In Figure 11.6, the size of the inflationary GDP is $Q_1 - Q_F$, which amounts to $200 billion (= $6.2 trillion − $6.0 trillion on the graph). If we want to restore price stability (P_F), however, we need to reduce aggregate demand by *more* than this GDP gap.

FIGURE 11.6

Excess Aggregate Demand

Too much aggregate demand (AD_1) causes the price level to rise (P_E) above its desired level (P_F). To restore price stability, the AD curve must shift leftward by *more* than the inflationary GDP gap: It must shift by the entire amount of the AD excess (here shown as $Q_1 - Q_2$). In this case, the AD excess amounts to $400 billion. If AD shifts by that much (from AD_1 to AD_2), the AD excess is eliminated and equilibrium moves from E_1 to E_2.

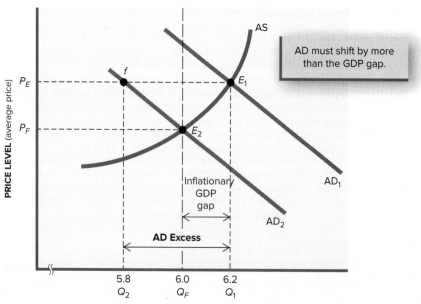

REAL OUTPUT (trillions of dollars per year)

The **AD excess**–like its counterpart, the AD shortfall–takes into account potential changes in the price level.

AD excess: The amount by which aggregate demand must be reduced to achieve full-employment equilibrium after allowing for price-level changes.

When we shift the AD_1 curve to the left (our policy goal), we can't assume prices will be unchanged. On the contrary, the sloped AS curve tells us that the price level will *fall* as aggregate demand declines. So, fiscal restraint, if properly designed, will move us from E_1 to E_2. At the equilibrium E_2, we have reined in the economy to its full-employment potential (Q_F).

How much fiscal restraint do we need to achieve this desired outcome? Notice that the AD_2 curve that passes through the E_2 intersection also passes through point f. Therefore, the initial AD_1 curve must be shifted far enough to the left to pass through point f. If it does, it will also pass through point E_2 and the economy will achieve the desired equilibrium.

The horizontal distance between the initial equilibrium at point E_1 and point f is our measure of the AD excess. It represents the amount by which aggregate demand must be reduced at the current price level in order to restrain inflation.

Observe that *the AD excess exceeds the inflationary GDP gap.* In Figure 11.6, the AD excess equals the horizontal distance from E_1 to point f, which amounts to $400 billion ($= \$6.2$ trillion $- \$5.8$ trillion). This excess aggregate demand is our fiscal policy target. To restore price stability, we must shift the AD curve leftward until it passes through point f. The AD_2 curve does this. The shift to AD_2 moves the economy to a new equilibrium at E_2. At E_2 we have less output but also a lower price level (less inflation).

Knowing how large the AD excess is allows us to plot a strategy for fiscal restraint. We once again call on the multiplier to help us. We need the multiplier because every dollar of fiscal restraint will set off a chain reaction of belt-tightening and associated AD shifts. Taking this multiplier process into account, we can compute the desired fiscal restraint as

$$\frac{\text{Desired}}{\text{fiscal restraint}} = \frac{\text{AD excess}}{\text{Multiplier}}$$

Notice the two distinct steps in this policy process. First we determine how far we want to shift the AD curve to the left–that is, the size of the AD excess. Then we compute how much government spending or taxes must be changed to achieve the desired shift, taking into account multiplier effects.

Budget Cuts

The first option to consider is budget cuts. By how much should we reduce government expenditure on goods and services? The answer is simple in this case: We first calculate the desired fiscal restraint with the equation just given. Then we cut government expenditure by that amount.

The AD Excess Target. The GDP gap in Figure 11.6 amounts to $200 billion ($= Q_1 - Q_F$). If aggregate demand is reduced by that amount, however, some of the restraint will be dissipated in price level reductions. To bring *equilibrium* GDP down to the full-employment (Q_F) level, even more of a spending reduction is needed. In this case, the AD excess amounts to $400 billion.

The Multiplier. We don't have to cut government spending by the full amount of the AD excess. Here again, the multiplier will come to our aid. If we assume a marginal propensity to consume of 0.75, the multiplier equals 4. In these circumstances, the desired fiscal restraint is

$$\frac{\text{Desired}}{\text{fiscal restraint}} = \frac{\text{AD excess}}{\text{Multiplier}}$$
$$= \frac{\$400 \text{ billion}}{4}$$
$$= \$100 \text{ billion}$$

Take a moment to see how this works. What would happen to aggregate demand if the federal government cut $100 billion out of the defense budget? Such a military cutback would throw a lot of aerospace employees out of work. Thousands of workers would get smaller paychecks, or perhaps none at all. These workers would be forced to cut back on their own spending. Hence, aggregate demand would take two hits: first a cut in government spending, then induced cutbacks in consumer spending. Front Page Economics "Defense Cuts Kill Jobs" highlights the impact of this *negative* multiplier process.

FRONT PAGE ECONOMICS

DEFENSE CUTS KILL JOBS

Cuts in defense spending are making it more difficult to restore full employment. Defense spending was slashed from $837 billion in 2011 to only $770 billion in 2013, following the mandates of the Budget Control Act of 2011 and President Obama's budget decisions. Hardware procurement, Department of Defense civilian employment, and active-duty forces have all been cut. As these defense cuts ripple through the economy, jobs are lost in an array of industries. The National Association of Manufacturers says the resulting loss of jobs and output is substantial: 261,000 fewer jobs in 2014 and 0.2 percentage point shaved off GDP.

Source: National Association of Manufacturers.

CRITICAL ANALYSIS: Reductions in governmental spending on goods and services directly decrease aggregate demand. **Multiplier effects** induce additional cutbacks in consumption, further reducing aggregate demand.

The marginal propensity to consume again reveals the power of the multiplier process. If the MPC is 0.75, the consumption of aerospace workers will drop by $75 billion when the government cutbacks reduce their income by $100 billion. (The rest of the income loss will be covered by a reduction in saving.)

From this point on, the story should sound familiar. The $100 billion government cutback will ultimately reduce consumer spending by $300 billion. The total drop in spending is thus $400 billion. Like their mirror image, *budget cuts have a multiplied effect on aggregate demand.* The total impact is equal to

$$\text{Cumulative reduction in spending} = \text{Multiplier} \times \frac{\text{Initial budget cut}}{\text{(fiscal restraint)}}$$

This cumulative reduction in spending would eliminate excess aggregate demand. We conclude, then, that *the budget cuts should equal the size of the desired fiscal restraint.*

Tax Hikes

Cuts in government spending aren't the only tool for restraining aggregate demand. Tax increases can also be used to shift the AD curve to the left. The direct effect of a tax increase is a reduction in disposable income. People will pay the higher taxes by reducing their consumption *and* saving less. Only the reduced consumption results in less aggregate demand. As consumers tighten their belts, they set off the multiplier process, leading again to a much larger, cumulative shift of aggregate demand.

Because people pay higher tax bills by reducing both consumption and saving (by MPC and MPS, respectively), *taxes must be increased more than a dollar to get a dollar of fiscal restraint.* This leads us to the following guideline:

$$\frac{\text{Desired increase}}{\text{in taxes}} = \frac{\text{Desired fiscal restraint}}{\text{MPC}}$$

In other words, changes in taxes must always be larger than the desired change in leakages or injections. How much larger depends on the marginal propensity to consume. In this case,

$$\frac{\text{Desired}}{\text{fiscal restraint}} = \frac{\text{AD excess}}{\text{Multiplier}}$$

Using the numbers from Figure 11.6 as an example, we see that

$$\frac{\text{Desired}}{\text{fiscal restraint}} = \frac{\$400 \text{ billion}}{4}$$
$$= \$100 \text{ billion}$$

Therefore, the appropriate tax increase is

$$\frac{\text{Desired}}{\text{tax hike}} = \frac{\text{Desired fiscal restraint}}{\text{MPC}}$$
$$= \frac{\$100 \text{ billion}}{\text{MPC}}$$
$$= \frac{\$100 \text{ billion}}{0.75}$$
$$= \$133 \text{ billion}$$

Were taxes increased by this amount, consumers would reduce their consumption by $100 billion (= 0.75 × $133 billion). This cutback in consumption would set off the multiplier, leading to a cumulative reduction in spending of $400 billion. In Figure 11.6, aggregate demand would shift from AD$_1$ to AD$_2$.

Tax increases have been used to "cool" the economy on several occasions. In 1968, for example, the economy was rapidly approaching full employment, and Vietnam War expenditures were helping to drive up prices. Congress responded by imposing a 10 percent surtax (temporary additional tax) on income, which took more than $10 billion in purchasing power away from consumers. Resultant multiplier effects reduced spending in 1969 more than $20 billion and thus helped restrain price pressures.

In 1982 there was great concern that the 1981 tax cuts had been excessive and that inflation was emerging. To reduce that inflationary pressure, Congress withdrew some of its earlier tax cuts. The net effect of the Tax Equity and Fiscal Responsibility Act of 1982 was to increase taxes roughly $90 billion for the years 1983 to 1985. This shifted aggregate demand leftward, thus reducing price level pressures.

Reduced Transfers

The third option for fiscal restraint is to reduce transfer payments. *A cut in transfer payments works like a tax hike, reducing the disposable income of transfer recipients.* With less income, consumers spend less, as reflected in the MPC. The appropriate size of the transfer cut can be computed exactly as the desired tax increase in the preceding formula.

Although transfer cuts have the same fiscal impact as a tax hike, they're seldom used. An outright cut in transfer payments has a direct and very visible impact on recipients, including the aged, the poor, the unemployed, and the disabled. Hence, this policy option smacks of "balancing the budget on the backs of the poor." In practice, *absolute* cuts in transfer payments are rarely proposed. Instead, this lever is sometimes used to reduce the rate of increase in transfer benefits. Then only *future* benefits are reduced, and not so visibly.

FISCAL GUIDELINES

The essence of fiscal policy entails deliberate shifting of the aggregate demand curve.

A Primer: Simple Rules

The steps required to formulate fiscal policy are straightforward:

* *Specify the amount of the desired AD shift* (AD excess or AD shortfall).
* *Select the policy tools needed to induce the desired shift.*

As we've seen, the fiscal policy toolbox contains a variety of tools for managing aggregate demand. When the economy is in a slump, the government can stimulate the economy with more government purchases, tax cuts, or an increase in transfer payments. When the economy is overheated, the government can reduce inflationary pressures by reducing government purchases, raising taxes, and cutting transfer payments. Table 11.3 summarizes the policy options and the desired use of each. As confusing as this list of options might at first appear, the guidelines are pretty simple. To use them, all one needs to know is the size of the AD shortfall or AD excess and the marginal propensity to consume.

A Warning: Crowding Out

The fiscal policy guidelines in Table 11.3 are a useful guide. However, they neglect a critical dimension of fiscal policy. Notice that we haven't said anything about how the government is going to *finance* its expenditures. Suppose the government wanted to stimulate the economy with a $50 billion increase in federal purchases. How would it pay for those purchases? If the government raised taxes for this purpose, the fiscal stimulus would be largely offset by resultant declines in consumption and investment. If, instead, the government *borrows* the money from the private sector, less credit may be available to finance consumption and investment,

TABLE 11.3

Fiscal Policy Primer

The goal of fiscal policy is to eliminate GDP gaps by shifting the AD curve rightward (to reduce unemployment) or leftward (to curb inflation). The desired shifts may be measured by the AD shortfall or the AD excess. In either case, the size of the fiscal initiative is equal to the desired shift divided by the multiplier. Once the size of the desired stimulus or restraint is known, the appropriate policy response is easily calculated.

Macro Problem: Weak Economy (Unemployment)
Policy Target: The AD Shortfall
Policy Strategy: Fiscal Stimulus (Rightward AD Shift)

$$\text{Desired fiscal stimulus} = \frac{\text{AD shortfall}}{\text{Multiplier}}$$

Policy Tools	Desired Amount
• Increase government purchases.	Desired fiscal stimulus
• Cut taxes.	$\dfrac{\text{Desired fiscal stimulus}}{\text{MPC}}$
• Increase transfer payments.	$\dfrac{\text{Desired fiscal stimulus}}{\text{MPC}}$

Macro Problem: Overheated Economy (Inflation)
Policy Target: The AD Excess
Policy Strategy: Fiscal Restraint (Leftward AD Shift)

$$\text{Desired fiscal restraint} = \frac{\text{AD excess}}{\text{Multiplier}}$$

Policy Tools	Desired Amount
• Reduce government purchases.	Desired fiscal restraint
• Increase taxes.	$\dfrac{\text{Desired fiscal restraint}}{\text{MPC}}$
• Reduce transfer payments.	$\dfrac{\text{Desired fiscal restraint}}{\text{MPC}}$

again creating an offsetting reduction in private demand. In either case, government spending may "crowd out" some private expenditure. If this happens, some of the intended fiscal stimulus may be offset by the **crowding out** of private expenditure. We examine this possibility further in Chapter 12 when we look at the budget deficits that help finance fiscal policy.

crowding out: A reduction in private sector borrowing (and spending) caused by increased government borrowing.

Time Lags

Another limitation on fiscal policy is *time*. In the real world it takes time to recognize that the economy is in trouble. A blip in the unemployment or inflation rate may not signal a trend. Before intervening, we may want to be more certain that a recessionary or inflationary GDP gap is emerging. Then it will take time to develop a policy strategy and to get Congress to pass it. That's why President-elect Obama prepared a stimulus package even *before* he took office. He wanted Congress to authorize a stimulus program within weeks of his inauguration. President-elect Trump did the same thing.

Once Congress authorizes fiscal policy initiatives, it still takes time to implement the policy. An increase in government spending on infrastructure, for example, doesn't actually occur until bids are obtained, contracts are signed, permits are issued, and resources are assembled. That can take months. Although President Obama targeted "shovel-ready" projects in his stimulus proposals, few infrastructure projects can be cranked up instantly. Even tax cuts can take months to implement.

Once a fiscal stimulus actually hits the economy, we have to wait for the many steps in the multiplier process to unfold. In the best of circumstances, the fiscal policy rescue may not arrive for quite a while. In the meantime, the very nature of our macro problems could change if the economy is hit with other internal or external shocks. We will examine these real-world impediments to "perfect" fiscal policy in Chapter 18.

Pork Barrel Politics

Before putting too much faith in fiscal policy, we should also remember who designs and implements tax and spending initiatives: the U.S. Congress. Once a tax or spending plan arrives at the Capitol, politics take over. However urgent fiscal restraint might be, members of Congress are reluctant to sacrifice any spending projects in their own districts. If taxes are to be cut, they want *their* constituents to get the biggest tax savings. And no one in Congress wants a tax hike or spending cut *before* the election. This kind of pork barrel politics can alter the content and timing of fiscal policy. We'll examine the *politics* of fiscal policy further in Chapters 12 and 18.

DECISIONS FOR TOMORROW

What Kind of Spending Should Be Targeted?

The guidelines for fiscal policy don't say anything about how the government spends its revenue or whom it taxes. The important thing is that the right amount of spending take place at the right time. In other words, insofar as our stabilization objectives are concerned, the *content* of total spending doesn't matter; the *level* of spending is the only thing that counts.

The "Second Crisis". But it does matter, of course, whether federal expenditures are devoted to military hardware, urban transit systems, or tennis courts. Our economic goals include not only full employment and price stability but also a desirable mix of output, an equitable distribution of income, and adequate economic growth. These other goals are directly affected by the content of total spending. The relative emphasis on, and sometimes exclusive concern for, stabilization objectives—to the neglect of related GDP

Continued

content—has been designated by Joan Robinson as the "second crisis of economic theory":

> The first crisis arose from the breakdown of a theory which could not account for the *level* of employment. The second crisis arises from a theory that cannot account for the *content* of employment.
>
> Keynes was arguing against the dominant orthodoxy which held that government expenditure could not increase employment. He had to prove, first of all, that it could. He had to show that an increase in investment will increase consumption—that more wages will be spent on more beer and boots whether the investment is useful or not. He had to show that the secondary increase in real income [the multiplier effect] is quite independent of the object of the primary outlay. Pay men to dig holes in the ground and fill them up again if you cannot do anything else.
>
> There was an enormous orthodox resistance to this idea. The whole weight of the argument had to be on this one obvious point.
>
> The war was a sharp lesson in Keynesism. Orthodoxy could not stand up any longer. Government accepted the responsibility to maintain a high and stable level of employment. Then economists took over Keynes and erected the new orthodoxy. Once the point had been established, the question should have changed. Now that we all agree that government expenditure can maintain employment, we should argue about what the expenditure should be for. Keynes did not *want* anyone to dig holes and fill them.[1]

The alternatives to paying people for digging and filling holes in the ground are virtually endless. With nearly $5 trillion to spend each year, the federal government has great influence not only on short-run prices and employment but also on the mix of output, the distribution of income, and the prospects for long-run growth. In other words, fiscal policy helps shape the dimensions of the economy tomorrow.

Public vs. Private Spending. One of the most debated issues in fiscal policy is the balance between the public and private sectors. Critics of Keynesian theory object to its apparent endorsement of government growth. They fear that using government spending to stabilize the economy will lead to an ever-larger public sector. They attribute the growth of the government's GDP share (from 10 percent in 1930 to 19 percent today) to the big-government bias of Keynesian fiscal policy.

In principle, this big-government bias doesn't exist. Keynes never said government spending was the only lever of fiscal policy. Even in 1934 he advised President Roosevelt to pursue only *temporary* increases in government spending. As we've seen, tax policy can be used to alter consumer and investor spending as well. Hence, fiscal policy can just as easily focus on changing the level of *private* sector spending as on changing *public* sector spending.

[1]Joan Robinson, "The Second Crisis of Economic Theory," *American Economic Review,* May 1972, p. 6.

SUMMARY

- The economy's short-run macro equilibrium may not coincide with full employment and price stability. Keynes advocated government intervention to shift the AD curve to a more desirable equilibrium. **LO11-1**
- Fiscal policy refers to the use of the government's tax and spending powers to achieve desired macro outcomes. The tools of fiscal stimulus include increasing government purchases, reducing taxes, and raising income transfers. **LO11-2**
- Fiscal restraint may originate in reductions in government purchases, increases in taxes, or cuts in income transfers. **LO11-4**

- Government purchases add directly to aggregate demand; taxes and transfers have an indirect effect by inducing changes in consumption and investment. This makes changes in government spending more powerful per dollar than changes in taxes or transfers. **LO11-5**
- Fiscal policy initiatives have a multiplied impact on total spending and output. An increase in government spending, for example, will result in more disposable income, which will be used to finance further consumer spending. **LO11-5**
- The objective of fiscal policy is to close GDP gaps. To do this, the aggregate demand curve must shift by *more* than

the size of the GDP gap to compensate for changing price levels. The desired shift is equal to the AD shortfall (or AD excess).   **LO11-3**

• Because of multiplier effects, the desired fiscal stimulus or restraint is always less than the size of the AD shortfall or AD excess.   **LO11-5**

• Time lags in the design, authorization, and implementation of fiscal policy reduce its effectiveness.   **LO11-5**

• Changes in government spending and taxes alter the content of GDP and thus influence what to produce. Fiscal policy affects the relative size of the public and private sectors.   **LO11-5**

Key Terms

aggregate demand (AD)	fiscal stimulus	disposable income
income transfers	aggregate supply (AS)	fiscal restraint
fiscal policy	AD shortfall	inflationary GDP gap
equilibrium (macro)	multiplier	AD excess
recessionary GDP gap	marginal propensity to consume (MPC)	crowding out

Questions for Discussion

1. How did the Sixteenth Amendment to the U.S. Constitution alter the federal government's ability to manage the macro economy?   **LO11-2**

2. How would you know whether the economy was in equilibrium? How would you know whether that equilibrium was desirable or not?   **LO11-1**

3. Recent stimulus programs have emphasized government spending (Obama, 2008), tax cuts (Trump, 2017), and income transfers (CARES, 2020). What are the advantages and disadvantages of each policy lever?   **LO11-2**

4. What happens to aggregate demand when transfer payments and the taxes to pay them both rise by the same amount?   **LO11-2**

5. Why are the AD shortfall and AD excess larger than their respective GDP gaps? Are they ever the same size as the GDP gap?   **LO11-3**

6. Will consumers always spend the same percentage of any tax cut? Why might they spend more or less than usual?   **LO11-2**

7. How does the slope of the AS curve affect the size of the AD shortfall? If the AS curve were horizontal, how large would the AD shortfall be in Figure 11.3?   **LO11-1**

8. Using Figure 11.3, explain why inflation accelerates when the economy moves back towards full employment.   **LO11-2**

9. Why do critics charge that fiscal policy has a "big-government bias"?   **LO11-2**

10. How did the 2017 tax cuts create more jobs in 2018-2019? (See Table 11.2.)   **LO11-5**

11. Which policy lever is more powerful in shifting AD, changes in military spending or changes in Social Security benefits?   **LO11-4**

LO11-2 1. Suppose the consumption function is

$$C = \$700 \text{ billion} + 0.8Y$$

and the government wants to stimulate the economy. By how much will aggregate demand at current prices shift initially (before multiplier effects) with

(a) A $30 billion increase in government purchases?

(b) A $30 billion tax cut?

(c) A $30 billion increase in income transfers?

What will the cumulative AD shift be for

(d) The increased G?

(e) The tax cut?

(f) The increased transfers?

LO11-2 2. Suppose the government decides to increase taxes by $50 billion to increase Social Security benefits by the same amount. By how much will this combined tax transfer policy affect aggregate demand at current prices if the MPC is 0.9?

LO11-3 3. On the accompanying graph, identify and label

(a) Macro equilibrium.

(b) The real GDP gap.

(c) The AD excess or AD shortfall.

(d) The new equilibrium that would occur with appropriate fiscal policy.

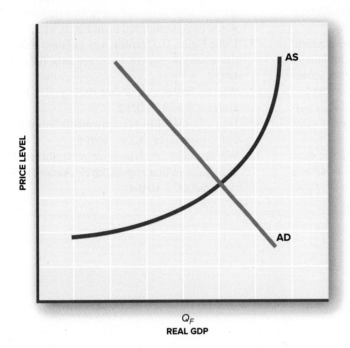

LO11-2 4. If the AD shortfall is $600 billion and the MPC is 0.95,

(a) How large is the desired fiscal stimulus?

(b) How large an income tax cut is needed?

(c) Alternatively, how much more government spending would achieve the target?

LO11-4 5. If the AD excess is $320 billion and the MPC is 0.75,

(a) How much fiscal restraint is desired?

(b) By how much do income taxes have to be increased to get that restraint?

(c) Alternatively, how much should government reduce its spending to achieve the target?

LO11-2 6. If the MPC in 2020 was 0.9,
   (*a*) How much would consumption increase initially as a result of the recovery rebates?
   (*b*) What would the ultimate impact of the rebates be on total spending?

   (See Front Page Economics "Congress OKs $2 Trillion Aid Package.")

LO11-5 7. According to CBO estimates (Table 11.2), how many jobs were created in 2018 and 2019 by the 2017 tax cuts? (Assume initial employment of 160 million.)

LO11-5 8. The 2020 budget included a $33 billion increase in military spending. By how much did this added spending shift the AD curve
   (*a*) Immediately?
   (*b*) Over time after all multiplier effects?

LO11-5 9. The tax cuts of 2017 increased the 2018 disposable income of households by roughly $200 billion. If the MPC were 0.9,
   (*a*) How much of this windfall was initially saved?
   (*b*) How much AD stimulus resulted over time after all multiplier effects?

LO11-2 10. Suppose that an increase in income transfers rather than government spending was the preferred policy for stimulating the economy depicted in Figure 11.4. By how much would transfers have to increase to attain the desired shift of AD?

LO11-4 11. If the marginal propensity to consume was 0.9, how large would each of the following need to be in order to restore a full-employment equilibrium in Figure 11.6?
   (*a*) A tax increase.
   (*b*) A government spending cut.
   (*c*) A cut in income transfers.

LO11-1 12. Use the following data to answer the following questions:

Price level	10	20	30	40	50	60	70	80	90	100
Real GDP supplied	$500	600	680	750	800	880	910	940	960	970
Real GDP demanded	$960	920	880	840	800	760	720	680	640	600

   (*a*) What is the rate of equilibrium GDP?
   (*b*) If full employment occurs at a real output rate of $910, how large is the real GDP gap?
   (*c*) If AD increases enough to restore full employment, what will the price level be?

LO11-2 13. *Decisions for Tomorrow:* The figure depicts an economy's production possibilities. Assume that the economy is currently at point *a*. How would the mix of output change if the economy was stimulated through increased highway construction?

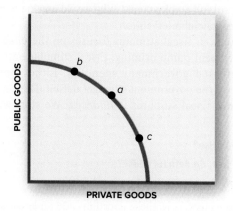

Design Credit: Shutterstock

12

Deficits and Debt

President Obama's massive 2009 stimulus package was designed to jump-start the recession-bound economy. Critics argued about both the content and size of that package. But the most controversial critique of Obama's fiscal stimulus was that it would ultimately do more harm than good. Those critics argued that the massive deficits generated by Obama's "American Recovery and Reinvestment Act" would undermine America's financial stability. To pay those deficits off, the government would later be forced to *raise* taxes and *cut* spending, taking the wind out of the economy's sails. Whatever short-term boost the economy got from the fiscal stimulus would be reversed in later years.

President Trump's 2017 tax cuts were subjected to the same critique (see Front Page Economics "Critics Decry Trump's 'Mountain of Debt'"). Those levers of fiscal stimulus boosted short-term economic growth, but they also increased the government's budget deficit and debt. How would that increased indebtedness affect longer-term growth? Would we be trading short-term gains for long-run losses?

The same questions arose during the coronavirus pandemic. Congress responded to the pandemic with a series of multi-trillion-dollar rescue packages of income transfers, tax cuts, and business subsidies. That fiscal intervention not only shifted the aggregate demand curve to the right, but also created an enormous increase in the government's 2020 budget deficit and a parallel jump in the government's debt. When, how, and by whom was that debt going to be repaid?

Why do these questions arise? Didn't the fiscal response both help stem the coronavirus pandemic and prop up an ailing economy? Didn't we just show how tax cuts shift aggregate demand rightward, propelling the economy toward full employment? Why would anyone have misgivings about such beneficial intervention?

The core critique of fiscal stimulus focuses on the *budget* consequences of government pump priming. Fiscal stimulus entails either tax cuts or increased government spending. Either option can increase the size of the government's budget deficit. Hence, we need to understand how fiscal stimulus is *financed*. We start with these questions:

- **How do deficits arise?**
- **What harm, if any, do deficits cause?**
- **Who will pay off the accumulated national debt?**

As you'll see, the answers to these questions add an essential dimension to fiscal policy debates.

FRONT PAGE ECONOMICS

CRITICS DECRY TRUMP'S "MOUNTAIN OF DEBT"

During the 2016 election campaign, candidate Trump accused President Obama of burdening the economy with a "mountain of debt." Now the tables are turned. President Trump's budget proposals call for a massive tax cut—"the biggest ever"—and increased spending on infrastructure, border security, national defense, and veterans' services. According to the conservative-leaning Tax Foundation, the tax cuts alone would add $4–6 trillion to the national debt over the next decade.

Source: Media reports, April 2017.

CRITICAL ANALYSIS: President Trump's initial budget entailed significant **fiscal stimulus**. Critics worried, though, that the tax cuts and spending plans would add significantly to the national debt, causing future economic problems.

BUDGET EFFECTS OF FISCAL POLICY

Keynesian theory highlights the potential of **fiscal policy** to solve our macro problems. The guidelines are simple. Use fiscal stimulus—stepped-up government spending, tax cuts, increased transfers—to eliminate unemployment. Use fiscal restraint—less spending, tax hikes, reduced transfers—to keep inflation under control. From this perspective, the federal budget is a key policy tool for controlling the economy.

fiscal policy: The use of government taxes and spending to alter macroeconomic outcomes.

Budget Surpluses and Deficits

Use of the budget to stabilize the economy implies that federal expenditures and receipts won't always be equal. In a recession, for example, the government has sound reasons both to cut taxes and to increase its own spending. By reducing tax revenues and increasing expenditures simultaneously, however, the federal government will throw its budget out of balance. This practice is called **deficit spending,** a situation in which the government borrows funds to pay for spending that exceeds tax revenues. The size of the resulting **budget deficit** is equal to the difference between expenditures and receipts:

deficit spending: The use of borrowed funds to finance government expenditures that exceed tax revenues.

$$\text{Budget deficit} = \text{Government spending} - \text{Tax revenues} > 0$$

Budget deficits are a staple of government behavior, as Table 12.1 illustrates. Notice that federal outlays (spending) exceeded federal revenues every year.

budget deficit: The amount by which government spending exceeds government revenue in a given time period.

Budget Total (in Billions of Dollars)	2006	2007	2008	2009	2010	2011	2012	2013	2014	2015	2016	2017	2018	2019	2020
Revenues	2,407	2,568	2,524	2,105	2,162	2,303	2,450	2,775	3,022	3,250	3,268	3,316	3,329	3,462	3,296
Outlays	−2,655	−2,729	−2,983	−3,518	−3,456	−3,603	−3,537	−3,455	−3,507	−3,689	−3,853	−3,981	−4,108	−4,446	−6,606
Surplus (deficit)	(248)	(161)	(459)	(1,413)	(1,294)	(1,300)	(1,087)	(680)	(485)	(439)	(585)	(665)	(779)	(984)	(3,310)

Source: Congressional Budget Office, September 2020.

TABLE 12.1

Budget Deficits and Surpluses

Budget deficits arise when government outlays (spending) exceed revenues (receipts). When revenues exceed outlays, a budget surplus exists.

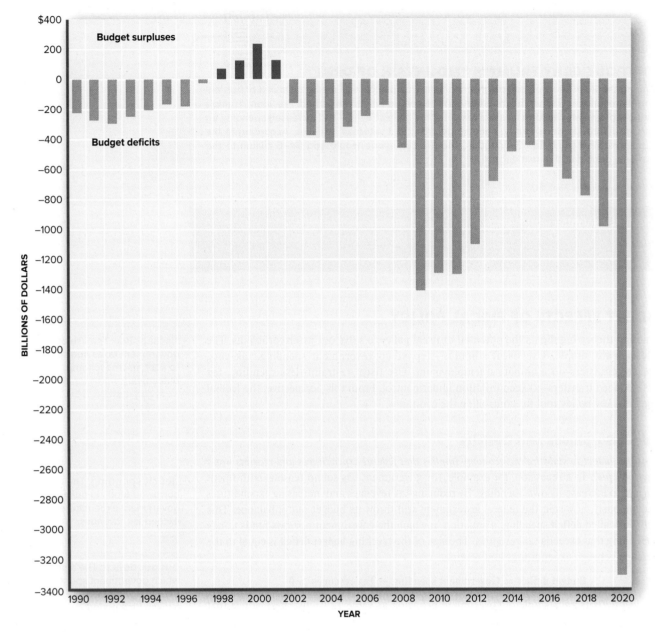

FIGURE 12.1

A String of Deficits

Budget deficits are the rule, not the exception. A budget surplus was achieved in only four years (1998–2001) since 1970. Deficits result from both cyclical slowdowns and discretionary policies.

Both forces contributed to the huge deficits of 2009-2011 and the massive deficit that emerged in 2020.

Source: Congressional Budget Office, September 2020.

---

budget surplus: An excess of government revenues over government expenditures in a given time period.

Looking closer at Table 12.1 gives us a first clue as to how these annual deficits arise. Notice that the federal government had a relatively small budget deficit ($161 billion) in 2007. But that deficit nearly *tripled* in 2008 and then almost *tripled* again in 2009. As a result, the 2009 deficit was nearly 9 times larger than the 2007 deficit!

Figure 12.1 illustrates how far out of line with prior experience these deficits were. While budget deficits arise nearly every year, prior deficits were small fractions of the trillion-dollar deficits incurred in 2009-2012 and 2020-2021. There were even a few years (1998-2001) in which the federal government managed a **budget surplus**—that is, it brought in more tax revenue than it spent.

The surge in the size of the budget deficit in 2009–2011 caused a lot of anxiety. In early 2011, opinion polls revealed that these huge deficits were the number one economic worry of Americans. As the deficit receded, so did worries about the deficit. But deficit anxiety started rising again as budget balances surged in 2017–2020. A Gallup poll in February 2020—just before the coronavirus eruption—revealed that government deficits and debt were again at the top of Americans' economic concerns.

Keynesian View. John Maynard Keynes wouldn't have been so worried. As far as he was concerned, budget deficits and surpluses are just a routine by-product of countercyclical fiscal policy. Deficits arise when the government uses **fiscal stimulus** to increase aggregate demand, just as **fiscal restraint** (tax hikes, spending cuts) may cause a budget surplus. As Keynes saw it, *the goal of macro policy is not to balance the budget but to balance the economy (at full employment).* If a budget deficit or surplus is needed to shift aggregate demand to the desired equilibrium, then so be it. In Keynes's view, a balanced budget would be appropriate only if all other injections and leakages were in balance and the economy was in full-employment equilibrium. As World View "Budget Imbalances Common" confirms, other nations evidently subscribe to that conclusion as well; budget deficits are common practice.

fiscal stimulus: Tax cuts or spending hikes intended to increase (shift) aggregate demand.

fiscal restraint: Tax hikes or spending cuts intended to reduce (shift) aggregate demand.

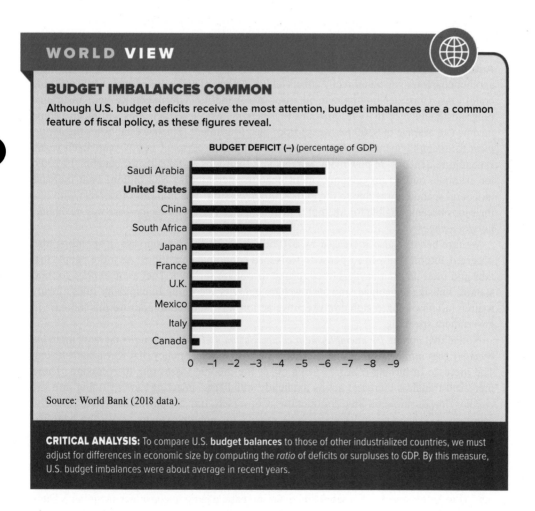

WORLD VIEW

BUDGET IMBALANCES COMMON

Although U.S. budget deficits receive the most attention, budget imbalances are a common feature of fiscal policy, as these figures reveal.

BUDGET DEFICIT (–) (percentage of GDP)

Source: World Bank (2018 data).

CRITICAL ANALYSIS: To compare U.S. **budget balances** to those of other industrialized countries, we must adjust for differences in economic size by computing the *ratio* of deficits or surpluses to GDP. By this measure, U.S. budget imbalances were about average in recent years.

Discretionary vs. Automatic Spending

Theory aside, budget analysts tell us that Congress couldn't balance the federal budget every year even if it wanted to. Congress doesn't have as much control over spending and revenues as people assume. To understand the limits of budget management, we have to take a closer look at how budget outlays and receipts are actually determined.

fiscal year (FY): The 12-month period used for accounting purposes; begins October 1 for the federal government.

discretionary fiscal spending: Those elements of the federal budget not determined by past legislative or executive commitments.

income transfers: Payments to individuals for which no current goods or services are exchanged, such as Social Security, welfare, and unemployment benefits.

automatic stabilizer: Federal expenditure or revenue item that automatically responds countercyclically to changes in national income, like unemployment benefits and income taxes.

At the beginning of each year, the president and Congress put together a budget blueprint for the next **fiscal year (FY).** They don't start from scratch, however. Most budget line items reflect commitments made in earlier years. In FY 2020, for example, the federal budget included $1 trillion in Social Security benefits. The FY 2020 budget also provided for $120 billion in veterans benefits, $390 billion for interest payments on the national debt, and many billions more for completion of projects begun in previous years. These expenditures are baked into the budget. Does anyone expect that Congress will just reduce Social Security benefits being paid to retired workers or refuse to pay the interest due on the accumulated debt? Or that it even has the legal authority to do so?

Short of repudiating all prior commitments, there's little that Congress or the president can do to alter these expenditures in any given year. *To a large extent, current revenues and expenditures are the result of decisions made in prior years.* In this sense, much of each year's budget is considered "uncontrollable."

At present, uncontrollables account for roughly 80 percent of the federal budget. This leaves only 20 percent for **discretionary fiscal spending**—that is, spending decisions not "locked in" by prior legislative commitments. In recent years, rising interest payments and increasing entitlements (Social Security, Medicare, civil service pensions, etc.) have reduced the discretionary share of the budget even further. This doesn't mean that discretionary fiscal policy is no longer important; it simply means that the potential for *changing* budget outlays in any year is much smaller than it might first appear.

Automatic Stabilizers. Most of the uncontrollable line items in the federal budget have another characteristic that directly affects budget deficits: Their value *changes* with economic conditions. Consider unemployment insurance benefits. The unemployment insurance program, established in 1935, provides that persons who lose their jobs will receive some income (an average of $300 per week) from the government. The law establishes the *entitlement* to unemployment benefits but not the amount to be spent in any year. Each year's expenditure depends on how many workers lose their jobs and qualify for benefits. In 2009, for example, outlays for unemployment benefits increased by $82 billion. That increase in federal spending was due to the 2008–2009 recession: The millions of workers who lost their jobs became eligible for unemployment benefits. The spending increase was *automatic,* not *discretionary*.

Welfare benefits also increased by $70 billion in 2009. This increase in spending also occurred automatically in response to worsened economic conditions. As more people lost jobs and used up their savings, they turned to welfare for help. They were *entitled* to food stamps, housing assistance, and cash welfare benefits according to eligibility rules already written; no new congressional or executive action was required to approve this increase in government spending.

Notice that *outlays for unemployment compensation and welfare benefits increase when the economy goes into recession.* This is exactly the kind of fiscal policy that Keynes advocated. The increase in **income transfers** helps offset the income losses due to recession. These increased transfers therefore act as **automatic stabilizers**—injecting new spending into the circular flow during economic contractions. Conversely, transfer payments *decline* when the economy is *expanding* and fewer people qualify for unemployment or welfare benefits. Hence, no one has to pull the fiscal policy lever to inject more or less entitlement spending into the circular flow; much of it happens automatically.

Automatic stabilizers also exist on the revenue side of the federal budget. Income taxes are an important stabilizer because they move up and down with the value of spending and output. As we've observed, if household incomes increase, a jump in consumer spending is likely to follow. The resultant multiplier effects might create some demand-pull inflation. The tax code lessens this inflationary pressure. When you get more income, you have to pay more taxes. Hence, income taxes siphon off some of the increased purchasing power that might have found its way to product markets. Progressive income taxes are particularly effective stabilizers because they siphon off increasing proportions of purchasing power when incomes are rising and decreasing proportions when aggregate demand and output are falling.

- *Changes in Real GDP Growth*

When the GDP growth rate decreases by one percentage point

1. Government spending (*G*) automatically increases for
    Unemployment insurance benefits.
    Food stamps.
    Welfare benefits.
    Social Security benefits.
    Medicaid.
2. Government tax revenues (*T*) automatically decline for
    Individual income taxes.
    Corporate income taxes.
    Social Security payroll taxes.
3. **The deficit increases by $67 billion.**

- *Changes in Inflation*

When the inflation rate increases by one percentage point

1. Government spending (*G*) automatically increases for
    Indexed retirement and Social Security benefits.
    Higher interest payments.
2. Government tax revenues (*T*) automatically increase for
    Corporate income taxes.
    Social Security payroll taxes.
2. **The deficit increases by $40 billion.**

Source: Congressional Budget Office (first-year effects only).

TABLE 12.2

The Budget Impact of Cyclical Forces (in 2020 dollars)

Changes in economic conditions alter federal revenue and spending. When GDP growth slows, tax revenues decline and income transfers increase. This widens the budget deficit.

Higher rates of inflation increase both outlays and revenues, but not equally.

The cyclical balance reflects the budget impacts of changing economic circumstances.

Cyclical Deficits

Automatic stabilizers imply that policymakers don't have total control of each year's budget. In reality, *the size of the federal budget deficit or surplus is sensitive to expansion and contraction of the macro economy.*

Effects of GDP Growth. Table 12.2 shows just how sensitive the budget is to cyclical forces. When the GDP growth rate slows, tax revenues decline. As the economy slows, more people turn to the government for income support: Unemployment benefits and other transfer payments increase. As a consequence, the budget deficit increases. This is exactly what happened in FY 2009: The recession increased the budget deficit by $225 billion *automatically* (see Table 12.3).

Effects of Inflation. Inflation also affects the budget. Because Social Security benefits are automatically adjusted to inflation, federal outlays increase as the price level rises. Interest rates also rise with inflation, forcing the government to pay more for debt services. Tax revenues also rise with inflation, but not as fast as expenditures. Table 12.2 shows that a one-point increase in the inflation rate *increases* the budget deficit by $40 billion in the first year (and more over time).

The most important implication of Table 12.2 is that neither the president nor the Congress has complete control of the federal deficit. *Actual budget deficits and surpluses may arise from economic conditions as well as policy.* Perhaps no one learned this better than President Reagan. In 1980 he campaigned on a promise to balance the budget. The 1981–1982 recession, however, caused the actual deficit to soar. The president later had to admit that actual deficits aren't solely the product of big spenders in Washington.

President Clinton had more luck with the deficit. Although he increased discretionary spending in his first two years, the annual budget deficit *shrank* by more than $90 billion between 1993 and 1995. Most of the deficit reduction was due to automatic stabilizers that kicked in as GDP growth accelerated and the unemployment rate fell. As the economy

TABLE 12.3

Cyclical vs. Structural Budget Balances (in billions of dollars)

The budget balance includes both cyclical and structural components. Changes in the structural component result from policy changes; changes in the cyclical component result from changes in the economy. In 2007 the cyclical surplus increased by $6 billion (from +11 billion to +17 billion) due to faster GDP growth. In 2009 the opposite occurred: The recession widened the cyclical deficit by $225 billion (from $−26 to $−251 billion).

Fiscal Year	Budget Balance	=	Cyclical Component	+	Structural Component
2000	+236		+58		+178
2001	+128		−1		+129
2002	−158		−83		−75
2003	−378		−107		−271
2004	−413		−58		−355
2005	−318		−20		−298
2006	−248		+11		−259
2007	−161		+17		−178
2008	−459		−26		−433
2009	−1,413		−251		−1,162
2010	−1,294		−300		−994
2011	−1,300		−264		−1,036
2012	−1,087		−208		−879
2013	−680		−207		−473
2014	−485		−168		−317
2015	−439		−86		−353
2016	−585		−76		−509
2017	−665		−53		−612
2018	−779		+11		−790
2019	−984		+53		−1,037
2020	−3,310		−403		−2,907

Source: Congressional Budget Office, September 2020.

continued to grow sharply, the unemployment rate fell to 4 percent. That surge in the economy increased tax revenues, reduced income transfers, and propelled the 1998 budget into surplus. It was primarily the economy, not the president or the Congress, that produced the first budget surplus in a generation.

President George W. Bush also benefited from GDP growth. From 2003 to 2007, economic growth raised both incomes and tax payments. Notice in Table 12.1 how tax revenue jumped from $2,407 billion in 2006 to $2,568 billion in 2007. Tax *rates* weren't increased during those years; people were simply earning more money. The *automatic* increase in revenues helped shrink the deficit from $248 billion in 2006 to $161 billion in 2007.

The recession of 2008–2009 reversed these favorable trends. Even before President Obama convinced Congress to cut taxes and increase government spending, the federal deficit was increasing. Tax receipts were declining as more and more workers lost paychecks. Federal spending was increasing as more workers sought unemployment benefits, welfare, and medical assistance.

The run-up in the deficit after 2016 was not due to another recession. This time the increase in the deficit was entirely due to discretionary policy. The Trump tax cuts of 2017 and his military build-up reduced revenues and increased spending at the same time, leading to the reemergence of a trillion-dollar deficit in 2019. Then came the COVID-19 shutdowns that not only reduced federal tax revenues but also motivated Congress to approve a massive increase in (discretionary) federal spending. The impact on the deficit was spectacular, *tripling* the deficit in 2020.

That part of the federal deficit attributable to cyclical disturbances (changes in unemployment and inflation) is referred to as the **cyclical deficit**. As we've observed,

cyclical deficit: That portion of the budget deficit attributable to unemployment or inflation.

- *The cyclical deficit widens when GDP growth slows or inflation increases.*
- *The cyclical deficit shrinks when GDP growth accelerates or inflation decreases.*

All of these cyclical changes in the budget occur automatically. Hence, we can't blame (or credit!) Congress or the president for every change in federal deficits. To assess the effect of *policy* decisions on the budget, we need another measure of budget dynamics.

Structural Deficits

To isolate the effects of fiscal policy, economists break down the actual budget balance into *cyclical* and *structural* components:

$$\frac{\text{Total budget}}{\text{balance}} = \frac{\text{Cyclical}}{\text{balance}} + \frac{\text{Structural}}{\text{balance}}$$

The cyclical portion of the budget balance reflects the impact of the business cycle on federal tax revenues and spending—the *automatic* changes we've discussed. The **structural deficit** reflects fiscal policy decisions. Rather than comparing actual outlays to actual receipts, the structural deficit compares the outlays and receipts that would occur if the economy were at full employment.[1] This technique eliminates budget distortions caused by cyclical conditions. Any remaining changes in spending or outlays must be due to policy decisions. Hence, ***part of the deficit arises from cyclical changes in the economy; the rest is the result of discretionary fiscal policy.***

Table 12.3 shows how the total, cyclical, and structural balances have behaved in recent years. Consider what happened to the federal budget in 2000–2001. In 2000 the federal surplus was $236 billion. In 2001 the surplus shrank to $128 billion. The shrinking surplus suggests that the government was trying to stimulate economic activity with expansionary fiscal policies (tax cuts, spending hikes). But this wasn't the case. The primary reason for the smaller 2001 surplus was an abrupt halt in GDP growth. As the economy slipped into recession, the *cyclical* component shifted from a *surplus* of $58 billion in 2000 to −$1 billion in 2001. This $59 billion swing in the cyclical budget accounted for most of the decrease in the total budget surplus. By contrast, the *structural* surplus shrank by only $49 billion, reflecting a fairly modest *discretionary* fiscal stimulus.

The distinction between the structural and cyclical components of the budget allows us to figure out who's to "blame" for deficit increases. This was a hot topic when the deficit soared in 2009–2011. According to CBO (Table 12.3), the trillion-dollar *increase* in the 2009 budget deficit was due in part to the economic downturn ($225 billion, i.e., the *change* in the cyclical component from −26 to −251) and the rest to discretionary fiscal policy ($729 billion). So, *policy decisions,* not cyclical changes in the economy, did most of the budget damage. This was clearly the case again in 2017–2019 when the deficit increased *despite* a growing economy. And then there was the massive policy response to the coronavirus pandemic in 2020 that tripled the deficit in a single year.

This CBO conclusion reflects the fact that both automatic stabilizers and policy initiatives affect the budget at the same time. To isolate the impact of policy decisions, we must focus on changes in the *structural* deficit, not the *total* deficit. Specifically,

- ***Fiscal stimulus is measured by an increase in the structural deficit*** (or shrinkage in the structural surplus).
- ***Fiscal restraint is gauged by a decrease in the structural deficit*** (or increase in the structural surplus).

According to this measure, fiscal policy was actually restrictive during the Great Depression, when fiscal stimulus was desperately needed (see Front Page Economics "Fiscal Policy in the Great Depression"). Both Presidents Hoover and Roosevelt thought the government should rein in its spending when tax revenues declined so as to keep the federal budget balanced. It took years of economic devastation before the fiscal policy lever was reversed. Since then, economists have focused on the state of the economy first, and then looked second at budget deficits.

structural deficit: Federal revenues at full employment minus expenditures at full employment under prevailing fiscal policy.

---

[1]The structural deficit is also referred to as the "full-employment," "high-employment," or "standardized" deficit.

FRONT PAGE ECONOMICS

FISCAL POLICY IN THE GREAT DEPRESSION

In 1931 President Herbert Hoover observed, "Business depressions have been recurrent in the life of our country and are but transitory." Rather than proposing fiscal stimulus, Hoover complained that expansion of public works programs had unbalanced the federal budget. In 1932 he proposed *cutbacks* in government spending and *higher* taxes. In his view, the "unquestioned balancing of the federal budget . . . is the first necessity of national stability and is the foundation of further recovery."

Franklin Roosevelt shared this view of fiscal policy. He criticized Hoover for not balancing the budget and in 1933 warned Congress that "all public works must be considered from the point of view of the ability of the government treasury to pay for them."

As the accompanying figure shows, the budget deficit persisted throughout the Great Depression. But these deficits were the result of a declining economy, not stimulative fiscal policy. The structural deficit actually *decreased* from 1931 to 1933 (see the figure), when fiscal *restraint* was pursued. This restraint reduced aggregate spending at a time when producers were desperate for increasing sales. Only when the structural deficit was expanded tremendously by spending during World War II did fiscal policy have a decidedly positive effect. Federal defense expenditures jumped from $2.2 billion in 1940 to $87.4 billion in 1944!

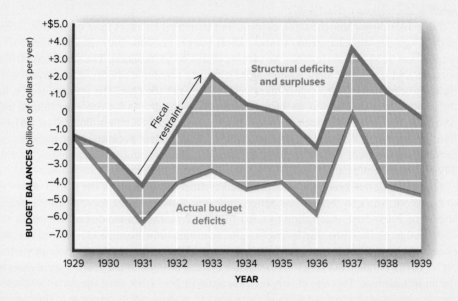

Source: E. Carey Brown, "Fiscal Policy in the Thirties: A Reappraisal," *American Economic Review,* December 1956, tab. 1 (The American Economic Association, 1956).

CRITICAL ANALYSIS: From 1931 to 1933, the **structural deficit** decreased from $4.5 billion to a $2 billion *surplus.* This fiscal restraint reduced aggregate demand and deepened the Great Depression.

ECONOMIC EFFECTS OF DEFICITS

No matter what the origins of budget deficits, most people are alarmed by them. Should they be? What are the *consequences* of budget deficits?

Crowding Out

crowding out: A reduction in private sector borrowing (and spending) caused by increased government borrowing.

We've already encountered one potential consequence of deficit financing: *If the government borrows funds to finance deficits, the availability of funds for private sector spending may be reduced.* This is the **crowding-out** problem first noted in Chapter 11. If crowding out

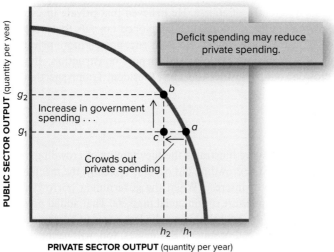

Deficit spending may reduce private spending.

FIGURE 12.2
Crowding Out

If the economy is fully employed, an increase in public sector expenditure (output) will reduce private sector expenditure (output).

In this case a deficit-financed increase in government expenditure moves the economy from point a to point b. In the process, the quantity $h_1 - h_2$ of private sector output is crowded out to make room for the increase in public sector output (from g_1 to g_2). If the economy started at point c, however, with unemployed resources, crowding out need not occur.

occurs, the increase in government expenditure will be at least partially offset by reductions in consumption and investment.

If the economy were operating at full employment, crowding out would be inevitable. At full employment, we'd be on the production possibilities curve, using all available resources. As Figure 12.2 reminds us, additional government purchases can occur only if private sector purchases are reduced. In real terms, *crowding out implies less private sector output.*

Crowding out is complete only if the economy is at full employment. If the economy is in recession, it's possible to get more public sector output (like highways, schools, defense) without cutbacks in private sector output. This possibility is illustrated by the move from point c to point b in Figure 12.2.

Tax cuts have crowding-out effects as well. The purpose of the 2017 tax cuts was to stimulate business and consumer spending. As the economy approaches full employment, however, how can more consumer output be produced? At the production possibilities limit, the added consumption will force cutbacks in either investment or government services.

What Figure 12.2 emphasizes is that *the risk of crowding out is greater the closer the economy is to full employment.* This implies that deficits are less appropriate at high levels of employment but more appropriate at low levels of employment.

Opportunity Cost

Even if crowding out does occur, that doesn't mean that deficits are necessarily too big. Crowding out simply reminds us that there's an **opportunity cost** to government spending. We still have to decide whether the private sector output crowded out by government expenditure is more or less desirable than the increased public sector output.

President Clinton defended government expenditure on education, training, and infrastructure as public "investment." He believed that any resulting crowding out of private sector expenditure wasn't necessarily an unwelcome trade-off. Public investments in education, health care, and transportation systems might even accelerate long-term economic growth.

President George W. Bush saw things differently. He preferred a mix of output that included less public sector output and more private sector output. Accordingly, he welcomed any crowding out of government spending that occurred as a result of tax cuts.

For his part, President Obama believed that government must play a leading role in education, health care, infrastructure, and the development of alternative energy sources. He viewed a shift of resources from the private sector to the public sector as a necessity to promote both short-run stimulus and long-term growth. Crowding out, if it occurred, wasn't a bad thing from his perspective.

opportunity cost: The most desired goods or services that are forgone in order to obtain something else.

President Trump saw things differently, of course. He believed that private investment was the premier source of growth and innovation. He championed tax cuts that were specifically tailored to encourage business investment. He even encouraged more private investment in public projects like highways, bridges, and airport construction. If some government spending was crowded out by business tax cuts, President Trump saw that as a mark of success.

Interest Rate Movements

Although the production possibilities curve illustrates the inevitability of crowding out at full employment, it doesn't explain *how* the crowding out occurs. Typically, the mechanism that enforces crowding out is the rate of interest. When the government borrows more funds to finance larger deficits, it puts pressure on financial markets. That added pressure may cause interest rates to rise. If they do, households will be less eager to borrow money to buy cars, houses, and other debt-financed products. Businesses, too, will be more hesitant to borrow and invest. Hence, *rising interest rates are both a symptom and a cause of crowding out.*

Rising interests may also crowd out *government* spending in the wake of tax cuts. As interest rates rise, government borrowing costs rise as well. According to the Congressional Budget Office, a one-point rise in interest rates increases Uncle Sam's debt expenses by more than $100 billion over four years. These higher interest costs leave less room in government budgets for financing new projects.

How much interest rates rise again depends on how close the economy is to its productive capacity. If there is a lot of excess capacity, interest rate–induced crowding out isn't very likely. This was the case in early 2009. Interest rates stayed low despite a run-up in government spending and new tax cuts. There was enough excess capacity in the economy to accommodate fiscal stimulus without crowding out. As capacity is approached, however, interest rates and crowding out are both likely to increase.

ECONOMIC EFFECTS OF SURPLUSES

Although budget deficits are clearly the norm, we might at least ponder the economic effects of budget *surpluses*. Essentially, they are the mirror image of those for deficits.

Crowding In

When the government takes in more revenue than it spends, it adds to leakage in the circular flow. But Uncle Sam doesn't hide the surplus under a mattress. And the sums involved (such as $236 billion in FY 2000) are too large to put in a bank. Were the government to buy corporate stock with the budget surplus, it would effectively be nationalizing private enterprises. So where does the surplus go?

There are really only four potential uses for a budget surplus:

- *Spend it on goods and services.*
- *Cut taxes.*
- *Increase income transfers.*
- *Pay off old debt ("save it").*

The first three options effectively wipe out the surplus by changing budget outlays or receipts. There are important differences here, though. The first option—increased government spending—not only reduces the surplus but enlarges the public sector. Cutting taxes or increasing income transfers, by contrast, puts the money into the hands of consumers and enlarges the private sector.

The fourth budget option is to use the surplus to pay off some of the debt accumulated from earlier deficits. This has a similar but less direct **crowding-in** effect. If Uncle Sam pays

crowding out: A reduction in private sector borrowing (and spending) caused by increased government borrowing.

off some of his accumulated debt, households that were holding that debt (government bonds) will end up with more money. If they use that money to buy goods and services, then private sector output will expand.

Even people who haven't lent any money to Uncle Sam will benefit from the debt reduction. When the government reduces its level of borrowing, it takes pressure off market interest rates. As interest rates drop, consumers will be more willing and able to purchase big-ticket items such as cars, appliances, and houses, thus changing the mix of output in favor of private sector production.

Cyclical Sensitivity

Like crowding out, the extent of crowding in depends on the state of the economy. In a recession, a surplus-induced decline in interest rates isn't likely to stimulate much spending. If consumer and investor confidence are low, even a surplus-financed tax cut might not lift private sector spending much.

THE ACCUMULATION OF DEBT

Because the U.S. government has had many more years of budget deficits than budget surpluses, Uncle Sam has accumulated a large **national debt.** In fact, the United States started out in debt. The Continental Congress needed to borrow money in 1777 to continue fighting the Revolutionary War. The Congress tried to raise tax revenues and even printed new money (the Continental dollar) to buy needed food, tents, guns, and ammunition. But by the winter of 1777, these mechanisms for financing the war were failing. To acquire needed supplies, the Continental Congress plunged the new nation into debt. The United States borrowed more than $8 million from France and $250,000 from Spain to help finance the Revolutionary War.

national debt: Accumulated debt of the federal government.

Debt Creation/Bonds

At the time it borrowed money from France and Spain, the Continental Congress promised to repay the loans at a later date. In effect, it gave France and Spain IOUs that contained those promises. We call those IOUs "bonds." Bonds spell out the amount to be repaid, when repayment will occur, and the interest rate that will be paid for the loan.

Today, the U.S. Treasury does the same thing. As the fiscal agent of the U.S. government, the Treasury collects tax revenues, signs checks for federal spending, and—when necessary—borrows funds to cover budget deficits. When the Treasury borrows funds, it issues **Treasury bonds;** these are IOUs of the federal government. As was the case with the Continental Congress, the Treasury's bonds spell out the amount borrowed and the terms of repayment (date, interest rate). People buy those bonds—lend money to the U.S. Treasury—because bonds pay interest and are a very safe haven for idle funds.

Treasury bonds: Promissory notes (IOUs) issued by the U.S. Treasury.

The total stock of all outstanding bonds represents the national debt. It's equal to the sum total of our accumulated deficits, less any repayments in those years when a budget surplus existed. In other words, *the national debt is a stock of IOUs created by annual deficit flows.* Whenever there's a budget deficit, the national debt increases. In years when a budget surplus exists, the national debt can be pared down.

Early History, 1790–1900

During the period 1790–1812, the United States often incurred debt but typically repaid it quickly. The War of 1812, however, caused a massive increase in the national debt. With neither a standing army nor an adequate source of tax revenues to acquire one, the U.S. government had to borrow money to repel the British. By 1816 the national debt was more than $129 million. Although that figure seems tiny by today's standards, it amounted to 13 percent of national income in 1816.

1835–1836: Debt-Free. After the War of 1812, the U.S. government used recurrent budget surpluses to repay its debt. These surpluses were so frequent that the U.S. government was completely out of debt by 1835. In 1835 and again in 1836, the government had neither national debt nor a budget deficit. The dilemma in those years was how to use the budget *surplus!* Because there was no accumulated debt, the option of using the surplus to reduce the debt didn't exist. In the end, Congress decided simply to distribute the surplus funds to the states. That was the last time the U.S. government was completely out of debt.

Civil War. The Mexican-American War (1846–1848) necessitated a sudden increase in federal spending. The deficits incurred to fight that war caused a fourfold increase in the debt. That debt was pared down the following decade. Then the Civil War (1861–1865) broke out, and both sides needed debt financing. By the end of the Civil War, the North owed more than $2.6 billion, or approximately half its national income. The South depended more heavily on newly printed Confederate currency to finance its side of the Civil War, relying on bond issues for only one-third of its financial needs. When the South lost, however, neither Confederate currency nor Confederate bonds had any value.[2]

Twentieth Century

The Spanish-American War (1898) also increased the national debt. But all prior debt was dwarfed by World War I, which increased the national debt from 3 percent of national income in 1917 to 41 percent at the war's end.

The national debt declined during the 1920s because the federal government was consistently spending less revenue than it took in. Budget surpluses disappeared quickly when the economy fell into the Great Depression, however, and the cyclical deficit widened (see Front Page Economics "Fiscal Policy in the Great Depression").

World War II. The most explosive jump in the national debt occurred during World War II, when the government had to mobilize all available resources. Rather than raise taxes to the fullest, the U.S. government restricted the availability of consumer goods. With consumer goods rationed, consumers had little choice but to increase their saving. Uncle Sam encouraged people to lend those idle funds to the U.S. Treasury by buying U.S. war bonds. The resulting bond purchases raised the national debt from 45 percent of GDP in 1940 to more than 125 percent of GDP in 1946 (see Figure 12.3).

The 1980s. During the 1980s, the national debt jumped again—by nearly $2 *trillion.* This 10-year increase in the debt exceeded all the net debt accumulation since the country was founded. This time, however, the debt increase wasn't war-related. Instead, the debt explosion of the 1980s originated in recessions (1980–1981 and 1981–1982), massive tax cuts (1981–1984), and increased defense spending. The recessions caused big jumps in the cyclical deficit while the Reagan tax cuts and military buildup caused the structural deficit to jump fourfold in only four years (1982–1986).

The 1990s. The early 1990s continued the same trend. Discretionary federal spending increased sharply in the first two years of the George H. Bush administration. The federal government was also forced to bail out hundreds of failed savings and loan associations. Although taxes were raised a bit and military spending was cut back, the structural deficit was little changed. Then the recession of 1990–1991 killed any chance of achieving smaller deficits. In only four years (1988–1992) the national debt increased by another $1 trillion.

[2]In anticipation of this situation, European leaders had forced the South to guarantee most of its loans with cotton. When the South was unable to repay its debts, these creditors could sell the cotton they had held as collateral. But most holders of Confederate bonds or currency received nothing.

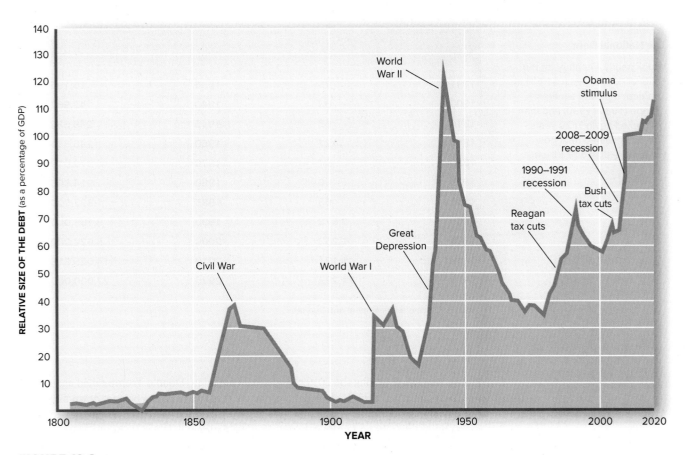

FIGURE 12.3

Historical View of the Debt/GDP Ratio

From 1790 to 1917, the national debt exceeded 10 percent of GDP during the Civil War years only. After 1917, however, the debt ratio grew sharply. World War I, the Great Depression, and World War II all caused major increases in the debt ratio. The tax cuts of 1981–1984 and 2001–2005 and the recessions of 1990–1991, 2001, and 2008–2009 caused further increases in the debt/GDP ratio. The Obama fiscal stimulus pushed the debt ratio still higher, as did the Trump tax cuts and the 2020 response to the coronavirus.

Source: Office of Management and Budget.

In 1993 the Clinton administration persuaded Congress to raise taxes, thereby reducing the structural deficit. Continuing recovery from the 1990-1991 recession also reduced the cyclical deficit. Nevertheless, the budget deficits of 1993-1996 pushed the national debt to more than $5 trillion.

Recent Years

Bush Tax Cuts, Defense Spending. After a couple of years of budget surplus, the accumulated debt still exceeded $5.6 trillion in 2002. Then the Bush tax cuts and the defense buildup kicked in, increasing the structural deficit by nearly $300 billion in only three years (FY 2002-2004) (Table 12.4). As a consequence, the national debt surged again. By January 2009—*before* the Obama stimulus plan was enacted—the debt exceeded $10 trillion.

Recession and Obama Stimulus. The Great Recession and the Obama fiscal stimulus caused a further surge in the national debt. The trillion-dollar-plus deficits of 2009-2012 (Table 12.1) increased the national debt to almost $20 trillion by the end of 2016. That works out to more than $61,000 of debt for every U.S. citizen. The thought of owing so much money is what worries people so much.

TABLE 12.4

The National Debt

It took nearly a century for the national debt to reach $1 trillion. The debt tripled in a mere decade (1980–1990) and then quintupled again in 20 years. The accumulated debt now totals more than $27 trillion.

Year	Total Debt Outstanding (Millions of Dollars)	Year	Total Debt Outstanding (Millions of Dollars)
1791	75	1930	16,185
1800	83	1940	42,967
1810	53	1945	258,682
1816	127	1960	286,331
1820	91	1970	370,919
1835	0	1980	914,300
1850	63	1985	1,827,500
1865	2,678	1990	3,163,000
1900	1,263	2000	5,629,000
1915	1,191	2010	14,025,615
1920	24,299	2020	27,000,000

Source: Office of Management and Budget.

Trump Stimulus. During the 2016 presidential campaign, Donald Trump railed against the $19 trillion national debt. If elected, he promised that "we're gonna bring it down big league and quickly." To do so, he vowed that "We're gonna stop our deficits." He envisioned eliminating budget deficits and ultimately reducing the national debt largely by shrinking or eliminating some government agencies like the Environmental Protection Agency and the Department of Education. Once he took office, though, he realized that reducing the deficit wasn't so easy. Indeed, the tax cuts and military spending he introduced actually *increased* the budget deficit, adding to the national debt.

Coronavirus Response. The deficit and the debt both increased abruptly with the federal response to the coronavirus in 2020. Mandatory shutdowns of factories, malls, stores, and entertainment venues reduced not only personal incomes, but federal tax revenues as well. Then federal spending increased dramatically, as Congress authorized increases in unemployment and sick-leave benefits, and initiated direct payments to both workers and businesses. By the end of 2020, the national debt had climbed to $27 trillion.

WHO OWNS THE DEBT?

To the average citizen, the accumulated national debt is both incomprehensible and frightening. Who can understand debts that are measured in *trillions* of dollars? Who can ever be expected to pay them?

Liabilities = Assets

liability: An obligation to make future payment; debt.

asset: Anything having exchange value in the marketplace; wealth.

The first thing to note about the national debt is that it represents not only a liability but an asset as well. When the U.S. Treasury borrows money, it issues bonds. Those bonds are a **liability** for the federal government because it must later repay the borrowed funds. But those same bonds are an **asset** to the people who hold them. Bondholders have a claim to future repayment. They can even convert that claim into cash by selling their bonds in the bond market. Therefore, *national debt creates as much wealth (for bondholders) as liabilities (for the U.S. Treasury).* Neither money nor any other form of wealth disappears when the government borrows money.

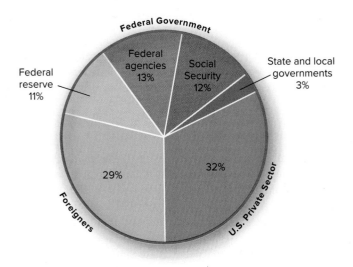

FIGURE 12.4

Debt Ownership

The bonds that create the national debt represent wealth that's owned by bondholders. About 40 percent of that wealth is held by the U.S. government itself. The private sector in the United States holds only 32 percent of the debt, and foreigners own 29 percent.

Source: U.S. Treasury Department, 2019 data.

The fact that total bond assets equal total bond liabilities is of little consolation to taxpayers confronted with $27 trillion of national debt and worried about when, if ever, they'll be able to repay it. The fear that either the U.S. government or its taxpayers will be "bankrupted" by the national debt always lurks in the shadows. How legitimate is that fear?

Ownership of the Debt

People are surprised when they discover who owns the bonds the U.S. Treasury has issued. As Figure 12.4 shows, the largest bondholder is the U.S. government itself: *Federal agencies hold nearly 40 percent of all outstanding Treasury bonds.* The Federal Reserve System, an independent agency of the U.S. government, acquires Treasury bonds in its conduct of monetary policy (see Chapters 14 and 15). Other agencies of the U.S. government also purchase bonds. The Social Security Administration, for example, maintains a trust fund balance to cover any shortfall between monthly payroll tax receipts and the retirement benefits it must pay out. Most of that balance is held in the form of interest-bearing Treasury bonds. Thus, one arm of the federal government (the U.S. Treasury) owes another arm (the U.S. Social Security Administration) a significant part of the national debt.

State and local governments hold another 3 percent of the national debt. This debt, too, arises when state and local governments use their own budget surpluses to purchase interest-bearing Treasury bonds.

The private sector in the United States owns about a third of the national debt. This private wealth is in the form of familiar U.S. savings bonds or other types of Treasury bonds. Few households own these bonds directly. Instead, most of this private wealth is held *indirectly* by banks, insurance companies, money market funds, corporations, and other institutions. These bonds are ultimately owned by the people who have deposits at the bank or in money market funds, who own stock in corporations, or who are insured by companies that hold Treasury bonds. Thus, *U.S. households hold about one-fifth of the national debt, either directly or indirectly.*

All the debt held by U.S. households, institutions, and government entities is referred to as **internal debt.** As Figure 12.4 illustrates, two-thirds of the national debt is internal. In other words, *we owe most of the national debt to ourselves.*

The remaining third of the national debt is held by foreign banks, corporations, households, and governments. U.S. Treasury bonds are attractive to global participants because of their relative security, the interest they pay, and the general acceptability of dollar-denominated assets in world trade. Bonds held by foreign households and institutions are referred to as **external debt.**

internal debt: U.S. government debt (Treasury bonds) held by U.S. households and institutions.

external debt: U.S. government debt (Treasury bonds) held by foreign households and institutions.

BURDEN OF THE DEBT

It may be comforting to know that most of our national debt is owned internally, and much of it by the government itself. Figure 12.4 won't still the fears of most taxpayers, however, especially those who don't hold any Treasury bonds. From their perspective, the total debt still looks frightening.

Refinancing

How much of a "burden" the debt really represents isn't so evident. For nearly 30 years (1970–1997), the federal government kept piling up more debt without apparent economic damage. The few years that the government had a budget surplus (1998–2001) weren't markedly different from the deficit years. As we saw earlier (Figure 12.3), deficits and debt stretched out over even longer periods in earlier decades without apparent economic damage.

How was the government able to pile debt upon debt? Quite simple: As debts have become due, the federal government has simply borrowed new funds to pay them off. New bonds have been issued to replace old bonds. This **refinancing** of the debt is a routine feature of the U.S. Treasury's debt management.

The ability of the U.S. Treasury to refinance its debt raises an intriguing question. What if the debt could be eternally refinanced? What if no one *ever* demanded to be paid off more than others were willing to lend Uncle Sam? Then the national debt would truly grow forever.

Two things are worrisome about this scenario. First, eternal refinancing seems like a chain letter that promises to make everyone rich. In this case, the chain requires that people hold ever-larger portions of their wealth in the form of Treasury bonds. People worry that the chain will be broken and that they'll be forced to repay all the outstanding debt. Parents worry that the scheme might break down in the next generation, unfairly burdening their own children or grandchildren.

Aside from its seeming implausibility, the notion of eternal refinancing seems to defy a basic maxim of economics—namely that "there ain't no free lunch." Eternal refinancing makes it look as though government borrowing has no cost, as though federal spending financed by the national debt is really a free lunch.

There are two flaws in this way of thinking. The first relates to the interest charges that accompany debt. The second, and more important, flaw relates to the real economic costs of government activity.

Debt Service

With more than $27 trillion in accumulated debt, the U.S. government must make enormous interest payments every year. **Debt service** refers to these annual interest payments. In FY 2020, the U.S. Treasury paid more than $390 billion in interest charges. These interest payments force the government to reduce outlays for other purposes or to finance a larger budget each year. In this respect, *interest payments restrict the government's ability to balance the budget or fund other public sector activities.*

Although the debt servicing requirements may pinch Uncle Sam's spending purse, the real economic consequences of interest payments are less evident. Who gets the interest payments? What economic resources are absorbed by those payments?

As we saw in Figure 12.4, most of the nation's outstanding debt is internal—that is, owned by domestic households and institutions. Therefore, most interest payments are made to people and institutions within the United States. *Most debt servicing is simply a redistribution of income from taxpayers to bondholders.* In many cases, the taxpayer and bondholder are the same person. In all cases, however, the income that leaks from the circular flow in the form of taxes to pay for debt servicing returns to the circular flow as interest payments. Total income is unchanged. Thus, debt servicing may not have any direct effect on the level of aggregate demand.

refinancing: The issuance of new debt in payment of debt issued earlier.

debt service: The interest required to be paid each year on outstanding debt.

Debt servicing also has little impact on the real resources of the economy. The collection of additional taxes and the processing of interest payments require the use of some land, labor, and capital. But the value of the resources used for the processing of debt service is trivial—a tiny fraction of the interest payments themselves. This means that *interest payments themselves have virtually no direct opportunity cost for the economy as a whole.* The amount of goods and services available for other purposes is virtually unchanged as a result of debt servicing.

Opportunity Costs

If debt servicing absorbs few economic resources, can we conclude that the national debt really does represent a free lunch? Unfortunately not. But the concept of opportunity cost provides a major clue about the true burden of the debt and who bears it.

Opportunity costs are incurred only when real resources (factors of production) are used. The amount of that cost is measured by the other goods and services that could have been produced with those resources, but weren't. As noted earlier, the *process* of debt servicing absorbs few resources and so has negligible opportunity cost. To understand the true burden of the national debt, we have to look at what that debt financed. *The true burden of the debt is the opportunity cost of the activities financed by the debt.* To assess that burden, we need to ask what the government did with the borrowed funds.

Government Purchases. Suppose Congress decides to upgrade our naval forces and borrows $10 billion for that purpose. What's the opportunity cost of that decision? The economic cost of the fleet upgrade is measured by the goods and services forgone in order to build more ships. The labor, land, and capital used to upgrade the fleet can't be used to produce something else. We give up the opportunity to produce another $10 billion worth of private goods and services when Congress upgrades the fleet.

The economic cost of the naval buildup is unaffected by the method of government finance. Whether the government borrows $10 billion or increases taxes by that amount, the forgone civilian output will still be $10 billion. *The opportunity cost of government purchases is the true burden of government activity, however financed.* The decision to finance such activity with debt rather than taxes doesn't materially alter that cost.

The Real Trade-offs

Although the national debt poses no special burden to the economy, the transactions it finances have a substantial impact on the basic questions of WHAT, HOW, and FOR WHOM to produce. Deficit financing allows the government to obtain more resources and change the mix of output. In general, *deficit financing changes the mix of output in the direction of more public sector goods.*

As noted earlier, the deficits of 2018–2020 helped finance a substantial military buildup. The same result could have been financed with higher taxes, but President Trump wanted to cut taxes, not raise them. Besides, tax hikes are more visible and always unpopular. By borrowing rather than taxing, the federal government's claim on scarce resources is less apparent. But the end result is the same: The public sector expands at the expense of the private sector. This resource reallocation reveals the true burden of the debt: *The burden of the debt is really the opportunity cost (crowding out) of deficit-financed government activity.* How large that burden is depends on how many unemployed resources are available and the behavioral responses of consumers and investors to increased government activity.

Timing of Burden. Notice also *when* that cost is incurred. If the military is upgraded this year, then the opportunity cost is incurred this year. It's only while resources are actually being used by the military that we give up the opportunity to use them elsewhere. Opportunity costs are incurred at the time a government activity takes place, not when the resultant debt is paid. In other words, *the primary burden of the debt is incurred when the debt-financed activity takes place.*

If the entire military buildup is completed this year, what costs are borne next year? None. The land, labor, and capital available next year can be used for whatever purposes are then desired. Once the military buildup is completed, no further resources are allocated to that purpose. The real costs of government projects can't be postponed until a later year. In other words, the real burden of the debt can't be passed on to future generations. On the contrary, future generations will benefit from the sacrifices made today to build ships, parks, highways, dams, and other public sector projects. Future taxpayers will be able to *use* these projects without incurring the opportunity costs of their construction.

Economic Growth. Although future generations may benefit from current government spending, they may also be adversely affected by today's opportunity costs. Of particular concern is the possibility that government deficits might crowd out private investment. Investment is essential to enlarging our production possibilities and attaining higher living standards in the future. If federal deficits and debt-servicing requirements crowd out private investment, the rate of economic growth may slow, leaving future generations with less productive capacity than they would otherwise have. Thus, *if debt-financed government spending crowds out private investment, future generations will bear some of the debt burden.* Their burden will take the form of smaller-than-anticipated productive capacity.

There's no certainty that such crowding out will occur. Also, any reduction in private investment may be offset by public works (such as highways, schools, defense systems) that benefit future generations. So future generations may not suffer a net loss in welfare even if the national debt slows private investment and economic growth. From this perspective, *the whole debate about the burden of the debt is really an argument over the* **optimal mix of output.** If we permit more deficit spending, we're promoting more public sector activity. On the other hand, limits on deficit financing curtail growth of the public sector. *Battles over deficits and debts are a proxy for the more fundamental issue of private versus public spending.*

Repayment. All this sounds a little too neat. Won't future generations have to pay interest on the debts we incur today? And might they even have to pay off some of the debt?

We've already observed that the collection of taxes and processing of interest payments absorb relatively few resources. Hence, the mechanisms of repayment entail little burden.

Notice also who *receives* future interest payments. When we die, we leave behind not only the national debt but also the bonds that represent ownership of that debt. Hence, future grandchildren will be both taxpayers *and* bondholders. If interest payments are made 30 years from today, only people who are alive and holding bonds at that time will receive interest payments. *Future interest payments entail a redistribution of income among taxpayers and bondholders living in the future.*

The same kind of redistribution occurs if and when our grandchildren decide to pay off the debt. Tax revenues will be used to pay off the debt. The debt payments will go to people then holding Treasury bonds. The entire redistribution will occur among people living in the future.

optimal mix of output: The most desirable combination of output attainable with existing resources, technology, and social values.

EXTERNAL DEBT

The nature of opportunity costs makes it difficult but not impossible to pass the debt burden on to future generations. The exception is the case of external debt.

No Crowding Out

When we borrow funds from abroad, we increase our ability to consume, invest, and finance government activity. In effect, other nations are lending us the income necessary to *import* more goods. If we can buy imports with borrowed funds (without offsetting exports), our real income will exceed our production possibilities. As Figure 12.5 illustrates, external borrowing allows us to enjoy a mix of output that lies *outside* our production possibilities curve. Specifically, *external financing allows us to get more public sector*

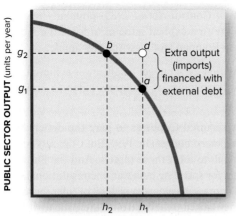

FIGURE 12.5
External Financing

A closed economy must forsake some private sector output to increase public sector output (see Figure 12.2). External financing temporarily eliminates that opportunity cost. Instead of having to move from *a* to *b*, external borrowing allows us to move from *a* to *d*. At point *d* we have more public output and no less private output.

goods without cutting back on private sector production (or vice versa) in the short run. When we use external debt to finance government spending, we move from point *a* to point *d* in Figure 12.5. Imported goods and services eliminate the need to cut back on private sector activity, a cutback that would otherwise force us to point *b*. External financing eliminates this opportunity cost. The move from point *a* to point *d* reflects the additional imports financed by external debt.

The imports needn't be public sector goods. A tax cut at point *b* might increase consumption and imports by $h_1 - h_2$, moving the economy to point *d*. At *d* we have *more* consumption and *no less* government activity.

External financing appears to offer the proverbial free lunch. It would be a free lunch if foreign lenders were willing to accumulate U.S. Treasury bonds forever. They would then own stacks of paper (Treasury bonds), and we'd consume some of their output (our imports) each year. *As long as outsiders are willing to hold U.S. bonds, external financing imposes no real cost.* No goods or services are given up to pay for the additional output received.

Repayment

Foreign investors may not be willing to hold U.S. bonds indefinitely. At some point they'll want to collect their bills. To do this, they'll cash in (sell) their bonds, and then use the proceeds to buy U.S. goods and services. When this happens, the United States will be *exporting* goods and services to pay off its debts. Recall that the external debt was used to acquire imported goods and services. Hence, *external debt must be repaid with exports of real goods and services.*

DEFICIT AND DEBT LIMITS

Although external and internal debts pose very different problems, most policy discussions overlook these distinctions. In policy debates, the aggregate size of the national debt is usually the only concern. The key policy questions are whether and how to limit or reduce the national debt.

Deficit Ceilings

The only way to stop the growth of the national debt is to eliminate the budget deficits that create debt. The first step in debt reduction, therefore, is a balanced annual budget. A balanced budget will at least stop the debt from growing further. **Deficit ceilings** are explicit limitations on the size of the annual budget deficit. A deficit ceiling of zero compels a balanced budget.

deficit ceiling: An explicit, legislated limitation on the size of the budget deficit.

The Balanced Budget and Emergency Deficit Control Act of 1985—popularly referred to as the Gramm-Rudman-Hollings Act—was the first explicit attempt to force the federal budget into balance. The essence of the Gramm-Rudman-Hollings Act was simple:

- First, it set a lower ceiling on each year's deficit until budget balance was achieved.
- Second, it called for automatic cutbacks in spending if Congress failed to keep the deficit below the ceiling.

The original Gramm-Rudman-Hollings law required Congress to pare the deficit from more than $200 billion in FY 1985 to zero (a balanced budget) by 1991. But Congress wasn't willing to cut spending and increase taxes enough to meet those targets. And the Supreme Court declared that the "automatic" mechanism for spending cuts was unconstitutional.

In 1990 President George H. Bush and the Congress developed a new set of rules for reducing the deficit. They first acknowledged that they lacked total control of the deficit. At best, Congress could close the *structural* deficit by limiting discretionary spending or raising taxes. The Budget Enforcement Act (BEA) of 1990 laid out a plan for doing exactly this. The BEA set separate limits on defense spending, discretionary domestic spending, and international spending. It also required that any new spending initiative be offset with increased taxes or cutbacks in other programs—a process called "pay as you go," or simply "paygo."

The Budget Enforcement Act was successful in reducing the structural deficit somewhat. But the political pain associated with spending cuts and higher taxes was too great for elected officials to bear. Since then, recurrent legislated deficit ceilings have proved to be more political ornaments than binding budget mandates.

Debt Ceilings

debt ceiling: An explicit, legislated limit on the amount of outstanding national debt.

Explicit **debt ceilings** are another mechanism for forcing Congress to adopt specific fiscal policies. A debt ceiling can be used either to stop the accumulation of debt or to force the federal government to start *reducing* the accumulated national debt. In effect, debt ceilings are a backdoor approach to deficit reduction. *Like deficit ceilings, debt ceilings are really just political mechanisms for forging compromises on how best to reduce budget deficits.*

This was evident in July 2019 when the national debt was again approaching its legislative limit ($22 trillion). Democrats wanted to raise taxes on the rich, reversing some of Trump's 2017 tax cuts. President Trump opposed any tax increases and suggested instead cutting federal benefit programs. Unable to strike a deal, the threat of a government shutdown convinced the two sides to *suspend* the debt ceiling for two years (until after the November 2020 elections). That suspension allowed the federal government to spend as much as Congress wanted, including huge outlays to offset the economic impact of the coronavirus.

DECISIONS FOR TOMORROW

Can We Keep Social Security Afloat?

The financing system for Social Security is simple. The payroll (FICA) tax generates revenue for the Social Security Trust Fund. The Fund, in turn, pays monthly benefits to retired workers.

Fund Surpluses. The revenue inflow (taxes) doesn't necessarily match the benefit outflow, however. Indeed, for more than 40 years the annual tax inflow has exceeded the benefit outflow. This annual surplus created an enormous pile of cash in the Social Security Trust Fund. That hoard became the "cash cow" of federal finance. Every year the Fund used its surplus revenues to purchase Treasury bonds. In the process, **Social Security Trust Fund surpluses helped finance federal government deficits.** As of 2019, the Fund was the largest creditor, holding nearly $2.9 trillion of Treasury bonds (see Figure 12.4).

Fund Deficits. The future of this cash cow isn't so rosy. The Baby Boomers who paid so much payroll tax are retiring in droves, and they are living longer in retirement. As a result, the annual flow of tax revenues and benefit outlays is changing direction (see Table 12.5).

As the Trust Fund balance shifts from annual surpluses to annual deficits, Social Security will be able to pay promised benefits only if (1) the U.S. Treasury pays all interest due on bonds held by the Trust Fund and, ultimately, (2) the U.S. Treasury redeems the bonds the Trust Fund will then be holding. This is what scares aging Baby Boomers (and should worry you).

The Baby Boomers wonder where the Treasury is going to get the funds needed to repay the Social Security Trust Fund. There really aren't many options. *To pay back Social Security loans, Congress will have to raise future taxes significantly, make substantial cuts in other (non–Social Security) programs, or sharply increase budget deficits.* None of these options is attractive. Worse yet, the budget squeeze created by the Social Security payback will severely limit the potential for discretionary fiscal policy.

Year	Workers per Beneficiary	Year	Workers per Beneficiary
1950	16.5	2000	3.4
1960	5.1	2015	2.7
1970	3.7	2030	2.0

Source: U.S. Social Security Administration.

TABLE 12.5

Changing Worker/Retiree Ratios

Seventy years ago there were more than 16 taxpaying workers for every retiree. Today there are only 2.7, and the ratio slips further as Baby Boomers retire. This demographic change will convert Social Security surpluses into deficits, causing future budget problems.

SUMMARY

- Budget deficits arise when government spending exceeds tax revenues. Budget surpluses are the reverse. **LO12-1**
- Budget deficits result from both discretionary fiscal policy (structural deficits) and cyclical changes in the economy (cyclical deficits). **LO12-1**
- Fiscal restraint is measured by the reduction in the structural deficit; fiscal stimulus occurs when the structural deficit increases. **LO12-1**
- Automatic stabilizers increase federal spending and reduce tax revenues during recessions, widening the cyclical deficit. When the economy expands, they have the reverse effect, shrinking the cyclical deficit. **LO12-1**
- Deficit financing of government expenditure may crowd out private investment and consumption. The risk of crowding out increases as the economy approaches full employment. **LO12-3**
- Crowding in refers to the increase in private sector output made possible by a decline in government borrowing. **LO12-3**
- Each year's deficit adds to the national debt. The national debt grew sporadically until World War II and then skyrocketed. Tax cuts, recessions, and increased government spending have increased the national debt to more than $23 trillion. **LO12-2**

- Budget surpluses may be used to finance tax cuts or more government spending, or used to reduce accumulated national debt. **LO12-1**
- Every dollar of national debt represents a dollar of assets to the people who hold U.S. Treasury bonds. Most U.S. bonds are held by U.S. government agencies, U.S. households, and U.S. banks, insurance companies, and other institutions, and are thus "internal debt." **LO12-4**
- The real burden of the debt is the opportunity cost of the activities financed by the debt. That cost is borne at the time the deficit-financed activity takes place. The benefits of debt-financed activity may extend into the future. **LO12-4**
- External debt (bonds held by foreigners) permits the public sector to expand without reducing private sector output. External debt also makes it possible to shift some of the real debt burden on to future generations. **LO12-4**
- Deficit and debt ceilings are largely symbolic efforts to force consideration of real trade-offs, to restrain government spending, and to change the mix of output. **LO12-4**
- The retirement of the Baby Boomers (born 1946–1960) is transforming Social Security surpluses into deficits, imposing new constraints on future fiscal policy. **LO12-1**

Key Terms

fiscal policy	automatic stabilizer	asset
deficit spending	cyclical deficit	internal debt
budget deficit	structural deficit	external debt
budget surplus	crowding out	refinancing
fiscal restraint	opportunity cost	debt service
fiscal stimulus	crowding in	optimal mix of output
fiscal year (FY)	national debt	deficit ceiling
discretionary fiscal spending	Treasury bonds	debt ceiling
income transfers	liability	

Questions for Discussion

1. Why do so many people worry about the size of federal deficits and debt? **LO12-4**
2. Who paid for the Revolutionary War? Did the deficit financing initiated by the Continental Congress pass the cost of the war on to future generations? **LO12-4**
3. What did President Hoover see as the "first priority" for fiscal policy in 1932? Was he right? **LO12-1**
4. When are larger deficits desirable? **LO12-1**
5. Can you forecast next year's deficit without knowing how fast GDP will grow? **LO12-1**
6. In what ways do *future* generations benefit from this generation's deficit spending? Cite three examples. **LO12-2, LO12-4**
7. If deficit spending "crowds out" some private investment, could future generations be worse off? If external financing eliminates crowding out, are future generations thereby protected? **LO12-3**
8. A constitutional amendment has been proposed that would require Congress to balance the budget each year. Is it possible to balance the budget each year? Is it desirable? **LO12-1**
9. What did the surge in defense spending from 1940 to 1944 crowd out? **LO12-3**
10. What are the "future problems" referred to in Front Page Economics "Critics Decry Trump's 'Mountain of Debt'"? **LO12-4**
11. Which of the following options do you favor for resolving future Social Security deficits? What are the advantages and disadvantages of each option? (*a*) cutting Social Security benefits, (*b*) raising payroll taxes, (*c*) cutting non–Social Security programs, and (*d*) raising income taxes. **LO12-1**

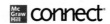
LO12-2 1. From 2016 to 2020, by how much did each of the following change?
(*a*) Tax revenues
(*b*) Government spending
(*c*) Budget deficit
(*Note:* See Table 12.1.)

LO12-2 2. Since 1994, in how many years has the federal budget had a surplus? (See Figure 12.1.)

LO12-2 3. What country had the largest budget deficit (as a percentage of GDP) in 2018 (World View "Budget Imbalances Common")?

LO12-1 4. What would happen to the budget deficit if the
(*a*) GDP growth rate jumped from 2 percent to 4 percent?
(*b*) Inflation rate increased by two percentage points?
(*Note:* See Table 12.2 for clues.)

LO12-1 5. From 2010 through 2020, in how many years was fiscal restraint initiated? (See Table 12.3.)

LO12-1 6. Use Table 12.3 to determine how much fiscal stimulus or restraint occurred between
(*a*) 2007 and 2008.
(*b*) 2017 and 2018.

LO12-1 7. According to Table 12.3, the federal deficit fell from $1,300 billion in 2011 to $680 billion in 2013. How much of this $620 billion deficit reduction was due to
(*a*) The growing economy?
(*b*) Fiscal restraint?

LO12-4 8. Suppose a government has no debt and a balanced budget. Suddenly it decides to spend $5 trillion while raising only $4 trillion worth of taxes.
(*a*) What will be the government's deficit?
(*b*) If the government finances the deficit by issuing bonds, what amount of bonds will it issue?
(*c*) At a 3 percent rate of interest, how much interest will the government pay each year?
(*d*) Add the interest payment to the government's $5 trillion expenditures for the next year, and assume that tax revenues remain at $4 trillion. In the second year, compute the
(*i*) Deficit.
(*ii*) Amount of new debt (bonds) issued.
(*iii*) Total debt at end of year.
(*iv*) Debt service requirement.

LO12-1 9. According to Front Page Economics "Fiscal Policy in the Great Depression,"
(*a*) How much fiscal restraint or stimulus occurred between 1931 and 1933?
(*b*) By how much did this policy reduce aggregate demand if the MPC was 0.75?

LO12-3 10. In Figure 12.5, what is the opportunity cost of increasing government spending from g_1 to g_2 if
(*a*) No external financing is available?
(*b*) Complete external financing is available?

LO12-4 11. (*a*) What percentage of U.S. debt do foreigners hold? (See Figure 12.4.)
(*b*) If the interest rate on U.S. Treasury debt is 3 percent, how much interest do foreigners collect each year from the U.S. Treasury? (Assume a *total* debt of $23 trillion.)

LO12-1 12. Use the data in Table 12.3 to answer questions about *changes* in the structural and cyclical deficits for fiscal years 2015–2020.
(*a*) In how many years do the two deficits change in *different* directions?
(*b*) In how many years was the government pursuing fiscal stimulus?

LO12-2 13. *Decisions for Tomorrow:* Using data in Table 12.5,
   (*a*) Use the figure below to graph workers per beneficiary since 1960.
   (*b*) Based on this change in demographics, what is the change in the relationship between payroll taxes and retirement benefits?

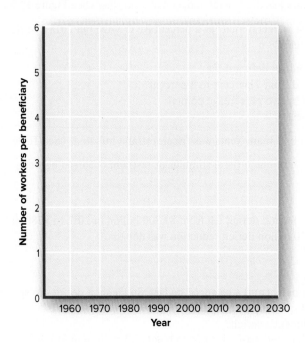

Design Credit: Shutterstock

MONETARY POLICY OPTIONS

Monetary policy tries to alter macro outcomes by managing the amount of money available in the economy. By changing the money supply and/or interest rates, monetary policy seeks to shift the aggregate demand curve in the desired direction. Chapters 13 through 15 illustrate how this policy tool works.

Anatolii Babii/Alamy Stock Photo

Pixtal/agefotostock

Paul J. Richards/AFP/Getty Images

CHAPTER 13

Money and Banks

LEARNING OBJECTIVES

After reading this chapter, you should know

LO13-1 What money is.

LO13-2 What a bank's assets and liabilities are.

LO13-3 How banks create money.

LO13-4 How the money multiplier works.

Sophocles, the ancient Greek playwright, had strong opinions about the role of money. As he saw it, "Of evils upon earth, the worst is money. It is money that sacks cities, and drives men forth from hearth and home; warps and seduces native intelligence, and breeds a habit of dishonesty."

In modern times, people may still be seduced by the lure of money and fashion their lives around its pursuit. Nevertheless, it's hard to imagine an economy functioning without money. Money affects not only morals and ideals but also the way an economy works.

This and the following two chapters examine the role of money in the economy today. We begin with a simple question:

• **What is money?**

As we'll discover, money isn't exactly what you might think it is. There's a lot more money in the economy than there is cash. And there's a lot more income out there than money. So money is something quite different from either cash or income.

Once we've established the characteristics of money, we go on to ask,

• **How is money created?**
• **What role do banks play in the circular flow of income and spending?**

In Chapter 14 we look at how the Federal Reserve System controls the amount of money created. In Chapter 15 we look at the implications for monetary policy, another tool in our macro policy toolbox.

WHAT IS "MONEY"?

To appreciate the significance of money for a modern economy, imagine for a moment that there were no such thing as money. How would you get something for breakfast? If you wanted eggs for breakfast, you'd have to tend your own chickens or go see Farmer Brown. But how would you pay Farmer Brown for his eggs? Without money, you'd have to offer him some goods or services that he could use. In other words, you'd have to engage in primitive **barter**—the direct exchange of one good for another—to get eggs for breakfast. You'd get those eggs only if Farmer Brown happened to want the particular goods or services you had to offer.

The use of money greatly simplifies market transactions. It's a lot easier to exchange money for eggs at the supermarket than to go into the country and barter with farmers every time you crave an omelet. Our ability to use money in market transactions, however, depends on the grocer's willingness to accept money as a *medium of exchange*. The grocer sells eggs for money only because he can use the same money to pay his help and buy the goods he himself desires. He too can exchange money for goods and services.

Without money, the process of acquiring goods and services would be much more difficult and time-consuming. This was evident when the value of the Venezuelan bolivar plummeted. Trading goods for Farmer Brown's eggs seems simple compared to the complicated barter deals Venezuelan consumers had to negotiate when paper money was no longer accepted (see World View "Trading Chickens for Diapers").

barter: The direct exchange of one good for another, without the use of money.

WORLD VIEW

TRADING CHICKENS FOR DIAPERS

Bartering for Survival in Venezuela

Caracas. February 28, 2017—Yeman needs diapers for her 16-month-old baby but can't find them in neighborhood stores. The stores in fact have very few goods to sell and run out of them quickly. So, she uses her smartphone to check the "United Moms" chat group on Facebook. There she discovers that someone has diapers that they are willing to trade for chicken. Luckily, Yeman has some chicken. She contacts the seller and arranges to meet, where she will swap her chicken for three packs of diapers.

Yeman's plight is commonplace in Venezuela these days. The nation's currency—the bolivar—has become worthless. Its market value has plummeted from 6.3 bolivars per U.S. dollar at the beginning of 2016 to 5,000 bolivars per U.S. dollar in early 2017. A bolivar doesn't buy much anymore.

Even if the bolivar were more valuable, there aren't many goods to buy in Venezuela's shrunken economy. People wait for hours in line to buy anything stores have to sell. Then they turn to Facebook, WhatsApp, or Instagram to trade the products they bought for goods they really want. Recent postings on Facebook revealed that a bag of flour could be traded for a bottle of shampoo and that a packet of diapers could be obtained for a kilo of pasta. Staples like sugar, coffee, corn flour, and rice are particularly hard to find.

Source: February 2017 news reports.

CRITICAL ANALYSIS: When the bolivar's value plummeted, its role as a medium of exchange evaporated. Venezuelans had to **barter** for the few goods that were available, a clumsy and time-consuming process.

THE MONEY SUPPLY

Although markets can't function well without money, they can get along without *dollars*.

Many Types of Money

In the early days of colonial America, there were no U.S. dollars; a lot of business was conducted with Spanish and Portuguese gold coins. Later, people used Indian wampum, then tobacco, grain, fish, and furs as media of exchange. Throughout the colonies, gunpowder and bullets were frequently used for small change. These forms of money weren't as convenient as U.S. dollars, but they did the job.

This historical perspective on money highlights its essential characteristics. *Anything that serves all the following purposes can be thought of as money:*

* *Medium of exchange:* is accepted as payment for goods and services (and debts).
* *Store of value:* can be held for future purchases.
* *Standard of value:* serves as a yardstick for measuring the prices of goods and services.

All the items used during the colonial days satisfied these conditions and were thus properly regarded as money.

After the colonies became an independent nation, the U.S. Constitution prohibited the federal government from issuing paper money. Money was instead issued by state-chartered banks. Between 1789 and 1865, more than 30,000 different paper bills were issued by 1,600 banks in 34 states. People often preferred to get paid in gold, silver, or other commodities rather than in one of these uncertain currencies.

The first paper money the federal government issued consisted of $10 million worth of "greenbacks," printed in 1861 to finance the Civil War. Soon thereafter, the National Banking Act of 1863 gave the federal government permanent authority to issue money.

Modern Concepts

The "greenbacks" we carry around today aren't the only form of "money" we use. Most people realize this when they offer to pay for goods with a check rather than cash. People do distinguish between "cash" and "money," and for good reason. The "money" you have in a checking account can be used to buy goods and services or to pay debts, or it can be retained for future use. In these respects, your checking account balance is as much a part of your "money" as are the coins and dollars in your pocket or purse. You can access your balance by writing a check or using an ATM or debit card. Checks are more convenient than cash because they eliminate trips to the bank. Checks are also safer: Lost or stolen cash is gone forever; checkbooks and debit cards are easily replaced at little or no cost. We might use checks and debit cards even more frequently if everyone accepted them.

There's nothing unique about cash, then, insofar as the market is concerned. *Checking accounts can and do perform the same market functions as cash.* Accordingly, we must include checking account balances in our concept of **money.** The essence of money isn't its taste, color, or feel but, rather, its ability to purchase goods and services.

Credit cards are another popular medium of exchange. People use credit cards for about one-third of all purchases greater than $100. This use is not sufficient, however, to qualify credit cards as a form of "money." Credit card balances must be paid by check or cash—that is, with *money.* The same holds true for balances in online electronic credit accounts ("e-cash"). Electronic purchases on the Internet, by Apple Pay, or online services are ultimately paid by withdrawals from a bank account (by check or computer). Online payment mechanisms and credit cards are a payment *service,* not a final form of payment (credit card companies charge fees and interest for this service). The cards themselves are not a store of value, in contrast to cash or bank account balances.

The Diversity of Bank Accounts. To determine how much money is available to purchase goods and services, we need to count not just our coins and currency, but also our bank account balances. This effort is complicated by the variety of bank accounts people have. In addition to simple no-interest checking accounts at full-service banks, people have bank accounts that pay interest, offer automatic transfers, require minimum holding periods, offer overdraft protection, or limit the number of checks that can be written. People also have "bank" accounts in credit unions, brokerage houses, and other nontraditional financial institutions.

Although all bank account balances can be spent, they're not all used the same way. People use regular checking accounts all the time to pay bills or make purchases. But consumers can't write checks on most savings accounts. And few people want to cash in a certificate of deposit just to go to the movies. Hence, *some bank accounts are better substitutes for cash than others.*

M1: Cash and Transactions Accounts

Several different measures of money have been developed to accommodate the diversity of bank accounts and other payment mechanisms. The narrowest definition of the **money supply** is designated **M1,** *which includes*

- *Currency in circulation.*
- *Transactions account balances.*
- *Traveler's checks.*

> **money:** Anything generally accepted as a medium of exchange.

> **money supply (M1):** Currency held by the public, plus balances in transactions accounts.

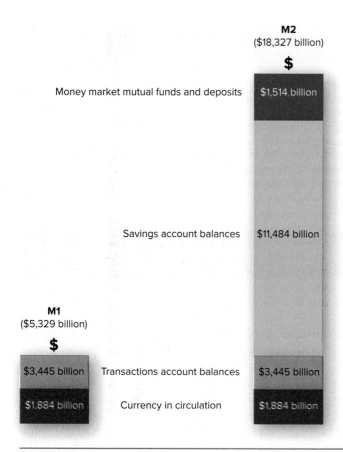

M2
($18,327 billion)

$

Money market mutual funds and deposits — $1,514 billion

Savings account balances — $11,484 billion

M1
($5,329 billion)

$

$3,445 billion | Transactions account balances | $3,445 billion

$1,884 billion | Currency in circulation | $1,884 billion

FIGURE 13.1

Composition of the Money Supply

Cash is only a part of the money supply. People also have easy access to transactions account balances by check or debit card. So M1 includes both cash and transactions accounts.

The much larger M2 includes savings accounts, CDs, and other less-used bank balances.

Source: Federal Reserve, July 2020 data.

As Figure 13.1 indicates, people hold much more money in **transactions accounts**—bank accounts that are readily accessed by check—than they do in cash. Most people refer to these simply as "checking accounts." The term "transactions account" is broader, however, including NOW accounts, ATS accounts, credit union share drafts, and demand deposits at mutual savings banks. *The distinguishing feature of all transactions accounts is that they permit direct payment to a third party (by check or debit card)* without requiring a trip to the bank to make a special withdrawal. Because of this feature, transactions accounts are the readiest substitutes for cash in market transactions. Traveler's checks issued by nonbank firms such as American Express can also be used directly in market transactions, just like good old-fashioned cash. But so few people use traveler's checks these days (around $1 billion) that they are included in the totals for demand deposits.

M2: M1 + Savings Accounts

Transactions accounts aren't the only substitute for cash. People can and do dip into savings accounts on occasion. People sometimes even cash in their certificates of deposit to buy something, despite the interest penalty associated with early withdrawal (see Front Page Economics "CDs Offer Little Interest"). And banks have made it easy to transfer funds from one type of account to another. Savings accounts can be transformed into transactions accounts with a phone call or computer instruction. As a result, *savings account balances are almost as good a substitute for cash as transactions account balances.*

Another popular way of holding money is to buy shares of money market mutual funds. Deposits into money market mutual funds are pooled and used to purchase interest-bearing securities such as Treasury bills. The interest rates paid on these funds are typically higher than those paid by banks. Moreover, the deposits made into the funds can often be

What do you pay with? Which one is *not* "money"?

Mark A. Dierker/McGraw-Hill Education

transactions account: A bank account that permits direct payment to a third party—for example, with a check or debit card.

CDs OFFER LITTLE INTEREST

Stash your money away for five years and you won't reap much of a reward. The highest rate offered by major banks in March 2020 on 5-year certificates of deposit (CDs) was only 1.80 percent. While that's better than the interest paid on checking accounts (0.23 percent), it's not much compensation for five years of thriftiness. Deposit $1,000 in a CD today at that rate and you'll end up with a paltry $1,093.30 in five years. And if you bail out of your CD before the five years are up, you pay an "early withdrawal" penalty that wipes out the little bit of interest earned. Might as well hold onto the cash.

Source: News reports, March 2020.

CRITICAL ANALYSIS: The interest rate paid on a CD account is higher if you promise to keep your money in the bank longer. Because people rarely use CD balances to buy things, CD balances are in **M2**, but not **M1**.

---

withdrawn immediately, just like those in transactions accounts. When interest rates are high, deposits move out of regular transactions accounts into money market mutual funds in order to earn a higher return.

Additional measures of the money supply have been constructed to account for the possibility of using savings account balances, money market mutual funds, and various other deposits to finance everyday spending. The most widely watched money measure is **M2,** which includes all of M1 *plus* balances in savings accounts, money market mutual funds, and some CDs ("time deposits"). As Figure 13.1 shows, M2 is four times larger than M1. Table 13.1 summarizes the content of these measures of money.

money supply (M2): M1 plus balances in most savings accounts and money market funds.

Purchasing Power. Our concern about the specific nature of money stems from our broader interest in **aggregate demand.** What we want to know is how much purchasing power consumers have because this affects their ability to purchase goods and services. What we've observed, however, is that money isn't so easily defined. How much spending power people have depends not only on the number of coins in their pockets but also on their willingness to write checks, make trips to the bank, or convert other assets into cash.

aggregate demand (AD): The total quantity of output (real GDP) demanded at alternative price levels in a given time period, *ceteris paribus.*

In an increasingly complex financial system, the core concept of "money" isn't easy to pin down. Nevertheless, the official measures of the money supply (M1 and M2) are fairly reliable benchmarks for gauging how much purchasing power market participants have.

TABLE 13.1

M1 versus M2

Measures of the money supply are intended to gauge the extent of purchasing power held by consumers. But the extent of purchasing power depends on how accessible assets are and how often people use them.

Measure	Components
M1	Currency in circulation outside bank vaults
	Demand deposits at commercial banks
	NOW and ATS accounts
	Credit union share drafts
	Demand deposits at mutual savings banks
	Traveler's checks (nonbank)
M2	M1 plus
	Savings accounts
	CDs of less than $100,000
	Money market mutual funds

CREATION OF MONEY

Once we've decided what money is, we still have to explain where it comes from. Part of the explanation is simple. Currency must be printed. Some nations use private printers for this purpose, but all U.S. currency is printed by the Bureau of Engraving and Printing in Washington, D.C., or Ft. Worth, Texas. Coins come from the U.S. mints located in Philadelphia and Denver. As we observed in Figure 13.1, however, currency is only a fraction of our total money supply. So we need to look elsewhere for the origins of most money. Specifically, where do all the transactions accounts come from? How do people acquire bank balances? How does the total amount of such deposits—and therefore the money supply of the economy—change?

The coins made here are a tiny fraction of the money supply.

Colin Smith/Alamy Stock Photo

Deposit Creation

Most people assume that all bank balances come from cash deposits. But this isn't the case. Direct deposits of paychecks, for example, are carried out by computer, not by the movement of cash. Moreover, the employer who issues the paycheck probably didn't make any cash deposits. It's more likely that she covered those paychecks with customers' checks that she deposited or with loans granted by the bank itself.

The ability of banks to lend money opens up a whole new set of possibilities for creating money. ***When a bank lends someone money, it simply credits that individual's bank account.*** The money appears in an account just as it would with a cash deposit. And the owner of the account is free to spend that money as with any positive balance. Hence, ***in making a loan, a bank effectively creates money. Why? Because transactions account balances are counted as part of the money supply.***

To understand the origins of our money supply, then, we must recognize two basic principles:

*   Transactions account balances are a large portion of the money supply.
*   Banks can create transactions account balances by making loans.

The following two sections examine this process of **deposit creation** more closely. We will see how banks actually create deposits and what forces might limit the process of deposit creation.

deposit creation: The creation of transactions deposits by bank lending.

Bank Regulation. Banks' deposit creation activities are regulated by the government. The most important agency in this regard is the Federal Reserve System. "The Fed" puts limits on the amount of bank lending, thereby controlling the basic money supply. We'll discuss the structure and functions of the Fed in the next chapter; here we focus on the process of deposit creation itself.

A Monopoly Bank

There are thousands of banks, of various sorts, in the United States. To understand how banks create money, however, we'll make life simple. We'll assume for the moment that there's only one bank in town, University Bank. Imagine also that you've been saving some of your income by putting loose change into a piggy bank. Now, after months of saving, you break the piggy bank and discover that your thrift has yielded $100. You immediately deposit this money in a new checking account at University Bank. How will this deposit affect the money supply?

Your initial deposit will have no immediate effect on the money supply. The coins in your piggy bank were already counted as part of the money supply (M1 and M2) because they represented cash held by the public. ***When you deposit cash or coins in a bank, you're only changing the composition of the money supply, not its size.*** The public (you) now holds $100 less of coins but $100 more of transactions deposits. Accordingly, no money is created by the demise of your piggy bank (the initial deposit). This transaction will be recorded on the books of the bank.

How do banks earn a profit?

Noam Galai/Getty Images

T-Accounts. The "books" the bank uses to record this transaction are called **T-accounts.** On the left side of the T-account, the bank keeps track of all its assets: things of value in its possession. On the right side of the ledger, the bank lists its liabilities: what it is obligated to pay to others. When you deposit your coins in the bank, the bank acquires an asset—your coins. It also acquires a liability—the promise to return your $100 when you so demand (your "demand deposit"). These two entries appear in the bank's T-account as shown here:

University Bank		Money Supply	
Assets	Liabilities	Cash held by the public	−$100
+$100 in coins	+$100 in deposits	Transactions deposits at bank	+$100
		Change in M	0

The total money supply is unaffected by your cash deposit because two components of the money supply change in opposite directions (i.e., $100 less cash, $100 more bank deposits). This initial deposit is just the beginning of the money creation process, however. Banks aren't in business for your convenience; they're in business to earn a profit. To earn a profit on your deposit, University Bank will have to put your money to work. This means using your deposit as the basis for making a loan to someone who's willing to pay the bank interest for use of money. If the function of banks was merely to store money, they wouldn't pay interest on their accounts or offer free checking services. Instead you'd have to pay them for these services. Banks pay you interest and offer free (or inexpensive) checking because *banks can use your money to make loans that earn interest.*

The Initial Loan. Typically a bank doesn't have much difficulty finding someone who wants to borrow money. Someone is always eager to borrow money. The question is, How much money can a bank lend? Can it lend your entire deposit? Or must University Bank keep some of your coins in reserve in case you want to withdraw them? The answer will surprise you.

Suppose University Bank decided to lend the entire $100 to Campus Radio. Campus Radio wants to buy a new antenna but doesn't have any money in its own checking account. To acquire the antenna, Campus Radio must take out a loan.

When University Bank agrees to lend Campus Radio $100, it does so by crediting the account of Campus Radio. Instead of giving Campus Radio $100 cash, University Bank simply adds an electronic $100 to Campus Radio's checking account balance. That is, the loan is made with a simple bookkeeping entry as follows:

University Bank		Money Supply	
Assets	Liabilities	Cash held by the public	No change
$100 in coins	$100 your account balance	Transactions deposits at bank	+$100
$100 in loans	$100 Campus Radio account	Change in M	+$100

Notice that the bank's assets have increased. It now has your $100 in coins *plus* an IOU worth $100 from Campus Radio ("loans"). On the right side of the T-account, deposit liabilities now include $100 in your account and $100 in the Campus Radio account.

Increased M. This simple bookkeeping procedure is the key to creating money. When University Bank lends $100 to the Campus Radio account, it "creates" money. Keep in mind that transactions deposits are counted as part of the money supply. Once the $100 loan is credited to its account, Campus Radio can use this new money to purchase its desired antenna, without worrying that its check will bounce.

Or can it? Once University Bank grants a loan to Campus Radio, both you and Campus Radio have $100 in your checking accounts to spend. But the bank is holding only $100 of **reserves** (your coins). In other words, the increased account balance obtained by Campus Radio doesn't limit *your* ability to write checks. There's been a net *increase* in the value of transactions deposits but no increase in bank reserves.

Secondary Deposits. What happens if Campus Radio actually spends the $100 on a new antenna? Won't this "use up all" the reserves held by the bank, endangering your check-writing privileges? The answer is no.

Consider what happens when Atlas Antenna receives the check from Campus Radio. What will Atlas do with the check? Atlas could go to University Bank and exchange the check for $100 of cash (your coins). But Atlas may prefer to deposit the check in its own checking account at University Bank (still the only bank in town). This way, Atlas not only avoids the necessity of going to the bank (it can deposit the check by mail or smartphone) but also keeps its money in a safe place. Should Atlas later want to spend the money, it can simply write a check. In the meantime, the bank continues to hold its entire reserves (your coins), and both you and Atlas have $100 to spend.

Fractional Reserves. Notice what's happened here. The money supply has increased by $100 as a result of deposit creation (the loan to Campus Radio). Moreover, the bank has been able to support $200 of transaction deposits (your account and either the Campus Radio or Atlas account) with only $100 of reserves (your coins). In other words, **bank reserves are only a fraction of total deposits.** In this case, University Bank's reserves (your $100 in coins) are only 50 percent of total deposits. Thus, the bank's **reserve ratio** is 50 percent—that is,

$$\frac{\text{Reserve}}{\text{ratio}} = \frac{\text{Bank reserves}}{\text{Total deposits}}$$

reserve ratio: The ratio of a bank's reserves to its total transactions deposits.

The ability of University Bank to hold reserves that are only a fraction of total deposits results from two facts: (1) people use checks and debit cards for most transactions and (2) there's no other bank. Accordingly, reserves are rarely withdrawn from this monopoly bank. In fact, if people *never* withdrew their deposits and *all* transactions accounts were held at University Bank, University Bank wouldn't need *any* reserves. In this most unusual case, University Bank could make as many loans as it wanted. Every loan it made would increase the supply of money.

In reality, many banks are available, and people both withdraw cash from their accounts and write checks to people who have accounts in other banks. In addition, bank lending practices are regulated by the Federal Reserve System. **The Federal Reserve System requires banks to maintain some minimum reserve ratio.** This reserve requirement directly limits banks' ability to grant new loans.

Required Reserves. The potential impact of Federal Reserve requirements on bank lending can be readily seen. Suppose that the Federal Reserve imposed a minimum reserve requirement of 75 percent on University Bank. Such a requirement would prohibit University Bank from lending $100 to Campus Radio. That loan would result in $200 of deposits, supported by only $100 of reserves. The actual ratio of reserves to deposits would be 50 percent ($100 of reserves ÷ $200 of deposits), which would violate the Fed's assumed 75 percent reserve requirement. A 75 percent reserve requirement means that University Bank must hold **required reserves** equal to 75 percent of *total* deposits, including those created through loans.

The bank's dilemma is evident in the following equation:

required reserves: The minimum amount of reserves a bank is required to hold; equal to required reserve ratio times transactions deposits.

$$\frac{\text{Required}}{\text{reserves}} = \frac{\text{Required reserve}}{\text{ratio}} \times \frac{\text{Total}}{\text{deposits}}$$

To support $200 of total deposits, University Bank would need to satisfy this equation:

$$\frac{\text{Required}}{\text{reserves}} = 0.75 \times \$200 = \$150$$

But the bank has only $100 of reserves (your coins) and so would violate the reserve requirement if it increased total deposits to $200 by lending $100 to Campus Radio.

University Bank can still issue a loan to Campus Radio, but the loan must be less than $100 to keep the bank within the limits of the required reserve formula. Thus, *a minimum reserve requirement directly limits deposit creation (lending) possibilities.* It's still true, however, as we'll now illustrate, that the banking system, taken as a whole, can create multiple loans (money) from a single deposit.

A Multibank World

Table 13.2 illustrates the process of deposit creation in a multibank world with a required reserve ratio. In this case, we assume that legally required reserves must equal at least 20 percent of transactions deposits. Now when you deposit $100 in your checking account, University Bank must hold at least $20 as required reserves.[1]

Excess Reserves. The remaining $80 the bank obtains from your deposit is regarded as **excess reserves.** These reserves are "excess" because your bank is *required* to hold in reserve only $20 (equal to 20 percent of your initial $100 deposit):

$$\frac{\text{Excess}}{\text{reserves}} = \frac{\text{Total}}{\text{reserves}} - \frac{\text{Required}}{\text{reserves}}$$

The $80 of excess reserves aren't required and may be used to support additional loans. Hence, the bank can now lend $80. In view of the fact that banks earn profits (interest) by making loans, we assume that University Bank will try to use these excess reserves as soon as possible.

To keep track of the changes in reserves, deposit balances, and loans that occur in a multibank world we'll have to do some more bookkeeping. For this purpose we'll again use the same balance sheet, or "T-account," that banks themselves use. Table 13.2 takes us down the accounting path.

Step 1: Cash Deposit. Notice how the balance of University Bank looks immediately after it receives your initial deposit (step 1, Table 13.2). Your deposit of coins is entered on *both* sides of University's balance sheet. On the left side of the bank's T-account, your deposit is regarded as an asset because your piggy bank's coins have an immediate market value. Those coins now appear as *reserves* on the left side. The reserves these coins represent are further divided into required reserves ($20, or 20 percent of your deposit) and excess reserves ($80).

On the right side of the balance sheet, the bank reminds itself that it has an obligation (liability) to return your deposit when you demand. Thus, the bank's accounts balance, with assets and liabilities being equal. In fact, *a bank's books must always balance because all the bank's assets must belong to someone (its depositors or the bank's owners).*

Step 2: Bank Loan. University Bank wants to do more than balance its books, however; it wants to earn profits. To do so, it will have to make loans—that is, put its excess reserves to work. Suppose that it lends $80 to Campus Radio.[2] As step 2 in Table 13.2 illustrates, this loan alters both sides of University Bank's balance sheet. On the right side, the bank creates a new transactions deposit for (credits the account of) Campus Radio; this item represents an additional liability (promise to pay). On the left side of the balance sheet, two things happen. First, the bank notes that Campus Radio owes it $80 ("loans"). Second, the bank recognizes that it's now required to hold $36 in *required* reserves, in accordance with its higher level of transactions deposits ($180). (Recall we're assuming that required reserves are 20 percent of total transactions deposits.) Because its total reserves are still $100, $64 is left as *excess* reserves. Note again that *excess reserves are reserves a bank isn't required to hold.*

Changes in the Money Supply. Before examining further changes in the balance sheet of University Bank, consider again what's happened to the economy's money supply during these first two steps. In the first step, you deposited $100 of cash in your checking account. This initial transaction didn't change the value of the money supply. Only the composition

---

[1]The reserves themselves may be held in the form of cash in the bank's vault but are usually held as credits with one of the regional Federal Reserve banks.
[2]Because of the Fed's assumed minimum reserve requirement (20 percent), University Bank can now lend only $80 rather than $100, as before.

excess reserves: Bank reserves in excess of required reserves.

Step 1: You deposit cash at University Bank. The deposit creates $100 of reserves, $20 of which are designated as required reserves. This leaves $80 of excess reserves.

University Bank				Banking System	
Assets		Liabilities		Change in Transactions Deposits	Change in M
Required reserves	$ 20	Your deposit	$100	+$100	$0
Excess reserves	80				
Total	$100		100		

Step 2: The bank uses its excess reserves ($80) to make a loan to Campus Radio. Total deposits now equal $180. The money supply has increased.

University Bank				Banking System	
Assets		Liabilities		Δ Deposits	Δ M
Required reserves	$ 36	Your account	$100	+$80	+$80
Excess reserves	64	Campus Radio account	80		
Loans	80				
Total	$180	Total	$180		

Step 3: Campus Radio buys an antenna. This depletes Campus Radio's account but increases Atlas's balance. Eternal Savings gets $80 of reserves when the Campus Radio check clears.

University Bank				Eternal Savings				Banking System	
Assets		Liabilities		Assets		Liabilities		Δ Deposits	Δ M
Required reserves	$ 20	Your account	$100	Required reserves	$16	Atlas Antenna account	$80	$0	$0
Excess reserves	0	Campus Radio account	0	Excess reserves	64				
Loan	80								
Total	$100	Total	$100	Total	$80	Total	$80		

Step 4: Eternal Savings lends money to Herman's Hardware. Deposits, loans, and M all increase by $64.

University Bank				Eternal Savings				Banking System	
Assets		Liabilities		Assets		Liabilities		Change in Transaction Deposits	Change in M
Required reserves	$ 20	Your account	$100	Required reserves	$28.80	Atlas Antenna account	$ 80	+$64	+$64
Excess reserves	0	Campus Radio account	0	Excess reserves	51.20	Herman's Hardware account	64		
Loan	80			Loans	64				
Total	$100	Total	$100		$ 144		$144		
⋮		⋮		⋮		⋮		⋮	⋮

***n*th step:** Some bank lends $1.00 · · · · +1 +1

Cumulative Change in Banking System

Bank Reserves	Transactions Deposits	Money Supply
+$100	+$500	+$400

TABLE 13.2

Deposit Creation

Excess reserves (step 1) are the basis of bank loans. When a bank uses its excess reserves to make a loan, it creates a deposit (step 2). When the loan is spent, a deposit will be made somewhere else (step 3). This new deposit creates additional excess reserves (step 3) that can be used for further loans (step 4, etc.). The process of deposit creation continues until the money supply has increased by a multiple of the initial deposit.

of the money supply (M1) was affected ($100 less cash held by the public, $100 more in transactions accounts).

Not until step 2—when the bank makes a loan—does all the excitement begin. In making a loan, the bank automatically increases the total money supply by $80. Why? Because someone (Campus Radio) now has more money (a transactions deposit) than it did before, *and no one else has any less.* And Campus Radio can use its money to buy goods and services, just like anybody else.

This second step is the heart of money creation. Money effectively appears out of thin air when a bank makes a loan. To understand how this works, you have to keep reminding yourself that money is more than the coins and currency we carry around. Transactions deposits are money too. Hence, *the creation of transactions deposits via new loans is the same thing as creating money.*

Step 3: Spending the Loan. Suppose again that Campus Radio actually uses its $80 loan to buy an antenna. The rest of Table 13.2 illustrates how this additional transaction leads to further changes in balance sheets and the money supply.

In step 3, we see that when Campus Radio buys the $80 antenna, the balance in its checking account at University Bank drops to zero because it has spent all its money. As University Bank's liabilities fall (from $180 to $100), so does the level of its required reserves (from $36 to $20). (Note that required reserves are still 20 percent of its remaining transactions deposits.) But University Bank's excess reserves have disappeared completely! This disappearance reflects the fact that Atlas Antenna keeps *its* transactions account at another bank (Eternal Savings). When Atlas deposits the check it received from Campus Radio, Eternal Savings does two things. First, it credits Atlas's account by $80. Second, it goes to University Bank to get the reserves that support the deposit.[3] The reserves later appear on the balance sheet of Eternal Savings as both required ($16) and excess ($64) reserves.

Observe that the money supply hasn't changed during step 3. The increase in the value of Atlas Antenna's transactions account balance exactly offsets the drop in the value of Campus Radio's transactions account. Ownership of the money supply is the only thing that has changed.

Step 4: More Deposit Creation. In step 4, Eternal Savings takes advantage of its newly acquired excess reserves by making a loan to Herman's Hardware. As before, the loan itself has two primary effects. First, it creates a transactions deposit of $64 for Herman's Hardware and thereby increases the money supply by the same amount. Second, it increases the required level of reserves at Eternal Savings. (To how much? Why?)

THE MONEY MULTIPLIER

By now it's perhaps obvious that the process of deposit creation won't come to an end quickly. On the contrary, it can continue indefinitely, just like the income multiplier process in Chapter 10. Indeed, people often refer to deposit creation as the money multiplier process, with the **money multiplier** expressed as the reciprocal of the required reserve ratio. That is,

$$\text{Money multiplier} = \frac{1}{\text{Required reserve ratio}}$$

money multiplier: The number of deposit (loan) dollars that the banking system can create from $1 of excess reserves; equal to 1 ÷ required reserve ratio.

Figure 13.2 illustrates the money multiplier process. When a new deposit enters the banking system, it creates both excess and required reserves. The required reserves represent leakage from the flow of money because they can't be used to create new loans. Excess reserves, on the other hand, can be used for new loans. Once those loans are made, they typically become transactions deposits elsewhere in the banking system. Then some additional leakage into required reserves occurs, and further loans are made. The process continues until all excess reserves have leaked into required reserves. Once excess reserves have

[3]In actuality, banks rarely "go" anywhere; such interbank reserve movements are handled by bank clearinghouses and regional Federal Reserve banks. The effect is the same, however. The nature and use of bank reserves are discussed more fully in Chapter 14.

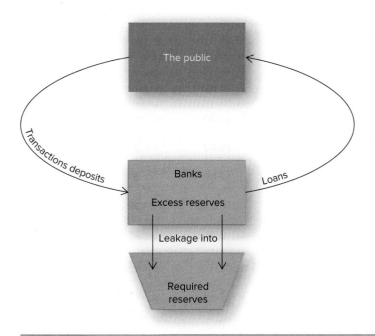

FIGURE 13.2
The Money Multiplier Process

Part of every new bank deposit leaks into required reserves. The rest—excess reserves—can be used to make loans. These loans, in turn, become deposits elsewhere. The process of money creation continues until all available reserves become required reserves.

completely disappeared, the total value of new loans will equal initial excess reserves multiplied by the money multiplier.

The potential of the money multiplier to create loans is summarized by the equation

$$\begin{matrix} \textbf{Excess} \\ \textbf{reserves} \\ \textbf{of banking} \\ \textbf{system} \end{matrix} \times \begin{matrix} \textbf{Money} \\ \textbf{multiplier} \end{matrix} = \begin{matrix} \textbf{Potential} \\ \textbf{deposit creation} \end{matrix}$$

Notice how the money multiplier worked in our previous example. The value of the money multiplier was equal to 5 because we assumed that the required reserve ratio was 0.20. Moreover, the initial level of excess reserves was $80 as a consequence of your original deposit (step 1). According to the money multiplier, then, the deposit creation potential of the banking system was

$$\begin{matrix} \text{Excess reserves} \\ (\$80) \end{matrix} \times \begin{matrix} \text{Money multiplier} \\ (5) \end{matrix} = \begin{matrix} \text{Potential} \\ \text{deposit} \\ \text{creation} (\$400) \end{matrix}$$

When all the banks fully utilized their excess reserves at each step of the money multiplier process, the ultimate increase in the money supply was in fact $400 (see the last row in Table 13.2).

Excess Reserves as Lending Power

While you're struggling through Table 13.2, notice the critical role that excess reserves play in the process of deposit creation. A bank can make additional loans only if it has excess reserves. Without excess reserves, all of a bank's reserves are required, and no further liabilities (transactions deposits) can be created with new loans. On the other hand, a bank with excess reserves can make additional loans. In fact,

•   *Each bank may lend an amount equal to its excess reserves and no more.*

As such loans enter the circular flow and become deposits elsewhere, they create new excess reserves and further lending capacity. As a consequence,

•   *The entire banking system can increase the volume of loans by the amount of excess reserves multiplied by the money multiplier.*

Required reserves = 0.20	Change in Transactions Deposits	Change in Total Reserves	Change in Required Reserves	Change in Excess Reserves	Change in Lending Capacity
If $100 in cash is deposited in Bank A, Bank A acquires	$100.00	$100.00	$ 20.00	$80.00	$ 80.00
If loan made and deposited elsewhere, Bank B acquires	80.00	80.00	16.00	64.00	64.00
If loan made and deposited elsewhere, Bank C acquires	64.00	64.00	12.80	51.20	51.20
If loan made and deposited elsewhere, Bank D acquires	51.20	51.20	10.24	40.96	40.96
If loan made and deposited elsewhere, Bank E acquires	40.96	40.96	8.19	32.77	32.77
If loan made and deposited elsewhere, Bank F acquires	32.77	32.77	6.55	26.22	26.22
If loan made and deposited elsewhere, Bank G acquires	26.22	26.22	5.24	20.98	20.98
If loan made and deposited elsewhere, Bank Z acquires	0.38	0.38	0.08	0.30	0.30
Cumulative, through Bank Z	$498.80	$100.00	$ 99.76	$ 0.24	$398.80
And if the process continues indefinitely	$500.00	$100.00	$100.00	$ 0.00	$400.00

Note: A $100 cash deposit creates $400 of new lending capacity when the required reserve ratio is 0.20. Initial excess reserves are $80 (= $100 deposit − $20 required reserves). The money multiplier is 5 (= 1 ÷ 0.20). New lending potential equals $400 (= $80 excess reserves × 5).

TABLE 13.3

The Money Multiplier at Work

The process of deposit creation continues as money passes through different banks in the form of multiple deposits and loans. At each step, excess reserves and new loans are created. The lending capacity of this system equals the money multiplier times excess reserves. In this case, initial excess reserves of $80 create the possibility of $400 of new loans when the reserve ratio is 0.20 (20 percent).

By keeping track of excess reserves, then, we can gauge the lending capacity of any bank or, with the aid of the money multiplier, the entire banking system.

Table 13.3 summarizes the entire money multiplier process. In this case, we assume that all banks are initially "loaned up"—that is, without any excess reserves. The money multiplier process begins when someone deposits $100 in cash into a transactions account at Bank A. If the required reserve ratio is 20 percent, this initial deposit creates $80 of excess reserves at Bank A while adding $100 to total transactions deposits.

If Bank A uses its newly acquired excess reserves to make a loan that ultimately ends up in Bank B, two things happen: Bank B acquires $64 in excess reserves (0.80 × $80) and total transactions deposits increase by $80 as well.

The money multiplier process continues with a series of loans and deposits. When the 26th loan is made (by Bank Z), total loans grow by only $0.30 and transactions deposits by an equal amount. Should the process continue further, the *cumulative* change in loans will ultimately equal $400—that is, the money multiplier times initial excess reserves. The money supply will increase by the same amount.

BANKS AND THE CIRCULAR FLOW

The bookkeeping details of bank deposits and loans are rarely exciting and often confusing. But they demonstrate convincingly that banks can create money. In that capacity, **banks perform two essential functions for the macro economy:**

- *Banks transfer money from savers to spenders by lending funds (reserves) held on deposit.*
- *The banking system creates additional money by making loans in excess of total reserves.*

In performing these two functions, banks change the size of the money supply—that is, the amount of purchasing power available for buying goods and services. Changes in the money supply may in turn alter *spending* behavior and thereby shift the aggregate demand curve.

Figure 13.3 is a simplified perspective on the role of banks in the circular flow. As before, income flows from product markets through business firms to factor markets and returns to consumers in the form of disposable income. Consumers spend most of their income but also save (don't spend) some of it.

Financing Injections

The leakage represented by consumer saving is a potential source of stabilization problems, particularly unemployment. If additional spending by business firms, foreigners, or governments doesn't compensate for consumer saving at full employment, a recessionary GDP gap will emerge, creating unemployment (see Chapters 9 and 10). Our interest here is in the role the banking system can play in encouraging such additional spending.

Suppose for the moment that *all* consumer saving was deposited in piggy banks rather than depository institutions (banks) and that no one used checks. Under these circumstances, banks couldn't transfer money from savers to spenders by holding deposits and making loans.

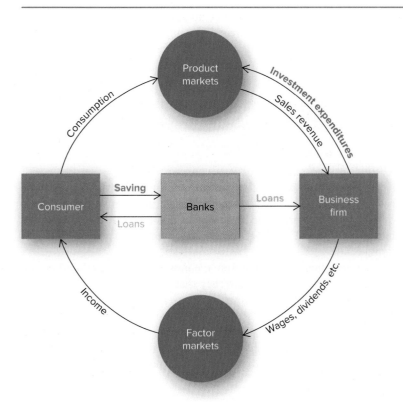

FIGURE 13.3

Banks in the Circular Flow

Banks help transfer income from savers to spenders by using their deposits to make loans to business firms and consumers who want to spend more money than they have. By lending money, banks help maintain any desired rate of aggregate demand.

In reality, a substantial portion of consumer saving *is* deposited in banks. These and other bank deposits can be used as the basis of loans, thereby returning purchasing power to the circular flow. In fact, **the primary economic function of banks isn't to store money but to transfer purchasing power from savers to spenders.** They do so by lending money to businesses for new plants and equipment, to consumers for new homes or cars, and to government entities to build sports stadiums and toll roads. Moreover, because the banking system can make *multiple* loans from available reserves, banks don't have to receive all consumer saving to carry out their function. On the contrary, *the banking system can create any desired level of money supply if allowed to expand or reduce loan activity at will.*

Constraints on Deposit Creation

There are four major constraints on the deposit creation of the banking system.

Deposits. The first constraint is the willingness of consumers and businesses to continue using and accepting checks or debit cards rather than cash in the marketplace. If people preferred to hold cash rather than bank balances, banks wouldn't be able to acquire or maintain the reserves that are the foundation of bank lending activity.

Willingness to Lend. Once banks are holding sufficient reserves, they must be willing to make new loans. In 2009–2010, this condition was violated. Banks had accumulated huge losses on previous mortgage loans. In addition, the economy was sliding into a deepening recession. So banks were reluctant to make new loans that might not get repaid. This put a serious crimp on aggregate demand.

Willingness to Borrow. The third constraint on deposit creation is the willingness of consumers, businesses, and governments to borrow the money that banks make available. The chain of events we've observed in deposit creation depends on the willingness of Campus Radio to borrow $80, of Herman's Hardware to borrow $64, and so on. If no one wanted to borrow any money, deposit creation would never begin. By the same reasoning, if all excess reserves aren't borrowed (lent), deposit creation won't live up to its theoretical potential.

Regulation. The fourth major constraint on deposit creation is the Federal Reserve System. As we've observed, the Fed may limit deposit creation by imposing reserve requirements. These and other tools of monetary policy are discussed in Chapter 14.

DECISIONS FOR TOMORROW

Is the World Ready for Libra?

On January 18, 2019, Facebook made an audacious announcement. It was working with a consortium of finance and tech companies to create a new global cryptocurrency, the Libra. The goals of the new currency included more efficient payment processing (without intermediaries like banks and credit-card companies), universal access (especially for the 1.7 billion households without financial access), lower costs, and greater privacy of market transactions.

Facebook's Libra faced serious opposition from the outset. Banks and other financial institutions didn't like the idea of a digital currency that would eliminate their role as intermediaries between buyers and sellers. Governments were concerned that an unregulated currency would restrict their ability to control the money supply (and, by implication, aggregate demand). And people were worried that Facebook could use or sell information on individual purchase behavior, violating their privacy. And others worried that a cryptocurrency could be hacked, similar to the experience with bitcoin.

Bitcoin Difference. Facebook was quick to point out that the proposed Libra was very different from bitcoin. The most important difference was their intrinsic value. Bitcoins never had any intrinsic value. Instead, there was only the assurance that the quantity of bitcoins would be fixed (limited) indefinitely. Their value would then depend on the *demand* for bitcoins. As it turned out, demand fluctuated enormously, creating wild swings in the value of a bitcoin. Therefore, bitcoins were not a stable store of value—one of the three essential characteristics required for "money."

Libra is very different. Its value is set by a basket of global currencies and U.S. Treasury securities. Further, Libra can be converted back into those currencies at any time. Therefore, Libra has both intrinsic value and easy convertibility. The global underpinnings of Libra also made it more likely to find acceptance in markets around the world—a widely used medium of exchange.

Faith in Money. As we've seen in this chapter, "money" isn't a simple concept. Most of our money is nothing more than an electronic blip in some financial institution. Ultimately, people use and accept money because they have faith in the governments that control it. That faith is not always justified, as experiences in the Weimar Republic, Venezuela, Zimbabwe, and other nations have shown. But the notion of bestowing responsibility for the money supply on a private organization like the Libra Association is a huge leap of faith. Libra is sure to confront a host of privacy, regulatory, and competitive obstacles as it tries to win market acceptance in the economy tomorrow.

SUMMARY

- In a market economy, money serves a critical function in *facilitating exchanges* and specialization, thus permitting increased output. **LO13-1**
- *Money* refers to any medium that's generally accepted in exchange, serves as a store of value, and acts as a standard of value. **LO13-1**
- Because people use bank account balances to buy goods and services (with checks or debit cards), such balances are also regarded as money. The money supply M1 includes cash plus transactions account (checkable) deposits. M2 adds savings account balances and other deposits to form a broader measure of the money supply. **LO13-1**
- The assets a bank holds must always equal its liabilities. **LO13-2**
- Banks have the power to create money by making loans. In making loans, banks create new transactions deposits, which become part of the money supply. **LO13-3**

- A bank's ability to make loans—create money—depends on its reserves. Only if a bank has excess reserves—reserves greater than those required by federal regulation—can it make new loans. **LO13-3**
- As loans are spent, they create deposits elsewhere, making it possible for other banks to make additional loans. The money multiplier (1 ÷ required reserve ratio) indicates the total value of deposits that can be created by the banking system from excess reserves. **LO13-4**
- The role of banks in creating money includes the transfer of money from savers to spenders as well as deposit creation in excess of deposit balances. Taken together, these two functions give banks direct control over the amount of purchasing power available in the marketplace. **LO13-3**
- The deposit creation potential of the banking system is limited by government regulation. It is also limited by the willingness of market participants to hold deposits or borrow money. **LO13-4**

Key Terms

barter	aggregate demand (AD)	required reserves
money	deposit creation	excess reserves
money supply (M1)	T-accounts	money multiplier
transactions account	bank reserves	
money supply (M2)	reserve ratio	

Questions for Discussion

1. Why are checking account balances, but not credit cards, regarded as "money"?   **LO13-1**
2. In what respects are modern forms of money superior to the colonial use of wampum as money?   **LO13-1**
3. How are an economy's production possibilities affected when barter replaces cash exchanges? (See World View "Trading Chickens for Diapers.")   **LO13-1**
4. Are digital wallets like ApplePay and GoogleWallet new forms of money?   **LO13-1**
5. What percentage of your monthly bills do you pay with (*a*) cash, (*b*) check, (*c*) credit card, and (*d*) automatic transfers? How do you pay off the credit card balance? How does your use of cash compare with the composition of the money supply (Figure 13.1)?   **LO13-1**
6. Why must a bank's assets always equal its liabilities?   **LO13-2**
7. Does the fact that your bank keeps only a fraction of your account balance in reserve make you uncomfortable? Why don't people rush to the bank and retrieve their money? What would happen if they did?   **LO13-3**
8. If people never withdrew cash from banks, how much money could the banking system potentially create? Could this really happen? What might limit deposit creation in this case?   **LO13-4**
9. If all banks heeded Shakespeare's admonition "Neither a borrower nor a lender be," what would happen to the circular flow?   **LO13-3**
10. Would you accept Libra in payment for something you were selling? Why is Facebook pushing the idea of a new digital currency?   **LO13-1**

PROBLEMS FOR CHAPTER 13

LO13-1 1. According to World View "Trading Chickens for Diapers," how many packs of diapers could a Venezuelan get in barter for one chicken?

LO13-1 2. What percent does cash account for in (refer to Figure 13.1)
  (*a*) M1?
  (*b*) M2?

LO13-2 3. A bank has $1,000 in deposits and the required reserve ratio is 10 percent. Based on this information
  (*a*) Enter the appropriate values in the T-account.

Assets	Liabilities

  (*b*) Calculate the potential total deposit creation of the bank.

LO13-1 4. If you withdraw $500 from your checking account and the required reserve ratio is 5 percent, initially how much do(es) the bank's
  (*a*) Total deposits change?
  (*b*) Required reserves change?
  (*c*) Excess reserves change?

  If you deposit a $200 check in your checking account and the required reserve ratio is 10 percent, initially how much do(es) the bank's
  (*d*) Total deposits change?
  (*e*) Required reserves change?
  (*f*) Excess reserves change?

LO13-2 5. If a bank has total deposits of $9,000,000 and reserves of $3,000,000
  (*a*) What is the current percentage of deposits held in reserve?
  (*b*) What percentage of deposits are currently loaned out?

LO13-2 6. Suppose a bank's balance sheet looks as follows:

Assets		Liabilities	
Reserves	$ 800	Deposits	$6,000
Loans	5,200		

  and banks are required to hold reserves equal to 10 percent of deposits.
  (*a*) How much excess reserves does the bank hold?
  (*b*) How much more can this bank lend?

LO13-3 7. Suppose a bank's balance sheet looks like this:

Assets		Liabilities	
Reserves		Deposits	$800
Required	$ 40		
Excess	140		
Loans	620		
Total	$800	Total	$800

  (*a*) What is the required reserve ratio?
  (*b*) How much money can this bank still lend?

LO13-4 8. What is the money multiplier when the required reserve ratio is
  (*a*) 2 percent?
  (*b*) 10 percent?

PROBLEMS FOR CHAPTER 13 (cont'd)

LO13-3 9. On January 10, 2017, a man in Lebanon, Virginia, frustrated with the DMV bureaucracy, paid his DMV bill with 300,000 pennies that he carted into the DMV office in five wheelbarrows. The DMV had to count all these pennies and deposit them into the DMV bank account. After the DMV deposit and assuming a 5 percent reserve requirement, calculate the initial change in
  (a) Money supply.
  (b) Deposits.
  (c) Total reserves.
  (d) Excess reserves.
  (e) Calculate the cumulative change for the banking system in lending capacity.

LO13-3 10. (a) When the reserve requirement changes, which of the following will change for an individual bank?
  Total deposits
  Total reserves
  Required reserves
  Excess reserves
  Unused lending capacity
  (b) When the reserve requirement changes, which of the following will change in the total banking system?
  Total deposits
  Total reserves
  Required reserves
  Excess reserves
  Unused lending capacity

LO13-4 11. Suppose a lottery winner deposits $8 million in cash into her transactions account at the Bank of America (B of A). Assume a reserve requirement of 20 percent and no excess reserves in the banking system prior to this deposit.
  (a) Use step 1 in the following T-accounts to show how her deposit initially affects the balance sheet at B of A.
  (b) Has the money supply been changed by her deposit?
  (c) Use step 2 in the following T-accounts to show the changes at B of A after the bank fully uses its new lending capacity.
  (d) Has the money supply been changed by step 2?
  (e) After the entire banking system uses the lending capacity of the initial ($8 million) deposit, by how much will the following have changed?
  Total reserves
  Total deposits
  Total loans
  The money supply

Step 1: Winnings Deposited
Bank of America

Assets (in Millions)		Liabilities (in Millions)	
Reserves:		Deposits	_____
Required	_____		
Excess	_____		
Loans	_____		
Total assets	_____	Total liabilities	_____

PROBLEMS FOR CHAPTER 13 (cont'd)

Step 2: Loans Made
Bank of America

Assets (in Millions)		Liabilities (in Millions)	
Reserves:		Deposits	_____
Required	_____		
Excess	_____		
Loans	_____		
Total assets	_____	Total liabilities	_____

LO13-1 12. *Decisions for Tomorrow:* How much does M1 and M2 change in the following situations?
    (*a*) $100 in coins is deposited into a checking account.
    (*b*) $500 is transferred from a savings to a checking account.
    (*c*) $300 is transferred into the cryptocurrency Libra.

The Federal Reserve building in Washington, D.C.
Pixtal/agefotostock

After reading this chapter, you should know

LO14-1 How the Federal Reserve is organized.

LO14-2 The Fed's major policy tools.

LO14-3 How open market operations work.

CHAPTER 14

The Federal Reserve System

We've seen how money is created with bank loans. We've also gotten a few clues about how the government limits money creation and thus aggregate demand. This chapter examines the mechanics of government control more closely:

- **Which government agency is responsible for controlling the money supply?**
- **What policy tools are used to control the amount of money in the economy?**
- **How are banks and bond markets affected by the government's policies?**

Most people have a ready answer for the first question. The popular view is that the government controls the amount of money in the economy by printing more or fewer dollar bills. But we've already observed that the concept of "money" isn't so simple. In Chapter 13 we demonstrated that banks, not printing presses, create most of our money. In making loans, banks create transactions deposits that are counted as part of the money supply.

Because bank lending activities are the primary source of money, the *government must regulate bank lending if it wants to control the amount of money in the economy.* That's exactly what the Federal Reserve System does. The Federal Reserve System—the "Fed"—not only limits the volume of loans that the banking system can make from available reserves; it can also alter the amount of reserves banks hold.

The Federal Reserve System's control over the supply of money is the key mechanism of **monetary policy.** The potential of this policy lever to alter macro outcomes (unemployment, inflation, etc.) is examined in Chapter 15. In this chapter, we focus on the *tools* of monetary policy.

STRUCTURE OF THE FED

In the absence of any government regulation, the supply of money would be determined by individual banks. Moreover, individual depositors would bear all the risks of bank failures. In fact, this is the way the banking system operated until 1914. The money supply was subject to abrupt changes, and consumers sometimes lost their savings in recurrent bank failures.

A series of bank failures resulted in a severe financial panic in 1907. Millions of depositors lost their savings, and the economy was thrown into a tailspin. In the wake of this panic, a National Monetary

Commission was established to examine ways of restructuring the banking system. The mandate of the commission was to find ways to prevent recurrent financial crises. After five years of study, the commission recommended the creation of a Federal Reserve System. Congress accepted the commission's recommendations, and President Wilson signed the Federal Reserve Act in December 1913.

monetary policy: The use of money and credit controls to influence macroeconomic outcomes.

Federal Reserve Banks

The core of the Federal Reserve System consists of 12 Federal Reserve banks. Each bank acts as a central banker for the private banks in its region. In this role, the regional Fed banks perform the following services:

- *Clearing checks between private banks.* Suppose that the Bank of America in San Francisco receives a deposit from one of its customers in the form of a share draft written on the New York State Employees Credit Union. The Bank of America doesn't have to go to New York to collect the cash or other reserves that support that draft. Instead the Bank of America can deposit the draft (check) at its account with the Federal Reserve Bank of San Francisco. The Fed then collects from the credit union. This vital clearinghouse service saves the Bank of America and other private banks a great deal of time and expense in processing the 5 *billion* checks that are written every year.
- *Holding bank reserves.* Notice that the Fed's clearinghouse service was facilitated by the fact that the Bank of America and the New York Employees Credit Union had their own accounts at the Fed. As we noted in Chapter 13, banks are *required* to hold some minimum fraction of their deposits in reserve. Only a small amount of reserves is held as cash in a bank's vaults. The rest is held in reserve accounts at the regional Federal Reserve banks. These accounts not only provide greater security and convenience for bank reserves but also enable the Fed to monitor the actual level of bank reserves.
- *Providing currency.* Before every major holiday there's a great demand for cash. People want some pocket money during holidays and know that it's difficult to cash checks on weekends or holidays, especially if they're going out of town. So they load up on cash at their bank or ATMs. After the holiday is over, most of this cash is returned to the banks, typically by the stores, gas stations, and restaurants that benefited from holiday spending. Because banks hold little cash in their vaults, they turn to the Fed to meet these sporadic cash demands. A private bank can simply call the regional Federal Reserve bank and order a supply of cash, to be delivered (by armored truck) before a weekend or holiday. The cash will be deducted from the bank's own account at the Fed. When all the cash comes back in after the holiday, the bank can reverse the process, sending the unneeded cash back to the Fed.
- *Providing loans.* The Federal Reserve banks may also lend reserves to private banks. This practice, called "discounting," is examined more closely in a moment.

The Board of Governors

At the top of the Federal Reserve System's organization chart (Figure 14.1) is the Board of Governors, which is responsible for setting monetary policy. The Board, located in Washington, D.C., consists of seven members ("governors"), appointed by the president of the United States and confirmed by the U.S. Senate. Board members are appointed for 14-year terms and can't be reappointed. Their exceptionally long appointments give the Fed governors a measure of political independence. They're not beholden to any elected official and will hold office longer than any president.

The intent of the Fed's independence is to keep control of the nation's money supply beyond the immediate reach of politicians (especially members of Congress, elected for two-year terms). The designers of the Fed system feared that political control of monetary policy would cause wild swings in the money supply and macro instability. Critics argue, however, that the Fed's independence makes it unresponsive to the majority will.

FIGURE 14.1

Structure of the Federal Reserve System

The Fed's broad policies are determined by the seven-member Board of Governors. The 12 Federal Reserve banks provide central banking services to individual banks in their respective regions. The Federal Open Market Committee directs Federal Reserve transactions in the money market. Various committees offer formal and informal advice to the Board of Governors.

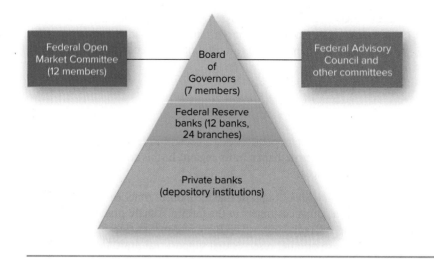

Jay Powell is the Chair of the Fed's Board of Governors.

Samuel Corum/Getty Images

The president selects one of the governors to serve as chair of the Board for four years. The current chair, Jay Powell, was nominated by President Trump in November 2017 and became chair in February 2018. He had been a Fed governor since 2012 and had previously served in the Treasury Department under President George H. Bush. He replaced Janet Yellen, who had been appointed by President Obama in 2014. Chair Powell is the primary spokesperson for Fed policy and reports to Congress every six months on the conduct of monetary policy.

The Federal Open Market Committee (FOMC)

A key arm of the Board is the Federal Open Market Committee (FOMC), which is responsible for the Fed's daily activity in financial markets. The FOMC plays a critical role in setting short-term interest rates and the level of reserves held by private banks. The membership of the FOMC includes all seven governors and 5 of the 12 regional Reserve bank presidents. The FOMC meets in Washington, D.C., every four or five weeks throughout the year to review the economy's performance. It decides whether the economy is growing fast enough (or too fast) and then adjusts monetary policy as needed.

MONETARY TOOLS

Our immediate interest isn't in the structure of the Federal Reserve but the way the Fed is able to alter the **money supply**. *The Fed's control of the money supply is exercised by use of three policy tools:*

money supply (M1): Currency held by the public, plus balances in transactions accounts.

- *Reserve requirements.*
- *Discount rates.*
- *Open market operations.*

Reserve Requirements

required reserves: The minimum amount of reserves a bank is required to hold; equal to required reserve ratio times transactions deposits.

The Fed's first policy tool focuses on reserve requirements. As noted in Chapter 13, the Fed requires private banks to keep some fraction of their deposits "in reserve." These **required reserves** are held either in the form of actual vault cash or, more commonly, as credits (deposits) in the bank's "reserve account" at a regional Federal Reserve bank. *By changing the reserve requirements, the Fed can directly alter the lending capacity of the banking system.*

Recall that the banking system's ability to make additional loans—create deposits—is determined by two factors: (1) the amount of excess reserves banks hold and (2) the money multiplier. Both factors are directly influenced by the Fed's required reserve ratio.

Computing Excess Reserves. Suppose, for example, that banks collectively hold $100 billion of deposits and total reserves of $30 billion. Assume too that the minimum reserve requirement is 20 percent. Under these circumstances, banks are holding more reserves than they have to. Recall that

$$\frac{\text{Required}}{\text{reserves}} = \frac{\text{Required}}{\text{reserve ratio}} \times \frac{\text{Total}}{\text{deposits}}$$

so in this case,

$$\frac{\text{Required}}{\text{reserves}} = 0.20 \times \$100 \text{ billion}$$
$$= \$20 \text{ billion}$$

Banks are *required* to hold $20 billion in reserve to meet Federal Reserve regulations on their deposit base ($100 billion). We've assumed, however, that they're actually holding $30 billion of reserves. The $10 billion difference between actual and required reserves is **excess reserves**—that is,

$$\frac{\text{Excess}}{\text{reserves}} = \frac{\text{Total}}{\text{reserves}} - \frac{\text{Required}}{\text{reserves}}$$

excess reserves: Bank reserves in excess of required reserves.

Lending Capacity. The existence of excess reserves implies that banks aren't fully utilizing their lending powers. With $10 billion of excess reserves and the help of the **money multiplier,** the banks *could* lend an additional $50 billion.

The potential for additional loans is calculated as

$$\frac{\text{Available lending capacity}}{\text{of banking system}} = \text{Excess reserves} \times \text{Money multiplier}$$

money multiplier: The number of deposit (loan) dollars that the banking system can create from $1 of excess reserves; equal to $1 \div$ required reserve ratio.

Recall that the money multiplier is equal to one divided by the reserve requirement. In this case, the money multiplier is 5 ($= 1 \div 0.20$). Thus, the available lending capacity of the banks is

$$\$10 \text{ billion} \times \frac{1}{0.20} = \$50 \text{ billion of unused lending capacity}$$

That is, the banking system could create another $50 billion of money (transactions account balances) without any additional reserves.

A simple way to confirm this—and thereby check your arithmetic—is to note what would happen to total deposits if the banks actually made further loans. Total deposits would increase to $150 billion in this case (the initial $100 billion of deposits plus the new loan-created deposits of $50 billion), an amount that could be supported with $30 billion in reserves (20 percent of $150 billion).

Soaking Up Excess Reserves. But what if the Fed doesn't want the money supply to increase this much? Maybe prices are rising and the Fed wants to restrain rather than stimulate total spending in the economy. Under such circumstances, the Fed would want to restrict the availability of credit (loans). Does it have the power to do so? Can the Fed reduce the lending capacity of the banking system?

The answer to both questions is clearly yes. ***By raising the required reserve ratio, the Fed can immediately reduce the lending capacity of the banking system.***

Table 14.1 summarizes the impact of an increase in the required reserve ratio. In this case, the required reserve ratio is increased from 20 to 25 percent. Notice that this change in the reserve requirement has no effect on the amount of deposits in the banking system (row 1, Table 14.1) or the amount of total reserves (row 2). They remain at $100 billion and $30 billion, respectively. What the increased reserve requirement does affect is the way those reserves can be used. Before the increase, only $20 billion in reserves were *required,* leaving $10 billion of *excess* reserves. Now, however, banks are required to hold $25 billion (0.25 × $100 billion) in reserves, leaving them with only $5 billion in excess reserves. Thus an increase in the reserve requirement immediately reduces excess reserves, as illustrated in row 4, Table 14.1.

TABLE 14.1

The Impact of an Increased Reserve Requirement

An increase in the required reserve ratio reduces both excess reserves (row 4) and the money multiplier (row 5). As a consequence, changes in the reserve requirement have a substantial impact on the lending capacity of the banking system (row 6).

	Required Reserve Ratio	
	If 20 Percent	If 25 Percent
1. Total deposits	$100 billion	$100 billion
2. Total reserves	30 billion	30 billion
3. Required reserves	20 billion	25 billion
4. Excess reserves	10 billion	5 billion
5. Money multiplier	5	4
6. Unused lending capacity	$ 50 billion	$ 20 billion

There's also a second effect. Notice what happens to the money multiplier (1 ÷ reserve ratio). Previously it was 5 (= 1 ÷ 0.20); now it's only 4 (= 1 ÷ 0.25). Consequently, a higher reserve requirement not only reduces excess reserves but diminishes their lending power as well.

A change in the reserve requirement, therefore, hits banks with a triple whammy. *A change in the reserve requirement causes a change in*

- *Excess reserves.*
- *The money multiplier.*
- *The lending capacity of the banking system.*

These changes sharply reduce bank lending power. Whereas the banking system initially had the power to increase the volume of loans by $50 billion ($10 billion of excess reserves × 5), it now has only $20 billion ($5 million × 4) of unused lending capacity, as noted in the last row in Table 14.1.

Changes in reserve requirements are a powerful tool for altering the lending capacity of the banking system. The Fed uses this tool sparingly so as not to cause abrupt changes in the money supply and severe disruptions of banking activity. From 1970 to 1980, for example, reserve requirements were changed only twice, and then by only half a percentage point each time (e.g., from 12.0 to 12.5 percent). The Fed last cut the reserve requirement from 12 to 10 percent in 1992 to increase bank profits and encourage more lending. In 2020 China did the same thing, hoping to restore economic growth in the wake of coronavirus losses (see World View "China Cuts Reserve Requirements").

WORLD VIEW

CHINA CUTS RESERVE REQUIREMENTS

The People's Bank of China (PBOC) has cut the reserve requirement for small and medium-sized banks. The cut from 7 percent to 6 percent will free up 400 billion yuan ($56 billion) in reserves for the country's 4,000 affected banks, many of which serve rural areas. The reserve cuts are seen as another response to the economic calamity caused by the coronavirus pandemic. Economic lockdowns in China and around the world have hit Chinese exports hard, with GDP stalling and unemployment rising. The PBOC's cuts are intended to encourage more lending and borrowing, especially among smaller enterprises.

Source: News reports, April 5–8, 2020.

CRITICAL ANALYSIS: A reduction in the **reserve requirement** transforms some of the banking system's required reserves into excess reserves, thus increasing potential lending activity and profits. It also increases the size of the money multiplier.

The Discount Rate

Banks have a tremendous incentive to maintain their reserves at or close to the minimum established by the Fed. Bank reserves held at the Fed earn lower rates of interest than banks could get from making loans or holding bonds. Hence, a profit-maximizing bank seeks to keep its excess reserves as low as possible, preferring to put its reserves to better, more profitable work. In fact, banks have demonstrated an uncanny ability to keep their reserves close to the minimum federal requirement. As Figure 14.2 illustrates, the few times banks held

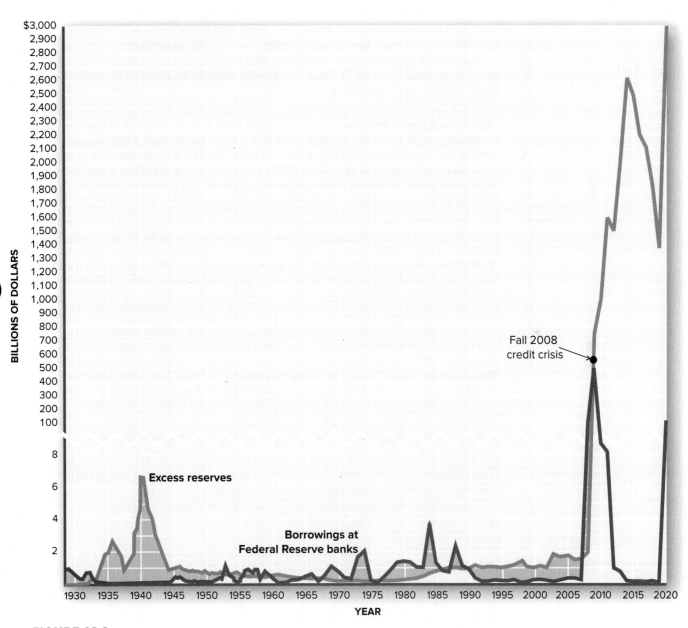

FIGURE 14.2

Excess Reserves and Borrowings

Excess reserves represent unused lending capacity. Hence, banks strive to keep excess reserves at a minimum. One exception to this practice occurred during the Great Depression, when banks were hesitant to make any loans. It happened even more dramatically during the Great Recession of 2008–2009, when bank assets lost value and new loans looked risky. By 2014 banks had stockpiled more than $2.5 trillion in excess reserves.

In early 2020 excess reserves again spiked when the coronavirus shut down businesses (potential borrowers).

In more normal circumstances, banks try to minimize excess reserves, occasionally falling short of required reserves in the process. At such times, they may borrow from other banks (the federal funds market), or they may borrow reserves directly from the Fed. Borrowing from the Fed is called "discounting."

huge excess reserves were in the Great Depression of the 1930s and during the 2008–2009 recession. The banks didn't want to make any more loans and were fearful of loan defaults and panicky customers withdrawing their deposits. Notice in Figure 14.2 the enormous jump in excess reserves in 2008–2009 when banks decided to curtail new lending activity. The 2020 spike in excess reserves was the result of the economic shutdowns in response to the coronavirus pandemic. At the same time banks increased their borrowings from the Fed to take advantage of the Fed's zero-rate interest policy.

Because banks continually seek to keep excess reserves at a minimum, they run the risk of falling below reserve requirements. A large borrower may be a little slow in repaying a loan, or the rate of deposit withdrawals and transfers may exceed expectations, or defaults and price declines may reduce the value of assets held by the bank. At such times, a bank may find that it doesn't have enough reserves to satisfy Fed requirements.

Banks could ensure continual compliance with reserve requirements by maintaining large amounts of excess reserves. But that's an unprofitable procedure, and a profit-maximizing bank will seek other alternatives.

The Federal Funds Market. A bank that finds itself short of reserves can turn to other banks for help. If a reserve-poor bank can borrow some reserves from a reserve-rich bank, it may be able to bridge its temporary deficit and satisfy the Fed. *Reserves borrowed by one bank from another are referred to as "federal funds" and are lent for short periods, usually overnight.* Although trips to the federal funds market—via telephone and computer—will usually satisfy Federal Reserve requirements, such trips aren't free. The lending bank will charge interest (the **federal funds rate**) on its interbank loan.[1] The use of the federal funds market to satisfy Federal Reserve requirements also depends on other banks having excess reserves to lend.

federal funds rate: The interest rate for interbank reserve loans.

Sale of Securities. Another option available to reserve-poor banks is the sale of securities. Banks use some of their excess reserves to buy government bonds, which pay interest. If a bank needs more reserves to satisfy federal regulations, it can sell these securities and deposit the proceeds at a regional Federal Reserve bank. Its reserve position thereby increases. This option also involves distinct costs, however, both in forgone interest-earning opportunities and in the possibility of capital losses when the bond is offered for quick sale.

Discounting. A third option for avoiding a reserve shortage lies in the structure of the Federal Reserve System itself. The Fed not only establishes certain rules of behavior for banks but also functions as a central bank, or banker's bank. Banks maintain accounts with the regional Federal Reserve banks, much the way you and I maintain accounts with a local bank. Individual banks deposit and withdraw "reserve credits" from these accounts, just as we deposit and withdraw dollars. Should a bank find itself short of reserves, it can go to the Fed's "discount window" and borrow some reserves. This process is called **discounting.** *Discounting means the Fed is lending reserves directly to private banks.*[2]

discounting: Federal Reserve lending of reserves to private banks.

The Fed's discounting operation provides private banks with an important source of reserves, but not without cost. The Fed too charges interest on the reserves it lends to banks, a rate of interest referred to as the **discount rate.**

discount rate: The rate of interest the Federal Reserve charges for lending reserves to private banks.

The discount window is a mechanism for directly influencing the size of bank reserves. *By raising or lowering the discount rate, the Fed changes the cost of money for banks and therewith the incentive to borrow reserves.* At high discount rates, borrowing from the Fed is expensive. High discount rates also signal the Fed's desire to restrain the money supply and an accompanying reluctance to lend reserves. Low discount rates, on the other hand, make it profitable to acquire additional reserves and exploit one's lending capacity to the fullest. Low discount rates also indicate the Fed's willingness to support credit expansion.

[1]An overnight loan of $1 million at 6 percent interest (per year) costs $165 in interest charges plus any service fees that might be added. Banks make multimillion-dollar loans in the federal funds market.
[2]In the past, banks had to present loan notes to the Fed in order to borrow reserves. The Fed "discounted" the notes by lending an amount equal to only a fraction of their face value. Although banks no longer have to present loans as collateral, the term "discounting" endures.

In the wake of the 2008 credit crisis, the Fed not only reduced the discount rate but urged banks to borrow more reserves. Notice in Figure 14.2 the spectacular increase in Fed-loaned reserves ("borrowings") in late 2008. The Fed wanted to reassure market participants that the banks had enough reserves to weather the economic storm.

Direct Commercial Lending. In 2020 the Fed acquired an even more powerful lending tool. The Coronavirus Aid, Relief, and Economic Security (CARES) Act gave the Fed temporary authority to lend money directly to private businesses. That option not only facilitated direct lending activity but helped assure market participants that the Fed was ready and willing to prop up the economy during the coronavirus pandemic.

Open Market Operations

Reserve requirements and discount window operations are important tools of monetary policy. But they don't come close to open market operations in day-to-day impact on the money supply. ***Open market operations are the principal mechanism for directly altering the reserves of the banking system.*** Because reserves are the lifeblood of the banking system, open market operations are of immediate and critical interest to private banks and the larger economy.

Portfolio Decisions. To appreciate the impact of open market operations, you have to think about the alternative uses for idle funds. All of us have some idle funds, even if they amount to just a few dollars in our pocket or a minimal balance in our checking account. Other consumers and corporations have great amounts of idle funds, even millions of dollars at any time. Here we're concerned with what people decide to do with such funds.

People (and corporations) don't hold all their idle funds in transactions accounts or cash. Idle funds are also used to purchase stocks, build up savings account balances, and purchase bonds. These alternative uses of idle funds are attractive because they promise some additional income in the form of interest, dividends, or capital appreciation, such as higher stock prices. Deciding where to place idle funds is referred to as the **portfolio decision.**

portfolio decision: The choice of how (where) to hold idle funds.

Hold Money or Bonds. The Fed's *open market operations focus on one of the portfolio choices people make: whether to deposit idle funds in bank accounts or purchase government bonds.* The Fed attempts to influence this choice by making bonds more or less attractive, as circumstances warrant. The Fed's goal is to encourage people to move funds from banks to bond markets or vice versa. In the process, reserves either enter or leave the banking system, thereby altering the lending capacity of banks.

Figure 14.3 depicts the general nature of the Fed's open market operations. As we first observed in Chapter 13 (Figure 13.2), the process of deposit creation begins when people deposit money in the banking system. But people may also hold their assets in the form of bonds. The fed's objective is to alter this portfolio decision by buying or selling bonds.

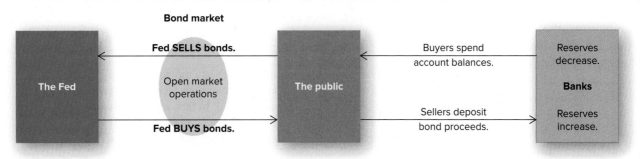

FIGURE 14.3

Open Market Operations

People may hold assets in the form of bank deposits (money) or bonds. When the Fed buys bonds from the public, it increases the flow of deposits (and reserves) to the banks. When the Fed sells bonds, it diminishes the flow of deposits and therewith the banks' capacity to lend (create money).

When the Fed buys bonds from the public, it increases the flow of deposits (reserves) to the banking system. Bond sales by the Fed reduce the inflow.

The Bond Market. To understand how open market operations work, let's look more closely at the bond market. Not all of us buy and sell bonds, but a lot of consumers and corporations do: Daily volume in bond markets exceeds $1 *trillion.* What's being exchanged in this market, and what factors influence decisions to buy or sell?

In our discussion thus far, we've portrayed banks as intermediaries between savers and spenders. Banks aren't the only mechanism available for transferring purchasing power from nonspenders to spenders. Funds are lent and borrowed in bond markets as well. In this case, a corporation may borrow money directly from consumers or other institutions. When it does so, it issues a bond as proof of its promise to repay the loan. A **bond** is simply a piece of paper certifying that someone has borrowed money and promises to pay it back at some future date. In other words, *a bond is nothing more than an IOU.* In the case of bond markets, however, the IOU is typically signed by a giant corporation or a government agency rather than a friend. It's therefore more widely accepted by lenders.

Because most corporations and government agencies that borrow money in the bond market are well known and able to repay their debts, their bonds are actively traded. If I lend $1,000 to General Motors on a 10-year bond, for example, I don't have to wait 10 years to get my money back; I can resell the bond to someone else at any time. If I do, that person will collect the face value of the bond (plus interest) from GM when it's due. The actual purchase and sale of bonds take place in the bond market. Although a good deal of the action occurs on Wall Street in New York, the bond market has no unique location. Like other markets we've discussed, the bond market exists whenever and however (electronically) bond buyers and sellers get together.

Bond Yields. People buy bonds because bonds pay interest. If you buy a General Motors bond, GM is obliged to pay you interest during the period of the loan. For example, an 8 percent 2035 GM bond in the amount of $1,000 states that GM will pay the bondholder $80 interest annually (8 percent of $1,000) until 2035. At that point, GM will repay the initial $1,000 loan (the "principal").

The current **yield** paid on a bond depends on the promised interest rate (8 percent in this case) and the actual purchase price of the bond. Specifically,

$$\text{Yield} = \frac{\text{Annual interest payment}}{\text{Price paid for bond}}$$

If you pay $1,000 for the bond, then the current yield is

$$\text{Yield} = \frac{\$80}{\$1,000} = 0.08, \text{ or } 8\%$$

which is the same as the interest rate printed on the face of the bond. But what if you pay only $900 for the bond? In this case, the interest rate paid by GM remains at 8 percent ($80 per year), but the *yield* jumps to

$$\text{Yield} = \frac{\$80}{\$900} = 0.089, \text{ or } 8.9\%$$

Buying a $1,000 bond for only $900 might seem like too good a bargain to be true. But bonds are often bought and sold at prices other than their face value (see Front Page Economics "Treasury Prices Rise on Recession Fears"). In fact, *a principal objective of Federal Reserve open market activity is to alter the price of bonds, and therewith their yields.* By doing so, the Fed makes bonds a more or less attractive alternative to holding money.

Open Market Activity. The basic premise of open market activity is that participants in the bond market will respond to changes in bond prices and yields. As we've observed, *the less you pay for a bond, the higher its yield.* Accordingly, the Fed can induce people to *buy* bonds by offering to sell them at a lower price (e.g., a $1,000, 8 percent bond for only $900). Similarly, the Fed can induce people to *sell* bonds by offering to buy them at higher prices.

bond: A certificate acknowledging a debt and the amount of interest to be paid each year until repayment; an IOU.

yield: The rate of return on a bond; the annual interest payment divided by the bond's price.

TREASURY PRICES RISE ON RECESSION FEARS

Increasing fears of a recession next year brought bond yields down dramatically in August. The yield on the Treasury's 1.75 percent 10-year bond fell from 2.0 percent at the beginning of August to 1.5 percent at month's end. In the process, the price of the 10-year bond rose from $875 to $1,167. Market analysts say that impending tariff hikes, the president's impeachment in the House, and lackluster manufacturing data have intensified fears of a recession.

Source: Market reports of September 2019.

CRITICAL ANALYSIS: Bond prices and yields move in opposite directions. If the Fed buys bonds, bond prices rise and **yields** (interest rates) fall.

In either case, the Fed hopes to move reserves into or out of the banking system. In other words, **open market operations** entail the purchase and sale of government securities (bonds) for the purpose of altering the flow of reserves into and out of the banking system.

open market operations: Federal Reserve purchases and sales of government bonds for the purpose of altering bank reserves.

Open Market Purchases. Suppose the Fed's goal is to increase the money supply. Its strategy is to provide the banking system with additional reserves. To do so, it must persuade people to deposit a larger share of their financial assets in banks and hold less in other forms, particularly government bonds. The tool for doing this is bond prices. *If the Fed offers to pay a higher price for bonds ("bids up bonds"), it will effectively lower bond yields and market interest rates.* The higher prices and lower yields will reduce the attractiveness of holding bonds. If the price offered by the Fed is high enough, people will sell some of their bonds to the Fed. What will they do with the proceeds of those bond sales? Deposit them in their bank accounts, of course. This influx of deposits into bank accounts will directly increase both the money supply and bank reserves—goal achieved.

Figure 14.4 illustrates the dynamics of open market operations in more detail. When the Fed buys a bond from the public, it pays with a check written on itself (step 1 in Figure 14.4). What will the bond seller do with the check? There really aren't any options. If the seller wants to use the proceeds of the bond sale, he or she will have to deposit the Fed check at a bank (step 2 in the figure). The bank, in turn, deposits the check at a regional Federal Reserve bank in exchange for a reserve credit (step 3). The bank's reserves are directly increased by the amount of the check. Thus, *by buying bonds, the Fed increases bank reserves.* These reserves can be used to expand the money supply still further as banks put their newly acquired reserves to work making loans.

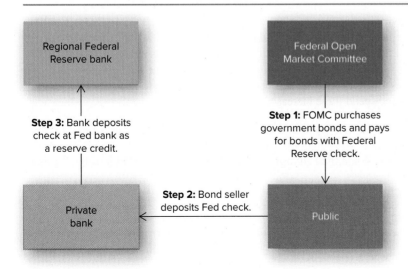

FIGURE 14.4

An Open Market Purchase

The Fed can increase bank reserves by buying bonds from the public. The Fed check used to buy bonds (step 1) gets deposited in a private bank (step 2). The bank returns the check to the Fed (step 3), thereby obtaining additional reserves. To decrease bank reserves, the Fed would sell bonds, thus reversing the flow of reserves.

Quantitative Easing. Federal Reserve open-market purchases were pursued so aggressively in 2009–2011 that they acquired a new name—"quantitative easing," or "QE." The Fed's QE program entailed two important changes in its traditional open market operations. First, it expanded the scope of Fed purchases beyond short-term government bonds to longer-term bonds and other securities (e.g., mortgage-backed securities). Second, the QE program allowed the Fed to purchase bonds directly from commercial banks rather than exclusively through the bond market. This gave the Fed more direct control of bank assets, reserves, and solvency. The Fed used its broadened powers to inject more reserves directly into the banking system and shore up confidence in bank solvency.

The first round of quantitative easing (QE1) began in November 2008 and continued through June 2010. During that period, the Fed purchased $1.5 trillion of securities, boosting bank reserves by the same amount (note the spike in excess reserves in Figure 14.2). When economic growth failed to accelerate as hoped, the Fed began a second round of asset purchases in November 2010 that continued to June 2011. A third round (QE3) was initiated in September 2012, with scheduled Fed purchases of $85 billion per month. By the end of the QE programs, the Fed had accumulated more than $2 trillion in bonds and other securities, and bank reserves had risen by a similar amount. These huge bond purchases helped to keep interest rates at historic lows.

Open Market Sales. Should the Fed desire to slow the growth in the money supply, it can reverse the whole process. Instead of offering to *buy* bonds, the Fed in this case will try to *sell* bonds. If the Fed "bids bonds down" (offers to sell them at low prices), bond yields will rise. In response, individuals, corporations, and government agencies will convert some of their transactions deposits into bonds. When they do so, they write a check, paying the Fed for the bonds.[3] The Fed then returns the check to the depositor's bank, taking payment through a reduction in the bank's reserve account. The reserves of the banking system are thereby diminished, as is the capacity to make loans. Thus, *by selling bonds, the Fed reduces bank reserves.*

The Fed Funds Rate

A market signal of these changing reserve flows is provided by the federal funds rate. Recall that "fed funds" are excess reserves traded among banks. If the Fed pumps more reserves into the banking system (by buying bonds), the interest rate charged for overnight reserve loans— the federal funds rate—will decline. Conversely, if the Fed is reducing bank reserves (by selling bonds), the federal funds rate will increase. Hence, *the federal funds rate is a highly visible signal of Federal Reserve open market operations.* When Alan Greenspan reduced the federal funds rate *11 times* in 2001, the Fed was underscoring the urgency of monetary stimulus to combat the recession and the aftereffects of the September 11 terrorist attacks.

Beginning in June 2004 the Fed used this same tool to *reduce* lending activity. In fact, the Fed completely reversed course and raised the fed funds rate *17 times* between June 2004 and June 2006.

The Fed changed course yet again in 2007. Between September 2007 and December 2008 the Fed lowered the federal funds rate *10 times*. The Fed's goal at that time was to push bond yields so low that people would prefer to hold their idle funds in banks rather than buy bonds. The result was a massive increase in excess reserves, as we saw in Figure 14.2. The lower interest rates that accompanied the Fed bond purchases were intended to encourage people to borrow and spend these increased excess reserves.

The Target Rate. When the Fed announces a change in the federal funds rate, it always refers to the "target" rate. The Fed doesn't actually *set* the fed funds rate. It only establishes a desired "target" rate. When the Fed lowers the target rate, it seeks to hit it by buying more bonds in the market.

---

[3]In actuality, the Fed deals directly with only 36 "primary" bond dealers. These intermediaries then trade with each other, "secondary" dealers, financial institutions, and individuals. These additional steps don't significantly alter the flow of funds depicted here. Using electronic transactions rather than paper checks doesn't alter the flow of funds either.

FRONT PAGE ECONOMICS

FED SLASHES RATES TO ZERO

The Federal Reserve announced on Sunday that it is cutting the federal funds rate to a range of 0–0.25 percent, a drop of a full percentage point. In its announcement, the Fed noted that the lower federal funds rate—the rate banks charge each other—should result in lower interest rates across the board. The Fed said the lower rates would ease the burden on consumers and businesses of existing debt and even encourage new borrowing. The rate cut was one more step in the Fed's attempt to contain the economic damage caused by the coronavirus pandemic.

Source: Media reports, March 15–17, 2020.

CRITICAL ANALYSIS: When the Fed changes its target for the **federal funds rate**, it uses open-market purchases and sales to achieve that target. Other interest rates tend to mirror changes in the federal funds rate.

This is exactly what the Fed did in March 2020 when it slashed the fed funds target rate to a low of zero percent (see Front Page Economics "Fed Slashes Interest Rates." The Fed drove interest rates down to the target range by buying massive quantities of bonds in the open market.

Volume of Activity. To appreciate the significance of open market operations, you need a sense of the magnitudes involved. As we noted earlier, the volume of trading in U.S. bond markets exceeds $1 *trillion* a day. The Fed alone owned more than $4 trillion worth of government securities at the beginning of 2020 and bought or sold enormous sums daily. Thus, open market operations involve tremendous amounts of money and, by implication, potential bank reserves. Each $1 of reserves represents something like $10 of potential lending capacity (via the money multiplier). Thus, open market operations can have a profound impact on the money supply.

INCREASING THE MONEY SUPPLY

The three major tools of monetary policy are reserve requirements, discount rates, and open market operations. The Fed can use these tools individually or in combination to change the money supply. This section illustrates the use of each tool to attain a specific policy goal.

Suppose that the policy goal is to increase the money supply from an assumed level of $340 billion to $400 billion. In surveying the nation's banks, the Fed discovers the facts shown in Table 14.2. On the basis of the facts presented in Table 14.2, it's evident that

- The banking system is "loaned up." Because excess reserves are zero (see row 5 in Table 14.2), there's no additional lending capacity.
- The required reserve ratio must be equal to 25 percent because this is the current ratio of required reserves ($60 billion) to total deposits ($240 billion).

Item	Amount
1. Cash held by public	$100 billion
2. Transactions deposits	240 billion
3. Total money supply (M1)	$340 billion
4. Required reserves	$ 60 billion
5. Excess reserves	0
6. Total reserves of banks	$ 60 billion
7. U.S. bonds held by public	$460 billion
8. Discount rate	5%

TABLE 14.2

How to Increase the Money Supply

The accompanying data depict a banking system that has $340 billion of money (M1) and no further lending capacity (excess reserves = 0). To enlarge M1 to $400 billion, the Fed can (1) lower the required reserve ratio, (2) reduce the discount rate, or (3) buy bonds held by the public.

Accordingly, if the Fed wants to increase the money supply, it will have to pump additional reserves into the banking system or lower the reserve requirement. *To increase the money supply, the Fed can*

- *Lower reserve requirements.*
- *Reduce the discount rate.*
- *Buy bonds.*

Lowering Reserve Requirements

Lowering the reserve requirements is an expedient way of increasing the lending capacity of the banking system. But by how much should the reserve requirement be reduced?

Recall that the Fed's goal here is to increase the money supply from $340 billion to $400 billion, an increase of $60 billion. If the public isn't willing to hold any additional cash, this entire increase in money supply will have to take the form of added transactions deposits. In other words, total deposits will have to increase from $240 billion to $300 billion. These additional deposits will have to be *created* by the banks in the form of new loans to consumers or business firms.

If the banking system is going to support $300 billion in transactions deposits with its *existing* reserves, the reserve requirement will have to be reduced from 25 percent. We can compute the desired reserve requirement as follows:

$$\frac{\text{Total reserves}}{\text{Desired level of deposits}} = \frac{\$60 \text{ billion}}{\$300 \text{ billion}} = 0.20$$

So the next move is to lower the reserve requirement from 0.25 to 0.20. At the moment the Fed lowers the minimum reserve ratio to 0.20, *total* reserves won't change. The banks' potential lending power will change, however. Required reserves will drop to $48 billion (0.20 × $240 billion), and excess reserves will jump from zero to $12 billion. These new excess reserves imply an additional lending capacity:

$$\underset{(\$12 \text{ billion})}{\textbf{Excess reserves}} \times \underset{(5)}{\textbf{Money multiplier}} = \underset{(\$60 \text{ billion})}{\textbf{Unused lending capacity}}$$

If the banks succeed in putting all this new lending power to work—actually make $60 billion in new loans—the Fed's objective of increasing the money supply will be attained.

Lowering the Discount Rate

The second monetary tool available to the Fed is the discount rate. We assumed it was 5 percent initially (see row 8 in Table 14.2). If the Fed lowers this rate, it will become cheaper for banks to borrow reserves from the Fed. The banks will be more willing to borrow (cheaper) reserves so long as they can make additional loans to their own customers at higher interest rates. The profitability of discounting depends on the *difference* between the discount rate and the interest rate the bank charges its loan customers. The Fed increases this difference when it lowers the discount rate.

There's no way to calculate the appropriate discount rate without more detailed knowledge of the banking system's willingness to borrow reserves from the Fed. Nevertheless, we can determine how much reserves the banks *must* borrow if the Fed's money supply target is to be attained. The Fed's objective is to increase transactions deposits by $60 billion. If these deposits are to be created by the banks—and the reserve requirement is unchanged at 0.25—the banks will have to borrow an additional $15 billion of reserves ($60 billion divided by 4, the money multiplier).

Buying Bonds

The Fed can also get additional reserves into the banking system by buying U.S. bonds in the open market. As row 7 in Table 14.2 indicates, the public holds $460 billion in U.S. bonds, none of which are counted as part of the money supply. If the Fed can persuade people to sell some of these bonds, bank reserves will surely rise.

To achieve its money supply target, the Fed will offer to buy $15 billion of U.S. bonds. It will pay for these bonds with checks written on its own account at the Fed. The people who sell the bonds will deposit these checks in their own transactions accounts. As they do so, they'll directly increase bank deposits and reserves by $15 billion.

Is $15 billion of open market purchases enough? Yes. The $15 billion is a direct addition to transactions deposits, and therefore to the money supply. The additional deposits bring in $15 billion of reserves, only $3.75 billion of which is required (0.25 × $15 billion). Hence, the new deposits bring in $11.25 billion of *excess* reserves. These new excess reserves themselves create additional lending capacity:

$$\underset{\text{($\$11.25$ billion)}}{\textbf{Excess reserves}} \times \underset{\text{(4)}}{\textbf{Money multiplier}} = \underset{\text{($\$45$ billion)}}{\textbf{Unused lending capacity}}$$

Thus, the $15 billion of open market purchases will eventually lead to a $60 billion increase in M1 as a consequence of both direct deposits ($15 billion) and subsequent loan activity ($45 billion).

Federal Funds Rate. When the Fed starts bidding up bonds, bond yields and market interest rates will start falling. So will the federal funds rate. This will give individual banks an incentive to borrow any excess reserves available, thereby accelerating deposit (loan) creation.

DECREASING THE MONEY SUPPLY

All the tools used to increase the money supply can also be used in reverse. *To reduce the money supply, the Fed can*

- *Raise reserve requirements.*
- *Increase the discount rate.*
- *Sell bonds.*

On a week-to-week basis, the Fed does occasionally seek to reduce the total amount of cash and transactions deposits held by the public. These are minor adjustments, however, to broader policies. A growing economy needs a steadily increasing supply of money to finance market exchanges. Hence, the Fed rarely seeks an outright reduction in the size of the money supply. What it does is regulate the *rate of growth* in the money supply.

When the Fed wants to slow the rate of consumer and investor spending, it restrains the *growth* of money and credit. Although many people talk about "reducing" the money supply, they're really talking about slowing its rate of growth. That was the goal of the Fed when it increased the federal funds rate in December 2018. Fearing that faster economic growth in 2019 might accelerate inflation, the Fed nudged interest rates just a bit higher (see Front Page Economics "Fed Raises Key Interest Rate").

FRONT PAGE ECONOMICS

FED RAISES KEY INTEREST RATE

Washington, D.C. The Fed, as expected, raised the target rate on federal funds from 2.25 to 2.5 percent today. Fed chair Jay Powell said the economy appeared "healthy" and "solid" enough to accommodate a small increase in interest rates. The Fed's goal is to keep inflation under control as the economy continues to grow and unemployment falls to historic levels.

President Trump reacted immediately to the Fed action, calling it "foolish" and "crazy"—an impediment to stronger growth and still more jobs.

Source: News reports of December 19–20, 2018.

CRITICAL ANALYSIS: The Fed pursues monetary restraint (**monetary policy**) by raising interest rates, increasing reserve requirements, or selling Treasury bonds in the open market.

DECISIONS FOR TOMORROW

Can We Crowdfund the Future?

As we have seen, banks play a critical role as intermediaries, moving money from savers to spenders. As such, they help plug leakage holes in the circular flow, keeping aggregate demand at or near its full-employment potential. The Federal Reserve, in turn, helps assure that banks have the right amount of lending capacity to stimulate or restrain aggregate demand, as needed.

The Fed's ability to control bank lending depends on its power to monitor and regulate bank reserves. But what about lending activity that doesn't pass through the banking system?

Sources: www.indiegogo.com, www.gofundme.com, www.kickstarter.com

In Chapter 13, we noted how Facebook is working on a digital currency (Libra) that would bypass traditional intermediaries like banks. If people make greater use of such cryptocurrencies, the power of banks and the Fed to control the money supply will diminish.

Another option for bypassing the banks arises with crowdfunding. The Internet creates the opportunity for savers and spenders to interact *directly,* without the involvement of banks. This kind of peer-to-peer lending is referred to as **crowdfunding.** If someone is rich in ideas, but low on cash, he or she can turn to the Internet for funding. Funds can be solicited by describing the project to be pursued, then asking for individuals to contribute. Typically, hundreds of individuals can contribute, allowing the project to proceed. In April 2013, writer Rob Thomas raised $5.7 million from 91,585 contributors to produce a feature film version of the discontinued *Veronica Mars* TV series. The musician Amanda Palmer raised $1.2 million from 24,833 backers to make a new album and an art book. In January 2017, a group on Kickstarter raised over $12 million from 19,264 backers to fund a board game called "Kingdom Death."

As crowdfunding has become more popular, more than 2,000 Internet sites have been created to serve as platforms for bringing project initiators and potential backers together. Among them are Kickstarter, gofundme, Indiegogo, Crowdrise, and Crowdfunder. Some focus on charitable activities like raising money for accident victims or people with dire health problems. Some, like appbacker, are designed for funding very specific products (new Internet applications). But the largest are intended to facilitate the funding of new business ventures. At these sites, backers (individual contributors) are typically given an equity share in the venture they are helping to fund. In 2019, over $40 billion of projects were crowdfunded.

Crowdfunding bypasses the banks. This alternative conduit of lending/investing potentially weakens the link between the money supply and aggregate demand. It also diminishes the importance of bank reserves as a measure of lending capacity. But the volume of crowdfunding ($40 billion) is so minuscule relative to the size of the money supply (M2 of $15 *trillion*) that traditional banks are still the dominant base for monetary policy.

crowdfunding: The financing of a project through individual contributions from a large number of people, typically via an Internet platform.

SUMMARY

- The Federal Reserve System controls the nation's money supply by regulating the loan activity (deposit creation) of private banks (depository institutions). **LO14-2**
- The core of the Federal Reserve System is the 12 regional Federal Reserve banks, which provide check clearance, reserve deposit, and loan ("discounting") services to individual banks. Private banks are required to maintain minimum reserves on deposit at the regional Federal Reserve banks. **LO14-1**
- The general policies of the Fed are set by its Board of Governors. The Board's chair is selected by the U.S. president and confirmed by the Senate. The chair serves as the chief spokesperson for monetary policy. The Fed's policy strategy is implemented by the Federal Open

Market Committee (FOMC), which directs open market sales and purchase of U.S. bonds.   **LO14-1**
- The Fed has three basic tools for changing the money supply: altering the required reserve ratio, altering discount rates, or using open-market operations.   **LO14-2**
- By altering the reserve requirement, the Fed can immediately change both the quantity of excess reserves in the banking system and the money multiplier, which limits banks' lending capacity.   **LO14-2**
- By altering discount rates (the rate of interest charged by the Fed for reserve borrowing), the Fed can also influence the amount of reserves maintained by banks.   **LO14-2**
- Finally, and most important, the Fed can increase or decrease the reserves of the banking system by buying or selling government bonds—that is, by engaging in open market operations.   **LO14-2**
- When the Fed buys bonds, it causes an increase in bank reserves (and lending capacity). When the Fed sells bonds, it induces a reduction in reserves (and lending capacity).   **LO14-3**
- The federal funds (interest) rate is a market signal of Fed open market activity and intentions.   **LO14-2**
- Crowdfunding is a source of lending and investing that bypasses the banking system, instead relying on direct peer-to-peer funding, typically via the Internet. Although crowdfunding lessens the importance of bank reserves, it is a tiny fraction of loan activity.   **LO14-2**

Key Terms

monetary policy
money supply (M1)
required reserves
excess reserves
money multiplier

federal funds rate
discounting
discount rate
portfolio decision
bond

yield
open market operations
crowdfunding

Questions for Discussion

1. Why do banks want to maintain as little excess reserves as possible? Under what circumstances might banks want to hold excess reserves? (*Hint:* See Figure 14.2.)   **LO14-2**
2. Why do people hold bonds rather than larger savings account or checking account balances? Under what circumstances might they change their portfolios, moving their funds out of bonds and into bank accounts?   **LO14-3**
3. Why did banks reduce their excess reserves so much after 2010 (refer to Figure 14.2)?   **LO14-2**
4. Why did China reduce reserve requirements in 2020? How did they expect consumers and businesses to respond? (See World View "China Cuts Reserve Requirements.")   **LO14-2**
5. Why did the Fed raise the federal funds rate in December 2018 (Front Page Economics "Fed Raises Key Interest Rate")? Why did President Trump call that action "crazy"?   **LO14-1**
6. Why did bond prices rise in August 2019? (See Front Page Economics "Treasury Prices Rise on Recession Fears.")   **LO14-3**
7. Why do bond prices decline when interest rates rise?   **LO14-3**
8. In 2020 the Fed reduced both the discount and federal fund rates dramatically, but bank loan volume didn't increase. What considerations might have constrained the market's response to Fed policy?   **LO14-2**
9. Between January 1 and July 1, 2020, the Fed purchased an additional $3 trillion of bonds. Why did it buy so many bonds? What impact did those open-market purchases have on the money supply and interest rates?   **LO14-3**
10. What are the advantages of crowdfunding over traditional bank lending? What are the disadvantages?   **LO14-2**

LO14-1 1. What is the money multiplier when the reserve requirement is
    (a) 0.05?
    (b) 0.10?
    (c) 0.125?
    (d) 0.111?

LO14-2 2. In Table 14.1, what would the following values be immediately if the required reserve ratio fell from 0.20 to 0.15?
    (a) Total deposits
    (b) Total reserves
    (c) Required reserves
    (d) Excess reserves
    (e) Money multiplier
    (f) Unused lending capacity

LO14-2 3. Assume that the following data describe the condition of the banking system:

Total reserves	$120 billion
Transactions deposits	$800 billion
Cash held by public	$300 billion
Reserve requirement	0.10

    (a) How large is the money supply (M1)?
    (b) How large are *required* reserves?
    (c) How large are *excess* reserves?
    (d) What is the money multiplier?
    (e) How much is the unused lending capacity?

LO14-2 4. In Problem 3, suppose the Fed wanted to stop further lending activity. To do this, what reserve requirement should the Fed impose?

LO14-2 5. According to World View "China Cuts Reserve Requirements," what was the money multiplier in China
    (a) Before the rate cut?
    (b) After the rate cut?

LO14-2 6. By how much did the following increase when China cut the reserve requirement (see World View "China Cuts Reserve Requirements"):
    (a) Excess reserves?
    (b) The lending capacity of the banking system?

LO14-2 7. Assume the banking system contains the following amounts:

Total reserves	$ 90 billion
Transactions deposits	$900 billion
Cash held by public	$100 billion
Reserve requirement	0.10

    (a) Are the banks currently fully utilizing their lending capacity?
    (b) What would happen to the money supply *initially* if the public deposited another $20 billion of cash in transactions accounts?
    (c) What would the lending capacity of the banking system be after this deposit?
    (d) How large would the money supply be if the banks fully utilized their lending capacity?
    (e) What three policy tools could the Fed use to offset that potential growth in M1?

LO14-3 8. According to Front Page Economics "Treasury Prices Rise on Recession Fears," what would the yield be on the Treasury bond if the market price of the bonds were:
    (a) $1,000?
    (b) $800?
    (c) $1,200?

LO14-3 9. Suppose a $1,000 bond pays $30 per year in interest.
   (a) What is the contractual interest rate ("coupon rate") on the bond?
   (b) If market interest rates rise to 4 percent, what price will the bond sell for?

LO14-3 10. According to Front Page Economics "Fed Raises Key Interest Rate,"
   (a) What was the Fed's target for the fed funds rate in late December 2018?
   (b) Was this an increase or a decrease from the previous period?
   (c) Would this rate change increase or decrease aggregate demand?

LO14-3 11. Suppose a banking system with the following balance sheet has no excess reserves. Assume that banks will make loans in the full amount of any excess reserves that they acquire.

Assets (in Billions)		Liabilities (in Billions)	
Total reserves	$ 30	Transactions accounts	$400
Securities	190		
Loans	180		
Total	$400	Total	$400

   (a) What is the reserve requirement?
   (b) Reconstruct the balance sheet of the total banking system if the requirement is changed to 5 percent and all banks have fully utilized their lending capacity.

Assets (in Billions)		Liabilities (in Billions)	
Total reserves	_____	Transactions accounts	_____
Securities	$190		
Loans	_____		
Total	_____	Total	_____

   (c) By how much has the money supply changed as a result of the lower reserve requirement (step b)?
   (d) Suppose the Fed now buys $10 billion of securities directly from the banks. What will the banks' books look like immediately after this purchase?

Assets (in Billions)		Liabilities (in Billions)	
Total reserves	_____	Transactions accounts	_____
Securities	_____		
Loans	_____		
Total	_____	Total	_____

   (e) How much excess reserves do the banks have now?
   (f) By how much can the money supply now increase due to this open market purchase?

LO14-2 12. *Decisions for Tomorrow:* Suppose a person who is developing a card game crowdfunds $40,000 and holds this as cash for future expenses. If this $40,000 comes from donors' checking accounts, by how much will the money supply fall if the reserve ratio is 10 percent?

Paul J. Richards/AFP/Getty Images

Monetary Policy

After reading this chapter, you should know

LO15-1 How interest rates are set in the money market.

LO15-2 How monetary policy affects macro outcomes.

LO15-3 The constraints on monetary policy impact.

LO15-4 The differences between Keynesian and monetarist monetary theories.

So what if the Federal Reserve System controls the nation's money supply? Why is this significant? Does it matter how much money is available?

Vladimir Lenin thought so. The first communist leader of the Soviet Union once remarked that the best way to destroy a society is to destroy its money. If a society's money became valueless, it would no longer be accepted in exchange for goods and services in product markets. People would have to resort to barter, and the economy's efficiency would be severely impaired. Adolf Hitler tried unsuccessfully to use this weapon against Great Britain during World War II. His plan was to counterfeit British currency, then drop it from planes flying over England. He believed that the sudden increase in the quantity of money, together with its suspect origins, would render the British pound valueless.

Even in peacetime, the quantity of money in circulation influences its value in the marketplace. Moreover, interest rates and access to credit (bank loans) are basic determinants of spending behavior. When credit becomes unavailable, the economy can grind to a halt. Consequently, control over the money supply is a critical policy tool for altering macroeconomic outcomes.

But how much influence does the money supply have on macro performance? Specifically,

- **What's the relationship between the money supply, interest rates, and aggregate demand?**
- **How can the Fed use its control of the money supply or interest rates to alter macro outcomes?**
- **How effective is monetary policy, compared to fiscal policy?**

Economists offer very different answers to these questions. Some argue that changes in the money supply directly affect macro outcomes; others argue that the effects of such changes are indirect and less certain.

Paralleling these arguments about *how* monetary policy works are debates over the relative effectiveness of monetary and fiscal policy. Some economists argue that monetary policy is more effective than fiscal policy; others contend the reverse is true. This chapter examines these different views of money and assesses their implications for macro policy.

THE MONEY MARKET

The best place to learn how **monetary policy** works is the money *market*. You must abandon any mystical notions you may harbor about money and view it like any other commodity that's traded in the marketplace.

Like other goods, there's a supply of money and a demand for money. Together they determine the "price" of money, or the **interest rate.**

At first glance, it may appear strange to call interest rates the price of money. But when you borrow money, the "price" you pay is measured by the interest rate you're charged. When interest rates are high, money is "expensive." When interest rates are low, money is "cheap."

Money Balances

Even people who don't borrow are affected by the price of money. People hold cash and maintain positive bank balances as part of the **money supply (M1, M2).** There's an opportunity cost associated with such money balances, however. Money held in transactions accounts earns little or no interest. Money held in savings accounts and money market mutual funds does earn interest but usually at relatively low rates. By contrast, money used to buy bonds or stocks or to make loans is likely to earn a higher rate of return, as Table 15.1 illustrates.

The Price of Money. The nature of the "price" of money should be apparent: People who hold *cash* are forgoing an opportunity to earn interest. So are people who hold money in checking accounts that pay no interest. In either case, *forgone interest is the opportunity cost (price) of money people choose to hold.* How high is that price? It's equal to the market rate of interest.

Money held in interest-paying bank accounts does earn some interest. In this case, the opportunity cost of holding money is the *difference* between the prevailing rate of interest and the rate paid on deposit balances. In Table 15.1 the opportunity cost of holding cash rather than Treasury bonds is 0.88 percent per year.

The Demand for Money

Once we recognize that money does have a price, we can formulate a *demand* for money. When we talk about the "demand" for money, we're not referring to your ceaseless craving for more income. Instead, the **demand for money** refers to the ability and willingness to *hold* money in the form of cash or bank balances. As is the case with all goods, the demand for money is a schedule (or curve) showing the quantity of money demanded at alternative prices (interest rates).

So why would anyone want to "hold" money? The decision to hold (demand) money balances is the kind of **portfolio decision** we examined in Chapter 14. While at first glance it might seem irrational to hold money balances that pay little or no interest, there are many good reasons for doing so.

Transactions Demand. Even people who have mastered the principles of economics hold money. They do so because they want to buy goods and services. To transact business in product or factor markets, we need money in the form of either cash or a positive bank account balance. Debit cards and ATM cards don't work unless there's money in the bank.

Option	Interest Rate
Cash	0.00%
Checking accounts	0.01
6-month CD	1.70
10-year Treasury bond	0.88
Corporate bond (Aaa)	2.67

Source: Federal Reserve (March 2020 rates).

---

monetary policy: The use of money and credit controls to influence macroeconomic outcomes.

interest rate: The price paid for the use of money.

money supply (M1): Currency held by the public, plus balances in transactions accounts.

money supply (M2): M1 plus balances in most savings accounts and money market funds.

demand for money: The quantities of money people are willing and able to hold at alternative interest rates, *ceteris paribus.*

portfolio decision: The choice of how (where) to hold idle funds.

TABLE 15.1
Portfolio Choices

Idle funds can be held in many forms. Holding funds in cash or checking accounts pays little or no interest. The "price" of holding money is the interest forgone from alternative portfolio choices. When that price is high, people hold (demand) less money.

transactions demand for
money: Money held for the
purpose of making everyday
market purchases.

precautionary demand for
money: Money held for
unexpected market transactions
or for emergencies.

speculative demand for
money: Money held for
speculative purposes, for later
financial opportunities.

equilibrium rate of interest:
The interest rate at which the
quantity of money demanded in
a given time period equals the
quantity of money supplied.

Payment by e-cash also requires a supporting bank balance. Even when we use credit cards (perhaps via a digital wallet), we're only postponing the date of payment by a few weeks or so. Some merchants won't even accept credit cards, especially for small purchases. Accordingly, we recognize the existence of a basic **transactions demand for money**—that is, money held in cash or bank accounts for everyday purchases.

Precautionary Demand. Another reason people hold money is their fear of the proverbial rainy day. A sudden emergency may require money purchases over and above normal transactions needs. Such needs may arise when the banks are closed or when you're in a community where your checks aren't accepted. Also, future income is uncertain and may diminish unexpectedly. Therefore, people hold a bit more money (cash or bank account balances) than they anticipate spending. This **precautionary demand for money** is the extra money being held as a safeguard against the unexpected.

Speculative Demand. People also hold money for speculative purposes. Suppose you were interested in buying stocks or bonds but hadn't yet picked the right ones or regarded their present prices as too high. In such circumstances, you might want to hold some money so that you could later buy a "hot" stock or bond at a price you think attractive. Thus, you'd be holding money in the hope that a better financial opportunity would later appear. In this sense, you'd be *speculating* with your money balances, forgoing present opportunities to earn interest in the hope of hitting a real jackpot later. These money balances represent a **speculative demand for money.**

The Market Demand Curve. These three motivations for holding money combine to create a *market demand* for money. What shape does this demand curve take? Does the quantity of money demanded decrease sharply as the rate of interest rises? Or do people tend to hold the same amount of money, regardless of its price?

People do cut down on their money balances when interest rates rise. At such times, the opportunity cost of holding money is simply too high. This explains why so many people move their money out of transactions deposits (M1) and into money market mutual funds (M2) when interest rates are extraordinarily high (e.g., in 1980-1982). Corporations are even more careful about managing their money when interest rates rise. Better money management requires watching checking account balances more closely and even making more frequent trips to the bank, but the opportunity costs are worth it.

Figure 15.1 illustrates the total market demand for money. Like nearly all demand curves, the market demand curve for money slopes downward. The downward slope indicates that *the quantity of money people are willing and able to hold (demand) increases as interest rates fall* (*ceteris paribus*).

The Money Supply. The money supply curve is assumed to be a vertical line. As we saw in Chapter 13, the Federal Reserve has the power to regulate the money supply through its reserve requirements, discount window, and open market operations. By using these policy tools, the Fed can target a specific quantity for the money supply (M1 or M2).

Equilibrium

Once a money demand curve and a money supply curve are available, the action in money markets is easy to follow. Figure 15.1 summarizes this action. The money demand curve in Figure 15.1 reflects existing demands for holding money. The money supply curve is drawn at an arbitrary level of g_1. In practice, its position depends on Federal Reserve policy (Chapter 14), the lending behavior of private banks, and the willingness of consumers and investors to borrow money.

The intersection of the money demand and money supply curves (E_1) establishes an **equilibrium rate of interest.** Only at this interest rate is the quantity of money supplied equal to the quantity demanded. In this case, we observe that an interest rate of 7 percent equates the desires of suppliers and demanders.

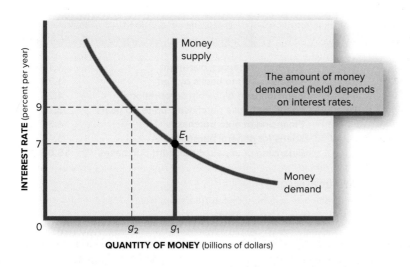

FIGURE 15.1
Money Market Equilibrium

All points on the money demand curve represent the quantity of money people are willing to hold (in cash or bank balances) at a specific interest rate.

The equilibrium interest rate occurs at the intersection (E_1) of the money supply and money demand curves. At that rate of interest, people are willing to hold as much money as is available. At any other interest rate (e.g., 9 percent), the quantity of money people are *willing* to hold won't equal the quantity available, and people will adjust their portfolios.

At any rate of interest other than 7 percent, the quantity of money demanded wouldn't equal the quantity supplied. Look at the imbalance that exists in Figure 15.1, for example, when the interest rate is 9 percent. At that rate, the quantity of money supplied (g_1 in Figure 15.1) exceeds the quantity demanded (g_2). All the money (g_1) must be held by someone, of course. But the demand curve indicates that people aren't *willing* to hold so much money at that interest rate (9 percent). People will adjust their portfolios by moving money out of cash and bank accounts into bonds or other assets that offer higher returns. This will tend to lower interest rates (recall that buying bonds tends to lower their yields). As interest rates drop, people are willing to hold more money. Ultimately we get to E_1, where the quantity of money demanded equals the quantity supplied. At that equilibrium, people are content with their portfolio choices.

Changing Interest Rates

The equilibrium rate of interest is subject to change. As we saw in Chapter 14, the Federal Reserve System can alter the money supply through changes in reserve requirements, changes in the discount rate, or open market operations. By implication, then, *the Fed can alter the equilibrium rate of interest.*

Figure 15.2 illustrates the potential impact of monetary policy on the equilibrium rate of interest. Assume that the money supply is initially at g_1 and the equilibrium interest rate is

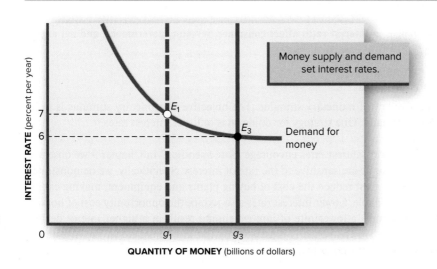

FIGURE 15.2
Changing the Rate of Interest

Changes in the money supply alter the equilibrium rate of interest. In this case, an increase in the money supply (from g_1 to g_3) lowers the equilibrium rate of interest (from 7 percent to 6 percent).

TABLE 15.2

The Hierarchy of Interest Rates

Interest rates reflect the risks and duration of loans. Because risks and loan terms vary greatly, dozens of different interest rates are available. Here are a few of the more common rates as of March 2020.

Interest Rate	Type of Loan	Rate
Federal funds rate	Interbank reserves, overnight	1.10%
Discount rate	Reserves lent to banks by Fed	1.75
Prime rate	Bank loans to blue-chip corporations	4.25
Mortgage rate	Loans for house purchases; up to 30 years	3.75
Auto loan	Financing of auto purchases	4.37
Consumer installment credit	Loans for general purposes	9.40
Credit cards	Financing of unpaid credit card purchases	15.05

Source: Federal Reserve (March 2020 rates).

7 percent, as indicated by point E_1. The Fed then increases the money supply to g_3 by lowering the reserve requirement, reducing the discount rate, or, most likely, purchasing additional bonds in the open market. This expansionary monetary policy brings about a new equilibrium at E_3. At this new intersection, the market rate of interest is only 6 percent. Hence, *by increasing the money supply, the Fed tends to lower the equilibrium rate of interest.* To put the matter differently, people are *willing* to hold larger money balances only at lower interest rates.

Were the Fed to reverse its policy and *reduce* the money supply, interest rates would rise. You can see this result in Figure 15.2 by observing the change in the rate of interest that occurs when the money supply *shrinks* from g_3 to g_1.

Federal Funds Rate. As we noted in Chapter 14, the most visible market signal of the Fed's activity is the **federal funds rate.** When the Fed injects or withdraws reserves from the banking system (via open market operations), the interest rate on interbank loans is most directly affected. Any change in the federal funds rate, moreover, is likely to affect a whole hierarchy of interest rates (see Table 15.2). *The federal funds rate reflects the cost of funds for banks.* When that cost decreases, banks respond by lowering the interest rates *they* charge to businesses (the prime rate), home buyers (the mortgage rate), and consumers (e.g., auto loans, installment credit, and credit cards).

federal funds rate: The interest rate for interbank reserve loans.

INTEREST RATES AND SPENDING

A change in interest rates isn't the end of this story. The ultimate goal of monetary policy is to alter macroeconomic outcomes: prices, output, employment. Those are the economic outcomes that we really care about. To alter them, the Fed must be able to shift aggregate demand. Hence, the next question is

- **How do changes in interest rates affect consumer, investor, government, and net export spending?**

Monetary Stimulus

Consider first a policy of monetary stimulus. The objective of monetary stimulus is to increase **aggregate demand.** One strategy for doing so is to lower interest rates.

aggregate demand (AD): The total quantity of output (real GDP) demanded at alternative price levels in a given time period, *ceteris paribus.*

Investment. Will lower interest rates encourage more spending? In Chapter 9 we observed that investment decisions are sensitive to the rate of interest. Specifically, we demonstrated that lower rates of interest reduce the cost of buying plants and equipment, making capital investment more profitable. Lower interest rates also reduce the opportunity cost of holding inventories. Accordingly, a lower rate of interest should result in a higher rate of desired investment spending. This response is illustrated by the movement down the investment demand curve in step 2 of Figure 15.3.

Step 1: An increase in the money supply lowers the rate of interest.

Step 2: Lower interest rates stimulate investment.

Step 3: More investment increases aggregate demand (including multiplier effects).

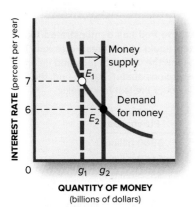
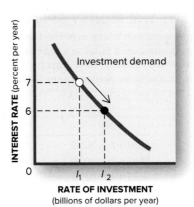
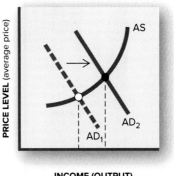

FIGURE 15.3

Monetary Stimulus

An increase in the money supply may reduce interest rates (step 1) and encourage more investment (step 2). The increase in investment will shift AD to the right and trigger multiplier effects that increase aggregate demand by an even larger amount (step 3).

Aggregate Demand. The increased investment brought about by lower interest rates represents an injection of new spending into the circular flow. That jump in spending will kick off multiplier effects and result in an even larger increase in aggregate demand. Step 3 in Figure 15.3 illustrates this increase by the rightward *shift* of the AD curve. Market participants, encouraged by lower interest rates, are now willing to buy more output at the prevailing price level.

Consumers too may change their behavior when interest rates fall. As interest rates fall, mortgage payments decline. Monthly payments on home equity and credit card balances may also decline. These lower interest changes free up billions of consumer dollars. This increased net cash flow and lower interest rates may encourage consumers to buy new cars, appliances, or other big-ticket items. State and local governments may also conclude that lower interest rates increase the desirability of bond-financed public works. All such responses add to aggregate demand.

From this perspective, *the Fed's goal of stimulating the economy is achieved in three distinct steps:*

- *An increase in the money supply.*
- *A reduction in interest rates.*
- *An increase in aggregate demand.*

This was the intent of the Fed's aggressive open market purchases in early 2020 (see Front Page Economics "Fed Opens the Money Spigots"). Note that the Fed announced it was *increasing* its purchases of bonds. As we observed in Chapter 14, increased open-market purchases by the Fed push bond prices *up* and their yields *down*. As bond yield declines, so do an array of interest rates (Table 15.2).

Quantitative Impact. Just how much stimulus can monetary policy create? According to former Fed Chairman Ben Bernanke, the impact of monetary policy can be impressive:

$$\text{Bernanke's policy guide:} \quad \frac{\frac{1}{4} \text{ point reduction in}}{\text{long-term interest rate}} = \frac{\$50 \text{ billion}}{\text{fiscal stimulus}}$$

By this rule of thumb, a full-point reduction in long-term interest rates would increase aggregate demand just as much as a $200 billion injection of new government spending.

FRONT PAGE ECONOMICS

FED OPENS THE MONEY SPIGOTS

In a series of bond purchases over the last few weeks, the Fed has demonstrated that it is willing to do whatever it takes to keep financial markets liquid and interest rates low. The Fed noted that "aggressive efforts must be taken . . . to limit the losses to jobs and incomes and to promote a swift recovery once the (COVID-19) disruptions abate." To that end, the Fed announced the following purchases of Treasury securities over the last few weeks:

Date	Purchases
March 24, 2020	$300 billion
March 30, 2020	$150 billion
April 1–6, 2020	$395 billion

These open-market purchases are flooding the financial markets with liquidity and bolstering investor confidence in the Fed as a strong backup to market disruptions.

Source: Federal Reserve news releases, March 24–April 7, 2020.

CRITICAL ANALYSIS: Open-market purchases reduce interest rates, encouraging market participants to borrow and spend more money. This **monetary stimulus** is intended to shift the AD curve rightward, setting off multiplier effects.

Monetary Restraint

Like fiscal policy, monetary policy is a two-edged sword, at times seeking to increase aggregate demand and at other times trying to restrain it. When inflation threatens, the goal of monetary policy is to reduce the rate of total spending, which puts the Fed in the position of "leaning against the wind." If successful, the resulting reduction in spending will keep aggregate demand from increasing inflationary pressures.

Higher Interest Rates. The mechanics of monetary policy designed to combat inflation are similar to those used to fight unemployment; only the direction is reversed. In this case, we seek to discourage spending by increasing the rate of interest. The Fed can push interest rates up by *selling* bonds, *increasing* the discount rate, or *raising* the reserve requirement. All these actions reduce the money supply and help establish a new and higher equilibrium rate of interest (e.g., g_3 to g_1 in Figure 15.2).

The ultimate objective of a restrictive monetary policy is to reduce aggregate demand. For monetary restraint to succeed, spending behavior must be responsive to interest rates.

Reduced Aggregate Demand. Figure 15.3 showed the impact of reduced interest rates on investment and aggregate demand. The same figure can be used in reverse. If the interest rate rises from 6 to 7 percent, investment declines from I_2 to I_1 and the AD curve shifts *leftward*. At higher rates of interest, many marginal investments will no longer be profitable. Likewise, many consumers will decide that they can't afford the higher monthly payments associated with increased interest rates; purchases of homes, cars, and household appliances will be postponed. State and local governments may also decide to cancel or postpone bond-financed projects. Thus, *monetary restraint is achieved with*

- *A decrease in the money supply.*
- *An increase in interest rates.*
- *A decrease in aggregate demand.*

The resulting leftward shift of the AD curve lessens inflationary pressures.

POLICY CONSTRAINTS

The mechanics of monetary policy are simple enough. They won't always work as well as we might hope, however. Several constraints can limit the Fed's ability to alter the money supply, interest rates, or aggregate demand.

Constraints on Monetary Stimulus

Short- vs. Long-Term Rates. One of the most visible constraints on monetary policy is the distinction between short-term interest rates and long-term interest rates. Bernanke's policy guide (see "Quantitative Impact" in the previous section) focuses on changes in *long-term* rates like mortgages and installment loans. Yet the Fed's open market operations have the most direct effect on *short-term* rates (e.g., the overnight federal funds rate). As a consequence, *the success of Fed intervention depends in part on how well changes in long-term interest rates mirror changes in short-term interest rates.*

In 2001 the Fed reduced the federal funds rate by three full percentage points between January and September, the biggest reduction in short-term rates since 1994. Long-term rates fell much less, however. The interest rate on 30-year mortgages, for example, fell less than half a percentage point in the first few months of monetary stimulus.

The same thing happened when the Fed reversed direction in 2004–2006. The *short-run* fed funds rate was ratcheted up from 1.0 to 5.25 percent during that period—a huge increase. But *long*-term rates (e.g., 10-year Treasury bonds and home mortgages) rose only modestly. Fed Chairman Alan Greenspan characterized these disparate trends as a "conundrum."

The same "conundrum" frustrated Fed Chairman Bernanke in 2008. The Fed was successful in pushing the short-term federal funds rate down from 4.25 percent at the start of 2008 to near zero at year's end, but long-term mortgage and bond rates didn't drop nearly as much. Hence, the aggregate demand stimulus was less than hoped for.

Reluctant Lenders. There are several reasons why long-term rates might not closely mirror cuts in short-term rates. The first potential constraint is the willingness of private banks to increase their lending activity. The Fed can reduce the cost of funds to the banking system; the Fed can even reduce reserve requirements. But *the money supply won't increase unless banks lend more money.*

If the banks instead choose to accumulate excess reserves, the money supply won't increase as much as intended. We saw this happen in the Great Depression (Figure 14.2). This happened again in 2008–2014, when the Fed was trying to stimulate the economy. Despite three rounds of quantitative easing (QE1, QE2, and QE3)—massive open market purchases—banks were reluctant to increase their loan activity. Banks were trying to shore up their own equity and were wary of making any new loans that might not get repaid in a weak economy. In such cases, long-term rates stay relatively high even when short-term rates are falling. Rather than making new loans, the banks simply stockpiled their excess reserves (see Figure 14.2). At the beginning of 2015, banks held more than $2 trillion of excess reserves—more than at any other time in history.

Liquidity Trap. There are circumstances in which even *short-term* rates may not fall when the Fed wants them to. The possibility that interest rates may not respond to changes in the money supply is illustrated by the "liquidity trap." When interest rates are low, the opportunity cost of holding money is cheap. At such times people may decide to hold all the money they can get, waiting for income-earning opportunities to improve. Bond prices, for example, may be high and their yields low. Buying bonds at such times entails the risk of capital losses (when bond prices fall) and little reward (because yields are low). Accordingly, market participants may decide just to hold any additional money the Fed supplies in cash or bank balances. At this juncture—a phenomenon Keynes called (*a*) A liquidity trap can stop interest rates from falling.

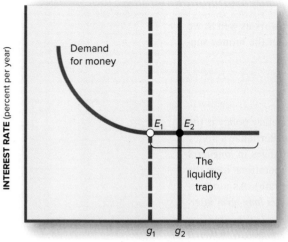

(*b*) Inelastic investment demand can also impede monetary policy.

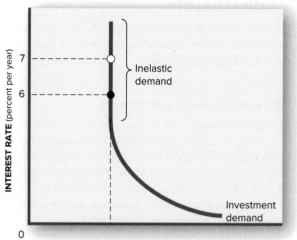

FIGURE 15.4

Constraints on Monetary Stimulus

(*a*) **Liquidity Trap** If people are willing to hold unlimited amounts of money (cash and bank balances) at the prevailing interest rate, increases in the money supply won't push interest rates lower. A liquidity trap—the horizontal segment of the money demand curve—prevents interest rates from falling (step 1 in Figure 15.3).

(*b*) **Inelastic Demand** A lower interest rate won't always stimulate investment. If investors have unfavorable expectations for future sales, small reductions in interest rates may not alter their investment decisions. Here the rate of investment remains constant when the interest rate drops from 7 to 6 percent. This kind of situation blocks the second step in the Keynesian approach to monetary policy (step 2 in Figure 15.3).

liquidity trap: The portion of the money demand curve that is horizontal; people are willing to hold unlimited amounts of money at some (low) interest rate.

the **liquidity trap**—further expansion of the money supply has no effect on the rate of interest. The horizontal section of the money demand curve in Figure 15.4*a* portrays this situation.

What happens to interest rates when the initial equilibrium falls into this trap? Nothing at all. Notice that the equilibrium rate of interest doesn't fall when the money supply is increased from g_1 to g_2 (Figure 15.4*a*). People are willing to hold all that additional money without a reduction in the rate of interest.

Low Expectations. Even if both short- and long-term interest rates do fall, we still have no assurance that aggregate demand will increase as expected. Keynes put great emphasis on *expectations*. Recall that **investment decisions are motivated not only by interest rates but by expectations as well.** During a recession—when unemployment is high and the rate of spending is low—corporations have little incentive to expand production capacity. With little expectation of future profit, investors are likely to be unimpressed by "cheap money" (low interest rates) and may decline to use the lending capacity that banks make available.

Investment demand that's slow to respond to the lure of cheap money is said to be *inelastic* because it won't expand. Consumers too are reluctant to borrow when current and future income prospects are uncertain or distinctly unfavorable. Accordingly, even if the Fed is successful in lowering interest rates, there's no assurance that lower interest rates will stimulate borrowing and spending. Such a reluctance to spend was evident in 2008–2014. Although the Fed managed to push interest rates down to historic lows, investors and consumers preferred to pay off old debts rather than incur new ones (see Front Page Economics "Consumers Not Responding to Low Interest Rates"). Expectations, not interest rates, dominated spending decisions.

Coronavirus Pandemic. Expectations played an even larger role during the coronavirus pandemic of early 2020. People were scared of contracting the virus in the marketplace. Furthermore, governments everywhere were telling people to stay at home and telling businesses to shut down. In that environment, lower interest rates weren't an effective incentive for coaxing consumers to spend more or businesses to invest more. Demand for money was pretty much inelastic.

The vertical portion of the investment demand curve in Figure 15.4b illustrates the possibility that investment spending may not respond at all to changes in the rate of interest. Notice that a reduction in the rate of interest from 7 percent to 6 percent doesn't increase investment spending. In this case, businesses are simply unwilling to invest any more funds. As a consequence, aggregate spending doesn't rise. The Fed's policy objective remains unfulfilled, even though the Fed has successfully lowered the rate of interest.

Time Lags. Even when expectations are good, businesses won't respond *instantly* to changes in interest rates. Lower interest rates make investments more profitable. But it still takes time to develop and implement new investments. Hence, *there is always a time lag between interest rate changes and investment responses.*

The same is true for consumers. Consumers don't rush out the door to refinance their homes or buy new ones the day the Fed reduces interest rates. They might start *thinking* about new financing, but they aren't likely to *do* anything for a while. It may take 6–12 months before market behavior responds to monetary policy.

Limits on Monetary Restraint

Expectations. Time lags and expectations could also limit the effectiveness of monetary restraint. In pursuit of "tight" money, the Fed can drain bank reserves and force interest rates higher. Yet market participants might continue to borrow and spend if high expectations for rising sales and profits overwhelm high interest rates in investment decisions. Consumers too might believe that future incomes will be sufficient to cover larger debts and higher interest charges. Both groups might foresee accelerating inflation that would make even high interest rates look cheap in the future.

Global Money. Market participants might also tap global sources of money. If money gets too tight in domestic markets, business may borrow funds from foreign banks or institutions. GM, Disney, ExxonMobil, Netflix, and other multinational corporations can borrow funds from foreign subsidiaries, banks, and even bond markets. As we saw in Chapter 14, market participants can also secure funds from nonbank sources in the United States. These nonbank and global lenders make it harder for the Fed to restrain aggregate demand.

How Effective? In view of all these constraints on monetary policies, some observers have concluded that monetary policy is an undependable policy lever. Keynes, for example, emphasized that monetary policy wouldn't be very effective in ending a deep recession. He believed that the combination of reluctant bankers, the liquidity trap, and low expectations would render monetary stimulus ineffective. Using monetary policy to stimulate the economy in such circumstances would be akin to "pushing on a string."

Alan Greenspan came to much the same conclusion in September 1992 when he said that further Fed stimulus would be ineffective in accelerating a recovery from the 1990–1991 recession. He believed, however, that earlier cuts in interest rates would help stimulate spending once banks, investors, and consumers gained confidence in the economic outlook.

The same kind of problem existed in 2001: The Fed's actions to reduce interest rates (11 times in as many months!) weren't enough to propel the economy forward in 2001–2002. Market participants had to recover their confidence in the future before they would start spending "cheap" money. The same lack of confidence limited the effectiveness of monetary stimulus in 2008–2016.

The COVID-19 pandemic created a different challenge for monetary policy. The Fed was successful in keeping interest rates at historically low levels by flooding financial markets with liquidity (via bond purchases). And those low interest rates were effective in maintaining demand for homes, cars, and other durable consumer products. But low interest rates alone weren't a sufficient incentive for consumers to resume shopping in the malls, going to nightclubs, attending concerts, dining in restaurants, or flying in airplanes. In fact, most of those activities were restricted by government fiat, imposing a *supply* constraint on market activity. Monetary stimulus alone couldn't push the economy out of a pandemic-caused recession.

The limitations on monetary *restraint* aren't considered as serious. The Fed has the power to reduce the money supply. If the money supply shrinks far enough, the rate of spending will have to slow down.

THE MONETARIST PERSPECTIVE

The Keynesian view of money emphasizes the role of interest rates in fulfilling the goals of monetary policy. *In the Keynesian model, changes in the money supply affect macro outcomes primarily through changes in interest rates.* The three-step sequence of (1) money supply change, (2) interest rate movement, and (3) aggregate demand shift makes monetary policy subject to several potential uncertainties. As we've seen, the economy doesn't always respond as expected to Fed policy.

An alternative view of monetary policy seizes on those occasional failures to offer a different explanation of how the money supply affects macro outcomes. The so-called *monetarist* school dismisses changes in short-term interest rates (e.g., the federal funds rate) as unpredictable and ineffective. They don't think real output levels are affected by monetary stimulus. As they see it, only the price level is affected by Fed policy, and then only by changes in the money supply. *Monetarists assert that monetary policy isn't an effective tool for fighting short-run business cycles, but it is a powerful tool for managing inflation.*

The Equation of Exchange

equation of exchange: Money supply (*M*) times velocity of circulation (*V*) equals level of aggregate spending (*P* × *Q*).

velocity of money (*V*): The number of times per year, on average, that a dollar is used to purchase final goods and services; *PQ* ÷ *M*.

Monetarists emphasize that the potential of monetary policy can be expressed in a simple equation called the **equation of exchange,** written as

$$MV = PQ$$

where *M* refers to the quantity of money in circulation and *V* to its **velocity** of circulation. Total spending in the economy is equal to the average price (*P*) of goods times the quantity

(*Q*) of goods sold in a period. This spending is financed by the supply of money (*M*) times the velocity of its circulation (*V*).

Suppose, for example, that only two participants are in the market and that the money supply consists of one crisp $20 bill. What's the limit to total spending in this case? If you answer "$20," you haven't yet grasped the nature of the circular flow.

Suppose I begin the circular flow by spending $20 on eggs, bacon, and a gallon of milk. The money I spend ends up in Farmer Brown's pocket because he is the only other market participant. Once in possession of the money, Farmer Brown may decide to satisfy his long-smoldering desire to learn something about economics and buy one of my books. If he acts on that decision, the $20 will return to me. At that point, both Farmer Brown and I have sold $20 worth of goods. Hence, $40 of total spending has been financed with one $20 bill.

As long as we keep using this $20 bill to buy goods and services from each other, we can continue to do business. Moreover, the faster we pass the money from hand to hand during any period of time, the greater the value of sales each of us can register. If the money is passed from hand to hand eight times, then I'll be able to sell $80 worth of textbooks and Farmer Brown will be able to sell $80 worth of produce during that period, for a total nominal output of $160. *The quantity of money in circulation and the velocity with which it travels (changes hands) in product markets will always be equal to the value of total spending and income (nominal GDP).* This relationship is summarized as

$$M \times V = P \times Q$$

In this case, the *equation of exchange* confirms that

$$\$20 \times 8 = \$160$$

The value of total sales for the year is $160.

Monetarists use the equation of exchange to simplify the explanation of how monetary policy works. There's no need, they argue, to follow the effects of changes in *M* through the money markets to interest rates and further to changes in total spending. The basic consequences of monetary policy are evident in the equation of exchange. The two sides of the equation of exchange must always be in balance. Hence, we can be absolutely certain that *if* **M** *increases, prices* (**P**) *or output* (**Q**) *must rise, or* **V** *must fall.*

The equation of exchange is an incontestable statement of how the money supply is related to macro outcomes. The equation itself, however, says nothing about *which* variables will respond to a change in the money supply. The *goal* of monetary policy is to change the macro outcomes on the right side of the equation. It's *possible,* however, that a change in *M* might be offset with a reverse change in *V,* leaving *P* and *Q* unaffected. Or it could happen that the *wrong* macro outcome is affected. Prices (*P*) might rise, for example, when we're trying to increase real output (*Q*).

Stable Velocity

Monetarists add some important assumptions to transform the equation of exchange from a simple identity to a behavioral *model* of macro performance. The first assumption is that the velocity of money (*V*) is stable. How fast people use their money balances depends on the institutional structure of money markets and people's habits. ATM machines on every corner and universal acceptance of Apple Pay would probably increase the rate of spending (velocity). But the institutional structure of markets doesn't change that fast. Nor are people's spending habits likely to change much in the short run. Accordingly, monetarists say a short-run increase in *M* won't be offset by a reduction in *V.* Instead the impact of an increased money supply will be transmitted to the right side of the equation of exchange, which means that **total spending must rise if the money supply (M) grows and V is stable.**

Money Supply Focus

From a monetarist perspective, there's no need to trace the impacts of monetary policy through interest rate movements. The focus on interest rates is a uniquely Keynesian perspective. Monetarists claim that interest rate movements are secondary to the major thrust of monetary policy. *As monetarists see it, changes in the money supply must alter total spending, regardless of how interest rates move.*

A monetarist perspective leads to a whole different strategy for the Fed. Because interest rates aren't part of the monetarist explanation of how monetary policy works, the Fed shouldn't try to manipulate interest rates; instead, it should focus on the money supply itself. Monetarists also argue that the Fed can't really control interest rates well because they depend on both the supply of and the demand for money. What the Fed *can* control is the supply of money, and the equation of exchange clearly shows that money matters.

Analysis: If the money supply shrinks (or its growth rate slows), price levels will rise less quickly. The Dropouts—Used by permission of The Estate of Howard Post.

"Natural" Rate of Unemployment

Some monetarists add yet another perspective to the equation of exchange. They assert that not only V but Q as well is stable. This is a pretty radical assertion. If it is true, then changes in the money supply (M) would affect only prices (P).

What does it mean for Q to be stable? The argument here is that the quantity of goods produced is primarily dependent on production capacity, labor market efficiency, and other "structural" forces. These structural forces establish a **"natural" rate of unemployment** that's fairly immune to short-run policy intervention. This is the *long-run* aggregate supply curve we first encountered in Chapter 8. From this perspective, there's no reason for producers to depart from this "natural" rate of output when the money supply increases. Producers are smart enough to know that both prices and costs will rise when spending increases. Hence, rising prices won't create any new profit incentives for increasing output. Firms will just continue producing at the "natural" rate with higher (nominal) prices and costs. As a result, increases in aggregate spending—whether financed by more M or faster V—aren't likely to alter real output levels. Q will stay constant.

If the quantity of real output is in fact stable, then P is the only thing that can change. Thus, *the most extreme monetarist perspective concludes that changes in the money supply affect prices only.* As the "simple economics" in the above cartoon suggests, a decrease in M should directly reduce the price level. When M increases, total spending rises, but the higher nominal value of spending is completely absorbed by higher prices. In this view, monetary policy affects only the rate of inflation. This is the kind of money-driven inflation that bedeviled George Washington's army (see Front Page Economics "'Not Worth a Continental': The U.S. Experience with Hyperinflation").

Figure 15.5 illustrates the extreme monetarist argument in the context of aggregate supply and demand. The assertion that real output is fixed at the natural rate of unemployment is reflected in the vertical, long-run aggregate supply curve. With real output stuck at Q^*, any increase in aggregate demand directly raises the price level.

natural rate of unemployment: The long-term rate of unemployment determined by structural forces in labor and product markets.

FRONT PAGE ECONOMICS

"NOT WORTH A CONTINENTAL": THE U.S. EXPERIENCE WITH HYPERINFLATION

The government of the United States had no means to pay for the Revolutionary War. Specifically, the federal government had no power to levy taxes that might transfer resources from the private sector to the public sector. Instead, it could only request the states to levy taxes of their own and contribute them to the war effort. The states were not very responsive, however: state contributions accounted for only 6 percent of federal revenues during the war years.

To pay for needed weapons and soldiers, the federal government had only two other options: either (1) borrow money or (2) create new money. When loans proved to be inadequate, the Continental Congress started issuing new paper money—the "Continental" dollar—in 1775. By the end of 1779, Congress had authorized issuance of more than $250 million in Continental dollars.

At first the paper money enabled George Washington's troops to acquire needed supplies, ammunition, and volunteers. But soon the flood of paper money inundated product markets. Wholesale prices of key commodities skyrocketed. Commodity prices *doubled* in 1776, in 1777, and again in 1778. Then prices increased *tenfold* in the next two years.

Many farmers and storekeepers refused to sell goods to the army in exchange for Continental dollars. Rapid inflation had taught them that the paper money George Washington's troops offered was nearly worthless. The expression "not worth a Continental" became a popular reference to things of little value.

The states tried price controls and even empowered themselves to seize needed war supplies. But nothing could stop the inflation fueled by the explosive increase in the money supply. Fortunately, the war ended before the economy collapsed. After the war, the U.S. Congress established a new form of money, and in 1787 it empowered the federal government to levy taxes and mint gold and silver coins.

—Sidney Ratner, James H. Soltow, and Richard Sylla

Source: Sidney Ratner, James H. Soltow, and Richard Sylla, *The Evolution of the American Economy,* 2nd ed. New York, NY: Macmillan Publishing Company, 1993. ©Richard Sylla. All rights reserved. Used with permission.

CRITICAL ANALYSIS: Rapid expansion of the **money supply** will push the price level up. As inflation accelerates, money becomes less valuable.

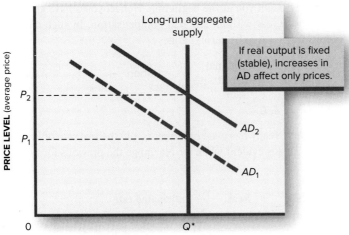

FIGURE 15.5
The Monetarist View

Monetarists argue that the rate of real output is set by structural factors. Furthermore, firms aren't likely to be fooled into producing more just because prices are rising because costs are likely to rise just as much. Hence, long-run aggregate supply remains at the "natural" level Q*. Any monetary-induced increases in aggregate demand, therefore, raise the price level (inflation) but not output.

Monetarist Policies

At first glance, the monetarist argument looks pretty slick. Keynesians worry about how the money supply affects interest rates, how interest rates affect spending, and how spending affects output. By contrast, monetarists point to a simple equation ($MV = PQ$) that produces straightforward responses to monetary policy.

There are fundamental differences between the two schools here, not only about how the economy works but also about how successful macro policy might be. To appreciate those differences, consider monetarist responses to inflationary and recessionary gaps.

Fighting Inflation. Consider again the options for fighting inflation. The policy goal is to reduce aggregate demand. From a Keynesian perspective, the way to achieve this reduction is to shrink the money supply and drive up interest rates. But monetarists argue that nominal interest rates are already likely to be high. Furthermore, if an effective anti-inflation policy is adopted, interest rates will come *down,* not go up. Yes, interest rates will come *down,* not go up, when the money supply is tightened, according to monetarists.

Real vs. Nominal Interest. To understand this monetarist conclusion, we have to distinguish between *nominal* interest rates and *real* ones. Nominal interest rates are the ones we actually see and pay. When a bank pays 5½ percent interest on your bank account, it's quoting (and paying) a nominal rate.

Real interest rates are never actually seen and rarely quoted. These are "inflation-adjusted" rates. Specifically, the **real interest rate** equals the nominal rate *minus* the anticipated rate of inflation; that is,

> **real interest rate:** The nominal interest rate minus the anticipated inflation rate.

$$\begin{matrix} \text{Real} & & \text{Nominal} & & \text{Anticipated} \\ \text{interest} & = & \text{interest} & - & \text{inflation} \\ \text{rate} & & \text{rate} & & \text{rate} \end{matrix}$$

Recall what inflation does to the purchasing power of the dollar: As inflation continues, each dollar purchases fewer goods and services. As a consequence, dollars borrowed today are of less real value when they're paid back later. The real rate of interest reflects this inflation adjustment.

Suppose that you lend someone $100 at the beginning of the year, at 8 percent interest. You expect to get more back at the end of the year than you start with. That "more" you expect refers to *real* goods and services, not just dollar bills. Specifically, you anticipate that when the loan is repaid with interest at the end of the year, you'll be able to buy more goods and services than you could at the beginning. This expectation of a *real* gain is at least part of the reason for making a loan.

Your expected gain won't materialize, however, if all prices rise by 8 percent during the year. If the inflation rate is 8 percent, you'll discover that $108 buys you no more at the end of the year than $100 would have bought you at the beginning. Hence, you'd have given up the use of your money for an entire year without any real compensation. In such circumstances, the *real* rate of interest turns out to be zero; that is,

$$\begin{matrix} \text{Real} & & 8\% \text{ nominal} & & 8\% \text{ inflation} \\ \text{interest} & = & \text{interest} & - & \text{rate} \\ \text{rate} & & \text{rate} & & \\ & = 0 & & & \end{matrix}$$

The nominal rate of interest, then, really has two components: (1) the real rate of interest and (2) an inflation adjustment. This is evident when we rearrange the previous formula as follows:

$$\begin{matrix} \text{Nominal} & & \text{Real} & & \text{Anticipated rate} \\ \text{interest rate} & = & \text{interest rate} & + & \text{of inflation} \end{matrix}$$

If the real rate of interest was 4 percent and an inflation rate of 9 percent was expected, the nominal rate of interest would be 13 percent. If inflationary expectations *declined,* the *nominal* interest rate would *fall.* If the real interest rate is 4 percent and anticipated inflation falls from 9 to 6 percent, the nominal interest rate would decline from 13 to 10 percent.

A central assumption of the monetarist perspective is that the real rate of interest is fairly stable. This is a critical point. *If the real rate of interest is stable, then changes in the nominal interest rate reflect only changes in anticipated inflation.* From this perspective, high nominal rates of interest are a symptom of inflation, not a cure. Indeed, high nominal rates may even look cheap if inflationary expectations are worsening faster than interest rates are rising. This was the case in Zimbabwe in 2019, when the nominal interest rate rose to 70 percent (see World View "Zimbabwe Raises Key Interest Rate to 70%").

WORLD VIEW

ZIMBABWE RAISES KEY INTEREST RATE TO 70%

Harare, Zimbabwe's central bank today raised its key interest rate from 50 percent to 70 percent. The governor of the Reserve Bank of Zimbabwe said the higher rate was intended to slow consumer spending, increase foreign buying of Zimbabwean dollars, and slow the rate of inflation, currently running at approximately 200 percent a year.

Source: News reports of September 12–15, 2019.

CRITICAL ANALYSIS: Higher interest rates are intended to discourage spending and shift the AD curve to the left. But higher **nominal interest rates** may not restrain spending if people expect higher inflation.

Consider the implications of all this for monetary policy. Suppose we want to close an inflationary GDP gap. Monetarists and Keynesians agree that a reduced money supply (*M*) will deflate total spending. But Keynesians rely on a "quick fix" of *higher* interest rates to slow consumption and investment spending. Monetarists, by contrast, assert that nominal interest rates will *fall* if the Fed tightens the money supply. Once market participants are convinced that the Fed is going to reduce money supply growth, inflationary expectations diminish. When inflationary expectations diminish, nominal interest rates will begin to fall.

Short- vs. Long-Term Rates (Again). The monetarist argument helps resolve the "conundrum" that puzzled former Fed Chairman Alan Greenspan and bedeviled his successor, Ben Bernanke—that is, the contradictory movements of short-term and long-term interest rates. As we observed earlier, short-run rates (like the federal funds rate) are very responsive to Fed intervention. But long-term rates are much slower to respond. This suggests that banks and borrowers look beyond current economic conditions in making long-term financial commitments.

If the Fed is reducing money supply growth, short-term rates may rise quickly. But long-term rates won't increase unless market participants expect inflation to worsen. Given the pivotal role of long-term rates in investment decisions, the Fed may have to stall GDP growth—even spark a recession—to restrain aggregate demand enough to stop prices from rising. Rather than take such risks, *monetarists advocate steady and predictable changes in the money supply.* Such a policy, they believe, would reduce uncertainties and thus stabilize both long-term interest rates and GDP growth.

Fighting Unemployment. The link between anticipated inflation and nominal interest rates also constrains monetary stimulus. The Keynesian cure for a recession is to expand M and lower interest rates. But monetarists fear that an increase in M will lead—via the equation of exchange—to *higher P.* If everyone believed this would happen, then an unexpectedly large increase in M would immediately raise people's inflationary expectations. Even if short-term interest rates fell, long-term interest rates might actually rise. This would defeat the purpose of monetary stimulus.

From a monetarist perspective, expansionary monetary policies aren't likely to lead us out of a recession. On the contrary, such policies might heap inflation problems on top of our unemployment woes. All monetary policy should do, say the monetarists, is ensure a stable and predictable rate of growth in the money supply. Then people could concentrate on real production decisions without worrying so much about fluctuating prices.

THE CONCERN FOR CONTENT

Monetary policy, like fiscal policy, can affect more than just the *level* of total spending. We must give some consideration to the impact of Federal Reserve actions on the *content* of the GDP if we're going to be responsive to the "second crisis" of economic theory.[1]

The Mix of Output

Both Keynesians and monetarists agree that monetary policy will affect nominal interest rates. When interest rates change, not all spending decisions will be affected equally. High interest rates don't deter consumers from buying pizzas, but they do deter purchases of homes, cars, and other big-ticket items typically financed with loans. Hence, the housing and auto industries bear a disproportionate burden of restrictive monetary policy. Accordingly, when the Fed pursues a policy of tight money—high interest rates and limited lending capacity—it not only restrains total spending but reduces the share of housing and autos in that spending. Utility industries, public works projects, and state and local finances are also disproportionately impacted by monetary policy.

In addition to altering the content of output, monetary policy affects the competitive structure of the market. When money is tight, banks must ration available credit among loan applicants. Large and powerful corporations aren't likely to run out of credit because banks will be hesitant to incur their displeasure and lose their business. Thus, General Motors and Google stand a much better chance of obtaining tight money than does the corner grocery store. Moreover, if bank lending capacity becomes too small, GM and Google can always resort to the bond market and borrow money directly from the public. Small businesses seldom have such an alternative.

Income Redistribution

Monetary policy also affects the distribution of income. When interest rates fall, borrowers pay smaller interest charges. On the other hand, lenders get smaller interest payments. Hence, a lower interest rate redistributes income from lenders to borrowers. When interest rates declined sharply in 2008–2009, home owners refinanced their mortgages and saved billions of dollars in interest payments. The decline in interest rates, however, *reduced* the income of retired persons, who depend heavily on interest payments from certificates of deposit, bonds, and other assets. Money supply increases also push up stock and bond prices, disproportionately benefiting higher-income households.

---

[1]See the quotation from Joan Robinson in Chapter 11, calling attention to the exclusive focus of economists on the level of economic activity (the "first crisis"), to the neglect of content (the "second crisis").

DECISIONS FOR TOMORROW

Which Policy Lever Should We Pull?

Our success in managing the macro economy of tomorrow depends on pulling the right policy levers at the right time. But which levers should be pulled? Keynesians and monetarists offer very different prescriptions for treating an ailing economy. Can we distill some usable policy guidelines from this discussion for policy decisions in the economy tomorrow?

The Policy Tools. The equation of exchange is a convenient summary of the differences between the Keynesian and monetarist perspectives. There's no disagreement about the equation itself: Aggregate spending ($M \times V$) *must* equal the value of total sales ($P \times Q$). *What Keynesians and monetarists argue about is which of the policy tools—M or V—is likely to be effective in altering aggregate spending.*

- *Monetarists* point to changes in the money supply (M) as the principal lever of macroeconomic policy. They assume V is reasonably stable.
- *Keynesian* fiscal policy *must* rely on changes in the velocity of money (V) because tax and expenditure policies have no direct impact on the money supply.

Crowding Out: Constant V. The extreme monetarist position that *only* money matters is based on the assumption that the velocity of money (V) is constant. *If V is constant, changes in total spending can come about only through changes in the money supply.* There are no other policy tools on the left side of the equation of exchange.

Think about an increase in government spending designed to stimulate the economy. How does the government pay for this fiscal policy stimulus? Monetarists argue that there are only two ways to pay for this increased expenditure (G): The government must either raise additional taxes or borrow more money. If the government raises taxes, the disposable income of consumers will be reduced, and private spending will fall. On the other hand, if the government *borrows* more money to pay for its expenditures, there will be less money available for loans to private consumers and investors. In either case, more government spending (G) implies less private spending (C or I). Thus, *increased G* effectively **"crowds out"** some C or I, leaving total spending unchanged. From this viewpoint, fiscal policy is ineffective; it can't even shift the aggregate demand curve. At best, fiscal policy can change the composition of demand and thus the mix of output. Only changes in M (monetary policy) can shift the aggregate demand curve.

Milton Friedman (1912-2006), formerly of the University of Chicago, championed the monetarist view with this argument:

> I believe that the state of the government budget matters; matters a great deal—for some things. The state of the government budget determines what fraction of the nation's income is spent through the government and what fraction is spent by individuals privately. The state of the government budget determines what the level of our taxes is, how much of our income we turn over to the government. The state of the government budget has a considerable effect on interest rates. If the federal government runs a large deficit, that means the government has to borrow in the market, which raises the demand for loanable funds and so tends to raise interest rates.
>
> If the government budget shifts to a surplus, that adds to the supply of loanable funds, which tends to lower interest rates. It was no surprise to those of us who stress money that enactment of the surtax was followed by a decline in interest rates. That's precisely what we had predicted and what our analysis leads us to predict. But—and I come to the main point—in my opinion, the state of the budget by itself has no significant effect on the course of nominal income, on inflation, on deflation, or on cyclical fluctuations.[2]

Continued

crowding out: A reduction in private sector borrowing (and spending) caused by increased government borrowing.

[2]Milton Friedman and Walter H. Heller, *Monetary vs. Fiscal Policy* (New York, NY: W.W. Norton & Company, 1969), pp. 50–51.

Keynes: *V* Changes. Keynesians reply that the alleged constant velocity of money is a monetarist's pipe dream. Some even argue that the velocity of money is so volatile that changes in *V* can completely offset changes in *M,* leaving us with the proposition that money doesn't matter.

The liquidity trap illustrates the potential for *V* to change. Keynes argued that people tend to accumulate money balances—slow their rate of spending—during recessions. *A slowdown in spending implies a reduction in the velocity of money.* Indeed, in the extreme case of the liquidity trap, the velocity of money falls toward zero. Under these circumstances, changes in *M* (monetary policy) won't influence total spending. The velocity of money falls as rapidly as *M* increases. On the other hand, increased government spending (fiscal policy) can stimulate aggregate spending by putting idle money balances to work (thereby increasing *V*). Changes in fiscal policy will also influence consumer and investor expectations, and thereby further alter the rate of aggregate spending.

How Fiscal Policy Works: Two Views. Tables 15.3 and 15.4 summarize these different perspectives on fiscal and monetary policy. The first table evaluates fiscal policy from both Keynesian and monetarist viewpoints. The central issue is whether and how a change in government spending (*G*) or taxes (*T*) will alter macroeconomic outcomes. Keynesians assert that aggregate demand will be affected as the velocity of money (*V*) changes. Monetarists say no because they anticipate an unchanged *V.*

If aggregate demand isn't affected by a change in *G* or *T,* then fiscal policy won't affect prices (*P*) or real output (*Q*). Thus monetarists conclude that fiscal policy isn't a viable tool for combating either inflation or unemployment. By contrast, Keynesians believe *V will* change and that output and prices will respond accordingly.

Insofar as interest rates are concerned, monetarists recognize that nominal interest rates will be affected (read Friedman's quote again), but *real* rates won't be. Real interest rates depend on real output and growth, both of which are seen as immune to fiscal policy. Keynesians see less impact on nominal interest rates and more on real interest rates.

Do Changes in G or T Affect	Monetarist View	Keynesian View
1. Aggregate demand?	No (stable *V* causes crowding out)	Yes (*V* changes)
2. Prices?	No (aggregate demand not affected)	Maybe (if at capacity)
3. Real output?	No (aggregate demand not affected)	Yes (output responds to demand)
4. Nominal interest rates?	Yes (crowding out)	Maybe (may alter demand for money)
5. Real interest rates?	No (determined by real growth)	Yes (real growth and expectations may vary)

TABLE 15.3

How Fiscal Policy Matters: Monetarist vs. Keynesian Views

Monetarists and Keynesians have very different views on the impact of fiscal policy. Monetarists assert that changes in government spending (G) and taxes (T) don't alter the velocity of money (V). As a result, fiscal policy alone can't alter total spending. Keynesians reject this view, arguing that V is changeable. They claim that tax cuts and increased government spending increase the velocity of money and so alter total spending.

Do Changes in *M* Affect	Monetarist View	Keynesian View
1. Aggregate demand?	Yes (*V* stable)	Maybe (*V* may change)
2. Prices?	Yes (*V* and *Q* stable)	Maybe (*V* and *Q* may change)
3. Real output?	No (rate of unemployment determined by structural forces)	Maybe (output responds to demand)
4. Nominal interest rates?	Yes (but direction unknown)	Maybe (liquidity trap)
5. Real interest rates?	No (depends on real growth)	Maybe (real growth may vary)

TABLE 15.4

How Money Matters: Monetarist vs. Keynesian Views

Because monetarists believe that *V* is stable, they assert that changes in the money supply (*M*) must alter total spending. But all the monetary impact is reflected in prices and nominal interest rates; *real* output and interest rates are unaffected.

Keynesians think that *V* is variable and thus that changes in *M* might *not* alter total spending. If monetary policy does alter aggregate spending, however, Keynesians expect all outcomes to be affected.

What all this boils down to is this: Fiscal policy, by itself, will be effective only if it can alter the velocity of money. *How well fiscal policy works depends on how much the velocity of money can be changed by government tax and spending decisions.*

How Monetary Policy Works: Two Views. Table 15.4 offers a similar summary of monetary policy. This time the positions of monetarists and Keynesians are reversed, or nearly so. Monetarists say a change in *M* must alter total spending ($P \times Q$) because *V* is stable. Keynesians assert that *V* may vary, so they aren't convinced that monetary policy will always work. The heart of the controversy is again the velocity of money. Monetary policy works as long as *V* is stable, or at least predictable. *How well monetary policy works depends on how stable or predictable* V *is.*

Once the central role of velocity is understood, everything else falls into place. Monetarists assert that prices but not output will be directly affected by a change in *M* because the right side of the equation of exchange contains only two variables (*P* and *Q*), and one of them (*Q*) is assumed to be unaffected by monetary policy. Keynesians, by contrast, aren't so sure that prices will be affected by *M* or that real output won't be. It all depends on *V* and the responsiveness of *P* and *Q* to changes in aggregate spending.

Finally, monetarists predict that nominal interest rates will respond to changes in *M*, although they're not sure in what direction. It depends on how inflationary expectations adapt to changes in the money supply. Keynesian economists aren't so sure nominal interest rates will change but are sure about the direction if they do.

Is Velocity Stable? Tables 15.3 and 15.4 highlight *the velocity of money as a critical determinant of policy impact.* The critical question appears to be whether *V* is stable. Why hasn't someone answered this simple question and resolved the debate over fiscal versus monetary policy?

Long-Run Stability. The velocity of money (*V*) turns out, in fact, to be quite stable over long periods of time. Over the past 30 years, the velocity of money (M2) has averaged

Continued

about 1.64, as Figure 15.6 illustrates. Moreover, the range of velocity has been fairly narrow, extending from a low of 1.56 in 1987 to a high of 2.05 in 1997. Monetarists conclude that the historical pattern justifies the assumption of a stable V.

Short-Run Instability. Keynesians reply that monetarists are farsighted and so fail to see significant short-run variations in V. The difference between a velocity of 1.56 and velocity of 2.05 translates into hundreds of billions of dollars in aggregate demand. Moreover, there's a pattern to short-run variations in V: Velocity tends to decline in recessions (see Figure 15.6). As the Great Recession of 2008–2009 unfolded, the velocity of money declined steadily from 1.90 in 2008 to a new low of 1.50 in 2015. That was a decline of more than 20 percent in the velocity of money. The magnitude of that decline in V outstripped the Fed's increase in M, rendering monetary policy fairly ineffective.

This velocity constraint was evident again during the COVID-19 pandemic. The Fed was flooding the markets with liquidity and low interest rates. But people were afraid – and even prohibited – to go shopping or attend entertainment events. They simply weren't spending their money as fast as usual. As a result, the velocity of money tumbled from 1.442 in 2019 to a historic low of 1.102 in early 2020 (see Figure 15.6). That 24 percent decline in velocity offset much of the increase in M. This was a situation in which fiscal stimulus was sorely needed to increase V.

Policy Targets. The differing views of monetarists and Keynesians clearly lead to different conclusions about which policy lever to pull.

Monetarist Advice: Target the Money Supply. The monetarists' policy advice to the Fed is straightforward. *Monetarists favor fixed money supply targets.* They believe that V is stable in the long run and unpredictable in the short run. Hence, the safest course of action is to focus on M. All the Fed has to do is announce its intention to increase the money supply by some fixed amount (such as 3 percent per year), then use its central banking powers to hit that money growth target.

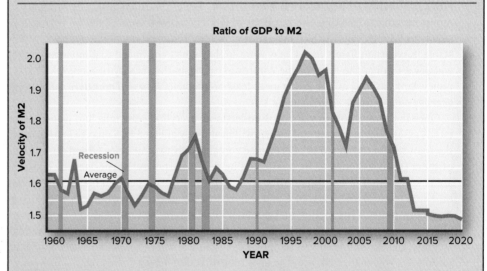

FIGURE 15.6
The Velocity of M2

The velocity of money (the ratio of GDP to M2) averages about 1.64. However, *V* appears to decline in recessions. Keynes urged the use of fiscal stimulus to boost *V*. Monetarists caution that short-run changes in *V* are too unpredictable.

Source: Federal Reserve Bank of St. Louis.

Keynesian Advice: Target Interest Rates. *Keynesians reject fixed money supply targets,* favoring more flexibility in control of the money supply. In their view, a fixed money supply target would render monetary policy useless in combating cyclical swings of the economy. Keynesians prefer the risks of occasional policy errors to the straitjacket of a fixed money supply target. *Keynesians advocate targeting interest rates, not the money supply.* Keynesians also advocate liberal use of the fiscal policy lever.

Inflation Targeting. In the past, the Fed has tried both monetarist and Keynesian strategies for managing aggregate demand, depending on the needs of the economy and the convictions of the Fed chair. The current chair, Jay Powell, isn't committed to either the monetarist or Keynesian perspective. Instead he tries to walk a thin line between these perspectives. Like his predecessors, Powell believes that price stability is the Fed's primary goal. The Fed's goal is to keep the inflation rate below the 2–3 percent range. If prices stay below that target, the Fed has typically put monetary policy on autopilot without worrying about constant adjustments of its policy tools.

What market participants like about this **inflation targeting** strategy is that it appears to offer greater predictability about whether and how the Fed will act. Critics point out, though, that *future* inflation, not *past* inflation, is the central policy concern. Because today's price movements may or may not be precursors of future inflation, the decision to pull monetary levers is still a judgment call.

inflation targeting: The use of an inflation ceiling ("target") to signal the need for monetary-policy adjustments.

Employment Targeting. Further complicating the Fed's task of fighting inflation is a second goal: full employment. It's not enough to keep prices from rising; we also want to create jobs and grow the economy. In the Great Recession of 2008–2009, inflation was a remote worry, but high unemployment was a huge problem. In response, the Fed decided to adopt **employment targeting** as a second component of its policy strategy. In December 2012, the Fed announced that its employment target was a 6.5 percent rate of unemployment. Over the next five years, the Fed kept the federal funds rate close to zero and the unemployment rate fell to below 4 percent.

employment targeting: The use of an unemployment-rate threshold (6.5 percent) to signal the need for monetary stimulus.

The twin guidelines of inflation targeting and employment targeting appear to simplify monetary policy. If inflation exceeds 2–3 percent, step on the monetary brakes. If unemployment exceeds 6.5 percent, step on the monetary accelerator. In reality, policy decisions aren't that easy. As we have seen (e.g., Figure 11.4), inflation can accelerate long before full employment is reached. So inflation targeting and employment targeting may give conflicting signals about what policy to pursue.

This was clearly the case in 2018: The Fed was worried about rising prices and began to tap on the monetary brakes. President Trump didn't think inflation was a problem and wanted more monetary stimulus. He claimed that "the Fed is way off-base with what they are doing" and even expressed regret about nominating Jay Powell to be the Fed chair. Such disagreements about monetary policy are sure to continue in the economy tomorrow, no matter who the president and the Fed chair are.

SUMMARY

- The essence of monetary policy lies in the Federal Reserve's control over the money supply. By altering the money supply, the Fed can determine the amount of purchasing power available.   **LO15-2**
- There are sharp disagreements about how monetary policy works. Keynesians argue that monetary policy works indirectly through its effects on interest rates and spending. Monetarists assert that monetary policy has more direct and more certain impacts, particularly on price levels.   **LO15-4**

- In the Keynesian view, the demand for money is important. This demand reflects desires to hold money (in cash or bank balances) for transactions, precautionary, and speculative purposes. The interaction of money supply and money demand determines the equilibrium rate of interest.   **LO15-1**
- From a Keynesian perspective, the impact of monetary policy on the economy occurs in three distinct steps: (1) changes in the money supply alter interest rates; (2) changes in interest rates alter spending plans; and (3) the change in desired spending alters (shifts) aggregate demand.   **LO15-2**

- For Keynesian monetary policy to be fully effective, interest rates must be responsive to changes in the money supply, and spending must be responsive to changes in interest rates. Neither condition is assured. In a liquidity trap, people are willing to hold unlimited amounts of money at some low rate of interest. The interest rate won't fall below this level as the money supply increases. Also, investor expectations of sales and profits may override interest rate considerations in investment decisions.   **LO15-3**
- Fed policy has the most direct impact on short-term interest rates, particularly the overnight federal funds rate. Long-term rates are less responsive to open market operations.   **LO15-3**
- The monetarist school emphasizes long-term linkages. Using the equation of exchange ($MV = PQ$) as a base, monetarists assert that the velocity of money (V) is stable, so that changes in M must influence ($P \times Q$). Monetarists focus on the money supply; Keynesians, on interest rates.   **LO15-4**
- Some monetarists also argue that the level of real output (Q) is set by structural forces, as illustrated by the vertical, long-run aggregate supply curve. Q is therefore insensitive to changes in aggregate spending. If both V and Q are constant, changes in M directly affect P.   **LO15-4**
- Monetary policy attempts to influence total expenditure by changing M and will be fully effective only if V is constant. Fiscal policy attempts to influence total expenditure by changing V and will be fully effective only if M doesn't change in the opposite direction. The controversy over the effectiveness of fiscal versus monetary policy depends on whether the velocity of money (V) is stable or, instead, is subject to policy influence.   **LO15-4**
- The velocity of money is more stable over long periods of time than over short periods. Keynesians conclude that this makes fiscal policy more powerful in the short run. Monetarists conclude that the unpredictability of short-run velocity makes any short-run policy risky.   **LO15-4**
- Inflation targeting signals monetary restraint when inflation rises above a policy-set ceiling ("target"), currently 2–3 percent.   **LO15-2**
- Employment targeting signals the need for monetary stimulus when the unemployment rate is above 6.5 percent.   **LO15-2**

Key Terms

monetary policy	speculative demand for money	natural rate of unemployment
interest rate	equilibrium rate of interest	real interest rate
money supply (M1, M2)	federal funds rate	crowding out
demand for money	aggregate demand (AD)	inflation targeting
portfolio decision	liquidity trap	employment targeting
transactions demand for money	equation of exchange	
precautionary demand for money	velocity of money (V)	

Questions for Discussion

1. What proportions of your money balance are held for transactions, precautionary, and speculative purposes? Can you think of any other purposes for holding money?   **LO15-1**
2. How would people "adjust their portfolios" in Figure 15.1?   **LO15-1**
3. Why do high interest rates so adversely affect the demand for housing and yet have so little influence on the demand for pizzas?   **LO15-2**
4. If the Federal Reserve banks mailed everyone a brand-new $100 bill, what would happen to prices, output, and income? Illustrate your answer by using the equation of exchange.   **LO15-2**
5. Can there be any inflation without an increase in the money supply? How?   **LO15-4**
6. When prices started doubling (see Front Page Economics "'Not Worth a Continental': The U.S. Experience with Hyperinflation"), why didn't the Continental Congress print even *more* money so Washington's army could continue to buy supplies? What brings an end to such "inflation financing"?   **LO15-2**
7. When the interest rate rose to 70 percent in Zimbabwe, why would anyone borrow money for investment or consumption (see World View "Zimbabwe Raises Key Interest Rate to 70%")?   **LO15-3**
8. Why did the stock market rally when the Fed announced that it was purchasing nearly $1 trillion in Treasury bonds (see Front Page Economics "Fed Opens the Money Spigots")?   **LO15-2**
9. When banks are reluctant to use their lending capacity as in 2012, what do they do with their increased reserves?   **LO15-3**
10. If mortgage rates fell to 0 percent ("free money"), why might consumers still hesitate to borrow money to buy a home?   **LO15-3**
11. What should the Fed do when prices are rising at a 3.5 percent rate and unemployment is at 7 percent?   **LO15-2**

PROBLEMS FOR CHAPTER 15

LO15-1 1. In Table 15.1, what is the implied price of holding money in a checking account rather than investing in Treasury bonds?

LO15-1 2. According to World View "Zimbabwe Raises Key Interest Rate to 70%," after the key interest rate was raised, what was:
  (*a*) The nominal interest rate?
  (*b*) The real interest rate?

LO15-2 3. Suppose home owners owe $8 trillion in mortgage loans.
  (*a*) If the mortgage interest rate is 4 percent, approximately how much are home owners paying in annual mortgage interest?
  (*b*) If the interest rate drops to 3.5 percent, by how much will annual interest payments decline?
  (*c*) How will this change in the interest rate impact aggregate demand?

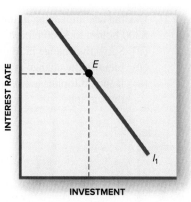

LO15-2 4. According to Bernanke's policy guide, what is the fiscal policy equivalent of a 0.25 percent cut in long-term interest rates?

LO15-2 5. Illustrate the effects on investment of
  (*a*) An interest rate cut (point *A*).
  (*b*) An interest rate cut accompanied by decreased sales expectations (point *B*).

LO15-2 6. How much would the Fed have had to reduce long-term interest rates to get the same stimulus as President Trump's planned $200 billion increase in government spending?

LO15-4 7. Suppose that an economy is characterized by
$$M = \$14 \text{ trillion}$$
$$V = 1.6$$
$$P = 1.0$$

  (*a*) What is the real value of output (*Q*)?

  Now assume that the Fed increases the money supply by 10 percent and velocity remains unchanged.
  (*b*) If the price level remains constant, by how much will real output increase?
  (*c*) If, instead, real output is fixed at the natural level of unemployment, by how much will prices rise?
  (*d*) By how much would *V* have to fall to offset the increase in *M*?

LO15-1 8. If the nominal rate of interest is 6 percent and the real rate of interest is 3 percent, what rate of inflation is anticipated?

LO15-2 9. Suppose that the Fed decided to purchase $100 billion worth of government securities in the open market. What impact would this action have on the economy? Specifically, answer the following questions:
  (*a*) How will M1 be affected initially?
  (*b*) By how much will the banking system's lending capacity increase if the reserve requirement is 20 percent?
  (*c*) Must interest rates rise or fall to induce investors to utilize this expanded lending capacity?
  (*d*) By how much will aggregate demand increase if investors borrow and spend all the newly available credit?
  (*e*) Under what circumstances ("recession" or "inflation") would the Fed be pursuing such an open market policy?
  (*f*) To attain those same objectives, what should the Fed do ("increase" or "decrease") with the
    (*i*) Discount rate?
    (*ii*) Reserve requirement?

LO15-3 10. The following data describe market conditions:

Money supply (in billions)	$100	$200	$300	$400	$ 500	$ 600	$ 700
Interest rate	8.0	7.5	7.0	6.5	6.0	5.5	5.5
Rate of investment (in billions)	$ 12	$ 12	$ 15	$ 16	$16.5	$16.5	$16.5

    (*a*) At what rate of interest does the liquidity trap emerge?
    (*b*) At what rate of interest does investment demand become totally inelastic?

LO15-3 11. Use the accompanying graphs to show what happens in the economy when *M* increases from
    $300 billion to $400 billion.
    (*a*) Show the change in *M* on the first graph.
    (*b*) Identify the change in interest rate on the second graph.
    (*c*) If the multiplier is 1.5, show the cumulative effect of this change in *M* on AD in the
    third graph.

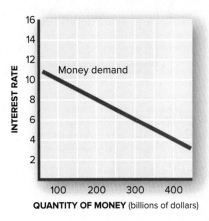 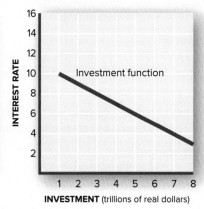 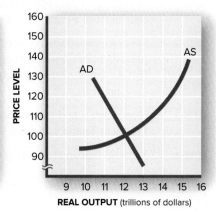

LO15-3 12. According to Figure 15.6, the velocity of money declined from 1.90 in 2008 to 1.40 in 2016. By
    what percent would *M* have to increase in order to fully offset this decline in *V*?

LO15-4 13. *Decisions for Tomorrow:* Match the statement with either a monetarist or Keynesian perspective.
    (*a*) The interest rate should be targeted, not the money supply.
    (*b*) A slowdown in spending implies a reduction in the velocity of money.
    (*c*) There should be fixed money supply targets.

PART

6

Comstock Images/Getty Images

Dennis MacDonald/Alamy Stock photo

SUPPLY-SIDE OPTIONS

Fiscal and monetary policies attempt to alter macro outcomes by managing aggregate demand. Supply-side policies focus instead on possibilities for shifting the aggregate *supply* curve. In the short run, any increase in aggregate supply promotes more output and less inflation. Supply-siders also emphasize how rightward shifts of aggregate supply are critical to long-run economic growth. Chapter 16 focuses on short-run supply-side options; Chapter 17 takes the long-run view.

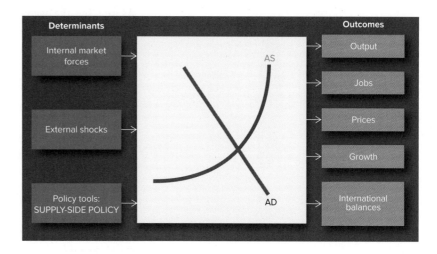

Supply-Side Policy: Short-Run Options

LEARNING OBJECTIVES

After reading this chapter, you should know

LO16-1 Why the short-run AS curve slopes upward.

LO16-2 How an unemployment–inflation trade-off arises.

LO16-3 How shifts of the aggregate supply curve affect macro outcomes.

LO16-4 The tools of supply-side policy.

The coronavirus pandemic of 2020 was a grim reminder that we can't solve all our macroeconomic problems with fiscal and monetary policies. The policy options that we have reviewed in the last few chapters focus on the *demand* side of the market. The basic premise of those policy approaches is that our macro goals can be achieved by shifting the aggregate demand curve to a desirable macro equilibrium. But what about the *supply* side of the market? The coronavirus forced companies to suspend production, transportation networks to shut down, schools to close, and workers to stay at home. In other words, the coronavirus was a shock to the *supply* side of the economy. No amount of fiscal or monetary stimulus could have overcome those supply disruptions.

What natural disasters like the coronavirus pandemic remind us is that the supply side of the economy merits our policy attention as well. The aggregate demand curve isn't the only game in town; the aggregate supply curve is important as well. In addition to natural disasters, lots of events and policies shape and shift the aggregate supply curve. Supply-side policy is focused on understanding how and why aggregate supply conditions change—and what policies can manipulate the aggregate supply curve to our macro advantage. Our focus is on two broad questions:

- **How does the aggregate supply curve affect macro outcomes?**
- **How can the aggregate supply curve be shifted?**

As we'll see, the aggregate supply curve plays a critical role in determining our ability to achieve the goals of full employment and price stability.

AGGREGATE SUPPLY

The impetus for examining the supply side of the macro economy sprang up in the stagflation of the 1970s. **Stagflation** occurs when both unemployment *and* inflation increase at the same time. From 1973 to 1974, for example, consumer price inflation surged from 8.7 to 12.3 percent. At the same time, the unemployment rate jumped from 4.9 to 5.6 percent. How could this happen? *No shift of the aggregate demand curve can increase inflation and unemployment at the same time.* If aggregate demand increases (shifts right), the price level may rise, but unemployment should decline with increased output. If aggregate demand decreases (shifts left), inflation should subside, but unemployment should increase. In other words, demand-side theories predict that inflation and unemployment move in *opposite* directions in the short run. When this didn't happen, an alternative explanation was sought. The explanation was found on the supply side of the macro economy. Two critical clues were (1) the shape of the **aggregate supply** curve and (2) potential AS shifts.

stagflation: The simultaneous occurrence of substantial unemployment and inflation.

SHAPE OF THE AS CURVE

As we've seen, the basic short-run objective of fiscal and monetary policy is to attain full employment and price stability. The strategy is to shift the aggregate demand curve to a more favorable position. Now the question turns to the *response* of producers to an aggregate demand shift. Will they increase real output? Raise prices? Or some combination of both?

The answer is reflected in the shape of the aggregate supply curve: *The response of producers to an AD shift is expressed in the slope and position of the aggregate supply curve.* Until now we've used a generally upward-sloping AS curve to depict aggregate supply. Now we'll consider a range of different supply responses.

aggregate supply (AS): The total quantity of output (real GDP) producers are willing and able to supply at alternative price levels in a given time period, *ceteris paribus.*

Three Views of AS

Figure 16.1 illustrates three very different supply behaviors.

Keynesian AS. Figure 16.1*a* depicts what we earlier called the "naive" Keynesian view. Recall that Keynes was primarily concerned with the problem of unemployment. He didn't think there was much risk of inflation in the depths of a recession. He expected producers to increase output, not prices, when aggregate demand expanded. This expectation is illustrated by a *horizontal* AS curve. When fiscal or monetary stimulus shifts the AD curve rightward (e.g., AD_1 to AD_2 in Figure 16.1*a*), output (Q) rises but not the price level (P). Only when capacity (Q^*) is reached do prices start rising abruptly (AD_2 to AD_3).

Monetarist AS. The monetarist view of supply behavior is very different. In the most extreme monetarist view, real output remains at its "natural" rate, regardless of fiscal or monetary interventions. Rising prices don't entice producers to increase output because costs are likely to rise just as fast. They instead make output decisions based on more fundamental factors like technology and market size. The monetarist AS curve is *vertical* because output doesn't respond to changing price levels. (This is the long-run AS curve we first encountered in Chapter 8.) With a vertical AS curve, only prices can respond to a shift in aggregate demand. In Figure 16.1*b*, the AS curve is anchored at the natural rate of unemployment Q_N. When aggregate demand increases from AD_4 to AD_5, the price level (P) rises, but output (Q) is unchanged.

Hybrid AS. Figure 16.1*c* blends these Keynesian and monetarist perspectives into a hybrid AS curve. At low rates of output, the curve is nearly horizontal; at high rates of output, the AS curve becomes nearly vertical. In the broad middle of the AS curve, the curve slopes gently upward. In this area, shifts of aggregate demand affect *both* prices and output. The message of this hybrid AS curve is that the outcomes of fiscal and monetary policy depend on how close the economy is to full employment. *The closer we are to capacity, the greater the risk that fiscal or monetary stimulus will spill over into price inflation.*

The Inflation–Unemployment Trade-Off

Because Figure 16.1*c* allows for varying output and price responses at different levels of economic activity, that hybrid AS curve is regarded as the most realistic for short-run outcomes. The reality it depicts, however, has some disturbing implications. If the AS curve slopes upward, then both prices and output increase when aggregate demand increases. This is not a good thing: The upward slope of the AS curve implies that we can't reduce both unemployment and inflation at the same time—at least not with fiscal and monetary policies. To see why this is the case, consider the simple geometry of policy stimulus and restraint.

FIGURE 16.1
Contrasting Views of Aggregate Supply

The effectiveness of fiscal and monetary policy depends on the shape of the AS curve. Some possibilities include these:

(a) Keynesian AS In the simple Keynesian model, the rate of output responds fully and automatically to increases in demand until full employment (Q^*) is reached. If demand increases from AD_1 to AD_2, equilibrium GDP will expand from Q_1 to Q^*, without any inflation. Inflation becomes a problem only if demand increases beyond capacity—to AD_3, for example.

(b) Monetarist AS Monetarists assert that changes in the money supply affect prices but not output. They regard aggregate supply as a fixed quantum, at the long-run, natural rate of unemployment (here noted as Q_N). Accordingly, a shift of demand (from AD_4 to AD_5) can affect only the price level (from P_4 to P_5).

(c) Hybrid AS The consensus view incorporates Keynesian and monetarist perspectives but emphasizes the upward slope that dominates the middle of the AS curve. When demand increases, both price levels and the rate of output increase. Hence, the slope and position of the AS curve limit the effectiveness of fiscal and monetary policies.

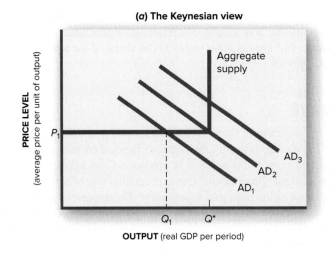

(a) The Keynesian view

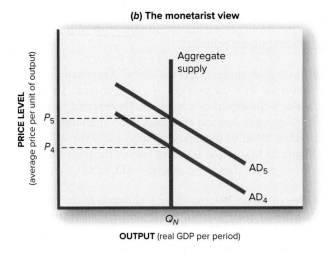

(b) The monetarist view

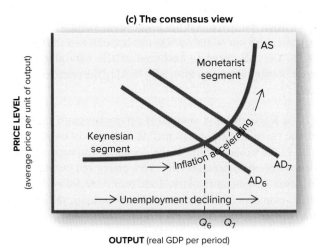

(c) The consensus view

Demand Stimulus. Successful monetary and fiscal stimulus will shift the aggregate demand curve rightward. This demand-side effect is illustrated by the AD_6 and AD_7 curves in Figure 16.1c. Output increases (from Q_6 to Q_7), but the price level increases as well. This is not what we want. Unfortunately, *all rightward shifts of the aggregate demand curve increase both prices and output if the aggregate supply curve is upward-sloping.* This implies that fiscal and monetary efforts to reduce unemployment will also cause some inflation. How much inflation occurs depends on the slope of the AS curve.

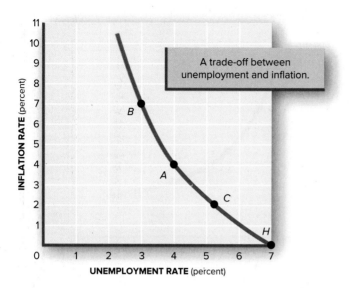

FIGURE 16.2
The Phillips Curve

The Phillips curve illustrates a trade-off between full employment and price stability. In the 1960s it appeared that efforts to reduce unemployment rates below 5.5 percent (point *C*) led to increasing rates of inflation (points *A* and *B*). Inflation threatened to reach unacceptable levels long before everyone was employed.

Demand Restraint. We have a similar dilemma with policy restraint. Monetary and fiscal restraint shifts the aggregate demand curve leftward. *If the aggregate supply curve is upward-sloping, leftward shifts of the aggregate demand curve cause both prices and output to fall.* Therefore, fiscal and monetary efforts to reduce inflation will also increase unemployment. How much unemployment increases depends again on the slope of the AS curve.

The Phillips Curve. The message of the upward-sloping aggregate supply curve is clear: *Demand-side policies alone can never succeed completely; they'll always cause some unwanted inflation or unemployment.*

Our macro track record provides ample evidence of this dilemma. Consider, for example, our experience with unemployment and inflation during the 1960s, as shown in Figure 16.2. This figure shows a **Phillips curve,** an inverse relationship between inflation and unemployment. Consider point *H* in the graph. At *H,* we have 7 percent unemployment but no inflation. Our goal is to reduce unemployment. As we reduce unemployment from 7 percent to 5 percent, however, prices start rising. We end up at point *C,* with lower unemployment but higher inflation. If we succeed in reducing unemployment further, inflation will accelerate (e.g., points *A* and *B*).

The Phillips curve was developed by a New Zealand economist, Alban W. Phillips, to summarize the relationship between unemployment and inflation in England for the years 1826–1957.[1] The Phillips curve was raised from the status of an obscure graph to that of a policy issue by the discovery that the same kind of relationship apparently existed in other countries and at other times. Paul Samuelson and Robert Solow of the Massachusetts Institute of Technology were among the first to observe that the Phillips curve was a reasonable description of U.S. economic performance for the years 1900–1960. A seesaw kind of relationship existed between inflation and unemployment: When one went up, the other fell.

The trade-off between unemployment and inflation originates in the upward-sloping AS curve. Figure 16.3a illustrates this point. Suppose the economy is initially at equilibrium *A,* with fairly stable prices but low output. When aggregate demand expands to AD_2, prices rise along with output, so we end up at point *B* with higher inflation but less unemployment. This is also shown in Figure 16.3b by the move from point *a* to point *b* on the Phillips curve. The move from point *a* to point *b* indicates a decline in unemployment (more output) but an increase in inflation (higher price level). If demand is increased further to AD_3, a still lower unemployment rate is achieved but at the cost of higher inflation (point *c*). This is the

Phillips curve: A historical (inverse) relationship between the rate of unemployment and the rate of inflation; commonly expresses a trade-off between the two.

[1]A. W. Phillips. "The Relationship between Unemployment and the Rate of Change of Money Wage Rates in the United Kingdom, 1826–1957," *Economica* (November 1958). Phillips's paper studied the relationship between unemployment and *wage* changes rather than *price* changes; most later formulations (and public policy) focus on prices.

(a) Increases in aggregate demand cause . . .

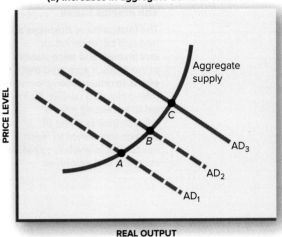

(b) A trade-off between unemployment and inflation.

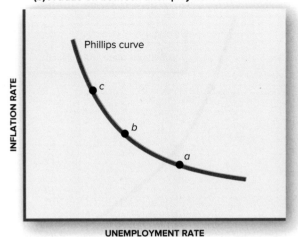

FIGURE 16.3

The Phillips Curve Trade-off

If the aggregate supply curve slopes upward, increases in aggregate demand always cause both prices and output to rise. Thus, higher inflation becomes a cost of achieving lower unemployment. In (a), increased demand moves the economy from point A to point B. At B, unemployment is lower, but prices are higher. This trade-off is illustrated on the Phillips curve in (b). Each point on the Phillips curve represents a different AS/AD equilibrium from the graph on the left.

kind of concern that prompted the Fed to increase interest rates in 2018, slowing economic growth and drawing a harsh rebuke from President Trump.

The Inflationary Flashpoint. The Phillips curve reminds us that there is bound to be a trade-off between unemployment and inflation at some point in economic expansions and contractions. But is there a *specific* point at which the trade-off becomes particularly worrisome? With the Keynesian AS curve (Figure 16.1a), there is *no* trade-off until full employment (Q^*) is reached, then inflation rockets upwards. Hence, the output level Q^* represents the **inflationary flashpoint**—the point at which inflationary pressures intensify—on the Keynesian AS curve.

The hybrid AS curve in Figure 16.1a doesn't have such a sharp flashpoint. The slope of the curve seems pretty smooth. In fact, however, inflationary pressures could bubble up as the economy expands. If that were to happen, the AS curve wouldn't be quite so smooth. Instead, at some rate of output, the slope of the AS curve would turn up sharply, as in Figure 16.4. That inflationary flashpoint represents the rate of output at which inflation begins to accelerate significantly. It is a point policymakers want to avoid.

inflationary flashpoint: The rate of output at which inflationary pressures intensify; the point on the AS curve where slope increases sharply.

FIGURE 16.4

The Inflationary Flashpoint

As the economy approaches capacity, inflationary pressures intensify. The point at which inflation noticeably accelerates is the "inflationary flashpoint"—a juncture policymakers want to avoid.

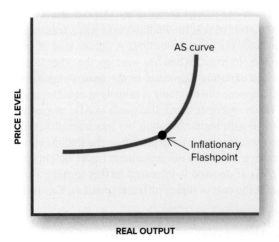

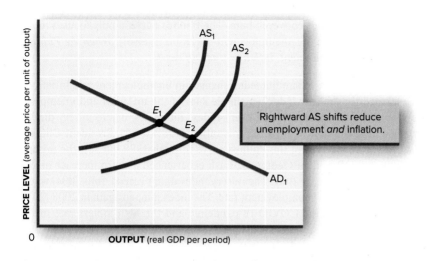

FIGURE 16.5
Shifts of Aggregate Supply

A rightward AS shift (AS$_1$ to AS$_2$) reduces both unemployment and inflation. A leftward shift has the opposite effect, creating stagflation.

SHIFTS OF THE AS CURVE

The unemployment–inflation trade-off implied by the upward-sloping AS curve is not etched in stone. Nor is the inflationary flashpoint unmovable. Many economists argue that the economy can attain lower levels of unemployment *without* higher inflation. This certainly appeared to be the case at times: Unemployment rates fell sharply from 2002 to 2008 and again from 2010 to 2016 without any increase in inflation. How could this have happened? There's no AD shift in any part of Figure 16.3 that would reduce both unemployment *and* inflation.

Rightward AS Shifts: All Good News

Only a rightward shift of the AS curve can reduce unemployment and inflation at the same time. When aggregate supply increases from AS$_1$ to AS$_2$ in Figure 16.5, macro equilibrium moves from E_1 to E_2. At E_2 real output is higher, so the unemployment rate must be lower. At E_2 the price level is also lower, indicating reduced inflation. Hence, a rightward shift of the AS curve offers the best of two worlds—something aggregate *demand* shifts (Figure 16.1) can't do.

Phillips Curve Shift. As we saw in Figure 16.3, the Phillips curve is a direct by-product of the AS curve. Accordingly, *when the AS curve shifts, the Phillips curve shifts as well.* As Figure 16.6 illustrates, the Phillips curve shifts to the left, the opposite of the AS shift in

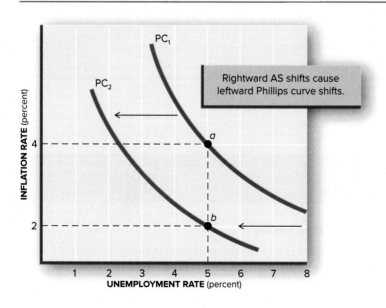

FIGURE 16.6
A Phillips Curve Shift

If the Phillips curve shifts leftward, the short-run unemployment–inflation trade-off eases. With PC$_1$, 5 percent unemployment ignites 4 percent inflation (point *a*). With PC$_2$, 5 percent unemployment causes only 2 percent inflation (point *b*).

Figure 16.5. No new information is conveyed here. The Phillips curve simply focuses more directly on the implied change in the unemployment-inflation trade-off. *When the Phillips curve shifts to the left, the unemployment-inflation trade-off eases.*

The Misery Index. To keep track of simultaneous changes in unemployment and inflation, Arthur Okun developed the "**misery index**"—a simple sum of the inflation and unemployment rates. As Front Page Economics "The Misery Index" illustrates, macro misery diminished substantially during the first Reagan administration (1981-1984). President Clinton also benefited from a leftward shift of the Phillips curve through 1998 but saw the misery index climb in 1999-2000. President George W. Bush experienced a sharp increase in the misery index during the recession of 2001. The misery index didn't recede until 2004, when strong output growth reduced the unemployment rate. The index jumped again in 2008-2011 and even further in 2020 when the COVID-19 pandemic and the high jobless rate made everybody miserable.

---

misery index: The sum of inflation and unemployment rates.

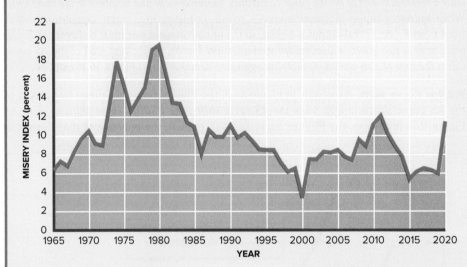

FRONT PAGE ECONOMICS

NEWS

THE MISERY INDEX

Unemployment is a problem, and so is inflation. Being burdened with both problems at the same time is real misery.

The late Arthur Okun proposed measuring the extent of misery by adding together the inflation and unemployment rates. He called the sum of the two rates the "discomfort index." Political pundits quickly renamed it the "misery index."

In essence, the misery index is a measure of stagflation—the simultaneous occurrence of inflation and unemployment. In 1980 the misery index peaked at 19.6 percent as a result of high inflation (12.5 percent) as well as high unemployment (7.1 percent). Stagflation—and the misery it causes—has since receded markedly.

Source: Economic Report of the President, 2020.

CRITICAL ANALYSIS: Stagflation refers to the simultaneous occurrence of inflation and unemployment. The "misery index" combines both problems into a single measure of macro performance.

Leftward AS Shifts: All Bad News

Whereas rightward AS shifts appear to be a dream come true, leftward AS shifts are a real nightmare. Imagine in Figure 16.5 that the AS shift is reversed—that is, from AS_2 to AS_1. What would happen? Output would decrease and prices would rise. In other words, nothing would go in the right direction. This would be rampant stagflation and widespread misery.

A natural disaster can trigger a leftward shift of the AS curve, especially in smaller nations. When a tsunami washed over nations in the Indian Ocean in December 2004, more than 200,000 people were killed. In Sri Lanka, 80 percent of the fishing fleet was destroyed, along with port facilities, railroads, highways, and communications systems. The huge loss of human and physical capital reduced Sri Lanka's production possibilities. This was reflected in a leftward shift of the AS curve. The same kind of devastation hit Mozambique in 2019, reducing that nation's potential output and intensifying inflationary pressures (see World View "Cyclone Idai Destroys Mozambique Port City").

WORLD VIEW

CYCLONE IDAI DESTROYS MOZAMBIQUE PORT CITY

BEIRA. The Red Cross estimates that cyclone Idai destroyed 90 percent of Beira, Mozambique's second-largest port city. The United Nations reported that when Idai struck Beira on March 14, it was the deadliest storm ever to hit Africa. Idai destroyed the port, roads, bridges, dams, and communications networks. It also flooded over 900,000 acres of cropland, destroying food supplies. Electricity was cut off, 17,000 homes were damaged, and 602 people died in the storm. Food prices jumped in the wake of the disruption to food supplies, worsening the already high malnutrition rate in this poor African nation. The World Bank lowered its growth estimate for the year from 3.9 percent to 2.1 percent and raised its inflation estimate from 5.5 to 8.1 percent.

Natural disasters destroy production facilities.
YASUYOSHI CHIBA/Getty Images

Source: News reports of March 15–21, 2019.

CRITICAL ANALYSIS: A natural disaster destroys production facilities, transportation routes, power sources, and people, causing a **leftward shift of the AS curve.**

In an economy as large as that of the United States, leftward shifts of aggregate supply are less dramatic. But Mother Nature can still push the AS curve around. Hurricanes Katrina and Rita, for example, destroyed vast amounts of production, transportation, and communications infrastructure in August 2005. Hurricane Mathew did similar damage to the supply side of the economy in October 2016. Hurricane Harvey was even more destructive when it struck Texas in August 2017. Then in August 2020 Louisiana got hit with the strongest hurricane (Laura) ever to make landfall in the United States. Roads were flooded, power supplies were shut down, oil refineries were closed, and all deliveries to the area were suspended. Factories were closed and people had no way to get to work. The resulting delays and cost increases were reflected in another leftward shift of the AS curve.

The 2020 coronavirus pandemic was a different kind of natural disaster. Unlike tsunamis, earthquakes, fires, and tornados, the coronavirus didn't destroy production or transportation infrastructure. It did, however, keep people from working. As factories, offices, and transportation networks shut down, the ability of the economy to produce goods fell sharply. The resulting leftward shift of the AS curve doomed the economies of the world to GDP shrinkage.

The September 11, 2001, terrorist attacks on the World Trade Center and Pentagon were another form of external shock. The attacks directly destroyed some production capacity (office space, telecommunications links, and transportation links). But they took an even greater toll on the *willingness* to supply goods and services. In the aftermath of the attacks, businesses, perceiving new risks to investment and production, held back from making new commitments. Increased security measures also made transporting goods more expensive. All of these responses shifted the AS curve leftward and the Phillips curve rightward, adding to macro misery.

Policy Tools

From the supply side of macro markets, the appropriate response to negative external shocks is clear: Shift the AS curve rightward. As the foregoing graphs have demonstrated, *rightward shifts of the aggregate supply curve always generate desirable macro outcomes.*

The next question, of course, is how to shift the aggregate supply curve in the desired (rightward) direction. Supply-side economists look for clues among the forces that influence the supply-side response to changes in demand. Among those forces, the following policy options for shifting the AS curve rightward have been emphasized:

- Tax incentives for saving, investment, and work.
- Human capital investment.
- Deregulation.
- Trade liberalization.
- Infrastructure development.

All these policies have the potential to change supply decisions *independently* of any changes in aggregate demand. If they're effective, they'll result in a rightward shift of the AS curve and an *improved* trade-off between unemployment and inflation.

TAX INCENTIVES

Tax cuts are one of the most familiar options for supply-side policy. Tax cuts are, of course, a staple of Keynesian economics. But tax cuts take on a whole new role on the supply side of the economy. *In Keynesian economics, tax cuts are used to increase aggregate demand.* By putting more disposable income in the hands of consumers, Keynesian economists seek to increase expenditure on goods and services. Output is expected to increase in response. From a Keynesian perspective, the form of the tax cut is not important as long as disposable income increases.

The supply side of the economy encourages a different view of taxes. *Taxes not only alter disposable income but also change incentives to work and produce.* High tax rates destroy incentives to work and produce, so they end up reducing total output. Low tax rates, by contrast, allow people to keep more of what they earn and so stimulate greater output. *The direct effects of taxes on the supply of goods are the concern of supply-side economists.* Figure 16.7 shows the difference between demand-side and supply-side perspectives on tax policy.

Marginal Tax Rates

marginal tax rate: The tax rate imposed on the last (marginal) dollar of income.

Supply-side theory places special emphasis on *marginal* tax rates. The **marginal tax rate** is the tax rate imposed on the last (marginal) dollar of income received. In our progressive income tax system, marginal tax rates increase as more income is received. Uncle Sam takes a larger share out of each additional dollar earned. In 2020, the highest marginal tax rate on personal income was 37 percent. That top tax rate was far below the 91 percent rate that existed in 1944, but it was also a lot higher than the 12 percent tax rate imposed in 1914 (see Figure 16.8).

In view of the wild history of tax rates, one might wonder whether the rate selected matters. Specifically, does the marginal tax rate affect supply decisions? Will people work and invest as much when the marginal tax rate is 91 percent as when it is only 12 percent? Doesn't seem likely, does it?

Labor Supply. The marginal tax rate directly changes the financial incentive to *increase* one's work. *If the marginal tax rate is high, there's less incentive to work more*—Uncle Sam will get most of the added income. Confronted with high marginal tax rates, workers may choose to stay home rather than work an extra shift. Families may decide that it doesn't pay to send both parents into the labor market. When marginal tax rates are low, by contrast, those extra work activities generate bigger increases in disposable income.

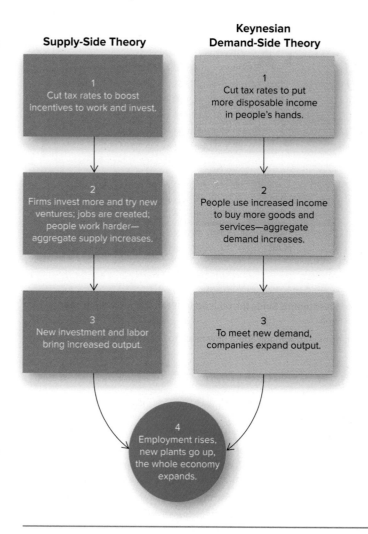

Supply-Side Theory

Keynesian
Demand-Side Theory

FIGURE 16.7

Two Theories for Getting the Economy Moving

Keynesians and supply-siders both advocate cutting taxes to reduce unemployment. But they have very different views on the kind of tax cuts required and the impact of any cuts enacted.

Entrepreneurship. Marginal tax rates affect not only labor supply decisions but also decisions on whether to start or expand a business. Most small businesses are organized as sole proprietorships or partnerships and are subject to *personal,* not *corporate,* tax rates. Hence, a decline in personal tax rates will affect the risk–reward balance for potential entrepreneurs. Columbia Business School professors William Gentry and Glenn Huber have demonstrated that progressive marginal tax rates discourage entry into self-employment. Syracuse professor Douglas Holtz-Eakin and Princeton economist Harvey Rosen have shown that the

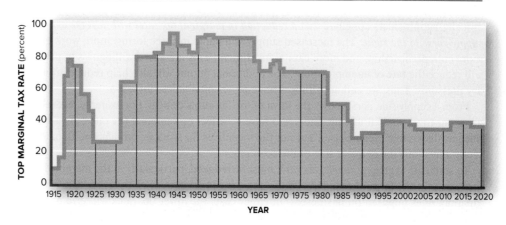

FIGURE 16.8

Changes in Marginal Tax Rates since 1915

The top marginal tax rate on personal income has varied from a low of 12 percent in 1914 to a high of 91 percent in 1944. Supply-side theory emphasizes how these varying tax rates affect work, investment, and production decisions—that is, aggregate supply.

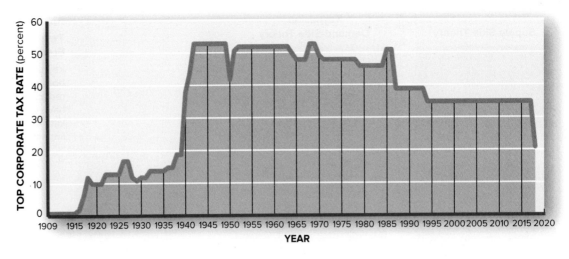

FIGURE 16.9

History of Corporate Tax Rates

Taxes are an important influence on corporate investment. Since introduced in 1909, the top corporate tax rate has varied from 1 percent to as high as 53 percent.

CRITICAL ANALYSIS: Tax rates affect the decisions of corporations about how much to invest in new plant, equipment, products, and ideas.

growth rate, investment, and employment of small businesses are also affected by marginal tax rates. As Holtz-Eakin concluded, "Taxes matter."

Investment. Taxes matter for corporations too. Corporate entities account for nearly 90 percent of business output and 84 percent of business assets. Like small proprietorships, corporations, too, are motivated by *after*-tax profits. Hence, corporate **investment** decisions will be affected by corporate tax rates. If Uncle Sam imposes a high tax rate on corporate profits, the payoff to investors will be diminished. Potential investors may decide to consume their income or to purchase tax-free bonds rather than invest in plants and equipment. If that happens, total investment will decline and output will suffer. Accordingly, *if high tax rates discourage investment, aggregate supply will be constrained.*

Like the personal income tax rate, the corporate income tax rate has been all over the map. When first introduced in 1909, the corporate tax rate was a measly 1 percent. Since then, it has been revised 30 times, hitting a high of 53 percent during World War II (see Figure 16.9). The Trump tax cuts of 2017 brought the top tax rate on corporations down to 21 percent, the lowest rate since the 1930s. President Biden vowed to push it back up a bit.

> **investment:** Expenditures on (production of) new plants, equipment, and structures (capital) in a given time period, plus changes in business inventories.

Tax-Induced Supply Shifts

If tax rates affect supply decisions, then *changes* in tax rates will shift aggregate supply. Specifically, supply-siders conclude that *a reduction in marginal tax rates will shift the aggregate supply curve to the right.* The increased supply will come in three forms: more work effort, more entrepreneurship, and more capital investment. This increased willingness to produce will reduce the rate of unemployment. The additional output will also help reduce inflationary pressures. Thus, we end up with less unemployment *and* less inflation.

From a supply-side perspective, the form of the tax cut is critical. For example, **tax rebates** are a one-time windfall to consumers and have no effect on marginal tax rates. As a consequence, disposable income rises, but not the incentives for work or production. Rebates directly affect only the demand side of the economy.

To stimulate aggregate *supply,* tax *rates* must be reduced, particularly at the margin. These cuts can take the form of reductions in personal income tax rates or reductions in the marginal tax rates imposed on businesses. In either case, the lower tax rates will give people a greater incentive to work, invest, and produce.

> **tax rebate:** A lump-sum refund of taxes paid.

Reagan Tax Cuts. No one understood the supply-side impact of tax rates better than Ronald Reagan. When he was working as an actor during World War II, he had to pay the highest marginal tax rate then in effect—a whopping 91 percent! He vowed that he would cut tax rates dramatically when he became president. And he did: He convinced Congress to cut the top rate on personal taxes from 71 percent in 1981 to a low of 28 percent in 1988. He also cut the top rate on corporate income from 46 percent to 34 percent.

Post-Reagan Rate Changes. The top tax rate on individuals didn't stay at 28 percent for long. President George H.W. Bush agreed with a Democrat-controlled Congress to increase the top rate to 31 percent in 1991. President Clinton raised it even higher—to 39.6 percent in 1993. George W. Bush succeeded in pushing the rate down to 35 percent during his presidency, but President Obama took it back to 39.6 percent in 2012. The top corporate tax rate stayed at 35 percent throughout these years.

Trump Tax Cuts. Donald Trump was convinced that high tax rates on individuals and businesses were a serious drag on U.S. economic growth. He emphasized that the 35 percent corporate tax rate was one of the highest in the world and discouraged businesses from starting or expanding in the United States. He succeeded in convincing Congress to chop the top corporate tax rate from 35 percent to 21 percent and drop the top personal tax rate from 39.6 to 37 percent (still 9 points higher than the Reagan low).

How Marginal Tax Rates Work. Clearly, marginal tax rates are the focus of both economic and political debate. It is important, therefore, to understand how cuts in marginal tax rates differ from other forms of tax cuts.

Table 16.1 illustrates the distinction between Keynesian and supply-side tax cuts. Under both tax systems (A and B), a person earning $200 pays $80 in taxes before the tax cut and

TABLE 16.1

Supply Side: Focus on Marginal Tax Rates

	Initial Alternatives				
Tax System	Initial Tax Schedule	Tax on Income of $200	Tax Rate Average	Tax Rate Marginal	Disposable Income
A	$30 + 50% of income over $100	$80	40%	50%	$120
B	$50 + 30% of income over $100	$80	40%	30%	$120

The same amount of taxes can be raised via two very different systems. Here a person earning $200 pays $80 in taxes under either system (A or B). Thus, the *average* tax rate (total tax ÷ total income) is the same in both cases ($80 ÷ $200 = 40%). The *marginal* tax rates are very different, however. System A has a high marginal tax rate (50%), whereas system B has a low marginal tax rate (30%). System B provides a greater incentive for people to earn over $100.

	Alternative Forms of Tax Cut				
Tax System	Initial Tax Schedule	Tax on Income of $200	Tax Rate Average	Tax Rate Marginal	Disposable Income
A	$10 + 50% of income over $100	$60	30%	50%	$140
B	$30 + 30% of income over $100	$60	30%	30%	$140

The *average tax rate* could be cut to 30 percent under either system. Under both systems, the revised tax would be $60 and disposable income would be increased to $140. Keynesians would be happy with either form of tax cut. But supply-siders would favor system B because the lower *marginal tax rate* gives people more incentive to earn higher incomes.

$60 after the tax cut. But under system A, the marginal tax rate is always 50 percent, which means that Uncle Sam is getting half of every dollar earned above $100. By contrast, system B imposes a marginal tax rate of only 30 percent—$0.30 of every dollar above $100 goes to the government. Under system B, people have a greater incentive to earn *more* than $100. Although both systems raise the same amount of taxes, system B offers greater incentives to work extra hours and produce more output.

Tax Elasticity of Supply

All economists agree that tax rates influence people's decisions to work, invest, and produce. But the policy-relevant question is, *how much* influence do taxes have? Do reductions in the marginal tax rate shift the aggregate supply curve far to the right? Or are the resultant shifts quite small?

The response of labor and capital to a change in tax rates is summarized by the **tax elasticity of supply.** Like other elasticities, this one measures the proportional response of supplies to a change in price (in this case a tax *rate*). Specifically, the tax elasticity of supply is the percentage change in quantity supplied divided by the percentage in tax rates; that is,

$$\frac{\text{Tax elasticity}}{\text{of supply}} = \frac{\text{\% change in quantity supplied}}{\text{\% change in tax rate}}$$

Normally we expect quantity supplied to go up when tax rates go down. Elasticity (E) is therefore negative, although it's usually expressed in absolute terms (without the minus sign). The (absolute) value of E must be greater than zero because we expect *some* response to a tax cut. That means that ***tax cuts—especially cuts in marginal tax rates—will shift the AS curve to the right.*** The policy issue boils down to the question of how large E actually is—how far AS will shift.

If the tax elasticity of supply were large enough, a tax cut might not only shift the AS curve but actually *increase* tax revenues. Suppose the tax elasticity were equal to 1.5. In that case a tax cut of 10 percent would cause output supplied to increase by 15 percent ($= 1.5 \times 10\%$). Such a large increase in the tax base (income) would result in *more* taxes being paid even though the tax *rate* was reduced. One of President Reagan's economic advisers, Arthur Laffer, actually thought such an outcome was possible. He predicted that tax revenues would *increase* after the Reagan supply-side tax cuts were made. In reality, the tax elasticity of supply turned out to be much smaller (around 0.15), and tax revenues fell substantially. The aggregate supply curve *did* shift to the right, but not very far, when marginal tax rates were cut.

According to a 2006 study by the Congressional Research Service, the 2001–2004 rate cuts initiated by President George W. Bush elicited a 0.20 tax elasticity of supply. In 2012, the Congressional Budget Office said the tax elasticity of supply might be higher still—at 0.27. Tax elasticities in that range underscore the significant potential of supply-side tax cuts to shift the aggregate supply curve and alter macroeconomic outcomes.

Savings Incentives

Supply-side economists emphasize the importance of *long-run* responses to changed tax incentives. On the demand side, an increase in income translates very quickly into increased spending. On the supply side, things don't happen so fast. It takes time to construct new plants and equipment. People are also slow to respond to new work and investment incentives. Hence, the full benefits of supply-side tax cuts—or the damage done by tax hikes—won't be immediately visible.

Of particular concern to supply-side economists is the rate of saving in the economy. Demand-side economists emphasize spending and tend to treat **saving** as a leakage problem. Supply-siders, by contrast, emphasize the importance of saving for financing investment and economic growth. At full employment, a greater volume of investment is possible only if the

---

tax elasticity of supply: The percentage change in quantity supplied divided by the percentage change in tax rates.

---

saving: That part of disposable income not spent on current consumption; disposable income less consumption.

rate of consumption is cut back. In other words, additional investment requires additional saving. Hence, *supply-side economists favor tax incentives that encourage saving as well as greater tax incentives for investment.* This kind of perspective contrasts sharply with the Keynesian emphasis on stimulating consumption.

Investment Incentives

An alternative lever for shifting aggregate supply is to offer tax incentives for investment. The 1981 tax cuts focused on *personal* income tax rates. By contrast, President George H. Bush advocated cutting capital gains taxes. A **capital gains tax** is a tax levied on the increase in the value of property, such as land, buildings, and corporate stock, when it's sold. It is different from the *income* taxes levied on the current incomes of individuals and businesses. The capital gains tax applies only when a piece of property (a building, shares of stock, gold, a house, a business, etc.) are sold. If the sales price exceeds the purchase price, then a capital gain exists. That gain is the focus of this tax.

capital gains tax: A tax levied on the profit from the sale of property.

The capital gains tax influences people's decision to start a business, to invest in corporate stocks, or to renovate homes, develop land, or make other investments. If the tax rate is low, then the anticipated after-tax profit will be higher. By contrast, higher capital gains tax rates make investment less profitable.

President Clinton's very first proposal for stimulating the economy was a temporary investment tax credit. Shortly thereafter, Congress cut the capital gains tax rate from 28 percent to 20 percent. President George Bush pushed the tax rate still lower, to 15 percent in 2003. During the 2008 campaign, Barack Obama vowed to reverse the Bush "tax cuts for the rich" by *raising* marginal income tax rates as well as capital gains and inheritance taxes. The Taxpayer Relief Act of 2012 pushed the capital gains tax rate back up to 20 percent, where it has remained.

The Trump tax cuts of 2017 entailed an enormous increase in investment incentives. The policy lever here was the corporate income tax, which was lowered from 35 percent to 21 percent, the lowest in 80 years (Figure 16.9). That dramatically increased the after-tax profits of corporate investments, thus enticing them to invest and produce more.

HUMAN CAPITAL INVESTMENT

A nation's ability to supply goods and services depends on its *human* capital as well as its *physical* capital. If the size of the labor force increased, more output could be produced in any given price level. Similarly, if the *quality* of the workforce were to increase, more output could be supplied at any given price level. In other words, increases in **human capital**—the skills and knowledge of the workforce—add to the nation's potential output.

human capital: The knowledge and skills possessed by the workforce.

Structural Unemployment

A mismatch between the skills of the workforce and the requirements of new jobs is a major cause of the unemployment–inflation trade-off. When aggregate demand increases, employers want to hire more workers. But the available (unemployed) workers may not have the skills employers require. This is the essence of **structural unemployment.** The consequence is that employers can't increase output as fast as they'd like to. Prices, rather than output, increase.

structural unemployment: Unemployment caused by a mismatch between the skills (or location) of job seekers and the requirements (or location) of available jobs.

The larger the skills gap between unemployed workers and the requirements of emerging jobs, the worse will be the Phillips curve trade-off. To improve the trade-off, the skills gap must be reduced. This is another supply-side imperative. *Investments in human capital reduce structural unemployment and shift the aggregate supply curve rightward.*

Worker Training

The tax code is a policy tool for increasing human capital investment as well as physical capital investment. In this case, tax credits are made available to employers who offer more worker training. Such credits reduce the employer's after-tax cost of training.

President Clinton proposed even stronger incentives for employer-based training. He wanted to *require* employers to spend at least 1.5 percent of their total payroll costs on training activities. Employers who didn't provide training activities directly would have to pay an equivalent sum into a public training fund. This "play-or-pay" approach would force employers to invest in the human capital of their employees.

Although the "play-or-pay" concept is intriguing, it might actually shift the aggregate supply curve the *wrong* way. The *costs* of employing workers would rise in the short run as employers shelled out more money for training or taxes. Hence, the aggregate supply curve would shift *leftward* in the short run, worsening the unemployment–inflation trade-off. Only later might AS shift rightward, and then only to the extent that training actually improved **labor productivity**.

labor productivity: Amount of output produced by a worker in a given period of time; output per hour (or day, etc.).

Education Spending

Another way to increase human capital is to expand and improve the efficacy of the education system. President George H. Bush encouraged local school systems to become more competitive. He suggested they experiment with vouchers that would allow students to attend the school of their choice. Schools would then have to offer services that attracted voucher-carrying students. Schools that didn't compete successfully wouldn't have enough funds (vouchers) to continue.

President Clinton advocated a more conventional approach. He urged Congress to allocate more funds to the school system, particularly programs for preschoolers, like Head Start, and for disadvantaged youth.

President George W. Bush characterized himself as the "education president." He increased federal spending on education and improved tax incentives for college savings accounts and tuition payments. His No Child Left Behind program also increased school accountability for human capital development. President Obama also emphasized educational improvements as a key to long-run growth. None of these educational tools generate a quick AS curve shift. Rather, any improvements in labor productivity are likely to emerge many years later.

Health Care

As the coronavirus pandemic reminded us, we need not only educated workers, but *healthy* workers as well. Illness and quarantines keep workers of all types and abilities from doing their jobs. To offset this natural disaster, public health resources had to be expanded dramatically. That surge in health care helped slow the leftward shift of the AS curve and ultimately helped reverse its direction. President Biden made the fight against COVID-19 his first priority, recognizing that a strong economy needed healthy workers and consumers.

Affirmative Action

Lack of skills and experience aren't the only reasons it's sometimes hard to find the "right" workers. The mismatch between employed workers and jobs is often less a matter of skills than of race, gender, or age. In other words, discrimination can create an artificial barrier between job seekers and available job openings.

If discrimination tends to shift the aggregate supply curve leftward, then reducing discriminatory barriers should shift it to the right. Equal opportunity programs are thus a natural extension of a supply-side approach to macro policy. However, critics are also quick to point out the risks inherent in government regulation of hiring decisions. From a supply-side perspective, laws that forbid discrimination are welcome and should be enforced. But aggressive affirmative action programs that require employers to hire specific numbers or types of workers limit productive capabilities and can lead to excessive costs.

Transfer Payments

Welfare programs also discourage workers from taking available jobs. Unemployment and welfare benefits provide an important source of income when a person isn't working.

Although these **transfer payments** are motivated by humanitarian goals, they also inhibit labor supply. Transfer recipients must give up some or all of their welfare payments when they take a job. That makes working less attractive and therefore reduces the number of available workers. The net result is a leftward shift of the aggregate supply curve.

In 1996 Congress reformed the nation's core welfare program. The supply-side emphasis of that reform was manifest in the very title of the reform legislation: the Personal Responsibility and Work Opportunity Act. Congress set time limits on how long people can draw welfare benefits. The act also required recipients to engage in job-related activities like job search and training while still receiving benefits.

The 1996 reforms had a dramatic effect on recipient behavior. Nationally, more than 5 million adults left welfare between 1996 and 2001. More than half of these ex-welfare recipients entered the labor force, thereby shifting the AS curve rightward.

Recognizing that income transfers reduce aggregate supply doesn't force us to eliminate all welfare programs. Welfare programs serve important social needs. The AS/AD framework reminds us, however, that the structure of such programs will affect aggregate supply. With more than 60 million Americans receiving income transfers, the effect on aggregate supply can be significant.

> **transfer payments:** Payments to individuals for which no current goods or services are exchanged, like Social Security, welfare, and unemployment benefits.

DEREGULATION

Government intervention affects the shape and position of the aggregate supply curve in other ways. The government intervenes directly in supply decisions by *regulating* employment and output behavior. In general, such regulations limit the flexibility of producers to respond to changes in demand. Government regulation also tends to raise production costs. The higher costs result not only from required changes in the production process but also from the expense of monitoring government regulations and filling out government forms. Thomas Hopkins, a Rochester Institute of Technology economist, estimates that the total costs of regulation exceed $700 billion a year. These added costs of production shift the aggregate supply curve to the left.

Factor Markets

Government intervention in factor markets increases the cost of supplying goods and services in many ways.

Minimum Wages. Minimum wage laws are one of the most familiar forms of factor market regulation. The Fair Labor Standards Act of 1938 required employers to pay workers a minimum of 25 cents per hour. Over time, Congress has increased the coverage of that act and the minimum wage itself repeatedly. Since 2009, however, the *federal* minimum wage has been stuck at $7.25 an hour, and 29 states have enacted higher *state* minimums (up to $13.50 in Washington in 2020).

The goal of all minimum wage laws is to ensure workers a decent standard of living. But the law has other effects as well. Quite simply, if labor becomes more expensive, employers will use less of it. This is the basic law of demand. What it means in labor markets is that fewer workers will be hired at higher wages. When the minimum wage goes up, some workers will actually lose jobs or hours. Teenagers especially may not have enough skills or experience to merit the minimum wage.

Here again, the issue is not whether minimum wage laws serve any social purposes but how they affect macro outcomes. By shifting the aggregate supply curve leftward, minimum wage laws make it more difficult to achieve full employment with stable prices.

Mandatory Benefits. Government-directed fringe benefits have the same kind of effect on aggregate supply. One of the first bills President Clinton signed into law was the Family and Medical Leave Act, which requires all businesses with 50 or more employees to grant leaves of absence for up to 12 weeks. The employer must continue to pay health benefits during such absences and must also incur the costs of recruiting and training temporary replacements.

The General Accounting Office (now the Government Accountability Office) estimated these benefits added nearly $700 million per year to payroll costs. These added payroll costs raise the costs of production, making producers less willing to supply output at any given price level.

Occupational Health and Safety. Government regulation of factor markets extends beyond wages and benefits. The government also sets standards for workplace safety and health. The Occupational Safety and Health Administration (OSHA), for example, issues very specific safety standards for all kinds of firms, including mandatory worker training in many areas. The standards include everything from eye protection to ergonomic design of assembly lines and computer workstations. In 2019 there were more than 75,000 federal and state inspections of individual work sites. Employers incur billions of dollars in costs learning about OSHA regulations, redesigning workplaces, training their workforce, responding to inspections, and paying fines. Here again, the point is not that the regulations are ineffective, but instead to recognize that all such interventions impose a cost—and therefore alter aggregate supply.

Product Markets

The government's regulation of factor markets tends to raise production costs and inhibit supply. The same is true of regulations imposed directly on product markets, as the following examples illustrate.

Transportation Costs. At the federal level, various agencies regulate the output and prices of transportation services. In 2013 the Federal Motor Carrier Safety Administration issued new regulations for the trucking industry's drivers. The new regulations specify how many hours a driver can work in a week, how much time must elapse between weeks, how often and for how long drivers must get off the road for a break, and even what hours of the night they must sleep. Although the regulators say the new rules will "ensure that drivers get the rest they need to be alert, safe, and awake," the industry says the new rules cut productivity and raise costs—that is, shift the AS curve to the left.

Similar problems continue to inflate intrastate trucking costs. All but eight states limit the routes, the loads, and the prices of intrastate trucking companies. These regulations promote inefficient transportation and protect producer profits. The net cost to the economy is at least $8 billion, or about $128 a year for a family of four.

Many cities and counties also limit the number of taxicabs and regulate their prices. Some also prohibit or constrain ride-sharing services like Uber and Lyft that offer cheaper transportation. The net effect of such regulation is to limit competition and drive up the cost of transportation.

Food and Drug Standards. The Food and Drug Administration (FDA) has a broad mandate to protect consumers from dangerous products. In fulfilling this responsibility, the FDA sets health standards for the content of specific foods. The FDA also sets standards for the testing of new drugs and evaluates the test results.

The goal of FDA regulation is to minimize health risks to consumers. Like all regulation, however, the FDA standards entail real costs. The tests required for new drugs are expensive and time-consuming. Getting a new drug approved for sale takes years of effort and requires multimillion-dollar investments. The net results are that (1) fewer new drugs are brought to market and (2) those that reach the market are more expensive. In other words, the aggregate supply of goods is shifted to the left.

Other examples of government regulation are commonplace. The Environmental Protection Agency (EPA) regulates auto emissions, the discharge of industrial wastes, and water pollution. The U.S. Congress restricts foreign imports and raises their prices. The Federal Trade Commission (FTC) limits firms' freedom to increase their output or advertise their products. The Consumer Product Safety Commission regulates toys, mandating expensive tests for the chemical content of materials and paint used in children's toys. Toy manufacturers complain that the required tests are unnecessary and too expensive, especially for the many small businesses that make, sell, or resell children's toys and clothes.

Reducing Costs

Many—perhaps most—of these regulatory activities are beneficial. In fact, all were originally designed to serve specific public purposes. As a result of such regulation, we get safer drugs, cleaner air, and less deceptive advertising. We must also consider the costs involved, however. All regulatory activities impose direct and indirect costs. These costs must be compared to the benefits received. ***The basic contention of supply-side economists is that regulatory costs are now too high.*** To improve our economic performance, they assert, we must *deregulate* the production process, thereby shifting the aggregate supply curve to the right again.

Regulation makes toys safer but also more expensive.

Steve Hix/Fuse

EASING TRADE BARRIERS

Government regulation of international trade also influences the shape and position of aggregate supply. Trade flows affect both factor and product markets.

Factor Markets

In factor markets, U.S. producers buy raw materials, equipment parts, and components from foreign suppliers. Tariffs (taxes on imported goods) make such inputs more expensive, thereby increasing the cost of U.S. production. Regulations or quotas that make foreign inputs less accessible or more expensive similarly constrain the U.S. aggregate supply curve. The quota on imported sugar, for example, increases the cost of U.S.-produced soda, cookies, and candy. Just that one trade barrier has cost U.S. consumers more than $2 billion in higher prices.

Product Markets

The same kind of trade barriers affect product markets directly. With completely unrestricted ("free") trade, foreign producers would be readily available to supply products to U.S. consumers. By increasing the quantity of output available at any given price level, foreign suppliers help flatten out the aggregate supply curve.

President Trump pursued trade policies that steepened rather than flattened the AS curve. Declaring China to be an "unfair" trading partner, he imposed a series of escalating tariffs on Chinese imports in 2018–2019. Those tariffs increased not only consumer prices but also the price of intermediate goods used to produce products in the United States. These higher input prices shifted the AS curve to the left, slowing economic growth and increasing inflation at the same time (see World View "Trump Tariffs Shave U.S. Growth").

WORLD VIEW

TRUMP TARIFFS SHAVE U.S. GROWTH

Declaring himself to be a "tariff man," President Trump imposed a series of escalating tariffs on Chinese goods. The tariff war started in early 2018 with a 25 percent tariff on 818 Chinese products and morphed into 10–25 percent tariffs on virtually all Chinese exports in late 2019. Economists estimate that the tariffs increased U.S. prices by 1 percent and shaved 0.26 percent off GDP growth in 2019.

Source: Media and research reports, December 2019.

CRITICAL ANALYSIS: Tariffs increase the price of imported products and inputs, making it more expensive to produce domestically. This results in a **leftward AS shift.**

Immigration

Another global supply-side policy lever is immigration policy. Skill shortages in U.S. labor markets can be overcome with education and training. But even faster relief is available in the vast pool of foreign workers. In 2000 Congress increased the quota for software engineers and other high-tech workers by 70 percent, to 195,000 workers. The intent was to relieve the skill shortage in high-tech industries, and with it the cost pressures that were increasing the slope of the aggregate supply curve. Temporary visas for farm workers also help avert cost-push inflation in the farm sector. By regulating the flow of immigrant workers, Congress has the potential to alter the shape and position of the short-run AS curve.

DECISIONS FOR TOMORROW

How Important Is Infrastructure?

infrastructure: The transportation, communications, education, judicial, and other institutional systems that facilitate market exchanges.

Another way to reduce the costs of supplying goods and services is to improve the nation's **infrastructure**—that is, the transportation, communications, judicial, and other systems that bind the pieces of the economy into a coherent whole. The interstate highway system, for example, enlarged the market for producers looking for new sales opportunities. Improved air traffic controls and larger airports have also made international markets and factors of production readily accessible. Without interstate highways and international airports, the process of supplying goods and services would be more localized and much more expensive.

It's easy to take infrastructure for granted until you have to make do without it. In recent years, U.S. producers have rushed into China, Russia, Eastern Europe, Cuba, and Africa looking for new profit opportunities. What they discovered is that even simple communication is difficult where Internet access and even telephones are often scarce. Imagine trying to start a food delivery service in Mozambique after cyclone Idai: no electricity, no roads, no telephone, and very-high-priced food.

Although the United States has a highly developed infrastructure, it too could be improved. There are roads and bridges to repair, more airports to be built, faster rail systems to construct, power grids to upgrade, water-treatment plants to modernize, and telecommunications networks to install. Even the basics need attention: 240,000 water mains break each year and both water and sewer pipes erode all the time. If we want to produce more efficiently, we've got to invest a lot more money in the nation's infrastructure.

Stagnant Infrastructure Investment. Over the last several decades, the United States has allocated about 2.5 percent of GDP to public infrastructure. About a fourth of this investment comes from the federal government, and the remainder from state and local governments. In 2019 total spending was about $450 billion, just 2.3 percent of GDP. At that rate of investment, the United States has barely been able to *maintain* existing infrastructure, much less *expand* it. The American Society of Civil Engineers says that 4,095 of the nation's 85,000 dams are in need of repair. They estimated that the nation's infrastructure—everything from highways to sewers—needs a $3.6 trillion upgrade.

Crumbling infrastructure constrains GDP growth.

Justin Sullivan/Getty Images News/ Getty Images

The Cost of Delay. The U.S. Department of Transportation estimates that people now spend nearly 3.5 billion hours a year in traffic delays. If the nation's highways don't improve, those delays will skyrocket to more than 4 billion hours a year a decade from now. That's a lot of labor resources to leave idle. Moreover, cars stuck on congested highways waste a lot of gasoline—nearly 4 billion gallons a year—and spew enormous amounts of carbon dioxide into our atmosphere.

Delays in air travel impose similar costs. The Federal Aviation Administration says air travel delays increase airline operating costs by more than $2 billion a year and idle more than $3 billion worth of passenger time. That time imposes a high opportunity cost in forgone business transactions and shortened vacations. Ultimately, all these costs are reflected in lower productivity, reduced output, higher prices, and greater environmental damage.

Resource Commitments. To alleviate these constraints on aggregate supply, Congress has voted several times to accelerate infrastructure spending. The Transportation Equity Act of 2000 raised federal spending to more than $600 billion in that decade. That clearly wasn't enough to stop the erosion of the nation's infrastructure. In his first year, president Trump proposed to increase federal spending on infrastructure by $200 billion over the next decade. But disagreements with Congressional Democrats about what to spend the money on kept those plans on hold. By the end of his term, no new infrastructure spending bill had passed Congress. President Biden was hoping to have more bipartisan success in funding infrastructure.

SUMMARY

- Fiscal and monetary policies seek to attain full employment and price stability by shifting the aggregate demand curve. Their success depends on microeconomic responses, as reflected in the price and output decisions of market participants. **LO16-1**
- The market's response to shifts in aggregate demand is reflected in the shape and position of the aggregate supply curve. If the AS curve slopes upward, a trade-off between unemployment and inflation exists. The Phillips curve illustrates the trade-off. **LO16-2**
- The inflationary flashpoint is the rate of output where inflation accelerates—where the unemployment–inflation trade-off becomes acute. **LO16-2**
- If the AS curve shifts to the left, the trade-off between unemployment and inflation worsens. Stagflation—a combination of substantial inflation and unemployment—results. This is illustrated by rightward shifts of the Phillips curve. **LO16-2**
- Supply-side policies attempt to alter price and output decisions directly. If successful, they'll shift the aggregate supply curve to the right. A rightward AS shift implies less inflation *and* less unemployment. **LO16-3**
- Marginal tax rates are a major concern of supply-side economists. High tax rates discourage extra work, investment,

and saving. A reduction in marginal tax rates should shift aggregate supply to the right. **LO16-3**
- The tax elasticity of supply measures the response of quantity supplied to changes in tax rates. Empirical evidence suggests that tax elasticity is modest but still triggers short-run shifts of the aggregate supply curve. **LO16-3**
- Investments in human capital increase productivity and therefore shift aggregate supply also. Workers' training, education, and health services are policy tools. **LO16-4**
- Government regulation often raises the cost of production and limits output. Deregulation is intended to reduce costly restrictions on price and output behavior, thereby shifting the AS curve to the right. **LO16-4**
- Public infrastructure is part of the economy's capital resources. Investments in infrastructure (such as transportation systems) facilitate market exchanges, expand production possibilities, and reduce environmental impacts. **LO16-4**
- Trade barriers shift the AS curve leftward by raising the cost of imported inputs and the price of imported products. Lowering trade barriers increases aggregate supply. **LO16-4**

Key Terms

stagflation	investment	structural unemployment
aggregate supply (AS)	tax rebate	labor productivity
Phillips curve	tax elasticity of supply	transfer payments
inflationary flashpoint	saving	infrastructure
misery index	capital gains tax	
marginal tax rate	human capital	

Questions for Discussion

1. Why might prices rise when aggregate demand increases? What factors might influence the extent of price inflation?   **LO16-1**

2. How did the 2019 cyclone alter aggregate supply and demand in Mozambique (World View "Cyclone Idai Destroys Mozambique Port City")?   **LO16-3**

3. Why did President Obama raise the top marginal tax rate to 39.6 percent if higher tax rates reduce aggregate supply?   **LO16-4**

4. Which of the following groups are likely to have the highest tax elasticity of labor supply: (*a*) college students, (*b*) single parents, (*c*) primary earners in two-parent families, and (*d*) secondary earners in two-parent families? Why are there differences?   **LO16-3**

5. How is the aggregate supply curve affected by (*a*) minimum wage laws, (*b*) Social Security payroll taxes, (*c*) Social Security retirement benefits, and (*d*) tighter border security?   **LO16-4**

6. If the government requires power companies to use "clean" energy sources rather than "dirty" ones, how would aggregate supply be affected?   **LO16-4**

7. How do traffic delays affect the nation's total output?   **LO16-3**

8. How does each of the following infrastructure items affect aggregate supply: (*a*) highways, (*b*) schools, (*c*) sewage systems, and (*d*) courts and prisons?   **LO16-4**

9. How would the volume and timing of capital investments be affected by (*a*) a permanent cut in the capital gains tax and (*b*) a temporary 10 percent tax credit?   **LO16-4**

10. How might the inflationary flashpoint affect policy decisions? How would you represent the flashpoint on the Phillips curve?   **LO16-2**

11. Why not spend a lot more on infrastructure? Why would anyone object to doubling our annual infrastructure spending?   **LO16-2**

PROBLEMS FOR CHAPTER 16

McGraw Hill connect

LO16-1 1. On the following graph, draw the (*A*) Keynesian, (*B*) monetarist, and (*C*) consensus hybrid AS curves, all intersecting AD at point *E*.

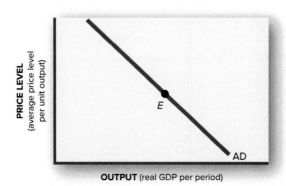

If AD shifts rightward, which AS curve (*A*, *B*, or *C*) generates
(*a*) The biggest increase in output?
(*b*) The biggest increase in prices?

LO16-1 2. Which AS curve (*a*, *b*, or *c*) in Figure 16.1 causes the least unemployment when fiscal or monetary restraint is pursued?

LO16-4 3. Suppose taxpayers are required to pay a base tax of $50 plus 30 percent on any income greater than $100, as in the initial tax system *B* in Table 16.1. Suppose further that the taxing authority wishes to raise the taxes of people with incomes of $200 by $40.
(*a*) If marginal tax rates are to remain unchanged, what will the new base tax have to be?
(*b*) If the base tax of $50 is to remain unchanged, what will the marginal tax rate have to be?

LO16-3 4. Suppose households supply 400 billion hours of labor per year and have a tax elasticity of supply of 0.15. If the tax rate is increased by 10 percent, by how many hours will the supply of labor decline?

LO16-4 5. By how much did the disposable income of rich people increase as a result of the 2017 drop in the top marginal tax rate from 39.6 to 37 percent? Assume rich people have $2 trillion of gross income in the highest bracket.

LO16-2 6. According to Figure 16.6, what inflation rate would occur if the unemployment rate rose to 6 percent, with
(*a*) PC_1?   (*b*) PC_2?

LO16-3 7. Illustrate the effect of a business tax cut on aggregate supply using the model of the macroeconomy. What happened to the
(*a*) Equilibrium rate of output?
(*b*) Equilibrium price level?
(*c*) Unemployment?

371

LO16-2 8. On the following graph, plot the unemployment and inflation rates for the years 2010–2019 using Data Tables at the end of the book. Is there any evidence of a Phillips curve trade-off?

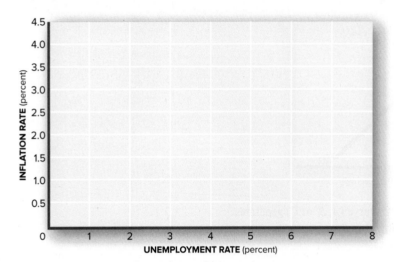

LO16-4 9. If the tax elasticity of labor supply is 0.24, by what percentage will the quantity of labor supplied increase in response to
(*a*) A $500 per person income tax rebate?
(*b*) A 9 percent reduction in marginal tax rates?

LO16-4 10. If the tax elasticity of labor supply is 0.17, by how much do tax rates have to be reduced to increase the labor supply by 2 percent?

LO16-3 11. If GDP grew by $831 billion in 2019,
(*a*) How much potential output was lost as a result of the Trump tariffs (World View "Trump Tariffs Shave U.S. Growth")?
(*b*) If a new house costs $150,000 to construct, how many houses could have been produced with that potential output?

LO16-1 12. *Decisions for Tomorrow:* This section provides estimates of time spent in traffic delays. If the average worker produces $110 of output per hour, what is the opportunity cost of
(*a*) Current traffic delays?
(*b*) Estimated delays in 10 years?

Dennis MacDonald/Alamy Stock photo

CHAPTER 17

Growth and Productivity: Long-Run Possibilities

LEARNING OBJECTIVES

After reading this chapter, you should know

LO17-1 The principal sources of economic growth.

LO17-2 The policy tools for accelerating growth.

LO17-3 The pros and cons of continued growth.

Economic growth is the fundamental determinant of the long-run success of any nation, the basic source of rising living standards, and the key to meeting the needs and desires of the American people.

—*Economic Report of the President, 1992*

Imagine a world with no smartphones, no satellite TV, no social media, and no digital sound. Such a world actually existed—only 40 years ago! At the time, personal computers were still on the drawing board, and laptops weren't even envisioned. Websites were a place where spiders gathered, not locations on the Internet. Home video hadn't been seen, and no one had yet popped any microwave popcorn. Biotechnology hadn't yet produced any blockbuster drugs, and people wore the same pair of athletic shoes for a wide variety of sports.

New products are evidence of economic progress. Over time, we produce not only *more* goods and services but also *new* and *better* goods and services. In the process, we get richer: Our material living standards rise.

Rising living standards aren't inevitable, however. According to World Bank estimates, over 2 *billion* people—more than a fourth of the world's population—continue to live in abject poverty with incomes of less than $3 per day. Worse still, living standards in many of the poorest countries have *fallen* in the last decade.

This chapter takes a longer-term view of economic performance. Chapters 8 to 16 were concerned with the business cycle—that is, *short-run* variations in output and prices. This chapter looks at the prospects for *long-run* growth and considers three questions:

- **How important is economic growth?**
- **How does an economy grow?**
- **Is continued economic growth possible? Is it desirable?**

We develop answers to these questions by first examining the nature of economic growth and then examining its sources and potential limits.

THE NATURE OF GROWTH

Economic growth refers to increases in the output of goods and services. But there are two distinct ways in which output increases, and they have different implications for our economic welfare.

Short-Run Changes in Capacity Utilization

The easiest kind of growth comes from increased use of our productive capabilities. In any given year there's a limit to an economy's potential output. This limit is determined by the quantity of resources available and our technological know-how. We've illustrated these short-run limits with a **production possibilities** curve, as in Figure 17.1a. By using all our available resources and our best expertise, we can produce any combination of goods and services on the production possibilities curve.

We don't always take full advantage of our productive capacity. The economy often produces a mix of output that lies *inside* our production possibilities, like point A in Figure 17.1a. This was our situation in the Great Recession of 2008–2009. When this happens, a major *short-run* goal of macro policy is to achieve full employment—to move us from point A to some point on the production possibilities curve (such as point B). In the process, we produce more output.

Long-Run Change in Capacity

Once we're fully utilizing our productive capacity, further increases in output are attainable only if we *expand* that capacity. To do so, we have to *shift* the production possibilities curve outward as in Figure 17.1b. Such shifts imply an increase in *potential* GDP—that is, our productive capacity.

Over time, increases in capacity are critical. Short-run increases in the utilization of existing capacity can generate only modest increases in output. Even high unemployment rates, such as 9 percent, leave little room for increased output. ***To achieve large and lasting increases in output, we must push our production possibilities outward.*** For this reason, economists often define **economic growth** in terms of changes in *potential* GDP.

The unique character of economic growth can also be illustrated with aggregate supply and demand curves. Figure 17.2 depicts both a sloped, *short-run* AS curve and a vertical, *long-run* AS curve. In the short run, macro stabilization policies try to shift the AD curve to a more desirable price–output equilibrium. Such demand-side policies are unlikely to change the country's long-run capacity to produce, however. At best they move the macro equilibrium to a more desirable point on the *short-run* AS curve (e.g., from E_1 to E_2 in Figure 17.2).

production possibilities: The alternative combinations of final goods and services that could be produced in a given period with all available resources and technology.

economic growth: An increase in output (real GDP); an expansion of production possibilities.

FIGURE 17.1

Two Types of Growth

Increases in output result from increased use of existing capacity or from increases in that capacity itself.

In part *a* the mix of output at point A doesn't make full use of production possibilities. We can get additional output by employing more of our available resources or using them more efficiently. This is illustrated by point B (or any other point on the curve).

Once we're on the production possibilities curve, we can get more output only by *increasing* our productive capacity. This is illustrated by the outward *shift* of the production possibilities curve in part *b*.

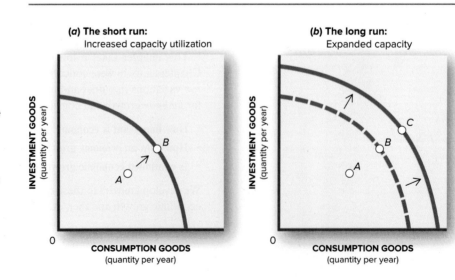

(a) The short run: Increased capacity utilization

(b) The long run: Expanded capacity

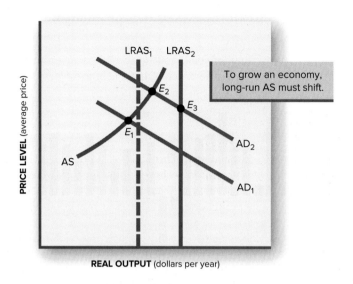

FIGURE 17.2

Shifts of Long-Run Supply

Macro stabilization policies try to shift the aggregate demand curve (e.g., from AD₁ to AD₂) to achieve greater output and employment in the short run.

The vertical long-run AS curve implies that these efforts will have no lasting impact on the natural rate of output, however. To achieve economic growth, the long-run aggregate supply curve must be shifted to the right (e.g., from LRAS₁ to LRAS₂).

Our productive capacity may increase nevertheless. If it does, the "natural" long-run AS curve will also shift. In this framework, *economic growth implies a rightward shift of the long-run aggregate supply curve.* Should that occur, the economy will be able to produce still more output with less inflationary pressure (e.g., as at E_3 in Figure 17.2).

Nominal vs. Real GDP

Notice that we refer to *real* GDP, not *nominal* GDP, in our concept of economic growth. Nominal GDP can rise even when the quantity of goods and services falls, as was the case in 2008. The total quantity of goods and services produced in 2008 was less than the quantity produced in 2007. Nevertheless, prices rose enough in 2008 to keep nominal GDP growing.

Real GDP refers to the actual quantity of goods and services produced. Real GDP avoids the distortions of inflation by adjusting for changing prices. By using 2012 prices as a **base year,** we observe that real GDP fell from $15,626 billion in 2007 to $15,605 billion in 2008 (a drop of $21 billion). Since then real GDP has increased another $4 trillion—impressive evidence of continuing economic growth.

real GDP: The value of final output produced in a given period, adjusted for changing prices.

base year: The year used for comparative analysis; the basis for indexing price changes.

MEASURES OF GROWTH

Typically, changes in real GDP are expressed in percentage terms, as a growth *rate.* The **growth rate** is simply the change in real output between two periods divided by total output in the base period. The percentage decline in real output during 2008 was thus $21 billion ÷ $15,626 billion, or just 0.13 percent. By contrast, real output grew in 2010 by 2.5 percent.

Figure 17.3 illustrates the recent growth experience of the U.S. economy. In the 1960s, real GDP grew by an average of 4.1 percent per year. Economic growth slowed to only 2.8 percent in the 1970s, however, with actual output declines in three years. The steep recession of 1982, as seen in Figure 17.3, reduced GDP growth in the 1980s to an even lower rate: 2.5 percent per year. After the Great Recession of 2008-2009 ended, the economy continued to grow at the more subdued pace of 2.5 percent a year until the coronavirus hit (the 2020 recession). Economists expected growth to continue at 2.5 percent or better after the pandemic ended.

growth rate: Percentage change in real output from one period to another.

The Exponential Process. Although the consequences of *negative* growth (e.g., job layoffs, unemployment, pay cuts, home foreclosures) merit headlines, variations in *positive* growth rates usually elicit yawns. Indeed, the whole subject of economic growth looks rather dull when you discover that "big" gains in economic growth are measured in fractions of a percent. However, this initial impression isn't fair. First, even one year's "low" growth implies lost output. If we had just *maintained* output in 2008 at its 2007 level—that is, "achieved" a

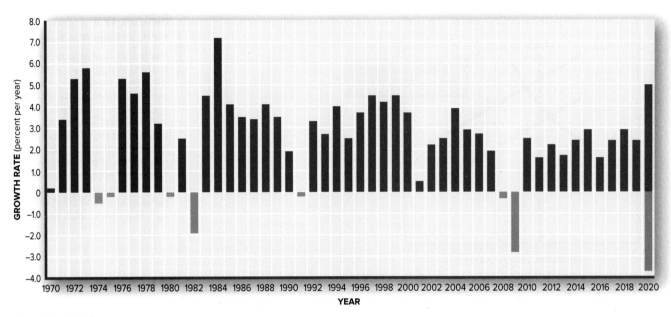

FIGURE 17.3

Recent U.S. Growth Rates

Total output typically increases from one year to another. The focus of policy is on the growth *rate*—that is, how fast real GDP increases from one year to the next. Annual growth rates since 1970 have ranged from a high of 7.2 percent (1984) to a low of *minus* 3.7 percent (2020).

Source: Economic Report of the President, 2020.

zero growth rate rather than an outright decline—we would have had $44 *billion* more worth of goods and services, which works out to nearly $140 worth of goods and services per person. In today's $22 trillion economy, each 1 percent of GDP growth translates into nearly $700 more output per person. Lots of people would like that extra output.

Second, economic growth is a *continuing* process. Gains made in one year accumulate in future years. It's like interest you earn at the bank: If you leave your money in the bank for several years, you begin to earn interest on your interest. Eventually you accumulate a nice little bankroll.

The process of economic growth works the same way. Each little shift of the production possibilities curve broadens the base for future GDP. As shifts accumulate over many years, the economy's productive capacity is greatly expanded. Ultimately we discover that those "little" differences in annual growth rates generate tremendous gains in GDP.

This cumulative process, whereby interest or growth is compounded from one year to the next, is called an "exponential process." At growth rates of 2.5 percent, GDP doubles in 29 years. With 3.5 percent growth, GDP doubles in only 21 years. In a single generation, the *difference* between 2.5 percent growth and 3.5 percent growth amounts to more than $15 trillion of output. That *difference* is roughly 60 percent of this year's total output. From this longer-term perspective, the difference between 2.5 percent and 3.5 percent growth begins to look very meaningful.

GDP per Capita: A Measure of Living Standards

The exponential process looks even more meaningful when we translate it into *per capita* terms. We can do so by looking at GDP *per capita* rather than total GDP. **GDP per capita** is simply total output divided by total population. In 2020, the total output of the U.S. economy was roughly $21 trillion. Because there were 330 million of us to share that output, GDP per capita was

GDP per capita: Total GDP divided by total population; average GDP.

$$\text{GDP per capita} \atop (2020) = \frac{\$21 \text{ trillion of output}}{330 \text{ million people}} = \$63,636$$

Net Growth Rate (%)		Doubling Time (Years)
0.0%	$\longrightarrow$	Never
0.5	$\longrightarrow$	144 years
1.0	$\longrightarrow$	72
1.5	$\longrightarrow$	48
2.0	$\longrightarrow$	36
2.5	$\longrightarrow$	29
3.0	$\longrightarrow$	24
3.5	$\longrightarrow$	21
4.0	$\longrightarrow$	18

TABLE 17.1

The Rule of 72

Small differences in annual growth rates cumulate into large differences in GDP. Shown here are the number of years it would take to double GDP per capita at various net growth rates. "Net" growth refers to the GDP growth rate minus the population growth rate.

Doubling times can be approximated by the "rule of 72." Seventy-two divided by the growth rate equals the number of years it takes to double.

This does not mean that every man, woman, and child in the United States received $63,636 worth of goods and services in 2020; it simply indicates how much output was potentially available to the "average" person. GDP per capita is often used as a basic measure of our standard of living.

Growth in GDP per capita is attained only when the growth of output exceeds population growth. In the United States, this condition is usually achieved. Even when *total* GDP growth slowed in the 1970s and 1980s, *per capita* GDP kept rising because the U.S. population was growing by only 1 percent a year. Hence, even relatively slow economic growth of 2.5 percent a year was enough to keep raising living standards.

The developing nations of the Third World aren't so fortunate. Many of these countries exhibit both slower *economic* growth and faster *population* growth. They have a difficult time *maintaining* living standards, much less increasing them. Central African Republic, for example, is one of the poorest countries in the world, with GDP per capita of roughly $450. Yet its population continues to grow rapidly (1.4 percent per year), putting constant pressure on living standards. In recent years, Central African Republic's GDP grew at a slower rate of only 0.4 percent. As a consequence, GDP per capita *declined* nearly 1.0 percent per year. As we'll see in the chapter titled "Global Poverty," many other poor nations are in similarly dire straits.

By comparison with these countries, the United States has been fortunate. Our GDP per capita has more than doubled since the 1980s, despite several recessions. This means that the average person today has twice as many goods and services as the average person had a generation ago.

What about the future? Will we continue to enjoy substantial gains in living standards? Many Americans harbor great doubts. A 2019 Pew research poll revealed that 6 out of 10 adults believe their children's living standards will be no higher than today's. That would happen only if population growth outstrips or equals GDP growth. That seems unlikely. Table 17.1 displays more optimistic scenarios in which GDP continues to grow faster than the population. If GDP *per capita* continues to grow at 2 percent per year—as it did in the 1990s—it will take 36 years to double our standard of living. If GDP per capita grows just half a percent faster, say, by 2.5 percent per year, our standard of living will double in only 29 years. Would you like to have that extra output when you're middle-aged?

GDP per Worker: A Measure of Productivity

The potential increases in living standards depicted in Table 17.1 won't occur automatically. Someone is going to have to produce more output if we want GDP per capita to rise. One reason our living standard rose in the 1980s is that the labor force grew faster than the population. Those in the World War II baby boom had reached maturity and were entering the **labor force** in droves. At the same time, more women took jobs outside the home, a trend that continued into the 1990s (see Figure 6.2). As a consequence, the **employment rate** increased significantly, as Figure 17.4 shows. With the number of workers growing faster than the population, GDP per capita was sure to rise.

labor force: All persons over age 16 who are either working for pay or actively seeking paid employment.

employment rate: The percentage of the adult population that is employed.

FIGURE 17.4

A Rising Employment Rate

The entry of Baby Boomers (born 1946–1960) into the labor force and increased labor force attachment of women caused the ratio of workers to total population (the employment rate) to rise from 1975 to 2000. This boosted per capita GDP. The trend reversed after 2000, however, making per capita income gains more difficult.

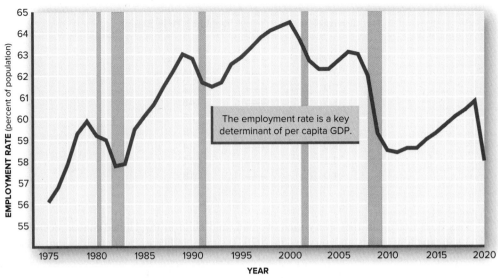

The employment rate is a key determinant of per capita GDP.

Note: Shaded areas indicate recessions.

productivity: Output per unit of input—for example, output per labor-hour.

The employment rate can't increase forever. At the limit, everyone would be in the labor market, and no further workers could be found. As Figure 17.4 reveals, the employment rate peaked in 2000, then dipped substantially in the 2001 recession and even further in the 2008–2009 recession. As the employment rate declines, increases in per capita income become more difficult. To offset the decline in the employment rate, we need to increase output per worker.

The most common measure of **productivity** is output per labor-hour, which is simply the ratio of total output to the number of hours worked. As noted earlier, total GDP in 2020 was roughly $21 trillion. In that same year, 150 million workers were employed. Hence, the average worker's productivity was

$$\frac{\text{productivity}}{\text{Labor}} = \frac{\text{Total output}}{\text{Total employment}}$$

$$= \frac{\$21 \text{ trillion}}{150 \text{ million workers}}$$

$$= \$140,000$$

This is a *lot* of output per worker! China has many more workers (800 million), but they produce much less output ($16,500) each. So Chinese living standards are far below American standards.

The *increase* in our GDP per capita in recent decades is directly related to the *rising* productivity of the average U.S. worker. The average worker today produces twice as many goods and services as the average worker did in 1983.

The Productivity Turnaround. For economic growth to continue, the productivity of the average U.S. worker must rise still further. Will it? As Figure 17.5 reveals, productivity grew at an average pace of 1.4 percent from 1973 to 1995. Along the way, however, there were many years (e.g., 1978–1984) in which productivity advances slowed to a snail's pace. This productivity slowdown constrained GDP growth.

After 1995 productivity advances accelerated sharply, as shown in Figure 17.5. This productivity jump was so impressive that it raised hopes for a "New Economy," in which technological breakthroughs, better management, and enlightened public policy would keep both productivity and GDP growing at faster rates. Although the economy did stumble into a steep recession in 2008–2009, worker productivity—and thus *potential* output—kept

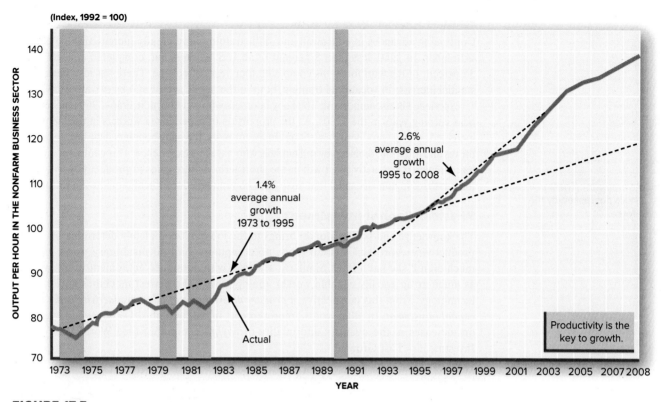

(Index, 1992 = 100)

OUTPUT PER HOUR IN THE NONFARM BUSINESS SECTOR

1.4%
average annual
growth
1973 to 1995

2.6%
average annual
growth
1995 to 2008

Actual

Productivity is the
key to growth.

YEAR

FIGURE 17.5
Productivity Gains

Increasing productivity (output per worker) is the critical factor in raising per capita GDP over time. Productivity advances slowed in 1978–1984 but accelerated sharply in 1995–2008.

Source: U.S. Department of Commerce.

increasing at a fast clip. Recent advances in cloud computing, artificial intelligence, 3D printing, and robotic manufacturing promise still further gains.

SOURCES OF GROWTH

The arithmetic of economic growth is simple. Future output growth depends on two factors:

$$\frac{\text{Growth rate of}}{\text{total output}} = \frac{\text{Growth rate of}}{\text{labor force}} + \frac{\text{Growth rate of}}{\text{productivity}}$$

Accordingly, how fast GDP increases in the future depends on how fast the labor force grows and how fast productivity advances. Because the long-run growth of the labor force has stabilized at around 1.1 percent, the real uncertainty about future economic growth originates in the unpredictability of productivity advances. Can worker productivity continue to increase at such a fast clip? Forever?

To assess the potential for future productivity gains, we need to examine the sources of productivity improvement. *The sources of productivity gains include*

- *Higher skills:* an increase in labor skills.
- *More capital:* an increase in the ratio of capital to labor.
- *Technological advance:* the development and use of better capital equipment and products.
- *Improved management:* better use of available resources in the production process.

Human Capital Investment

Continuing advances in education and skills training have greatly increased the quality of U.S. labor. In 1950, less than 8 percent of all U.S. workers had completed college. Today 35 percent of the workforce has completed four years of college. There has also been a substantial increase in vocational training, both in the public sector and by private firms.

Experience is also important. The baby boomers who were born in 1946–1960 reached their peak earning years in the 1990s. As the proportion of experienced workers in the labor force increased, average productivity went up. In recent years, the baby boomers have been retiring in droves and are being replaced by millennials, who have less experience. This demographic trend has dampened productivity growth in the short term. Future gains in productivity will reflect the increases in **human capital** that arise from continuing education and on-the-job learning.

human capital: The knowledge and skills possessed by the workforce.

Physical Capital Investment

The knowledge and skills a worker brings to the job don't completely determine his or her productivity. A worker with no tools, no computers, and no machinery won't produce much even if she has a PhD. Similarly, a worker with outmoded equipment won't produce as much as an equally capable worker equipped with the newest machines and the best technology. From this perspective, ***a primary determinant of labor productivity is the rate of capital investment.*** In other words, improvements in output per *worker* depend in large part on increases in the quantity and quality of *capital* equipment (see World View "High Investment = Fast Growth").

WORLD VIEW

HIGH INVESTMENT = FAST GROWTH

Investment in new plants and equipment is essential for economic growth. In general, countries that allocate a larger share of output to investment will grow more rapidly. In recent years, China has had one of the world's fastest GDP growth rates, and also one of the highest investment rates.

Country	Gross Investment as Percentage of GDP (2008–2012)	Growth Rate of GDP (Average, 2000–2018)
China	44	9.5
India	34	6.8
Vietnam	36	6.3
Singapore	35	5.6
Sweden	19	2.0
United States	19	1.8
Greece	18	−0.9

Source: The World Bank.

CRITICAL ANALYSIS: Investment increases production possibilities. Countries that devote a larger share of output to investment tend to grow faster.

U.S. workers are outfitted with an exceptional amount of capital equipment. As we first saw in Chapter 2, U.S. productivity is buttressed by huge investments in equipment and technology. The average U.S. worker is supported by more than $100,000 of capital inputs. To *increase* productivity, however, the quality and quantity of capital available to the average worker must continue to increase. That requires capital spending to increase faster than the labor force. With the labor force growing at 1.1 percent a year, that's not a hard standard to beat. How *much* faster capital investment grows is nevertheless a decisive factor in productivity gains.

Saving and Investment Rates. The dependence of productivity gains on capital investment puts a new perspective on consumption and saving. In the short run, the primary concern of macroeconomic policy is to balance aggregate demand and aggregate supply. In this context, savings are a form of leakage that requires offsetting injections of investment or government spending. From the longer-run perspective of economic growth, saving and investment take on added importance. ***Savings aren't just a form of leakage but a basic source of investment financing.*** If we use all our resources to produce consumer, export, and public sector goods, there won't be any investment. In that case, we might not face a short-run stabilization problem—our productive capacity might be fully utilized—but we'd confront a long-run *growth* problem. Indeed, if we consumed our entire output, our productive capacity would actually shrink because we wouldn't even be replacing worn-out plants and equipment. We must have at least enough savings to finance **net investment.**

net investment: Gross investment less depreciation.

Household and Business Saving. Household saving rates in the United States have been notoriously low. In 2000 and again in 2006, U.S. households actually *dis*saved—spending more on consumption than their disposable incomes. In recent years the household saving rate has averaged around 5.5 percent.

Fortunately, household saving is not the only source of investment financing. Businesses themselves generate a lot of cash they can use for further investment. The retained earnings and depreciation allowances that create business savings generated a huge cash flow for investment in the 1990s. The same cash-rich situation emerged in 2012–2016, setting the stage for another investment surge and faster GDP growth.

Foreign investors also continue to pour money into U.S. plants, equipment, software, and financial assets. Maintaining—and growing—these saving flows are essential to financing future investment.

Management Training

The accumulation of more and better capital equipment does not itself guarantee higher productivity or faster GDP growth. The human factor is still critical: How well resources are organized and managed will affect the rate of growth. Hence, entrepreneurship and the quality of continuing management are also major determinants of economic growth.

It's difficult to characterize differences in management techniques or to measure their effectiveness. However, much attention has been focused in recent years on the alleged shortsightedness of U.S. managers. U.S. firms, it is said, focus too narrowly on short-run profits, neglecting long-term productivity. There is little evidence of such a failure, however. The spreading use of stock options in management ranks ties executives' compensation to multiyear performance. Moreover, productivity trends in the United States not only have accelerated in recent years but also have consistently surpassed productivity gains in other industrial nations. To maintain that advantage, U.S. corporations spend billions of dollars each year on continuing management training.

Research and Development

A fourth and vital source of productivity advance is research and development (R&D), a broad concept that includes scientific research, product development, innovations in production techniques, and the development of management improvements. R&D activity may be a specific, identifiable activity such as in a research lab, or it may be part of the process of learning by doing. In either case, the insights developed from R&D generally lead to new products and cheaper ways of producing them. Over time, R&D is credited with the greatest contributions to economic growth. In his study of U.S. growth during the period 1929–1982, Edward Denison concluded that 26 percent of *total* growth was due to "advances in knowledge." Gordon Moore, the cofounder of Intel, doesn't see an end to research-based productivity advance. His "Moore's Law" predicts a *doubling* of computer power every 18 months.

Research and development is critical for economic growth.

Gorodenkoff/Shutterstock

New Growth Theory. The evident contribution of "advances in knowledge" to economic growth has spawned a new perspective called "new growth theory." "Old growth theory," it is said, emphasized the importance of bricks and mortar—that is, saving and investing in new plants and equipment. By contrast, "new" growth theory emphasizes the importance of investing in ideas. Paul Romer, a Stanford economist, asserts that new ideas and the spread of knowledge are the primary engines of growth. Unfortunately, neither Romer nor anyone else is exactly sure how one spawns new ideas or best disseminates knowledge. The only evident policy lever appears to be the support of research and development, a staple of "old" growth theory.

There's an important link between R&D and capital investment. As noted earlier, part of each year's gross investment compensates for the depreciation of existing plants and equipment. However, new machines are rarely identical to the ones they replace. When you get a new computer, you're not just *replacing* an old one; you're *upgrading* your computing capabilities with more memory, faster speed, and a lot of new features. Indeed, the availability of *better* technology is often the motive for such capital investment. The same kind of motivation spurs businesses to upgrade machines and structures. Hence, ***advances in technology and capital investment typically go hand in hand.***

POLICY TOOLS

As we've observed, economic growth depends on rightward shifts of the long-run aggregate supply curve (Figure 17.2). It should not surprise you, then, that growth policy makes liberal use of the tools in the supply-side toolbox (Chapter 16). The challenge for growth policy is to select those tools that will give the economy *long*-run increases in productive capacity.

Increasing Human Capital Investment

Because *workers* are the ultimate source of output and productivity growth, the first place to look for growth-accelerating tools is in the area of human capital development.

Education. Governments at all levels already play a tremendous role in human capital development by building, operating, and subsidizing schools. The quantity and quality of continuing investments in America's schools will have a major effect on future productivity. Government policy also plays an *indirect* role in schooling decisions by offering subsidized loans for college and vocational education.

Immigration. Immigration policy is also a determinant of the nation's stock of human capital. At least 1 million immigrants enter the United States every year. Most of the *legal* immigrants are relatives of people already living in the United States as permanent residents (with green cards) or naturalized citizens. In addition to these *family-based* visas, the United

States also grants a much smaller number of *employment-based* visas. The H-1B program offers temporary (three-year) visas to highly skilled foreigners who want to work in U.S. firms. Only 65,000 H-1B visas are available each year, however—a tiny percent of the U.S. labor force. Temporary visas for agricultural (H-2A) and other less-skilled workers (H-2B) are fewer still. To accelerate our productivity and GDP growth, observers urge us to expand these programs.

Increasing Physical Capital Investment

As in the case of human capital, the possibilities for increasing physical capital investment are also many and diverse.

Investment Incentives. The tax code is a mechanism for stimulating investment. Faster depreciation schedules, tax credits for new investments, and lower business tax rates all encourage increased investment in physical capital. The 2002 and 2003 tax cuts were designed for this purpose. President Obama's 2011 stimulus program also provided increased tax incentives (100 percent expensing) for investment in physical capital. President Trump's 2017 cut in the corporate income tax rate was explicitly designed to increase domestic investment.

Savings Incentives. In principle, the government can also deepen the savings pool that finances investment. Here again, the tax code offers some policy levers. Tax preferences for individual retirement accounts and other pension savings may increase the marginal propensity to save or at least redirect savings flows to longer-term investments. The Bush 2001 tax package (Chapter 11) included not only a *short-run* fiscal stimulus (e.g., tax rebates) but also enhanced incentives for *long-term* savings (retirement and college savings accounts).

Infrastructure Development. The government also directly affects the level of physical capital through its public works spending. As we observed in Chapter 16, the $2 trillion already invested in bridges, highways, airports, sewer systems, and other infrastructure is an important part of America's capital stock. President Obama's 2009 stimulus program vastly increased spending on roads, bridges, power sources, and educational facilities. President Trump's infrastructure plans are even more ambitious. Investments of that sort reduce transportation costs, increase market efficiency, reduce environmental impact, and expand potential output.

Fiscal Responsibility. In addition to these many supply-side interventions, the government's *macro* policies also affect the rate of investment and growth. Of particular interest in this regard is the federal government's budget balance. As we've seen, budget deficits may be a useful mechanism for attaining short-run macro stability. Those same deficits, however, may have negative long-run effects. If Uncle Sam borrows more funds from the national savings pool, other borrowers may end up with less. As we saw in Chapter 12, there's no guarantee that federal deficits will result in the **crowding out** of private investment. Let's recognize the risk of such an outcome, however. Hence, *fiscal and monetary policies must be evaluated in terms of their impact not only on (short-run) aggregate demand but also on long-run aggregate supply.*

crowding out: A reduction in private sector borrowing (and spending) caused by increased government borrowing.

Many people fear that the enormous deficits created by the Obama and Trump budgets will ultimately raise interest rates and crowd out private investment (see Front Page Economics "Paying for Trump's Infrastructure Spending").

Maintaining Stable Expectations

The position of the long-run AS curve also depends on a broader assessment of the economic outlook. Expectations are a critical factor in both consumption and investment behavior. People who expect to lose their jobs next year are unlikely to buy a new car or house this year. Likewise, if investors expect interest rates to jump next year, they may be less willing to initiate long-run capital projects.

FRONT PAGE ECONOMICS

PAYING FOR TRUMP'S INFRASTRUCTURE SPENDING

WASHINGTON, D.C. The conservative Tax Foundation has estimated the economic effects of President Trump's proposed infrastructure spending. They estimate that a $500 billion increase in infrastructure spread out over ten years will indeed create jobs, boost productivity, and increase GDP. But if that spending is funded by deficit borrowing, interest rates will rise and those higher rates will dampen the pro-growth effects of the fiscal stimulus. The net effects will be a modest 0.11 percent increase in the GDP growth rate, an additional 21,400 jobs, $25 billion in productivity gains, and an increase in the government's budget deficit of $21.5–26 billion per year.

Source: Tax Foundation.

CRITICAL ANALYSIS: Any increase in pro-growth government spending must be financed with higher taxes or increased borrowing (deficits), either of which might result in **crowding out** of private spending. The *net* impact of such spending incorporates both the positive and negative effects of the budget changes.

A sense of political and economic stability is critical to any long-run current trend. Within that context, however, specific perceptions of government policy may also alter investment plans. Investors may look to the Fed for a sense of monetary stability. They may be looking for a greater commitment to long-run price stability than to short-run adjustments of aggregate demand. In the fiscal policy area, the same kind of commitment to long-run fiscal discipline rather than to short-run stimulus may be sought. Such possibilities imply that macro policy must be sensitive to long-run expectations.

Institutional Context

Last, but not least, the prospects for economic growth depend on the institutional context of a nation's economy. We first encountered this proposition in Chapter 1. In World View "Index of Economic Freedom," nations were ranked on the basis of an Index of Freedom. Studies have shown how greater economic freedom—secure property rights, open trade, lower taxes, less regulation—typically fosters faster growth. In less-regulated economies, there's more scope for entrepreneurship and more opportunity to invest. Recognizing this, nations around the world, from India to China, to Russia, to Latin America, have deregulated industries, privatized state enterprises, and promoted more open trade and investment.

DECISIONS FOR TOMORROW

Are There Any Limits to Future Growth?

Suppose we pulled all the right policy levers and were able to keep the economy on a fast-paced growth track. Could the economy keep growing forever? Wouldn't we use up all available resources and ruin the environment in the process? How much long-term growth is really possible—or even desirable?

The Malthusian Formula for Destruction. The prospect of an eventual limit to economic growth originated in the 18th-century warnings of the Reverend Thomas Malthus. Malthus argued that continued economic growth was impossible because food production couldn't keep pace with population growth. His dire projections earned the economics profession its characterization as the "dismal science."

When Malthus first issued his warnings, in 1798, the population of England (including Wales) was about 9 million. Annual production of barley, oats, and related grains was approximately 162 million bushels, and wheat production was around 50 million bushels, just about enough to feed the English population (a little had to be imported from other countries). Although the relationship between food and population was satisfactory in

1798, Malthus reasoned that starvation was not far off. First of all, he observed that "population, when unchecked, goes on doubling itself every 25 years, or increases in a geometrical ratio."[1] Thus, he foresaw the English population increasing to 36 million people by 1850, 144 million by 1900, and more than 1 billion by 1975, unless some social or natural restraints were imposed on population growth.

Limits to Food Production. One natural population check that Malthus foresaw was a scarcity of food. England had only a limited amount of land available for cultivation and was already farming the most fertile tracts. Before long, all available land would be in use, and only improvements in agricultural productivity (output per acre) could increase food supplies. Some productivity increases were possible, Malthus concluded, but "the means of subsistence, under circumstances the most favorable to human industry, could not possibly be made to increase faster than in an arithmetical ratio."[2]

With population increasing at a *geometric* rate and food supplies at an *arithmetic* rate, the eventual outcome is evident. Figure 17.6 illustrates how the difference between a **geometric growth** path and an **arithmetic growth** path ultimately leads to starvation. As Malthus calculated it, per capita wheat output would decline from 5.5 bushels in 1800 to only 1.7 bushels in

geometric growth: An increase in quantity by a constant proportion each year.

arithmetic growth: An increase in quantity by a constant amount each year.

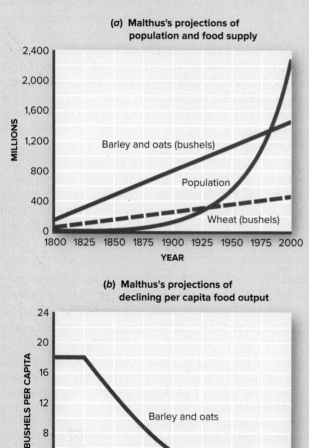

(a) Malthus's projections of population and food supply

(b) Malthus's projections of declining per capita food output

FIGURE 17.6

The Malthusian Doomsday

By projecting the growth rates of population and food output into the future, Malthus foresaw England's doomsday. At that time, the amount of available food per capita would be too small to sustain human life. Fortunately, Malthus overestimated population growth and underestimated productivity growth.

Source: Malthus's arithmetic applied to actual data for 1800.

Continued

[1]Thomas Malthus, *An Essay on the Principle of Population* (1798; reprint ed., Homewood, IL: Richard D. Irwin, 1963), p. 4.
[2]Ibid., p. 5.

1900 (Figure 17.6*b*). This wasn't enough food to feed the English people. According to Malthus's projections, either England died off about 100 years ago, or it has been maintained at the brink of starvation for more than a century only by recurrent plagues, wars, or the kind of "moral restraint" that's commonly associated with Victorian preachments.

Malthus's logic was impeccable. As long as population increased at a geometric rate while output increased at an arithmetic rate, England's doomsday was as certain as two plus two equals four. Malthus's error was not in his logic but in his empirical assumptions. He didn't know how fast output would increase over time, any more than we know whether people will be wearing electronic wings in the year 2203. He had to make an educated guess about future productivity trends. He based his estimates on his own experiences at the very beginning of the Industrial Revolution. As it turned out (fortunately), he had no knowledge of the innovations that would change the world, and he grossly underestimated the rate at which productivity would increase. *Output, including agricultural products, has increased at a geometric rate, not at the much slower arithmetic rate foreseen by Malthus.* As we observed earlier, U.S. output has grown at a long-term rate of roughly 3 percent a year. This *geometric* growth has doubled output every 25 years or so. That rate of economic growth is more than enough to raise living standards for a population growing by only 1 percent a year.

Resource Constraints. As Yale historian Paul Kennedy has suggested, maybe Malthus's doomsday predictions were just premature, not wrong. Maybe growth will come to a screeching halt when we run out of arable land, water, oil, or some other vital resource.

Malthus focused on arable land as the ultimate resource constraint. Other doomsday prophets have focused on the supply of whale oil, coal, oil, potatoes, and other "essential" resources. All such predictions ignore **the role of markets in both promoting more efficient uses of scarce resources and finding substitutes for them.** If, for example, the world were really running out of oil, what would happen to oil prices? Oil prices would rise substantially, prompting consumers to use oil more efficiently and prompting producers to develop alternative fuel sources.

If productivity and the availability of substitutes increase fast enough, the price of "scarce" resources might actually fall rather than rise. This possibility prompted a famous "doomsday bet" between University of Maryland business professor Julian Simon and Stanford ecologist Paul Ehrlich. In 1980 Paul Ehrlich identified five metals that he predicted would become so scarce as to slow economic growth. Simon wagered that the price of those metals would actually *decline* over the ensuing decade as productivity and available substitutes increased. In 1990 their prices had fallen, and Ehrlich paid Simon for the bet.

Environmental Destruction. The market's ability to circumvent resource constraints would seem to augur well for our future. Doomsayers warn, though, that other limits to growth will emerge, even in a world of "unlimited" resources and unending productivity advance. The villain this time is pollution. More than 40 years ago, Paul Ehrlich warned about this second problem:

> Attempts to increase food production further will tend to accelerate the deterioration of our environment, which in turn will eventually *reduce* the capacity of the Earth to produce food. It is not clear whether environmental decay has now gone so far as to be essentially irreversible; it is possible that the capacity of the planet to support human life has been permanently impaired. Such technological "successes" as automobiles, pesticides, and inorganic nitrogen fertilizers are major contributors to environmental deterioration.[3]

The "inevitability" of environmental destruction led G. Evelyn Hutchinson to conclude in 1970 that the limits of habitable existence on Earth would be measured "in decades."[4]

It's not difficult for anyone with the basic five senses to comprehend the pollution problem. Pollution is as close these days as the air we breathe. Moreover, we can't fail to observe a distinct tendency for pollution levels to rise along with GDP and population

[3]Paul Erhlich and Anne H. Erhlich, *Population Resources Environment: Issues in Human Ecology,* 2nd ed. (San Francisco, CA: W.H. Freeman, 1972), p. 442.
[4]Evelyn Hutchinson, "The Biosphere," *Scientific American,* September 1970, p. 53; Dennis L. Meadows et al., *The Limits to Growth* (New York: Universe Books, 1972), ch. 4.

expansion. Scientists are also alarmed by the climate changes that have accompanied population and output growth. If one projects past climate change and pollution trends into the future, things are bound to look pretty ugly.

Although pollution is universally acknowledged to be an important and annoying problem, we can't assume that the *rate* of pollution will continue unabated. On the contrary, the growing awareness of the pollution problem has prompted significant abatement efforts. The Environmental Protection Agency (EPA), for example, is unquestionably a force working for cleaner air and water. Indeed, active policies to curb pollution are as familiar as auto exhaust controls, DDT bans, and tradable CO_2 and SO_2 permits. A computer programmed 10 or 20 years ago to forecast pollution levels wouldn't have foreseen these abatement efforts and would thus have overestimated current pollution levels.

This isn't to say that we have in any final way solved the pollution problem or that we're even doing the best job we possibly can. It simply says that geometric increases in pollution aren't inevitable. There's no compelling reason why we have to continue polluting the environment; if we stop, another doomsday can be averted.

The Possibility of Growth. The misplaced focus on doomsday scenarios has a distinct opportunity cost. As Robert Solow summed up the issue,

> My real complaint about the Doomsday school [is that] it diverts attention from the really important things that can actually be done, step by step, to make things better. The end of the world *is* at hand—the earth, if you take the long view, will fall into the sun in a few billion years anyway, unless some other disaster happens first. In the meantime, I think we'd be better off passing a strong sulfur emissions tax, or getting some Highway Trust Fund money allocated to mass transit, or building a humane and decent floor under family incomes, or overriding President Nixon's veto of a strong Water Quality Act, or reforming the tax system, or fending off starvation in Bengal—instead of worrying about the generalized "predicament of mankind."[5]

Karl Marx expressed these same thoughts nearly a century earlier. Marx chastised "the contemptible Malthus" for turning the attention of the working class away from what he regarded as the immediate problem of capitalist exploitation to some distant and ill-founded anxiety about "natural" disaster.[6]

The Desirability of Growth. Let's concede, then, that continued, perhaps even "limitless," growth is *possible*. Can we also agree that it's *desirable?* Those of us who commute on congested highways, worry about climate change, breathe foul air, and can't find a secluded camping site may raise a loud chorus of nos. But before reaching a conclusion, let's at least determine what it is people don't like about the prospect of continued growth. Is it really economic growth per se that people object to, or instead the specific ways GDP has grown in the past?

First of all, let's distinguish clearly between economic growth and population growth. Congested neighborhoods, dining halls, and highways are the consequence of too many people, not of too many goods and services. Indeed, if we had *more* goods and services— if we had more houses and transit systems—much of the population congestion we now experience might be relieved. Maybe if we had enough resources to meet our existing demands *and* to build a solar-generated "new town" in the middle of Montana, people might move out of the crowded neighborhoods of Chicago and St. Louis. Well, probably not, but at least one thing is certain: With fewer goods and services, more people will have to share any given quantity of output.

This brings us back to the really essential measure of growth: **GDP per capita.** Are there any serious grounds for desiring *less* GDP per capita, a reduced standard of living? Don't say yes just because you think we already have too many cars on our roads or calories in our bellies. That argument refers to the *mix* of output again and doesn't answer the question of whether we want *any* more goods or services per person. Increasing GDP per capita can take a million forms, including the educational services you're now consuming. The rejection of economic growth per se implies that none of those forms is desirable in the economy tomorrow.

---

[5] Robert M. Solow, "Is the End of the World at Hand?," *Challenge* 16, no. 1 (March/April 1973), p. 50.
[6] Cited by John Maddox in *The Doomsday Syndrome* (New York: McGraw-Hill, 1972), pp. 40 and 45.

SUMMARY

- Economic growth refers to increases in real GDP. Short-run growth may result from increases in capacity utilization (like less unemployment). In the long run, however, growth requires increases in capacity itself—rightward shifts of the long-run aggregate supply curve.   **LO17-1**
- The U.S. economy has grown an average of 3 percent a year, a rate that doubles total output every 24 years.   **LO17-1**
- GDP per capita is a basic measure of living standards. GDP per capita will continue to increase as long as output growth exceeds population growth.   **LO17-1**
- GDP per worker is a basic measure of productivity.   **LO17-1**
- The rate of economic growth is set by the growth rate of the labor force *plus* the growth rate of output per worker (productivity). Over time, increases in productivity have been the primary cause of rising living standards.   **LO17-1**
- Productivity gains come from many sources, including better labor quality, increased capital investment, research and development, improved management, and supportive government policies.   **LO17-2**
- Supply-side policies increase both the short- and long-run capacity to produce. Monetary and fiscal policies may also affect capital investment and thus the rate of economic growth.   **LO17-2**
- Recent U.S. investment growth has been financed primarily with business saving and foreign investment. U.S. households save very little.   **LO17-1**
- The argument that there are identifiable and imminent limits to growth—perhaps even a cataclysmic doomsday—are founded on one of two concerns: (1) the depletion of resources and (2) pollution of the ecosystem.   **LO17-3**
- The flaw in doomsday arguments is that they regard existing patterns of resource use or pollution as unalterable. They consistently underestimate the possibilities for technological advance or market adaptation.   **LO17-3**
- Continued economic growth is desirable as long as it brings a higher standard of living for people and an increased ability to produce and consume socially desirable goods and services.   **LO17-3**

Key Terms

production possibilities
economic growth
real GDP
base year
growth rate

GDP per capita
labor force
employment rate
productivity
human capital

net investment
crowding out
geometric growth
arithmetic growth

Questions for Discussion

1. In what specific ways (if any) does a college education increase a worker's productivity?   **LO17-1**
2. How does international trade affect economic growth? (See World View "Trump Tariffs Shave U.S. Growth" in Chapter 16.)   **LO17-2**
3. Why don't we consume all our current output instead of sacrificing some present consumption for investment?   **LO17-1**
4. How might economic growth be impeded by (*a*) high levels of national debt and/or (*b*) fiscal restraint designed to reduce that national debt?   **LO17-2**
5. Should fiscal policy encourage more consumption or more saving? Does it matter?   **LO17-2**
6. In 1866 Stanley Jevons predicted that economic growth would come to a halt when England ran out of coal, a doomsday that he reckoned would occur in the mid-1970s. How did we avert that projection? Will we avert an "oil crisis" in the same way?   **LO17-3**
7. Fertility rates in the United States have dropped so low that we're approaching zero population growth, a condition that France has maintained for decades. How will this affect our economic growth? Our standard of living?   **LO17-1**
8. Is limitless growth really possible? What forces do you think will be most important in slowing or halting economic growth?   **LO17-3**
9. Why do some nations grow and prosper while others stagnate?   **LO17-1**
10. Real resources are needed to produce products (e.g., solar panels, charging stations, smokestack filters) that protect the environment. If the economy doesn't grow, where will we get these resources?   **LO17-3**

PROBLEMS FOR CHAPTER 17

LO17-1 1. According to the Rule of 72 (Table 17.1), how many years will it take for GDP to double if the economy is growing at
  (*a*) 2.5 percent a year?
  (*b*) 3 percent a year?

LO17-1 2. According to the Rule of 72 (Table 17.1) and recent growth rates (World View "High Investment = Fast Growth"), how long will it be before GDP doubles in
  (*a*) The United States?
  (*b*) China?
  (*c*) Sweden?

LO17-1 3. How much *more* output will the average American (U.S. population = 330 million) have a year from now if the $22 trillion GDP grows by
  (*a*) 0 percent?
  (*b*) 1 percent?
  (*c*) 3 percent?

LO17-3 4. According to Figure 17.3, in how many years since 1990 has GDP grown
  (*a*) Faster than the population (1 percent growth)?
  (*b*) Slower than the population?

LO17-1 5. If the labor force increases by 1.1 percent each year and productivity increases by 2.7 percent, how fast will output grow?

LO17-1 6. In 2019, 61 percent of the adult population (260 million) was employed. If the employment rate increased to 62 percent,
  (*a*) How many more people would be working?
  (*b*) By how much would total output increase if per worker GDP were $140,000?

LO17-1 7. If output per worker is now $140,000 per year, how much will the average worker produce next year if productivity improves by
  (*a*) 2.0 percent per year?
  (*b*) 3.0 percent per year?

LO17-1 8. The real (inflation-adjusted) value of U.S. manufacturing output and related manufacturing employment was

	Output	Employment
2000	$1.541 trillion	17,321,000
2018	$2.330 trillion	12,700,000

  (*a*) How many manufacturing jobs were lost between 2000 and 2018?
  (*b*) How much did output increase?
  (*c*) What was average manufacturing productivity (output per worker) in
    (*i*) 2000?
    (*ii*) 2018?

LO17-2 9. Suppose that every additional four percentage points in the investment rate ($I \div$ GDP) boost economic growth by one percentage point. Assume also that all investment must be financed with consumer saving. The economy is now assumed to be fully employed at

GDP	$8 trillion
Consumption	6 trillion
Saving	1 trillion
Investment	1 trillion

If the goal is to raise the growth rate by 1 percent,

    (*a*) By how much must investment increase?

    (*b*) By how much must consumption decline for this to occur?

LO17-1 10. Using the Data Tables at the end of the book, graph the real GDP growth rates for 2010–2019.

LO17-1 11. Using the Data Tables at the end of the book, graph Tables, calculate nominal GDP per capita for 2010–2019.

LO17-2 12. ***Decisions for Tomorrow:*** Suppose a country's GDP is \$12 billion and the population is 3 million this year.

    (*a*) Calculate GDP per capita for this year.

    (b) Calculate GDP per capita for next year if the population grows by 5 percent and there is no change in output.

    (*c*) Calculate GDP per capita for next year if the population grows by 1 percent and output grows by 3 percent.

PART

7

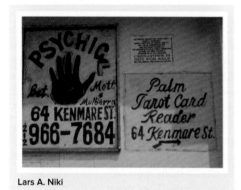

Lars A. Niki

POLICY CONSTRAINTS

Macro theories often provide conflicting advice about whether and how the government ought to intervene. To make matters worse, the information needed to make a decision is typically incomplete. Politics muddies the waters too by changing priorities and restricting the use of policy tools. Finally, there's the inescapable reality that everything changes at once—there's no *ceteris paribus* in the real world. Chapter 18 surveys the real-world obstacles to better policy decisions and macro outcomes.

Lars A. Niki

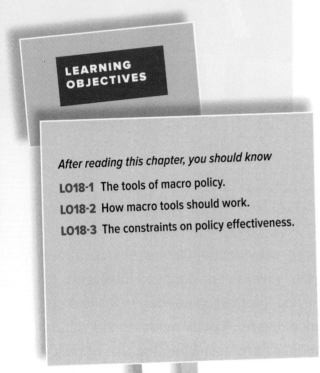

Theory versus Reality

There are no all-powerful, all-knowing superheroes ... who can rescue ... the economy all by themselves. You might think that the federal government could revive the economy quickly ... or that the Fed could fix it. ... But Washington has far less power over the economy ... than many people think. We always think there's a person who holds the magic wand. But this society and this economy are far too complex to be susceptible to magic wands.

—**Senator Judd Gregg,** *Fortune,* **November 1, 2010**

Macroeconomic theory is supposed to explain the business cycle and show policymakers how to control it. But something is obviously wrong. Despite our relative prosperity, we haven't consistently achieved the goals of full employment, price stability, and vigorous economic growth. All too often, either unemployment or inflation surges or economic growth slows down. No matter how hard we try to eliminate it, the business cycle seems to persist.

What accounts for this gap between the promises of economic theory and the reality of economic performance? Are the theories inadequate? Or is sound economic advice being ignored?

Many people blame the economists. They point to the conflicting advice of Keynesians, monetarists, and supply-siders and wonder what theory is supposed to be followed. If economists themselves can't agree, it is asked, why should anyone else listen to them?

Not surprisingly, economists see things a bit differently. First, they point out, the **business cycle** isn't as bad as it used to be. Since World War II, the economy has had many ups and downs, but none as severe as the Great Depression or earlier catastrophes. Second, economists complain that politics often takes precedence over good economic advice. Politicians are reluctant, for example, to raise taxes, cut spending, or slow money growth to control inflation. Their concern is winning the next election, not solving the country's economic problems.

When President Jimmy Carter was in office, he anguished over another problem: the complexity of economic decision making. In the real world, neither theory nor politics can keep up with all our economic goals. As President Carter observed, "We cannot concentrate just on inflation or just on unemployment or just on deficits in the federal budget or our international payments. Nor can we act in isolation from other countries. We must deal with all of these problems simultaneously and on a worldwide basis."

No president learned this lesson faster or more forcefully than George W. Bush. Just as he was putting the final touches on a bipartisan consensus on taxes, spending, and debt reduction, terrorists destroyed the World

Trade Center and damaged the Pentagon. In response to those attacks, all major economic policy decisions had to be revised. President Obama also had to revise his economic plans as soon as he took office. An acceleration of the 2008–2009 downturn forced him to abandon promised tax increases on the rich and instead fashion a fiscal stimulus package. President Trump confronted an even sharper reversal of fortunes. He was trumpeting the success of his economic policy as late as January 2020. Then the coronavirus pandemic erupted, forcing him to deal with not only a health crisis, but also production shutdowns and a spike in unemployment.

As if the burdens of a continuously changing world weren't enough, the president must also contend with sharply differing economic theories and advice, a slow and frequently hostile Congress, a massive and often unresponsive bureaucracy, and a complete lack of knowledge about the future.

This chapter confronts these and other frustrations of the real world head on. In so doing, we provide answers to the following questions:

- **What's the ideal "package" of macro policies?**
- **How well does our macro performance live up to the promises of that package?**
- **What kinds of obstacles prevent us from doing better?**

The answers to these questions may shed some light on a broader concern that has long troubled students and policymakers alike—namely, "If economists are so smart, why is the economy always in such a mess?"

business cycle: Alternating periods of economic growth and contraction.

POLICY TOOLS

Table 18.1 summarizes the macroeconomic tools available to policymakers. Although this list is brief, we hardly need a reminder at this point of how powerful each instrument can be. Every one of these major policy instruments can significantly change our answers to the basic economic questions of WHAT, HOW, and FOR WHOM to produce.

Fiscal Policy

The basic tools of **fiscal policy** are contained in the federal budget. Tax cuts are supposed to increase aggregate demand by putting more income in the hands of consumers and businesses. Tax increases are intended to curtail spending and reduce inflationary pressures. Table 18.2 summarizes some of the major tax changes of recent years.

The expenditure side of the federal budget is another fiscal policy tool. From a Keynesian perspective, increases in government spending raise aggregate demand and so encourage more production. A slowdown in government spending is supposed to restrain aggregate demand and lessen inflationary pressures.

fiscal policy: The use of government taxes and spending to alter macroeconomic outcomes.

Type of Policy	Policy Tools
Fiscal policy	• Tax cuts and increases. • Changes in government spending. • Transfer cuts and increases.
Monetary policy	• Open market operations. • Changes in reserve requirements. • Changes in the discount rate.
Supply-side policy	• Tax incentives for investment and saving. • Deregulation. • Human capital investment. • Infrastructure development. • Free trade. • Changes to immigration policy.

TABLE 18.1

The Policy Tools

Economic policymakers have access to a variety of policy instruments. The challenge is to choose the right tools at the right time.

TABLE 18.2

Fiscal Policy Milestones

Fiscal policy is contained in tax and spending legislation approved by Congress. These are some significant decisions.

Year	Act	Description
1986	Tax Reform Act	Major reduction in tax rates coupled with broadening of tax base.
1990	Budget Enforcement Act	Limits set on discretionary spending; pay-as-you-go financing required.
1993	Clinton "New Direction"	Tax increases and spending cuts to achieve $300 billion deficit reduction.
1994	Contract with America	Republican-led Congress cuts spending, sets seven-year target for balanced budget.
1997	Balanced Budget Act, Taxpayer Relief Act	Package of tax cuts and spending cuts to balance budget by 2002.
2001	Economic Growth and Tax Relief Act	Eight-year, $1.35 trillion in personal tax cuts.
2002	Job Creation and Worker Assistance Act	Business investment tax cuts.
2003	Jobs and Growth Tax Relief Act	Cuts in dividend and capital gains taxes.
2008	Economic Stimulus Act	$168 billion of tax rebates.
2009	American Recovery and Reinvestment Act	$787 billion package of spending and tax cuts.
2010	Continuing Resolution	Extension of tax cuts, unemployment benefits, spending until 2012, plus one-year payroll tax cut.
2011	Deficit Reduction	Package of spending cuts and tax hikes to reduce deficit.
2013	Taxpayer Relief Act	Increased top tax rate on personal income and on capital gains.
2015	Bipartisan Budget Act	Increased discretionary spending by $80 billion for 2016–2017.
2017	Tax Cuts and Jobs Act	Huge cut in corporate taxes and small cuts in personal income taxes.
2020	Coronavirus Aid, Relief, and Economic Security (CARES) Act	$2 trillion package of rebates, unemployment benefits, and business subsidies

automatic stabilizer: Federal expenditure or revenue item that automatically responds countercyclically to changes in national income, like unemployment benefits and income taxes.

structural deficit: Federal revenues at full employment minus expenditures at full employment under prevailing fiscal policy.

fiscal stimulus: Tax cuts or spending hikes intended to increase (shift) aggregate demand.

fiscal restraint: Tax hikes or spending cuts intended to reduce (shift) aggregate demand.

monetary policy: The use of money and credit controls to influence macroeconomic outcomes.

Who Makes Fiscal Policy? As we first observed in Chapter 11, changes in taxes and government spending originate in both economic events and explicit policy decisions. When the economy slows, tax revenues decline, and government spending increases automatically. Conversely, when real GDP grows, tax revenues automatically rise, and government transfer payments decline. These **automatic stabilizers** are a basic countercyclical feature of the federal budget. They don't represent active fiscal policy. On the contrary, *fiscal policy refers to deliberate changes in tax or spending legislation.* These changes can be made only by the U.S. Congress. Every year the president proposes specific budget and tax changes, negotiates with Congress, then accepts or vetoes specific acts that Congress has passed. The resulting policy decisions represent "discretionary" fiscal policy. Those policy decisions expand or shrink the **structural deficit** and thus give the economy a shot of **fiscal stimulus** or **fiscal restraint.** That was the intent of the trillion-dollar package of increased spending Congress authorized in March 2020 to help mitigate the economic effects of the coronavirus.

Monetary Policy

The policy arsenal in Table 18.1 also contains monetary tools. Tools of **monetary policy** include open market operations, discount rate changes, and reserve requirements.

As we saw in Chapter 15, there are disagreements over how these monetary tools should be used. Keynesians believe that interest rates are the critical policy lever. In their view, the money supply should be expanded or curtailed to achieve whatever interest rate is needed to shift aggregate demand. Monetarists, on the other hand, contend that the money supply

October 1979	Fed adopts monetarist approach, focusing exclusively on money supply; interest rates soar.
July 1982	Deep into recession, Fed votes to ease monetary restraint.
October 1982	Fed abandons pure monetarist approach and expands money supply rapidly.
May 1983	Fed reverses policy and begins slowing money supply growth.
1985	Fed increases money supply with discount rate cuts and open market purchases.
1987	Fed abandons money supply targets as policy guides; money supply growth decreases; discount rate increases.
1989	Greenspan announces goal of "zero inflation," tightens policy.
1991	Deep in recession, the Fed begins to ease monetary restraint.
1994	Fed slows M2 growth to 1 percent; raises federal funds rate by three percentage points as economy nears full employment.
1995	Greenspan trumpets "soft landing" and eases monetary restraint.
1998	Fed cuts interest rates to cushion the United States from Asian crisis.
1999–2000	Fed raises interest rates 6 times.
2001–2003	Fed cuts interest rates 13 times.
2004–2006	Fed raises fed funds rate 17 times.
2007–2008	Fed cuts interest rates 10 times.
2008–2014	Three rounds of "quantitative easing": Fed buys more than $2 trillion of bonds and securities directly from banks.
November 2014	Quantitative easing ends.
2015–2018	Fed increases federal funds rate 9 times.
2019	Fed cuts federal funds rate 3 times.
2020	Fed cuts federal funds rate to zero; undertakes massive bond purchases

TABLE 18.3

Monetary Policy Milestones

Monetary policy is set by the Federal Reserve Board of Governors.

itself is the critical policy tool and that it should be expanded at a steady and predictable rate. This policy, they believe, will ensure price stability and a **natural rate of unemployment.**

Who Makes Monetary Policy? Actual monetary policy decisions are made by the Federal Reserve's Board of Governors. Twice a year the Fed provides Congress with a broad over-view of the economic outlook and monetary objectives. The Fed's assessment of the econ-omy is updated at meetings of the Federal Open Market Committee (FOMC). The FOMC decides which monetary policy levers to pull.

Table 18.3 depicts milestones in recent monetary policy. Of particular interest is the Oc-tober 1979 decision to adopt a pure monetarist approach. This involved an exclusive focus on the money supply, without regard for interest rates. After interest rates soared and the economy appeared on the brink of a depression, the Fed abandoned the monetarist ap-proach and again began keeping an eye on both interest rates (the Keynesian focus) and the money supply.

Monetarists contend that the Fed never fully embraced their policy. The money supply grew at a very uneven pace in 1980, they argue, not at the steady, predictable rate that they demanded. Nevertheless, the policy shifts of 1979 and 1982 were distinctive and had dramatic effects.

A quick review of Table 18.3 reveals that such monetary policy reversals have been quite frequent. There were U-turns in monetary policy between 1982 and 1983, 1989 and 1991, 1998 and 1999, 2000 and 2001, 2003 and 2004, 2007 and 2008, and again in 2017 and 2019.

In November 2008 the Fed began massive purchases of long-term Treasury bonds and other securities, hoping to bring down long-term interest rates (especially mortgage rates). This first round of "quantitative easing" (QE1) ended in March 2010. When the economic recovery started to look wobbly later that year, the Fed pursued a second round (QE2) of massive ($600 billion) bond purchases from November 2010 to June 2011 and a third round (QE3) from September 2012 to the end of 2014. Monetarists were horrified, fearing that such a huge increase in *M* would ultimately ignite inflation (*P*).

natural rate of unemployment: the long-term rate of unemployment determined by structural forces in labor and product markets.

The Fed kept interest rates at record low levels for more than six years. When the unemployment rate got very low and prices started to rise, the Fed tapped on the brakes a bit. In December 2016, the Fed raised the federal funds target rate slightly (from 0.25–0.50 percent to 0.50–0.75 percent) and continued raising it to 2.25–2.50 percent in December 2018. The Fed reversed course in 2019, bringing the federal funds rate down to a low of 1.50–1.75 percent by the year's end. When the coronavirus brought the U.S. economy to a near standstill, the Fed cut the funds rate all the way down to zero! It also bought over a trillion dollars' worth of market securities.

Supply-Side Policy

supply-side policy: The use of tax incentives, (de)regulation, and other mechanisms to increase the ability and willingness to produce goods and services.

Supply-side theory offers the third major set of policy tools. The focus of **supply-side policy** is to provide incentives to work, invest, and produce. Of particular concern are high tax rates and regulations that reduce supply incentives. Supply-siders argue that marginal tax rates and government regulation must be reduced to get more output without added inflation.

In the 1980s tax rates were reduced dramatically. The maximum marginal tax rate on individuals was cut from 70 to 50 percent in 1981, and then still further, to 28 percent, in 1987. The 1980s also witnessed major milestones in the deregulation of airlines, trucking, telephone service, and other industries.

Some of the momentum toward less regulation was reversed during the 1990s (see Table 18.4). New regulatory costs on business were created by the Americans with Disabilities Act, the 1990 amendments to the Clean Air Act, and the Family and Medical Leave Act of 1993. All three laws provide important benefits to workers or the environment. At the same time, however, they make supplying goods and services more expensive.

The Obama administration broadened supply-side efforts to include infrastructure development and increased investment in human capital (through education and skill training programs). These activities increase the capacity to produce and so shift the aggregate supply curve rightward. The Obama administration also toughened environmental regulation, however, and introduced new regulations on bank lending (Dodd-Frank) and health care (Affordable Care Act), and paid family leave that shifted the aggregate supply curve leftward. Increases in marginal tax rates on personal income, capital gains, and dividends further diminished incentives to work and invest.

President Trump reversed the shifts of the AS curve, particularly with a huge drop in the tax rate on corporations (from 35 to 21 percent). The same Tax Cuts and Jobs Act of 2017 also reduced the top marginal tax rate on personal incomes from 39.6 to 37 percent. The Trump administration also pursued a vigorous policy of deregulation, significantly scaling back the regulatory costs of doing business. However, some of these rightward shifts of the AS curve were offset by a trade war with China that increased the cost and reduced the availability of imported goods and parts.

Who Makes Supply-Side Policy? Because tax rates are a basic tool of supply-side policy, fiscal and supply-side policies are often intertwined. When Congress changes the tax laws, it almost always alters marginal tax rates and thus changes production incentives. Notice, for example, that tax legislation appears in Table 18.4 as well as in Table 18.2. The Taxpayer Relief Act of 2012 not only changed total tax revenues (fiscal policy) but also restructured production and investment incentives (supply-side policy). The 2017 tax cuts likewise had both aggregate demand (more disposable income) and aggregate supply (lower marginal tax rates) effects.

Supply-side and fiscal policies also interact on the outlay side of the budget. The Transportation Equity Act of 2000, for example, authorized accelerated public works spending (fiscal stimulus) on infrastructure development (increase in supply capacity). The 2020 CARES Act not only stimulated demand with income transfers but also provided federal subsidies for health care that helped maintain the labor force (AS). *Deciding whether to increase spending is a fiscal policy decision; deciding how to spend available funds may entail supply-side policy.*

1990	Social Security Act amendments	Increased payroll tax to 7.65 percent.
	Americans with Disabiliuals Act	Required employers to provide greater access for disabled individuals.
	Immigration Act	Increased immigration, especially for highly skilled workers.
	Clean Air Act amendments	Increased pollution controls.
1993	Rebuild America Program	Increased spending on infrastructure and human capital investment.
	Family and Medical Leave Act	Required employers to provide unpaid leaves of absence for workers.
	NAFTA	Lowered North American trade barriers.
1994	GATT renewed	Lowered world trade barriers.
1996	Telecommunications Act	Permitted greater competition in cable and telephone industries.
	Personal Responsibility and Work Opportunity Act	Required more welfare recipients to work.
1997	Taxpayer Relief Act	Created tuition tax credits; cut capital gains tax.
1998	Workforce Investment Act	Increased funds for skills training.
2000	Transportation Equity Act	Provided new funding for highways, rails.
2001	Economic Growth and Tax Relief Act	Increased savings incentives; reduced marginal tax rates.
2002	Job Creation and Worker Assistance Act	Provided more tax incentives for investment.
2003	Jobs and Growth Tax Relief Act	Reduced taxes on capital gains and dividends.
2007	Minimum wage hike	Raised from $5.15 to $7.25 in 2009.
2009	American Recovery and Reinvestment Act	Infrastructure and energy development.
2010	Affordable Care and Dodd-Frank Acts	Raised costs and reduced incentives for labor supply, labor demand, and bank lending.
2013	Taxpayer Relief Act	Raised top marginal tax rate on personal incomes (39.6%), capital gains, and dividends (to 20% from 15%).
2017	Tax Cuts and Jobs Act	Reduced corporate tax rate from 35% to 21% and shaved marginal tax rates on personal income.
2018–2019	Increased tariffs	Increased import tariffs, especially on Chinese goods.
2018–2020	Deregulation	Substantial decline in growth of federal regulations.

Regulatory policy is also fashioned by Congress. The president and executive agencies play a critical role in this supply-side area in the day-to-day decisions on how to interpret and enforce regulatory policies.

IDEALIZED USES

These fiscal, monetary, and supply-side tools are potentially powerful levers for controlling the economy. In principle, they can cure the excesses of the business cycle and promote faster economic growth. To see how, let's review their use in three distinct macroeconomic settings.

Case 1: Recession

When output and employment levels fall far short of the economy's full-employment potential, the mandate for public policy is clear. Aggregate demand must be increased so that producers can sell more goods, hire more workers, and move the economy toward its

recessionary GDP gap: The amount by which equilibrium GDP falls short of full-employment GDP.

multiplier: The multiple by which an initial change in aggregate spending will alter total expenditure after an infinite number of spending cycles; $1/(1 - MPC)$.

velocity of money (V): The number of times per year, on average, that a dollar is used to purchase final goods and services; $PQ \div M$.

inflationary GDP gap: The amount by which equilibrium GDP exceeds full-employment GDP.

stagflation: The simultaneous occurrence of substantial unemployment and inflation.

productive capacity. At such times, the most urgent need is to get people back to work and close the **recessionary GDP gap.**

How can the government end a recession? Keynesians emphasize the need to increase aggregate demand by cutting taxes or boosting government spending. The resulting stimulus will set off a **multiplier** reaction. If the initial stimulus and multiplier are large enough, the recessionary GDP gap can be closed, propelling the economy to full employment.

Modern Keynesians acknowledge that monetary policy might also help. Specifically, increases in the money supply may lower interest rates and thus give investment spending a further boost. To give the economy a really powerful stimulus, we might want to pull all these policy levers at the same time. That's what the government did in early 2001—using tax cuts, lower interest rates, and increased spending to jump-start the economy. The same one-two punch was used again, on a much more massive scale, in 2008–2010 and 2020.

Monetarists would proceed differently. First, they see no point in toying with the federal budget. In the pure monetarist model, changes in taxes or government spending may alter the mix of output but not its level. So long as the **velocity of money (V)** is constant, fiscal policy doesn't matter. In this view, the appropriate policy response to a recession is patience. As sales and output slow, interest rates will decline, and new investment will be stimulated.

Supply-siders emphasize the need to improve production incentives. They urge cuts in marginal tax rates on investment and labor. They also look for ways to reduce government regulation. Finally, they urge that any increase in government spending (fiscal stimulus) focus on long-run capacity expansion such as infrastructure development.

Case 2: Inflation

An overheated economy provides as clear a policy mandate as does a sluggish one. In this case, the immediate goal is to restrain aggregate demand until the rate of total expenditure is compatible with the productive capacity of the economy. This entails shifting the aggregate demand curve to the left to close the **inflationary GDP gap.** Keynesians would do this by raising taxes and cutting government spending. Keynesians would also see the desirability of increasing interest rates to curb investment spending.

Monetarists would simply cut the money supply. In their view, the short-run aggregate supply curve is unknown and unstable. The only predictable response is reflected in the vertical, long-run aggregate supply curve. According to this view, changes in the money supply alter prices, not output. Inflation is seen simply as "too much money chasing too few goods." Monetarists would turn off the money spigot. The Fed's job in this situation isn't only to reduce money supply growth but to convince market participants that a more cautious monetary policy will be continued.

Supply-siders would point out that inflation implies both "too much money" *and* "not enough goods." They'd look at the supply side of the market for ways to expand productive capacity. In a highly inflationary setting, they'd propose more incentives to save. The additional savings would automatically reduce consumption while creating a larger pool of investable funds. Supply-siders would also cut taxes and regulations that raise production costs and lower import barriers that keep out cheaper foreign goods.

Case 3: Stagflation

Although serious inflations and recessions provide clear mandates for economic policy, there's a vast gray area between these extremes. Occasionally the economy suffers from both inflation and unemployment at the same time, a condition called **stagflation.** In 1980, for example, the unemployment rate (7.1 percent) and the inflation rate (12.5 percent) were both too high. With an upward-sloping aggregate supply curve, the easy policy options were foreclosed. If aggregate demand were stimulated to reduce unemployment, the resultant pressure on prices might fuel the existing inflation. And if fiscal and monetary restraints were used to reduce inflationary pressures, unemployment might worsen. In such a situation, there are no simple solutions.

Knowing the causes of stagflation will help achieve the desired balance. If prices are rising before full employment is reached, some degree of structural unemployment is likely. An appropriate policy response might include more vocational training in skill shortage areas as well as a redirection of aggregate demand toward labor surplus sectors.

High tax rates or costly regulations might also contribute to stagflation. If either constraint exists, high prices (inflation) may not be a sufficient incentive for increased output. In this case, reductions in tax rates and regulation might help reduce both unemployment and inflation, which is the basic strategy of supply-side policies.

Stagflation may also arise from a temporary contraction of aggregate supply that both reduces output and drives up prices. In this case, neither structural unemployment nor excessive demand is the culprit. Rather, an "external shock" (such as a natural disaster or a terrorist attack) or an abrupt change in world trade (such as a spike in oil prices) is likely to be the cause of the policy dilemma. Accordingly, none of our familiar policy tools is likely to provide a complete "cure." In most cases, the economy simply has to adjust to a temporary setback.

Fine-Tuning

The apparently inexhaustible potential of public policy to alter the economy's performance has often generated optimistic expectations about the efficacy of fiscal, monetary, and supply-side tools. In the early 1960s, such optimism pervaded even the highest levels of government. Those were the days when prices were relatively stable, unemployment rates were falling, the economy was growing rapidly, and preparations were being made for the first trip into space. The potential of economic policy looked great indeed. It was also during the 1960s that a lot of people (mostly economists) spoke of the potential for **fine-tuning,** or altering economic outcomes to fit very exacting specifications. Flexible responses to changing market conditions, it was argued, could ensure fulfillment of our economic goals. The prescription was simple: When unemployment is the problem, simply give the economy a jolt of fiscal or monetary stimulus; when inflation is worrisome, simply tap on the fiscal or monetary brakes. To fulfill our goals for content and distribution, simply pick the right target for stimulus or restraint. With a little attention and experience, the right speed could be found and the economy guided successfully down the road to prosperity. As the economic expansion of the 1990s stretched into the record books, the same kind of economic mastery was claimed. More than a few prominent economists claimed the business cycle was dead.

fine-tuning: Adjustments in economic policy designed to counteract small changes in economic outcomes; continuous responses to changing economic conditions.

THE ECONOMIC RECORD

The economy's track record doesn't live up to these high expectations. To be sure, the economy has continued to grow, and we've attained an impressive standard of living. We can't lose sight of the fact that our per capita income greatly exceeds the realities and even the expectations in most other countries of the world. Nevertheless, we must also recognize that our economic history is punctuated by periods of recession, high unemployment, inflation, and recurring concern for the distribution of income and mix of output. The recession of 2008–2009 was a lesson in humility. And the coronavirus pandemic of 2020 was a stark reminder of how we can't predict external shocks or the extent of disruption they will cause.

The graphs in Figure 18.1 provide a quick summary of the gap between the theory and reality of economic policy. The Employment Act of 1946 committed the federal government to macro stability. It's evident that we haven't kept that commitment. In the 1970s we rarely came close. Although we approached all three goals in the mid-1980s, our achievements were short-lived. Economic growth ground to a halt in 1989, and the economy slipped into yet another recession in 1990. Although inflation stayed low, unemployment rates jumped.

The economy performed very well again from 1992 until early 2000. After that, however, growth came to an abrupt halt again. With the economy teetering on recession, the unemployment rate started rising in mid-2000. Some of the people who had proclaimed the business cycle to be dead were out of work. Then the economy was hit by the external shock of a terrorist attack that suspended economic activity and shook investor and consumer confidence.

FIGURE 18.1

The Economic Record

The Full Employment and Balanced Growth Act of 1978 established specific goals for unemployment (4 percent), inflation (3 percent), and economic growth (4 percent). We've rarely attained those goals, however, as these graphs illustrate. Measurement, design, and policy implementation problems help explain these shortcomings.

Source: U.S. Bureau of Labor Statistics, Bureau of Economic Analysis, and Congressional Budget Office.

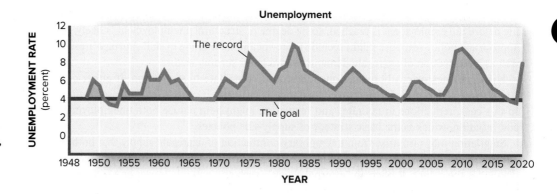

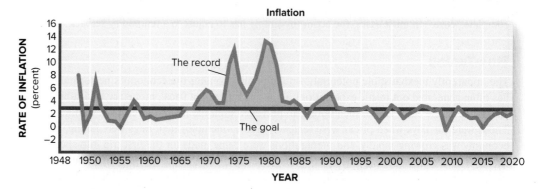

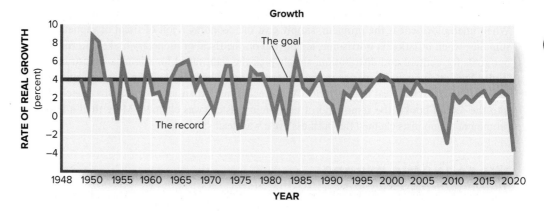

It took two years to get unemployment rates back down into the "full-employment" range (4–6 percent). The cycle began to reverse at the end of 2007, leading to the recession of 2008–2009. Unemployment rose to 10 percent and stayed very high for five years. From 2015 through 2019 the economy performed quite well. Unemployment trended down to a low of 3.5 percent and inflation remained subdued, just inching above 2 percent on occasion. But GDP growth remained below the long-run average. Then the 2020 coronavirus pandemic brought virtually all world economies to a near standstill for several months.

Looking back over the entire postwar (1946–) period, the record includes 12 years of outright recession (actual declines in output) and another 24 years of **growth recession** (growth of less than 3 percent). That adds up to a 49 percent macro failure rate. Moreover, the distribution of income in 2020 looked worse than that of 1946, and nearly 40 million people were still officially counted as poor in the later year.

Despite many setbacks, recent economic performance of the United States has been better than that of other Western nations. Other economies haven't grown as fast as the United States nor reduced unemployment as much. But as World View "Comparative Macro Performance" shows, some countries did a better job of restraining prices.

growth recession: A period during which real GDP grows but at a rate below the long-term trend of 3 percent.

WORLD VIEW

COMPARATIVE MACRO PERFORMANCE

The performance of the U.S. economy in the 2000s was better than that of most developed economies. Japan had the greatest success in restraining inflation (0.4 percent) but suffered from sluggish growth (0.7 percent). The United States grew faster and also experienced less unemployment than most European countries.

Performance, 2000–2018	U.S.	Japan	Germany	U.K.	France	Canada
Real growth (annual average)	1.8	0.7	1.3	1.5	1.1	1.9
Inflation (annual average)	2.2	0.4	1.4	2.0	1.4	1.9
Unemployment (annual average)	6.1	4.3	6.8	5.9	9.2	7.1

Source: International Monetary Fund and OECD.

CRITICAL ANALYSIS: Macroeconomic performance (**growth, inflation,** and **unemployment**) varies a lot, both over time and across countries. In the 2000s the U.S. performed well on most measures.

WHY THINGS DON'T ALWAYS WORK

There's plenty of blame to go around for the many blemishes on our economic record. Some people blame the president; others blame the Fed or Congress; still others blame China or Mexico. Some forces, however, constrain economic policy even when no one is specifically to blame. In this regard, we can distinguish *four obstacles to policy success:*

- *Goal conflicts.*
- *Measurement problems.*
- *Design problems.*
- *Implementation problems.*

Goal Conflicts

The first factor to take note of is potential conflicts in policy priorities. President Clinton had to confront this problem his first day in office. He had pledged to create new jobs by increasing public infrastructure spending and offering a middle-class tax cut. He had also promised to reduce the deficit, however. This created a clear goal conflict. In the end, President Clinton had to settle for a smaller increase in infrastructure spending and a tax *increase.*

President George W. Bush confronted similar problems. In the 2000 presidential campaign he had promised a big increase in federal spending on education. By the time he took office, however, the federal budget surplus was rapidly shrinking, and the goal of preserving the surplus took precedence. The conflict between spending priorities and budget balancing became much more intense when President Bush decided to attack Iraq. We also noted earlier how President Obama had to set aside some campaign promises (e.g., raising taxes on capital gains, estates, and "the rich") when confronted on day 1 with the urgent need to stimulate aggregate demand. For his part, President Trump had to figure out how to reconcile his ambitious spending plans for infrastructure and the military with his promise to end deficit spending.

These and other goal conflicts have their roots in the short-run trade-off between unemployment and inflation. With aggressive use of fiscal and monetary stimulus, we can surely increase AD and move the economy toward full employment. But we might set off a multiplier process that pushes the economy past its **inflationary flashpoint.** In view of that risk, should we try to cure inflation, unemployment, or just a bit of both? Answers are likely to vary. Unemployed people put the highest priority on attaining full employment. Labor unions press for faster economic growth. Bankers, creditors, and people on fixed incomes demand an end to inflation.

inflationary flashpoint:
The rate of output at which inflationary pressures intensify; the point on the AS curve where slope increases sharply.

This goal conflict is often institutionalized in the decision-making process. The Fed is traditionally viewed as the guardian of price stability. The president and Congress worry more about people's jobs and government programs, so they are less willing to raise taxes or cut spending.

Distributional goals may also conflict with macro objectives. Anti-inflationary policies may require cutbacks in programs for the poor, the elderly, or needy students. These cutbacks may be politically impossible. Likewise, tight-money policies may be viewed as too great a burden for small businesses, home builders, and auto manufacturers.

Although the policy tools in Table 18.1 are powerful, they can't grant all our wishes. Because we still live in a world of scarce resources, *all policy decisions entail opportunity costs,* which means that we'll always be confronted with trade-offs. The best we can hope for is a set of compromises that yields *optimal* outcomes, not ideal ones.

Measurement Problems

One reason firefighters are pretty successful in putting out fires before entire cities burn down is that fires are highly visible phenomena. But such visibility isn't characteristic of economic problems. An increase in the unemployment rate from 5 to 6 percent, for example, isn't the kind of thing you notice while crossing the street. Unless you work in the unemployment insurance office or lose your own job, the increase in unemployment isn't likely to attract your attention. The same is true of prices; small increases in product prices aren't likely to ring many alarms. Hence, both inflation and unemployment may worsen considerably before anyone takes serious notice. Were we as slow and ill-equipped to notice fires, whole neighborhoods would burn before someone rang the alarm.

Measurement problems are a very basic policy constraint. To formulate appropriate economic policy, we must first determine the nature of our problems. To do so, we must measure employment changes, output changes, price changes, and other macro outcomes. The old adage that governments are willing and able to solve only those problems they can measure is relevant here. Indeed, before the Great Depression, a fundamental constraint on public policy was the lack of statistics on what was happening in the economy. One lasting benefit of that experience is that we now try to keep informed on changing economic conditions. The information at hand, however, is always dated and incomplete. *At best, we know what was happening in the economy last month or last week.* The processes of data collection, assembly, and presentation take time, even in this age of high-speed computers. The average recession lasts about 11 months, but official data generally don't even confirm the existence of a recession until 8 months after a downturn starts! As Front Page Economics "Great

FRONT PAGE ECONOMICS

GREAT RECESSION OFFICIALLY ENDED LAST YEAR

CAMBRIDGE. September 20, 2010—The Business Cycle Dating Committee of the National Bureau of Economic Research met yesterday by conference call. At its meeting, the committee determined that a trough in business activity occurred in the U.S. economy in June 2009. The trough marks the end of the recession that began in December 2007 and the beginning of an expansion. The recession lasted 18 months, which makes it the longest of any recession since World War II. Previously the longest postwar recessions were those of 1973–75 and 1981–82, both of which lasted 16 months. ...

A recession is a period of falling economic activity spread across the economy, lasting more than a few months, normally visible in real GDP, real income, employment, industrial production, and wholesale-retail sales. The trough marks the end of the declining phase and the start of the rising phase of the business cycle.

Source: National Bureau of Economic Research, September 20, 2010.

CRITICAL ANALYSIS: In the absence of timely information, today's policy decisions are inevitably based on yesterday's perceptions. This **measurement problem** can decrease the efficacy of policy.

Recession Officially Ended Last Year" reveals, the 2008–2009 recession ended 15 months before researchers confirmed its demise!

Forecasts. In an ideal world, policymakers wouldn't just *respond* to economic problems but would also *anticipate* their occurrence. If an inflationary GDP gap is emerging, for example, we want to take immediate action to keep aggregate spending from increasing. That is, the successful firefighter not only responds to a fire but also looks for hazards that might start one.

Unfortunately, economic policymakers are again at a disadvantage. Their knowledge of future problems is even worse than their knowledge of current problems. *In designing policy, policymakers must depend on economic forecasts*—that is, informed guesses about what the economy will look like in future periods.

Macro Models. Those guesses are often based on complex computer models of how the economy works. These models—referred to as *econometric macro models*—are mathematical summaries of the economy's performance. The models try to identify the key determinants of macro performance and then show what happens to macro outcomes when they change. The apparent precision of such computer models may disguise inherent guesswork, however.

An economist "feeds" the computer two essential inputs. One is a quantitative model of how the economy allegedly works. A Keynesian model, for example, includes equations that show multiplier spending responses to tax cuts. A monetarist model shows that tax cuts raise interest rates, not total spending ("crowding out"), and a supply-side model stipulates labor supply and production responses. The computer can't tell which theory is right; it just predicts what it's programmed to see. In other words, the computer sees the world through the eyes of its economic master.

The second essential input in a computer forecast is the assumed values for critical variables. A Keynesian model, for example, must specify how large a multiplier to expect. All the computer does is carry out the required mathematical routines, once it's told that the multiplier is relevant and what its value is. It can't discern the true multiplier any better than it can pick the right theory.

Given the dependence of computers on the theories and perceptions of their economic masters, it's not surprising that computer forecasts often differ greatly. It's also not surprising that they're often wrong. Even policymakers who are familiar with both economic theory and computer models can make some pretty bad calls. In January 1990 Fed Chairman Alan Greenspan assured Congress that the risk of a recession was as low as 20 percent. Although he said he "wouldn't bet the ranch" on such a low probability, he was confident that the odds of a recession were below 50 percent. Five months after his testimony, the 1990–1991 recession began. Greenspan's successor, Ben Bernanke, lost the same bet in 2008 (see Front Page Economics "Fed Chief Sees No Recession").

FRONT PAGE ECONOMICS

FED CHIEF SEES NO RECESSION

WASHINGTON, D.C. Fed Chairman Ben Bernanke says fears of a recession are overblown. In his testimony before the Senate Banking Committee yesterday Bernanke acknowledged that rising unemployment, declining home prices, and high energy prices were weighing on consumers. But he sees no recession on the horizon.

"My baseline outlook involves a period of sluggish growth, followed by a somewhat stronger pace of growth starting later this year as the effects of (Fed) and fiscal stimulus begin to be felt," Bernanke told committee members. ...

—Barbara Hagenbaugh

Source: Media reports, February 15, 2008.

CRITICAL ANALYSIS: Policy decisions are based on **forecasts** of economic performance. Bad forecasts can lead to delayed or wrong policy actions.

The Council of Economic Advisers has made similar blunders. The CEA was forecasting 2–3 percent growth just as the economy was falling into the 2001 recession. In early 2008 the Bush White House was predicting a growth pickup later in the year. In fact, the downturn *accelerated* in the final months of that year. And in February 2009 Obama's CEA predicted that the unemployment rate would drop from 7.6 percent to 7.0 percent by 2010. Instead it rose to 10 percent.

President Trump made similarly bad predictions. Touting "the biggest ever" tax cuts, he predicted that the Tax Cuts and Jobs Act of 2017 would create millions of jobs, accelerate growth to above 3 percent, and even pay for itself through the added tax receipts generated by faster growth. In early 2019 the Congressional Research Service debunked those claims. At best, the tax cuts had added about 0.3 percent to 2018 GDP growth (which came in at 2.9 percent). And the tax cuts didn't come close to paying for themselves; they instead widened the federal budget deficits by tens of billions of dollars.

Leading Indicators. Given the complexity of macro models, many people prefer to use simpler tools for divining the future. One of the most popular is the Leading Economic Index. As noted in Chapter 9 (see Table 9.2), the Leading Indicators are things we can observe today that are logically linked to future production (e.g., orders for new equipment). Unfortunately the logical sequence of events doesn't always unfold as anticipated. All too often, the links in the chain of Leading Indicators are broken by changing expectations and unanticipated events.

Crystal Balls. In view of the fragile foundations and spotty record of computer and index-based forecasts, many people shun them altogether, preferring to use their own "crystal balls." The Foundation for the Study of Cycles has identified 4,000 different crystal balls that people use to gauge the health of the economy, including the ratio of used car to new car sales (it rises in recession); the number of divorce petitions (it rises in bad times); animal population cycles (they peak just before economic downturns); and even the optimism/pessimism content of popular music (a reflection of consumer confidence). Corporate executives claim that such crystal balls are as valuable as professional economic forecasts. In a Gallup survey of CEOs, most respondents said economists' forecasts had little or no influence on company plans or policies. The head of one large company said, "I go out of my way to ignore them." The general public apparently shares this view, giving higher marks to the forecasts of sportswriters and weather forecasters than to those of economists.

Economic forecasters defend themselves in two ways. First, they note that economic policy decisions are inevitably based on anticipated changes in the economy's performance. The decision to stimulate or restrain the economy can't be made by a flip of a coin; *someone* must try to foresee the future course of the economy. Second, forecasters claim that their quantitative approach is the only honest one. Because forecasting models require specific behavioral assumptions and estimates, they force people to spell out their versions of the future. Less rigorous ("gut feeling") approaches are too ambiguous and often inconsistent.

These are valid arguments. Still, one must be careful to distinguish the precision of computers from the inevitable uncertainties of their spoon-fed models. The basic law of the computer is GIGO: garbage in, garbage out. If the underlying models and assumptions are no good, the computer's forecasts won't be any better.

Policy and Forecasts. The task of forecasting the economic future is made still more complex by the interdependence of forecasts, policy decisions, and economic outcomes (see Figure 18.2). First, a forecast is made, based on current economic conditions, likely disturbances to the economy, and anticipated economic policy. These forecasts are then used to project likely budget deficits and other policy variables. Congress and the president react to these projections by revising fiscal, monetary, or supply-side policies. These changes, in turn, alter the basis for the initial forecasts.

This interdependence among forecasts, budget projections, and policy decisions was superbly illustrated in the early months of the George W. Bush presidency. At the beginning

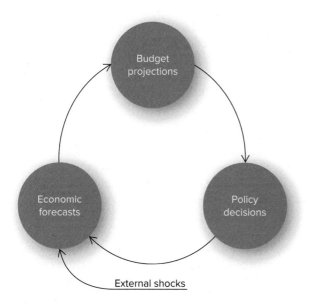

FIGURE 18.2

The Interdependance of Forecasts and Policy

Because tax revenues and government spending are sensitive to economic conditions, budget projections *must* rely on economic forecasts. The budget projections may alter policy decisions, however, and so change the basis for the initial forecasts. This interdependence among macro forecasts, budget projections, and policy decisions is inevitable.

of 2001, both the White House and the Congress were forecasting enormous budget surpluses. The central policy debate focused on what to do with those surpluses. The Democrats wanted to spend the surplus; the Republicans wanted to give it back to households with larger tax cuts. As the debate dragged on, however, the weakening economy shrank the surplus. In August 2001 the Congressional Budget Office (CBO) announced that the surplus it had forecast just seven months earlier had vanished. This forced both political parties to change their policy proposals. Protecting the vanishing surplus became the political priority. Spending proposals were scaled back, as were hopes of debt repayment.

President Obama used dire forecasts of the economy to build support for his stimulus proposals. He claimed that the 2008–2009 recession was the worst since the Great Depression and that the economy might *never* recover unless his stimulus package was implemented. The resulting fear and uncertainty increased public support for his stimulus plan, which Congress authorized within the first month of his presidency.

External Shocks. Even accurate forecasts can be knocked astray by external shocks. The budget decisions reached in early 2001 didn't anticipate the September 11 terrorist attacks. And budget and economic forecasts made in early 2020 had no way of anticipating the destructive force of the coronavirus on our production capacity. The very nature of external *shocks* is that they are *unanticipated*. Hence, even if we knew enough about the economy to forecast "shockless" outcomes perfectly, an external shock could always disrupt the economy and ruin our forecasts.

Design Problems

Assume for the moment that we somehow are able to get a reliable forecast of where the economy is headed. The outlook, let's suppose, is bad. Now we're in the driver's seat to steer the economy past looming dangers. We need to chart our course—to design an economic plan. What action should we take? Which theory of macro behavior should guide us? How will the marketplace respond to any specific action we take?

Suppose, for example, that we adopt a Keynesian approach to ending a recession. Specifically, we want to use fiscal policy to boost aggregate demand. Should we cut taxes or increase government spending? This was a core decision President Obama confronted as he developed his stimulus program. The choice depends in part on the efficacy of either policy tool. Will tax cuts stimulate aggregate demand? In 1998 Japanese households used their tax cut to increase *savings* rather than consumption. In 2001 U.S. households were also slow to spend their tax rebates. In 2018 corporations were skeptical about investing their tax savings in new plants, equipment, and ventures. And in 2020 consumers and businesses alike were too absorbed with COVID-19 fears to respond as usual to fiscal and monetary incentives. When market participants don't respond as anticipated, the intended fiscal stimulus doesn't materialize. Such behavioral responses frustrate even the best-intentioned policy.

Implementation Problems

Measurement and design problems can break the spirit of even the best policymaker (or the policymaker's economic advisers). Yet measurement and design problems are only part of the story. A good idea is of little value unless someone puts it to use. Accordingly, to understand fully why things go wrong, we must also consider the difficulties of *implementing* a well-designed policy.

Congressional Deliberations. Suppose that the president decides that a tax cut is necessary to stimulate demand for goods and services. Can he simply go ahead and cut tax rates? No, because only Congress can legislate tax changes. Once the president decides on the appropriate policy, he must ask Congress for authority to take the required action, which means a delay in implementing policy or possibly no policy at all.

At the very least, the president must convince Congress of the wisdom of his proposed policy. The tax proposal must work its way through separate committees of both the House of Representatives and the Senate, get on the congressional calendar, and be approved in each chamber. If there are important differences in Senate and House versions of the tax cut legislation, they must be compromised in a joint conference. The modified proposal must then be returned to each chamber for approval.

The same kind of process applies to the outlay side of the budget. Once the president has submitted his budget proposals (in January), Congress reviews them, then sets its own spending goals. After that, the budget is broken down into 13 different categories, and a separate appropriations bill is written for each one. These bills spell out in detail how much can be spent and for what purposes. Once Congress passes them, they go to the president for acceptance or veto.

Budget legislation requires Congress to finish these deliberations by October 1 (the beginning of the federal fiscal year), but Congress rarely meets this deadline. In most years, the budget debate continues well into the fiscal year. In some years, the budget debate isn't resolved until the fiscal year is nearly over! The final budget legislation is typically more than 1,000 pages long and so complex that few people understand all its dimensions.

Time Lags. This description of congressional activity isn't an outline for a civics course; rather, it's an important explanation of why economic policy isn't fully effective. ***Even if the right policy is formulated to solve an emerging economic problem, there's no assurance that it will be implemented. And if it's implemented, there's no assurance that it will take effect at the right time.*** One of the most frightening prospects for economic policy is that a policy design intended to serve a specific problem will be implemented much later, when economic conditions have changed. This isn't a remote danger. According to economists Christina Romer and Paul Romer, the Fed doesn't pull the monetary stimulus lever until a recession is under way, and Congress is even slower in responding to an economic downturn. Indeed, a U.S. Treasury Department study concluded that almost every postwar fiscal stimulus package was enacted well after the end of the recession it was intended to cure!

Figure 18.3 is a schematic view of why macro policies don't always work as intended. There are always delays between the time a problem emerges and the time it's recognized. There are additional delays between recognition and response design, between design and implementation, and finally between implementation and impact. Not only may mistakes be made at each juncture, but even correct decisions may be overcome by changing economic conditions.

FIGURE 18.3

Policy Response: A Series of Time Lags

Even the best-intentioned economic policy can be frustrated by time lags. It takes time for a problem to be recognized, time to formulate a policy response, and still more time to implement that policy. By the time the policy begins to affect the economy, the underlying problem may have changed.

Politics vs. Economics. Politics often contributes to delayed and ill-designed policy interventions. Especially noteworthy in this regard is the potential conflict of economic policy with political objectives. The president and Congress are always reluctant to impose fiscal restraint (tax increases or budget cutbacks) in election years, regardless of economic circumstances. Fiscal restraint is never popular.

The tendency of Congress to hold fiscal policy hostage to electoral concerns has created a pattern of short-run stops and starts—a kind of policy-induced business cycle. Indeed, some argue that the business cycle has been replaced with the political cycle: The economy is stimulated in the year of an election and then restrained in the postelection year. The conflict between the urgent need to get reelected and the necessity to manage the economy results in a seesaw kind of instability.

Finally, we must recognize that policy design is obstructed by a certain attention deficit. Neither people on the street nor elected public officials focus constantly on economic goals and activities. Even students enrolled in economics courses have a hard time keeping their minds on the economy and its problems. The executive and legislative branches of government, for their part, are likely to focus on economic concerns only when economic problems become serious or voters demand action.

DECISIONS FOR TOMORROW

Hands On or Hands Off?

In view of the goal conflicts and the measurement, design, and implementation problems that policymakers confront, it's less surprising that things sometimes go wrong than that things ever work out right. The maze of obstacles through which theory must pass before it becomes policy explains many economic disappointments. On this basis alone, we may conclude that *consistent fine-tuning of the economy isn't compatible with either our design capabilities or our decision-making procedures.* We have exhibited a strong capability to avoid or contain major economic disruptions in the last four decades. We haven't, however, been able to make all the minor adjustments necessary to fulfill our goals completely. As Arthur Burns, former chairman of the Fed's Board of Governors, said nearly half a century ago

There has been much loose talk of when the state of knowledge permits us to predict only within a fairly broad level the course of economic development and the results of policy actions.[1]

Continued

[1]Arthur Burns, as quoted in Milton Friedman, "The Inflationary Fed," *Newsweek,* August 27, 1973, p. 74.

Hands Off. Some critics of economic policy take this argument a few steps further. If fine-tuning isn't really possible, they say, we should abandon discretionary policies altogether and follow fixed rules for fiscal and monetary intervention.

As we saw in Chapter 15, pure monetarism would require the Fed to increase the money supply at a constant rate. Critics of fiscal policy would require the government to maintain balanced budgets, or at least to offset deficits in sluggish years with surpluses in years of high growth. Such rules would prevent policymakers from over- or understimulating the economy. Such rules would also add a dose of certainty to the economic outlook.

Milton Friedman was one of the most persistent advocates of fixed policy rules. With discretionary authority, Friedman argued,

> the wrong decision is likely to be made in a large fraction of cases because the decision makers are examining only a limited area and not taking into account the cumulative consequences of the policy as a whole. On the other hand, if a general rule is adopted for a group of cases as a bundle, the existence of that rule has favorable effects on people's attitudes and beliefs and expectations that would not follow even from the discretionary adoption of precisely the same policy on a series of separate occasions.[2]

The case for a hands-off policy stance is based on practical, not theoretical, arguments. *Everyone agrees that flexible, discretionary policies* **could** *result in better economic performance. But Friedman and others argue that the practical requirements of monetary and fiscal management are too demanding and thus prone to failure.* Even former Fed Chairman Alan Greenspan, an advocate of hands-on discretion, later admitted he erred 30 percent of the time. Critics of activist policy say that is too high an error rate.

New Classical Economics. Monetarist critiques of discretionary policy are echoed by a new perspective referred to as new classical economics (NCE). Classical economists saw no need for discretionary macro policy. In their view, the private sector is inherently stable, and government intervention serves no purpose. New classical economics reaches the same conclusion. As Robert Barro, a proponent of NCE, put it, "It is best for the government to provide a stable environment, and then mainly stay out of the way."[3] Barro and other NCE economists based this laissez-faire conclusion on the intriguing notion of **rational expectations**. This notion contends that people make decisions on the basis of all available information, including the *future* effects of *current* government policy.

Suppose, for example, that the Fed decided to increase the money supply to boost output. If people had rational expectations, they'd anticipate that this money supply growth will fuel later inflation. To protect themselves, they'd immediately demand higher prices and wages. As a result, the stimulative monetary policy would fail to boost real output.

Discretionary fiscal policy could be equally ineffective. Suppose Congress accelerated government spending in an effort to boost aggregate demand. Monetarists contend that the accompanying increase in the deficit would push interest rates up and crowd out private investment and consumption. New classical economists again reach the same conclusion via a different route. They contend that people with rational expectations would anticipate that a larger deficit now will necessitate tax increases in later years. To prepare for later tax bills, consumers will reduce spending now, thereby saving more. This "rational" reduction in consumption will offset the increased government expenditure, thus rendering fiscal policy ineffective.

If the new classical economists are right, the only policy that works is one that surprises people—one that consumers and investors don't anticipate. But a policy based on

rational expectations: Hypothesis that people's spending decisions are based on all available information, including the anticipated effects of government intervention.

[2]Milton Friedman, *Capitalism and Freedom* (Chicago, IL: University of Chicago Press, 1962), p. 53.
[3]Robert Barro, "Don't Fool with Money, Cut Taxes," *The Wall Street Journal,* November 21, 1991, p. A14.

Keynesians	Keynesians believe that the private sector is inherently unstable and prone to stagnate at low levels of output and employment. They want the government to manage aggregate demand with changes in taxes and government's spending.
Modern ("neo") Keynesians	Post–World War II followers of Keynes worry about inflation as well as recession. They urge budgetary restraint to cool an overheated economy. They also use monetary policy to change interest rates.
Monetarists	The money supply is their only heavy hitter. By changing the money supply, they can raise or lower the price level. Pure monetarists shun active policy, believing that it destabilizes the otherwise stable private sector. Output and employment gravitate to their natural levels.
Supply-siders	Incentives to work, invest, and produce are the key to their plays. Cuts in marginal tax rates and government regulation are used to expand production capacity, thereby increasing output and reducing inflationary pressures.
New classical economists	They say fine-tuning won't work because once the private sector realizes what the government is doing, it will act to offset it. They also question the credibility of quick-fix promises. They favor steady, predictable policies.

TABLE 18.5

Who's on First? Labeling Economists

It's sometimes hard to tell who's on what side in economic debates. Although some economists are proud to wear the colors of monetarists, Keynesians, or other teams, many economists shun such allegiances. Indeed, economists are often accused of playing on one team one day and on another team the next, making it hard to tell which team is at bat. To simplify matters, this guide may be used for quick identification of the players. Closer observation is advised, however, before choosing up teams.

surprises isn't practical. Accordingly, new classical economists conclude that minimal policy intervention is best. This conclusion provides yet another guideline for policy decisions. See Table 18.5 for a roster of competing theories.

Hands On. *Proponents of a hands-on policy strategy acknowledge the possibility of occasional blunders. They emphasize, however, the greater risks of doing nothing when the economy is faltering.* Some proponents of the quick fix even turn the new classical economics argument on its head. Even the wrong policy, they argue, might be better than doing nothing if enough market participants believe that *change* implied *progress*. They cite the jump in consumer confidence that followed the election of Bill Clinton, who had emphasized the need for a *change* in policy but hadn't spelled out the details of that change. The surge in confidence itself stimulated consumer purchases even before President Clinton took office. The same kind of response occurred after the September 11, 2001, terrorist attacks. Consumers were dazed and insecure. There was a serious risk that they would curtail spending if the government didn't *do something*. Details aside, they just wanted reassurance that someone was taking charge of events. Quick responses by the Fed (increasing the money supply), the Congress (authorizing more spending), and President Bush (mobilizing security and military forces) kept consumer confidence from plunging. President Obama argued that a similar situation existed in early 2009. Claiming that the economy would slide into another Depression if Congress didn't act, he said doing *something*—even if not perfect—was better than doing *nothing*.

Just doing *something* isn't the purpose of a hands-on policy, of course. Policy activists believe that we have enough knowledge about how the economy works to pull the right policy levers most of the time. They also point to the historical record. Our economic track record may not be perfect, but the historical record of prices, employment, and growth has improved since active fiscal and monetary policies were adopted: Recessions have gotten shorter and economic expansions longer.

SUMMARY

- The government possesses an array of macro policy tools, each of which can significantly alter economic outcomes. **LO18-1**
- To end a recession, we can cut taxes, expand the money supply, or increase government spending. To curb inflation, we can reverse each of these policy tools. To overcome stagflation, we can combine fiscal and monetary levers with improved supply-side incentives. **LO18-2**
- Although the potential of economic theory seems impressive, the economic record doesn't look as good. Persistent unemployment, recurring economic slowdowns, and nagging inflation suggest that the realities of policymaking are more difficult than theory implies. **LO18-3**
- To some extent, the failures of economic policy are a reflection of scarce resources and competing goals. Even when consensus exists, however, serious obstacles

to effective economic policy remain. These obstacles include
- (a) Measurement problems. Our knowledge of economic performance is always dated and incomplete.
- (b) Design problems. We don't know exactly how the economy will respond to specific policies.
- (c) Implementation problems. It takes time for Congress and the president to agree on an appropriate plan of action. Moreover, political needs may take precedence over economic needs.

For all these reasons, discretionary policy rarely lives up to its theoretical potential. **LO18-3**
- Monetarists and new classical economists favor rules rather than discretionary macro policies. They argue that discretionary policies are unlikely to work and risk being wrong. Critics respond that discretionary policies are needed to cope with ever-changing economic circumstances. **LO18-3**

Key Terms

business cycle	monetary policy	inflationary GDP gap
fiscal policy	natural rate of unemployment	stagflation
automatic stabilizer	supply-side policy	fine-tuning
structural deficit	recessionary GDP gap	growth recession
fiscal stimulus	multiplier	inflationary flashpoint
fiscal restraint	velocity of money (V)	rational expectations

Questions for Discussion

1. What policies would Keynesians, monetarists, and supply-siders advocate for (a) restraining inflation and (b) reducing unemployment? **LO18-1**
2. Why did Fed Chairman Bernanke expect there would be no recession in 2008 (see Front Page Economics "Fed Chief Sees No Recession")? Why was he wrong? **LO18-3**
3. If policymakers had instant data on the economy's performance, should they respond immediately? Why or why not? **LO18-3**
4. Suppose it's an election year and aggregate demand is growing so fast that it threatens to accelerate inflation. Why might Congress and the president hesitate to cut government spending or raise taxes, as theory suggests? **LO18-3**
5. Should military spending be subject to macroeconomic constraints? What programs should be expanded or contracted to bring about needed changes in the budget? **LO18-2**
6. Why was the investment response to the Trump tax cuts so muted? **LO18-3**

7. Suppose the government proposes to cut taxes while maintaining the current level of government expenditures. To finance this deficit, it may either (i) sell bonds to the public or (ii) ask the Fed to increase the money supply. What are the likely effects of these financing alternatives on each of the following? Would Keynesians, monetarists, and supply-siders give the same answers? **LO18-2**
   - (a) Interest rates.
   - (b) Consumer spending.
   - (c) Business investment.
   - (d) Aggregate demand.
8. How would the economy have fared during the coronavirus pandemic if the government had not pursued such massive fiscal and monetary stimulus? **LO18-2**
9. What are the pros and cons of tax cuts or increased government spending as stimulative tools? **LO18-3**
10. Which nation in the World View "Comparative Macro Performance" had the best record? **LO18-3**

PROBLEMS FOR CHAPTER 18

LO18-3 1. The Congressional Budget Office admits that its forecasts of next year's GDP are off by an average of 0.5 percent. If the Congressional Budget Office makes its average error, by how much could it under- and overestimate next year's GDP in a $23 trillion economy?

LO18-1 2. In 2011 the unemployment rate was 8.9 percent, far above the full-employment threshold (4 percent).
   (*a*) How many jobs were lost, as a result, in a labor force of 140 million?
   (*b*) If the average worker produced $100,000 of output, how much output was lost?
   (*c*) By how much did GDP per capita decline as a result (310 million people)?

LO18-1 3. According to World View "Comparative Macro Performance"
   (*a*) Which country had the greatest macro misery in the 2000s? (Compute the "misery index" from Chapter 16.)
   (*b*) Which country had the fastest growth?

LO18-1 4. If infrastructure spending increases by $200 billion and taxes are raised by the same amount, by how much will aggregate demand change if the MPC is 0.90?

LO18-3 5. The CBO said it was 66.7 percent confident that the GDP growth rate for 2016–2020 would be between 0.7 and 3.2 percent. In a $20 trillion economy, what is the implied range of forecasted GDP for a single year?

LO18-3 6. The following table displays Congressional Budget Office forecasts made in January 2015 of future federal budget deficits. Compare these forecasts with *actual* deficits for those same years (see Table 12.3 for data).

Year:	2015	2016	2017	2018	2019	2020
Deficit forecast (in billions of dollars)	−468	−467	−489	−540	−652	−739

   (*a*) In how many years was the CBO too optimistic (underestimating the deficit)?
   (*b*) In how many years was the CBO too pessimistic?

LO18-2 7. Complete the following chart by summarizing the policy prescriptions of various economic theories:

Policy Approach	Policy Prescription for	
	Recession	**Inflation**
Fiscal		
Classical	_____	_____
Keynesian	_____	_____
Monetarist	_____	_____
Monetary		
Keynesian	_____	_____
Monetarist	_____	_____
Supply side	_____	_____

LO18-2   8. *Decisions for Tomorrow:* Match the statement with the school of economic thought:

Statement	School of Thought
Money supply should be grown at a steady pace.	Keynesians
Fine-tuning does not work because the private sector will act to offset government policy.	Modern Keynesians (Neo-Keynesians)
Government should manage aggregate demand with changes in taxes and spending.	Monetarists
Inflation is just as much of a concern as recessions.	Supply-siders
Marginal tax rates should be cut to stimulate the economy in times of recession.	New classical economists

INTERNATIONAL ECONOMICS

Our interactions with the rest of the world have a profound impact on the mix of output (WHAT), the methods of production (HOW), and the distribution of income (FOR WHOM). Trade and global money flows can also affect the stability of the macro economy. Chapters 19 and 20 explore the motives, the nature, and the effects of international trade and finance.

Chapter 21 examines one of the world's most urgent problems—the deprivation that afflicts nearly 3 billion people worldwide. In this last chapter, the dimensions, causes, and potential cures for global poverty are discussed.

Ingram Publishing

Don Tonge/Alamy Stock Photo

AFP/Getty Images

International Trade

LEARNING OBJECTIVES

After reading this chapter, you should know

LO19-1 What comparative advantage is.

LO19-2 What the gains from trade are.

LO19-3 How trade barriers and trade pacts affect prices, output, and incomes.

The 2020 World Series between the Los Angeles Dodgers and the Tampa Bay Rays was played with Japanese gloves, baseballs made in Costa Rica, and Mexican bats. Most of the players were wearing shoes made in Korea or China. And during the regular season, many of the games throughout the major leagues were played on artificial grass made in Taiwan. Baseball, it seems, has become something less than the "all-American" game.

Imported goods have made inroads into other activities as well. All smartphones and video game consoles are imported, as are most televisions, fax machines, personal computers, and iPads. Most of these imported goods could have been produced in the United States. Why did we purchase them from other countries? For that matter, why does the rest of the world buy computers, tractors, chemicals, airplanes, and wheat from us rather than produce such products for themselves? Wouldn't we all be better off relying on ourselves for the goods we consume (and the jobs we need) rather than buying and selling products in international markets? Or is there some advantage to be gained from international trade?

This chapter begins with a survey of international trade patterns—what goods and services we trade, and with whom. Then we address basic issues related to such trade:

- **What benefit, if any, do we get from international trade?**
- **How much harm do imports cause, and to whom?**
- **Should we protect ourselves from "unfair" trade by limiting imports?**

After examining the arguments for and against international trade, we draw some general conclusions about trade policy. As we'll see, international trade tends to increase *average* incomes, although it may diminish the job and income opportunities for specific industries and workers.

U.S. TRADE PATTERNS

The United States is the largest player in global product and resource markets. In 2019 we purchased 13 percent of the world's exports and sold 11 percent of the same total.

Imports

In dollar terms, our imports in 2019 exceeded $3 trillion. These **imports** included the consumer items mentioned earlier as well as capital equipment, raw materials, and food. Table 19.1 identifies some of the goods and services we purchase from foreign suppliers.

Although imports represent only 15 percent of total GDP, they account for larger shares of specific product markets. Coffee is a familiar

TABLE 19.1

A U.S. Trade Sampler

The United States imports and exports a staggering array of goods and services. Shown here are some of the top exports and imports with various countries. Notice that we export many of the same goods we import (such as cars and computers). What's the purpose of trading goods we produce ourselves?

Country	Imports from	Exports to
Australia	Beef Alumina Pharmaceuticals	Airplanes Computers Auto parts
Belgium	Jewelry Pharmaceuticals Optical glass	Cigarettes Airplanes Diamonds
Canada	Cars Trucks Paper	Auto parts Cars Computers
China	Computers Clothes Toys	Soybeans Airplanes Cars
Germany	Cars Engines Auto parts	Airplanes Computers Cars
Japan	Cars Computers Telephones	Airplanes Computers Timber
Mexico	Cars Computers Appliances	Computers Cars Chemicals
Russia	Oil Platinum Artworks	Corn Wheat Oil seeds
South Korea	Shoes Cars Computers	Airplanes Leather Iron ingots and oxides

Source: U.S. Department of Commerce.

example. Because virtually all coffee is imported (except for a tiny amount produced in Hawaii), Americans would have a harder time staying awake without imports. Likewise, there'd be no aluminum if we didn't import bauxite, no chrome bumpers if we didn't import chromium, no tin cans without imported tin, no smartphones, and a lot fewer computers without imported components. We couldn't even play the all-American game of baseball without imports because baseballs are no longer made in the United States.

We import *services* as well as *goods.* If you fly to Europe on Virgin Airways, you're importing transportation services. If you stay in a London hotel, you're importing lodging services. When you go to Barclay's Bank to cash traveler's checks, you're importing foreign financial services. If you go to Mexico for spring break, you are importing tourism services. These and other services now account for one-sixth of U.S. imports.

imports: Goods and services purchased from international sources.

Exports

While we're buying goods (merchandise) and services from the rest of the world, global consumers are buying our **exports.** In 2019 we exported $1.6 trillion of *goods,* including farm products (wheat, corn, soybeans), tobacco, machinery (computers), aircraft, automobiles and auto parts, raw materials (lumber, iron ore), and chemicals (see Table 19.1 for a sample of U.S. merchandise exports). We also exported $845 billion of services (movies, software licenses, tourism, engineering, financial services, etc.).

exports: Goods and services sold to foreign buyers.

Where do the coffee beans come from?

limpido/Getty Images

Although the United States is the world's second largest exporter of goods and services, exports represent a relatively modest fraction of our total output. As World View "Export Ratios" illustrates, other nations export much larger proportions of their GDP. Belgium is one of the most export-oriented countries, with tourist services and diamond exports pushing its export ratio to an incredible 70 percent. By contrast, Afghanistan is basically a closed economy with few exports (other than opium and other drugs traded in the black market).

The low U.S. export ratio (12 percent) disguises our heavy dependence on exports in specific industries. We export 25 to 50 percent of our rice, corn, and wheat production each year, and still more of our soybeans. Clearly a decision by international consumers to stop eating U.S. agricultural products could devastate a lot of American farmers. Such companies as Boeing (planes), Caterpillar Tractor (construction and farm machinery), Weyerhaeuser (logs, lumber), Dow (chemicals), and Oracle (computer workstations) sell more than one-fourth of their output in foreign markets. McDonald's sells hamburgers to nearly 70 million people a day in 120 countries around the world; to do so, the company exports management and marketing services (as well as frozen food) from the United States. The Walt Disney Company produces the most popular TV shows in Russia and Germany,

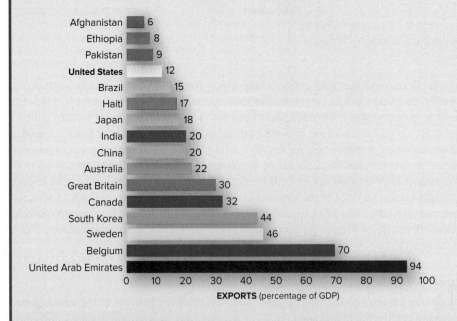

WORLD VIEW

EXPORT RATIOS

Very poor countries often have little to export and thus low export ratios. Saudi Arabia, by contrast, depends heavily on its oil exports. Fast-developing countries in Asia also rely on exports to enlarge their markets and raise incomes. The U.S. export ratio is low by international standards.

Country	Exports (percentage of GDP)
Afghanistan	6
Ethiopia	8
Pakistan	9
United States	12
Brazil	15
Haiti	17
Japan	18
India	20
China	20
Australia	22
Great Britain	30
Canada	32
South Korea	44
Sweden	46
Belgium	70
United Arab Emirates	94

EXPORTS (percentage of GDP)

Source: The World Bank, *WDI2019 Data Set.*

CRITICAL ANALYSIS: The relatively low U.S. export ratio reflects the vast size of our domestic market and our relative self-sufficiency in food and resources. European nations are smaller and highly interdependent.

Product Category	Exports ($ billions)	Imports ($ billions)	Surplus (Deficit) ($ billions)
Merchandise	$1,653	$2,519	$(866)
Services	845	595	250
Total trade	$2,498	$3,114	$(616)

Source: U.S. Department of Commerce.

TABLE 19.2

Trade Balances

Both merchandise (goods) and services are traded between countries. The United States typically has a merchandise deficit and a services surplus. When combined, an overall trade deficit remained in 2019.

publishes Italy's best-selling weekly magazine, and has the most popular tourist attraction in Japan (Tokyo Disneyland). The 500,000 foreign students attending U.S. universities are purchasing $5 billion of American educational services. All these activities are part of America's service exports.

Trade Balances

Although we export a lot of products, we usually have an imbalance in our trade flows. The trade balance is the difference between the value of exports and imports:

$$\text{Trade balance} = \text{Exports} - \text{Imports}$$

During 2019 we imported much more than we exported and so had a *negative* trade balance. A negative trade balance is called a **trade deficit.**

Although the overall trade balance includes both goods and services, these flows are usually reported separately, with the *merchandise* trade balance distinguished from the *services* trade balance. As Table 19.2 shows, the United States had a merchandise (goods) trade deficit of $866 billion in 2019 and a *services* trade *surplus* of $250 billion, leaving the overall trade balance in the red.

When the United States has a trade deficit with the rest of the world, other countries must have an offsetting **trade surplus.** On a global scale, imports must equal exports because every good exported by one country must be imported by another. Hence, *any imbalance in America's trade must be offset by reverse imbalances elsewhere.*

Whatever the overall balance in our trade accounts, bilateral balances vary greatly. Table 19.3 shows, for example, that our 2019 aggregate trade deficit ($615 billion) incorporated huge bilateral merchandise trade deficits with China, Germany, Japan, and Mexico. In the same year, however, we had trade surpluses with Brazil, the Netherlands, and Hong Kong.

trade deficit: The amount by which the value of imports exceeds the value of exports in a given time period (negative net exports).

trade surplus: The amount by which the value of exports exceeds the value of imports in a given time period (positive net exports).

Country	Merchandise Exports to ($ billions)	Merchandise Imports from ($ billions)	Trade Balance ($ billions)
Top Deficit Countries			
China	$106	$451	−$345
Mexico	291	399	−108
Japan	124	194	−70
Germany	96	164	−68
Canada	356	390	−32
Top Surplus Countries			
Hong Kong	$ 46	$ 20	+$26
The Netherlands	51	30	+21
Brazil	69	57	+12
United Kingdom	114	138	+6
Singapore	54	49	+5

Source: U.S. Census Bureau (2019 data).

TABLE 19.3

Bilateral Trade Balances

The U.S. trade deficit is the net result of bilateral deficits and surpluses. We had huge trade deficits with China, Germany, and Japan in 2019, for example, but small trade surpluses with Brazil, the Netherlands, and Hong Kong. International trade is *multi*national, with surpluses in some countries being offset by trade deficits elsewhere.

MOTIVATION TO TRADE

Many people wonder why we trade so much, particularly because (1) we import many of the things we also export (like computers, airplanes, cars, clothes), (2) we *could* produce many of the other things we import, and (3) we worry so much about trade imbalances. Why not just import those few things that we can't produce ourselves, and export just enough to balance that trade?

Specialization

Although it might seem strange to be importing goods we could produce ourselves, such trade is entirely rational. Our decision to trade with other countries arises from the same considerations that motivate individuals to specialize in production: satisfying their remaining needs in the marketplace. Why don't you become self-sufficient—growing all your own food, building your own shelter, and recording your own songs? Presumably because you've found that you can enjoy a much higher standard of living (and better music) by working at just one job and then buying other goods in the marketplace. When you do so, you're no longer self-sufficient. Instead you are *specializing* in production, relying on others to produce the array of goods and services you want. When countries trade goods and services, they are doing the same thing—*specializing* in production and then *trading* for other desired goods. Why do they do this? Because **specialization increases total output.**

To see how nations benefit from trade, we'll examine the production possibilities of two countries. We want to demonstrate that two countries that trade can together produce more output than they could in the absence of trade. If they can, **the gain from trade is increased world output and a higher standard of living in all trading countries.** This is the essential message of the *theory of comparative advantage.*

Production and Consumption without Trade

Consider the production and consumption possibilities of just two countries—say, the United States and France. For the sake of illustration, assume that both countries produce only two goods: bread and wine. Let's also set aside worries about the law of diminishing returns and the substitutability of resources, thus transforming the familiar **production possibilities** curve into a straight line, as in Figure 19.1.

The "curves" in Figure 19.1 suggest that the United States is capable of producing much more bread than France. With our greater abundance of labor, land, and other resources, we assume that the United States is capable of producing up to 100 zillion loaves of bread per year. To do so, we'd have to devote all our resources to that purpose. This capability is indicated by point *A* in Figure 19.1*a* and in row *A* of the accompanying production possibilities schedule.

France (Figure 19.1*b*), on the other hand, confronts a *maximum* bread production of only 15 zillion loaves per year (point *G*) because it has little available land, less fuel, and fewer potential workers.

The capacities of the two countries for wine production are 50 zillion barrels for us (point *F*) and 60 zillion for France (point *L*), largely reflecting France's greater experience in tending vines. Both countries are also capable of producing alternative *combinations* of bread and wine, as evidenced by their respective production possibilities curves (points *A–F* for the United States and *G–L* for France).

A nation that doesn't trade with other countries is called a **closed economy.** In the absence of contact with the outside world, the production possibilities curve for a closed economy also defines its **consumption possibilities.** Without imports, a country cannot consume more than it produces. Thus, the only immediate issue in a closed economy is which mix of output to choose—*what* to produce and consume—out of the domestic choices available.

Assume that Americans choose point *D* on their production possibilities curve, producing and consuming 40 zillion loaves of bread and 30 zillion barrels of wine. The French, on the other hand, prefer the mix of output represented by point *I* on their production possibilities curve. At that point they produce and consume 9 zillion loaves of bread and 24 zillion barrels of wine.

---

production possibilities: The alternative combinations of final goods and services that could be produced in a given period with all available resources and technology.

---

closed economy: A nation that doesn't engage in international trade.

---

consumption possibilities: The alternative combinations of goods and services that a country could consume in a given time period.

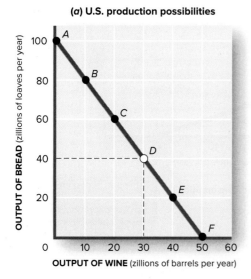

(a) U.S. production possibilities

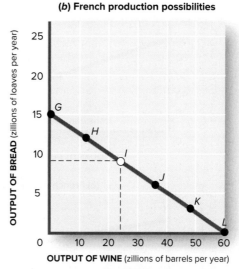

(b) French production possibilities

FIGURE 19.1

Consumption Possibilities without Trade

In the absence of trade, a country's consumption possibilities are identical to its production possibilities. The assumed production possibilities of the United States and France are illustrated in the graphs and the corresponding schedules. Before entering into trade, the United States chose to produce and consume at point *D,* with 40 zillion loaves of bread and 30 zillion barrels of wine. France chose point *I* on its own production possibilities curve. By trading, each country hopes to increase its consumption beyond these levels.

In a closed economy, production possibilities and consumption possibilities are identical.

U.S. Production Possibilities				French Production Possibilities			
	Bread (Zillions of Loaves)	+	Wine (Zillions of Barrels)		Bread (Zillions of Loaves)	+	Wine (Zillions of Barrels)
A	100	+	0	G	15	+	0
B	80	+	10	H	12	+	12
C	60	+	20	I	9	+	24
D	40	+	30	J	6	+	36
E	20	+	40	K	3	+	48
F	0	+	50	L	0	+	60

To assess the potential gain from trade, we must focus the *combined* output of the United States and France. In this case, total world output (points *D* and *I*) comes to 49 zillion loaves of bread and 54 zillion barrels of wine. What we want to know is whether world output would increase if France and the United States abandoned their isolation and started trading. Could either country, or both, consume *more* output by engaging in a little trade?

Production and Consumption with Trade

Because both countries are saddled with limited production possibilities, trying to eke out a little extra wine and bread from this situation might not seem possible. Such a conclusion is unwarranted, however.

Change U.S. Production. Take another look at the production possibilities confronting the United States, as reproduced in Figure 19.2. Suppose the United States were to produce at point *C* rather than point *D*. At point *C* we could produce 60 zillion loaves of bread and 20 zillion barrels of wine. That combination is clearly *possible* because it lies on the production possibilities curve. We didn't choose that point earlier because we assumed the mix of output at point *D* was preferable. The mix of output at point *C could* be produced, however.

FIGURE 19.2

Consumption Possibilities with Trade

A country can increase its consumption possibilities through international trade. Each country alters its mix of domestic output to produce more of the good it produces best. As it does so, total world output increases, and each country enjoys more consumption. In this case, trade allows U.S. consumption to move from point *D* to point *N*. France moves from point *I* to point *M*.

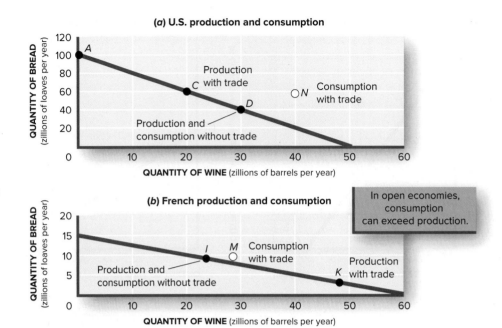

(a) U.S. production and consumption

(b) French production and consumption

In open economies, consumption can exceed production.

Change French Production. We could also change the mix of output in France. Assume that France moved from point *I* to point *K*, producing 48 zillion barrels of wine and only 3 zillion loaves of bread.

Increased World Output. Two observations are now called for. The first is simply that output mixes have changed in each country. The second, and more interesting, is that total world output has *increased*. Notice how this works. When the United States and France were at points *D* and *I*, their *combined* output consisted of

A: Initial Production Choices		
	Bread (Zillions of Loaves)	Wine (Zillions of Barrels)
United States (at point D)	40	30
France (at point I)	9	24
Total pre-trade output	49	54

After they moved along their respective production possibilities curves to points *C* and *K*, the combined world output became

B: Revised Production Choices		
	Bread (Zillions of Loaves)	Wine (Zillions of Barrels)
United States (at point C)	60	20
France (at point K)	3	48
Total output with trade	63	68

Total world output has increased by 14 zillion loaves of bread and 14 zillion barrels of wine. *Just by changing the mix of output in each country, we've increased total world output.* This additional output creates the potential for making both countries better off than they were in the absence of trade.

This almost seems like a magic trick, but it isn't. Here's what happened. The United States and France weren't initially producing at points *C* and *K* before because they simply didn't want to *consume* those particular output combinations. Nevertheless, our discovery that points *C* and *K* allow us to produce *more* output suggests that everybody can consume more goods and services if we change the mix of output in each country. This is our first clue as to how specialization and trade can benefit an **open economy**—a nation that engages in international trade.

open economy: A nation that engages in international trade.

Start Trading. Suppose that we Americans are the first to discover the potential benefits from trade. Using Figure 19.2 as our guide, we suggest to the French that they move their mix of output from point *I* to point *K*. As an incentive for making such a move, we promise to give them 6 zillion loaves of bread in exchange for 20 zillion barrels of wine. This would leave them at point *M*, with as much bread to consume as they used to have, plus an extra 4 zillion barrels of wine. At point *I* they had 9 zillion loaves of bread and 24 zillion barrels of wine. At point *M* they can have 9 zillion loaves of bread and 28 zillion barrels of wine. Thus, by altering their mix of output (from point *I* to point *K*) and then trading (point *K* to point *M*), the French end up with more goods and services than they had in the beginning. Notice in particular that this new consumption possibility (point *M*) lies *outside* France's domestic production possibilities curve.

The French will be quite pleased with the extra output they get from trading. But where does this leave us? Does France's gain imply a loss for us? Or do we gain from trade as well?

Mutual Gains

As it turns out, *both* the United States and France gain by trading. The United States, too, ends up consuming a mix of output that lies outside our production possibilities curve.

Note that at point *C* we *produce* 60 zillion loaves of bread per year and 20 zillion barrels of wine. We then *export* 6 zillion loaves to France. This leaves us with 54 zillion loaves of bread to *consume*.

In return for our exported bread, the French give us 20 zillion barrels of wine. These imports, plus our domestic production, permit us to *consume* 40 zillion barrels of wine. Hence, we end up consuming at point *N*, enjoying 54 zillion loaves of bread and 40 zillion barrels of wine. Thus, by first changing our mix of output (from point *D* to point *C*), then trading (point *C* to point *N*), we end up with 14 zillion more loaves of bread and 10 zillion more barrels of wine than we started with. Time to celebrate! International trade has made us better off, too.

Table 19.4 recaps the gains from trade for both countries. Notice that U.S. imports match French exports and vice versa. Also notice how the ***trade-facilitated consumption in each country exceeds no-trade levels.***

	Production and Consumption with Trade						Production and Consumption with No Trade
	Production	+ Imports	− Exports	= Consumption			
United States at	Point *C*				Point *N*		Point *D*
Bread	60	+ 0	− 6	= 54		compare	40
Wine	20	+ 20	− 0	= 40			30
France at	Point *K*				Point *M*		Point *I*
Bread	3	+ 6	− 0	= 9		compare	9
Wine	48	+ 0	− 20	= 28			24

TABLE 19.4

Gains from Trade

When nations specialize in production, they can export one good and import another and end up with *more* total goods to consume than they had without trade. In this case, the United States specializes in bread production. Notice how

U.S. *consumption* of both goods increases (compare total U.S. consumption of bread and wine at point *N* [with trade] to consumption at point *D* [no trade]).

Specialization Is the Key. All these numbers do indeed look like some kind of magic trick, but there's no sleight of hand going on here; the gains from trade are due to specialization in production. When each country goes it alone, it's a prisoner of its own production possibilities curve; it must make production decisions on the basis of its own consumption desires. When international trade is permitted, however, each country can concentrate on the exploitation of its production capabilities. *Each country produces those goods it makes best and then trades with other countries to acquire the goods it desires to consume.*

The resultant specialization increases total world output. In the process, each country is able to escape the confines of its own production possibilities curve, to reach beyond it for a larger basket of consumption goods. *When a country engages in international trade, its consumption possibilities always exceed its production possibilities.* These enhanced consumption possibilities are emphasized by the positions of points *N* and *M outside* the production possibilities curves (Figure 19.2). If it weren't possible for countries to increase their consumption by trading, there'd be no incentive for trading, and thus no trade.

PURSUIT OF COMPARATIVE ADVANTAGE

Although international trade can make everyone better off, it's not so obvious which goods should be traded, or on what terms. In our previous illustration, the United States ended up trading bread for wine in terms that were decidedly favorable to us. Why did we export bread rather than wine, and how did we end up getting such a good deal?

Opportunity Costs

comparative advantage: The ability of a country to produce a specific good at a lower opportunity cost than its trading partners.

opportunity cost: The most desired goods or services that are forgone in order to obtain something else.

The decision to export bread is based on **comparative advantage**—that is, the *relative* cost of producing different goods. Recall that we can produce a maximum of 100 zillion loaves of bread per year or 50 zillion barrels of wine. Thus, the domestic **opportunity cost** of producing 100 zillion loaves of bread is the 50 zillion barrels of wine we forsake in order to devote all our resources to bread production. In fact, at every point on the U.S. production possibilities curve (Figure 19.2a), the opportunity cost of a loaf of bread is ½ barrel of wine. We're effectively paying half a barrel of wine to get a loaf of bread.

Although the cost of bread production in the United States might appear outrageous, even higher opportunity costs prevail in France. According to Figure 19.2b, the opportunity cost of producing a loaf of bread in France is a staggering 4 barrels of wine. To produce a loaf of bread, the French must use factors of production that could otherwise be used to produce 4 barrels of wine.

How much bread is a bottle of wine worth?

robeo/Getty Images

Comparative Advantage. A comparison of the opportunity costs prevailing in each country exposes the nature of comparative advantage. The United States has a comparative advantage in bread production because less wine has to be given up to produce bread in the United States than in France. In other words, the opportunity costs of bread production are lower in the United States than in France. *Comparative advantage refers to the relative (opportunity) costs of producing particular goods.*

A country should specialize in what it's *relatively* efficient at producing—that is, goods for which it has the lowest opportunity costs. In this case, the United States should produce bread because its opportunity cost (½ barrel of wine) is less than France's (4 barrels of wine). Were you the production manager for the whole world, you'd certainly want each country to exploit its relative abilities, thus maximizing world output. Each country can arrive at that same decision itself by comparing its own opportunity costs to those prevailing elsewhere.

CHAPTER 19: INTERNATIONAL TRADE

World output, and thus the potential gains from trade, will be maximized when each country pursues its comparative advantage. To do so, each country

- *Exports goods with relatively low opportunity costs.*
- *Imports goods with relatively high opportunity costs.*

That's the kind of situation depicted in Table 19.4.

Absolute Costs Don't Count

In assessing the nature of comparative advantage, notice that we needn't know anything about the actual costs involved in production. Have you seen any data suggesting how much labor, land, or capital is required to produce a loaf of bread in either France or the United States? For all you and I know, the French may be able to produce both bread and wine with fewer resources than we're using. Such an **absolute advantage** in production might exist because of their much longer experience in cultivating both grapes and wheat or simply because they have more talent.

We can envy such productivity, and even try to emulate it, but it shouldn't alter our production or trade decisions. All we really care about are *opportunity costs*—what *we* have to give up in order to get more of a desired good. If we can get a barrel of wine for less bread in trade than in production, we have a comparative advantage in producing bread. As long as we have a *comparative* advantage in bread production, we should exploit it. It doesn't matter to us whether France could produce either good with fewer resources. For that matter, even if France had an absolute advantage in *both* goods, we'd still have a *comparative* advantage in bread production, as we've already confirmed. The absolute costs of production were omitted from the previous illustration because they were irrelevant.

To clarify the distinction between absolute advantage and comparative advantage, consider this example. When Charlie Osgood joined the Willamette Warriors football team, he was the fastest runner ever to play football in Willamette. He could also throw the ball farther than most people could see. In other words, he had an *absolute advantage* in both throwing and running. Charlie would have made the greatest quarterback or the greatest end ever to play football. *Would have.* The problem was that he could play only one position at a time. Thus, the Willamette coach had to play Charlie either as a quarterback or as an end. He reasoned that Charlie could throw only a bit farther than some of the other top quarterbacks but could far outdistance all the other ends. In other words, Charlie had a *comparative advantage* in running and was assigned to play as an end.

absolute advantage: The ability of a country to produce a specific good with fewer resources (per unit of output) than other countries.

TERMS OF TRADE

It definitely pays to pursue one's comparative advantage by specializing in production. It may not yet be clear, however, how we got such a good deal with France. We're clever traders; but beyond that, is there any way to determine the **terms of trade**—the quantity of good A that must be given up in exchange for good B? In our previous illustration, the terms of trade were very favorable to us; we exchanged only 6 zillion loaves of bread for 20 zillion barrels of wine (Table 19.4). The terms of trade were thus 6 loaves = 20 barrels.

terms of trade: The rate at which goods are exchanged; the amount of good A given up for good B in trade.

Limits to the Terms of Trade

The terms of trade with France were determined by our offer and France's ready acceptance. But why did France accept those terms?

France was willing to accept our offer because the terms of trade permitted France to increase its wine consumption without giving up any bread consumption. Our offer of 6 loaves for 20 barrels was an improvement over France's domestic opportunity costs. France's domestic possibilities required it to give up 24 barrels of wine in order to produce 6 loaves of bread (see Figure 19.2b). Getting bread via trade was simply cheaper for France than producing bread at home. France ended up with an extra 4 zillion barrels of wine (take another look at the last two columns in Table 19.4).

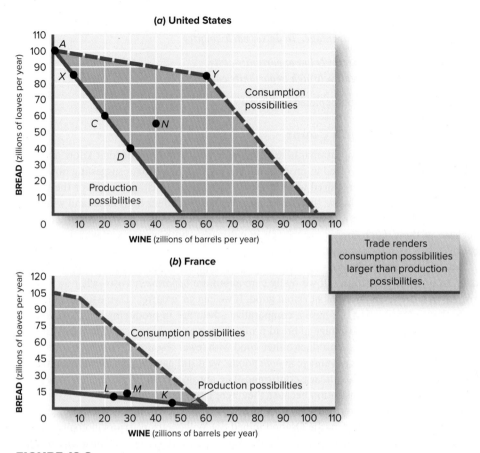

(a) United States

(b) France

Trade renders consumption possibilities larger than production possibilities.

FIGURE 19.3

Searching for the Terms of Trade

Assume the United States can produce 100 zillion loaves of bread per year (point *A*). If we reduce output to only 85 zillion loaves, we could move to point *X*. At point *X* we have 7.5 zillion barrels of wine and 85 zillion loaves of bread.

Trade increases consumption possibilities. If we continued to produce 100 zillion loaves of bread, we could trade 15 zillion loaves to France in exchange for as much as 60 zillion barrels of wine. This would leave us *producing* at point *A* but *consuming* at point *Y*. At point *Y* we have more wine and no less bread than we had at point *X*. This is our motivation to trade.

A country will end up on its consumption possibilities curve only if it gets *all* the gains from trade. It will remain on its production possibilities curve only if it gets *none* of the gains from trade. The terms of trade determine how the gains from trade are distributed, and thus at what point in the shaded area each country ends up.

Note: The kink in the consumption possibilities curve at point Y occurs because France is unable to produce more than 60 zillion barrels of wine.

Our first clue to the terms of trade, then, lies in each country's domestic opportunity costs. *A country won't trade unless the terms of trade are superior to domestic opportunities.* In our example, the opportunity cost of 1 barrel of wine in the United States is 2 loaves of bread. Accordingly, we won't *export* bread unless we get at least 1 barrel of wine in exchange for every 2 loaves of bread we ship overseas.

All countries want to gain from trade. Hence, we can predict that *the terms of trade between any two countries will lie somewhere between their respective opportunity costs in production.* That is, a loaf of bread in international trade will be worth at least ½ barrel of wine (the U.S. opportunity cost), but no more than 4 barrels (the French opportunity cost). In our example, the terms of trade ended up at 1 loaf = 3.33 barrels (that is, at 6 loaves = 20 barrels). This represented a very large gain for the United States and a small gain for France. Figure 19.3 illustrates this outcome and several other possibilities.

The Role of Markets and Prices

Relatively little trade is subject to such direct negotiations between countries. More often than not, the decision to import or export a particular good is left up to the market decisions of individual consumers and producers.

Individual consumers and producers aren't much impressed by such abstractions as comparative advantage. Market participants tend to focus on prices, always trying to allocate their resources in order to maximize profits or personal satisfaction. Consumers tend to buy the products that deliver the most utility per dollar of expenditure, while producers try to get the most output per dollar of cost. Everybody's looking for a bargain.

The Lone Trader. So what does this have to do with international trade? Well, suppose that Henri, an enterprising Frenchman, visited the United States before the advent of international trade. He observed that bread was relatively cheap while wine was relatively expensive—the opposite of the price relationship prevailing in France. These price comparisons brought to his mind the opportunity for making a fast euro. All he had to do was bring over some French wine and trade it in the United States for a large quantity of bread. Then he could return to France and exchange the bread for a greater quantity of wine. *Alors!* Were he to do this a few times, he'd amass substantial profits.

Trade "Winners". Henri's entrepreneurial exploits will not only enrich him but also move each country toward its comparative advantage. The United States ends up exporting bread to France, and France ends up exporting wine to the United States, exactly as the theory of comparative advantage suggests. The activating agent isn't the Ministry of Trade and its 620 trained economists but simply one enterprising French trader. He's aided and encouraged, of course, by consumers and producers in each country. American consumers are happy to trade their bread for his wines. They thereby end up paying less for wine (in terms of bread) than they'd otherwise have to. In other words, the terms of trade Henri offers are more attractive than the prevailing (domestic) relative prices. On the other side of the Atlantic, Henri's welcome is equally warm. French consumers are able to get a better deal by trading their wine for his imported bread than by trading with the local bakers.

Even some producers are happy. The wheat farmers and bakers in the United States are eager to deal with Henri. He's willing to buy a lot of bread and even to pay a premium price for it. Indeed, bread production has become so profitable in the United States that a lot of people who used to grow and mash grapes are now growing wheat and kneading dough. This alters the mix of U.S. output in the direction of more bread, exactly as suggested in Figure 19.2a.

In France the opposite kind of production shift is taking place. French wheat farmers are planting more grape vines so they can take advantage of Henri's generous purchases. Thus, Henri is able to lead each country in the direction of its comparative advantage while raking in a substantial profit for himself along the way.

Where the terms of trade and the volume of exports and imports end up depends partly on how good a trader Henri is. It will also depend on the behavior of the thousands of individual consumers and producers who participate in the market exchanges. In other words, trade flows depend on both the supply and the demand for bread and wine in each country. *The terms of trade, like the price of any good, depend on the willingness of market participants to buy or sell at various prices.* All we know for sure is that the terms of trade will end up somewhere between the limits set by each country's opportunity costs.

....

PROTECTIONIST PRESSURES

Although the potential gains from world trade are impressive, not everyone will be cheering at the Franco-American trade celebration. On the contrary, some people will be upset about the trade routes that Henri has established. They'll not only boycott the celebration but actively seek to discourage us from continuing to trade with France.

Trade "Losers"

Consider, for example, the winegrowers in western New York. Do you think they're going to be happy about Henri's entrepreneurship? Americans can now buy wine more cheaply from France than they can from New York. Before long we may hear talk about unfair foreign competition or about the greater nutritional value of American grapes (see World View "Imported Wine Squeezing U.S. Vintners"). The New York winegrowers may also emphasize the importance of maintaining an adequate grape supply and a strong wine industry at home, just in case of terrorist attacks.

WORLD VIEW

IMPORTED WINE SQUEEZING U.S. VINTNERS

American consumers are sipping increasing quantities of Italian and French wines. In 2018 U.S. wine consumption barely inched up to 348 million cases, an increase of less than 1 percent. Imports accounted for 23.7 percent of that total consumption, up 1.7 percent from 2017. That increasing import competition is keeping wine prices low and encouraging domestic vintners to convert their vineyards into almond or avocado farms.

Source: Industry reports, November 2019–February 2020.

CRITICAL ANALYSIS: Although **trade** increases consumption possibilities, imports typically compete with a domestic industry. The affected industries will try to restrict imports in order to preserve their own jobs and incomes.

Import-Competing Industries. Joining with the growers will be the farmworkers and the other merchants whose livelihood depends on the New York wine industry. If they're clever enough, the growers will also get the governor of the state to join their demonstration. After all, the governor must recognize the needs of his people, and his people definitely don't include the wheat farmers in Kansas who are making a bundle from international trade, much less French vintners. New York consumers are, of course, benefiting from lower wine prices, but they're unlikely to demonstrate over a few cents a bottle. On the other hand, those few extra pennies translate into millions of dollars for domestic wine producers.

The wheat farmers in France are no happier about international trade than are the winegrowers in the United States. They'd dearly love to sink all those boats bringing cheap wheat from America, thereby protecting their own market position.

If we're to make sense of trade policies, then we must recognize one central fact of life: Some producers have a vested interest in restricting international trade. In particular, *workers and producers who compete with imported products—who work in import-competing industries—have an economic interest in restricting trade.* This helps explain why GM, Ford, and Chrysler are unhappy about auto imports and why shoe workers in Massachusetts want to end the importation of Italian shoes. It also explains why textile producers in South Carolina think China is behaving irresponsibly when it sells cheap cotton shirts and dresses in the United States.

Export Industries. Although imports typically mean fewer jobs and less income for some domestic industries, exports represent increased jobs and income for other industries. Producers and workers in export industries gain from trade. Thus, on a microeconomic level there are identifiable gainers and losers from international trade. *Trade not only alters the mix of output but also redistributes income from import-competing industries to export industries.* This potential redistribution is the source of political and economic friction.

Net Gain. We must be careful to note, however, that the microeconomic gains from trade are greater than the microeconomic losses. It's not simply a question of robbing Peter to enrich Paul. We must remind ourselves that consumers enjoy a higher standard of living as a result of international trade. As we saw earlier, trade increases world efficiency and total output. Accordingly, we end up slicing up a larger pie rather than just reslicing the same old smaller pie.

The gains from trade will mean little to workers who end up with a smaller slice of the (larger) pie. It's important to remember, however, that the gains from trade are large enough to make everybody better off. Whether we actually choose to distribute the gains from trade in this way is a separate question, to which we shall return shortly. Note here, however, that *trade restrictions designed to protect specific microeconomic interests reduce the total gains from trade.* Trade restrictions leave us with a smaller pie to split up.

Additional Pressures

Import-competing industries are the principal obstacle to expanded international trade. Selfish micro interests aren't the only source of trade restrictions, however. Other arguments are also used to restrict trade.

National Security. The national security argument for trade restrictions is twofold. We can't depend on foreign suppliers to provide us with essential defense-related goods, it is said, because that would leave us vulnerable in time of war. The machine tool industry used this argument to protect itself from imports. In 1991 the Pentagon again sided with the tool-makers, citing the need for the United States to "gear up military production quickly in case of war," a contingency that couldn't be assured if weapons manufacturers relied on imported lathes, milling machines, and other tools. After the September 11, 2001, terrorist attacks on the World Trade Center and Pentagon, U.S. farmers convinced Congress to safeguard the nation's food supply with additional subsidies. The steel industry emphasized the importance of not depending on foreign suppliers.

The national security argument surfaced again in 2019. Huawei Technologies is the world's largest producer of telecommunications equipment and a leader in the development of base stations for 5G networks. But it is closely affiliated with the Chinese government. This raised concerns that Huawei's equipment could be used to facilitate cyber espionage or, worse, cripple a nation's telecommunications network in a time of crisis. Several nations, including the United States, have restricted the use (imports) of Huawei equipment.

Variants of the national security argument arose in 2020. The COVID-19 pandemic increased the need for medical supplies dramatically and abruptly. As it turned out, a high percentage of the needed face masks, gloves, swabs, and even medicines needed to fight the pandemic were manufactured in China, then imported into the United States. Trade hawks used that situation to demand that America limit future dependence on imported medical supplies by restricting imports and building up American production capacity. The Trump also used the national security argument to block access to the popular TikTok video-sharing app. President Trump said he was worried that the personal data of TikTok users would be accessible to the Chinese government, which was the majority owner of the app's corporate structure.

Dumping. Another argument against free trade arises from the practice of **dumping.** Foreign producers "dump" their goods when they sell them in the United States at prices lower than those prevailing in their own country, perhaps even below the costs of production.

Dumping may be unfair to import-competing producers, but it isn't necessarily unwelcome to the rest of us. As long as foreign producers continue dumping, we're getting foreign products at low prices. How bad can that be? There's a legitimate worry, however. Foreign producers might hold prices down only until domestic producers are driven out of business. Then we might be compelled to pay the foreign producers higher prices for their products. In that case, dumping could consolidate market power and lead to monopoly-type pricing. The fear of dumping, then, is analogous to the fear of predatory pricing.

dumping: The sale of goods in export markets at prices below domestic prices.

The potential costs of dumping are serious. It's not always easy to determine when dumping occurs, however. Those who compete with imports have an uncanny ability to associate any and all low prices with predatory dumping. The United States has used dumping *charges* to restrict imports of Chinese shrimp, furniture, lingerie, solar panels, and other products in which China has an evident comparative advantage. The Chinese have retaliated with dozens of their own dumping investigations, including the fiber optic cable case. In 2020 the U.S. Commerce Department launched an investigation of alleged dumping by South Korean cigarette manufacturers (see World View "U.S. Accuses South Korea of Dumping Cigarettes").

WORLD VIEW

U.S. ACCUSES SOUTH KOREA OF DUMPING CIGARETTES

The U.S. Commerce Department is investigating charges that the Korean Tobacco and Ginseng Corporation (KT&G) is illegally selling cigarettes in the United States at unfair prices. Sales of the company's THIS brand have skyrocketed from 1.36 million packs in December 2017 to over 220 million packs in December 2019. Domestic competitors claim KT&G is selling its Carnival, THIS, and other brands—a total of $80 million in 2019—at prices "below fair value." If the charge is corroborated, the U.S Trade Representative will propose countervailing duties.

Source: Media reports, January 2020.

CRITICAL ANALYSIS: Dumping means that a foreign producer is selling exports at prices below cost or below prices in the home market, putting import-competing industries at a competitive disadvantage. Accusations of dumping are an effective trade barrier.

Infant Industries. Actual dumping threatens to damage already established domestic industries. Even normal import prices, however, may make it difficult or impossible for a new domestic industry to develop. Infant industries are often burdened with abnormally high start-up costs. These high costs may arise from the need to train a whole workforce, build production infrastructure, and establish new marketing channels. With time to grow, however, an infant industry might experience substantial cost reductions and establish a comparative advantage. When this is the case, trade restrictions might help nurture an industry in its infancy. Trade restrictions are justified, however, only if there's tangible evidence that the industry can develop a comparative advantage reasonably quickly.

Improving the Terms of Trade. A final argument for restricting trade rests on how the gains from trade are distributed. As we observed, the distribution of the gains from trade depends on the terms of trade. If we were to buy fewer imports, foreign producers might lower their prices. If that happened, the terms of trade would move in our favor, and we'd end up with a larger share of the gains from trade.

One way to bring about this sequence of events is to put restrictions on imports, making it more difficult or expensive for Americans to buy foreign products. Such restrictions will reduce the volume of imports, thereby inducing foreign producers to lower their prices. Unfortunately, this strategy can easily backfire. Retaliatory restrictions on imports, each designed to improve the terms of trade, will ultimately eliminate all trade and therewith all the gains people were competing for in the first place.

BARRIERS TO TRADE

The microeconomic losses associated with imports give rise to a constant clamor for trade restrictions. People whose jobs and incomes are threatened by international trade tend to organize quickly and air their grievances. When France signed new trade deals with Canada,

Brazil, and Argentina in October 2019, French farmers drove their tractors into Paris, clogging major highways and dumping hay on critical thoroughfares (see World View "French Tractors Roll into Paris"). Within days, the French government agreed to respond to farmers' concerns about cheap imports. More often than not, governments grant the wishes of these well-organized and well-financed special interests.

WORLD VIEW

FRENCH TRACTORS ROLL INTO PARIS

French farmers drove 1,000 tractors into Paris to protest new trade deals that threaten their livelihood. Trade deals with Canada, Brazil, and Argentina threaten to bring in wheat imports that will crush French farmers. As Joffrey Beaudot, president of the Young Farmers of Saone-et-Loire lamented, "The cost of production for French farmers is higher than that of South American countries; we can't compete, so we will disappear." Farmers used their tractors to clog the highway ring around Paris and to disrupt major arteries in central Paris.

Julien Mattia/ Getty Images

Source: Media reports, November 27–29, 2019.

CRITICAL ANALYSIS: Import-competing industries cite lots of reasons for restricting trade. Their primary concern, however, is to protect their own jobs and profits.

Embargoes

The surefire way to restrict trade is simply to eliminate it. To do so, a country need only impose an embargo on exports or imports, or both. An **embargo** is nothing more than a prohibition against trading particular goods.

In 1951 Senator Joseph McCarthy convinced the U.S. Senate to impose an embargo on Soviet mink, fox, and five other furs. He argued that such imports helped finance world communism. Senator McCarthy also represented the state of Wisconsin, where most U.S. minks are raised. The Reagan administration tried to end the fur embargo in 1987 but met with stiff congressional opposition. By then U.S. mink ranchers had developed a $120 million per year industry.

The United States has also maintained an embargo on Cuban goods since 1959, when Fidel Castro took power there. This embargo severely damaged Cuba's sugar industry and deprived American smokers of the famed Havana cigars. It also fostered the development of U.S. sugar beet and tobacco farmers, who now have a vested interest in maintaining the embargo.

embargo: A prohibition on exports or imports.

tariff: A tax (duty) imposed on imported goods.

Tariffs

A more frequent trade restriction is a **tariff,** a special tax imposed on imported goods. Tariffs, also called *customs duties,* were once the principal source of revenue for governments. In the 18th century, tariffs on tea, glass, wine, lead, and paper were imposed on the American colonies to provide extra revenue for the British government. The tariff on tea led to the Boston Tea Party in 1773 and gave added momentum to the American independence movement.

In modern times, tariffs have been used primarily as a means to protect specific industries from import competition. The current U.S. tariff code specifies tariffs on more than 9,000 different products—nearly 50 percent of all U.S. imports. Although the average tariff is less than 5 percent, individual tariffs vary widely. The tariff on cars, for example, is only 2.5 percent, while cotton sweaters confront a 17.8 percent tariff.

The attraction of tariffs to import-competing industries should be obvious. *A tariff on imported goods makes them more expensive to domestic consumers and thus less competitive with domestically produced goods.* Among familiar tariffs in effect in 2020 were 50 cents per gallon on Scotch whisky and 76 cents per gallon on imported champagne. These tariffs made American-produced spirits look relatively cheap and thus contributed to higher sales and profits for domestic distillers and grape growers. In the same manner, imported baby food is taxed at 34.6 percent, maple sugar at 9.4 percent, golf shoes at 8.5 percent, and imported sailboats at 1.5 percent. In 2009 President Obama imposed a 35 percent tariff on imported Chinese tires and a 26 percent tariff on Chinese solar panels in 2014. In 2017, President Trump announced a 24 percent tariff on Canadian lumber. In each case, domestic producers in import-competing industries gain. The losers are domestic consumers, who end up paying higher prices. The tariff on orange juice, for example, raises the price of drinking orange juice by $525 million a year. The tariff on Canadian lumber raises the price of a new home by $3,000. Tariffs also hurt foreign producers, who lose business, and world efficiency, as trade is reduced.

"Beggar Thy Neighbor". Microeconomic interests aren't the only source of pressure for tariff protection. Imports represent leakage from the domestic circular flow and a potential loss of jobs at home. From this perspective, reducing imports looks like an easy solution to the problem of domestic unemployment. Just get people to "buy American" instead of buying imported products, so the argument goes, and domestic output and employment will surely expand. President Obama used this argument to include "buy American" rules in his 2009 stimulus package. President Trump was even more insistent about "bringing jobs home" by restricting imports and signing "buy American" orders.

Congressman Willis Hawley used this same argument in 1930. He assured his colleagues that higher tariffs would "bring about the growth and development in this country that has followed every other tariff bill, bringing as it does a new prosperity in which all people, in all sections, will increase their comforts, their enjoyment, and their happiness."[1] Congress responded by passing the Smoot-Hawley Tariff Act of 1930, which raised tariffs to an average of nearly 60 percent, effectively cutting off most imports.

Tariffs designed to expand domestic employment are more likely to fail than to succeed. If a tariff wall does stem the flow of imports, it effectively transfers the unemployment problem to other countries, a phenomenon often referred to as "beggar thy neighbor." The resultant loss of business in other countries leaves them less able to purchase our exports. The imported unemployment also creates intense political pressures for retaliatory action. That's exactly what happened in the 1930s. Other countries erected trade barriers to compensate for the effects of the Smoot-Hawley tariff. World trade subsequently fell from $60 billion in 1928 to a mere $25 billion in 1938. This trade contraction increased the severity of the Great Depression (see World View "'Beggar-Thy-Neighbor' Policies in the 1930s").

The same kind of macroeconomic threat surfaced in 2009. The "buy American" provisions introduced by the Obama administration angered foreign nations that would lose export sales. When they threatened to retaliate with trade barriers of their own, President Obama had to offer reassurances about America's commitment to "free trade." When

[1]*The New York Times,* June 15, 1930, p. 25.

WORLD VIEW

"BEGGAR-THY-NEIGHBOR" POLICIES IN THE 1930S

President Herbert Hoover signed the Smoot-Hawley Tariff Act on June 17, 1930, despite the pleas from 1,028 economists to veto it. The Act raised the effective tariff on imports by 50 percent between 1929 and 1932. Although designed to limit import competition and boost domestic employment, the Act triggered quick retaliation from America's trading partners:

- Spain passed the Wais tariff in July in reaction to U.S. tariffs on grapes, oranges, cork, and onions.
- Switzerland, objecting to new U.S. tariffs on watches, embroideries, and shoes, boycotted American exports.
- Italy retaliated against tariffs on hats and olive oil with high tariffs on U.S. and French automobiles in June 1930.
- Canada reacted to high duties on many food products, logs, and timber by raising tariffs threefold in August 1932.
- Australia, Cuba, France, Mexico, and New Zealand also joined in the tariff wars.

From 1930 to 1931 U.S. imports dropped 29 percent, but U.S. exports fell even more, 33 percent, and continued their collapse to a modern-day low of $2.4 billion in 1933. World trade contracted by similar proportions, spreading unemployment around the globe.

In 1934 the U.S. Congress passed the Reciprocal Trade Agreements Act to empower the president to reduce tariffs by half the 1930 rates in return for like cuts in foreign duties on U.S. goods. The "beggar-thy-neighbor" policy was dead. Since then, the nations of the world have been reducing tariffs and other trade barriers.

Source: "'Beggar-Thy-Neighbor' Policies in the 1930s," *World Development Report 1987,* p. 139, box 8.4.

CRITICAL ANALYSIS: Tariffs inflict harm on foreign producers. If foreign countries retaliate with tariffs of their own, world trade will shrink and unemployment will increase in all countries.

President Trump imposed tariffs on Chinese goods in 2018 in order to "bring jobs home," China retaliated in kind, igniting a trade war between the two nations.

Quotas

Tariffs reduce the flow of imports by raising import prices. The same outcome can be attained more directly by imposing import **quotas,** numerical restrictions on the quantity of a particular good that may be imported. The United States limits the quantity of ice cream imported from Jamaica to 950 gallons a year. Only 1.4 million kilograms of Australian cheddar cheese and no more than 7,730 tons of Haitian sugar can be imported. Additional quotas are imposed on brooms, tuna, tobacco, and cotton. Textile quotas are imposed on every country that wants to ship textiles to the U.S. market. According to the U.S. Department of State, approximately 12 percent of our imports are subject to import quotas.

quota: A limit on the quantity of a good that may be imported in a given time period.

Comparative Effects

Quotas, like all barriers to trade, reduce world efficiency and invite retaliatory action. Moreover, their impact can be even more damaging than tariffs. To see this, we may compare market outcomes in four different contexts: no trade, free trade, tariff-restricted trade, and quota-restricted trade.

No-Trade Equilibrium. Figure 19.4*a* depicts the supply-and-demand relationships that would prevail in an economy that imposed a trade *embargo* on foreign textiles. In this situation, the **equilibrium price** of textiles is completely determined by domestic demand and supply curves. The no-trade equilibrium price is p_1, and the quantity of textiles consumed is q_1.

FIGURE 19.4

The Impact of Trade Restrictions

In the *absence of trade,* the domestic price and sales of a good will be determined by domestic supply and demand curves (point *A* in part *a*). Once trade is permitted, the market supply curve will be altered by the availability of imports. With *free trade* and unlimited availability of imports at price p_2, a new market equilibrium will be established at world prices (point *B*).

   Tariffs raise domestic prices and reduce the quantity sold (point *C*). *Quotas* put an absolute limit on imported sales and thus give domestic producers a great opportunity to raise the market price (point *D*).

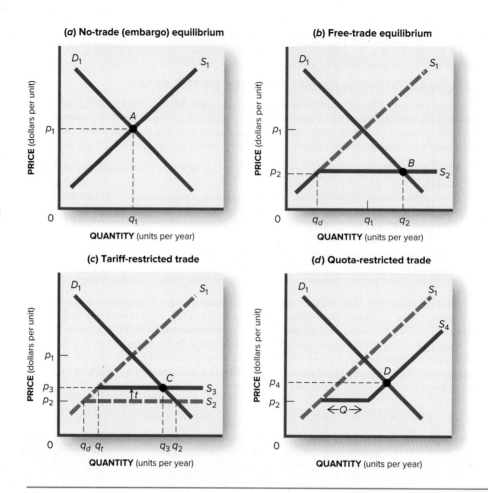

(a) No-trade (embargo) equilibrium

(b) Free-trade equilibrium

(c) Tariff-restricted trade

(d) Quota-restricted trade

Free-Trade Equilibrium. Suppose now that the embargo is lifted. The immediate effect of this decision will be a rightward shift of the market supply curve, as foreign supplies are added to domestic supplies (Figure 19.4*b*). If an unlimited quantity of textiles can be bought in world markets at a price of p_2, the new supply curve will look like S_2 (infinitely elastic at p_2). The new supply curve (S_2) intersects the old demand curve (D_1) at a new equilibrium price of p_2 and an expanded consumption of q_2. At this new equilibrium, domestic producers are supplying the quantity q_d while foreign producers are supplying the rest ($q_2 - q_d$). Comparing the new equilibrium to the old one, we see that *free trade results in reduced prices and increased consumption.*

   Domestic textile producers are unhappy, of course, with their foreign competition. In the absence of trade, the domestic producers would sell more output (q_1) and get higher prices (p_1). Once trade is opened up, the willingness of foreign producers to sell unlimited quantities of textiles at the price p_2 puts a lid on domestic prices. Domestic producers hate this.

Tariff-Restricted Trade. Figure 19.4*c* illustrates what would happen to prices and sales if the United Textile Producers were successful in persuading the government to impose a tariff. Assume that the tariff raises imported textile prices from p_2 to p_3, making it more difficult for foreign producers to undersell domestic producers. Domestic production expands from q_d to q_t, imports are reduced from $q_2 - q_d$ to $q_3 - q_t$, and the market price of textiles rises. Domestic textile producers are clearly better off. So is the U.S. Treasury, which will collect increased tariff revenues. Unfortunately, domestic consumers are worse off (higher prices), as are foreign producers (reduced sales).

Quota-Restricted Trade. Now consider the impact of a textile *quota.* Suppose we eliminate tariffs but decree that imports can't exceed the quantity *Q*. Because the quantity of imports can never exceed *Q*, the supply curve is effectively shifted to the right by that amount. The new curve S_4 (Figure 19.4d) indicates that no imports will occur below the world price p_2 and above that price the quantity Q will be imported. Thus, the *domestic* demand curve determines subsequent prices. Foreign producers are precluded from selling greater quantities as prices rise further. This outcome is in marked contrast to that of tariff-restricted trade (Figure 19.4c), which at least permits foreign producers to respond to rising prices. Accordingly, ***quotas are a greater threat to competition than tariffs because quotas preclude additional imports at any price.*** The actual quotas on textile imports raise the prices of shirts, towels, and other textile products by 58 percent. As a result, a $10 shirt ends up costing consumers $15.80. All told, U.S. consumers end up paying an extra $25 billion a year for textile products.

The sugar industry is one of the greatest beneficiaries of quota restrictions. By limiting imports to 15 percent of domestic consumption, sugar quotas keep U.S. prices artificially high (see Front Page Economics "Sugar Quotas a Sour Deal for U.S. Consumers"). This costs consumers nearly $3 billion a year in higher prices. Candy and soda producers lose sales and profits. According to the U.S. Department of Commerce, more than 6,000 jobs have been lost in sugar-using industries (e.g., candy manufacturing) due to high sugar costs. Hershey alone closed plants in Pennsylvania, Colorado, and California and moved candy production to Canada. Foreign sugar producers (mainly in poor nations) also lose sales, profits, and jobs. Who gains? Domestic sugar producers—who, coincidentally, are highly concentrated in key electoral states like Florida.

FRONT PAGE ECONOMICS

SUGAR QUOTAS A SOUR DEAL FOR U.S. CONSUMERS

U.S. sugar farmers have enjoyed protection from imports since 1789 when Congress enacted the first tariff on imported sugar. The Sugar Act of 1934 gave U.S. farmers an even better deal by creating a quota on the amount of sugar that can be imported into the United States. The Farm Bill of 2018 continued that protection, limiting sugar imports to 1.2 million tons per year—just a fraction of the 11 million tons Americans consume. As a result of that quota, U.S. sugar prices in early 2020 were about 10 cents a pound higher than world prices.

That's great news for America's 4,700 sugar farmers but a sour deal for U.S. consumers and manufacturers, who pay more for all sugar products. U.S. candy producers have cut thousands of jobs and moved manufacturing plants to Canada and elsewhere, where sugar is cheaper. Analysts estimate that 3 manufacturing jobs have been lost for every 1 sugar job saved and consumers are paying more than $2 billion a year in higher sugar prices.

Source: Industry and media reports, January 2020.

CRITICAL ANALYSIS: Import quotas preclude increased foreign competition when domestic prices rise. Protected domestic producers enjoy higher prices and profits while consumers pay higher prices.

Voluntary Restraint Agreements

A slight variant of quotas has been used in recent years. Rather than impose quotas on imports, the U.S. government asks foreign producers to "voluntarily" limit their exports. These so-called **voluntary restraint agreements** have been negotiated with producers in Japan, South Korea, Taiwan, China, the European Union, and other countries. Korea, for example, agreed to reduce its annual shoe exports to the United States from 44 million pairs to 33 million pairs. Taiwan reduced its shoe exports from 156 million pairs to 122 million pairs per year. In 2005 China agreed to slow its exports of clothing, limiting its sales growth to 8–17 percent a year. For their part, the Japanese agreed to reduce sales of color TV sets in the United States from 2.8 million to 1.75 million per year. In 2006 Mexico agreed to limit its cement exports to the United States to 3 million tons a year. In 2014 Mexico also agreed to curtail its sugar exports to the United States, forsaking its unique treaty rights to unrestricted exports.

voluntary restraint agreement (VRA): An agreement to reduce the volume of trade in a specific good; a "voluntary" quota.

All these voluntary export restraints, as they're often called, represent an informal type of quota. The only difference is that they're negotiated rather than imposed. But these differences are lost on consumers, who end up paying higher prices for these goods. The voluntary limit on Japanese auto exports to the United States alone cost consumers $15.7 billion in only four years.

Nontariff Barriers

Tariffs and quotas are the most visible barriers to trade, but they're only the tip of the iceberg. Indeed, the variety of protectionist measures that have been devised is testimony to the ingenuity of the human mind. At the turn of the century, the Germans were committed to a most-favored-nation policy: a policy of extending equal treatment to all trading partners. The Germans, however, wanted to lower the tariff on cattle imports from Denmark without extending the same break to Switzerland. Such a preferential tariff would have violated the most-favored-nation policy. Accordingly, the Germans created a new and higher tariff on "brown and dappled cows reared at a level of at least 300 meters above sea level and passing at least one month in every summer at an altitude of at least 800 meters." The new tariff was, of course, applied equally to all countries. But Danish cows never climb that high, so they weren't burdened with the new tariff.

With the decline in tariffs over the last 20 years, nontariff barriers have increased. The United States uses product standards, licensing restrictions, restrictive procurement practices, and other nontariff barriers to restrict roughly 15 percent of imports. In 1999–2000 the European Union banned imports of U.S. beef, arguing that the use of hormones on U.S. ranches created a health hazard for European consumers. Although both the U.S. government and the World Trade Organization disputed that claim, the ban was a highly effective nontariff trade barrier. The United States responded by slapping 100 percent tariffs on dozens of European products.

Mexican Trucks. One of the more flagrant examples of nontariff barriers is the use of safety regulations to block Mexican trucking companies from using U.S. roads to deliver goods. The resulting trade barrier forced Mexican trucks to unload their cargoes at the U.S. border, and then reload them into U.S. (Teamster-driven) trucks for shipment to U.S. destinations. The U.S. agreed to lift that restriction in 1995, but didn't. In 2009 President Obama actually solidified the Mexican roadblock, despite the fact that Mexican trucks passed all 22 safety (nontariff) regulations the U.S. Department of Transportation had imposed. In so doing, President Obama secured more jobs for Teamster-union drivers but raised costs for U.S. shippers and consumers and drove down sales and employment for Mexican trucking companies. Fed up with U.S. protectionism, Mexico retaliated by slapping tariffs on 90 U.S. export products. By early 2011, U.S. exports to Mexico of those products had declined by 81 percent. This prompted President Obama to offer Mexico a new round of negotiations, which ended in January 2015 with the U.S. declaring Mexican trucks to be safe enough to travel U.S. roads and Mexico repealing the tariffs on U.S. exports. The 2019 U.S-Mexico-Canada Agreement (USMCA) ratified that understanding, prompting a significant increase in cross-border trade.

MULTILATERAL TRADE DEALS

Proponents of free trade and import-competing industries are in constant conflict. Most of the time the trade policy deck seems stacked in favor of the special interests. Because import-competing firms and workers are highly concentrated, they're quick to mobilize politically. By contrast, the benefits of freer trade are less direct and spread over millions of consumers. As a consequence, the beneficiaries of freer trade are less likely to monitor trade policy—much less lobby actively to change it. Hence, the political odds favor the spread of trade barriers.

Multilateral Trade Pacts

Despite these odds, the long-term trend is toward *lowering* trade barriers, thereby increasing global competition. Two forces encourage this trend. ***The principal barrier to protectionist*** *policies is worldwide recognition of the gains from freer trade.* Because world nations now understand that trade barriers are ultimately self-defeating, they're more willing to rise above the din of protectionist cries and dismantle trade barriers. They diffuse political opposition by creating across-the-board trade pacts that seem to spread the pain (and gain) from freer trade across a broad swath of industries. Such pacts also incorporate multiyear timetables that give affected industries time to adjust.

Trade liberalization has also been encouraged by firms that *export* products or use imported inputs in their own production. Candy manufacturers don't want to pay more for sugar, auto companies don't want to pay more for steel, and shippers don't want to pay more for transportation. They, too, can organize and petition governments for relief from trade barriers.

Global Pacts: GATT and WTO

The granddaddy of the multilateral, multiyear free-trade pacts was the 1947 *General Agreement on Tariffs and Trade (GATT)*. Twenty-three nations pledged to reduce trade barriers and give all GATT nations equal access to their domestic markets.

Since the first GATT pact, seven more "rounds" of negotiations have expanded the scope of GATT; 117 nations signed the 1994 pact. As a result of these GATT pacts, average tariff rates in developed countries have fallen from 40 percent in 1948 to less than 4 percent today.

WTO

The 1994 GATT pact also created the *World Trade Organization (WTO)* to enforce free-trade rules. If a nation feels its exports are being unfairly excluded from another country's market, it can file a complaint with the WTO. This is exactly what the United States did when the EU banned U.S. beef imports. The WTO ruled in favor of the United States. When the EU failed to lift its import ban, the WTO authorized the United States to impose retaliatory tariffs on European exports.

The EU turned the tables on the United States in 2003. It complained to the WTO that U.S. tariffs on imported steel violated trade rules. The WTO agreed and gave the EU permission to impose retaliatory tariffs on $2.2 billion of U.S. exports. That prompted the Bush administration to scale back the tariffs in December 2003. The U.S. was chastised again in September 2020 for unfairly imposing tariffs on Chinese goods in 2018.

In effect, the WTO is now the world's trade police force. It is empowered to cite nations that violate trade agreements and even to impose remedial action when violations persist. Why do sovereign nations give the WTO such power? Because they are all convinced that free trade is the surest route to GDP growth.

Regional Pacts

Because worldwide trade pacts are so complex, many nations have also pursued *regional* free-trade agreements.

NAFTA. In December 1992 the United States, Canada, and Mexico signed the *North American Free Trade Agreement (NAFTA)*, a 1,000-page document covering more than 9,000 products. The ultimate goal of NAFTA was to eliminate all trade barriers between these three countries. At the time of signing, intraregional tariffs averaged 11 percent in Mexico, 5 percent in Canada, and 4 percent in the United States.

The NAFTA-initiated reduction in trade barriers substantially increased trade flows between Mexico, Canada, and the United States. It also prompted a wave of foreign investment in Mexico, where both cheap labor and NAFTA access were available. Overall, NAFTA accelerated economic growth and reduced inflationary pressures in all three nations. Some industries (like construction and apparel) suffered from the freer trade, but others (like trucking, farming, and finance) reaped huge gains.

USMCA. NAFTA was revised and updated with a new trade agreement called the U.S.-Mexico-Canada Agreement (USMCA), signed by President Trump in January 2020. The USMCA continued the free-trade commitments of NAFTA, while adding more labor and environmental standards. It also gives U.S. dairy farmers more access to Canada's market and increases country-of-origin requirements for autos. The International Trade Commission estimated that the new regional pact will add 0.35 percent to U.S. GDP growth over its first six years.

TPP. The Trans-Pacific Partnership was intended to be another regional trade pact, linking 12 nations that border the Pacific Ocean in a multiyear commitment to freer trade. After eight years of negotiations, those 12 nations signed a tentative TPP agreement in February 2016. That 2,000-page agreement not only called for reductions in tariffs and nontariff trade barriers among the member nations, but also sought greater coordination of policies on environmental protection, workers' rights, and regulatory practices. To become effective, the legislatures of the 12 nations had to ratify the agreement by February 2018. President Trump called TPP a particularly "bad deal" and vowed to kill it. He kept that vow by officially withdrawing the United States from the TPP on his very first day of office. Henceforth, he said, he only wanted bilateral deals that "put America first." Critics warned that he was ignoring the benefits of freer trade and risking the perception that America was an unreliable trading partner.

DECISIONS FOR TOMORROW

WHO WINS TRADE WARS?

President Trump's "America first" approach to trade policy put him at odds with the global trend toward lower trade barriers. Indeed, he proclaimed himself to be "a tariff man" who had long advocated using tariffs to offset the "unfair trade practices" of other nations. He singled out China as one of the worst trading partners, claiming that it unfairly promoted huge bilateral trade deficits, engaged in theft of intellectual property, and forced U.S. companies doing business in China to transfer technology secrets.

Retaliatory Tariff Rounds. On March 22, 2018, President Trump announced that he was imposing tariffs on as many as 1,300 Chinese products as "a response to the unfair trade practices of China over the years." Those tariffs, he argued, would force China to reform its trade practices, "leveling the field" for American companies to compete. Advised that China might retaliate with tariffs on American goods, President Trump shrugged that "trade wars are good and easy to win."

China did retaliate. After the U.S. tacked on tariffs to $34 billion of Chinese exports, China did the same to $34 billion of U.S. exports. Three additional rounds of tariffs initiated by Trump made over $250 billion of Chinese products subject to tariffs as high as 25 percent in early 2019. In June 2019 China responded again with 25 percent tariffs on another $60 billion of U.S. exports.

Economic Effects. The tariff escalations sharply reduced trade flows between the United States and China. U.S. agricultural exports to China were particularly hard hit as China sharply cut purchases of American soybeans, pork, and wheat. The uncertainties created by the trade war also caused businesses to defer investment. The Congressional Budget Office estimated that the trade war reduced GDP growth in 2019 by 0.3 percent, trimmed investment spending by 1.3 percent, and reduced the income of the average U.S. household by $580. The International Monetary Fund noted that the effects of the U.S.-China trade war spilled over to other nations, causing a global GDP slowdown from 3.6 percent to 3.3 percent.

A Cease Fire. Recognizing the increasing damage inflicted on both countries, the U.S. and China called for a truce in December 2019. In "Phase One" of that truce, signed on January 15, 2020, the two nations agreed to roll back some of their tariffs, resume some bilateral purchases, and rethink disputed trade practices. As a November 2019 United Nations report noted, there was no winner in the U.S.-China trade war.

SUMMARY

- International trade permits each country to specialize in areas of relative efficiency, increasing world output. For each country, the gains from trade are reflected in consumption possibilities that exceed production possibilities. **LO19-2**
- One way to determine where comparative advantage lies is to compare the quantity of good A that must be given up in order to get a given quantity of good B from domestic production. If the same quantity of B can be obtained for less A by engaging in world trade, we have a comparative advantage in the production of good A. Comparative advantage rests on a comparison of relative opportunity costs. **LO19-1**
- The terms of trade—the rate at which goods are exchanged—are subject to the forces of international supply and demand. The terms of trade will lie somewhere between the opportunity costs of the trading partners. The terms of trade determine how the gains from trade are shared. **LO19-2**

- Resistance to trade emanates from workers and firms that must compete with imports. Even though the country as a whole stands to benefit from trade, these individuals and companies may lose jobs and incomes in the process. **LO19-3**
- Trade barriers take many forms. Embargoes are outright prohibitions against import or export of particular goods. Quotas limit the quantity of a good imported or exported. Tariffs discourage imports by making them more expensive. Other nontariff barriers make trade too costly or time-consuming. **LO19-3**
- The World Trade Organization (WTO) seeks to reduce worldwide trade barriers and enforce trade rules. Regional accords such as the USMCA pursue similar objectives among fewer countries. **LO19-3**
- Trade wars inflict economic losses on the feuding nations and the broader global economy. Such losses create an incentive to resolve disputed issues. **LO19-3**

Key Terms

imports
exports
trade deficit
trade surplus
production possibilities
closed economy

consumption possibilities
open economy
comparative advantage
opportunity cost
absolute advantage
terms of trade

dumping
embargo
tariff
quota
equilibrium price
voluntary restraint agreement (VRA)

Questions for Discussion

1. Suppose a lawyer can type faster than any secretary. Should the lawyer do her own typing? Can you demonstrate the validity of your answer? **LO19-1**
2. What would be the effects of a law requiring bilateral trade balances? **LO19-2**
3. If a nation exported much of its output but imported little, would it be better or worse off? How about the reverse—that is, exporting little but importing a lot? **LO19-2**
4. How does international trade restrain the price behavior of domestic firms? **LO19-3**
5. Suppose we refused to sell goods to any country that reduced or halted its exports to us. Who would benefit and who would lose from such retaliation? **LO19-2**
6. Domestic producers often base their demands for import protection on the fact that workers in country X are paid substandard wages. Is this a valid argument for protection? **LO19-1**
7. Who will benefit or gain if the U.S. slaps tariffs on South Korean cigarettes (see World View "U.S. Accuses South Korea of Dumping Cigarettes")? **LO19-3**
8. According to the National Association of Home Builders, the 2017 tariff on Canadian lumber resulted in the loss of 8,000 U.S. construction jobs. How does this happen? **LO19-3**
9. Would France be better or worse off importing cheap Argentinian wheat? (see World View "French Tractors Roll into Paris")? **LO19-2**
10. If trade wars inflict economic damage on both nations, why do they occur? **LO19-3**

PROBLEMS FOR CHAPTER 19

LO19-2 1. Which countries are
   (*a*) The two largest export markets for the United States? (See Table 19.3.)
   (*b*) The two biggest sources of imports?

LO19-1 2. Suppose a country can produce a maximum of 12,000 jumbo airliners or 2,000 aircraft carriers.
   (*a*) What is the opportunity cost of an aircraft carrier?
   (*b*) If another country offers to trade eight planes for one aircraft carrier, should the offer be accepted?
   (*c*) What is the implied "price" of the carrier in trade?

LO19-1 3. If it takes 10 farmworkers to harvest 1 ton of strawberries and 3 farmworkers to harvest 1 ton of wheat, what is the opportunity cost of 6 tons of strawberries?

LO19-2 4. Alpha and Beta, two tiny islands in the Pacific, produce pearls and pineapples. The following production possibilities schedules describe their potential output in tons per year:

Alpha		Beta	
Pearls	**Pineapples**	**Pearls**	**Pineapples**
0	30	0	20
2	25	10	16
4	20	20	12
6	15	30	8
8	10	40	4
10	5	45	2
12	0	50	0

   (*a*) Graph the production possibilities confronting each island.
   (*b*) What is the opportunity cost of pineapples on each island (before trade)?
   (*c*) Which island has a comparative advantage in pineapple production?
   (*d*) Which island has a comparative advantage in pearl production?
   Now suppose Alpha and Beta specialize according to their comparative advantages and trade.
   If one pearl is traded for 1.5 pineapples,
   (*e*) How many pearls would have to be exported to get 15 pineapples in return?
   After this trade,
   (*f*) What is Alpha's consumption?
   (*g*) What is Beta's consumption?

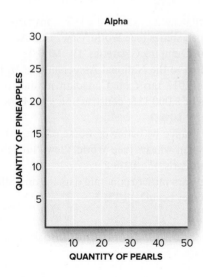

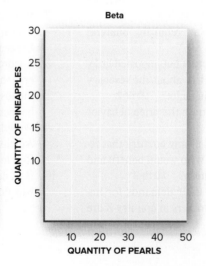

438

PROBLEMS FOR CHAPTER 19 (cont'd)

LO19-3 5. (*a*) How much more are U.S. consumers paying for the 11 million tons of sugar they consume each year as a result of the quotas on sugar imports? (See Front Page Economics "Sugar Quotas a Sour Deal.")
   (*b*) How much is this per person (population = 330 million)?
   (*c*) How much would each person save if the quota was lifted?

LO19-2 6. Suppose the two islands in Problem 4 agree that the terms of trade will be one for one and exchange 10 pearls for 10 pineapples.
   (*a*) If Alpha produced 6 pearls and 15 pineapples while Beta produced 30 pearls and 8 pineapples before they decided to trade, how many pearls would each be producing after trade? Assume that the two countries specialize according to their comparative advantage.
   (*b*) How much would the combined production of pineapples increase for the two islands due to specialization?
   (*c*) How much would the combined production of pearls increase?
   (*d*) What is the post trade consumption for each island?

LO19-3 7. If there are 12 bottles in a case of wine,
   (*a*) How many bottles of wine did Americans consume in 2018?
   (*b*) How many of those were imported? (See World View "Imported Wine Squeezing U.S. Vintners.")

LO19-3 8. Suppose the following table reflects the domestic supply and demand for Bluetooth headphones:

Price ($)	60	55	50	45	40	35	30	25
Quantity supplied (in millions per year)	8	7	6	5	4	3	2	1
Quantity demanded (in millions per year)	2	4	6	8	10	12	14	16

   (*a*) Graph these market conditions and identify
      (*i*) The equilibrium price.
      (*ii*) The equilibrium quantity.
   (*b*) Now suppose that foreigners enter the market, offering to sell an unlimited supply of Bluetooth headphones for $35 apiece. Illustrate and identify
      (*i*) The new market price.
      (*ii*) Domestic consumption.
      (*iii*) Domestic production.
   (*c*) If a tariff of $5 per unit is imposed, what will be
      (*i*) The market price?
      (*ii*) Domestic consumption?
      (*iii*) Domestic production?
   Graph your answers.

LO19-3 9. (*a*) Which regional trade pact was in force in 2015 among Canada, the United States, and Mexico?
   (*b*) Which industries have gained from this trade pact?
   (*c*) Which industries have lost from this trade pact?

LO19-3 10. *Decisions for Tomorrow:*
   (*a*) Graphically show the impact of the retaliatory tariff in the Chinese market for soybeans.
   (*b*) What happened to the market price in China for these imported soybeans from the U.S.?

Design Credit: Shutterstock

Don Tonge/Alamy Stock Photo

CHAPTER 20

International Finance

Textile, furniture, and shrimp producers in the United States want China to increase the value of the yuan. They say China's undervalued currency makes Chinese exports too cheap, undercutting American firms. President Trump agreed, calling China a "currency manipulator" that kept its currency cheap to undercut American producers. He demanded that China increase the value of its currency so as to "bring jobs back from China."

Walmart disagrees. Walmart thinks a cheap yuan is a good thing because it keeps prices low for the *$100 billion* of toys, tools, linens, and other goods it buys from China each year. Those low import prices help Walmart keep its own prices low and its sales volume high. Walmart is also the largest employer in the United States, providing more than 1.5 million jobs.

This chapter examines how currency values affect trade patterns and ultimately the core questions of WHAT, HOW, and FOR WHOM to produce. We focus on the following questions:

- **What determines the value of one country's money compared to the value of another's?**
- **What causes the international value of currencies to change?**
- **How and why do governments intervene to alter currency values?**

EXCHANGE RATES: THE GLOBAL LINK

As we saw in Chapter 19, the United States exports and imports a staggering volume of goods and services. Although we trade with nearly 200 nations around the world, we seldom give much thought to where imports come from and how we acquire them. Most of the time, all we want to know is which products are available and at what price.

Suppose that you want to buy Apple AirPods. You don't have to know that AirPods are manufactured in China. And you certainly don't have to fly to China to pick them up. All you have to do is drive to the nearest electronics store; or you can just "click and buy" at the Internet's virtual mall.

But you may wonder how the purchase of an imported product was so simple. Chinese companies sell their products in yuan, the currency of China. But you purchase the AirPods in dollars. How is this possible?

There's a chain of distribution between your dollar purchase in the United States and the yuan-denominated sale in China. Somewhere along that chain someone has to convert your dollars into yuan. The critical question for everybody concerned is how many yuan we can get for our dollars—that is, what the **exchange rate** is. If we can get eight yuan for every dollar, the exchange rate is 8 yuan = 1 dollar. Alternatively, we could note that the price of a yuan is 12.5 U.S. cents when the exchange rate is 8 to 1. Thus, *an exchange rate is the price of one currency in terms of another.*

How do AirPods (made in China) end up selling for U.S. dollars?

Photographer and videographer/ iStock/Getty Images

FOREIGN EXCHANGE MARKETS

Most exchange rates are determined in foreign exchange markets. Stop thinking of money as some sort of magical substance, and instead view it as a useful commodity that facilitates market exchanges. From that perspective, an exchange rate—the price of money—is subject to the same influences that determine all market prices: demand and supply.

exchange rate: The price of one country's currency expressed in terms of another's; the domestic price of a foreign currency.

The Demand for Dollars

When the Chinese company Shuanghui International bought Smithfield Foods in 2013, it paid $4.7 billion. When Belgian beer maker InBev bought Anheuser-Busch (Budweiser, etc.) in 2008, it also needed dollars—more than 50 billion of them. When Fiat acquired control of Chrysler in 2011, it also needed U.S. dollars. In all three cases, the objective of the foreign investor was to acquire an American business. To attain their objectives, however, the buyers first had to buy *dollars.* The Chinese, Belgian, and Italian buyers had to exchange their own currency for American dollars.

Which currency is most valuable? It depends on exchange rates.

Maria Toutoudaki/Getty Images

Canadian tourists also need American dollars. Few American restaurants or hotels accept Canadian currency as payment for goods and services; they want to be paid in U.S. dollars. Accordingly, Canadian tourists must buy American dollars if they want to warm up in Florida.

Some foreign investors also buy U.S. dollars for speculative purposes. When Argentina's peso started losing value in 2012–2013, many Argentinians feared that its value would drop further and preferred to hold U.S. dollars; they *demanded* U.S. dollars. Ukrainians clamored for U.S. dollars when Russia invaded its territory in 2014. In 2017 Venezuelans were desperately trying to sell their worthless bolivars for pennies.

All these motivations give rise to a demand for U.S. dollars. Specifically, *the market demand for U.S. dollars originates in*

- *Foreign demand for American exports* (including tourism).
- *Foreign demand for American investments.*
- *Speculation.*

Governments also create a demand for dollars when they operate embassies, undertake cultural exchanges, or engage in intergovernment financial transactions.

The Supply of Dollars

The *supply* of dollars arises from similar sources. On the supply side, however, it's Americans who initiate most of the exchanges. Suppose you take a trip to Mexico. You'll need to buy Mexican pesos at some point. When you do, you'll be offering to *buy* pesos by offering to *sell* dollars. In other words, *the* **demand** *for foreign currency represents a* **supply** *of U.S. dollars.*

When Americans buy BMW cars, they also supply U.S. dollars. American consumers pay for their BMWs in dollars. Somewhere down the road, however, those dollars will be exchanged for European euros. At that exchange, dollars are being *supplied* and euros *demanded.*

American corporations demand foreign exchange too. General Motors builds cars in Germany, Coca-Cola produces Coke in China, and Exxon produces and refines oil all over the world. In nearly every such case, the U.S. firm must first build or buy some plants and equipment, using another country's factors of production. This activity requires foreign currency and thus becomes another component of our demand for foreign currency. When Elon Musk wanted to build a gigafactory in Shanghai in 2019, he needed $2 billion worth of Chinese yuan to pay construction companies, workers, and suppliers. Now that the factory is open, he needs a constant stream of yuan to pay local Tesla workers and suppliers.

We may summarize these market activities by noting that *the supply of dollars originates in*

- *American demand for imports* (including tourism).
- *American investments in foreign countries.*
- *Speculation.*

As on the demand side, government intervention can also contribute to the supply of dollars.

The Value of the Dollar

Whether American consumers will choose to buy an imported BMW depends partly on what the car costs. The price tag isn't always apparent in international transactions. Remember that the German BMW producer and workers want to be paid in their own currency, the euro. Hence, the *dollar* price of an imported BMW depends on two factors: (1) the German price of a BMW and (2) the *exchange rate* between U.S. dollars and euros. Specifically, the U.S. price of a BMW is

$$\frac{\text{Dollar price}}{\text{of BMW}} = \frac{\text{Euro price}}{\text{of BMW}} \times \frac{\text{Dollar price}}{\text{of euro}}$$

Suppose the BMW company is prepared to sell a German-built BMW for 100,000 euros and that the current exchange rate is 2 euros = \$1. At these rates, a BMW will cost you

$$\frac{\text{Dollar price}}{\text{of BMW}} = 100{,}000 \text{ euros} \times \frac{\$1}{2 \text{ euros}}$$
$$= \$50{,}000$$

If you're willing to pay this much for a shiny new German-built BMW, you may do so at current exchange rates.

Now suppose the exchange rate changes from 2 euros = \$1 to 1 euro = \$1. Now you're getting only 1 euro for your dollar rather than 2 euros. In other words, euros have become more expensive. *A higher dollar price for euros will raise the dollar costs of European goods.* In this case, the dollar price of a euro increases from \$0.50 to \$1. At this new exchange rate, the BMW plant in Germany is still willing to sell BMWs at 100,000 euros apiece. And German consumers continue to buy BMWs at that price. But this constant euro price now translates into a higher *dollar* price. That same BMW that you previously could buy for \$50,000 now costs you \$100,000—not because the cost of manufacturing the car in Germany went up, but simply because the exchange rate changed.

As the dollar price of a BMW rises, the number of BMWs sold in the United States will decline. As BMW sales decline, the quantity of euros demanded may decline as well. Thus, the quantity of foreign currency demanded declines when the exchange rate rises because foreign goods become more expensive and imports decline. When the dollar price of European currencies actually increased in 1992, BMW decided to start producing cars in South Carolina. A year later, Mercedes-Benz decided to produce cars in the United States as well. Sales of American-made BMWs and Mercedes no longer depend on the exchange rate of the U.S. dollar. But the dollar price of German-made Audis, French wine, and Italian shoes does.

The Supply Curve. These market responses suggest that the supply of dollars is upward-sloping. If the value of the dollar rises, Americans will be able to buy more euros. As a result, the dollar price of imported BMWs will decline. American consumers will respond by demanding more imports, thereby supplying a larger quantity of dollars. The supply curve in Figure 20.1 shows how the quantity of dollars supplied rises as the value of the dollar increases.

The Demand Curve. The demand for dollars can be explained in similar terms. Remember that the demand for dollars arises from the foreign demand for U.S. exports and investments. If the exchange rate moves from 2 euros = \$1 to 1 euro = \$1, the euro price of dollars falls. As

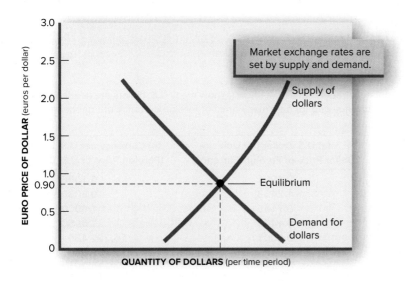

dollars become cheaper for Germans, all American exports effectively fall in price. Germans will buy more American products (including trips to Disney World) and therefore demand a greater quantity of dollars. In addition, foreign investors will perceive in a cheaper dollar the opportunity to buy U.S. stocks, businesses, and property at fire-sale prices. Accordingly, they join foreign consumers in demanding more dollars. Not all these behavioral responses will occur overnight, but they're reasonably predictable over a brief period of time.

Equilibrium

Given market demand and supply curves, we can predict the **equilibrium price** of any commodity—that is, the price at which the quantity demanded will equal the quantity supplied. This occurs in Figure 20.1 where the two curves cross. At that equilibrium, the value of the dollar (the exchange rate) is established. In this case, the euro price of the dollar turns out to be 0.90.

The value of the dollar can also be expressed in terms of other currencies. World View "Foreign Exchange Rates" displays a sampling of dollar exchange rates in March 2020. Notice how many Indonesian rupiah you could buy for $1: A dollar was worth 16,222 rupiah. By contrast, a U.S. dollar was worth only 0.90 euro. **The *average* value of the dollar is a weighted mean of the exchange rates between the U.S. dollar and all these currencies.** The value of the dollar is "high" when its foreign exchange price is above recent levels, and it is "low" when it is below recent averages.

equilibrium price: The price at which the quantity of a good demanded in a given time period equals the quantity supplied.

The Balance of Payments

The equilibrium depicted in Figure 20.1 determines not only the *price* of the dollar, but also a specific *quantity* of international transactions. Those transactions include the exports, imports, international investments, and other sources of dollar supply and demand. A summary of all those international money flows is contained in the **balance of payments**—an accounting statement of all international money flows in a given period of time.

balance of payments: A summary record of a country's international economic transactions in a given period of time.

Trade Balance. Table 20.1 depicts the U.S. balance of payments for 2019. Notice first how the millions of separate transactions are classified into a few summary measures. The trade balance is the difference between exports and imports of goods (merchandise) and services. In 2019 the United States imported more than $3.1 trillion of goods and services but exported only $2.5 trillion. This created a **trade deficit** of $616 billion. That trade deficit represents a net outflow of dollars to the rest of the world.

trade deficit: The amount by which the value of imports exceeds the value of exports in a given time period (negative net exports).

$$\text{Trade balance} = \text{Exports} - \text{Imports}$$

WORLD VIEW

FOREIGN EXCHANGE RATES

The foreign exchange midrange rates here show (a) how many U.S. dollars are needed to buy one unit of foreign currency and (b) how many units of foreign currency are needed to buy one U.S. dollar.

Country	(a) U.S. Dollar per Unit (Dollar Price of Foreign Currency)	(b) Currency per U.S. Dollar (Foreign Price of U.S. Dollar)
Brazil (real)	0.1961	5.1006
Britain (pound)	1.2453	0.8030
Canada (dollar)	0.7145	1.4000
China (yuan)	0.1409	7.0950
Indonesia (rupiah)	0.0001	16,222.435
Japan (yen)	0.0092	107.9112
Mexico (peso)	0.0429	23.3313
Russia (ruble)	0.0127	78.7265
Eurozone (euro)	1.1144	0.8973
Venezuela (bolivar)	0.1001	9.9875

Source: March 2020 data from Federal Reserve Board of Governors.

CRITICAL ANALYSIS: The exchange rates between currencies are determined by supply and demand in foreign exchange markets. The rates reported here represent the equilibrium exchange rates on a particular day.

Current Account Balance. The current account balance is a second subtotal in Table 20.1. It includes the trade balance as well as private transfers such as wages sent home by foreign citizens working in the United States (like Mexican strawberry pickers in California). It also includes the income flows from international investments.

$$\frac{\text{Current account}}{\text{balance}} = \frac{\text{Trade}}{\text{balance}} + \frac{\text{Unilateral}}{\text{transfers}} + \frac{\text{Net investment}}{\text{income}}$$

The current account balance is the most comprehensive summary of our trade relations. As indicated in Table 20.1, the United States had a current account deficit of $498 billion in 2019.

TABLE 20.1

The U.S. Balance of Payments

The balance of payments is a summary statement of a country's international transactions. The major components of that activity are the trade balance (merchandise exports minus merchandise imports), the current account balance (trade, services, and transfers), and the capital account balance. The net total of these balances must equal zero because the quantity of dollars paid must equal the quantity received.

Item		Amount ($ billions)
1.	Merchandise exports	$1,653
2.	Merchandise imports	(2,519)
3.	Service exports	845
4.	Service imports	(595)
	Trade balance (items 1–4)	−616
5.	Income from U.S. overseas investments	1,123
6.	Income outflow for foreign-owned U.S. investments	(866)
7.	Net transfers and pensions	(139)
	Current account balance (items 1–7)	−498
8.	U.S. capital inflow	822
9.	U.S. capital outflow	(427)
	Capital account balance (items 8–9)	395
10.	Statistical discrepancy	103
	Net balance (items 1–10)	0

Source: U.S. Department of Commerce (2019 data).

Capital Account Balance. The current account deficit is offset by the capital account surplus. The capital account balance takes into consideration assets bought and sold across international borders:

$$\text{Capital account balance} = \text{Foreign purchases of U.S. assets} - \text{U.S. purchases of foreign assets}$$

As Table 20.1 shows, foreign consumers demanded $822 billion in 2019 to buy farms and factories as well as U.S. bonds, stocks, and other investments (item 8). This exceeded the flow of U.S. dollars going overseas to purchase foreign assets (item 9).

The net capital inflows were essential in financing the U.S. trade deficit (negative trade balance). As in any market, the number of dollars demanded must equal the number of dollars supplied. Thus, **the capital account surplus must equal the current account deficit.** In other words, there can't be any dollars left lying around unaccounted for. Item 10 in Table 20.1 reminds us that our accounting system isn't perfect—we can't identify every transaction. Nevertheless, all the accounts must eventually "balance out":

$$\text{Net balance of payments} = \text{Current account balance} + \text{Capital account balance} = 0$$

That's the character of a market *equilibrium:* The quantity of dollars demanded equals the quantity of dollars supplied.

MARKET DYNAMICS

The interesting thing about markets isn't their character in equilibrium but the fact that prices and quantities are always changing in response to shifts in demand and supply. The U.S. demand for BMWs shifted overnight when Japan introduced a new line of sleek, competitively priced cars (e.g., Lexus). The reduced demand for BMWs shifted the supply of dollars leftward. That supply shift raised the value of the dollar vis-à-vis the euro, as illustrated in Figure 20.2. (It also increased the demand for Japanese yen, causing the yen value of the dollar to *fall.*)

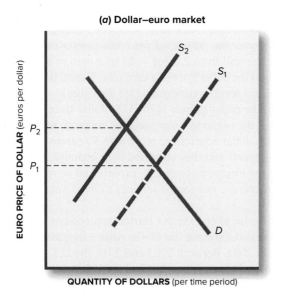

(a) Dollar–euro market

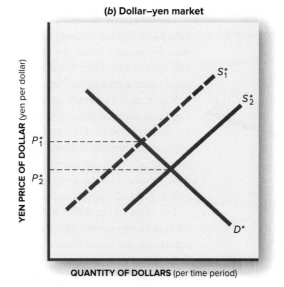

(b) Dollar–yen market

FIGURE 20.2

Shifts in Foreign Exchange Markets

When the Japanese introduced luxury autos into the United States, the American demand for German cars fell. As a consequence, the supply of dollars in the dollar–euro market (part *a*) shifted to the left and the euro value of the dollar rose.

At the same time, the increased American demand for Japanese cars shifted the dollar supply curve in the yen market (part *b*) to the right, reducing the yen price of the dollar.

FIGURE 20.3
Changing Values of U.S. Dollar

Since 1973, exchange rates have been flexible. As a result, the value of the U.S. dollar has fluctuated with international differences in inflation, interest rates, and economic growth. Between 2010 and 2020, the value of the U.S. dollar rose by roughly 30 percent.

Source: Federal Reserve Bank of St. Louis.

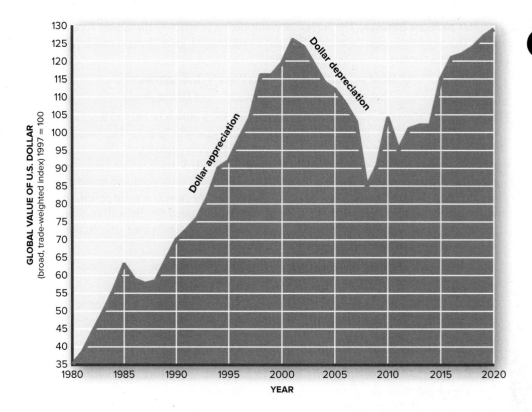

---

depreciation (currency): A fall in the price of one currency relative to another.

---

appreciation: A rise in the price of one currency relative to another.

If the dollar is rising in value (appreciating), the euro must be depreciating.

Depreciation and Appreciation

Exchange rate changes have their own terminology. **Depreciation** of a currency occurs when one currency becomes cheaper in terms of another currency. In our earlier discussion of exchange rates, for example, we assumed that the exchange rate between euros and dollars changed from 2 euros = $1 to 1 euro = $1, making the euro price of a dollar cheaper. In this case, the dollar *depreciated* with respect to the euro.

The other side of depreciation is **appreciation,** an increase in value of one currency as expressed in another country's currency. ***Whenever one currency depreciates, another currency must appreciate.*** When the exchange rate changed from 2 euros = $1 to 1 euro = $1, not only did the euro price of a dollar fall, but also the dollar price of a euro rose. Hence, the euro appreciated as the dollar depreciated. It's like a seesaw relationship (see the figure).

Figure 20.3 illustrates actual changes in the exchange rate of the U.S. dollar since 1980. The trade-adjusted value of the U.S. dollar is the (weighted) average of all exchange rates for the dollar. Between 1980 and 1985, the U.S. dollar appreciated more than 80 percent. This appreciation greatly reduced the price of imports and thus increased their quantity. At the same time, the dollar appreciation raised the foreign price of U.S. exports and so reduced their volume. U.S. farmers, aircraft manufacturers, and tourist services suffered huge sales losses. The trade deficit ballooned.

The value of the dollar briefly reversed course after 1985 but started appreciating again, slowing export growth and increasing imports throughout the 1990s. After a long steep appreciation, the dollar started losing value in 2003. Between 2003 and 2011, the U.S. dollar depreciated by 25 percent. This was good for U.S. exporters but bad for U.S. tourists and foreign producers.

The value of the U.S. dollar reversed course again in 2014. From 2014 to 2020 the dollar appreciated by 25 percent. This put a lot of pressure on U.S. companies that competed with imported products. It also made winter vacations in Florida more expensive for Canadians. But Walmart loved the stronger dollar, as it made the price of the imported goods that it sells much less expensive (see World View "Who Gains, Who Loses from Strong Dollar").

WORLD VIEW

WHO GAINS, WHO LOSES FROM STRONG DOLLAR

Between 2014 and 2020, the international value of the U.S. dollar increased by 25 percent. Was that dollar appreciation a good thing? It depends where you were positioned in global markets. Here is a sampling of winners and losers in the United States:

The winners:
Consumers of imported goods
Producers like Apple that use imported parts and equipment
Retailers like Walmart that sell imported goods
Investors in foreign stocks and production facilities
American tourists

The losers:
U.S. exporters like Boeing, Caterpillar, farmers
Import-competing industries like steel, autos, solar panels
Companies like Disney that attract foreign visitors
Companies with overseas factories and outlets

CRITICAL ANALYSIS: Depreciation of a nation's currency is good for that nation's exporters but bad for that nation's importers (including its tourists).

Market Forces

Exchange rates change for the same reasons that any market price changes: The underlying supply or demand (or both) has shifted. Among the more important sources of such shifts are

- *Relative income changes.* If incomes are increasing faster in country A than in country B, consumers in A will tend to spend more, thus increasing the demand for B's exports and currency. B's currency will appreciate (and A's will depreciate).
- *Relative price changes.* If domestic prices are rising rapidly in country A, consumers will seek out lower-priced imports. The demand for B's exports and currency will increase. B's currency will appreciate (and A's will depreciate).
- *Changes in product availability.* If country A experiences a disastrous wheat crop failure, it will have to increase its food imports. B's currency will appreciate.
- *Relative interest rate changes.* If interest rates rise in country A, people in country B will want to move their deposits to A. Demand for A's currency will rise and it will appreciate.
- *Speculation.* If speculators anticipate an increase in the price of A's currency, for the preceding reasons or any other, they'll begin buying it, thus pushing its price up. A's currency will appreciate.

All these various changes are taking place every minute of every day, thus keeping **foreign exchange markets** active. On an average day, more than *$5 trillion* of foreign exchange is bought and sold in the market. Significant changes occur in currency values, however, only when several of these forces move in the same direction at the same time.

foreign exchange markets: Places where foreign currencies are bought and sold.

Ukraine Crisis of 2014

Exchange values are also subject to abrupt changes when an unexpected political or natural upheaval occurs. The Russian invasion of Ukraine in early 2014 was a classic case of an external shock. Foreign exchange markets reacted quickly, sending the value of the hryvnia (Ukraine's currency) into a prolonged depreciation. The dollar value of the hryvnia plunged from 12.3 cents to 7.6 cents in a couple of months. That 40 percent depreciation in the value of the hryvnia substantially increased the cost of badly needed food, oil, and weapons imports.

Venezuelan Currency Collapse, 2016–2018

The collapse of the Venezuelan bolivar was a bit less abrupt, but no less dramatic. Hyper-inflation in 2016 eroded the value of the bolivar. People needed wads of bolivars just to buy everyday staples like bread. Worse yet, few goods were available to buy as the economy contracted. People needed U.S. dollars to buy goods from other countries or in the black markets. Venezuelans were desperate to buy U.S. dollars at any price. In 2016 Venezuelans could buy one U.S. dollar for 10 bolivars. By mid-2018 a single dollar cost a staggering 248,210 bolivars! The bolivar was all but worthless. The Venezuelan government then created a new currency, the bolivar soberano, that was worth 100,000 of the old currency (bolivar fuerte).

RESISTANCE TO EXCHANGE RATE CHANGES

Given the scope and depth of currency crises, it's easy to understand why people crave *stable* exchange rates. The resistance to exchange rate fluctuations originates in various micro- and macroeconomic interests.

Micro Interests

The microeconomic resistance to changes in the value of the dollar arises from two concerns. First, people who trade or invest in world markets want a solid basis for forecasting future costs, prices, and profits. Forecasts are always uncertain, but they're even less dependable when the value of money is subject to change. An American firm that invests $2 million in a ski factory in Sweden expects not only to make a profit on the production there but also to return that profit to the United States. If the Swedish krona depreciates sharply in the interim, however, the profits amassed in Sweden may dwindle to a mere trickle, or even a loss, when the kronor are exchanged back into dollars. Imagine how devastated foreign investors in Venezuela were when the bolivar collapsed: They saw not only their profits but their investments evaporate. General Motors recorded a loss of $720 million on its Venezuelan factory due to the abrupt depreciation of the bolivar.

The World View "Weakest Currencies of 2019" illustrates how much some other currencies depreciated in 2019. The new Venezuelan currency essentially became worthless in that year. But a lot of other nations experienced substantial weakness in their currencies, making exports cheaper but needed imports more expensive. For international investors and travelers, these kinds of currency fluctuations are an unwanted headache.

WORLD VIEW

WEAKEST CURRENCIES OF 2019

The U.S. dollar continued its upward move in 2019, gaining strength against most other currencies. But the global 2 percent appreciation of the dollar disguised dramatic changes in the exchange rates for specific countries. These are some of the biggest depreciations of 2019:

Venezuela	Argentina	Haiti	Pakistan	Sweden	South Korea
bolivar	peso	gourde	rupee	krona	won
−97.7%	−31.9%	−19.0%	−10.4%	−7.9%	−6.6%

Source: Forex market, January–September 2019.

CRITICAL ANALYSIS: The global value of a currency changes with shifts of demand and supply. The appreciation of the U.S. dollar is reflected in the **depreciation** of other currencies.

Even when the direction of an exchange rate move is certain, those who stand to lose from the change are prone to resist. *A change in the price of a country's money automatically alters the price of all its exports and imports.* When the Russian ruble and Japanese yen depreciated in 2015–2016, for example, the dollar price of Russian and Japanese steel declined as well. This prompted U.S. steelmakers to accuse Russia and Japan of "dumping" steel. Steel companies and unions appealed to Washington to protect their sales and jobs.

Even in the country whose currency becomes cheaper, there will be opposition to exchange rate movements. When the U.S. dollar appreciates, Americans buy more foreign products. This increased U.S. demand for imports may drive up prices in other countries. In addition, foreign firms may take advantage of the reduced American competition by raising their prices. In either case, some inflation will result. The consumer's insistence that the government "do something" about rising prices may turn into a political force for "correcting" foreign exchange rates.

Macro Interests

Any microeconomic problem that becomes widespread enough can turn into a macroeconomic problem. The huge U.S. trade deficits of the 1980s effectively exported jobs to foreign nations. Although the U.S. economy expanded rapidly in 1983–1985, the unemployment rate stayed high, partly because American consumers were spending more of their income on imports.

This is the kind of scenario that prompted President Trump to castigate "currency manipulators" like China. In his view, the strong dollar of 2014–2017 was in part due to other nations keeping their currencies artificially low. Those low values encouraged American consumers to buy more imports and American businesses to build more factories abroad. He vowed "to bring jobs back to America" by imposing tariffs (Chapter 19) that would offset the cheap price of foreign currencies.

The U.S. trade deficits are typically offset by capital account surpluses. Foreign investors participate in the U.S. economic expansion by buying land, plants, and equipment and by lending money in U.S. financial markets. These capital inflows complicate monetary policy, however, and increase U.S. foreign debt and interest costs.

U.S. a Net Debtor

The inflow of foreign investment also raised anxieties about "selling off" America. When Japanese and other foreign investors increased their purchases of farmland, factories, and real estate (e.g., Rockefeller Center), many Americans worried that foreign investors were taking control of the U.S. economy.

Fueling these fears was the dramatic change in America's international financial position. From 1914 to 1984, the United States had been a net creditor in the world economy. We owned more assets abroad than foreign investors owned in the United States. Our financial position changed in 1985. Continuing trade deficits and offsetting capital inflows transformed the United States into a net debtor in that year. Since then foreigners have owned more U.S. assets than Americans own of foreign assets.

America's debtor status can complicate domestic policy. A sudden flight from U.S. assets could severely weaken the dollar and disrupt the domestic economy. To prevent that from occurring, policymakers must consider the impact of their decisions on foreign investors. This may necessitate difficult policy choices.

There's a silver lining to this cloud, however. The inflow of foreign investment is a reflection of confidence in the U.S. economy. Foreign investors want to share in our growth and profitability. In the process, their investments (like BMW's auto plant) expand America's production possibilities and stimulate still more economic growth.

Foreign investors actually assume substantial risk when they invest in the United States. If the dollar falls, the foreign value of *their* U.S. investments will decline. Hence, foreigners who've already invested in the United States have no incentive to start a flight from the dollar. On the contrary, a strong dollar protects the value of their U.S. holdings.

EXCHANGE RATE INTERVENTION

Given the potential opposition to exchange rate movements, governments often feel compelled to intervene in foreign exchange markets. The intervention is usually intended to achieve greater exchange rate stability. But such stability may itself give rise to undesirable micro- and macroeconomic effects.

Fixed Exchange Rates

One way to eliminate fluctuations in exchange rates is to fix a currency's value. The easiest way to do this is for each country to define the worth of its currency in terms of some common standard. Under a **gold standard,** each country declares that its currency is worth so much gold. In so doing, it implicitly defines the worth of its currency in terms of all other currencies that also have a fixed gold value. In 1944 the major trading nations met at Bretton Woods, New Hampshire, and agreed that each currency was worth so much gold. The value of the U.S. dollar was defined as being equal to 0.0294 ounce of gold, while the British pound was defined as being worth 0.0823 ounce of gold. Thus, the exchange rate between British pounds and U.S. dollars was effectively fixed at $1 = 0.357 pound, or 1 pound = $2.80 (or $2.80/0.0823 = $1/0.0294).

Balance-of-Payments Problems. It's one thing to proclaim the worth of a country's currency; it's quite another to *maintain* the fixed rate of exchange. As we've observed, foreign exchange rates are subject to continual and often unpredictable changes in supply and demand. Hence, two countries that seek to stabilize their exchange rate at some fixed value will have to somehow neutralize such foreign exchange market pressures.

Suppose the exchange rate officially established by the United States and Great Britain is equal to e_1, as illustrated in Figure 20.4. As is apparent, that particular exchange rate is consistent with the then-prevailing demand and supply conditions in the foreign exchange market (as indicated by curves D_1 and S_1).

Now suppose that Americans suddenly acquire a greater taste for British cars and start spending more income on Jaguars, Bentleys, and Mini Coopers. This increased desire for British goods will *shift* the demand for British currency from D_1 to D_2 in Figure 20.4. Were exchange rates allowed to respond to market influences, the dollar price of a British pound would rise, in this case to the rate e_2. But we've assumed that government intervention has *fixed* the exchange rate at e_1. Unfortunately, at e_1, American consumers want to buy more pounds (q_D) than the British are willing to supply (q_S). The difference between the quantity demanded and the quantity supplied in the market at the rate e_1 represents a **market shortage** of British pounds.

---

gold standard: An agreement by countries to fix the price of their currencies in terms of gold; a mechanism for fixing exchange rates.

---

market shortage: The amount by which the quantity demanded exceeds the quantity supplied at a given price; excess demand.

FIGURE 20.4
Fixed Rates and Market Imbalance

If exchange rates are fixed, they can't adjust to changes in market supply and demand. Suppose the exchange rate is initially fixed at e_1. When the demand for British pounds increases (shifts to the right), an excess demand for pounds emerges. More pounds are demanded (q_D) at the rate e_1 than are supplied (q_S). This causes a balance-of-payments deficit for the United States.

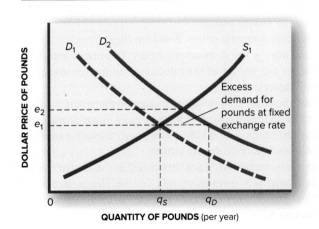

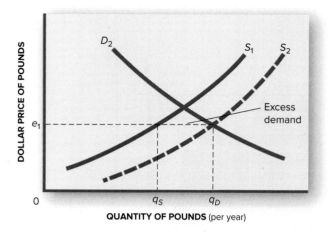

FIGURE 20.5
The Impact of Monetary Intervention

If the U.S. Treasury holds reserves of British pounds, it can use them to buy U.S. dollars in foreign exchange markets. As it does so, the supply of pounds will shift to the right, to S_2, thereby maintaining the desired exchange rate, e_1. The Bank of England could bring about the same result by offering to buy U.S. dollars with pounds (i.e., *supplying* pounds).

The excess demand for pounds implies a **balance-of-payments deficit** for the United States: More dollars are flowing out of the country than into it. The same disequilibrium represents a **balance-of-payments surplus** for Britain because its outward flow of pounds is less than its incoming flow.

Basically, there are only two solutions to balance-of-payments problems brought about by the attempt to fix exchange rates:

- Allow exchange rates to rise to e_2 (Figure 20.4), thereby eliminating the excess demand for pounds.
- Alter market supply or demand so they intersect at the fixed rate e_1.

Because fixed exchange rates were the initial objective of this intervention, only the second alternative is of immediate interest.

The Need for Reserves. One way to alter market conditions would be for someone simply to supply British pounds to American consumers. The U.S. Treasury could have accumulated a reserve of foreign currency in earlier periods. By selling some of those **foreign exchange reserves** now, the Treasury would be *supplying* British pounds, helping to offset excess demand. The rightward shift of the pound supply curve in Figure 20.5 illustrates the sale of accumulated British pounds—and related purchase of U.S. dollars—by the U.S. Treasury.

Although foreign exchange reserves can be used to fix exchange rates, such reserves may not be adequate. Indeed, Figure 20.6 should be testimony enough to the fact that today's deficit isn't always offset by tomorrow's surplus. A principal reason that fixed exchange rates didn't live up to their expectations is that the United States had balance-of-payments deficits for 22 consecutive years. This long-term deficit overwhelmed the government's stock of foreign exchange reserves.

The Role of Gold. Gold reserves are a potential substitute for foreign exchange reserves. As long as each country's money has a value defined in terms of gold, we can use gold to buy British pounds, thereby restocking our foreign exchange reserves. Or we can simply use the gold to purchase U.S. dollars in foreign exchange markets. In either case, the exchange value of the dollar will tend to rise. However, we must have **gold reserves** available for this purpose. Unfortunately, the continuing U.S. balance-of-payments deficits recorded in Figure 20.6 exceeded even the hoards of gold buried under Fort Knox. As a consequence, our gold reserves lost their credibility as a guarantor of fixed exchange rates. When it appeared that foreigners would demand more gold than the U.S. government possessed, President Nixon simply ended the link between the U.S. dollar and gold. As of August 15, 1971, the U.S. dollar had no guaranteed value.

balance-of-payments deficit: An excess demand for foreign currency at current exchange rates.

balance-of-payments surplus: An excess demand for domestic currency at current exchange rates.

foreign exchange reserves: Holdings of foreign currencies by official government agencies, usually the central bank or treasury.

gold reserves: Stocks of gold held by a government to purchase foreign exchange.

FIGURE 20.6

The U.S. Balance of Payments, 1950–1973

The United States had a balance-of-payments deficit for 22 consecutive years. During this period, the foreign exchange reserves of the U.S. Treasury were sharply reduced. Fixed exchange rates were maintained by the willingness of foreign countries to accumulate large reserves of U.S. dollars. However, neither the Treasury's reserves nor the willingness of foreigners to accumulate dollars was unlimited. In 1973 fixed exchange rates were abandoned.

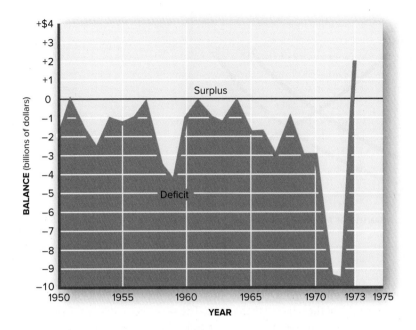

Domestic Adjustments. Government can also use fiscal, monetary, and trade policies to achieve a desired exchange rate. With respect to trade policy, *trade protection can be used to prop up fixed exchange rates.* We could eliminate the excess demand for pounds (Figure 20.4), for example, by imposing quotas and tariffs on British goods. Such trade restrictions would reduce British imports to the United States and thus the demand for British pounds. In August 1971 President Nixon imposed an emergency 10 percent surcharge on all imported goods to help reduce the payments deficit that fixed exchange rates had spawned. Such restrictions on international trade, however, violate the principle of comparative advantage and thus reduce total world output. Trade protection also invites retaliatory trade restrictions.

Fiscal policy is another way out of the imbalance. An increase in U.S. income tax rates will reduce disposable income and have a negative effect on the demand for all goods, including imports. A reduction in government spending will have similar effects. In general, *deflationary (or restrictive) policies help correct a balance-of-payments deficit by lowering domestic incomes and thus the demand for imports.*

Monetary policies in a deficit country could follow the same restrictive course. A reduction in the money supply raises interest rates. The balance of payments will benefit in two ways. The resultant slowdown in spending will reduce import demand. In addition, higher interest rates may induce international investors to move more of their funds into the deficit country. Such moves will provide immediate relief to the payments imbalance.[1] Russia tried this strategy in 1998, tripling key interest rates (to as much as 150 percent). But even that wasn't enough to restore confidence in the ruble, which kept depreciating. Within three months of the monetary policy tightening, the ruble lost half its value.

A surplus country could help solve the balance-of-payments problem. By pursuing expansionary—even inflationary—fiscal and monetary policies, a surplus country could stimulate the demand for imports. Moreover, any inflation at home will reduce the competitiveness of exports, thereby helping to restrain the inflow of foreign demand. Taken together, such efforts would help reverse an international payments imbalance.

---

[1]Before 1930, not only were foreign exchange rates fixed, but domestic monetary supplies were tied to gold stocks as well. Countries experiencing a balance-of-payments deficit were thus forced to contract their money supply, and countries experiencing a payments surplus were forced to expand their money supply by a set amount. Monetary authorities were powerless to control domestic money supplies except by erecting barriers to trade. The system was abandoned when the world economy collapsed into the Great Depression.

Even under the best of circumstances, domestic economic adjustments entail significant costs. In effect, *domestic adjustments to payments imbalances require a deficit country to forsake full employment and a surplus country to forsake price stability.* China has had to grapple with these domestic consequences of fixing the value of its currency. The artificially low value of the yuan promoted Chinese exports and accelerated China's GDP growth. But it also created serious macro problems. To keep the value of the yuan low, the Chinese had to keep buying dollars. By 2020 China had more than $3 trillion of foreign currency reserves. It paid for those dollars with yuan, adding to China's money supply. All that money stoked inflation in China. Ultimately, the Chinese government had to adopt restrictive monetary and fiscal policies to keep inflation in check. The Chinese government also had to be willing to keep accumulating U.S. dollars and other currencies.

As we noted earlier, President Trump pursued another approach to correct market imbalances. He blamed the huge trade deficit with China on the intentional manipulation of the value of the yuan by the Chinese government. He called China the "grand champion of currency manipulation" for its alleged role in keeping the value of the yuan low. To offset that "unfair" exchange rate, Trump imposed tariffs on all Chinese imports. He was hoping that the resulting economic pain would force China to appreciate its currency. But China retaliated with tariffs on U.S. exports, and a trade war ensued (Chapter 19). China maintained that it was not manipulating its currency; the cheap yuan was a product of market forces.

There's no easy way out of this impasse. Market imbalances caused by fixed exchange rates can be corrected only with abundant supplies of foreign exchange reserves or deliberate changes in fiscal, monetary, or trade policies. At some point, it may become easier to let a currency adjust to market equilibrium.

The Euro Fix. The original 12 nations of the European Monetary Union (EMU) fixed their exchange rates in 1999. They went far beyond the kind of exchange rate fix we're discussing here. Members of the EMU *eliminated* their national currencies, making the euro the common currency of Euroland. They don't have to worry about reserve balances or domestic adjustments. However, they do have to reconcile their varied national interests to a single monetary authority, which has proven to be difficult politically in times of economic stress.

Flexible Exchange Rates

Balance-of-payments problems wouldn't arise in the first place if exchange rates were allowed to respond to market forces. Under a system of **flexible exchange rates** (often called floating exchange rates), the exchange rate moves up or down to choke off any excess supply of or demand for foreign exchange. Notice again in Figure 20.4 that the exchange rate move from e_1 to e_2 prevents any excess demand from emerging. *With flexible exchange rates, the quantity of foreign exchange demanded always equals the quantity supplied,* and there's no imbalance. For the same reason, there's no need for foreign exchange reserves.

Although flexible exchange rates eliminate balance-of-payments and foreign exchange reserves problems, they don't solve all of a country's international trade problems. *Exchange rate movements associated with flexible rates alter relative prices and may disrupt import and export flows.* As noted before, depreciation of the dollar raises the price of all imported goods, contributing to domestic cost-push inflation. Also, domestic businesses that sell imported goods or use them as production inputs may suffer sales losses. On the other hand, appreciation of the dollar raises the foreign price of U.S. goods and reduces the sales of American exporters. Hence, *someone is always hurt, and others are helped, by exchange rate movements.* The resistance to flexible exchange rates originates in these potential losses. Such resistance creates pressure for official intervention in foreign exchange markets or increased trade barriers.

The United States and its major trading partners abandoned fixed exchange rates in 1973. Although exchange rates are now able to fluctuate freely, it shouldn't be assumed that they necessarily undergo wild gyrations. On the contrary, experience with flexible rates since 1973 suggests that some semblance of stability is possible even when exchange rates are free to change in response to market forces.

flexible exchange rates: A system in which exchange rates are permitted to vary with market supply-and-demand conditions; floating exchange rates.

Speculation. One force that often helps maintain stability in a flexible exchange rate system is—surprisingly—speculation. Speculators often counteract short-term changes in foreign exchange supply and demand. If a currency temporarily rises above its long-term equilibrium, speculators will move in to sell it. By selling at high prices and later buying at lower prices, speculators hope to make a profit. In the process, they also help stabilize foreign exchange rates.

Speculation isn't always stabilizing, however. Speculators may not correctly gauge the long-term equilibrium. Instead they may move "with the market" and help push exchange rates far out of kilter. This kind of destabilizing speculation sharply lowered the international value of the U.S. dollar in 1987, forcing the Reagan administration to intervene in foreign exchange markets, borrowing foreign currencies to buy U.S. dollars. In 1997 the Clinton administration intervened for the opposite purpose: stemming the rise in the U.S. dollar. The Bush administration was more willing to stay on the sidelines, letting global markets set the exchange rates for the U.S. dollar.

These kinds of interventions are intended to *narrow* rather than *eliminate* exchange rate movements. Such limited intervention in foreign exchange markets is often referred to as **managed exchange rates,** or, popularly, "dirty floats."

Although managed exchange rates would seem to be an ideal compromise between fixed rates and flexible rates, they can work only when some acceptable "rules of the game" and mutual trust have been established. As Sherman Maisel, a former governor of the Federal Reserve Board, put it, "Monetary systems are based on credit and faith: If these are lacking, a . . . crisis occurs."[2]

managed exchange rates: A system in which governments intervene in foreign exchange markets to limit but not eliminate exchange rate fluctuations; "dirty floats."

DECISIONS FOR TOMORROW

Are Currency Bailouts a Good Thing?

The world has witnessed a string of currency crises, including the one in Asia during 1997-1998, the Brazilian crisis of 1999, the Argentine crisis of 2001-2002, the Greek and Portuguese crises of 2010-2012, Venezuela in 2016-2018, and recurrent ruble crises in Russia. In every instance, the country in trouble pleads for external help. In most cases, a currency "bailout" is arranged, whereby global monetary authorities lend the troubled nation enough reserves (such as U.S. dollars) to defend its currency. Typically the International Monetary Fund (IMF) heads the rescue party, joined by the central banks of the strongest economies.

The Case for Bailouts. The argument for currency bailouts typically rests on the domino theory. Weakness in one currency can undermine another. This seemed to be the case during the 1997-1998 Asian crisis. After the **devaluation** of the Thai baht, global investors began worrying about currency values in other Asian nations. Choosing to be safe rather than sorry, they moved funds out of Korea, Malaysia, and the Philippines and invested in U.S. and European markets (notice in Figure 20.3 the 1997-1998 appreciation of the U.S. dollar).

The initial baht devaluation also weakened the competitive trade position of these same economies. Thai exports became cheaper, diverting export demand from other Asian nations. To prevent loss of export markets, Thailand's neighbors felt they had to devalue as well. Speculators who foresaw these effects accelerated the domino effect by selling the region's currencies.

When Brazil devalued its currency (the *real*) in January 1999, global investors worried that a "samba effect" might sweep across Latin America. The domino effect could reach

devaluation: An abrupt depreciation of a currency whose value was fixed or managed by the government.

[2]Sherman Maisel, *Managing the Dollar* (New York: W. W. Norton, 1973), p. 196.

across the ocean and damage U.S. and European exports as well. The Greek crisis of 2010 threatened the common currency (euro) of 28 nations. Hence, richer, more stable countries often offer a currency bailout as a form of self-defense.

The Case against Bailouts. Critics of bailouts argue that such interventions are ultimately self-defeating. They say that once a country knows for sure that currency bailouts are in the wings, it doesn't have to pursue the domestic policy adjustments that might stabilize its currency. A nation can avoid politically unpopular options such as high interest rates, tax hikes, or cutbacks in government spending. It can also turn a blind eye to trade barriers, monopoly power, lax lending policies, and other constraints on productive growth. Hence, the expectation of readily available bailouts may foster the very conditions that cause currency crises.

Future Bailouts? The decision to bail out a depreciating currency isn't as simple as it appears. To minimize the ill effects of bailouts, the IMF and other institutions typically require the nation in crisis to pledge more prudent monetary, fiscal, and trade policies. Usually there's a lot of debate about what kinds of adjustments will be made—and how soon. As long as the nation in crisis is confident of an eventual bailout, however, it has a lot of bargaining power to resist policy changes. Only after the IMF finally said no to further bailouts in Greece did the Greek parliament pass austerity measures that reduced its fiscal imbalances.

SUMMARY

- Money serves the same purposes in international trade as it does in the domestic economy—namely, to facilitate specialization and market exchanges. The basic challenge of international finance is to create acceptable standards of value from the various currencies maintained by separate countries.   **LO20-1**

- Exchange rates are the mechanism for translating the value of one national currency into the equivalent value of another. An exchange rate of $1 = 2 euros means that one dollar is worth two euros in foreign exchange markets.   **LO20-1**

- Foreign currencies have value because they can be used to acquire goods and resources from other countries. Accordingly, the supply of and demand for foreign currency reflect the demands for imports and exports, for international investment, and for overseas activities of governments.   **LO20-2**

- The balance of payments summarizes a country's international transactions. Its components are the trade balance, the current account balance, and the capital account balance. The current and capital accounts must offset each other.   **LO20-2**

- The equilibrium exchange rate is subject to any and all shifts of supply and demand for foreign exchange. If relative incomes, prices, or interest rates change, the demand for foreign exchange will be affected. A depreciation is a change in market exchange rates that makes one country's currency cheaper in terms of another currency. An appreciation is the opposite kind of change.   **LO20-3**

- Changes in exchange rates are often resisted. Producers of export goods don't want their currencies to rise in value (appreciate); importers and tourists dislike it when their currencies fall in value (depreciate).   **LO20-4**

- Under a system of fixed exchange rates, changes in the supply and demand for a specific currency can't be expressed in exchange rate movements. Instead, such shifts will be reflected in excess demand for or supply of that currency. Such market imbalances are referred to as balance-of-payments deficits or surpluses.   **LO20-3**

- To maintain fixed exchange rates, monetary authorities must enter the market to buy and sell foreign exchange. To do so, deficit countries must have foreign exchange reserves. In the absence of sufficient reserves, a country can maintain fixed exchange rates only if it's willing to alter basic fiscal, monetary, or trade policies.   **LO20-4**

- Flexible exchange rates eliminate balance-of-payments problems and the crises that accompany them. But complete flexibility can lead to disruptive changes. To avoid this contingency, many countries prefer to adopt managed exchange rates—that is, rates determined by the market but subject to government intervention.   **LO20-4**

Key Terms

exchange rate
equilibrium price
balance of payments
trade deficit
depreciation (currency)
appreciation

foreign exchange markets
gold standard
market shortage
balance-of-payments deficit
balance-of-payments surplus
foreign exchange reserves

gold reserves
flexible exchange rates
managed exchange rates
devaluation

Questions for Discussion

1. Why would a rise in the value of the dollar prompt U.S. manufacturers to build production plants in Mexico? **LO20-4**
2. How do changes in the value of the U.S. dollar affect foreign enrollments at U.S. colleges? **LO20-4**
3. How would rapid inflation in Canada affect U.S. tourism travel to Canada? Does it make any difference whether the exchange rate between Canadian and U.S. dollars is fixed or flexible? **LO20-3**
4. Under what conditions would a country welcome a balance-of-payments deficit? When would it *not* want a deficit? **LO20-4**
5. In what sense do fixed exchange rates permit a country to "export its inflation"? **LO20-4**
6. Why did the value of the Ukrainian hryvnia depreciate so much when Russia invaded (see section Ukraine Crisis of 2014)? **LO20-3**

7. If a nation's currency depreciates, are the reduced export prices that result "unfair"? **LO20-4**
8. How would each of these events affect the supply or demand for Japanese yen? **LO20-3**
    (*a*) Stronger U.S. economic growth.
    (*b*) A decline in Japanese interest rates.
    (*c*) Higher inflation in the United States.
    (*d*) A Japanese tsunami.
9. According to the World View "Weakest Currencies of 2019," which nation got the cheapest for American tourists in 2019? Why did it get so cheap? **LO20-4**
10. How could Venezuela have slowed the depreciation of the bolivar? Would an international bailout have solved the problem? **LO20-3**

PROBLEMS FOR CHAPTER 20

LO20-1 1. According to World View "Foreign Exchange Rates," which nation had
    (*a*) The cheapest currency?
    (*b*) The most expensive currency?

LO20-1 2. If a euro is worth $1.20, what is the euro price of a dollar?

LO20-3 3. How many Ukrainian hryvnia (see section Ukraine Crisis of 2014) could you buy with one U.S. dollar
    (*a*) Before the Russian invasion?
    (*b*) After the Russian invasion?

LO20-1 4. If a McDonald's Big Mac meal sold for $5.00 in March 2020, how much would it cost in the currencies of
    (*a*) Brazil?
    (*b*) Japan?
    (*c*) Indonesia?
    (See World View "Foreign Exchange Rates.")

LO20-3 5. By what percent did the cost of visiting Argentina decline in 2019 for American tourists? (See World View "Weakest Currencies of 2019.")

LO20-4 6. If an admission ticket to Disney World in Florida costs $120, how much more expensive was the ticket to a person from Sweden after the 2019 currency depreciation (see World View "Weakest Currencies of 2019")?

LO20-1 7. Between 2014 and 2017, did the U.S. dollar appreciate or depreciate (see Figure 20.3)?

LO20-1 8. If a PlayStation 5 costs 40,000 yen in Japan, how much will it cost in U.S. dollars if the exchange rate is
    (*a*) 110 yen = $1?
    (*b*) 1 yen = $0.009?
    (*c*) 100 yen = $1?

LO20-1 9. Between 1990 and 2000, by how much did the dollar appreciate (Figure 20.3)?

LO20-1 10. If inflation raises U.S. prices by 2 percent and the U.S. dollar appreciates by 3 percent, by how much does the foreign price of U.S. exports change?

LO20-1 11. According to World View "Foreign Exchange Rates," what was the peso price of a euro in March 2020?

LO20-2 12. For each of the following possible events, indicate whether the global value of the U.S. dollar will rise or fall.
    (*a*) American cars become suddenly more popular abroad.
    (*b*) Inflation in the United States accelerates.
    (*c*) The United States falls into a recession.
    (*d*) Interest rates in the United States drop.
    (*e*) The United States experiences rapid increases in productivity.

LO20-3 13. The following schedules summarize the supply and demand for trifflings, the national currency of Tricoli:

Triffling price (U.S. dollars per triffling)	0	$4	$8	$12	$16	$20	$24
Quantity demanded (per year)	40	38	36	34	32	30	28
Quantity supplied (per year)	1	11	21	31	41	51	61

Use these schedules for the following:
(*a*) Graph the supply and demand curves.
(*b*) Determine the equilibrium exchange rate.

(*c*) Determine the size of the excess supply or excess demand that would exist if the Tricolian government fixed the exchange rate at $20 = 1 triffling.

(*d*) Which of the following events would help reduce the payments imbalance? Which would not?

  (*i*) Domestic inflation.
  (*ii*) Foreign inflation.
  (*iii*) Slower domestic growth.
  (*iv*) Faster domestic growth.

LO20-3 14. ***Decisions for Tomorrow:*** Show graphically the impact on the South Korean currency (won) when the Thai baht was devalued.

AFP/Getty Images

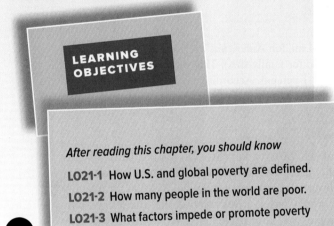

CHAPTER 21

Global Poverty

Bono, the lead singer for the rock group U2, has performed concerts around the world to raise awareness of global poverty. He doesn't have a specific agenda for eradicating poverty. He does believe, though, that greater awareness of global poverty will raise assistance levels and spawn more ideas for combating global hunger, disease, and isolation.

The dimensions of global poverty are staggering. According to the World Bank, more than a third of the world's population lacks even the barest of life's necessities. *Billions* of people are persistently malnourished, poorly sheltered, minimally clothed, and at constant risk of debilitating diseases. Life expectancies among the globally poor population still hover in the range of 40–50 years, far below the norm (70–80 years) of the rich, developed nations.

In this chapter we follow Bono's suggestion and take a closer look at global poverty. We address the following issues:

- **What income thresholds define "poverty"?**
- **How many people are poor?**
- **What actions can be taken to reduce global poverty?**

In the process of answering these questions, we get another opportunity to examine what makes economies "tick"—particularly what forces foster faster economic growth for some nations and slower economic growth for others.

LEARNING OBJECTIVES

After reading this chapter, you should know

LO21-1 How U.S. and global poverty are defined.

LO21-2 How many people in the world are poor.

LO21-3 What factors impede or promote poverty reduction.

AMERICAN POVERTY

Poverty, like beauty, is often in the eye of the beholder. Many Americans feel "poor" if they can't buy a new car, live in a fancy home, or take an exotic vacation. Indeed, the average American asserts that a family needs at least $58,000 a year "just to get by." With that much income, however, few people would go hungry or be forced to live in the streets.

Official Poverty Thresholds

To develop a more objective standard of poverty, the U.S. government assessed how much money a U.S. family needs to purchase a "minimally adequate" diet. Back in 1963 it concluded that $1,000 per year was needed for that purpose alone. Then it asked how much income was needed to purchase other basic necessities like housing, clothes, transportation, and so on. It figured all those *non*food necessities would cost twice as much as the food staples. So it concluded that a budget of $3,000 per year would fund a "minimally adequate" living standard for a U.S. family of four. That standard became the official **U.S. poverty threshold** in 1963.

poverty threshold (U.S.):
Annual income of less than
$26,200 for a family of four
(2020).

Inflation Adjustments. Since 1963, prices have risen every year. As a result, the price of the poverty "basket" has risen as well. In 2020, it cost roughly $26,000 to purchase those same basic necessities for a family of four that cost only $3,000 in 1963.

Twenty-six thousand dollars might sound like a lot of money, especially if you're not paying your own rent or feeding a family. If you break the budget down, however, it doesn't look so generous. Only a third of the budget goes for food. And that portion has to feed four people. So the official U.S. poverty standard provides less than $6 per day for an individual's food. That just about covers a single Big Mac combo at McDonald's. There's no money in the poverty budget for dining out. And the implied rent money is only $850 a month (for the whole family). So the official U.S. poverty standard isn't that generous—certainly not by *American* standards (where the *average* family has an income of nearly $85,000 per year and eats outside their $250,000 home three times a week).

U.S. Poverty Count

poverty rate: Percentage of
the population counted as poor.

The Census Bureau counted more than 34 million Americans as "poor" in 2019 according to the official U.S. thresholds (as adjusted for family size). This was one out of nine U.S. households, for a **poverty rate** of roughly 11 percent. According to the Census Bureau, the official U.S. poverty rate has been in a narrow range of 11-15 percent for the last 40 years.

How Poor Is U.S. "Poor"?

Many observers criticize these official U.S. poverty statistics. On the one hand, liberals assert that the official poverty thresholds are ridiculously low. They also contend that the number of households in "near poverty" (incomes of $26,000–$34,000 for a family of four) is too high and too often ignored. Conservatives respond that the official poverty count is overstated—that there are far fewer poor people in America than the Census Bureau claims.

in-kind transfers: Direct
transfers of goods and services
rather than cash, such as food
stamps, Medicaid benefits, and
housing subsidies.

In-Kind Income. A major flaw in the official tally is that the government counts only *cash* income in defining poverty. Since the 1960s, however, the United States has developed an extensive system of **in-kind transfers** that augment cash incomes. Food stamps, for example, can be used just as easily as cash to purchase groceries. Medicaid and Medicare pay doctor and hospital bills, reducing the need for cash income. Government rent subsidies and public housing allow poor families to have more housing than their cash incomes would permit. These in-kind transfers allow "poor" families to enjoy a higher living standard than their cash incomes imply. Adding those transfers to cash incomes would bring the U.S. poverty count down into the 8-10 percent range.

Material Possessions. Even those families who remain "poor" after counting in-kind transfers aren't necessarily destitute. More than 40 percent of America's "poor" families own their homes, 70 percent own a car or truck, and 30 percent own at least *two* vehicles. Telephones, color TVs, dishwashers, clothes dryers, air conditioners, and microwave ovens are commonplace in America's poor households.

America's poor families themselves report few acute problems in everyday living. Fewer than 14 percent report missing a rent or mortgage payment, and fewer than 8 percent report a food deficiency. So American poverty isn't synonymous with homelessness, malnutrition, chronic illness, or even social isolation. These problems exist among America's poverty population, but they don't define American poverty.

GLOBAL POVERTY

Poverty in the rest of the world is much different from poverty in America. *American poverty is more about* relative *deprivation than* absolute *deprivation. In the rest of the world, poverty is all about* absolute *deprivation.*

Low Average Incomes

As a starting point for assessing global poverty, consider how *average* incomes in the rest of the world stack up against U.S. levels. By global standards, the United States is unquestionably a very rich nation. As we observed in Chapter 2 (see World View "GDP per Capita around the World"), U.S. GDP per capita is five times larger than the world average. More than three-fourths of the world's population lives in what the World Bank calls "low-income" or "lower-middle-income" nations. In those nations the *average* income is under $4,000 a year, less than *one-tenth* of America's per capita GDP. Average incomes are lower yet in Haiti, Nigeria, Ethiopia, and other desperately poor nations. By American standards, virtually all the people in these nations would be poor. By *their* standards, no American would be poor.

World Bank Poverty Thresholds

Because national poverty lines are so diverse and culture-bound, the World Bank decided to establish a uniform standard for assessing global poverty. And it set the bar amazingly low. In fact, the World Bank regularly uses two thresholds, namely $1.90 per day for **"extreme" poverty** and a higher $3.10 per day standard for less **"severe" poverty**.

The World Bank thresholds are incomprehensibly low by American standards. The $1.90 standard works out to $2,774 per year for a family of four—a mere tenth of America's poverty standard. Think about it. How much could you buy for $1.90 a day? A little rice, maybe, and perhaps some milk? Certainly not a Big Mac. Not even a grande coffee at Starbucks. And part of that $1.90 would have to go for rent. Clearly this isn't going to work. Raising the World Bank standard to $3.10 per day (severe poverty) doesn't reach a whole lot further.

The World Bank, of course, wasn't defining "poverty" in the context of American affluence. They were instead trying to define a rock-bottom threshold of absolute poverty—a threshold of physical deprivation that people everywhere would acknowledge as the barest "minimum"—a condition of "unacceptable deprivation."

Global Poverty Counts

On the basis of household surveys in more than 100 nations, *the World Bank classifies 700 million people as being in "extreme" poverty (<$1.90/day) and nearly 2 billion people as being in "severe" poverty (<$3.10/day).*

Figure 21.1 shows where concentrations of extreme poverty are the greatest. Concentrations of extreme poverty are alarmingly high in dozens of smaller, less developed nations like Mali, Haiti, and Zambia, where average incomes are also shockingly low. However, the greatest *number* of extremely poor people reside in the world's largest countries.

Table 21.1 reveals that the distribution of severe poverty (<$3.10/day) is similar. The incidence of this higher poverty threshold is, of course, much greater. Severe poverty afflicts more than 80 percent of the population in dozens of nations and even reaches more than 90 percent of the population in some (e.g., Burundi). By contrast, less than 15 percent of the U.S. population falls below the official *American* poverty threshold, and *virtually no American household has an income below the* **global** *poverty threshold.*

extreme poverty (world): World Bank income standard of less than $1.90 per day per person (inflation adjusted).

severe poverty (world): World Bank income standard of $3.10 per day per person (inflation adjusted).

Analysis: Global poverty is defined in terms of absolute deprivation.
Stockbyte/Getty Images

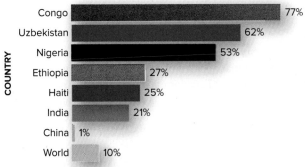

POPULATION IN EXTREME POVERTY (<$1.90/DAY)

FIGURE 21.1

Geography of Extreme Poverty

Over 700 million people around the world are in "extreme" poverty. In smaller, poor nations, deprivation is commonplace.

Source: The World Bank, *WDR2019 Data Set.*

TABLE 21.1

Population in Severe Poverty (<$3.10/day)

A fourth of the world's population has income of less than $3.10 per person per day. Such poverty is pervasive in low-income nations.

Country	Living in Severe Poverty (Percent)
Congo	91%
Burundi	89
Uzbekistan	86
Sierra Leone	81
Nigeria	78
Ethiopia	62
India	60
Haiti	51
China	7
United States	1.5
World	**25%**

Source: The World Bank, *WDR2019 Data Set.*

The COVID-19 Surge

The coronavirus pandemic that swept across the globe in 2020 made an already desperate situation worse for the global poor. The United Nations estimated that the illnesses, deaths, and economic disruptions caused by COVID-19 pushed an additional 71 million people into extreme poverty in 2020. That was the first increase in global poverty since 1998. The pandemic also caused significant setbacks in education and health for the world's poor.

Social Indicators

The levels of poverty depicted in Figure 21.1 and Table 21.1 imply levels of physical and social deprivation few Americans can comprehend. Living on less than two or three dollars a day means always being hungry, malnourished, ill-clothed, dirty, and unhealthy. The problems associated with such deprivation begin even before birth. Pregnant women often fail to get enough nutrition or medical attention. In low-income countries, only a third of all births are attended by a skilled health practitioner. If something goes awry, both the mother and the baby are at fatal risk. Nearly all of the children in global poverty are in a state of chronic malnutrition. At least 1 out of 10 children in low-income nations will actually die before reaching age 5. In the poorest sectors of the population, infant and child mortality rates are often two to three times higher than that. Children often remain unimmunized to preventable diseases. And AIDS is rampant among both children and adults in the poorest nations. All of these factors contribute to a frighteningly short life expectancy—less than half that in the developed nations.

Fewer than one out of two children from extremely poor households is likely to stay in school past the eighth grade. Women and minority ethnic and religious groups are often wholly excluded from educational opportunities. As a consequence, great stocks of human capital remain undeveloped: In low-income nations, only one out of two women and only two out of three men are literate.

Persistent Poverty

Global poverty is not only more desperate than American poverty, but also more permanent. In India a rigid caste system still defines differential opportunities for millions of rich and poor villagers. Studies in Brazil, South Africa, Peru, and Ecuador document barriers that block access to health care, education, and jobs for children of poor families. Hence, inequalities in poor nations not only are more severe than in developed nations but also tend to be more permanent.

Economic stagnation also keeps a lid on upward mobility. President John F. Kennedy observed that "a rising tide lifts all boats," referring to the power of a growing economy to raise everyone's income. In a growing economy, one person's income *gain* is not another person's *loss*. By contrast, a stagnant economy intensifies class warfare, with everyone jealously protecting whatever gains they have made. The *haves* strive to keep the *have-nots* at bay. Unfortunately, this is the reality in many low-income nations. As we observed in Chapter 2 (Table 2.1), in some of the poorest nations in the world, output grows more slowly than the population, intensifying the competition for resources.

GOALS AND STRATEGIES

Global poverty is so extensive that no policy approach offers a quick solution. Even the World Bank doesn't see an end to global poverty. The United Nations set a much more modest goal back in 2000.

The UN Millennium Goals

The UN established a Millennium Poverty Goal of cutting the incidence of extreme global poverty in half by 2015 (from 30 percent in 1990 to 15 percent in 2015). That goal was attained. But that didn't significantly decrease the *number* of people in poverty. The world's population keeps growing at upward of 80–100 million people a year. In 2020, there were 7.8 billion people on this planet. Fifteen percent of that population would still have left more than a *billion* people in extreme global poverty. In 2015, the World Bank set a new and more ambitious goal of *eliminating* extreme poverty by 2030.

Why should we care? After all, America has its own poverty problems and a slew of other domestic concerns. So why should an American—or, for that matter, an affluent Canadian, French, or German citizen—embrace the UN **and World Bank Poverty Goal?**

For starters, one might embrace the notion that a poor child in sub-Saharan Africa or Borneo is no less worthy than a poor child elsewhere. And a child's death in Bangladesh is just as tragic as a child's death in Buffalo, New York. In other words, humanitarianism is a starting point for *global* concern for poor people.

Then there are pragmatic concerns. Poverty and inequality sow the seeds of social tension both within and across national borders. Poverty in other nations also limits potential markets for international trade. Last but not least, undeveloped human capital anywhere limits human creativity. For all these reasons, the World Bank feels its Poverty Goal should be universally embraced.

> **UN and World Bank Poverty Goal:** UN goal of eliminating extreme poverty by 2030.

Policy Strategies

Eliminating severe poverty around the world won't be easy. In principle, ***there are only two general approaches to global poverty reduction:***

*   *Redistribution* of incomes within and across nations.
*   *Economic growth* that raises average incomes.

The following sections explore the potential of these strategies for eliminating global poverty.

INCOME REDISTRIBUTION

Many people suggest that the quickest route to eliminating global poverty is simply to *redistribute* incomes and assets, both within and across countries. The potential for redistribution is often exaggerated, however, and its risks are underestimated.

Within-Nation Redistribution

Take another look at those nations with the highest concentrations of extreme poverty. Nigeria is near the top of the list in Figure 21.1 and Table 21.1, with an incredible 54 percent of its population in extreme poverty and 78 percent in severe poverty. Yet the other 22 percent of the population lives fairly well, taking more than half of that nation's income. So what would happen if we somehow forced Nigeria's richest households to share that wealth? Sure,

WORLD VIEW

GLARING INEQUALITIES

Inequality tends to diminish as a country develops. In some developing nations, the richest tenth of the population can get 40 to 50 percent of all income—sometimes even more. In more developed countries, the richest tenth gets 20 to 30 percent of total income.

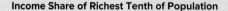

Income Share of Richest Tenth of Population

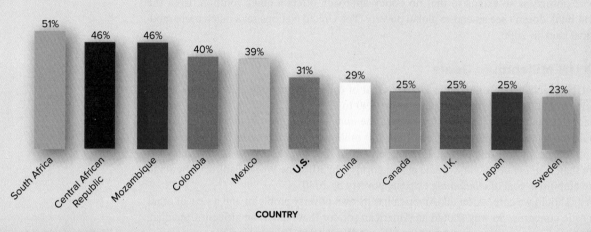

Source: The World Bank, *WDI2019 Data Set,* data.worldbank.org.

CRITICAL ANALYSIS: The FOR WHOM question is reflected in the distribution of income. Although the U.S. income distribution is very unequal, inequalities loom even larger in most poor countries.

Nigeria's poorest households would be better off. But the gains wouldn't be spectacular: The *average* income in Nigeria is only $5,500 a year. Haiti, Zambia, and Madagascar also have such low *average* incomes that outright redistribution doesn't hold great hope for income gains by the poor. (See World View "Glaring Inequalities.")

Economic Risks. Then there's the downside to direct redistribution. How is the income pie going to be resliced? Will the incomes or assets of the rich be confiscated? How will underlying jobs, stocks, land, and businesses be distributed to the poor? How will *total* output (and income) be affected by the redistribution?

If savings are confiscated, people will no longer want to save and invest. If large, efficient farms are divided up into small parcels, who will manage them? After Zimbabwe confiscated and fragmented that nation's farms in 2000, its agricultural productivity plummeted and the economy collapsed. Cuba experienced the same kind of economic decline after the government seized and fragmented sugar and tobacco plantations. If the government expropriates factories, mills, farms, or businesses, who will run them? If the *rewards* to saving, investment, entrepreneurship, and management are expropriated, who will undertake these economic activities?

This is not to suggest that *no* redistribution of income or assets is appropriate. More progressive taxes and land reforms can reduce inequalities and poverty. But the potential of direct withinnation redistribution is often exaggerated. Historically, nations have often been forced to reverse land, tax, and property reforms that have slowed economic growth and reduced average incomes.

Expenditure Reallocation. In addition to directly redistributing private income and wealth, governments can also reduce poverty by reallocating direct government expenditures. As we observed in Chapter 1 (Figure 1.3), some poor nations devote a large share of output to the military. If more of those resources were channeled into schools, health services, and infrastructure, the poor would surely benefit. Governments in poor nations

Country	Total Aid ($ billions)	Percentage of Donor Total Income
United States	$ 34	0.17%
United Kingdom	19	0.70
Germany	25	0.61
France	12	0.43
Japan	14	0.28
Sweden	6	1.04
Canada	5	0.28
Italy	5	0.19
Australia	3	0.23
24-Nation Total	$153	0.31%

Source: OECD (2018 data).

TABLE 21.2

Foreign Aid

Rich nations give roughly $150 billion to poor nations every year. This is a tiny fraction of donor GDP, however.

also tend to give priority to urban development (where the government and middle class reside), to the neglect of rural development (where the poor reside). Redirecting more resources to rural development and core infrastructure (roads, electricity, and water) would accelerate poverty reduction.

Across-Nation Redistribution

Redistribution *across* national borders could make even bigger dents in global poverty. After all, the United States and other industrialized nations are so rich that they could transfer a lot of income to the globally poor if they chose to.

Foreign Aid. Currently, developed nations give poorer nations around $150 billion a year in "official development assistance." That's a lot of money. But even if it were distributed exclusively to globally poor households, it would amount to only $50 per year per person.

Developed nations have set a goal of delivering more aid. The United Nations' **Millennium Aid Goal** is to raise foreign aid levels to 0.7 percent of donor-country GDP. That may not sound too ambitious, but it's a much larger flow than at present. As Table 21.2 reveals, few "rich" nations now come close to this goal. Although the United States is by far the world's largest aid donor, its aid equals only 0.17 percent of U.S. total output. For all developed nations, the aid ratio averages 0.31 percent.

Given the history of foreign aid, the UN goal is unlikely to be met anytime soon. But what if it were? What if foreign aid *tripled?* Would that cure global poverty? No. Tripling foreign aid would generate only $200 a year for each of the 2 billion people now in global poverty. Even that figure is optimistic, as it assumes all aid is distributed to the poor in a form (e.g., food, clothes, and medicine) that directly addresses their basic needs.

Millennium Aid Goal: United Nations goal of raising foreign aid levels to 0.7 percent of donor-country GDP.

Nongovernmental Aid. Official development assistance is augmented by private charities and other nongovernmental organizations (NGOs). The Gates Foundation, for example, spends upward of $1 billion a year on health care for the globally poor, focusing on treatable diseases like malaria, tuberculosis, and HIV infection (see World View "The Way We Give"). Religious organizations operate schools and health clinics in areas of extreme poverty. The International Red Cross brings medical care, shelter, and food in emergencies.

As with official development assistance, the content of NGO aid can be as important as its level. Relatively low-cost immunizations, for example, can improve health conditions more than an expensive, high-tech health clinic can. Teaching basic literacy to a community of young children can be more effective than equipping a single high school with Internet capabilities. Distributing drought-resistant seeds to farmers can be more effective than donating advanced farm equipment (which may become useless when it needs to be repaired).

WORLD VIEW

THE WAY WE GIVE

Philanthropy Can Step in Where Market Forces Don't

One day my wife Melinda and I were reading about millions of children dying from diseases in poor countries that were eliminated in this country. . . .

Malaria has been known for a long time. In 1902, in 1907, Nobel Prizes were given for advances in understanding the malaria parasite and how it was transmitted. But here we are a hundred years later and malaria is setting new records, infecting more than 400 million people every year, and killing more than a million people every year. That's a number that's increasing every year, and every day it's more than 2,000 African children. . . .

And this would extend to tuberculosis, yellow fever, AIDS vaccine, acute diarrheal illnesses, respiratory illnesses; you know, millions of children die from these things every year, and yet the advances we have in biology have not been applied because rich countries don't have these diseases. The private sector really isn't involved in developing vaccines and medicines for these diseases because the developing countries can't buy them. . . .

And so if left to themselves, these market forces create a world, which is the situation today, where more than 90 percent of the money spent on health research is spent on those who are the healthiest. An example of that is the billion a year spent on combating baldness. That's great for some people, but perhaps it should get behind malaria in terms of its priority ranking. . . .

So philanthropy can step in where market forces are not there. . . . It can get the people who have the expertise and draw them in. It can use awards, it can use novel arrangements with private companies, it can partner with the universities. . . . And every year the platform of science that we have to do this on gets better.

—Bill Gates

Source: Gates, Bill. "Speech at The Tech Museum." Bill & Melinda Gates Foundation, November 15, 2006.

CRITICAL ANALYSIS: When markets fail to provide for basic human needs, additional institutions and incentives may be needed (such as **nongovernmental aid**).

ECONOMIC GROWTH

No matter how well designed foreign aid and philanthropy might be, across-nation transfers alone cannot eliminate global poverty. As Bill Gates observed, the entire endowment of the Gates Foundation would meet the health needs of the globally poor for only one year. The World Bank concurs: "Developing nations hold the keys to their prosperity; global action cannot substitute for equitable and efficient domestic policies and institutions."[1] So as important as international assistance is, it will never fully suffice.

Increasing Total Income

economic growth: An increase in output (real GDP); an expansion of production possibilities.

The "key" to ending global poverty is, of course, **economic growth.** As we've observed, *redistributing existing incomes doesn't do the job;* total *income has to increase.* This is what economic growth is all about.

Unique Needs. The generic prescription for economic growth is simple: more resources and better technology. But this growth formula takes on a new meaning in the poorest nations. Rich nations can focus on research, technology, and the spread of "brain power." Poor nations need the basics—the "bricks and mortar" elements of an economy such as water systems, roads, schools, and legal systems. Bill Gates learned this firsthand in his early philanthropic efforts. In 1996 Microsoft donated a computer for a community center in Soweto, one of the poorest areas in South Africa. When he visited the center in 1997, he

[1]World Bank, *World Development Report, 2006* (Washington, DC: World Bank, 2006), p. 206.

discovered the center had no electricity. He quickly realized that growth policy priorities for poor nations are different from those for rich nations.

Growth Potential

The potential of economic growth to reduce poverty in poor nations is impressive. The 40 nations classified as "low-income" by the World Bank have a combined output of only $600 billion. That's just a shade more than the annual sales revenue of Walmart. "Lower-middle-income" nations like China, Brazil, Egypt, and Sri Lanka produce another $7 trillion or so of annual output. Hence, every percentage point of economic growth increases total income in these combined nations by nearly $75 billion. According to the World Bank, if these nations could grow their economies by just 3.8 percent a year, that would generate an extra $285 billion of output in the first year and increasing thereafter. That "growth dividend" is twice the amount of foreign aid (Table 21.2).

China has demonstrated just how effective economic growth can be in reducing poverty. Since 1990 China has been the world's fastest-growing economy, with annual GDP growth rates routinely in the 8–10 percent range. This sensational growth has not only raised *average* incomes but has also dramatically reduced the incidence of poverty. In fact, ***the observed success in reducing extreme global poverty from 30 percent in 1990 to 10 percent in 2019 is almost entirely due to the decline in Chinese poverty.*** By contrast, slow economic growth in Africa, Latin America, and South Asia has *increased* their respective poverty populations.

Growth of Per Capita Output

The really critical factor in reducing poverty is the relationship of output growth to population growth. China has been spectacularly successful in this regard: Not only does it have one of the fastest GDP growth rates, but it also has one of the world's slowest population growth rates. As a result, its per capita output has grown by an incredible 9 percent a year.

Notice in Table 21.3 how slow population growth rates in high-income nations allow them to achieve ever-rising living standards. Japan is the ultimate example: With zero population growth, it is pretty easy to achieve an increase in per capita income.

	Average Annual Growth Rate (2000–2018) of		
	GDP	Population	Per Capita GDP
High-income countries			
United States	1.7	0.8	0.9
Canada	1.9	1.0	0.9
Japan	0.7	0.0	0.7
France	1.1	0.6	0.5
Middle-income countries			
China	9.5	0.5	9.0
India	6.8	1.4	5.4
West Bank/Gaza	5.2	2.5	2.7
Libya	−1.2	1.2	−2.4
Zimbabwe	1.4	1.1	0.3
Low-income countries			
Burundi	3.1	3.1	0.0
Madagascar	2.9	2.8	0.1
Haiti	1.4	1.5	−0.1
Central African Republic	0.4	1.4	−1.0
Ethiopia	9.8	2.8	7.0

Source: The World Bank, *WDR2019 Data Set.*

TABLE 21.3

Growth Rates in Selected Countries, 2000–2018

The relationship between GDP growth and population growth is very different in rich and poor countries. The populations of rich countries are growing very slowly, and gains in per capita GDP are easily achieved. In the poorest countries, population is still increasing rapidly, making it difficult to raise living standards. Notice how per capita incomes are declining in many poor countries (such as Libya and Haiti).

Libya, Haiti, and the Central African Republic don't fare so well. Their output didn't grow as fast as their populations. As a consequence, the average citizen had *less* output to consume every year: extreme poverty spread.

Investing in Human Capital

human capital: The knowledge and skills possessed by the workforce.

While the math of global poverty is simple, the strategies for reducing poverty are many and diverse. A common observation, however, is the need to invest more in **human capital.**

Education. In poor nations, the need for human capital development is evident. Only 71 percent of the population in low-income nations completes even elementary school. Even fewer people are *literate*—that is, able to read and write a short, simple statement about everyday life (e.g., "We ate rice for breakfast"). Educational deficiencies are greatest for females, who are often prevented from attending school by cultural, social, or economic concerns (see World View "The Female 'Inequality Trap'"). In Chad and Liberia, fewer than one out of six girls completes primary school. Primary school completion rates for girls are in the 25–35 percent range in most of the poor nations of sub-Saharan Africa.

WORLD VIEW

THE FEMALE "INEQUALITY TRAP"

In many poor nations, women are viewed as such a financial liability that female fetuses are aborted, female infants are killed, and female children are so neglected that they have significantly higher mortality rates. The "burden" females pose results from social norms that restrict the ability of women to earn income, accumulate wealth, or even decide their own marital status. In many of the poorest nations, women

- Have restricted property rights.
- Can't inherit wealth.
- Are prohibited or discouraged from working outside the home.
- Are prohibited or discouraged from going to school.
- Are prevented from voting.
- Are denied the right to divorce.
- Are paid less than men if they do work outside the home.
- Are often expected to bring a financial dowry to the marriage.
- May be beaten if they fail to obey their husbands.

These social practices create an "inequality trap" that keeps returns on female human capital investment low. Without adequate education or training, they can't get productive jobs. Without access to good jobs, they have no incentive to get an education or training. This kind of vicious cycle creates an inequality trap that keeps women and their communities poor.

Source: The World Bank, *World Development Report 2006*, pp. 51–54.

CRITICAL ANALYSIS: Denying women economic rights not only is discriminatory but reduces the amount of **human capital** available for economic growth.

inequality trap: Institutional barriers that impede human and physical capital investment, particularly by the poorest segments of society.

In Niger and Mali, only one out of five *teenage* girls is literate. This lack of literacy creates an **inequality trap** that restricts the employment opportunities for young women to simple, routine, manual jobs (e.g., carpet weaving and sewing). With so few skills and little education, they are destined to remain poor.

The already low levels of *average* education are compounded by unequal access to schools. Families in extreme poverty typically live in rural areas, with primitive transportation and communication facilities. *Physical* access to school itself is problematic. On top of that, the poorest families often need their children to work, either within the family or in paid employment. In Somalia, only 8 percent of poor young children attend primary schools; in Ethiopia, Yemen, and Mali, about 50 percent attend. These forces often foreclose school attendance for the poorest children.

Health. In poor nations, basic health care is also a critical dimension of human capital development. Immunizations against measles, diphtheria, and tetanus are more the exception than the rule in Somalia, Nigeria, Afghanistan, Congo, the Central African Republic, and many other poor nations. For all low-income nations taken together, the child immunization rate is only 67 percent (versus 96 percent in the United States). Access and education—not money—are the principal barriers to greater immunizations.

Water and sanitation facilities are also in short supply. The World Bank defines "adequate water access" as a protected water source of at least 20 liters per person a day within 1 kilometer of the home dwelling. We're not limited to indoor plumbing with this definition: A public water pipe a half mile from one's home is considered adequate. Yet only three out of four households in low-income nations meet even this minimum threshold of water adequacy. In Afghanistan, Ethiopia, and Somalia, only one out of four households has even that much water access. Access to sanitation facilities (ranging from pit latrines to flush toilets) is less common still (on average one out of three low-income-nation households). In Ethiopia only 6 percent of the population is so privileged.

When illness strikes, professional health care is hard to find. In the United States, there is one doctor for every 180 people. In Sierra Leone, there is one doctor for every 10,000 people! For low-income nations as a group, there are 2,500 people for every available doctor.

These glaring inadequacies in health conditions breed high rates of illness and death. In the United States, only 8 out of every 1,000 children die before age 5. In Angola, 260 of every 1,000 children die that young. For all low-income nations, the under-5 mortality rate is 13.5 percent (nearly one out of seven). Those children who live are commonly so malnourished (severely underweight and/or short) that they can't develop fully (another inequality trap).

AIDS takes a huge toll as well. Only 0.6 percent of the U.S. adult population has HIV. In Botswana, Lesotho, Swaziland, and Zimbabwe, more than 25 percent of the adult population is HIV-infected. As a result of these problems, life expectancies are inordinately low. In Zambia, only 16 percent of the population lives to age 65. In the Central African Republic, life expectancy at birth is 52 years (versus 79 years in the United States). For low-income nations as a group, life expectancy is a mere 63 years.

Analysis: Unsafe water is a common problem for the globally poor.
Frank Bienewald/Getty Images

Capital Investment

If they are ever going to eradicate poverty and its related social ills, poor nations need sharply increased capital investment in both the public and private sectors. Transportation and communications systems must be expanded and upgraded so markets can function. Capital equipment and upgraded technology must flow into both agricultural and industrial enterprises.

Internal Financing. Acquiring the capital resources needed to boost productivity and accelerate economic growth is not an easy task. Domestically, freeing up scarce resources for capital investment requires cutbacks in domestic consumption. In the 1920s Stalin used near-totalitarian powers to cut domestic consumption in Russia (by limiting output of consumer goods) and raise Russia's **investment rate** to as much as 30 percent of output. This elevated rate of investment accelerated capacity growth, but at a high cost in terms of consumer deprivation.

Other nations haven't had the power or the desire to make such a sacrifice. China spent two decades trying to raise consumption standards before it gave higher priority to investment. Once it did so, however, economic growth accelerated sharply. Unfortunately, low investment rates continue to plague other poor nations.

Pervasive poverty in poor nations sharply limits the potential for increased savings. Nevertheless, governments can encourage more saving with improved banking facilities, transparent capital markets, and education and saving incentives. And there is mounting evidence that even small dabs of financing can make a big difference. Extending a small loan that

investment rate: The percentage of total output (GDP) allocated to the production of new plants, equipment, and structures.

microfinance: The granting of small ("micro"), unsecured loans to small businesses and entrepreneurs.

enables a poor farmer to buy improved seeds or a plow can have substantial effects on productivity. Financing small equipment or inventory for an entrepreneur can get a new business rolling. Such **microfinance** can be a critical key to escaping poverty. The Bangladesh economist Muhammad Yunus won the Nobel Peace Prize for his early demonstrations of how micro lending could create "development from below" in poor, rural areas.

Some nations have also used inflation as a tool for shifting resources from consumption to investment. By financing public works projects and private investment with an increased money supply, governments can increase the inflation rate. As prices rise faster than consumer incomes, households are forced to curtail their purchases. This "inflation tax" ultimately backfires, however, when both domestic and foreign market participants lose confidence in the nation's currency. Periodic currency collapses have destabilized many South and Central American economies and governments. Inflation financing also fails to distinguish good investment ideas from bad ones.

External Financing. Given the constraints on internal financing, poor nations have to seek external funding to lift their investment rate. In fact, Columbia University economist Jeffrey Sachs has argued that external financing is not only necessary but, if generous enough, also sufficient for *eliminating* global poverty (see World View "Jeffrey Sachs: Big Money, Big Plans"). As we've observed, however, actual foreign aid flows are far below the "Big Money" threshold that Sachs envisions. Skeptics also question whether more foreign aid would really solve the problem, given the mixed results of previous foreign aid flows. They suggest that more emphasis should be placed on increasing *private* investment flows. Private investment typically entails *direct foreign investment* in new plants, equipment, and technology, or the purchase of ownership stakes in existing enterprises.

WORLD VIEW

JEFFREY SACHS: BIG MONEY, BIG PLANS

Columbia University economics professor Jeffrey Sachs has seen the ravages of poverty around the world. As director of the UN Millennium Project, he is committed to attaining the UN's goal of reducing global poverty rates by half by 2015. In fact, Professor Sachs thinks we can do even better: the complete *elimination* of extreme poverty by 2025.

How will the world do this? First, rich nations must double their foreign aid flows now, and then double them again in 10 years. Second, poor nations must develop full-scale, comprehensive plans for poverty reduction. This "shock therapy" approach must address all dimensions of the poverty problem simultaneously and quickly, sweeping all inequality traps out of the way.

Critics have called Sachs's vision utopian. They point to the spotty history of foreign aid projects and the failure of many top-down, Big Plan development initiatives. But they still applaud Sachs for mobilizing public opinion and economic resources to fight global poverty.

Source: Jeffrey Sachs, *The End of Poverty* (New York, NY: Penguin Random House, 2006).

CRITICAL ANALYSIS: World poverty can't be eliminated without committing far more resources. Jeffrey Sachs favors an **external finance** option: the comprehensive Big Plan approach.

Agricultural Development

When we think about capital investment, we tend to picture new factories, gleaming office buildings, and computerized machinery. In discussing global poverty, however, we have to remind ourselves of how dependent poor nations are on agriculture. As Figure 21.2 illustrates, nearly 50 percent of Somalia's income originates in agriculture. Agricultural shares in the range of 30–45 percent are common in the poorest nations. By contrast, only 1 percent of America's output now comes from farms.

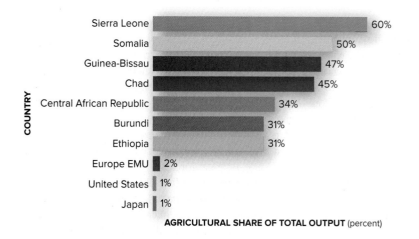

AGRICULTURAL SHARE OF TOTAL OUTPUT (percent)

FIGURE 21.2

Agricultural Share of Output

In poor nations, agriculture accounts for a very large share of total output.

Source: The World Bank, *WDR2019 Data Set.*

Low Farm Productivity.

Low Farm Productivity. What keeps poor nations so dependent on agriculture is their incredibly low **productivity**. Subsistence farmers are often forced to plow their own fields by hand with wooden plows. Irrigation systems are primitive and farm machinery is scarce or nonexistent. While high-tech U.S. farms produce nearly $100,000 of output per worker, Ugandan farms produce a shockingly low $690 of output per worker (see Figure 21.3). Farmers in Somalia produce only 500 kilograms of cereal per hectare, compared with 8,200 kilos per hectare in the United States.

To grow their economies, poor nations have to invest in agricultural development. Farm productivity has to rise beyond subsistence levels so that workers can migrate to other industries and expand production possibilities. One of the catapults to China's growth was an exponential increase in farm productivity that freed up labor for industrial production. (China now produces 6,000 kilos of cereal per hectare.) To achieve greater farm productivity, poor nations need capital investment, technological know-how, and improved infrastructure.

productivity: Output per unit of input—for example, output per labor-hour.

Analysis: Lack of capital, technology, and markets keeps farm productivity low.

Barry Barker/McGraw Hill

Institutional Reform

Clearly, poor nations need a lot more investment. But more resources alone may not suffice. To attract and keep capital, **a** *nation needs an institutional structure that promotes economic growth.*

Property Rights. Land, property, and contract rights have to be established before farmers will voluntarily improve their land or invest in agricultural technology. China saw how agricultural productivity jumped when it transformed government-run communal farms into local enterprises and privately managed farms, beginning in 1978. China is using the lessons of that experience to now extend ownership rights to farmers.

VALUE OF FARM OUTPUT PER WORKER (2020 U.S. dollars)

Country	Value
Burundi	$220
Madagascar	$310
Zimbabwe	$380
Uganda	$690
Bangladesh	$1,100
China	$4,000
United States	$100,000

FIGURE 21.3

Low Agricultural Productivity

Farmers in poor nations suffer from low productivity. They are handicapped by low education, inferior technology, primitive infrastructure, and a lack of machinery.

Source: The World Bank, *WDR2019 Data Set.*

Entrepreneurial Incentives. Unleashing the "animal spirits" of the marketplace is also critical. People *do* respond to incentives. If farmers see the potential for profit—and the opportunity to keep that profit—they will pursue productivity gains with more vigor. To encourage that response, governments need to assure the legitimacy of profits and their fair tax treatment. In 1992 the Chinese government acknowledged the role of profits and entrepreneurship in fostering economic advancement. Before then, successful entrepreneurs ran the risk of offending the government with conspicuous consumption that highlighted growing inequalities. The government even punished some entrepreneurs and confiscated their wealth. Once "profits" were legitimized, however, entrepreneurship and foreign investment accelerated, raising China's growth rate significantly.

Cuba stopped short of legitimizing private property and profits. Although Fidel Castro periodically permitted some private enterprises (e.g., family restaurants), he always withdrew that permission when entrepreneurial ventures succeeded. As a consequence, Cuba's economy stagnated for decades. Venezuela has recently moved further in that direction, expropriating and nationalizing private enterprises (see World View "Maduro: 'Bourgeois Parasites' Thwart Growth"), thereby discouraging private investment and entrepreneurship. In the first five years of the Maduro presidency, Venezuela's GDP contracted by more than 50 percent.

WORLD VIEW

MADURO: "BOURGEOIS PARASITES" THWART GROWTH

When he won a third presidential term in 2006, Hugo Chávez made his intentions clear. Venezuela, he said, is "heading toward socialism, and no one can prevent it." He embarked on a policy of nationalization, price controls, and a political takeover of Venezuela's central bank. Since then, the Venezuelan economy has stalled; factories, oil fields, and farms have shut down; inflation has soared; and food and energy shortages have become commonplace.

Chávez's successor, Nicolas Maduro, blames the nation's economic woes not on government policy but on the "bourgeois parasites" who have conspired to raise prices, hoard commodities, and strangle the economy. He ordered the nation's largest electronic retailer, Daka, to cut its prices in half and sent the military into its stores to enforce those price cuts. He urged Venezuelans to "leave nothing on the shelves, nothing in the warehouses" and threatened store managers with arrest if they interfered. Critics called the action "government-sanctioned looting." Maduro also levied fines and threatened jail sentences for General Motors executives who he accused of cutting back production and charging "exploitive" prices for new cars.

President Maduro's policies drove the Venezuelan economy into a downward spiral. Output shrank every year and inflation skyrocketed. In the wake of increasing popular protests and a disputed election, President Maduro in late 2019 agreed to relax some of his most anti-capitalism rhetoric and policies.

Source: News reports, September 2014 and January 2020.

CRITICAL ANALYSIS: By restricting private ownership and market freedom, governments curb the **entrepreneurship** and investment that may be essential for economic development.

Equity. What disturbed both Castro and Venezuelan President Chávez was the way capitalism intensified income inequalities. Entrepreneurs got rich while the mass of people remained poor. For Castro, the goal of equity was more important than the goal of efficiency. A nation where everyone was equally poor was preferred to a nation of haves and have-nots.

In many of today's poorest nations, policy interests are not so noble. A small elite often holds extraordinary political power and uses that power to protect its privileges. Greed

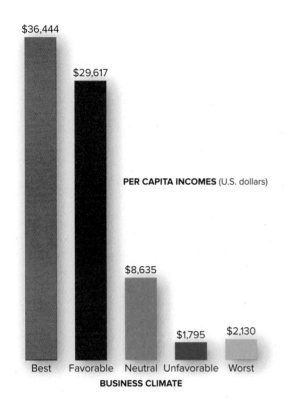

$36,444

$29,617

PER CAPITA INCOMES (U.S. dollars)

$8,635

$1,795 $2,130

Best   Favorable   Neutral Unfavorable Worst
BUSINESS CLIMATE

FIGURE 21.4

Business Climates Affect Growth

Nations that offer more secure property rights, less regulation, and lower taxes grow faster and enjoy higher per capita incomes.

Note: Business climate in 183 nations gauged by 50 measures of government tax, regulatory, and legal policy.

2011 Index of Economic Freedom, Washington, DC: The Heritage Foundation, p. 7, 2011.

restricts the flow of resources to the poorest segments of the population, leaving them to fend for themselves. These inequalities in power, wealth, and opportunity create inequality traps that restrain human capital development, capital investment, entrepreneurship, and ultimately economic growth.

Business Climate. To encourage capital investment and entrepreneurship, governments have to assure a secure and supportive business climate. Investors and business start-ups want to know what the rules of the game are and how they will be enforced. They also want assurances that contracts will be enforced and that debts can be collected. They want their property protected from crime and government corruption. They want minimal interference from government regulation and taxes.

As the annual surveys by the Heritage Foundation document, nations that offer a more receptive business climate grow at a faster pace. Figure 21.4 illustrates this connection. Notice that nations with the most pro-business climate (e.g., Hong Kong, Singapore, Iceland, the United States, and Denmark) enjoy living standards far superior to those in nations with hostile business climates (e.g., North Korea, Cuba, Congo, Sudan, Zimbabwe, and Myanmar). This is no accident; *pro-business climates encourage the capital investment, the entrepreneurship, and the human capital investment that drive economic growth.*

Unfortunately, some of the poorest nations still fail to provide a pro-business environment. Figure 21.5 illustrates how specific dimensions of the business climate differ across fast-growing nations (China) and perpetually poor ones (Cambodia and Kenya). A biannual survey of 26,000 international firms elicits their views of how different government policies restrain their investment decisions. Notice how China offers a more certain policy environment, less corruption, more secure property rights, and less crime. Given these business conditions, where would you invest?

The good news about the business climate is that it doesn't require huge investments to fix. It does require, however, a lot of political capital.

FIGURE 21.5

Investment Climate

International investors gravitate toward nations with business-friendly policies. Shown here are the percentages of international firms citing specific elements of the business climate that deter their investment in the named countries.

Source: The World Bank, *World Development Indicators 2006.*

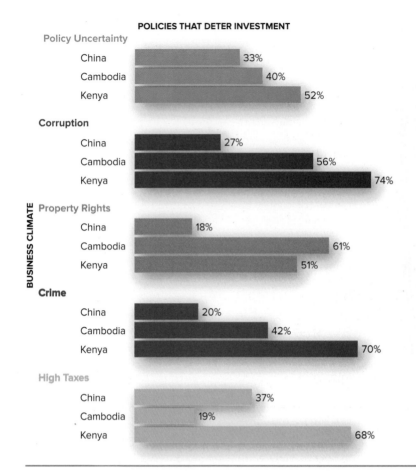

POLICIES THAT DETER INVESTMENT

Policy Uncertainty
China 33%
Cambodia 40%
Kenya 52%

Corruption
China 27%
Cambodia 56%
Kenya 74%

Property Rights
China 18%
Cambodia 61%
Kenya 51%

Crime
China 20%
Cambodia 42%
Kenya 70%

High Taxes
China 37%
Cambodia 19%
Kenya 68%

BUSINESS CLIMATE

World Trade

When it comes to political capital, poor nations have a complaint of their own. They say that rich nations lock them out of their most important markets—particularly agricultural export markets. Poor nations typically have a **comparative advantage** in the production of agricultural products. Their farm productivity may be low (see Figure 21.3), but their low labor costs keep their farm output competitive. They can't fully exploit that advantage in export markets, however. The United States, the European Union, and Japan heavily subsidize their own farmers. This keeps farm prices low in the rich nations, eliminating the cost advantage of farmers in poor nations. To further protect their own farmers from global competition, rich nations erect trade barriers to stem the inflow of Third World products. The United States, for example, enforces an **import quota** on foreign sugar. This trade barrier has fostered a high-cost, domestic beet sugar industry while denying poor nations the opportunity to sell more sugar and grow their economies faster.

Poor nations need export markets. Export sales generate the hard currency (dollars, euros, and yen) that is needed to purchase capital equipment in global markets. Export sales also allow farmers in poor nations to expand production, exploit economies of scale, and invest in improved technology. Ironically, *trade barriers in rich nations impede poor nations from pursuing the agricultural development that is a **prerequisite** for growth.* The latest round of multilateral trade negotiations dragged on forever because of the resistance of rich nations to opening their agricultural markets. Poor nations plead that "trade, not aid" is their surest path to economic growth.

comparative advantage: The ability of a country to produce a specific good at a lower opportunity cost than its trading partners.

import quota: A limit on the quantity of a good that may be imported in a given time period.

DECISIONS FOR TOMORROW

Can Entrepreneurship Alleviate Poverty?

The traditional approach to economic development emphasizes the potential for government policy to reallocate resources and increase capital investment. External financing of capital investment was always at or near the top of the policy agenda (see World View "Jeffrey Sachs: Big Money, Big Plans"). This approach has been criticized for neglecting the power of people and markets.

Analysis: Markets exist but struggle in poor nations.
Lissa Harrison

One of the most influential critics is the Peruvian economist Hernando de Soto. When he returned to his native Peru after years of commercial success in Europe, he was struck by the dichotomy in his country. The "official" economy was mired in bureaucratic red tape and stagnant. Most of the vitality of the Peruvian economy was contained in the unofficial "underground" economy. The underground economy included trade in drugs but was overwhelmingly oriented to meeting the everyday demands of Peruvian consumers and households. The underground economy wasn't hidden from view; it flourished on the streets, in outdoor markets, and in transport services. The only thing that forced this thriving economy underground was the failure of the government to recognize it and give it legitimate status. Government restrictions on prices, business activities, finance, and trade—a slew of inequality traps—forced entrepreneurs to operate "underground."

De Soto concluded that countries like Peru could grow more quickly if governments encouraged rather than suppressed these entrepreneurial resources. In his best-selling book *The Other Path,* he urged poor countries to refocus their development policies. This "other path" entails improving the business climate by

- Reducing bureaucratic barriers to free enterprise.
- Spreading private ownership.
- Developing and enforcing legal safeguards for property, income, and wealth.
- Developing infrastructure that facilitates business activity.

Muhammad Yunus's "microloans" would also fit comfortably on this other path.

De Soto's book has been translated into several languages and has encouraged market-oriented reforms in Peru, Argentina, Mexico, Russia, Vietnam, and elsewhere. In India the government is drastically reducing both regulation and taxes to pursue De Soto's other path. The basic message of his other path is that poor nations should exploit the one resource that is abundant in even the poorest countries—entrepreneurship.

SUMMARY

- Definitions of "poverty" are culturally based. Poverty in the United States is defined largely in *relative* terms, whereas global poverty is tied more to *absolute* levels of subsistence. **LO21-1**

- About 11 percent of the U.S. population (more than 37 million people) is officially counted as poor. Poor people in America suffer from *relative* deprivation, not *absolute* deprivation, as in global poverty. **LO21-1**

- Global poverty thresholds are about one-tenth of U.S. standards. "Extreme" poverty is defined as less than $1.90 per day per person; "severe" poverty is less than $3.10 per day (inflation adjusted). **LO21-1**
- More than 700 million people around the world are in extreme poverty; 2 billion are in severe poverty. In low-income nations, global poverty rates are as high as 70–90 percent. **LO21-2**
- The United Nations' Millennium Poverty Goal is to eliminate severe poverty by 2030. **LO21-3**
- Redistribution of incomes *within* poor nations doesn't have much potential for reducing poverty, given their low *average* incomes. *Across*-nation redistributions (e.g., foreign aid) can make a small dent, however. **LO21-3**

- Economic growth is the key to global poverty reduction. Many poor nations are held back by undeveloped human capital, primitive infrastructure, and subsistence agriculture. To grow more quickly, they need to meet basic human needs (health and education), increase agricultural productivity, and encourage investment. **LO21-3**
- To move into sustained economic growth, poor nations need capital investment and institutional reforms that promote both equity and entrepreneurship. **LO21-3**
- Poor nations also need "trade, not aid"—that is, access to rich nation markets, particularly in farm products. **LO21-3**

Key Terms

poverty threshold (U.S.)	UN and World Bank Poverty Goal	investment rate
poverty rate	Millennium Aid Goal	microfinance
in-kind transfers	economic growth	productivity
extreme poverty (world)	human capital	comparative advantage
severe poverty (world)	inequality trap	import quota

Questions for Discussion

1. Why should Americans care about extreme poverty in Haiti, Ethiopia, or Bangladesh? **LO21-2**
2. If you had only $18 to spend per day (the U.S. poverty threshold), how would you spend it? What if you had only $1.90 a day (the World Bank "extreme poverty" threshold)? **LO21-1**
3. If a poor nation must choose between building an airport, some schools, or a steel plant, which one should it choose? Why? **LO21-3**
4. How do more children per family either restrain or expand income-earning potential? **LO21-3**
5. Are property rights a prerequisite for economic growth? Explain. **LO21-3**
6. How do unequal rights for women affect economic growth? **LO21-3**
7. How does microfinance alter prospects for economic growth? The distribution of political power? **LO21-3**
8. Why is the agricultural share of total output so high in poor nations? (See Figure 21.2.) **LO21-3**
9. Would you invest in Cambodia or Kenya on the basis of the information in Figure 21.5? **LO21-3**
10. Why do economists put so much emphasis on entrepreneurship? How can poor nations encourage it? **LO21-3**
11. If economic growth reduced poverty but widened inequalities, would it still be desirable? **LO21-3**

PROBLEMS FOR CHAPTER 21

LO21-1 1. The World Bank's threshold for "extreme" poverty is $1.90 per person per day.
   (*a*) How much *annual* income does this imply for a family of four?
   (*b*) What portion of the official U.S. poverty threshold (roughly $26,000 for a family of four) is met by the World Bank's measure?

LO21-2 2. There are 2 billion people in "severe" poverty with less than $3.10 of income per day.
   (*a*) What is the maximum *combined* income of this "severely" poor population?
   (*b*) What percentage of the world's *total* income (roughly $90 trillion) does this represent?

LO21-2 3. In Mozambique,
   (*a*) What percentage of total output is received by the richest 10 percent of households? (See World View "Glaring Inequalities.")
   (*b*) How much output did this share amount to in 2018, when Mozambique's GDP was $14 billion?
   (*c*) With a total population of 30 million, what was the implied per capita income of
      (*i*) The richest 10 percent of the population?
      (*ii*) The remaining 90 percent?

LO21-3 4. (*a*) How much foreign aid did the United States provide in 2018? (See Table 21.2.)
   (*b*) How much more is required to satisfy the UN's Millennium Aid Goal if U.S. GDP was $20 trillion?

LO21-3 5. If the 24 industrialized nations were to satisfy the UN's Millennium Aid Goal, how much *more* foreign aid would they give annually? (See Table 21.2.)

LO21-3 6. According to Table 21.3, how many years will it take for per capita GDP to double in
   (*a*) China?
   (*b*) Madagascar?
   (*c*) Burundi?

LO21-3 7. According to World View "The Way We Give,"
   (*a*) How much money is spent annually to combat baldness?
   (*b*) How much medical care would that money buy for each child who dies from malaria each year?

LO21-3 8. Foreign aid to poor nations amounted to $20 per year per person. What percentage did this aid cover of
   (*a*) The extreme poverty annual budget?
   (*b*) The severe poverty annual budget?

LO21-3 9. *Decisions for Tomorrow:* Identify the four key paths identified by De Soto to improve business climate in less-developed countries.

Design Credit: Shutterstock

GLOSSARY

A

absolute advantage: The ability of a country to produce a specific good with fewer resources (per unit of output) than other countries.

acreage set-aside: Land withdrawn from production as part of policy to increase crop prices.

AD excess: The amount by which aggregate demand must be reduced to achieve full-employment equilibrium after allowing for price-level changes.

AD shortfall: The amount of additional aggregate demand needed to achieve full employment after allowing for price-level changes.

adjustable-rate mortgage (ARM): A mortgage (home loan) that adjusts the nominal interest rate to changing rates of inflation.

aggregate demand (AD): The total quantity of output (real GDP) demanded at alternative price levels in a given time period, *ceteris paribus*.

aggregate expenditure: The rate of total expenditure desired at alternative levels of income, *ceteris paribus*.

aggregate supply (AS): The total quantity of output (real GDP) producers are willing and able to supply at alternative price levels in a given time period, *ceteris paribus*.

antitrust: Government intervention to alter market structure or prevent abuse of market power.

appreciation: A rise in the price of one currency relative to another.

arithmetic growth: An increase in quantity by a constant amount each year.

asset: Anything having exchange value in the marketplace; wealth.

automatic stabilizer: Federal expenditure or revenue item that automatically responds countercyclically to changes in national income, like unemployment benefits and income taxes.

autonomous consumption: Consumer spending not dependent on current income.

average fixed cost (AFC): Total fixed cost divided by the quantity produced in a given time period.

average propensity to consume (APC): Total consumption in a given period divided by total disposable income.

average total cost (ATC): Total cost divided by the quantity produced in a given time period.

average variable cost (AVC): Total variable cost divided by the quantity produced in a given time period.

B

balance of payments: A summary record of a country's international economic transactions in a given period of time.

balance-of-payments deficit: An excess demand for foreign currency at current exchange rates.

balance-of-payments surplus: An excess demand for domestic currency at current exchange rates.

bank reserves: Assets held by a bank to fulfill its deposit obligations.

barriers to entry: Obstacles such as patents that make it difficult or impossible for would-be producers to enter a particular market.

barter: The direct exchange of one good for another, without the use of money.

base year: The year used for comparative analysis; the basis for indexing price changes.

bilateral monopoly: A market with only one buyer (a monopsonist) and one seller (a monopolist).

bond: A certificate acknowledging a debt and the amount of interest to be paid each year until repayment; an IOU.

bracket creep: The movement of taxpayers into higher tax brackets (rates) as nominal incomes grow.

breakeven level of income: The income level at which welfare eligibility ceases.

budget constraint: A line depicting all combinations of goods that are affordable with a given income and given prices.

budget deficit: The amount by which government spending exceeds government revenue in a given time period.

budget surplus: An excess of government revenues over government expenditures in a given time period.

business cycle: Alternating periods of economic growth and contraction.

C

capital: Final goods produced for use in the production of other goods, such as equipment and structures.

capital gain: An increase in the market value of an asset.

capital gains tax: A tax levied on the profit from the sale of property.

capital-intensive: Production processes that use a high ratio of capital to labor inputs.

capitalization: Market value of a publicly traded company; equals number of shares multiplied by the price of the share.

cartel: A group of firms with an explicit, formal agreement to fix prices and output shares in a particular market.

cash transfers: Income transfers that entail direct cash payments to recipients, such as Social Security, welfare, and unemployment benefits.

ceteris paribus: The assumption of nothing else changing.

closed economy: A nation that doesn't engage in international trade.

collective bargaining: Direct negotiations between employers and unions to determine labor market outcomes.

comparative advantage: The ability of a country to produce a specific good at a lower opportunity cost than its trading partners.

competitive firm: A firm without market power, with no ability to alter the market price of the goods it produces.

competitive market: A market in which no buyer or seller has market power.

complementary goods: Goods frequently consumed in combination; when the price of good *x* rises, the demand for good *y* falls, *ceteris paribus*.

concentration ratio: The proportion of total industry output produced by the largest firms (usually the four largest).

constant returns to scale: Increases in plant size do not affect minimum average cost; minimum per-unit costs are identical for small plants and large plants.

Consumer Price Index (CPI): A measure (index) of changes in the average price of consumer goods and services.

consumer surplus: The difference between the maximum price a person is willing to pay and the price paid.

consumption: Expenditure by consumers on final goods and services.

consumption function: A mathematical relationship indicating the rate of desired consumer spending at various income levels.

consumption possibilities: The alternative combinations of goods and services that a country could consume in a given time period.

contestable market: An imperfectly competitive industry subject to potential entry if prices or profits increase.

core inflation rate: Changes in the CPI, excluding food and energy prices.

corporate stock: Shares of ownership in a corporation.

corporation: A business organization having a continuous existence independent of its members (owners) and power and liabilities distinct from those of its members.

cost efficiency: The amount of output associated with an additional dollar spent on input; the MPP of an input divided by its price (cost).

cost-of-living adjustment (COLA): Automatic adjustments of nominal income to the rate of inflation.

coupon rate: Interest rate set for a bond at time of issuance.

cross-price elasticity of demand: Percentage change in the quantity demanded of X divided by the percentage change in the price of Y.

cross-subsidization: Use of high prices and profits on one product to subsidize low prices on another product.

crowdfunding: The financing of a project through individual contributions from a large number of people, typically via an Internet platform.

crowdfunding: An internet-based method of raising funds from a large number of people.

crowding in: An increase in private sector borrowing (and spending) caused by decreased government borrowing.

crowding out: A reduction in private sector borrowing (and spending) caused by increased government borrowing.

current yield: The rate of return on a bond; the annual interest payment divided by the bond's price.

cyclical deficit: That portion of the budget deficit attributable to unemployment or inflation.

cyclical unemployment: Unemployment attributable to a lack of job vacancies—that is, to an inadequate level of aggregate demand.

D

debt ceiling: An explicit, legislated limit on the amount of outstanding national debt.

debt service: The interest required to be paid each year on outstanding debt.

default: Failure to make scheduled payments of interest or principal on a bond.

deficit ceiling: An explicit, legislated limitation on the size of the budget deficit.

deficit spending: The use of borrowed funds to finance government expenditures that exceed tax revenues.

deflation: A decrease in the average level of prices of goods and services.

demand: The willingness and ability to buy specific quantities of a good at alternative prices in a given time period, *ceteris paribus*.

demand curve: A curve describing the quantities of a good a consumer is willing and able

to buy at alternative prices in a given time period, *ceteris paribus*.

demand for labor: The quantities of labor employers are willing and able to hire at alternative wage rates in a given time period, *ceteris paribus*.

demand for money: The quantities of money people are willing and able to hold at alternative interest rates, *ceteris paribus*.

demand schedule: A table showing the quantities of a good a consumer is willing and able to buy at alternative prices in a given time period, *ceteris paribus*.

demand-pull inflation: An increase in the price level initiated by excessive aggregate demand.

deposit creation: The creation of transactions deposits by bank lending.

depreciation: The consumption of capital in the production process; the wearing out of plant and equipment.

depreciation (currency): A fall in the price of one currency relative to another.

derived demand: The demand for labor and other factors of production results from (depends on) the demand for final goods and services produced by these factors.

devaluation: An abrupt depreciation of a currency whose value was fixed or managed by the government.

discount rate: The rate of interest the Federal Reserve charges for lending reserves to private banks.

discounting: Federal Reserve lending of reserves to private banks.

discouraged worker: An individual who isn't actively seeking employment but would look for or accept a job if one were available.

discretionary fiscal spending: Those elements of the federal budget not determined by past legislative or executive commitments.

disposable income (DI): After-tax income of households; personal income less personal taxes.

dissaving: Consumption expenditure in excess of disposable income; a negative saving flow.

dividend: Amount of corporate profits paid out for each share of stock.

dumping: The sale of goods in export markets at prices below domestic prices.

E

economic cost: The value of all resources used to produce a good or service; opportunity cost.

economic growth: An increase in output (real GDP); an expansion of production possibilities.

economic profit: The difference between total revenues and total economic costs.

economics: The study of how best to allocate scarce resources among competing uses.

economies of scale: Reductions in minimum average costs that come about through increases in the size (scale) of plant and equipment.

effective tax rate: Taxes paid divided by total (gross) income.

efficiency: Maximum output of a good from the resources used in production.

efficiency decision: The choice of a production process for any given rate of output.

elasticity of labor supply: The percentage change in the quantity of labor supplied divided by the percentage change in wage rate.

embargo: A prohibition on exports or imports.

emission charge: A fee imposed on polluters, based on the quantity of pollution.

employment rate: The percentage of the adult population that is employed.

employment targeting: The use of an unemployment-rate threshold (6.5 percent) to signal the need for monetary stimulus.

entrepreneurship: The assembling of resources to produce new or improved products and technologies.

equation of exchange: Money supply (M) times velocity of circulation (V) equals level of aggregate spending ($P \times Q$).

equilibrium (macro): The combination of price level and real output that is compatible with both aggregate demand and aggregate supply.

equilibrium GDP: The value of total output (real GDP) produced at macro equilibrium (AS = AD).

equilibrium price: The price at which the quantity of a good demanded in a given time period equals the quantity supplied.

equilibrium rate of interest: The interest rate at which the quantity of money demanded in a given time period equals the quantity of money supplied.

equilibrium wage: The wage rate at which the quantity of labor supplied in a given time period equals the quantity of labor demanded.

excess reserves: Bank reserves in excess of required reserves.

exchange rate: The price of one country's currency expressed in terms of another's; the domestic price of a foreign currency.

expected value: The probable value of a future payment, including the risk of nonpayment.

expenditure equilibrium: The rate of output at which desired spending equals the value of output.

explicit costs: A payment made for the use of a resource.

exports: Goods and services sold to foreign buyers.

external costs: Costs of a market activity borne by a third party; the difference between the social and private costs of a market activity.

external debt: U.S. government debt (Treasury bonds) held by foreign households and institutions.

externalities: Costs (or benefits) of a market activity borne by a third party; the difference between the social and private costs (benefits) of a market activity.

extreme poverty (world): World Bank income standard of less than $1.90 per day per person (inflation adjusted).

F

factor market: Any place where factors of production (e.g., land, labor, capital) are bought and sold.

factors of production: Resource inputs used to produce goods and services, e.g., land, labor, capital, entrepreneurship.

federal funds rate: The interest rate for interbank reserve loans.

financial intermediary: Institution (e.g., a bank or the stock market) that makes savings available to dissavers (e.g., investors).

fine-tuning: Adjustments in economic policy designed to counteract small changes in economic outcomes; continuous responses to changing economic conditions.

fiscal policy: The use of government taxes and spending to alter macroeconomic outcomes.

fiscal restraint: Tax hikes or spending cuts intended to reduce (shift) aggregate demand.

fiscal stimulus: Tax cuts or spending hikes intended to increase (shift) aggregate demand.

fiscal year (FY): The 12-month period used for accounting purposes; begins October 1 for the federal government.

fixed costs: Costs of production that don't change when the rate of output is altered, such as the cost of basic plants and equipment.

flexible exchange rates: A system in which exchange rates are permitted to vary with market supply-and-demand conditions; floating exchange rates.

foreign exchange markets: Places where foreign currencies are bought and sold.

foreign exchange reserves: Holdings of foreign currencies by official government agencies, usually the central bank or treasury.

free rider: An individual who reaps direct benefits from someone else's purchase (consumption) of a public good.

frictional unemployment: Brief periods of unemployment experienced by people moving between jobs or into the labor market.

full employment: The lowest rate of unemployment compatible with price stability, variously estimated at between 4 percent and 6 percent unemployment.

full-employment GDP: The value of total market output (real GDP) produced at full employment.

G

game theory: The study of decision making in situations where strategic interaction (moves and countermoves) occurs between rivals.

GDP deflator: A price index that refers to all goods and services included in GDP.

GDP per capita: Total GDP divided by total population; average GDP.

geometric growth: An increase in quantity by a constant proportion each year.

Gini coefficient: A mathematical summary of inequality based on the Lorenz curve.

gold reserves: Stocks of gold held by a government to purchase foreign exchange.

gold standard: An agreement by countries to fix the price of their currencies in terms of gold; a mechanism for fixing exchange rates.

government failure: Government intervention that fails to improve economic outcomes.

gross business saving: Depreciation allowances and retained earnings.

gross domestic product (GDP): The total market value of all final goods and services produced within a nation's borders in a given time period.

gross investment: Total investment expenditure in a given time period.

growth rate: Percentage change in real output from one period to another.

growth recession: A period during which real GDP grows but at a rate below the long-term trend of 3 percent.

H

Herfindahl-Hirshman Index (HHI): Measure of industry concentration that accounts for number of firms and size of each.

horizontal equity: Principle that people with equal incomes should pay equal taxes.

human capital: The knowledge and skills possessed by the workforce.

hyperinflation: Inflation rate in excess of 200 percent, lasting at least one year.

I

implicit cost: The value of resources used, for which no direct payment is made.

import quota: A limit on the quantity of a good that may be imported in a given time period.

imports: Goods and services purchased from international sources.

in-kind income: Goods and services received directly, without payment, in a market transaction.

in-kind transfers: Direct transfers of goods and services rather than cash, such as food stamps, Medicaid benefits, and housing subsidies.

income effect of higher wages: An increased wage rate allows a person to reduce hours worked without losing income.

income elasticity of demand: Percentage change in quantity demanded divided by percentage change in income.

income quintile: One-fifth of the population, rank-ordered by income (e.g., top fifth).

income share: The proportion of total income received by a particular group.

income transfers: Payments to individuals for which no current goods or services are exchanged, such as Social Security, welfare, and unemployment benefits.

indifference curve: A curve depicting alternative combinations of goods that yield equal satisfaction.

indifference map: The set of indifference curves that depicts all possible levels of utility attainable from various combinations of goods.

inequality trap: Institutional barriers that impede human and physical capital investment, particularly by the poorest segments of society.

inferior good: Goods for which demand decreases when income rises.

inflation: An increase in the average level of prices of goods and services.

inflation rate: The annual percentage rate of increase in the average price level; (Price $\text{Level}_{\text{Year 2}} - \text{Price Level}_{\text{Year 1}})/\text{Price Level}_{\text{Year 1}}$.

inflation targeting: The use of an inflation ceiling ("target") to signal the need for monetary-policy adjustments.

inflationary flashpoint: The rate of output at which inflationary pressures intensify; the point on the AS curve where slope increases sharply.

inflationary gap: The amount by which aggregate spending at full employment exceeds full-employment output.

inflationary GDP gap: The amount by which equilibrium GDP exceeds full-employment GDP.

infrastructure: The transportation, communications, education, judicial, and other institutional systems that facilitate market exchanges.

initial public offering (IPO): The first issuance (sale) to the general public of stock in a corporation.

injection: An addition of spending to the circular flow of income.

interest rate: The price paid for the use of money.

intermediate goods: Goods or services purchased for use as input in the production of final goods or in services.

internal debt: U.S. government debt (Treasury bonds) held by U.S. households and institutions.

investment: Expenditures on (production of) new plants, equipment, and structures (capital) in a given time period, plus changes in business inventories.

investment decision: The decision to build, buy, or lease plants and equipment; to enter or exit an industry.

investment rate: The percentage of total output (GDP) allocated to the production of new plants, equipment, and structures.

item weight: The percentage of total expenditure spent on a specific product; used to compute inflation indexes.

L

labor force: All persons over age 16 who are either working for pay or actively seeking paid employment.

labor force participation rate: The percentage of the working-age population working or seeking employment.

labor productivity: Amount of output produced by a worker in a given period of time; output per hour (or day, etc.).

labor supply: The willingness and ability to work specific amounts of time at alternative wage rates in a given time period, *ceteris paribus*.

laissez faire: The doctrine of "leave it alone," of nonintervention by government in the market mechanism.

law of demand: The quantity of a good demanded in a given time period increases as its price falls, *ceteris paribus*.

law of diminishing marginal utility: The marginal utility of a good declines as more of it is consumed in a given time period.

law of diminishing returns: The marginal physical product of a variable input declines as more of it is employed with a given quantity of other (fixed) inputs.

law of supply: The quantity of a good supplied in a given time period increases as its price increases, *ceteris paribus*.

leakage: Income not spent directly on domestic output but instead diverted from the circular flow—for example, saving, imports, taxes.

liability: An obligation to make future payment; debt.

liquidity: The ability of an asset to be converted into cash.

liquidity trap: The portion of the money demand curve that is horizontal; people are willing to hold unlimited amounts of money at some (low) interest rate.

loan rate: The implicit price paid by the government for surplus crops taken as collateral for loans to farmers.

long run: A period of time long enough for all inputs to be varied (no fixed costs).

long-run competitive equilibrium: $p = \text{MC} = $ minimum ATC.

Lorenz curve: A graphic illustration of the cumulative size distribution of income; contrasts complete equality with the actual distribution of income.

M

macroeconomics: The study of aggregate economic behavior, of the economy as a whole.

managed exchange rates: A system in which governments intervene in foreign exchange markets to limit but not eliminate exchange rate fluctuations; "dirty floats."

marginal cost (MC): The increase in total cost associated with a one-unit increase in production.

marginal cost pricing: The offer (supply) of goods at prices equal to their marginal cost.

marginal factor cost (MFC): The change in total costs that results from a one-unit increase in the quantity of a factor employed.

marginal physical product (MPP): The change in total output associated with one additional unit of input.

marginal propensity to consume (MPC): The fraction of each additional (marginal) dollar of disposable income spent on consumption; the change in consumption divided by the change in disposable income.

marginal propensity to save (MPS): The fraction of each additional (marginal) dollar of disposable income not spent on consumption; $1 - \text{MPC}$.

marginal rate of substitution: The rate at which a consumer is willing to exchange one good for another; the relative marginal utilities of two goods.

marginal revenue (MR): The change in total revenue that results from a one-unit increase in the quantity sold.

marginal revenue product (MRP): The change in total revenue associated with one additional unit of input.

marginal tax rate: The tax rate imposed on the last (marginal) dollar of income.

marginal utility: The change in total utility obtained by consuming one additional (marginal) unit of a good or service.

marginal wage: The change in total wages paid associated with a one-unit increase in the quantity of labor employed.

market demand: The total quantities of a good or service people are willing and able to buy at alternative prices in a given time period; the sum of individual demands.

market failure: An imperfection in the market mechanism that prevents optimal outcomes.

market mechanism: The use of market prices and sales to signal desired outputs (or resource allocations).

market power: The ability to alter the market price of a good or service.

market share: The percentage of total market output produced by a single firm.

market shortage: The amount by which the quantity demanded exceeds the quantity supplied at a given price; excess demand.

market structure: The number and relative size of firms in an industry.

market supply: The total quantities of a good that sellers are willing and able to sell at alternative prices in a given time period, *ceteris paribus*.

market supply of labor: The total quantity of labor that workers are willing and able to supply at alternative wage rates in a given time period, *ceteris paribus*.

market surplus: The amount by which the quantity supplied exceeds the quantity demanded at a given price; excess supply.

merit good: A good or service society deems everyone is entitled to some minimal quantity of.

microeconomics: The study of individual behavior in the economy, of the components of the larger economy.

microfinance: The granting of small ("micro"), unsecured loans to small businesses and entrepreneurs.

Millennium Aid Goal: United Nations goal of raising foreign aid levels to 0.7 percent of donor-country GDP.

misery index: The sum of inflation and unemployment rates.

mixed economy: An economy that uses both market signals and government directives to allocate goods and resources.

monetary policy: The use of money and credit controls to influence macroeconomic outcomes.

money: Anything generally accepted as a medium of exchange.

money illusion: The use of nominal dollars rather than real dollars to gauge changes in one's income or wealth.

money multiplier: The number of deposit (loan) dollars that the banking system can create from $1 of excess reserves; equal to 1 ÷ required reserve ratio.

money supply (M1): Currency held by the public, plus balances in transactions accounts.

money supply (M2): M1 plus balances in most savings accounts and money market funds.

monopolistic competition: A market in which many firms produce similar goods or services but each maintains some independent control of its own price.

monopoly: A firm that produces the entire market supply of a particular good or service.

monopsony: A market in which there's only one buyer.

moral hazard: An incentive to engage in undesirable behavior.

multiplier: The multiple by which an initial change in aggregate spending will alter total expenditure after an infinite number of spending cycles; $1/(1 - MPC)$.

N

national debt: Accumulated debt of the federal government.

national income (NI): Total income earned by current factors of production: GDP less depreciation and indirect business taxes, plus net foreign factor income.

national income accounting: The measurement of aggregate economic activity, particularly national income and its components.

natural monopoly: An industry in which one firm can achieve economies of scale over the entire range of market supply.

natural rate of unemployment: The long-term rate of unemployment determined by structural forces in labor and product markets.

net domestic product (NDP): GDP less depreciation.

net exports: The value of exports minus the value of imports: $(X - M)$.

net investment: Gross investment less depreciation.

nominal GDP: The value of final output produced in a given period, measured in the prices of that period (current prices).

nominal income: The amount of money income received in a given time period, measured in current dollars.

nominal tax rate: Taxes paid divided by taxable income.

normal good: Good for which demand increases when income rises.

normal profit: The opportunity cost of capital; zero economic profit.

O

Okun's law: One percent more unemployment is estimated to equal 2 percent less output.

oligopolist: One of the dominant firms in an oligopoly.

oligopoly: A market in which a few firms produce all or most of the market supply of a particular good or service.

open economy: A nation that engages in international trade.

open market operations: Federal Reserve purchases and sales of government bonds for the purpose of altering bank reserves.

opportunity cost: The most desired goods or services that are forgone in order to obtain something else.

opportunity wage: The highest wage an individual would earn in his or her best alternative job.

optimal consumption: The mix of consumer purchases that maximizes the utility attainable from available income.

optimal mix of output: The most desirable combination of output attainable with existing resources, technology, and social values.

optimal rate of pollution: The rate of pollution that occurs when the marginal social benefit of pollution control equals its marginal social cost.

outsourcing: The relocation of production to foreign countries.

P

par value: The face value of a bond; the amount to be repaid when the bond is due.

parity: The relative price of farm products in the period 1910-1914.

payoff matrix: A table showing the risks and rewards of alternative decision options.

per capita GDP: The dollar value of GDP divided by total population; average GDP.

perfect competition: A market in which no buyer or seller has market power.

personal income (PI): Income received by households before payment of personal taxes.

Phillips curve: A historical (inverse) relationship between the rate of unemployment and the rate of inflation; commonly expresses a trade-off between the two.

portfolio decision: The choice of how (where) to hold idle funds.

poverty gap: The shortfall between actual income and the poverty threshold.

poverty rate: Percentage of the population counted as poor.

poverty threshold (U.S.): Annual income of less than $26,200 for a family of 4 (2020).

precautionary demand for money: Money held for unexpected market transactions or for emergencies.

predatory pricing: Temporary price reductions designed to alter market shares or drive out competition.

present discounted value (PDV): The value today of future payments, adjusted for interest accrual.

price ceiling: An upper limit imposed on the price of a good.

price discrimination: The sale of an individual good at different prices to different consumers.

price elasticity of demand: The percentage change in quantity demanded divided by the percentage change in price.

price elasticity of supply: The percentage change in quantity supplied divided by the percentage change in price.

price floor: Lower limit set for the price of a good.

price leadership: An oligopolistic pricing pattern that allows one firm to establish the (market) price for all firms in the industry.

price stability: The absence of significant changes in the average price level; officially defined as a rate of inflation of less than 3 percent.

price-fixing: Explicit agreements among producers regarding the price(s) at which a good is to be sold.

price/earnings (P/E) ratio: The price of a stock share divided by earnings (profit) per share.

private costs: The costs of an economic activity directly borne by the immediate producer or consumer (excluding externalities).

private good: A good or service whose consumption by one person excludes consumption by others.

product differentiation: Features that make one product appear different from competing products in the same market.

product market: Any place where finished goods and services (products) are bought and sold.

production decision: The selection of the short-run rate of output (with existing plants and equipment).

production function: A technological relationship expressing the maximum quantity of a good attainable from different combinations of factor inputs.

production possibilities: The alternative combinations of final goods and services that could be produced in a given period with all available resources and technology.

production process: A specific combination of resources used to produce a good or service.

productivity: Output per unit of input—for example, output per labor-hour.

profit: The difference between total revenue and total cost.

profit per unit: Total profit divided by the quantity produced in a given time period; price minus average total cost.

profit-maximization rule: Produce at that rate of output where marginal revenue equals marginal cost.

progressive tax: A tax system in which tax rates rise as incomes rise.

proportional tax: A tax that levies the same rate on every dollar of income.

public choice: Theory of public sector behavior emphasizing rational self-interest of decision makers and voters.

public good: A good or service whose consumption by one person does not exclude consumption by others.

Q

quota: A limit on the quantity of a good that may be imported in a given time period.

R

rational expectations: Hypothesis that people's spending decisions are based on all available information, including the anticipated effects of government intervention.

real GDP: The value of final output produced in a given period, adjusted for changing prices.

real income: Income in constant dollars; nominal income adjusted for inflation.

real interest rate: The nominal interest rate minus the anticipated inflation rate.

recession: A decline in total output (real GDP) for two or more consecutive quarters.

recessionary gap: The amount by which aggregate spending at full employment falls short of full-employment output.

recessionary GDP gap: The amount by which equilibrium GDP falls short of full-employment GDP.

reference price: Government-guaranteed price floor for specific agricultural commodities.

refinancing: The issuance of new debt in payment of debt issued earlier.

regressive tax: A tax system in which tax rates fall as incomes rise.

regulation: Government intervention to alter the behavior of firms—for example, in pricing, output, or advertising.

relative price: The price of one good in comparison with the price of other goods.

required reserves: The minimum amount of reserves a bank is required to hold; equal to required reserve ratio times transactions deposits.

reserve ratio: The ratio of a bank's reserves to its total transactions deposits.

retained earnings: Amount of corporate profits not paid out in dividends.

risk premium: The difference in rates of return on risky (uncertain) and safe (certain) investments.

S

saving: That part of disposable income not spent on current consumption; disposable income less consumption.

Say's law: Supply creates its own demand.

scarcity: Lack of enough resources to satisfy all desired uses of those resources.

seasonal unemployment: Unemployment due to seasonal changes in employment or labor supply.

severe poverty (world): World Bank income standard of $3.10 per day per person (inflation adjusted).

shift in demand: A change in the quantity demanded at any (every) price.

short run: The period in which the quantity (and quality) of some inputs can't be changed.

short-run competitive equilibrium: $p = \text{MC}$.

shutdown point: The rate of output where price equals minimum AVC.

size distribution of income: The way total personal income is divided up among households or income classes.

social costs: The full resource costs of an economic activity, including externalities.

social insurance programs: Event-conditioned income transfers intended to reduce the costs of specific problems, such as Social Security and unemployment insurance.

speculative demand for money: Money held for speculative purposes, for later financial opportunities.

stagflation: The simultaneous occurrence of substantial unemployment and inflation.

structural deficit: Federal revenues at full employment minus expenditures at full employment under prevailing fiscal policy.

structural unemployment: Unemployment caused by a mismatch between the skills (or location) of job seekers and the requirements (or location) of available jobs.

substitute goods: Goods that substitute for each other; when the price of good x rises, the demand for good y increases, *ceteris paribus.*

substitution effect of higher wages: An increased wage rate encourages people to work more hours (to substitute labor for leisure).

supply: The ability and willingness to sell (produce) specific quantities of a good at alternative prices in a given time period, *ceteris paribus.*

supply curve: A curve describing the quantities of a good a producer is willing and able to sell (produce) at alternative prices in a given time period, *ceteris paribus.*

supply-side policy: The use of tax incentives, (de)regulation, and other mechanisms to increase the ability and willingness to produce goods and services.

T

T-accounts: The accounting ledgers used by banks to track assets and liabilities.

target efficiency: The percentage of income transfers that go to the intended recipients and purposes.

tariff: A tax (duty) imposed on imported goods.

tax base: The amount of income or property directly subject to nominal tax rates.

tax elasticity of labor supply: The percentage change in quantity of labor supplied divided by the percentage change in tax rates.

tax elasticity of supply: The percentage change in quantity supplied divided by the percentage change in tax rates.

tax incidence: Distribution of the real burden of a tax.

tax rebate: A lump-sum refund of taxes paid.

terms of trade: The rate at which goods are exchanged; the amount of good A given up for good B in trade.

total cost: The market value of all resources used to produce a good or service.

total revenue: The price of a product multiplied by the quantity sold in a given time period: $p \times q$.

total utility: The amount of satisfaction obtained from entire consumption of a product.

trade deficit: The amount by which the value of imports exceeds the value of exports in a given time period (negative net exports).

trade surplus: The amount by which the value of exports exceeds the value of imports in a given time period (positive net exports).

transactions account: A bank account that permits direct payment to a third party—for example, with a check or debit card.

transactions demand for money: Money held for the purpose of making everyday market purchases.

transfer payments: Payments to individuals for which no current goods or services are exchanged, like Social Security, welfare, and unemployment benefits.

Treasury bonds: Promissory notes (IOUs) issued by the U.S. Treasury.

U

UN and World Bank Poverty Goal: UN goal of eliminating extreme poverty by 2030.

underemployment: People seeking full-time paid employment who work only part-time or are employed at jobs below their capability.

unemployment: The inability of labor force participants to find jobs.

unemployment rate: The proportion of the labor force that is unemployed.

union shop: An employment setting in which all workers must join the union within 30 days after being employed.

unionization rate: The percentage of the labor force belonging to a union.

unit labor cost: Hourly wage rate divided by output per labor-hour.

utility: The pleasure or satisfaction obtained from a good or service.

V

value added: The increase in the market value of a product that takes place at each stage of the production process.

variable costs: Costs of production that change when the rate of output is altered, such as labor and material costs.

velocity of money (V): The number of times per year, on average, that a dollar is used to purchase final goods and services; $PQ \div M$.

vertical equity: Principle that people with higher incomes should pay more taxes.

voluntary restraint agreement (VRA): An agreement to reduce the volume of trade in a specific good; a "voluntary" quota.

W

wage replacement rate: The percentage of base wages paid out in benefits.

wealth: The market value of assets.

wealth effect: A change in consumer spending caused by a change in the value of owned assets.

welfare programs: Means-tested income transfer programs, such as welfare and food stamps.

Y

yield: The rate of return on a bond; the annual interest payment divided by the bond's price.

Note: **Bold** page numbers indicate definitions; page numbers followed by *n* indicate material in notes.

Employment targeting, 345
EMU (European Monetary Union), 453
Ends vs. means, 19
Entrepreneurship
  defined, **5**
  economic growth and, 472-473
  as factor of production, 5, 36
  marginal tax rates and, 359-360
  microfinance and, 470, 475
Environmental protection
  climate change and, 21, 386-387
  government intervention for, 37-38
  pollution and, 386-387
  secondhand smoke and, 77
Environmental Protection Agency, U.S.
  (EPA), 366, 387
Equal opportunity programs, 364
Equation of exchange, 334-336, 341
Equilibrium. *See also* Equilibrium (macro)
  changes in, 63-65
  expenditure, 212-213
  international trade and, 431-432
  market clearing and, 61
  market shortages and, 62
  market surpluses and, 61
  in money market, 326-327
  self-adjusting prices and, 63
  in supply and demand, 60-65, 170-171
Equilibrium GDP, 200-202, **221**
Equilibrium (macro)
  in AS/AD model, 170-171, 184
  defined, **171, 184, 240**
  desired adjustment in, 184
  disequilibrium vs., 171
  fiscal policy and, 240
  market responses to, 171
  self-adjustment and, 225-228
  undesired, 172, 199-202
  unstable, 172, 202
Equilibrium price, 61, 63-65, 172, **431, 443**
Equilibrium rate of interest, 326-328
Equity. *See* Inequity; Stock market
Ethiopia, development patterns in, 35
Ethnicity, unemployment and, 122-123
European Monetary Union (EMU), 453
European Union (EU). *See also*
    specific countries
  gross domestic product of, 31
  nontariff barriers and, 434
  trade patterns of, 474
  voluntary restraint agreements with, 433
Excess reserves, 294, 297-298, **309**-310
Exchange rates. *See also* Foreign
    exchange markets
  appreciation, 446
  currency bailouts, 454-455
  defined, **441**
  depreciation, 446
  fixed, 450-453
  flexible, 453-454
  international comparison of, 444
  resistance to changes, 448-449

Excise taxes, 85
Expectations
  consumption and, 188-189, 192-193
  as demand determinant, 52
  investment and, 195-196
  maintaining stable expectations,
    383-384
  monetary restraint and, 333
  monetary stimulus and, 332-333
  rational, 408
  self-adjustment and, 218
  as supply determinant, 57
Expenditure equilibrium, 212-213
Export industries, 426
Exports
  aggregate demand and, 169
  comparative export ratios, 416
  defined, **107, 415**
  net, 107, 185, 198
  trade balances and, 417
  in U.S. trade patterns, 415-417
  voluntary restraint agreements for,
    433-434
External benefits, 79-80
External costs, 78-79
External debt, 275, 278-279
External financing, 470, 475
Externalities
  benefits from, 79-80
  costs generated by, 78-79
  defined, **37, 77**
  environmental protection and, 37-38
  market failure and, 77-80
External shocks, 166-167, 399, 405
Extreme poverty, 461
ExxonMobil, 333

Facebook, 3, 36, 300-301
Factor markets
  in circular flow, 47-48
  defined, **48**
  deregulation of, 365-366
  mandatory benefits in, 365-366
  minimum wages in, 365
  occupational health and safety in, 366
  trade barrier easing in, 367
Factor mobility, 36
Factors of production. *See also* Capital;
    Entrepreneurship; Labor force
  cost of, 57
  defined, **4, 35**
  HOW decisions and, 35-38
  land, 5, 36
  role of government in, 37-38
  in United States, 35-38
Fair Labor Standards Act of 1938, 365
Family and Medical Leave Act of 1993,
  365-366, 396
FAO (Food and Agriculture
  Organization), 62
Farm Bill of 2018, 433

Farming. *See* Agriculture
FDA (Food and Drug Administration,
  U.S.), 366
Federal Aviation Administration, U.S.,
  368-369
Federal Express, 36
Federal funds rate, 312, 316-317, 319,
  328, 396
Federal government
  countercyclical spending by, 198
  direct expenditures of, 83
  growth of, 82-84
  income transfers and, 83-84, 239, 264
  taxation by, 84-85, 238-239
Federal income taxes, 84-85, 144
Federal Motor Carrier Safety
  Administration (FMCSA), 366
Federal Open Market Committee (FOMC),
  308, 395
Federal Reserve Act of 1913, 307
Federal Reserve System, 306-319
  Board of Governors, 307-308, 395
  discounting and, 313
  discount rate and, 311-313, 318, 328
  federal funds rate and, 312, 316-317, 319,
    328, 396
  open market operations, 313-316,
    330-331, 395
  ownership of national debt, 275
  regulation by, 291, 300
  reserve requirements, 293-294, 308-310,
    318-319
  structure of, 306-308
Federal Trade Commission, U.S. (FTC),
  38, 366
Females. *See* Gender
Final goods, 102
Financial markets, 188, 194, 469-470
Financing injections, 299-300
Fine-tuning, 399
Firefighting services, as public good, 75-76
Fiscal policy, 238-256. *See also* Fiscal
    restraint; Fiscal stimulus
  aggregate demand and, 240-253, 263,
    352-353
  budget effects of, 251-252, 261-268,
    279-280
  concern for content of, 255-256
  in COVID-19 pandemic, 249-250, 260,
    280, 394
  crowding out and, 254-255
  debt accumulation and, 271-274
  debt burden and, 276-278
  debt ceilings in, 280
  debt ownership and, 274-275
  deficits and, 261-263, 268-270, 279-280
  defined, **179, 239, 261, 393**
  development of, 394
  external debt and, 275, 278-279
  fine-tuning, 399
  government spending and, 239, 242-244,
    251-252, 255-256, 261-268

NOMINAL GROSS DOMESTIC PRODUCT, Selected Years, 1929–2020 (billions of dollars)

Year	GDP	Personal Consumption Expenditures Total	Gross Private Domestic Investment Total	Net Exports			Government Purchases					Percent Change from Prior Year GDP
				Net	Exports	Imports	Total	Federal			State and Local	
								Total	National Defense	Non-defense		
1929	103	77	16	0	6	6	8	1	—	—	7	—
1930	90	70	10	0	4	4	9	1	—	—	7	−12.4
1931	75	60	5	0	2	2	9	1	—	—	7	−18.2
1932	58	48	1	0	2	1	8	1	—	—	6	−23.5
1933	55	45	1	0	2	1	7	2	—	—	5	−4.1
1934	65	61	3	0	2	2	9	3	—	—	6	17.1
1935	72	55	6	−2	2	3	10	3	—	—	6	11.1
1936	82	82	8	−2	3	3	12	5	—	—	6	14.4
1937	90	68	12	0	4	4	11	4	—	—	7	9.8
1938	84	64	7	1	3	2	12	5	—	—	7	−6.5
1939	90	67	9	1	3	3	13	5	1	4	8	7.0
1940	100	71	13	1	4	3	13	8	2	3	7	10.2
1941	125	81	18	1	5	4	24	17	13	3	7	25.0
1942	158	88	10	0	4	4	58	52	49	2	7	28.8
1943	192	99	6	−3	4	7	88	61	60	1	7	21.3
1944	211	108	7	−2	4	7	96	89	58	1	7	9.7
1945	213	119	10	−1	6	7	83	75	74	1	7	1.0
1946	211	144	31	7	14	7	29	19	16	2	9	−.8
1947	234	182	36	11	19	8	28	13	10	3	12	10.6
1948	260	173	48	3	13	10	31	16	10	5	14	11.1
1949	259	178	36	5	14	9	38	21	13	7	17	−.4
1980	2,795	1,762	477	−14	278	293	569	245	169	75	324	8.9
1981	3,131	1,944	570	−15	302	317	631	281	197	84	349	12.0
1982	3,259	2,079	516	−20	282	303	684	312	228	84	371	4.1
1983	3,534	2,286	564	−51	277	328	735	344	252	92	391	8.5
1984	3,932	2,498	735	−102	303	405	800	376	283	92	424	11.3
1985	4,213	2,712	736	−114	303	417	878	413	312	101	464	7.1
1986	4,452	2,895	747	−131	320	452	942	438	332	106	503	5.7
1987	4,742	3,105	781	−142	365	507	997	460	351	109	537	6.5
1988	5,108	3,356	821	−106	446	553	1,036	462	355	106	574	7.7
1989	5,489	3,596	872	−80	509	589	1,100	482	363	119	617	7.5
1990	5,803	3,839	846	−78	552	630	1,180	508	374	134	671	5.8
1991	5,995	3,986	803	−27	596	624	1,234	527	383	144	706	3.3
1992	6,337	4,235	848	−33	635	668	1,271	533	376	157	737	5.7
1993	6,657	4,477	932	−65	655	720	1,291	525	362	162	766	5.0
1994	7,072	4,743	1,033	−93	720	814	1,325	519	353	165	806	6.2
1995	7,397	4,975	1,112	−91	812	903	1,369	519	348	170	850	4.6
1996	7,816	5,256	1,209	−96	868	964	1,416	527	354	172	888	5.7
1997	8,304	5,547	1,317	−101	955	1,056	1,468	530	349	181	937	6.2
1998	8,747	5,879	1,438	−159	955	1,115	1,518	530	345	184	987	5.3
1999	9,268	6,282	1,558	−260	991	1,251	1,620	555	360	195	1,065	6.0
2000	9,817	6,739	1,679	−379	1,096	1,475	1,721	578	370	208	1,142	6.5
2001	10,128	7,055	1,646	−367	1,032	1,399	1,825	612	392	220	1,212	3.3
2002	10,469	7,350	1,570	−424	1,005	1,430	1,961	679	437	242	1,281	3.3
2003	10,960	7,703	1,649	−499	1,040	1,540	2,092	756	497	259	1,336	4.9
2004	11,685	8,196	1,889	−615	1,152	1,798	2,217	826	551	275	1,391	6.6
2005	12,422	8,694	2,086	−714	1,312	2,025	2,355	876	588	287	1,480	6.7
2006	13,178	9,207	2,220	−757	1,481	2,238	2,508	932	624	308	1,576	5.8
2007	13,808	9,710	2,130	−708	1,662	2,370	2,675	979	662	317	1,696	4.5
2008	14,291	10,035	2,087	−710	1,849	2,557	2,878	1,080	738	342	1,798	1.7
2009	13,939	9,866	1,547	−392	1,583	518	2,918	1,143	775	368	1,775	−2.0
2010	14,527	10,246	1,795	−517	1,840	562	3,000	1,223	819	404	1,780	3.8
2011	15,518	10,689	2,240	−580	2,106	2,686	3,169	1,304	837	467	1,865	3.7
2012	16,163	11,083	2,479	−568	2,194	2,763	3,169	1,291	818	473	1,878	4.2
2013	16,768	11,484	2,648	−508	2,262	2,770	3,143	1,232	770	462	1,912	3.7
2014	17,393	11,863	2,887	−509	2,375	2,884	3,152	1,219	746	473	1,933	3.7
2015	18,037	12,284	3,057	−522	2,264	2,786	3,218	1,225	732	493	1,933	3.7
2016	18,754	12,770	3,188	−513	2,227	2,740	3,299	1,235	729	506	2,065	2.9
2017	19,543	13,340	3,351	−556	2,375	2,930	3,407	1,264	747	517	2,143	4.3
2018	20,612	13,993	3,633	−610	2,529	3,138	3,595	1,339	794	545	2,256	5.5
2019	21,433	14,545	3,751	−611	2,515	3,125	3,748	1,419	852	567	2,329	4.0

Source: U.S. Department of Commerce.

REAL GROSS DOMESTIC PRODUCT IN CHAIN-WEIGHTED DOLLARS, Selected Decades, 1929–2020 (2012 = 100)

Year	GDP	Personal Consumption Expenditures Total	Gross Private Domestic Investment Total	Exports	Imports	Government Purchases Total	Percent Change from Prior Year GDP
1929	1,109	831	120	44	58	180	—
1930	1015	786	82	36	51	199	−8.5
1931	950	762	53	30	44	207	−6.4
1932	828	694	20	23	37	200	−12.9
1933	817	678	27	24	38	194	−1.3
1934	906	727	44	26	39	218	10.8
1935	786	771	77	28	51	225	8.9
1936	1,113	849	97	29	50	260	12.9
1937	1,170	881	119	37	57	250	5.1
1938	1,132	867	82	36	44	269	−3.3
1939	1,222	915	103	38	46	292	8.0
1940	1,330	962	140	43	47	303	8.8
1941	1,566	1,031	172	45	58	510	17.7
1942	1,862	1,006	96	29	53	1,184	18.9
1943	2,178	1,034	60	25	67	1,775	17.0
1944	2,352	1,064	71	27	70	1,992	8.0
1945	2,329	1,129	92	37	74	1,750	−1.0
1946	2,058	1,269	220	81	62	616	−11.6
1947	2,035	1,293	212	92	58	523	−1.1
1948	2,119	1,322	267	72	68	552	4.1
1949	2,107	1,359	207	72	66	611	−0.5
1980	6,759	4,243	864	404	407	1,732	−.2
1981	6,931	4,302	940	409	418	1,749	2.6
1982	6,806	4,365	822	378	413	1,780	−1.9
1983	7,118	4,612	899	368	465	1,846	4.6
1984	7,633	4,854	1,144	398	578	1,911	7.3
1985	7,951	5,106	1,143	411	615	2,038	4.2
1986	8,226	5,317	1,145	443	668	2,150	3.5
1987	8,511	5,497	1,178	491	707	2,212	3.5
1988	8,867	5,727	1,207	571	735	2,239	4.2
1989	9,192	5,894	1,255	637	767	2,303	3.7
1990	9,366	6,012	1,223	693	795	2,377	1.9
1991	9,355	6,023	1,142	739	794	2,405	−.1
1992	9,685	6,245	1,225	790	849	2,416	3.6
1993	9,952	6,462	1,323	816	923	2,397	2.7
1994	10,352	6,713	1,480	888	1,033	2,399	4.0
1995	10,630	6,911	1,527	979	1,115	2,411	2.7
1996	11,031	7,151	1,661	1,059	1,212	2,433	3.8
1997	11,522	7,420	1,850	1,185	1,376	2,473	4.5
1998	12,038	7,814	2,026	1,213	1,536	2,533	4.5
1999	12,611	8,225	2,199	1,273	1,710	2,615	4.7
2000	13,131	8,643	2,347	1,379	1,930	2,663	4.1
2001	13,262	8,861	2,215	1,300	1,876	2,762	1.0
2002	13,493	9,089	2,196	1,277	1,944	2,885	1.7
2003	13,879	9,378	2,290	1,305	2,040	2,947	2.9
2004	14,406	9,729	2,503	1,431	2,273	2,993	3.8
2005	14,913	10,076	2,671	1,533	2,421	3,016	3.5
2006	15,338	10,385	2,752	1,676	2,582	3,063	2.9
2007	15,626	10,615	2,684	1,822	2,646	3,119	1.9
2008	15,605	10,593	2,463	1,925	2,587	3,196	−0.1
2009	15,209	10,460	1,942	1,764	2,249	3,307	−2.5
2010	15,599	10,643	2,217	1,978	2,544	3,307	2.6
2011	15,841	16,844	2,362	2,119	2,687	3,203	1.6
2012	16,197	11,007	2,622	2,191	2,760	3,137	2.2
2013	16,495	11,167	2,802	2,270	2,802	3,081	1.8
2014	16,912	11,497	2,959	2,365	2,943	3,033	2.5
2015	17,432	11,934	3,122	2,375	3,095	3,088	3.1
2016	17,731	12,265	3,075	2,382	3,146	3,144	1.7
2017	18,144	12,587	3,183	2,476	3,292	3,172	2.3
2018	18,688	12,928	3,385	2,550	3,427	3,230	3.0
2019	19,091	13,240	3,443	2,547	3,464	3,304	2.2

Source: U.S. Department of Commerce.

CONSUMER PRICE INDEX, 1925–2020 (1982–84=100)

Year	Index (all items)	Percent Change
1925	17.5	3.5
1926	17.7	−1.1
1927	17.4	−2.3
1928	17.1	−1.2
1929	17.1	0.6
1930	16.7	−6.4
1931	15.2	−9.3
1932	13.7	−10.3
1933	13.0	0.8
1934	13.4	1.5
1935	13.7	3.0
1936	13.9	1.4
1937	14.4	2.9
1938	14.1	−2.8
1939	13.9	0.0
1940	14.0	0.7
1941	14.7	9.9
1942	16.3	9.0
1943	17.3	3.0
1944	17.6	2.3
1945	18.0	2.2
1946	19.5	18.1
1947	22.3	8.8
1948	24.1	3.0
1949	23.8	−2.1
1970	38.8	5.6
1971	40.5	3.3
1972	41.8	3.4
1973	44.4	8.7
1974	49.3	12.3
1975	53.8	6.9
1976	56.9	4.9
1977	60.6	6.7
1978	65.2	9.0
1979	72.6	13.3
1980	82.4	12.5
1981	90.9	8.9
1982	96.5	3.8
1983	99.6	3.8
1984	103.9	3.9
1985	107.6	3.8
1986	109.6	1.1
1987	113.6	4.4
1988	118.3	4.6
1989	124.0	4.6
1990	130.7	6.1
1991	136.2	3.1
1992	140.3	2.9
1993	144.5	2.7
1994	148.2	2.7
1995	152.4	2.5
1996	156.9	3.3
1997	160.5	1.7
1998	163.0	1.6
1999	166.6	2.7
2000	172.2	3.4
2001	177.1	2.8
2002	179.7	1.6
2003	184.0	2.6
2004	188.9	2.7
2005	195.3	3.4
2006	201.6	3.2
2007	207.3	2.8
2008	215.3	3.8
2009	214.5	−0.4
2010	218.1	1.6
2011	224.9	3.2
2012	229.6	2.1
2013	233.0	1.5
2014	236.7	1.6
2015	237.0	0.1
2016	240.0	1.3
2017	245.1	2.1

(continued)

Year	Index (all items)	Percent Change
2018	251.1	2.4
2019	255.7	1.8
2020	259.1	1.0

Note: Data beginning 1978 are for all urban consumers I; earlier data are for urban wage earners and clerical workers.

Source: U.S. Department of Labor, Bureau of Statistics.

CHAIN-WEIGHTED PRICE DEFLATORS FOR GROSS DOMESTIC PRODUCT, 1970–2020 (2012=100)

Year	Index (all items)	Percent Change
1970	21.7	5.3
1971	22.8	5.0
1972	23.8	4.3
1973	25.0	5.5
1974	27.3	9.0
1975	29.8	9.5
1976	31.5	5.7
1977	33.4	6.4
1978	35.8	7.0
1979	38.8	8.3
1980	42.3	9.1
1981	46.3	9.4
1982	49.1	6.1
1983	51.1	3.9
1984	52.9	3.8
1985	54.6	3.0
1986	55.7	2.2
1987	57.0	2.8
1988	59.1	3.4
1989	61.4	3.8
1990	63.7	3.9
1991	65.8	3.5
1992	67.3	2.4
1993	68.9	2.2
1994	70.4	2.1
1995	71.9	2.1
1996	73.2	1.9
1997	74.4	1.8
1998	75.3	1.1
1999	76.3	1.5
2000	78.1	2.2
2001	77.8	2.3
2002	81.0	1.6
2003	82.6	2.2
2004	84.8	2.8
2005	87.4	3.3
2006	90.1	3.3
2007	92.5	2.9
2008	94.3	2.2
2009	95.0	0.9
2010	96.1	1.0
2011	98.1	2.1
2012	100.0	1.8
2013	101.8	1.4
2014	103.6	2.0
2015	104.6	1.1
2016	105.7	1.3
2017	107.8	2.0
2018	110.3	2.3
2019	112.3	1.8
2020	113.4	1.0

Source: U.S. Department of Commerce, Bureau of Economic Analysis.

INTEREST RATES, 1929–2020 (percent per annum)

Year	Prime Rate Charged by Banks	Discount Rate, Federal Reserve Bank of New York
1929	5.50–6.00	5.16
1933	1.50–4.00	2.56
1939	1.50	1.00
1940	1.50	1.00
1941	1.50	1.00
1942	1.50	1.00
1943	1.50	1.00
1944	1.50	1.00
1945	1.50	1.00
1946	1.50	1.00
1947	1.50–1.75	1.00
1948	1.75–2.00	1.34
1949	2.00	1.50
1970	7.91	5.95
1971	5.72	4.88
1972	5.25	4.50
1973	8.03	6.44
1974	10.81	7.83
1975	7.86	6.25
1976	6.84	5.50
1977	6.83	5.46
1978	9.06	7.46
1979	12.67	10.28
1980	15.27	11.77
1981	18.87	13.42
1982	14.86	11.02
1983	10.79	8.50
1984	12.04	8.80
1985	9.93	7.69
1986	8.83	6.33
1987	8.21	5.66
1988	9.32	6.20
1989	10.87	6.93
1990	10.01	6.98
1991	8.46	5.45
1992	6.25	3.25
1993	6.00	3.00
1994	7.15	3.60
1995	8.83	5.21
1996	8.27	5.02
1997	8.44	5.00
1998	8.35	4.92
1999	8.00	4.62
2000	9.23	5.73
2001	6.91	3.40
2002	4.67	1.17
2003	4.12	1.15
2004	4.34	2.34
2005	6.19	4.19
2006	7.96	5.96
2007	8.05	5.86
2008	5.09	2.39
2009	3.25	0.50
2010	3.25	0.75
2011	3.25	0.75
2012	3.25	0.75
2013	3.25	0.75
2014	3.25	0.75
2015	3.26	0.76
2016	3.51	1.01
2017	4.25	1.63
2018	5.00	2.46
2019	5.25	2.75
2020	3.25	0.25

Source: Board of Governors of the Federal Reserve System.

POPULATION AND THE LABOR FORCE, 1929–2020

Year	Total Population	Civilian Noninstitutional Population	Armed Forces	Civilian Labor Force	Civilian Unemployment	Unemployment Rate	Civilian Labor-Force Participation Rate	Employment Population Ratio
							(Percent)	
		Thousands of Persons 14 Years of Age and Over					**Percent**	
1929	121,767	—	—	49,180	1,550	3.2	—	—
1933	125,579	—	—	51,590	12,830	24.9	—	—
1939	130,880	—	—	55,230	9,480	17.2	—	—
1940	132,122	99,840	—	55,640	8,120	14.6	55.7	47.6
1941	133,402	99,900	—	55,910	5,560	9.9	56.0	50.4
1942	134,860	98,640	—	56,410	2,660	4.7	57.2	54.5
1943	136,739	94,640	—	55,540	1,070	1.9	58.7	57.6
1944	138,397	93,220	—	54,630	670	1.2	58.6	57.9
1945	139,928	94,090	—	53,860	1,040	1.9	57.2	56.1
1946	141,389	103,070	—	57,520	2,270	3.9	55.8	53.6
1947	144,126	106,018	—	60,168	2,356	3.9	56.8	54.5
		Thousands of Persons 16 Years of Age and Over						
1947	144,083	101,827	—	59,350	2,311	3.9	58.3	56.0
1948	146,631	103,068	—	60,621	2,276	3.8	58.8	56.6
1949	149,188	103,994	—	61,286	3,637	5.9	58.9	55.4
1970	205,052	137,085	2,118	82,771	4,093	4.9	60.4	57.4
1971	207,661	140,216	1,973	84,382	5,016	5.9	60.2	56.6
1972	209,896	144,126	1,813	87,034	4,882	5.6	60.4	57.0
1973	211,909	147,096	1,774	89,429	4,365	4.9	60.8	57.8
1974	213,854	150,120	1,721	91,949	5,156	5.6	61.3	57.8
1975	215,973	153,153	1,678	93,775	7,929	8.5	61.2	56.1
1976	218,035	156,150	1,668	96,158	7,406	7.7	61.6	56.8
1977	220,239	159,033	1,656	99,009	6,991	7.1	62.3	57.9
1978	222,585	161,910	1,631	102,251	6,202	6.1	63.2	59.3
1979	225,055	164,863	1,597	104,962	6,137	5.8	63.7	59.9
1980	227,726	167,745	1,604	106,940	7,637	7.1	63.8	59.2
1981	229,966	170,130	1,645	108,670	8,273	7.6	63.9	59.0
1982	232,188	172,271	1,668	110,204	10,678	9.7	64.0	57.8
1983	234,307	174,215	1,676	111,550	10,717	9.6	64.0	57.9
1984	236,348	176,383	1,697	113,544	8,539	7.5	64.4	59.5
1985	238,466	178,206	1,706	115,461	8,312	7.2	64.8	60.1
1986	240,651	180,587	1,706	117,834	8,237	7.0	65.3	60.7
1987	242,804	182,753	1,737	119,865	7,425	6.2	65.6	61.5
1988	245,021	184,613	1,709	121,669	6,701	5.5	65.9	62.3
1989	247,342	186,393	1,668	123,869	6,528	5.3	66.5	63.0
1990	249,924	188,049	1,637	124,787	6,874	5.5	66.4	62.7
1991	252,688	189,765	1,564	125,303	8,426	6.7	66.0	61.6
1992	255,414	191,576	1,566	126,982	9,384	7.4	66.3	61.4
1993	258,137	193,550	1,705	128,040	8,734	6.8	66.2	61.6
1994	260,660	196,814	1,610	131,056	7,996	6.1	66.6	62.5
1995	263,034	198,584	1,533	132,304	7,404	5.6	66.6	62.9
1996	265,453	200,591	1,479	133,943	7,236	5.4	66.8	63.2
1997	267,901	203,133	1,437	136,297	6,739	4.9	67.1	63.8
1998	270,290	205,220	1,401	137,673	6,210	4.5	67.1	64.1
1999	272,945	207,753	1,411	139,368	5,880	4.2	67.1	64.3
2000	282,434	212,573	1,423	142,583	5,692	4.0	67.1	64.4
2001	285,545	215,092	1,387	143,734	6,801	4.7	66.8	63.7
2002	288,600	217,570	1,416	144,863	8,378	5.8	66.6	62.7
2003	291,049	221,168	1,390	146,510	8,774	6.0	66.2	62.3
2004	293,708	223,357	1,411	149,401	8,149	5.5	66.0	62.3
2005	296,639	226,082	1,387	149,320	7,591	5.1	66.0	62.7
2006	299,801	228,815	1,414	151,428	7,001	4.6	66.2	63.1
2007	302,045	231,867	1,380	153,124	7,078	4.6	66.0	63.0
2008	304,906	233,788	1,455	154,287	8,924	5.8	66.0	62.2
2009	307,007	235,801	1,443	154,142	14,265	9.3	65.4	59.3
2010	309,438	237,830	1,430	153,889	14,825	9.6	64.7	58.5
2011	311,663	239,618	1,425	153,617	13,747	8.9	64.1	58.4
2012	313,998	243,284	1,400	154,975	12,506	8.1	63.7	58.6
2013	316,205	245,679	1,370	155,389	11,460	7.4	63.2	58.6
2014	318,563	247,947	1,354	155,922	9,617	6.2	62.9	59.0
2015	320,897	250,801	1,320	157,130	8,296	5.3	62.7	59.3
2016	323,127	253,538	1,301	159,187	7,751	4.9	62.8	59.7
2017	325,085	255,079	1,359	160,320	6,982	4.4	62.9	60.1
2018	327,096	257,791	1,347	162,075	6,314	3.9	62.9	60.4
2019	329,065	259,175	1,383	163,539	6,001	3.7	63.1	60.8

Source: U.S. Department of Labor, Bureau of Labor Statistics.